DESIGN & THE DECORATIVE ARTS
BRITAIN 1500-1900

DESIGN & THE DECORATIVE ARTS

BRITAIN 1500-1900

Michael Snodin and John Styles

V&A Publications

Distributed by Harry N. Abrams, Inc., Publishers

Contents

Foreword

This book is published to coincide with the opening of the Victoria and Albert Museum's new 'British Galleries 1500–1900' and to take the subject of the galleries to an audience beyond the Museum's walls. The British Galleries form the largest project that the V&A has undertaken since its staff reinstalled the entire Museum in 1947–52, after the evacuation of objects to safe storage during the Second World War. Indeed, in terms of floor space and number of objects, these galleries are larger than many museums in Britain or elsewhere. This book, fittingly, is also the largest and most ambitious that the Museum has ever published. However, it is not only size and chronological scope that distinguish the British Galleries and this publication – both represent fundamentally new approaches to their subject matter.

To do justice to the subject in its various aspects and to give structure to the chronological narrative in both book and galleries, four distinct but complementary questions are addressed: What were the formal aesthetics of different styles? Who led taste? How did new modes of living lead to the design of new types of objects or the increased consumption of existing ones? What was new? These themes were originally conceived for the gallery visitor and their wording on the page reflects this. But they are equally valid for the book, addressing, as they do, fundamental matters of aesthetics, cultural authority, taste and innovation. They reveal some of the important stories that emerge from a consideration of design in Britain, and enable those stories to be traced over four centuries. Different questions might have been asked, but these four themes would inevitably form the core of them.

Book and galleries echo one another in fundamental ways, but the book is able to provide a deeper historical context by providing chapters about the wider history of each period as an introduction to each of the book's three sections. The book cannot illustrate all the objects displayed in the galleries, but it is able to address a somewhat wider range of objects, including those that the V&A cannot or has chosen not to collect, such as ships and railway locomotives, as well as illustrating the original settings for objects, including the wider built and landscaped environment. Nevertheless the book remains firmly rooted in the Museum. Its two principal authors and editors are long-standing members of the Museum's staff. The other contributors all work, or have worked, at the Museum.

The V&A is Britain's National Museum of Art and Design. Its collections represent what people at various periods in the past – patrons, consumers, collectors, curators – have considered to be the best of their kind in aesthetic terms. Inevitably, both the book and the galleries reflect this sometimes partial history of institutional collecting, although not uncritically. As a consequence, both deal principally with what are referred to as high-design objects. These were objects that embodied a deliberate striving after the most prized aesthetic effects of their era. They were made to be used by the economically and socially privileged, whose tastes dictated what was considered beautiful and fashionable at any time. It was they who commanded the resources necessary to procure the most expensive materials and to enjoy the fruits of the most skilled techniques of manufacture. Nevertheless, the book acknowledges that these high-design objects were only one element in the wider visual culture that prevailed in Britain, a visual culture that in many of its more everyday aspects remains poorly recorded or understood for much of the period. Where appropriate and possible, the book makes reference to such everyday objects and to the people for whom, and by whom, they were made.

The book and galleries concern themselves with those apparently functional, but often deliberately aesthetically pleasing, objects that fall between the traditional concerns of the fine arts and architecture. They include furniture, ceramics, metalwares, textiles and clothing, graphic works of various kinds, as well as the immensely varied products of modern manufacturing that we associate with the phrase 'industrial design'. These are the objects that have come to constitute the territory of design in its most familiar modern usage. It is such objects that constitute the bulk of the collections of the V&A and that figure most prominently in this book, rooted as it is in the Museum's collections.

Nevertheless, architecture and the fine arts appear with regularity in this book, as they do in the galleries. Architecture was crucial for the formulation of many of the design ideas that were most influential in Britain between 1500 and 1900, although unusually the book places as much emphasis on interior as on exterior architecture. The fine arts (traditionally defined as painting and sculpture, together with drawing and especially print-making) also figure in the book, but their role is as part of the narrative of the designed world rather than as a distinct history of their own. For example, when considering the role of landscape in having fostered a sense of Britishness in the early nineteenth century, paintings and drawings are not treated separately from the use of similar imagery in other media, including ceramics and glass. In other instances, such as consideration of the growth of portraiture in the eighteenth century or the spread of the private sculpture gallery in the early nineteenth, the fine arts are integrated into the story in numerous ways: as part of the formation of new types of interiors, as part of the story of collecting, as integral to the transmission of style as well as to the formation of taste, including their role in the spread of refinement and politeness in British society.

This is not a book about the history of Britain, nor is it a history of British designers. While book and galleries attempt to present what was distinctively British about British design, they also demonstrate ways in which 'Britishness' was constructed, more often than not, by the creative adaptation of objects and visual ideas that originated elsewhere. This was motivated by the desire to replace the imported object with a domestically produced version of it. The book and the galleries make explicit a story of British design that is based on the conscious appropriation of non-British objects, craftspeople, visual sources, designers, architects and artists. Tapestry making in sixteenth-century Britain would have developed quite differently if William Sheldon had not brought Flemish weavers to teach the craft; the grandeur of the Melville State Bed (c. 1700) would have been inconceivable without the design ideas of Daniel Marot, a Frenchman active in Holland; lacquer from Japan provoked imitation in British painted, 'japanned' furniture; it was the early training of Nicholas Sprimont in the Low Countries that led to the success of the Chelsea porcelain factory under his management from the 1740s; and in Scotland the entire nineteenth-century industry of paisley shawls was based on the desire to emulate the fine weaving of imported Kashmir shawls.

British design is, therefore, defined in this book and in the galleries not in a narrow, nationalistic way, but as the product of lengthy, complex and often fruitful international and colonial relationships arising out of commerce, cultural exchange and geopolitical conflict. And, of course, during the period covered by this book, Britain ceased to be predominantly a taker of design from others. It became one of the world's leading suppliers of designed objects and design ideas.

As far as geography is concerned, Britain is taken to mean the territory of Great Britain: in other words, England, Scotland and Wales. Questions of nationhood and national identity through design are actively debated subjects at the moment of writing, as they have been, episodically, throughout the period covered by this book. As early as the sixteenth century, a politician complained of England being 'overburdened with unnecessary foreign wares'; in the seventeenth century, the threat of luxury goods to the national character was the source of public argument; in the mid-eighteenth century, intense – indeed virulent – rivalry with France encouraged the promotion of higher standards of design education and a new self-consciousness, which propelled Britain to international prominence in design; and in the Victorian period, the intensity of debates about good and bad design, indeed the morality of design, distinguished Britain from other design cultures.

Within Britain, while London has usually enjoyed a pivotal place in matters of design, production and taste, the specialist regional centres of production, such as Stoke-on-Trent, Birmingham and Sheffield, have played key roles within the design economy of the nation. Designers and makers from throughout Britain are well represented in these pages and in the galleries. Moreover, products distributed from centres like London, Edinburgh and Bristol, whether made in Britain or imported from abroad, have, via a network of traders and local taste makers, found a place throughout England, Scotland and Wales.

The time-span covered in the book and galleries is the period from the end of the fifteenth century to the turn of the twentieth century, from the reigns of Henry VII in England and James IV in Scotland to the death of Queen Victoria. It covers the epoch that saw the rise of Britain from a position of relative international insignificance at the end of the Middle Ages to one of huge international influence in Victoria's reign, not simply in design, but also in great power politics and economics. It ends at the moment when international leadership in design was about to pass to the advocates of twentieth-century aesthetic Modernism. This movement, with its many manifestations, was a development that Britain, of all the major world powers, was to find the most difficulty in accommodating.

The question of design is central to both galleries and book. The earliest meaning of the word in Britain was close to the Italian term *disegno* and was intimately linked to the activity of drawing. Thus a design was a drawing or print, and the activity of designing was to make a drawing that would enable a two- or three-dimensional object to be made, whether by hand, machine, or a combination of the two. More recently, the term design has often been used to refer exclusively to modern objects, especially those whose appearance was shaped by architects, industrial or product designers, by the tenets of twentieth-century Modernism or the imperatives of industrial mass production. In this context the focus is on the final look of the object – its design. By contrast, historical objects like those in the V&A have been described as decorative, or applied, art. These are nineteenth-century terms, which aimed to associate decorative, practical or utilitarian objects with the status of the fine arts, while continuing to differentiate them from it. The term decorative art, unlike applied art, still has popular currency and is therefore used in the title of this book.

Yet even before the nineteenth century, the word design could have the broader meaning of an intention, a plan or a conception. Today it is this meaning that prevails when we use the word design in relation to objects. When we speak of an object's design we mean its overall characteristics and the processes that have taken place in order to create it. It is in this sense that the word design is employed in this book. The authors identify design as a complex and multi-layered process, including research, experimentation, manufacture, marketing and use, rather than concerning themselves solely with the history of drawn or printed designs, or with the appearance of the finished object.

This book and the British Galleries at the V&A have the same approach to the interpretation of design as an historical phenomenon and offer new perspectives on design and the decorative arts in Britain. The scope of both is more extensive, international and complex than any surveys previously attempted. Each offers complementary versions of this survey. Whereas the book can present readers with a deeper and wider historical context for design in Britain, the galleries allow visitors to the V&A the experience of more than 3,000 objects made and used in Britain over 400 years.

Christopher Wilk

Chief Curator

British Galleries Project

March 2001

Acknowledgements

Planning, writing and editing this book has taken the best part of three years. From the start, it has been an integral part of the wider British Galleries project at the V&A. As the book's editors and principal authors, we owe a great debt of gratitude to Christopher Wilk, who has led the British Galleries project and has been unwavering in his support for the book. Alan Borg, former Director of the V&A, and Gwyn Miles, Director of Projects, were instrumental in supporting a publication of this scope and scale. We would also like to register our thanks to the rest of the staff of the British Galleries project for many kindnesses, in particular to the three Gallery Team Co-Ordinators – Nick Humphrey, Karen Livingstone and Leela Meinertas – who remained astonishingly calm and efficient in the face of our countless requests for information and assistance.

For ideas, references and advice on illustrations we are grateful to Cathy Arbuthnot, Philip Atkins, Elizabeth Bonython, Justin Champion, Quentin Colville, Rosemany Crill, Richard Edgcumbe, Clive Edwards, Hazel Forsyth, Werner Freundel, Eileen Harris, Anthony Kersting, Roger Knight, Reino Liefkes, Sarah Medlam, Julia Muir, Christopher Nicholson, Anthony North, Michael Sonenscher, the late Clive Wainwright, Alex Werner, Michael Whiteway, James Yorke and Jonathan Zeitlin as well as to all our fellow contributors. Thanks are also due to the many students on the V&A/RCA MA Course in the History of Design who have written relevant essays and dissertations, from which we learned much. We are grateful to Michael Braddick, Anthony Burton, Martin Daunton, Maurice Howard, Joanna Innes, Peter Mandler and Amanda Vickery for reading sections of the text and commenting on them. Responsibility for the final outcome remains our own.

Melanie Brooks, Jennifer Eiss, Jack Hinton, Nina Jacobson, Antonia Salt and Mary Wessel managed the almost impossible task of bringing together nearly 1,000 illustrations and their captions. Without the V&A's photographers and the staff of the V&A Picture Library this book would simply not have been possible. Kim Smith checked the chronologies, bibliographies and personal dates. We owe a special debt to Alicia Weisberg-Roberts, Samuel H. Kress Curatorial Fellow at the V&A, who made an outstanding contribution to almost every aspect of the book.

The book was written and put together mainly in the Research Department at the V&A, to very tight deadlines. We would like to thank Paul Greenhalgh and Carolyn Sargentson, who successively headed the Department, for their support and understanding. Thanks are also due to those many colleagues with whom we shared the Research Department's wonderful facilities and who helped us, sometimes without knowing it.

To say that a book could not have been completed without the efforts of publishers, editors and designers is an authorial cliché, but in the case of this book it is emphatically true. The book would not have seen the light of day without the extraordinary hard work, persistence and patience of Mary Butler at V&A Publications and the team that she assembled, especially Geoff Barlow, the book's project manager; Clare Davis, V&A Publications' production manager; Mandy Greenfield, the book's copy editor; Janet James, its designer; and John Noble, its indexer.

Finally we must register our gratitude to those whom we have neglected in order to bring this enormous project to completion. First, to our long-suffering colleagues in the Department of Prints, Drawings and Paintings at the V&A and on the V&A/RCA MA Course in the History of Design. Second, and most important, to our families. For them, living with this book has not always been a pleasure, its progress measured in long hours at the office and bedtime stories and school meetings foregone. Thank you.

The book is dedicated to our fathers.

Michael Snodin and John Styles

2001

List of Contributors

Malcolm Baker is Deputy Head, Research Department, V&A.

Julia Bigham is Assistant Curator, Prints, Drawings and Paintings Department, V&A.

Christopher Breward is Professor in Historical and Cultural Studies at the London College of Fashion, The London Institute. He was previously a Course Tutor on the V&A/RCA MA Course in the History of Design at the Royal College of Art.

Clare Browne is Assistant Curator, Textiles and Dress Department, V&A.

Jim Cheshire is Lecturer in the History of Art and Material Culture at the University of Lincoln. He was previously Research Assistant, British Galleries Project, V&A.

Helen Clifford is Course Tutor on the V&A/RCA MA Course in the History of Design, Research Department, V&A.

Frances Collard is Deputy Curator, Furniture and Woodwork Department, V&A.

Ann Eatwell is Assistant Curator, Metalwork, Silver and Jewellery Department, V&A.

Suzanne Fagence Cooper is Lecturer in the History of Art and Design at Buckinghamshire Chilterns University College, and High Wycombe Research Fellow at the V&A, responsible for co-curating the exhibition 'Inventing New Britain: the Victorian Vision'.

Paul Greenhalgh is President of the Nova Scotia College of Art and Design, Canada. He was previously Head of Research at the V&A.

Mark Haworth-Booth is Head of Photographs in the Prints, Drawings and Paintings Department, V&A.

Robin Hildyard is Assistant Curator, Ceramics and Glass Department, V&A.

Laura Houliston is Assistant Curator, British Galleries Project, V&A.

Maurice Howard is Professor of the History of Art at the University of Sussex. He has been Sussex Exchange Fellow at the V&A and is senior specialist advisor for the Tudor and Stuart sections of the British Galleries.

Nick Humphrey is British Galleries Team Co-Ordinator, V&A.

Rachel Kennedy is an independent researcher and writer. She was previously Research Assistant, British Galleries Project, V&A.

Karen Livingstone is British Galleries Team Co-Ordinator, V&A.

Elizabeth Miller is Assistant Curator, Prints, Drawings and Paintings Department, V&A.

Tessa Murdoch is Acting Chief Curator, Furniture and Woodwork Department, V&A.

Kate Newnham is Curator of Eastern Art and Culture at Bristol City Museum. She was previously Assistant Curator, British Galleries Project, V&A.

Susan North is Deputy Curator, Textiles and Dress Department, V&A.

Linda Parry is Acting Chief Curator, Textiles and Dress Department, V&A.

Sara Pennell is an independent researcher and writer. She was previously Research Assistant, British Galleries Project, V&A.

Michael Snodin is Head of the Designs Section, Prints, Drawings and Paintings Department, V&A.

John Styles is Head of Postgraduate Studies, Research Department, V&A.

Rowan Watson is Head of Collections Development, National Art Library, V&A.

Dinah Winch is Assistant Curator, British Galleries Project, V&A.

Hilary Young is Assistant Curator, Ceramics and Glass Department, V&A.

Tudor and Stuart Britain

1500–1714

CHAPTER 1

Tudor and Stuart Britain, 1500–1714

Introduction

JOHN STYLES

1. Stability and change

The rulers of Tudor and Stuart Britain prized order, hierarchy and stability, and yet the experience of the Tudor and Stuart period was one of profound change. The Protestant faith replaced the Catholic faith as the national religion; a civil war was fought and a king beheaded; the British Isles were brought together under a single ruler; plantations and trading posts were established in the Americas and Asia, across previously unsailed seas. Such changes, and the heightened sense of both impermanence and opportunity that they provoked, were not confined to the spheres of religion, politics and international relations. They extended to the material world inhabited by British men and women, to the works of art and the everyday things that shaped their lives. Britain's rulers tried intermittently to hold back the tide of material change, but in vain. Parliament enacted laws to confine the wearing of fashionable clothes to limited categories of people; monarchs issued royal proclamations to prevent the fields on the edges of London disappearing under new houses. Yet in the course of the sixteenth and seventeenth centuries the fashion cycle achieved an unprecedented intensity and London expanded to become the largest city in western Europe.

It is the mushrooming growth of London that offers the most vivid illustration of the material changes that transformed Tudor and Stuart Britain. London was the phenomenon of the age. In 1500, under the rule of the first Tudor king, Henry VII, it was a middle-ranking medieval capital city, inhabited by some 40,000 people. Its houses were built of timber, clay and plaster; its streets were narrow. In population, it was less than half the size of leading continental cities like Paris and Venice. In commerce, it was subservient to the vibrant mercantile centres of the Low Countries, particularly Bruges and Antwerp. In the course of the next hundred years London boomed, as trade, manufacturing and government all expanded. The sixteenth century

1 previous pages (left):
Chinese porcelain jar with English mounts; jar 1630–40, mounts 1660–70. Marked WH, probably for Wolfgang Howzer. Porcelain and silver-gilt mounts. VAM M. 308-1962.

2 previous pages (right):
Detail of a glove, 1600–49. Metal threads, coloured silks on satin. VAM T.42-1954.

3 Detail of *Edward VI's processional entry into the City of London in 1547*. Painted in 1787 by Samuel Hieronymous Grimm after a wall painting at Cowdray House, Sussex, now lost. Watercolour. Society of Antiquaries of London.

witnessed what the 1615 edition of John Stow's *Annales, or, a General Chronicle of England* described as 'the unimaginable enlarging of London, and the suburbs, within the space of fiftie years'. By the time the last Tudor monarch, Elizabeth I, died in 1603, the city had more than quadrupled in size, housing approximately 180,000 people.

But in its physical appearance Shakespeare's London was still a medieval city, not a Renaissance one. It resembled its smaller, early-Tudor predecessor of a century before more than it did contemporary continental cities like Antwerp, Venice or even Paris. Despite spectacular growth in the city's population, buildings in new architectural styles, like the Royal Exchange in Cornhill, closely modelled on the bourse in Antwerp, or the classical façade of Somerset House on the Strand, were the exception, not the rule. In the case of the Royal Exchange, it was not simply the design but also the designer, Hendrick van Paesschen, and much of the building material that came from Flanders. Few London houses were built of brick, and the formal entrances to the city – its gates – were old-fashioned and lacked magnificence, while its parish churches were outdated and in poor repair. In 1561 the spire of St Paul's Cathedral had been struck by lightning and burned; by 1603 it had still not

4 Detail of *Londinium*, a design for a triumphal arch made for the procession of James I and VI through the City of London in March 1604. Engraved by William Kip and published by Stephen Harrison as part of the set, *Arch's of Triumph*, 1604. The scene depicted is London at the start of the 17th century. Engraving. VAM 14006.

5 *Byrsa Londinensis vulgo the Royal Exchange*, 1647. Engraved by Wenceslaus Hollar. Building designed by Hendrick van Paesschen. The engraving shows the Exchange as built in 1566–71, before its destruction in the Great Fire of 1666. Engraving. VAM E.2203-1948.

been replaced. The city lacked fine vistas and public spaces like those that had recently been created in Antwerp, Rome and Paris.

When Queen Anne, the last Stuart monarch, died in 1714, all this had changed. London had overtaken Paris as the largest city in western Europe, with a population of nearly 600,000. It was about to displace Amsterdam as the centre of the world's trading economy. Moreover, London had been physically transformed. A guide book published in 1708 could describe the city as 'the most spatious, populous, rich, beautiful, renowned and noble that we know of at this day in the world'. The journalist and author Daniel Defoe, writing shortly after Queen Anne's death, observed 'new squares and new streets rising up every day to such a prodigy of buildings that nothing in the world does, or ever did, equal it, except old Rome in Trajan's time'.

In part, this physical transformation was a consequence of the Great Fire of London, which razed vast tracts of the city in 1666. The speed with which the burned-out areas were rebuilt is testimony to London's astonishing wealth in the second half of the seventeenth century. The quality of the public buildings that replaced those destroyed in the Fire, most prominently the 52 new churches, demonstrates the mastery of the classical style achieved by native British architects, in particular Christopher Wren. But the ravages of the Fire accounted for only some of the new building that changed the face of London in the half-century after 1660. The distinctive new residential squares extolled by Defoe – Panton Square, Soho Square, St James's Square, Red Lion Square, Leicester Square, Bloomsbury Square – were developed principally in the West End of the metropolis, which the Fire never reached.

This new London, this new world city, was not a planned exercise in baroque pomp and magnificence, the brainchild of an absolute monarch. It lacked the monuments and palaces, the vistas of cathedrals and citadels that were to typify the aesthetics of royal absolutism in Turin, Karlsruhe and Berlin. Moreover, there was no British Versailles, no purpose-built royal seat of government located at a safe but accessible distance from the capital. In these and many other of its physical characteristics, Queen Anne's London was a reflection of the chequered history of the nation and its capital under the

6 *Sohoe or King's Square,* 1754. Drawn by Edward Days, engraved by Sutton Nicholls. Originally known as King's Square, Soho Square was developed in the 1680s. Engraving. VAM E.624-1976.

Tudors and Stuarts. That history was one of sustained economic expansion, combined with political inconsistency and often discord, which foreigners found baffling. The city's out-of-date and half-completed royal palaces were testimony to the way in which the power and wealth of successive monarchs had waxed and waned. It was Wren's new churches that dominated the city's skyline, proclaiming the hard-won but still qualified ascendancy of that peculiarly British brand of Protestantism embodied in the Church of England. The mercantile heart of the city, quickly reconstructed after the Fire in a piecemeal fashion, ignoring the grand formal replanning advocated by Wren and others, attested to the overwhelming priority that London's merchant rulers accorded to the continuation of business as usual. The elegant new streets and squares of the West End were evidence of the commercial disposition of the British nobility, eager to turn a profit from its landed property on the fringes of the city by providing wealthy people from across the British Isles with the smart London residences they craved.

8

7

---

7 *The Thames at Horseferry*, about 1706–10. By Jan Griffier the Elder. In the background is the City of London, where the spires of Wren's churches flank the newly completed dome of St Paul's Cathedral. Oil on canvas. The Museum of London.

8 *The Palace of Whitehall*, after a mid-17th-century engraving by Wenceslaus Hollar. Published by William Herbert, 1809. The Banqueting House on the left was built in 1619–22 to a design by Inigo Jones. Subsequently, Charles I planned a new royal palace around it in the same classical style, but it was never built. The Banqueting House was still surrounded by much older buildings when Charles I was beheaded in 1649 on a scaffold erected in front of it. Engraving. VAM E.416-1898.

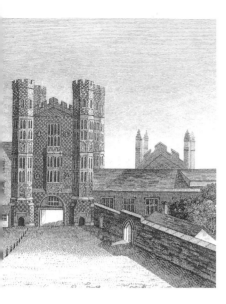

2. The medieval legacy

In 1500, at the end of what we now call the Middle Ages, Britain played a peripheral role in the affairs of Europe. What contemporaries saw as the great centres of European art and culture, of wealth and power, lay elsewhere. It was the beautiful objects created in places like Venice and Florence, Antwerp and Bruges that were coveted throughout western Europe, not those made in London. Foreigners saw little that was admirable – or even worthy of comment – in English decorative art and design. What we now perceive as the triumphs of the visual arts in fifteenth-century England, particularly the Perpendicular style in architecture, were uniquely English and had negligible influence elsewhere in Europe. What was true of England was even more true of Scotland and Wales, which had far smaller populations.

If England held a peripheral place in European cultural affairs at the end of the Middle Ages, this state of affairs reflected its marginality in economic and political matters. The centres of gravity of European trade and urban life lay in the Low Countries and the Mediterranean. Indeed, the British Isles lay towards the geographical margins of the world as it was then understood by Europeans. The Atlantic Ocean was perceived as the boundary of the known world, not as a gateway to global intercourse. It was only in 1492 that Christopher Columbus, financed by the King and Queen of Spain, landed in the Americas; it was only in 1498 that the Portuguese Vasco da Gama reached India by sea. In 1500, moreover, England's direct stake in continental European affairs was much reduced. The vast swathes of French territory that the kings of England had controlled during most of the later Middle Ages were entirely lost in the course of the fifteenth

9

century. By 1500 England had been stripped of all its possessions in continental Europe, with the single exception of Calais. In 1529, Henry VIII, not known for his modesty, described himself as 'a small king in a corner' of Europe. At home, the political turmoil of the Wars of the Roses between 1455 and 1487 limited the capacity of court and nobility to exercise cultural leadership. England enjoyed fertile soils and mineral wealth, but it was thinly populated. Its population in 1500, at under two and a half million, had hardly recovered from the losses inflicted by the 'Black Death' of more than a century before. Foreigners commented on the country's natural wealth, but criticized its people's reluctance to exert themselves to enhance it.

9 King's College chapel, Cambridge, built 1446–1515. The Perpendicular style of architecture at its grandest.

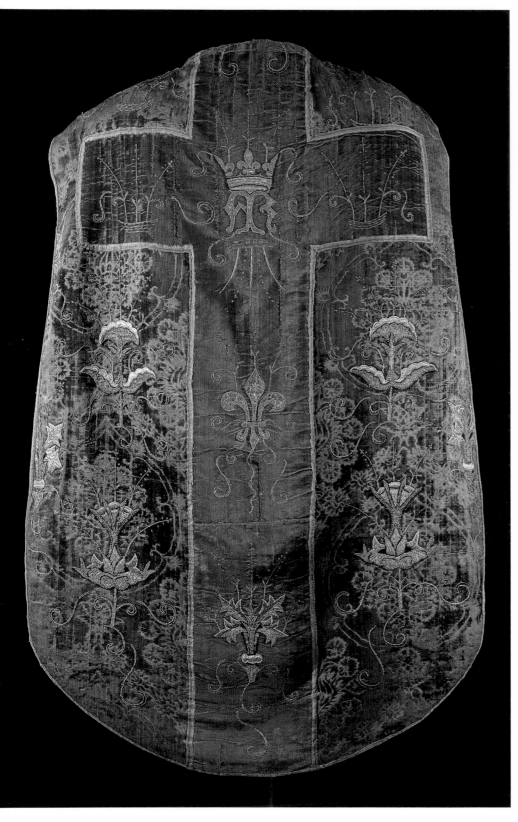

In both manufactures and trade England was underdeveloped compared with the leading European centres. Her economy was overwhelmingly agricultural and her towns were small. She was Europe's main supplier of woollen cloth, but the cloth was exported in an undyed, semi-finished state, and trade in this staple commodity was becoming entirely controlled from Antwerp. Woollen cloth was the country's only major export. The highest-quality luxury goods were largely imported. In 1436 the English were already complaining about 'the great galees of Venees and Florence' that brought 'thynges wyth whiche they fetely blere oure eye, wyth thynges not endurynge that we bye'. This flow of foreign luxuries testifies to the country's wealth and the desire of the wealthy to spend on fine goods. But to secure them the wealthy, including the King, had to rely on the skills of immigrants from continental Europe. Native English producers of such goods were largely incapable of performing to the highest western European standards of technique and aesthetic quality. The range of goods that they could make was narrow and the techniques they employed were limited. Innovation came predominantly from abroad.

10 Chasuble, 1480–1538. A pre-Reformation priest's vestment made partly of imported Italian silk. Silk velvet; embroidery on linen applied to the velvet, with silver-gilt and silk threads with sequins. The silk velvet probably made in Italy, embroidered in England. VAM Loan: Butler-Bowden.3.

11 *Henry VII*, about 1509–11. Sculpted in London by the Florentine sculptor Pietro Torrigiani. Painted terracotta. VAM A.49-1935.

12 The Heneage ('Armada') Jewel, about 1600. The medallic image portrays Elizabeth I. Gold and enamel, with diamonds and rubies. VAM M.81-1935.

3. Authority

In the course of the sixteenth and seventeenth centuries, the marginal position occupied by Britain in European cultural affairs at the end of the Middle Ages was reversed. By the early eighteenth century British makers of a range of high-design goods could perform to the highest European standards. London had become one of the continent's leading centres for design and the decorative arts. This cultural transformation did not take place in isolation. It went hand-in-hand with the rise of British political and economic influence in Europe and beyond. But Britain's acquisition of political and economic power was hard-won. Political life in Tudor and Stuart Britain was turbulent, unpredictable and could be bloody. Foreigners found British politics confusing, inconsistent and sometimes incomprehensible. 'Since the time of Queen Elizabeth,' Johan de Witt, the leading Dutch politician of his age, was quoted as saying in 1668, there had been 'only a continual fluctuation in the conduct of England, with which one could not concert measures for two years at a time'. Nevertheless, it is possible to identify three fundamental political issues that had particular significance for developments in design and the decorative arts under the Tudors and Stuarts. The first was the problem of

constitutional authority, the second the problem of religion, and the third the problem of international relations. Each was intimately linked to the others.

For most of the sixteenth and seventeenth centuries Britain was subject to a system of government in which the monarch was pivotal. Indeed, under the Tudors the powers of the English Crown increased. The experience of turmoil during the Wars of the Roses had rendered a strong monarchy attractive to many of the great landowners as a guarantee of order and privilege. In the sixteenth century persistent threats from abroad – from Scotland, France, the Pope and Spain – added to the appeal of strong leadership. The Protestant Reformation under Henry VIII made the monarch the spiritual as well as the secular head of the realm. Order and obedience became an obsession among the governing classes; the sovereign power of the monarch was exalted as the fount of all authority. By the end of the sixteenth century writers could describe the Queen, Elizabeth I, as an absolute monarch. Her successor, James I and VI, claimed to rule by divine right.

The power of the monarchy under the Tudors and Stuarts was not unlimited, however, either in theory or in practice. Even in theory, it had long been the prevailing view that England's was a mixed constitution, under which the King was expected to rule in cooperation with his subjects as represented in Parliament. That Parliament was far from being a democratically elected body, but in a rough and ready manner it did represent the wealthier and more powerful sections of the population across the realm. By continental European standards, the powers of the English Parliament were already considerable at the start of the sixteenth century. Parliament's authority grew under the Tudors, in particular because Henry VIII relied on it to force through the Protestant Reformation. By the seventeenth century, when continental monarchs increasingly chose to disregard whatever institutions existed to represent their subjects, the authority exercised by the English Parliament had become exceptional, even if it was not unique.

13 *James I and VI and his family*, 1612–14. Painted in the studios of Nicholas Hilliard and Isaac Oliver and assembled about 1625–50. These portraits were painted separately, but framed together soon afterwards. From top left: *James*; *Anne of Denmark*, his queen; *Prince Henry*, his son and heir who died in 1612; *Prince Charles*; *Frederick King of Bohemia*, his son-in-law; and *Elizabeth*, *Queen of Bohemia*, his daughter. Watercolour on vellum, in a 17th-century frame of ebony veneered onto oak. VAM P.147-152-1910.

TUDOR AND STUART MONARCHS, 1485–1714

John Styles

Henry VII   *m.*   Elizabeth of York
1485–1509   daughter of Edward IV
                   d.1503

Henry VIII
1509–47

m.

1	Catherine of Aragon m.1509, divorced 1533, d.1536	➤ **Mary I** 1553–8
2	Anne Boleyn m.1533, executed 1536	➤ **Elizabeth I** 1558–1603
3	Jane Seymour m.1536, d.1537	➤ **Edward VI** 1547–53
4	Anne of Cleves m.1540, divorced 1541, d.1557	
5	Katherine Howard m.1541, executed 1542	
6	Catherine Parr m.1543, d.1548	

James IV   *m.*   Margaret Tudor
of Scotland   d.1541
1473–1513

James V   *m.*   Mary of Guise
of Scotland   d.1560
1513–42

Mary   *m.*   Henry, Lord Darnley
Queen of Scots   d.1567
1542–68,
executed 1587

James I/James VI . . .

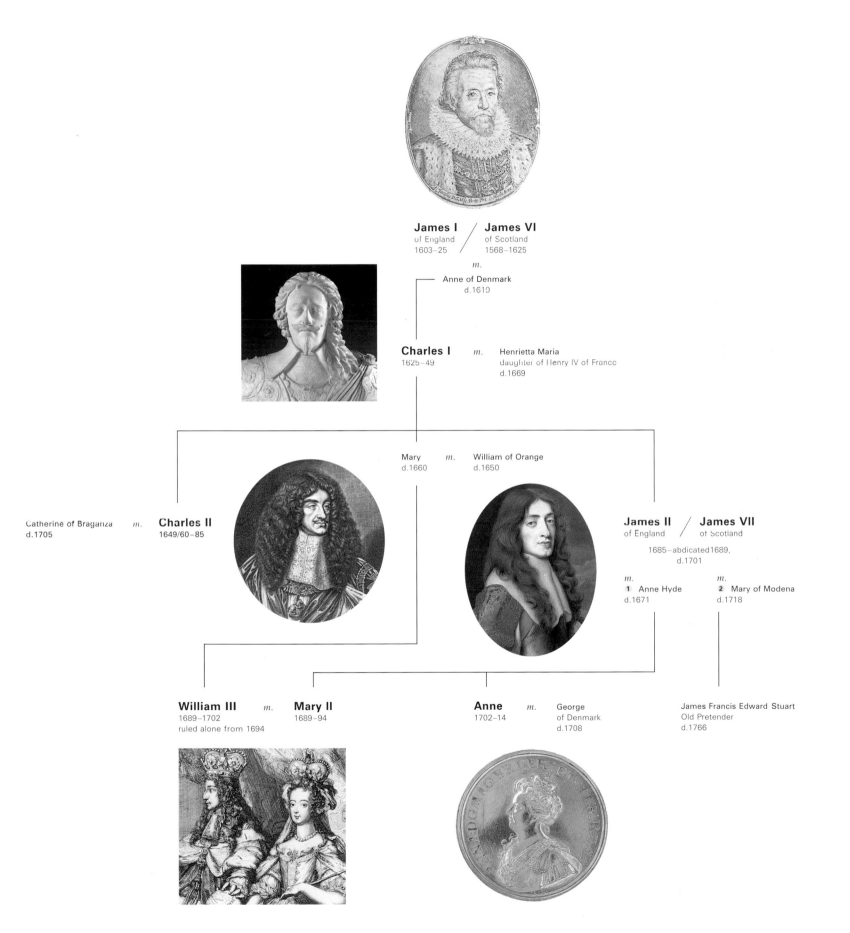

James I / **James VI**
of England / of Scotland
1603–25 / 1568–1625

m.

Anne of Denmark
d.1619

Charles I   *m.*   Henrietta Maria
1625–49   daughter of Henry IV of France
                   d.1669

Mary   *m.*   William of Orange
d.1660   d.1650

Catherine of Braganza   *m.*   **Charles II**
d.1705   1649/60–85

James II / **James VII**
of England / of Scotland

1685–abdicated1689,
d.1701

m.   *m.*
1 Anne Hyde   **2** Mary of Modena
d.1671   d.1718

William III   *m.*   **Mary II**
1689–1702   1689–94
ruled alone from 1694

Anne   *m.*   George
1702–14   of Denmark
                    d.1708

James Francis Edward Stuart
Old Pretender
d.1766

Parliament, moreover, was not the only constraint on the power of the Crown. In contrast to continental monarchs like Philip II of Spain and Louis XIII of France, the Tudors and their immediate Stuart successors in England had no professional army and no professional civil service to impose their will. For most of the period these were luxuries they could not afford. Henry VIII had inherited vast landed estates. He supplemented their income with that of the lands he confiscated from the monasteries dissolved in 1536 and 1539. But this carefully assembled royal wealth was rapidly dissipated in that most expensive of royal pursuits – warfare. Henry's own wars with France, his daughter Elizabeth's war with Spain and her campaigns in Ireland left the royal coffers almost bare. Parliament could, and did, grant additional revenue from taxation for war and other emergencies, but it did so only reluctantly and with conditions attached, which monarchs often found irksome. Nevertheless, expectations of government continued to grow, as did the cost of warfare as firearms replaced longbows and pikes. By the early seventeenth century the Stuart kings could make ends meet only if they avoided expensive wars and extravagant expenditure at court. For much of the 1630s Charles I's income was as little as one-tenth of Louis XIII's.

Charles I's ineptitude in managing these problems of royal authority and finance helped bring about the civil war of the 1640s, but neither the war nor Charles's beheading in 1649, nor even Oliver Cromwell's republican regime in the 1650s, successfully resolved them. For all the enthusiastic royalism displayed by Parliament in the aftermath of the restoration of Charles II in 1660, similar problems quickly re-emerged. They were finally resolved only after the overthrow of Charles II's brother, James II and VII, in what its victorious supporters called the 'Glorious Revolution' of 1688. James was toppled from the throne in that year by an invasion of Dutch troops led by his son-in-law, William of Orange, military leader of the Netherlands. William's

His Excellencie, Oliuer Cromwell, Generall of all the Forces of England Scotland, & Ireland, Chancelour of the Vniversity of Oxford, Lord Protector of England, Scotland and Ireland

R.G. fecit

Peter Stent Exc: 1653.

15

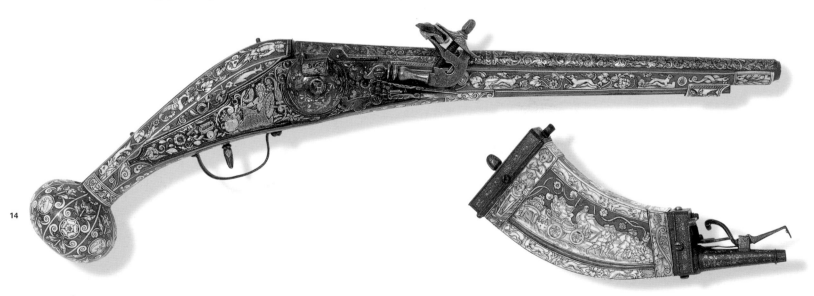

14 Wheel-lock pistol and powder-flask, about 1580. Made in England. Steel, wooden stock inlaid with engraved staghorn, and barrel mounts damascened in gold and silver. VAM M.949-1983 and M.950 1983.

15 *Oliver Cromwell*, 1653. After a drawing by Robert Gaywood. Etching. VAM E.1348-1960.

priority was to secure British support in his war with Louis XIV's France. In return for that support, he was prepared to accept a dramatic and, as it turned out, decisive tilting of the balance of constitutional authority in Britain away from the monarch towards Parliament. Henceforth British monarchs ruled on terms dictated by the legislature. Parliament had become the ultimate source of political authority. Claims to absolute monarchy and the divine right of kings could no longer be sustained. The ceremonial life of the royal court continued, but it was no longer to be the focus of authority, either political or cultural.

16 James II and VII crowned by Peace and Justice, about 1685. By Jacobus Constantin. Ivory; frame of tortoiseshell and ebony. VAM A.13-1937.

17 Terracotta model of William III, about 1695. By Jan van Nost the Elder. This figure is a model for a full-size statue of the King that was erected in 1695 at the Royal Exchange in London. Modelled terracotta. VAM A.35-1939.

For much of the Tudor and Stuart period, therefore, there was a mismatch between the authority that British monarchs believed they should exercise and their capacity to do so. This was as true of the artistic realm as it was in matters of domestic governance or foreign policy. In art, as in war, expectations were set not in Britain, but in continental Europe. Rulers in Italy, Germany, Spain and France, many of them uninhibited by the constitutional limitations that applied in England, established new and ever more costly standards of royal splendour. Renaissance and baroque kingship was extraordinarily theatrical. Monarchs and their courtiers lavished their subjects' wealth on palaces and paintings, furnishings and festivals designed to outshine their rivals, both at home and abroad. Displays of material magnificence and aloof grandeur were deliberately contrived to inspire awe, to project authority and to foster obedience. The impresarios of this orgy of courtly display were artists and craftspeople, architects and designers; its settings were royal palaces and royal progresses.

However much Britain's Tudor and Stuart monarchs aspired to match the leading European kings and emperors in splendour and magnificence, few of them succeeded. The monarch who came closest was Henry VIII, who regarded himself as the equal of major European rulers like Francis I of France and enjoyed, at some points in his reign at least, financial resources sufficient to compete aesthetically as well as diplomatically and militarily. His expensive new palaces were lavishly decorated by foreign artists, adopting elements of new styles derived from continental Europe. But in the first half of the sixteenth century the royal court numbered only about 1,000 people and the costs of international competition in architectural and artistic magnificence were still limited. None of Henry's Tudor or Stuart successors was as successful in matching the aesthetic grandeur achieved by their foremost continental rivals. Whether through lack of money, lack of will or lack of time, none of them managed to complete the building of an entirely new royal palace. Yet the physical need for such a palace became all the more pressing as the size of the court, 'greater and more gallant' than before, grew to nearly 2,000 people by the 1630s.

Of all Henry VIII's successors, it was the ill-fated Charles I who came closest to the Renaissance ideal of kingship in his aesthetic policy. Profoundly conscious of the capacity of art, architecture and design to project the dignity and majesty of monarchy, Charles built, commissioned and collected. He was himself a connoisseur and, like many of his courtiers, displayed a knowledge of continental art and design that was unprecedented in its sophistication. In 1629 the Flemish artist Peter Paul Rubens was struck by the 'incredible quality of excellent pictures, statues and ancient inscriptions

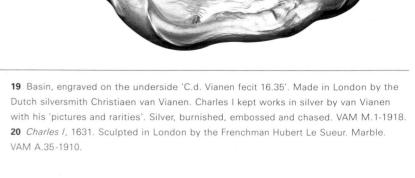

18 Writing box painted with the arms and devices of Henry VIII and Catherine of Aragon, about 1525. The figures of Venus and Mars are based on woodcuts by the German Hans Burgkmair, published in 1510. Walnut and oak lined with painted and gilded leather; later covering in shagreen. VAM W.29-1932.

19 Basin, engraved on the underside 'C.d. Vianen fecit 16.35'. Made in London by the Dutch silversmith Christiaen van Vianen. Charles I kept works in silver by van Vianen with his 'pictures and rarities'. Silver, burnished, embossed and chased. VAM M.1-1918. **20** *Charles I*, 1631. Sculpted in London by the Frenchman Hubert Le Sueur. Marble. VAM A.35-1910.

which are to be found in this court'. He found 'none of the crudeness which one might expect from a place so remote from Italian elegance'. Charles's principal designer, Inigo Jones, and other leading courtiers had been to Italy and studied Italian design. The King spent on architecture and high design even when his resources were pinched, laying out £133,000 to complete the Queen's House at Greenwich at a time in the 1630s when his debts were rising. But the money and effort that Charles invested in the aesthetics of royal power entirely failed to prevent his own downfall and, at least temporarily, that of the monarchy. Under the Cromwellian republic, royal palaces were sold off, as was most of Charles's prized collection of paintings.

21 The south front of the Queen's House, Greenwich, London, built 1616–35. Designed by Inigo Jones.

22 Cabinet, 1644–50. Made in Florence for John Evelyn with panels by Domenico Benotti and bronze plaques by Francesco Fanelli. Evelyn, an active royalist, travelled extensively in France and Italy between 1643 and 1652. In Florence he bought hard-stone floral panels and had them incorporated into this cabinet, possibly adding the bronze plaques later. Collecting was a new, fashionable activity at Charles I's court, and cabinets were display cases for art treasures and curiosities. Ebony veneer on a pine carcase with panels of pietra dura, oak drawers, gilt-bronze mounts and plaques; later brass strawberry-leaf cresting. VAM W. 24-1977.

BRITAIN AND ITS RULERS, 1485-1714

John Styles

In 1485 Henry Tudor defeated and killed Richard III at the Battle of Bosworth to become King Henry VII of England (1485–1509) and establish the Tudor dynasty on the English throne. At this date the different political entities that made up the British Isles – England, Ireland, Scotland and Wales – were politically quite distinct. England and Scotland were entirely separate kingdoms, with different royal families (the Tudors in England and the Stewarts in Scotland), although there was a long-standing claim of overlordship in Scotland by the Kings of England. Wales comprised a principality and a march under English control. The Kings of England claimed the Lordship of Ireland, but in practice their authority was limited to areas in the east and south of that country.

Two hundred and thirty years later, on the death of Queen Anne (1702–14), the last Stuart monarch, the political organization of the British Isles had been transformed. A single monarch ruled all the territories in the British archipelago and the work of governing those territories was subject to effective central oversight from London, although distinct political institutions still operated in Scotland and Ireland.

The process of integration was begun by the second Tudor King of England, Henry VIII (1509–47). Laws were made in England in 1536 and 1543 to unite England and Wales as a single kingdom. Wales was divided into counties and granted representation in the English Parliament. This was not an act of union ratified by both parties, but rather an imposition by the English of their law and customs. Wales became part of England as far as its political institutions were concerned, although the Tudors (who had Welsh roots) did go on to promote the idea of Britain, with its links to Arthurian legend and the pre-Saxon era. In addition, in 1541 Henry VIII had Ireland designated a kingdom and himself proclaimed its king. The kingdom of Ireland remained, however, an entity separate from England, with its own council, parliament and courts in Dublin. It was to remain so until the nineteenth century.

When Elizabeth I (1558–1603), the last Tudor monarch of England and Ireland, died without children, her successor was James VI of Scotland (1568–1625). He became James I of England and Ireland and anglicized the spelling of his family name to Stuart. The uniting of the Scottish and English crowns was accompanied by the use of the term 'Great Britain' to describe the new joint entity. James was anxious to move rapidly towards a full political union of the two kingdoms, to be symbolized by the creation of a new union flag combining the crosses of St George for England and St Andrew for Scotland. Various designs were proposed, but it was one that superimposed the cross of St George on the cross of St Andrew that was eventually adopted in 1606. It still forms the basis of the modern Union Jack.

Choosing a design for the new flag proved easier than creating an effective political union between the two nations. The English Parliament refused to support James's desire for steps towards a full political union of the kingdoms of England and Scotland and there the matter rested for half a century. A political union of the two countries was imposed briefly between 1654 and 1660 by the republican government of Oliver Cromwell, which came to power in the aftermath of the English civil war (1642–6) and the execution of James I's son, Charles I (1625–49). With the Restoration of the monarchy in 1660, the two kingdoms became, once again, separate entities sharing only a monarch. The final union of Scotland and England to form the kingdom of Great Britain was agreed by the parliaments of the two countries in 1707.

23. Designs for an Anglo-Scottish union flag commissioned by Lord Admiral Nottingham, about 1604. Nottingham preferred the one that showed the crosses of St George and St Andrew side by side, 'for this is like man and wife, without blemish on to other', although none of them was adopted. Pen, ink and wash. National Library of Scotland.

24

25

4. Religion

The civil war that led to Charles I's execution was not, of course, simply the outcome of long-standing constitutional tensions between Crown and Parliament. It was also the product of disagreements about religion, which were equally deep-seated. The sixteenth century saw the adoption of the reformed, Protestant form of Christianity in England, Wales and Scotland. Reformation involved a rejection of the authority of the Pope in Rome, but it did not inaugurate freedom of conscience in religious affairs. One state-enforced religious monopoly was replaced by another. The beliefs and practices of the medieval Catholic Church centred on priestly rituals employing objects and images. Protestantism substituted forms of religious observance that centred on the word of God.

At the heart of sixteenth-century Protestantism was the Bible, printed in the vernacular using the technology of movable type, itself relatively new to Britain. Reformation, especially for its most enthusiastic devotees, required the destruction of the apparatus of Catholic ritual – the smashing and confiscation of the candlesticks, statues, altars, crucifixes, vestments and chalices in which popular belief and artistic skill had been invested in the Middle Ages. Iconoclasm fostered by the new Bible-based religion was more limited in England than it was in Scotland. In England the churches were not entirely stripped of ritual objects. Indeed, many English churches at the end of the sixteenth century retained elements of the look of their Catholic predecessors. Nevertheless, the Reformation fundamentally changed the nature of the rituals in which religious objects were employed, and worked to undermine belief in their spiritual potency. By doing so, it contributed to a secularization of design and the decorative arts. Never again would church patronage and the production of religious objects loom so large in the work of both artists and designers.

Protestantism had originated in the protests against the Roman Church started in 1517 in Germany by Martin Luther. In England and Scotland the new faith was imposed on the mass of the population without their consent, but it arrived in the two countries by different means and took different forms. In Scotland, Protestantism spread among sections of the population from the 1530s, but the decisive moment came in 1560 when Protestant nobles seized control of government in an anti-Catholic revolt that led to the expulsion of the Catholic Mary, Queen of Scots. During the long minority of her young son, James VI, the ruling nobles imposed a militant Presbyterian Protestantism as the state religion. The new Scottish church was organized around congregations. It was suspicious of interference from worldly authority, whether royal or ecclesiastical, and extremely hostile to religious images and icons. In England, by contrast, the reformed church was the creation of a king – Henry VIII – who had at first been hostile to Luther. Henry's break with Rome in 1533 was driven principally by his desire to divorce his first wife,

---

24 *St Agatha and St William of Norwich*. Part of a rood screen painted 1450–70 for the Chapel of St Mary in St John's Church, Maddermarket, Norwich. In a pre-Reformation church the whole congregation looked towards the rood screen, which separated priest and altar from the people. Tempera on oak panel. VAM 24-1894.

25 Communion cup and cover, with the royal arms, with London hallmarks for 1549–50. Maker's mark of W. An early example of post-Reformation church plate, from the period when plain Protestant communion cups began to replace the ornate chalices used in the Catholic mass. Silver-gilt and champlevé enamel. VAM Loan Aldermary 1&a.

26

27

26 Title page to *The Bible in Englyshe*, 1540. Henry VIII is depicted as supreme head of the Church of England, enthroned beneath a tiny God the Father. He distributes copies of the Bible to the Archbishop of Canterbury and his chief minister, Thomas Cromwell, who pass them on to the bishops and lords. The crowds at the bottom of the page acclaim the King. Woodcut. The British Library.

27 Defaced painting of the Annunciation, 1470–90. From the Church of the Holy Innocents, Great Barton, Suffolk. Adapted from a traditional composition of the Virgin Mary enthroned, to represent the Annunciation by the addition of the words 'Ecce ancilla domini'. The careful erasing of the face may represent a post-Reformation effort to rob the traditional image of its power, while leaving it in its original position in the church. Tempera or oil on panel. VAM W.50-1921.

30

either sympathized with the outlawed Catholic faith or, in the case of James, professed it. The sons of a Catholic mother, Charles and James had spent time in exile in Catholic Europe in the aftermath of the English civil war. They were admirers of the absolutist style of baroque Catholic monarchy practised by their cousin Louis XIV in France. James's authoritarian attempt to re-establish Catholicism in the mainstream of British life led directly to his forced abdication and return to exile in the 'Glorious Revolution' of 1688.

In its aftermath the assumption that all the King's subjects must profess the same faith was abandoned. Under William and Mary, freedom of worship was extended to all Protestants. Britain became in effect a multi-denominational society. This did not mean religious equality. A state church continued to exist, enjoying enormous political, economic and organizational privileges. Other Protestant denominations had to finance their own clergy and premises. In England, the state church was Anglican; in Scotland it was Presbyterian – a cynical but realistic accommodation to national differences in theology that marked a retreat from the commitment to religious uniformity of previous generations. Henceforth even the tiny minority of Catholics, who remained subject to legal proscription, were by and large left in peace.

30 *Charles II giving audience to the Governors, masters and children of Christ's Hospital*, about 1680. By Antonio Verrio. Preliminary sketch for the 'Great Picture' at Christ's Hospital, a charity school. Oil on canvas. VAM P.2-1956.

5. Britain in the wider world

Western Europe in the sixteenth and seventeenth centuries was a dangerous place. Divided then, much more than it is now, into a multiplicity of different states, the continent was beset with rivalries and conflicts that intermingled domestic and foreign affairs in a peculiarly intimate way. Religious hostility between Protestant and Catholic was rife both within states and between them, as the Reformation swept northern Europe and the Counter-Reformation then strove to extirpate it. Absolute monarchs were pitted against representative institutions at home and abroad. In a Europe where most states were monarchies and the various royal families, disdainful of inferiors, intermarried endlessly, the claims and counter-claims of competing royal dynasties were a constant theme of domestic and international politics. Economic rivalries, driven by the spiralling costs of warfare and inspired by dreams of unimaginable riches in the newly explored world beyond Europe, led to a merging of trade, war and overseas expansion on a global scale.

The disputes over constitutional authority and religion that bedevilled Tudor and Stuart Britain were all the more potent, therefore, because they involved choices that had international as well as domestic ramifications. Choosing Protestantism came to mean antagonizing Catholic Spain, the most powerful state in western Europe in the sixteenth century, fuelled by wealth from its American conquests. Upholding a mixed, parliamentary constitution meant rejecting the alternative – the authoritarian, absolutist form of kingship, which seemed to many Europeans the most modern and effective form of government, especially as practised by Louis XIV of France in the later seventeenth century. The expansion of trade and colonies involved conflict not only with Catholic, absolutist Spain, which claimed a monopoly in the Americas, but also with the Protestant, anti-absolutist Dutch, who became the

dominant commercial power in the seventeenth century. The outcomes of these difficult and often contradictory choices were not simply religious, political and economic. For most of this period Britain played a peripheral role in the setting of international trends in design and the decorative arts. It was a taker rather than a setter of fashion and taste. Religious, economic or political choices could influence which foreign aesthetic influences prevailed in Britain – French rather than Spanish styles in dress, Protestant rather than Catholic refugee craftspeople.

Despite all the confusing twists and turns of British policy, the long-term trajectory of Britain's international position is clear enough. At the start of the sixteenth century England was a small-to-middling European power. Its only overseas territory, Calais, was lost in 1557. Britain as a whole played only a minor part in the spectacular sixteenth-century projection of European power into Africa, Asia and the Americas, which was undertaken principally by Portugal and Spain. Two centuries later Great Britain was, along with France, one of the two leading contenders for world power. Underpinned by the growth of agriculture, trade and manufactures evident from the mid-sixteenth century onwards, British military capacity began to make an impact on the world stage under Oliver Cromwell in the 1650s. After the Glorious Revolution, the new constitutional settlement enabled Britain's economic resources to be translated into military might much more effectively. By 1714, after some twenty years of warfare, the armies of the British and their allies, led by the Duke of Marlborough, had defeated Louis XIV's expansionist, aggressively Catholic France, the largest and most powerful state in continental Europe. In the course of the seventeenth century Britain had also acquired an extra-European empire – Barbados and Jamaica in the West Indies; a string of colonies along the eastern seaboard of North America, from Newfoundland in

the north to the Carolinas in the south; Bombay and Madras in India; and, early in the eighteenth century, a semi-permanent trading presence at Canton in China.

Britain's international standing in design and the decorative arts followed a parallel trajectory. At the start of the sixteenth century they exhibited a provincialism characterized by an overwhelming dependence on ideas, people and objects from the Low Countries. In the course of the sixteenth and especially the seventeenth centuries provincialism gradually came to be replaced by a cosmopolitan confidence, which saw Britain acquire, rework and increasingly re-market aesthetic ideas from across Europe and the world.

31

31 *H.M.S. Royal Prince and other vessels at the Four Days Battle, 1–4 June, 1666.* By Abraham Storck. The painting depicts a bloody engagement off the East Anglian coast between English and Dutch ships of the line during the second Anglo-Dutch War of 1665–7, one of three wars that the two countries fought in the seventeenth century for commercial and naval supremacy. Oil on canvas. © National Maritime Museum, London.

32 Printed handkerchief depicting the victories of England and her allies in the War of Spanish Succession, 1707. Lettering engraved by Robert Spofforth. After the Duke of Marlborough's military successes in 1703 and 1704 he began to be portrayed as a hero, his victories celebrated in popular prints, songs and on decorative objects. Silk, printed from an engraved plate. VAM T.85-1934.

6. Trade and manufactures

This transformation of design and the decorative arts in Britain owed much to the expansion of trade and manufactures. Britain was one of the principal beneficiaries of the broad shift in the balance of Europe's economy away from the Mediterranean towards the north-western seaboard, between the end of the Middle Ages and the beginning of the eighteenth century, reflecting the rise of Atlantic commerce and global sea routes. This brought stagnation to Venice and Genoa, boom to Amsterdam and London. Nevertheless, it was only in the seventeenth century that the impact of this shift on British commercial life became really marked. Under the Tudors, Britain's trade remained narrowly focused on the Low Countries. Her exports grew, but they continued to consist overwhelmingly of semi-finished woollen cloth. It was craftspeople and merchants in the Low Countries who undertook the immensely skilled and lucrative work of dyeing and finishing the cloth. It was their command of information about international fashion and taste that enabled them to reap the profits of supplying the finished, dyed English cloth to eager customers throughout Europe.

The Low Countries, too, were the source of most of the high-quality manufactured goods that the British imported in growing quantities in return for their cloth throughout the sixteenth century – even when, like Turkish carpets or Italian silks, they originated much further afield. It was principally through the Low Countries that the British became acquainted with Italian silks, lace, glass, tin-glazed ceramics and paper, German swords, armour and textiles, as well as a host of high-design goods made locally, including metalwares, furniture, textiles and leather goods. It is not surprising, therefore, that Netherlandish styles so dominated British design in the period, or that it was in a Netherlandish guise that the stylistic ideas of the Italian Renaissance so often arrived in Britain.

34

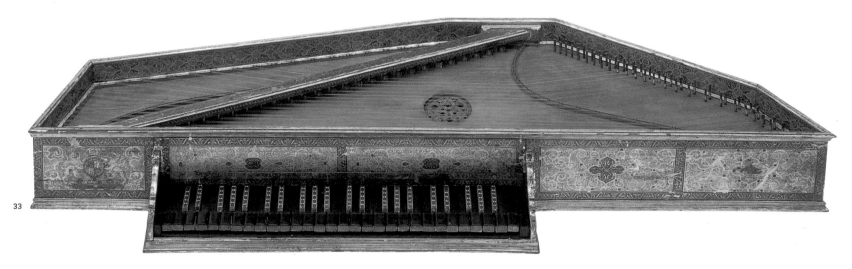

33

33 Spinet, 1570–80. Probably made by Benedictus Florianus in Venice. Possibly commissioned by Elizabeth I and popularly known as 'Queen Elizabeth's virginals'. Cypress case, soundboard and jacks, decorated with parchment, gilding, painting and inlay. VAM 19-1887.

34 Turkish 'Lotto' carpet, about 1550–90. Carpets of this kind are named after the 16th-century Italian artist Lorenzo Lotto, because they appear in some of his paintings. Hand-knotted woollen pile. VAM 903-1897.

It was from the Low Countries, too, that many of the skilled craftspeople came who began to establish the manufacture in Britain of some of the high-design goods previously imported from across the North Sea. Protestant refugees from religious persecution in Antwerp and its hinterland were particularly important in the years after 1560. British-made artefacts replaced more and more European imports, although initially not at the highest levels of the market. The later sixteenth and early seventeenth centuries saw the establishment in London of large-scale production of a wide range of new products, including drinking glasses, tin-glazed ceramics, silk cloth, coaches and watches. Yet the pool of mainly immigrant craftspeople in London, working to the highest international standards of aesthetic and technical quality, remained a small one at the start of the seventeenth century. For its supply of high-design goods, the royal court and other wealthy purchasers continued to depend heavily on imports.

Nevertheless, London was becoming an increasingly important international centre for luxury goods. In the early seventeenth century England began to participate substantially in the new intercontinental trades with Asia and the Americas, which had in the previous century been virtually monopolized by the Portuguese and Spanish. The English East India Company was founded in 1600. The first permanent English settlement in the Americas, at Jamestown in Virginia, was established in 1607. Luxury goods like Indian decorated cottons and Japanese lacquer began to arrive direct from Asia, albeit in small quantities. The playwright Ben Jonson caught the mood in an entertainment that he wrote for the opening of the New Exchange in 1609. A shopboy shouts, 'What doe you lacke? What is't you buy? Veary fine China stuffes, of all kindes and quallityes? China chaynes, China braceletts, China scarfes, China fannes, China girdles, China knives, China boxes, China cabinetts.'

As the seventeenth century progressed, the direct intercontinental trade between London and the Americas and Asia underwent massive growth. It was accompanied by a corresponding acceleration in the pace at which exotic new commodities – tobacco, sugar, coffee, tea, cotton textiles – arrived in the city. By the end of the century the re-export of exotic goods to other parts of Europe had became a significant element of Britain's trade. Britain had become one of the principal gateways through which Europeans secured the products of a wider world.

Otherwise, British exports in the seventeenth century continued to consist predominantly of woollen textiles, but there was a striking change in the kind of cloth being made and in its destination, which signalled the increasing sophistication of British manufacturing and commerce. Trade shifted away from the supply to merchants in the Low Countries of undyed, semi-finished cloth towards the export of a diverse range of lighter, often colourful finished

35 Italian silk fabric, 1600–20. The design and colouring of this silk are very similar to that of the silk used in a dress worn by Queen Anne, wife of James I and VI, as portrayed in a painting by Marcus Gheeraerts the Younger, about 1605–10. Woven silk brocaded with metal thread. VAM T.361-1970.

36 Chinese porcelain ewer with English mounts; ewer 1560–85, mounts with hallmarks for 1585–6. Porcelain was a great rarity at this period and, in common with other decorative curiosities, was often mounted in precious metal. Wanli porcelain and silver-gilt mounts. [h. 25.6cm]. VAM 7915-1862.

37 Jug, about 1620. Made in London, probably in Southwark. Tin-glazed earthenware was made in London from the 1570s, having previously been imported from Italy and the Low Countries. Tin-glazed earthenware, painted in oxide colours. [h. 32.2cm]. VAM C.5-1974.

cloths direct to new markets in Italy, Spain and Portugal. At the same time the process of import substitution begun in the sixteenth century continued. It was assisted by the continuing arrival of foreign craftspeople. They included the Protestant Huguenot refugees, exiled from Catholic France as a result of the Revocation of the Edict of Nantes in 1685, who brought new skills across the whole range of the decorative arts. With the help of these foreigners, London rapidly evolved in the course of the seventeenth century from a city with a manufacturing capacity that was limited, both in the range and the quality of its products, into a centre of production capable of performing in many manufacturing trades to the highest western European standards of technique and aesthetics, approaching the same level as, for example, Paris or Amsterdam. By the end of the Stuart era Britain was manufacturing virtually the whole range of high-design products that the country had previously imported, from stoneware to decorated cotton textiles, although there remained a few notable exceptions, such as porcelain. In addition, Britain had begun to acquire an unprecedented European-wide reputation as a leader in a range of sophisticated manufactures, most notably scientific instruments, clocks and watches.

The international standing of British manufactures at the end of the seventeenth century was summed up by the Swiss visitor Béat-Louis de Muralt. 'English artisans have acquired a great reputation in the world, in many things with reason; they excel in watchmaking, carpentry, in making saddles and all sorts of tools.' But he also noted their limitations. 'On the whole, in jewellery and all sorts of frivolities more curious than necessary, they are surpassed by the French, and for these things their masters come from Paris.'

38 Watch and case, about 1700. Made in London by Daniel Quare. Quare invented a repeating mechanism for watches, which was awarded a patent by James II. Engraved silver cases, silver dial; quarter-repeating movement with verge escapement. VAM 1362-1904.

39 *Design for a balustrade and two details for screens*, 1693. Designed by the French Huguenot ironsmith Jean Tijou (active in England 1688–1712). Engraved in London by Michael Vandergucht, a native of Antwerp, Belgium. Plate from *A New Book of Drawings, Invented and Designed by Jean Tijou*, the earliest English publication of designs for ironwork, 1693. Engraving. VAM 25082:9.

41

7. People

Britain was one of the great economic success stories of sixteenth- and seventeenth-century Europe. Trade grew, manufacturing flourished and, crucially in a country that remained predominantly rural, agriculture thrived. The population doubled to about six and a half million in 1700, but by and large the growing number of inhabitants did not outrun the country's capacity to feed itself. Yet British men and women did not benefit equally from the nation's growing prosperity. The numbers of poor and landless multiplied during the period of rapid population growth between 1550 and 1650, when resources shifted towards the better-off. But in the upper echelons of the social pyramid, among those who formed the principal market for high-design goods, the gulf between the few great noble magnates and other, lesser property owners was much less marked in 1700 than it had been in 1500.

The 160 English noble families of 1688 were just as fabulously rich as their 62 predecessors in 1559. Almost all enjoyed incomes of several thousand pounds a year. It was members of the nobility who constituted the core of the royal court. It was they who built prodigy houses on their rural estates and the great London palaces that came to line the Strand under the early Stuarts. It was they who were the leading collectors of antique and continental art and were among the earliest cultural tourists to Italy. But immediately beneath the nobility in the social hierarchy a great deal changed in the course of the sixteenth and seventeenth centuries. The numbers of lesser rural landowners – the gentry – grew faster than the nobility, while in both London and the provinces there were increasing numbers of prosperous merchants, manufacturers and professionals, whose numbers had been very small at the end of the Middle Ages. At the end of the seventeenth century the English nobility remained tiny by continental European standards, but immediately beneath it on the social

42

---

40 Printed handkerchief depicting a map of the road network of England and Wales and listing market towns and days, about 1686–8. By William Berry. The design testifies to the vitality of inland trade in the late 17th century. Silk handkerchiefs printed with non-washable printer's ink were first produced in the 1650s. Silk, printed from an engraved plate. VAM T.223-1931.

41 *Dudley, 3rd Baron North*, about 1630. By an unknown artist. Dudley North was a leading nobleman at the court of James I. Oil on canvas. VAM P.4-1948.

42 Portraits, probably of Henry Holme of Paul Holme, Yorkshire, his wife Dorothy and their two children, 1628. By an unknown artist. Provincial gentry families were often portrayed in this manner, well dressed, but not in the height of fashion. Oil on panel. VAM W.5-1951.

ladder lay the massed ranks of the moderately wealthy, who numbered many tens of thousands. With incomes at the end of the seventeenth century extending upwards from about £100 a year, their wealth might derive from land, trade or the professions. It was these people, above all, who sustained the businesses of that growing multitude of makers producing high-design objects. Already, in his *Description of England* of 1577, the social commentator and clergyman William Harrison noted that knights, gentlemen, merchants and some other wealthy townspeople far exceeded their predecessors in the ownership of luxury goods. According to Harrison, it was not unusual 'to behold generally their great provision of tapestry, Turkey work, pewter, brass, fine linen, and thereto costly cupboards of plate'.

Harrison was also struck by the growing range of decorative objects that was coming to be owned by people still further down the social scale: the group that was known at the time as the 'middling sort'. It consisted of artisans and shopkeepers, as well as the farmers who had profited from rising prices for agricultural produce. Costly household goods like silver plate and decorative woven textiles had, Harrison reported, 'descended yet lower, even unto the inferior artificers and many farmers'. Initially it was the 'middling sort' in London and prosperous parts of south-east England, like Radwinter, Harrison's own Essex village, who enjoyed these material improvements. In the course of the seventeenth century, however, they became much more widely spread across England. Even among the labouring poor, the seventeenth century saw the acquisition of a growing range of colourful clothing fabrics, as well as access to the first of the exotic new commodities from beyond Europe to secure anything resembling a mass market – tobacco.

8. Ideas

This proliferation of material possessions sat uneasily with the dictates of Christian morality. Religion infused every aspect of people's thinking about their world in the sixteenth and seventeenth centuries. There was a powerful and long-standing tradition in Christian thought that disapproved of luxury, overindulgence and wasteful expenditure on superfluities, emphasizing instead charity and the husbanding of God's gifts to mankind. Puritans, in particular, disapproved of anything that might distract attention from God. They preached relentlessly against the sins of covetousness and vanity, pride and envy, so easily aroused by the allure of worldly things, especially those that were beautiful and fashionable. This view found its most complete expression among the Quakers, the extreme (though not strictly Puritan) sect that emerged in the 1650s. Quakers refused to wear the elaborate fashions of the mid-seventeenth century, sometimes burning in public fashionable accessories like ribbons. Their insistence on plainness extended to decorative goods of all kinds. In 1656 the leading Quaker, George Fox, called on 'all you makers of images, and makers of baubles and toys to please the lusts and vanity of people' to repent, 'lest God lay you in the dust with them, and make you like unto them'.

For Protestants, of course, suspicion of ornament was fuelled by the enthusiastic use of the decorative arts by the Counter-Reformation Catholic Church on the continent. Protestants feared the visceral power of beautiful objects to lure the vulnerable into Catholic superstition. Hence the anxieties expressed in 1624 by the diplomat and art collector, Sir Henry Wotton, that 'there may be a lascivious and there may be likewise a superstitious use, both

---

43 Fragment of a wall painting, 1632. Based on a suite of prints of *The Five Senses*, engraved by Johannes Barra about 1625. Painted for William Sparrow of Park Farm, Hilton, Huntingdonshire. The well-dressed woman depicted here is indulging in the fashionable activity of tobacco-smoking. Painted plaster. VAM W.28-1946.

44 *Thomas Baker*, about 1638. Made in the Roman workshop of Gianlorenzo Bernini. It was unusual at this date for Englishmen, even wealthy ones, to have themselves sculpted by leading Italian artists. Baker was a Suffolk landed gentleman who is believed to have delivered Van Dyck's triple portrait of Charles I to Bernini in Rome and, while there, commissioned this portrait bust of himself. Marble. VAM A.63-1921.

of picture and of sculpture'. Hence the Puritan hostility to Charles I's church reforms of the 1630s. His reforms suggested an almost Catholic conviction that believers could be seduced into reverence and obedience by wrapping the sacred in beautiful things.

It should be emphasized, however, that although Puritans had profound reservations about some aspects of art and culture, particularly religious images and the theatre, these rarely extended to the decorative arts as a whole. Most Protestants accepted the God-given nature of the social hierarchy and its inequality. Even the Quaker Robert Barclay denied in 1678 that 'we intend to destroy the mutual relation that either is betwixt *prince* and *people*, *master* and *servants*, *parents* and *children*'. Most Protestants expected people to own the things that were appropriate to their stations in life. Kings were expected to be magnificent; labourers to be plain. It was extravagance, excess and overindulgence that were disapproved of. And because many Protestants believed that God rewarded those who followed him in this world as well as in the next, it was possible to interpret material well-being, whether displayed by individuals or by the nation as a whole, as the sign of a lively faith and God's providence.

45 Detail of *A Quakers' meeting*, late 17th century. Probably by Egbert van Heemskirk. This painting caricatures the Quakers' plain dress and their unusual forms of religious observance, particularly their practice of allowing women to preach. Oil on canvas. Library of the Religious Society of Friends.

46 *The dole ceremony at Tichborne House, Hampshire*, 1670. By Gillis van Tilborch. The Catholic landed gentleman Sir Henry Tichborne, his family and servants distribute bread to the local poor. The painting presents an idealization of social hierarchy in which the participants know their place and duty, and behave and dress appropriately. Oil on canvas. Tichborne Park, Hampshire.

By the later Stuart years this kind of providential justification for the ownership of fine things was supplemented by more utilitarian, secular arguments. Sometimes these were shocking in their unabashed materialism. In attempting to account for the dizzying growth of British commercial wealth in the later years of the seventeenth century, economic writers began to turn traditional Christian morality on its head. For the tea dealer and journalist John Houghton, the deadly sins could become economic virtues. 'Our high-living is so far from prejudicing the nation, that it enriches it,' he wrote in the early 1680s. 'Those who are guilty of prodigality, pride, vanity, and luxury, do cause more wealth to the kingdom, than loss to their own estates.' The most lyrical exponent of the disturbing new view that individual greed was good for national wealth was, appropriately, the leading developer of London's West End streets and squares, Nicholas Barbon. In 1690 he argued that the economy would prosper if mankind's natural propensity to acquire attractive things was accepted and encouraged:

> The wants of the mind are infinite, man naturally aspires, and as his mind is elevated, his senses grow more refined, and more capable of delight; his desires are inlarged, and his wants increase with his wishes, which is for everything that is rare, can gratifie his senses, adorn his body, and promote the ease, pleasure, and pomp of life.

It was a view that was to haunt debates about design and the decorative arts for the next century.

47 *The Yarmouth Collection*, about 1676–9. Possibly painted by the Dutch artist Peter Gerritsz van Roestraten. Commissioned by the courtier Robert Paston, first Earl of Yarmouth, of Oxnead Hall, Norfolk. The painting depicts part of Paston's spectacular collection of valuable curiosities, several of them with precious-metal mounts, in a manner that juxtaposes symbols of wealth and luxury with those representing vanity and transience. Oil on canvas. Norwich Castle Museum.

CHAPTER 2

Tudor and Stuart Britain, 1500–1714

Style

MICHAEL SNODIN

1. The Perpendicular Gothic style

The year 1503 saw the start of the most splendid royal building of the early sixteenth century, the chapel of King Henry VII at the east end of Westminster Abbey. Originally intended as a chantry chapel for the King's uncle, Henry VI, it became the burial place of a number of his successors, including his granddaughter Queen Elizabeth I. But what are we to make of the style, or look, that it presents to us? The chapel's architecture, with its wonderful fan-vaulted roof and complex exterior, is the finest surviving expression of the Perpendicular Gothic style. Perpendicular was among the last developments of the Gothic style, which, in various forms, had dominated European architecture since its birth in France in the middle of the twelfth century. However, unlike all other expressions of Gothic in England, it was not a variation on a French model, but a distinctively English development, which in the case of the chapel was designed and put together by English masons. The same cannot be said for the stained glass, which was made by Flemish painters; or for the 107 carved figures of saints, which were also made by craftspeople from the Low Countries.

The most remarkable foreign contribution, however, was the great bronze and marble tomb of Henry and his queen, centred on the altar and completed in about 1518. This was made by the Florentine sculptor Pietro Torrigiani, a pupil – with Michelangelo (whose nose he broke fighting) – of the Florentine painter Domenico Ghirlandaio. Now we might have expected an Italian sculptor to produce a work in the classically based Italian Renaissance style, which was sweeping up through northern Europe during these very years. We can certainly find Renaissance elements in the putti, figures and ornaments of the sarcophagus, as well as in the human realism of King and Queen, but there, interestingly, it stops. Taken all in all, the tomb, with its reclining figures and Perpendicular-style bronze screen, is a reflection of the Gothic style.

2

1 The Chapel of Henry VII, Westminster Abbey, London, completed 1519.

2 The tomb of Henry VII and Elizabeth of York, Westminster Abbey, London. Made by Pietro Torrigiani and completed about 1518.

2. Mixtures and changes

The stylistic mix presented by Henry VII's chapel, with its foreign and local contributions, was characteristic of much of the story of style in British design and architecture over the next 200 years. In one sense that story was already an old one, for style and design in Britain continued to reflect, as before, new ideas from continental Europe, while the flow of imported goods from abroad not only continued but increased. Thus the Tudor 'antique' work of the period of Henry VIII was dependent on Italian early Renaissance design ideas; the Elizabethan and Jacobean styles on Italian High Renaissance architectural ideas and Mannerist decorative motifs from the Low Countries; and the style of the period of Charles II and William and Mary at the end of the seventeenth century on baroque motifs from France and Holland. In another sense, however, the story was crucially different, for the two centuries from 1500 saw, for the first time, the emergence of peculiarly British varieties of style and design in which local interpretations of foreign styles displayed a new individuality and followed their own paths.

What do we mean when we talk about the style of an object? Style in the widest sense is the 'look' of something – what makes it different from other things. That 'look' has something to do with its shape (or shapes, and how they are handled), its texture and colour, or what we might now call its design.

It is also to do with its decoration, or ornamentation. In the sixteenth and seventeenth centuries ornamentation was the main element in design and the chief indicator of style. Changes in ornament are therefore the main subject of this chapter.

The rapid changes in style that we see today, as in the ebb and flow of modern fashion, might suggest that such shifts are the result of mere whim. In fact, they are usually linked to outside forces: social, ideological and economic. What happened to style in Britain between about 1500 and 1700 was no exception, and a number of major trends can be identified. Firstly, objects made in identifiable styles became available to increasing numbers of people, reflecting the gradual advance of surplus money across British society. The wooden platters, few pots and single rough chair in a typical yeoman farmer's house of about 1500 would probably not have carried any decorative motifs, but the joined furniture, pewter, ceramics and possibly even silver in such a house in 1700 would all have reflected particular styles. In addition, the house itself would probably have shown at least some of the architectural ideas visible in the great house up the road.

Secondly, over this period there was a marked increase in types of styled object, from forks to armchairs, as social etiquette (and its architectural setting) became more complex and domestic comfort increased. Matching this last

3 Swakeleys, Hillingdon, London, built 1629–38 for Edmund Wright. The house is in the 'Artisan Mannerist' style, combining several foreign influences.

trend was a move, towards the end of the seventeenth century, for the same style to be carried across objects of all types, from wallpapers to ceramics, reflecting French ideas of the totally designed interior.

Thirdly, not only were novel types of objects in demand, but the styles of these objects, and the interiors in which they were used, had to reflect the desires and social aspirations of the new consumers. At the start of the Tudor and Stuart period these styles were not the same all over Britain. In architecture, Scotland, England and Wales were distinct, while in England itself there were wide regional variations. By 1700, however, national styles had emerged, in architecture, interior decoration and movable objects, to which large numbers of consumers aspired.

5

3. Renaissance styles and the persistence of Gothic

It was not until the later 1520s that the Italian Renaissance elements first seen in the royal environment of Henry VII's chapel began to reach beyond court circles. Even then they by no means swept the board, as recognizably Gothic forms and ornamental motifs remained in use long after that date, both on their own and combined with Renaissance ideas. It is also possible to see the persistence of Gothic habits of design in the broader sense, not only in the continuing love of botanical ornament and grotesque human and animal forms, but in a persistent interest, especially up to about 1620, in dense masses of confused ornament.

Such stylistic conservatism is perhaps unexpected in the context of the boom in building and the consumption of goods after about 1570. Thus we find the linenfold panelling typical of the late-Gothic interior in about 1500 in wide use into the second half of the sixteenth century, while the shallow, four-centred arch and characteristic mouldings of Perpendicular Gothic were used in windows and doors well into the seventeenth century and in some areas, like the Cotswolds and northern England, even later. West Country stone buildings offer useful examples, combining Gothic details with simple elevations linked to symmetrical plans ultimately derived from Italian examples. The resulting building type, ideally suited to the smaller manor house,

4

4 Barrington Court, Somerset, built 1552–64, for William Clifton.

5 A cup known as the Howard Grace Cup, with London hallmarks for 1525–6. Mark of a bundle of implements. The bands of ornament are in the Renaissance style, but the cresting on the foot is Gothic. Turned elephant ivory bowl with silver-gilt mounts, set with gemstones and pearls. [h. 27.3cm]. VAM M.2680-1931.

'RENAISSANCE': CLASSICAL OR GOTHIC?

Maurice Howard

In Britain the new interest in the classical past emanating from Italy was first shown in experimentation with forms of ornament. The potential for new decorative ideas was understood long before there was a full grasp of the abstract principles of symmetry and decorum that underlay classical design. The term 'Renaissance' was not used by contemporaries in connection with this ornament, but rather the terms 'antique', 'all'antica' or 'antiques of the latest fashion'. Its formal visual vocabulary included piled-up candelabrum forms, shaped and sculpted into the new invention of the baluster, along with naked cherubs, exotic birds, military trophies, and floral and leaf ornament, especially the acanthus.

The new forms became the starting point for invention and fantasy. Wherever it first appeared, Italian ornament was squashed into irregularly shaped spaces and used alongside local forms. So the 'antique' is found cheek-by-jowl with Gothic tracery and the ogee arch. At first craftspeople in England seemed able to use new forms in a flat and decorative manner, but without restraint or any sense of the need for appropriate mouldings. This first phase was governed by the assumption that ornament had to be lavishly applied or, for small portable objects, made in highly expensive materials. Buildings of traditional design, as well as some tombs and church screens, were covered in *all'antica* ornament made in terracotta cast from moulds so that it could be replicated as much as possible. Small-scale luxury items met the demands of both courtier and merchant patrons.

6. Screen in the Bedingfield chantry chapel, St John the Evangelist, Oxburgh, Norfolk, about 1525–30. Moulded terracotta.

The language of the antique, particularly the use of column and pilaster, was used as a natural framing device in these smaller items, notably the frontispieces of books, medals, seals and small, engraved implements in gold. There was a growing awareness that the more restrained the ornament, the more dignified was its supportive role for heraldry – then the most significant message of lavish decoration. Equally contributive to the richness of new ornament at this time were motifs originating not from Italy but from the Islamic world. The 'moresque', which was associated with the Moors of North Africa who had only recently been expelled from Spain, provided a different means of covering the decorative field, with complex interlaced and knot patterns.

7. Fragment of a frieze, 1518–22. Made in London. From Suffolk Place, Southwark, London, the house of Charles Brandon, Duke of Suffolk. Terracotta. VAM A.28-1938.

8. Candle snuffers, 1547–53. Made for the Privy Council of Edward VI. Silver-gilt. VAM M.837-1928.

9. Bedpost, about 1520. Oak.
[h. 184.5cm]. VAM W.4A-1920.

10. Portion of panelling, about 1520–30. Photographed about 1899. Probably formed part of the decoration of the Abbey-house at Waltham Abbey, Essex. Oak. [h. 63.4cm]. VAM 2011-1899.

11. Stained glass showing the arms of the Piggott family, 1562. Clear, flashed and pot-metal glass painted with yellow stain and brown enamel. [h. 62cm]. VAM C.126-1929.

12. Detail of a valance from a bed, with moresque ornament, mid-16th century. Embroidered, velvet with gold thread. [h. 137.2cm]. VAM 4513-1858.

Bellin, an Italian sculptor who had also worked in France. Royal portraits contained Renaissance elements taken from illustrations in architectural books, which also supplied designs for actual ceilings. In Scotland dynastic alliances with France (King James V married two French princesses in succession) led to the French Renaissance façade of Falkland Palace, erected by French masons from 1539.

In England, in the 1540s, other French court models were being emulated. Although all such royal interiors have been lost, drawings show that they were related in design to those at Francis I's palace at Fontainebleau, which used thick, belt-like sculptural elements in a decorative form now known as strapwork. This was to dominate advanced design in Britain for the next 50 years or more, but its main source was not to be the example of the French court but innumerable printed designs coming out of Antwerp.

A little later than 'antique' work, another imported form of ornament arrived in Britain. Called the moresque, after the Muslim Moors of North Africa, it was itself an Italian adaptation of interlaced decorative patterns from the eastern Mediterranean. It was used especially for black-and-white embroidery on clothing; indeed, the first ever pattern book of designs to be

remained fashionable into the early years of the eighteenth century. In Scotland, meanwhile, a Gothic tradition of building, combined with ideas brought directly from French manor houses and châteaux, created a distinct 'Scottish Baronial' style.

By the same token, half-timbered buildings – which, with their elaborate and striking black-and-white pattern effects in wood and plaster, we now think of as typically Tudor – owed nothing (except sometimes their carved details) to ideas from abroad, but were developed from earlier medieval forms of house building. What made them typical products of the Tudor (and Jacobean) age was their extravagance of effect and delight in elaboration, reflecting the desire of their builders to show off their new-found wealth.

In English court circles Renaissance decorative elements were part of a battle for splendour, in which courts all over Europe took part, taking their lead from France (which had itself invaded Italy). Thus at the Field of Cloth of Gold, in 1520, the camps of King Henry VIII and the French King, Francis I, displayed a true unity of style in their Italian tents and temporary palaces (*see 3:10*). The painter Hans Holbein the Younger, brought to England twice by Henry VIII (in 1526 and from 1532), designed jewellery, silver and other precious objects in a German version of the Italian style. The exterior walls of Henry's palace of Nonsuch were sheathed in a dazzling system of painted stucco reliefs of classical figures and carved slate ornament made by Nicholas

13 Craigievar Castle, Grampian region, built 1610–26 for William Forbes. French angle turrets with conical roofs and gables combine with the Scottish tower-house form.

14 *Design for moresque ornament.* 1548. From *Morysse and Damashin renewed and encreased Very profitable for Goldsmythes and Embroderars* by Thomas Geminus. Engraving. VAM 19009.

15

published in England was a book of moresques aimed at embroiderers and goldsmiths. The book was put out in 1548 by Thomas Geminus, an artist from France, who had arrived in England in about 1540. Moresque became the chief ornament on the standard model of communion cup developed after the Reformation. Copied from secular drinking cups from Germany and Flanders, these were very different from the chalices of the Catholic Church, from whose melted silver they were made, and a rare instance of the new Renaissance style being used as a signal of change and reform.

15 *Design for an interior*, about 1545. Intended for Henry VIII, perhaps for Whitehall Palace, London. The figures and strapwork are very similar to work carried out for King Francis I at Fontainebleau: it is drawn in the French style and may show work to be carried out by French craftspeople. Pen and ink. Musée du Louvre.

4. Going classical

The years around 1550 saw the beginnings of a greater interest in the true nature of classical design in architecture, with its emphasis on proportion, symmetry and balance, and the systematic use of the classical orders. In 1550 the Duke of Northumberland sent John Shute, a painter and member of his household, to Rome to 'confer with the doings of the skilful masters in architecture, and also to view such ancient monuments thereof as are still extant'. In 1563 Shute published the *First and Chief Grounds of Architecture*, the first architectural book in English. It was but a weak reflection of what might have been. A slim volume, published too late, it was largely derived from other architectural works, especially those of the Italian architect Sebastiano Serlio, whose illustrated architectural publications, put out between 1537 and 1551, were among the most influential in Europe.

By contrast, direct experience of contemporary French classical building was probably the chief spur behind the design of Somerset House in London, built from 1547. Although composed in a traditional Tudor Gothic manner, its façade on the Strand (made of stone rather than brick) was the first classically proportioned symmetrical structure in England (*see 3:23*). Its pedimented windows were arranged symmetrically and not according to internal needs. At the centre was a gatehouse based on a Roman triumphal arch, with the classical orders correctly disposed. The general flavour, however, was French.

For all its pioneering elements, Somerset House was a rather unsatisfactory composition. Longleat in Wiltshire, one of the earliest of the great 'prodigy houses' built by the nobles and new magnates of the Elizabethan and Jacobean period, is by contrast a masterpiece of symmetry, balance and control, with its four glittering façades – at least half glass – all turned outwards.

16 View of Longleat House, Wiltshire, 1678.
By Jan Siberechts. The house was built in
1567–80, incorporating work from 1554 for
Sir John Thynne, with the masons Robert
Smythson and Allan Maynard. Oil on canvas.
Government Art Collection.

Longleat was the first great house to abandon the inward-turning courtyard plan for something recognizably modern. With its sparse French-style ornament, it was a model of restraint compared with later prodigy houses like Burghley, near Stamford (begun in 1575), and Wollaton Hall in Nottinghamshire (begun in 1580). These displayed outside, and more especially inside, a delight in densely applied integrated ornament that was unparalleled up to the nineteenth century (which, interestingly enough, saw an intense revival of interest in the 'Elizabethan' style), with the aim of producing maximum splendour.

5. Flemish Mannerism

At Wollaton, a plan taken from Serlio was combined with a mass of crestings, turrets and applied ornament that are classical in detail. Taken together, they nevertheless manage to suggest a castle out of an Arthurian romance, matching the chivalric mood of Queen Elizabeth's court. The idea of massed and confused ornament was, however, not in itself some sort of revival of medieval forms, for this approach to design was a characteristic of the Mannerist style sweeping northern Europe, driven by the designers and architects of Antwerp, then its commercial centre.

In Britain Mannerism not only found its way on to and into prodigy houses, but could just as easily be used for silver, jewellery, textiles, carved woodwork, moulded plaster, book title-pages, church monuments and even garden design. Indeed, the earliest surviving appearance of the style in England was in silver, in a ewer made in 1554, probably by one of the many Flemish craftspeople at work in London; similar ewers, made in Flanders, were in the royal collection by 1550. The style continued in many fields, including architecture, in a progressively simplified form, up to the 1620s; and in furniture made in the north of England even longer.

---

17 The east front of Wollaton Hall, Nottinghamshire, built 1580–8. Designed by Robert Smythson for Sir Francis Willoughby.

18 The Wyndham ewer, with London hallmarks for 1554–5. Mark of intersecting triangles. Silver gilt. [h. 35cm]. The British Museum.

JACOBEAN EXTRAVAGANCE

Maurice Howard

Well-established, inherited stylistic conventions dominated royal patronage during the early years of the Jacobean court. On the accession of James VI of Scotland to the throne of England, as James I in 1603, his consort, Anne of Denmark, inherited the vast wardrobe of Elizabeth I. Court fashions, especially the French farthingale for women's dress, remained unchanged for more than 15 years, probably because of this legacy. In buildings, the lead was at first taken by great courtiers rather than by the Crown. In 1607 James forced the swap of the old royal palace of Hatfield for the most glamorous of all late-Elizabethan courtier houses, Lord Burghley's Theobalds in Hertfordshire.

This dependence on the Elizabethan past, but regrouped to create ever-richer effects, is reflected throughout the decorative arts of the period. The great pattern books of the 1580s and 1590s, especially those of the German Wendel Dietterlin and the Netherlander Hans Vredeman de Vries, remained major source books. In architecture, work on churches, civic buildings, country houses and the colleges at Oxford and Cambridge often concentrated the most elaborate effects on entrance porches, where the classical orders were multiplied and stacked on top of each other to frame the heraldry of either individuals or institutions.

In his portraits, Richard Sackville, the third Earl of Dorset, exhibited his lifestyle and his patronage, both key features of contemporary extravagance. He continued the great schemes of decoration and furnishing begun by his grandfather, the first Earl, at the family seat of Knole in Kent. He spent enormous sums in London, a magnet for all aspiring young courtiers, where, as his wife noted in her diary, 'He went much abroad to Cocking, to Bowling Alleys, to Plays and Horse Races.' He dressed lavishly to match, as recorded in the more than 100 items in his wardrobe inventoried in 1617, the year after his death.

The last decade of James's reign, after about 1615, was to see significant changes in fashion, as discerning and well-travelled patrons like the second (Howard) Earl of Arundel and the first Duke of Buckingham shaped new tastes in collecting and commissioning painting. And the work of Inigo Jones, with his scrupulous examination of Italian classical and Renaissance architecture, initiated a new phase in the country's absorption of foreign styles of building.

19. The loggia at Hatfield House, Hertfordshire, about 1611. Possibly designed by Inigo Jones for Robert Cecil, first Earl of Salisbury.

20. Reproduction of a ewer in the form of a leopard of 1600-1, made for Queen Elizabeth I; the original in the Kremlin, Moscow. Made by Elkington's of Birmingham in 1884. Electrotype. [h. 93cm]. VAM M.51-1996.

22. The great staircase at Knole, Kent, 1605–8. Made for Thomas Sackville, first Earl of Dorset. Probably painted by Paul Isaacson. The paintings represent the Ages of Man and the Virtues. They and the ornament are adapted from Flemish prints.

21. *Richard Sackville, third Earl of Dorset*, 1616. By Isaac Oliver. Watercolour on vellum, stuck to card. VAM 721-1882.

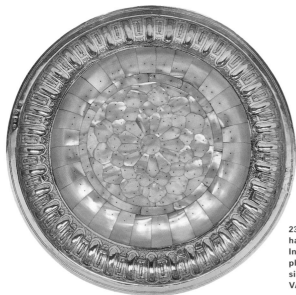

23. Bowl, with London hallmarks for 1621–2. Indian mother-of-pearl plaques, mounted in silver-gilt. [diam. 33.9cm]. VAM M.17-1968.

24. Basin, with London hallmarks for 1607–8. Sponsor's mark 'RS' over a device in a plain shield. Silver-gilt. [diam. 56.7cm]. VAM M.6-1961.

25

The Antwerp style brought with it the notion that architectural treatments could be applied to objects other than architecture. This can be seen especially clearly in furniture, particularly large fixed pieces like beds and court cupboards. In silver, salts were architecturally treated, and classical obelisk finials marked out a distinct group of vessels now known as 'steeple' cups, created to make an effect on architecturally designed dining-room buffets (*see 5:70*).

By the same token, a unified style was brought to the decoration of rooms through the introduction of classical architectural elements. The Bromley by Bow room (from the 'Old Palace' at Bromley by Bow, London, and now in the Victoria and Albert Museum), created in about 1606, is typical, with its panelling set off by decorated pilasters – all, however, put in the shade by the dominating chimneypiece and elaborate plaster ceiling. Such architectural elements would also have been echoed in the motifs found on tapestries and hanging painted cloths that gave these rooms warmth. At Hardwick Hall in Derbyshire are tapestries dating from before 1591 specially woven to size in Flanders to fit above the panelling that was characteristic of the English interior, reminding us that many objects in the new style must have been imported.

The rich density of ornament that characterized strapwork was typical of the whole approach to style around 1600. The same density characterized the flat patterns of fruit and flowers in sprigs and continuous foliage that continued to be popular into the eighteenth century. Although this botanical ornament absorbed from time to time ideas from the mainstream of European ornament, it never quite threw off a love of detail over proportion, which sometimes gave it the naïve quality of folk art. This was probably a true reflection of its use on objects that were at one remove from the highest status, including painted cloths, wall paintings, carved or painted oak, delftware, pewter, beadwork and, above all, embroidered and other worked textiles, the last of which were often made by amateurs following printed and other patterns.

We know very little of how people regarded these new styles, or indeed of attitudes to style in general, although old-fashioned styles were sometimes used to convey traditionalist meanings. Inventories, such as those listing silver, show clerks abandoning the catch-all 'antique work' (for the earlier Renaissance style) and noting down 'crotiske' (grotesque work), personages, marine subjects or snails in their efforts to encompass the complexities of Flemish Mannerism. Far more attention was devoted to recording coats of arms, reflecting the general interest in signs, symbols, emblems and complex devices that dominated European culture. This stimulated the incorporation into Mannerist ornament of allegorical and other figures and figurative scenes on surfaces of all kinds, from silver to wall painting. Such scenes formed part of a complex programme of meaning that was intended to be consciously 'read' by the visitor.

The essential elements of the Mannerist style were strapwork and the moresque, combined with the classical grotesque – a framework of plants and fantastic and other creatures derived from ancient Roman wall paintings. The grotesque had re-emerged as a decorative device in Rome in about 1500, with the discovery of these paintings, and was further developed by Raphael and his school in the decorations of the Vatican in the 1520s. It became the basis of most European flat decoration up to the start of the nineteenth century. The heavy strapwork grotesques of Fontainebleau were developed in Antwerp in the 1540s into a dense, all-over system of real or fictive three-dimensional ornament of immense versatility. While many of the craftspeople and decorators using this complex style came from abroad, the real secret of its widespread use in Britain, especially in architecture and interior decoration, lay in the fact that it was frequently copied or adapted from the prints of ornament that were pouring out of Antwerp.

25 Panel, about 1590–1610. With strapwork in the form of a grotesque, this is similar to a design by Hans Vredeman de Vries, published in *Exercitatio Alphabetica Nova et Utilissima*, Antwerp, 1569. The arms are of the Moule family of Northampton and the Hawkins family of Rushall, Staffordshire. Carved and painted oak, the paint not original. VAM 404-1872.

26 Part of a room, 1606. From the 'Old Palace' at Bromley by Bow, London. Oak, limestone and plaster. VAM 248-1894.

27 Woman's jacket. Made about 1610, altered about 1620. Worn by Margaret Laton, wife of Francis Laton, Master Yeoman of the Jewel House during the reigns of James I and VI, Charles I and Charles II (*see 4:41*). The embroidered design is taken from printed pattern books and herbals, but was probably by a professional embroiderer. Linen, embroidered with silver and silver-gilt thread, coloured silks, sequins, bobbin lace and spangles. VAM T.228-1994.

28 Spice bowl, with London hallmarks for 1573–4. Mark of RF, possibly for Roger Flynt. From a set of dessert plates engraved with scenes from the story of Abraham. This one, 'The Triumph of Isaac', was taken from a print in the engraved set *The Triumph of Patience*, 1559, by Maarten van Heemskerk. The borders were copied from other prints. Engraved silver-gilt. VAM M55:B-1946.

'THE GREAT BED OF WARE'

Maurice Howard

29. The Great Bed of Ware, about 1590–1600. Oak, carved and originally painted, with panels of marquetry; modern textile hangings. [h. 267cm]. VAM W.47-1931.

This celebrated bed takes its name from the town of Ware in Hertfordshire. It was perhaps made for a country house, but more probably for one of the great inns at Ware, a busy staging post on the north road out of London. By 1596, when it was adorning such an inn, it was famous enough to be mentioned by a German visitor to England, while Shakespeare refers to it in *Twelfth Night*, which was first performed in 1601. The bed, twice the size of any other great bed of the period, is rumoured to have slept half a dozen couples, yet it shares both form and decoration with more normal beds of the period.

Unlike today, beds were highly prized. They were the site of some of the most significant events of people's lives, often made to celebrate a marriage, accompanied by the ritualistic but ribald ceremony of 'bedding' the newly-weds. Childbirth, too, was attended by celebrative ritual. Among the upper classes, witnesses at the birth were a necessary proof of legitimacy. At the close of life, to die with dignity and appropriate leave-taking in your own bed afforded a welcome degree of control over death. In the royal palaces, distinguished foreign visitors would be shown beds in which kings and queens had died.

The style and content of the decoration of beds was therefore of great significance. Their overall architectural form and decorative elements were taken from the repertoire of Flemish Mannerism. Their carving, inlay and colour combined to give them an exceptional richness and ritualistic significance. Originally richly painted (although only traces now remain), the bed of Ware would also have been lavishly dressed with hangings. When closed, these created a room within the greater room, with the corners of the bed, half-concealed, half-revealed, forming the boundary between public and private worlds.

30. *The Life and Death of Sir Henry Unton* (detail), about 1596. By an anonymous artist. Oil on panel. National Portrait Gallery, London.

The foreposts of the bed of Ware are virtuoso pieces of woodcarving from which decorated columns rise up to support the tester. At the other end, the corners of the headboard display satyrs: half-human, half-animal forms surmounting mask-like heads, indicating the potential for sexual pleasure and procreation.

On the bedhead itself, one female and two male terminal figures frame panels of marquetry inlay with perspective scenes of fantastical architecture, derived from prints after the Netherlandish designer, Hans Vredeman de Vries.

31. Detail of the headboard of the Great Bed of Ware, about 1590–1600. The marquetry decoration derived from engravings after designs by Hans Vredeman de Vries.

32. Satyr figure on the Great Bed of Ware, about 1590–1600.

6. Inigo Jones and the revival of classicism

With few exceptions, the buildings and artefacts we have discussed so far used the ancient classical orders and ornament as a decorative device, a glorious mix-and-match, in their striving for maximum splendour. The idea that such classical elements were part of a system dependent on balance and proportion was of course well known, but was either ignored or adapted to fit local customs. It is against this background that we must see the architectural and stylistic innovations of Inigo Jones. The first British architect and designer of international significance in our story so far, his life and career are more fully described in Chapter 3. Jones's two trips to Italy (before 1603 and in 1613–14) enabled him to experience Italian architecture at first hand, notably that of his hero, the sixteenth-century architect Andrea Palladio.

Placed in charge of the royal buildings from 1615, Jones immediately started designing and erecting buildings that showed a profound understanding of the principles of classical architecture. For the first time in Britain, buildings were designed from the ground up, as unified three-dimensional compositions, their plans and exteriors properly coordinated. The earliest of these was the Queen's House at Greenwich, begun in 1616 but not completed until the 1630s (*see 1:21*). The second, the Banqueting House at the Palace of Whitehall, was built in 1619–22. Even in its earliest form, the Queen's House, at Greenwich, with its unadorned walls and carefully spaced windows, was startlingly plain – we need only compare it with Charlton House nearby, built a little earlier.

34

33

In fact contemporary commentators failed to spot its revolutionary aesthetic qualities, one describing the Queen's House as 'some curious device of Inigo Jones' – in other words, one of those occasional buildings (like the earlier Lyveden New Bield in Northamptonshire) that was intended to convey hidden messages through their odd design.

The Banqueting House, which today hardly draws a glance embedded in the rather monotonous classical grandeur of Whitehall, was equally revolutionary. For the first time the façade of a complete building was controlled by correctly composed, superimposed classical orders. It was developed from a *palazzo* design by Palladio. The interior was no less remarkable. The single room, a vast galleried hall in the proportions of a double cube, like the basilica form advocated by Palladio following the ancient Roman architect Vitruvius, was the first great classical space to be made in Britain (*see 3:40*).

33 The west front of Charlton House, Greenwich, London, built 1607–12 for Sir Adam Newton, tutor to Henry, Prince of Wales.

34 The Banqueting House, Whitehall, London, built 1619–22. Designed by Inigo Jones.

During Jones's lifetime (he died in 1652) his style was very largely restricted to the court and its circles. However, in the theatre and its close relation, interior decoration, Jones's work for the court had a major national effect. For these areas he developed a style that combined ideas from late sixteenth-century Italy and mid-sixteenth-century France, the latter taken largely from prints. After the arrival in 1625 of Henrietta Maria, daughter of the King of France, a significant modern French element was imported, not only in the form of artists and craftspeople, but in terms of style. Interiors took on elements, often very literally translated, from the early baroque style that was emerging in France on the back of ideas from Italy. While very few such interiors by Jones survive, the work of his pupil John Webb is instructive. For the famous double-cube room at Wilton House near Salisbury, made in 1649, Webb designed a space richly French in style, with panelled walls and a deeply coved ceiling painted with figure scenes and swags of flowers and fruit, all to become major themes over the next 50 years.

35 *Design for a chimneypiece at the Queen's House, Greenwich*, London, 1636. Designed by Inigo Jones in the French style. Pen and ink. RIBA Library Drawings Collection.

36 The double-cube room, Wilton House, Wiltshire, made about 1649. Designed by John Webb. The ceiling cove painted by Edward Pierce.

A good idea of the French-influenced court style of the 1630s at a slightly more modest level is to be obtained at Ham House, London, decorated for William Murray, Gentleman of the Bedchamber to Charles I and first Earl of Dysart, with its French ceremonial staircase (one of the first in England) and its painted decoration by Franz Cleyn from Germany. Cleyn also designed furniture carrying Jones's characteristic mask motifs, and the tapestries for the London tapestry works at Mortlake, founded in 1619. The tapestries and Cleyn's own ornament prints show the same type of smoothed-out grotesque ornament as at Ham, and reflect the fleshy, fat cartouches characteristic of the auricular style, which began in Holland in about 1600 and was named after its resemblance to the forms of the ear. This style was especially promoted by the van Vianen goldsmithing family of Utrecht, one of whose members, Christiaen, came to London in about 1630 to work for Charles I and returned in 1660. The auricular style continued to be popular until after 1660, becoming incorporated into mainstream baroque botanical ornament, especially in carving in both stone (church monuments) and wood, notably in the so-called 'Sunderland' picture-frame type.

By the 1650s the French-style elements of the Jonesian interiors had spread well beyond court level to gentry houses far from London, no doubt aided by a set of prints first published by Cleyn and the painter Edward Pierce the Elder (who had worked for Jones) in 1640. This combined style was, however, most clearly shown in the work of immigrant artists, such as the tomb of the Duke of Buckingham in Westminster Abbey, carved by Isaac Besnier, with bronze work by the sculptor Hubert le Sueur.

37 Chair, about 1625. Possibly designed by Francis Cleyn. The design is based on Italian models. Carved oak and beech, with traces of gilding. VAM W9-1953.

38 Standish (inkstand), with London hallmarks for 1639–40. Mark of AI, possibly for Alexander Jackson. Probably made in the London workshop of Christiaen van Vianen. Silver. VAM. Anonymous loan.

40

7. 'Artisan Mannerism'

Outside court circles, architecture from the 1620s to the 1640s was experiencing the gradual spread of Mannerism from the great prodigy houses to smaller country houses, and finally to street architecture in towns. But the forms were changing under the impact of new ideas. In London the newest buildings were of brick and were more regular and symmetrical in their proportions. Both owed much to royal proclamations on building begun by James I and VI, who declared in 1615 'that we found our cities and suburbs of sticks and left them of brick, being a material far more durable, safe from fire and beautiful and magnificent'. The proclamations, administered and devised in detail by Jones and the Commissioners of New Building of the 1630s, ordained specifically classical forms, such as windows taller than they were broad. But in areas without such controls, timber buildings became ever larger and more elaborate and remained Jacobean in style. The new London houses were built with shaped scrolling gables and 'pergulas' (iron balconies), an innovation from Italy, both developments perhaps first introduced by Jones (*see 2:3*).

His influence also lay behind the building of the first English terraced houses, a row in London's Great Queen Street erected in 1637, evidently inspired by his arcaded building at Covent Garden. The giant classical pilasters on their façades were widely copied and can still be found on the front of Lindsey House in Lincoln's Inn Fields, a remarkable survivor of about 1640. The interiors of such houses might contain elements in the Jacobean style mixed with more recent notions.

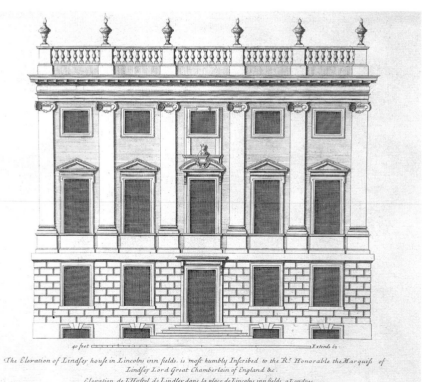

The Elevation of Lindsey house in Lincolns inn fields. is most humbly Inscribed to the R! Honorable the Marquiss of Lindsey Lord Great Chamberlain of England &c.
Elevation de L'Hostel de Lindsey dans la place de Lincolns inn fields a Londres.
In: Campbell Delin:

41

---

39 The staircase, Ham House, London. Built 1637–8.

40 Design for a frieze, 1668. Copied from a frieze design by Edward Pierce the Elder from a set first published in 1640. Published by Edward Tooker. Engraving. VAM E.3617-1907.

41 *Lindsey House, Lincoln's Inn Fields, London*, built about 1640. Plate from *Vitruvius Britannicus* by Colen Campbell, second edition 1725 (first published 1715). Lindsey House was in 1715 believed to have been designed by Inigo Jones. It was perhaps designed by the sculptor/mason Nicholas Stone, a friend of the owner of the house, Sir David Cunningham. Engraving. VAM 64.H.93.

THE BAROQUE IN ENGLAND

Tessa Murdoch

As heir to the English throne, Charles II spent 12 years in exile absorbing continental design, which was then developing into the baroque style. On his Restoration in 1660, he embarked on the refurbishment of his royal palaces. The architect Hugh May, who also spent four years in Holland, was responsible for Windsor Castle. The Royal Chapel there, said to be the finest baroque interior in England, was painted by the Italian artist Antonio Verrio in *trompe l'oeil* with twisted columns framing scenes of the Last Supper and Christ healing the sick, below a cloud-filled ceiling depicting the Resurrection. The decorative painting appeared to dissolve the rectilinear structure of the building. In the same way, the dramatic baroque portrait of the monarch by the French sculptor Honoré Pelle invades the viewer's space with its twisted pose and dramatic swirling drapery.

An interest in technical developments promoted the use of characteristic baroque forms. Lathe-turning produced spirally twisted forms in wood, which were used as effective supports for furniture and architectural

47. *Charles II*, 1684. By Honoré Pelle. Carved in Genoa. Marble. [h. 128.9cm]. VAM 239-1881.

woodwork. A general fascination with artistic virtuosity aided the career of the young Dutch-trained carver Grinling Gibbons, who provided naturalistic decoration for both secular and ecclesiastical interiors. Also inspired by continental example, the practice of marquetry, introduced in the 1660s, provided a novel form of decoration for furniture, imitating the Italian use of inlaid hardstones, yet satisfying contemporary interest in the texture of native woods.

In the 1690s the role of court designer became, in imitation of the French example, an important means of ensuring unity of design across interiors. Daniel Marot, designer to William and Mary, guided the production of decorative painting, sculpture, furnishings, upholstery and ceramics. Courtiers swiftly imitated the royal example. In upholstered furniture, richness of colour and texture was impressively combined with new forms. Continental craftspeople settled in Britain, bringing innovative styles and standards of excellence. They were eagerly commissioned by the monarchs, their courtiers, officers of state and military leaders.

46. Musical trophy, about 1692. Designed and carved by Grinling Gibbons, at Petworth House, Sussex. Limewood.

48. Table, the top showing a view of Wingerworth Hall, Derbyshire, about 1674. Made to commemorate the marriage of Sir Henry Hunloke and Katherine Tyrwhitt in 1673/4. Elm and walnut veneer with marquetry of various woods on oak and pine carcase. VAM W.53-1948.

49. Settee, 1690–1700.
From Hampton Court,
Herefordshire. Walnut legs,
the frame upholstered in
embroidery of wool and silk,
the back and sides covered
in glazed wool; cushions
lined with kidskin, and silk
trimmings. [h. 137.8cm].
VAM W.15-1945.

50. Cabinet, about 1700.
Possibly made in London
by John Byfield. Made
to commemorate the
marriage between
Margaret Trotter and
George Lawson, probably
for East Harsley Castle,
Yorkshire. Walnut veneer,
marquetry of burr walnut,
sycamore, holly, pine and
oak carcase. [h. 240cm].
VAM W.136-1928.

Baroque architecture became fully
developed in the early eighteenth century. Sir
Christopher Wren's St Paul's Cathedral was
completed in 1710; other London churches
included Nicholas Hawksmoor's Christ Church,
Spitalfields (1714–29) and James Gibbs's St
Martin-in-the-Fields (1722–6). Great houses
built for the nobility included the palace-like
Castle Howard, described by its architect
Sir John Vanbrugh as 'the top seat and garden
in England'.

51. The Royal Chapel,
Windsor Castle, Berkshire.
Designed by Hugh May,
the painted decoration by
Antonio Verrio, about
1675–84. Watercolour by
Charles Wild, 1815–18
© The Royal Collection.

Catherine of Aragon. He became supreme governor of a church that retained a full ecclesiastical hierarchy with most of its powers. The King's commitment to Protestant ideas remained half-hearted. For the rest of the sixteenth century the reformed English church continued to display many features that disappointed Protestant militants.

It was governments that set the process of Reformation in motion, but, on both sides of the Anglo-Scottish border, inculcating Protestant belief among the population at large took time. Despite sustained persecution, pockets of Catholic resistance persisted, especially where local lords and gentry remained loyal to the old faith. Nevertheless, by the early seventeenth century large sections of the population of both countries were coming to consider themselves Protestants. In the face of bitter hostility from the Catholic powers of Europe – especially Spain – English popular nationalism began to take on that aggressively Protestant aspect that was to persist into the twentieth century. Foreigners came to regard the people of Britain as stridently Protestant. Protestant refugees, including many skilled craftspeople, flocked to Britain to escape persecution by Catholic rulers on the continent.

But the Reformation's legacy in terms of organization and doctrine was an inconsistent one. The militantly Presbyterian state church in Scotland existed alongside a hierarchical English church in which Protestant beliefs of various degrees coexisted, sometimes uneasily. In a world where it was commonly believed that good government required the enforcement of religious truth, these inconsistencies were disturbing. The union of the crowns of England and Scotland in 1603 highlighted them. The accession of Charles I, a king of deeply autocratic instincts, rendered them unsustainable. Charles sought to impose on both the English and Scottish churches a form of high-church Protestantism that extolled hierarchy, ritual and the divine right of monarchs. It involved a renewed emphasis on the trappings of worship, as opposed to preaching the word of God. This version of Protestantism, though still distinct from the Roman faith, did not seem very different from Catholicism to Scottish Presbyterians and their ultra-Protestant

sympathizers in England, the Puritans. Their concern was heightened by the success in turning back the tide of Protestantism enjoyed by a re-invigorated, Counter-Reformation Catholicism on the continent. British Protestants' suspicion of a Catholic conspiracy at Charles I's court was reinforced by Charles's marriage to Henrietta Maria, a French Catholic princess, for reasons of international dynastic politics. Hostility and paranoia provoked by Charles's religious policy, especially in Scotland, helped precipitate the civil war.

The religious policies of the Puritan victors in the civil war were no more successful than those of their royal predecessors, and they lost many supporters both by tolerating Protestant extremists and by attempting to reform morals and manners. With the restoration of Charles II in 1660, his father's brand of high-church Protestantism was re-established as the doctrine of the Church of England, to wide acclaim. It was soon to find impressive physical expression in Wren's new London churches. The Puritans and others, like the Quakers, who could not stomach the new religious order withdrew from the Church of England to establish their own dissenting congregations, which faced intermittent persecution. They comprised perhaps one-tenth of the population. Yet at the same time the two men who were the supreme rulers of the Church of England between 1660 and 1688, Charles II and James II and VII,

28

29

By the 1640s dense, three-dimensional vegetable ornament had become the leading theme in France and was used in a new type of rich but soberly designed interior, ultimately derived from Italian baroque examples. By the 1660s this design approach had become the official French style, in Paris and at Versailles, and was playing a key role in the propaganda for Louis XIV. It was this interior style, which combined botanical (and especially leaf) ornament in plaster and carved wood with figurative wall and ceiling painting showing allegorical or symbolic subjects, that was taken up in Britain in the 1660s in direct emulation of the court of Louis. It is significant that it was at this moment that the London publisher John Overton chose to reissue sets of leaf ornament by Edward Pierce the Elder and others, as well as a copy (in 1672) of a set of acanthus scrolls first published in Italy in the 1620s.

This period saw the height of development of the panelled interior, with rooms commonly being lined with large fielded panels thrust forward on bulbous bolection mouldings. In elaborate schemes such panelling would be set off by deeply undercut naturalistic ornament and three-dimensional figures carried out in a style derived from slightly earlier Dutch and possibly German precedents. The great master of this style, and its chief promoter, was the famous woodcarver and sculptor Grinling Gibbons, whose work matured in the mid-1670s, although there were many others working in the same manner.

52

The undercut wood was frequently matched by ceilings in which deeply projecting mouldings arranged along Jonesian patterns were embellished with startlingly naturalistic leafage, made possible by the new technique of attaching individual elements in hard plaster. The third decorative element, large-scale illusionistic wall painting, was introduced with the arrival in about 1672 of the Italian painter Antonio Verrio. He was the first of a number of painters, chiefly French and Italian, but including the Englishman Sir James Thornhill, who supplied the need for large allegorical or symbolic wall or ceiling paintings up to the mid-eighteenth century.

The vegetable naturalism seen in interiors from the 1660s was echoed to some extent in the smaller objects of the house; by the 1680s it had developed into a generalized form of scrolling acanthus that was applied to goods of all sorts. In the 1660s it appears to have been strongest in silver embossed with fruit and flowers, perhaps because so many of the earliest surviving pieces in the style were made by immigrant silversmiths; it was also often combined with the auricular style.

At a less luxurious level, the characteristic tulip appeared on delftware and enamelled brass. The deeply undercut naturalism of decorative woodcarving was to be found on pieces integral to the room, such as mirrors, while other items such as bookcases (a new form, perhaps from Holland) matched in their mouldings the acanthus carving on the room's cornices and dado rails (see 5:47). Other types of furniture, notably chairs, had legs in a spiral form taken from French or Dutch precedents. Such baroque-style furniture only became usual in the 1670s, for much furniture of the 1660s still followed the old Flemish Mannerist styles.

52 The State Bedroom, Powis Castle, Powis, about 1668. The furniture from about 1725.

53 Tile from a set probably made for the Water Gallery, Hampton Court Palace, London, about 1694. Made in Delft, the Netherlands, at the 'Greek A' factory and marked with the monogram of its proprietor from 1686 to 1701, Adrianus Kocx. From a design by Daniel Marot. Tin-glazed earthenware, painted in blue (delftware). [h. 61cm]. VAM C.13-1956.

10. Daniel Marot and a new style

While the scrolling acanthus continued to be an underlying ornamental theme, from the 1680s a new style from France began to make itself felt, especially after the accession of William and Mary in 1688. It reflected a revived concentration on the grotesque, notably in the work of the French court designer Jean Berain, who developed a new form of grotesque in which the clear, light strapwork structures were adorned with acanthus and varied figures, animals and other motifs. This type of grotesque not only found its way on to flat decorations, painted panels and textiles, carved mouldings, stamped leathers, wallpapers and even ironwork, but was matched by new forms of vessel and vase design in which clearly expressed mouldings divided up plain but bold shapes. Foreign designers and craftspeople played a central role in the introduction of the style to Britain. One of the key figures was William and Mary's court *dessinateur*, Daniel Marot, a French Huguenot and son of a designer to Louis XIV, who had emigrated to Holland. He was in England between the mid-1690s and about 1700 and is known to have worked for the Queen, laying out the garden at Hampton Court. The Dutch delftware tiles from the Water Gallery at Hampton Court, of about 1694, followed his designs. Other rooms in the Water Gallery were lined in lacquer, mirrors and marble and were filled with massed displays of East Asian porcelain, blue-and-white delftware on brackets, and flower vases and Delft flower-pyramids on the floor. The style now associated with Marot's name spread well beyond the court, notably to a group of noblemen who both built and furnished in an especially French manner.

54 Dish, about 1670–85. Probably made in London. Earthenware, tin- and lead-glaze painted in colours (delftware). [diam. 33.7cm]. VAM C.244-1911.

55 Looking glass, 1665–72. The frame possibly made by a Dutch or Flemish carver in London. Painted with the arms of Gough of Old Fallings Hall and Perry Hall, Staffordshire. Pine wood, carved and decorated with gesso and silver leaf, retaining traces of red glaze, later paint and gilding. [h.176.5cm]. VAM W.37-1949.

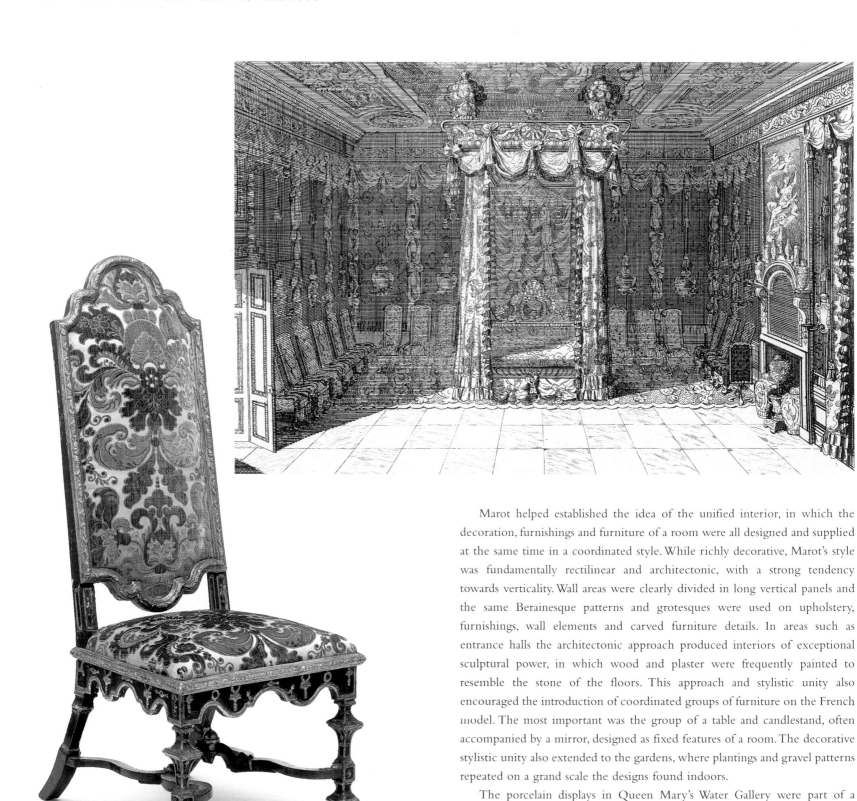

Marot helped established the idea of the unified interior, in which the decoration, furnishings and furniture of a room were all designed and supplied at the same time in a coordinated style. While richly decorative, Marot's style was fundamentally rectilinear and architectonic, with a strong tendency towards verticality. Wall areas were clearly divided in long vertical panels and the same Berainesque patterns and grotesques were used on upholstery, furnishings, wall elements and carved furniture details. In areas such as entrance halls the architectonic approach produced interiors of exceptional sculptural power, in which wood and plaster were frequently painted to resemble the stone of the floors. This approach and stylistic unity also encouraged the introduction of coordinated groups of furniture on the French model. The most important was the group of a table and candlestand, often accompanied by a mirror, designed as fixed features of a room. The decorative stylistic unity also extended to the gardens, where plantings and gravel patterns repeated on a grand scale the designs found indoors.

The porcelain displays in Queen Mary's Water Gallery were part of a European-wide craze for goods from the Indies (see pp. 134–5). In the porcelain cabinets created from the 1680s onwards, hundreds of pieces were

56 Chair, about 1700. Beech carved, painted and gilded; modern cut-velvet upholstery. The original upholstery was Genoa velvet in red, blue and black on a buff background. VAM W.11-1964.

57 *Design for a state bedroom*, 1702. Reversed copy, probably published in Holland 1712–84, of a plate in the *Second Livre Dappartements* by Daniel Marot (first published 1702). The chimneypiece is decorated with East Asian porcelain. Etching. VAM E.5914-1905.

58 Embroidery, about 1710–20. From a set hung at Stoke Edith, Herefordshire, built in 1697 for Paul Foley, Speaker of the House of Commons. The embroidery may show the garden at Stoke Edith, laid out by George London from 1692. Linen canvas embroidered with silk and wool, with some details in appliqué. VAM T.568-1996.

58

59

60

arranged in patterns on classically designed walls. The British interest in blue-and-white was greatly increased by Queen Mary's, whose own particular passion was porcelain. At her palace at Kensington she had 787 pieces of porcelain, 154 of which were in her bedchamber.

Such decorative displays were frequently accommodated on the corner chimneypieces that were characteristic of English interiors. Rooms were also lined in real or imitation lacquer, hung with real or imitation Chinese wallpaper or decorated with tapestries showing Chinese scenes adapted from designs on lacquer and porcelain. Such scenes marked the transition to true chinoiserie – that is, the creation of a distinctly European style based on an evocation of China, in colourful and often playful counterpoint to the high seriousness of the classical baroque.

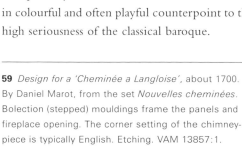

59 *Design for a 'Cheminée a Langloise'*, about 1700. By Daniel Marot, from the set *Nouvelles cheminées*. Bolection (stepped) mouldings frame the panels and fireplace opening. The corner setting of the chimney-piece is typically English. Etching. VAM 13857:1.

60 Cabinet on a stand, about 1690–1700. Once the property of Sir Richard Hill. The cabinet has been painted ('japanned') to look like Japanese lacquer. The stand is in the style of Daniel Marot. Stand of carved and silvered pine and lime. VAM W.20-1959.

It was only to be expected that the French influence would also be felt in architecture. At Hampton Court Palace, built in 1690–6, Wren created for William and Mary a scheme that went at least some way towards providing the version of Versailles that all European rulers craved, although in this case with a strongly domestic Dutch feel. More directly French in design were the great houses of some of William and Mary's courtiers, such as Boughton House in Northamptonshire, begun in 1688 for the Duke of Montagu (and Montagu House in London, now demolished), and Petworth in Sussex for the Duke of Somerset. For the east front at Chatsworth in Derbyshire, William Talman designed for the Earl of Devonshire from 1686 a composition that used French

elements such as heavy keystones and a giant order, but treated them in a dramatic and emotional manner. This makes it the first British architectural composition that can be called baroque.

The architectural style first fully introduced at Chatsworth saw its complete development in the years around and immediately after 1700, in a series of exceptional great houses, including Castle Howard in Yorkshire and Blenheim Palace in Oxfordshire. At the former, designed by Sir John Vanbrugh from 1698 for the Earl of Carlisle, a great dome rides for the first time over an English country house. It is a baroque palace fit to match any on the continent. While most of the rooms (where they have survived) show

61 The park front of Hampton Court Palace, London, 1690–6. Designed by Sir Christopher Wren.

62 Castle Howard, North Yorkshire, built 1698–1726. Designed by Sir John Vanbrugh, assisted by Nicholas Hawksmoor, for the Earl of Carlisle.

63 The south front of Chatsworth House, Derbyshire, begun 1686. Designed by William Talman.

themselves as modest exercises in the Marot manner, Castle Howard's hall and flanking paired staircases together form a fantastic piece of baroque spatial design with the feeling of an Italian chapel. Many of the craftspeople were indeed Italian, including the mural painter Giovanni Pellegrini (from Venice) and the first of many Italian-Swiss plasterers to come to Britain, Plura and Giovanni Bagutti.

At Beningbrough Hall nearby, the far less wealthy John Bourchier built from about 1710 another exercise in the baroque. Its exterior is a curious mix of elements taken from Italian pattern books (probably gathered by Bourchier on his Grand Tour) and the interior is almost entirely panelled in wood, with fine Marot-style carving. But the hall and corridors, as at Castle Howard, are grand spatial exercises in plaster and stone.

64

65

64 The hall, Castle Howard, North Yorkshire, created 1709–12. Designed by Sir John Vanbrugh. The chimneypiece probably by Plura and Giovanni Bagutti, the wall painted by Giovanni Antonio Pellegrini, the overdoors by Marco Ricci.

65 Looking through the state apartment from the dressing room at Beningbrough Hall, North Yorkshire, built about 1710–16.

CHAPTER 3

Tudor and Stuart Britain, 1500–1714

Who led taste?

MICHAEL SNODIN

1. Taste and power

For most people between 1485 and 1714 visual choices were not, as they are today, simply 'a matter of taste', or of changing fashion, available to anyone with the money to indulge them. Fashions did, of course, exist, and changing styles were just as prevalent as they are today. But the business of visual culture, of architecture, design, public displays and the visual arts, existed chiefly to service and reinforce a highly stratified social and political system in which power came from the top. As a result, changes in taste also tended to come from the top. Around 1500 this meant both the Church and the royal court. After the Reformation in the 1530s the court was the dominant authority. Unlike today's monarchy, it was the real centre of government. Henry VIII took a personal lead in royal building and furnishing, while Elizabeth I's political methods and manipulation of her courtiers produced a rich culture of building and furnishing outside the royal palaces, but one that was linked to her person.

By 1700 the court's central influence on taste had weakened noticeably, matching the emergence of the mechanisms of modern government. At one end, courtiers and court officials, like the royal architect Sir Christopher Wren, now took the lead; at the other, the beginning of a recognizably modern system of retail shopping, rapid fashion changes and the spread of visual culture through prints, newspapers and other printed media meant that the visual arts could much more easily be acquired by the new group of high-consuming, more numerous and increasingly important, non-aristocratic 'middling sort' in society.

Maintaining a direct link between social rank and visual culture was essential, especially during a time of increasing wealth. A nobleman could not be more magnificent in his building, furnishing or dress than his sovereign, nor could a servant outdo his master: every rank had its appropriate degree of display. Correspondingly, movement up the social ladder was marked by the acquisition of new, more expensive objects and demotion of the old. In 1577 the commentator William Harrison noted the widespread replacement of wooden plates by pewter ones, which were imitations of those in silver. By 1700 those country yeomen who aspired to the degree of the lesser gentry were sending their pewter to the kitchen and stocking their eating rooms with silver.

Such shifts in consumption were often seen as a threat. Law makers attempted to control inappropriate consumption, not only because of its social effect, but to prevent the import of foreign luxury goods and discourage private luxury on moral grounds. A series of sumptuary laws between 1510 and 1554 set limits on the consumption of luxuries, especially fine clothing, for all except the nobility. Other methods of control were also possible. A subject's over-pretension could, for instance, lead to the confiscation of property, as happened to Cardinal Wolsey and the Duke of Buckingham. Queen Elizabeth, who took great pride in her own magnificent clothes, kept a very sharp eye on those of the ladies at court, on one occasion taking the particularly splendid dress of Lady Mary Howard and trying it on herself. On finding it too short, she said to Lady Mary, '. . . if it become not me as being too short, I am minded it shall never become thee, as being too fine'.

1 *Henry VIII*, 1669. By Remigius van Leemput, derived from a fresco painted by Hans Holbein the Younger at Whitehall Palace, 1537. Henry VIII's portrait reflected not only his worldly power, but also the sumptuous and up-to-date nature of design at court. Oil on canvas. The National Trust, Petworth House.

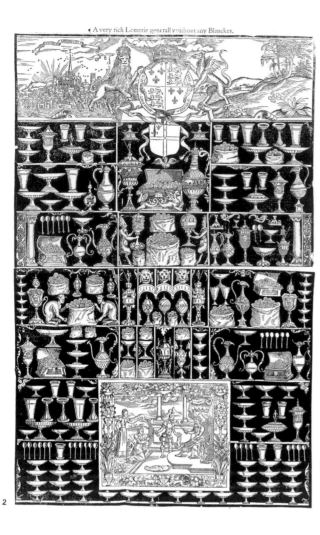

2. How taste travelled

The extent to which changing tastes passed in a 'trickle-down' manner from the court or nobility to other social groups varied greatly and is now often difficult to track. Enterprising craftspeople certainly adapted stylistic court fashions, such as that for Flemish Mannerism, to suit the pockets of burghers and the gentry. Many items were not specially commissioned, but were of standard design and from the start of the Tudor period were available ready-made from a variety of shops and other retailers. In terms of precious metals, before about 1660, it is overwhelmingly this type of lesser object that has survived for our inspection, with only one piece from Elizabeth I's own contributions to her jewel house remaining to give any idea of the splendours that it contained.

The same is true of surviving furniture before about 1660, which consists almost entirely of carved pieces in the Gothic style or more or less crude interpretations of Flemish Mannerism. Only a few pieces, like the famous sea-dog table at Hardwick Hall, which is a French import, survive to give us an idea of the appearance of fine carved furniture at court level, while court-level portrait paintings up to 1650 emphasize instead the luxury world of cloth and comfort, notably the upholstered state chair (no early examples of which survive). Other forms of adaptation as ideas moved down the social scale involved the imitation of expensive objects in cheaper materials. Tapestries were imitated in painted (or 'stained') cloths or replicated as wall paintings, while silver forms were imitated in pewter and ceramics.

2 *A very rich Lotterie generall without any Blanckes*, 1567. Advertising sheet by an anonymous artist. While the first prize was a very expensive tapestry, most of the prizes were smaller objects of a standardized type. Woodcut, The Folger Shakespeare Library.

3 Table, made about 1580 in France. Recorded in the inventory of Hardwick Hall, Derbyshire, compiled in 1601. Walnut. The National Trust, Hardwick Hall.

4 *Portrait of an unknown lady*, about 1630. By an unknown English artist. An expensively upholstered chair is prominently displayed. Oil on canvas. VAM 565-1882.

5

5 Candlestick, dated 1648. Made in Southwark, London, probably at the Pickleherring factory, for William Withers. The design imitates a metal original. Tin-glazed earthenware, painted. VAM 4752-1901.

4

Attitudes to taste before about 1650, as well as design decisions and processes, are perhaps most clearly shown in the design of buildings. In an age before the emergence of the professional architect, the lead in design was usually taken by the builder himself, in consultation with the mason or other craftsman (often referred to as the 'architect' in contemporary records) who was to erect the building. Typically ideas for the design were gleaned from local and other buildings. In 1603 Henry Percy, Duke of Northumberland, who was planning building works at Syon, wrote that he was 'ready to go, and see Copthall, for now that I am a builder I must borrow of my knowledge somewhat out of Tibbals [Theobalds, Hertfordshire] somewhat out of every place of mark where curiosities are used'.

Sir Robert Townshend, the builder of Raynham Hall in Norfolk, made a tour in 1619, with his mason, of notable English houses, including Hatfield House and Audley End; Townshend even, very exceptionally, took him abroad to the Low Countries. Further down the social scale, John Smythson, from a notable family of surveyors, made careful drawings of Italian 'pergulas' or balconies and other architectural novelties in London in 1619. Builders and, more rarely, masons and surveyors also

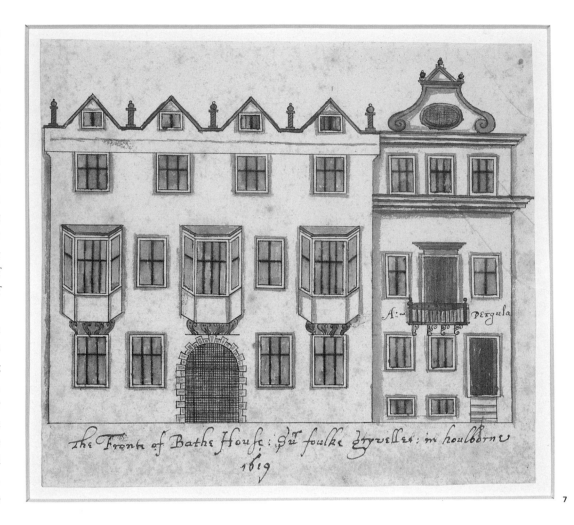

the Front of Bathe House: S^r foulke Gryuelles: in houlborne
1619

7

owned architectural books and prints from which ideas could be drawn: Townshend was reported to have 'many Italian and French books of architecture'. Masons working on several houses carried ideas and personal stylistic mannerisms from job to job. Finally there was the purpose of the building to be considered: show was necessary where social position needed to be maintained; otherwise simple forms sufficed. But the design process was not yet over, for even during building changes could be made.

The results of such a process naturally varied from the conservative to the novel. Raynham reflected the latest London city building styles, as well as incorporating a remarkable Ionic portico closely modelled on the ideas of the royal architect Inigo Jones. In most cases, however, the design process resulted in the emergence of distinctive local and regional styles, which took on the characteristics of court and aristocratic architecture to varying degrees. By 1700 such differences had become minor, marking the emergence of a national architectural style.

6

6 Raynham Hall, Norfolk, begun 1621, finished about 1635.

7 *Bath House and Sir Fulke Greville's house, Holborn, London*, 1619. By John Smythson. Pen, ink and wash. RIBA Library Drawings Collection.

3. The Church

The power and wealth of the Roman Catholic Church before the Reformation are hard to grasp today. In terms of wealth it exceeded that of the Crown, while its churchmen often played a major role in government. As patrons of architecture and the arts, the great churchmen of the later fifteenth and early sixteenth centuries were very active, often in fields beyond the strictly ecclesiastical, building themselves palaces as well as numerous lesser residences, founding colleges, maintaining great households and finally making themselves magnificent tombs. A good example is Richard Fox, successively Bishop of Exeter, Bath and Wells, Durham and Winchester, who founded Corpus Christi College, Oxford (endowing it with splendid silver), and built a palace at Norham, in Northumberland, as well as beginning a major rebuilding of the cathedral at Winchester.

The last and greatest of them all, both in terms of power and expenditure, was Cardinal Wolsey, who rose from obscurity to become the Pope's ambassador and Henry VIII's Lord Chancellor. Amassing vast sums from numerous ecclesiastical appointments and other sources, he built on a scale unmatched in his time. His projects included Hampton Court Palace (begun in 1514), York Place in London (later called Whitehall), the houses known as The More and Tyttenhanger in Hertfordshire, as well as colleges in Oxford and Ipswich. Wolsey was accused by contemporary critics of flaunting his wealth, while the scale of his building activities eventually led to them being taken into the royal domain. Only then did Henry VIII's own property begin to match that of his former Chancellor. To some extent Wolsey's building activities were justified, and in keeping with his status. The vast works at Hampton were designed to host the whole royal court (some 1,000 people) on its journeys, as well as great foreign embassies and rulers; for the highest officers of state proximity to the sovereign and helping to fulfil state business were everything.

8

9

8 The head of Bishop Fox's crozier, probably 1487–90. Silver-gilt and enamel. Corpus Christi College, Oxford.

9 Hampton Court Palace, London. Cardinal Wolsey's Hampton Court consisted of the present base court (at the bottom of this view), and the first inner court. The second inner court (greatly enlarged in 1689–95) was built by Henry VIII, who also built a new great hall (on the left).

4. Royal households and magnificence

Magnificence was the key concept of building, household and ceremony in the royal context. Henry VII built much, including Richmond Palace and chapels at Westminster and King's College, Cambridge, but his son Henry VIII built more than any other English monarch before or since. By his death he had 68 houses, amassed from dissolved monasteries and out-of-favour courtiers. While only a tiny handful of objects have survived from his court, its splendour is amply shown by the inventories. Henry's collection of tapestries was probably the biggest ever assembled, while his jewel house contained 997 items of gold, silver and jewellery at his death. In addition he had collections (then novel) of musical instruments and glass, as well as a considerable library. Much of the magnificence of the court was expressed in ephemeral events, such as masques, tournaments and other celebrations. Henry is known to have taken a close personal interest in the design and detailed arrangements of his buildings at court, especially after 1529 and Wolsey's departure from the scene, when his expenditure and building activities suddenly increased.

10 *The temporary palace at the Field of Cloth of Gold*, about 1545. Detail of a larger painting by an anonymous artist, recording the event of 1520.
© The Royal Collection.

5. Wolsey and Henry VIII as style innovators

We know from the accounts of contemporaries that the true test of magnificence in art and architecture in the first half of the sixteenth century was quite simply its total visual impact. It was a matter of monetary value, of complexity and curiosity of design and execution, and of sheer size. Stylistic innovation on a purely aesthetic level was unimportant and usually went unremarked. It is in this context that we should view the arrival in England of Italian Renaissance design elements and 'antique' ornament, upon which so much emphasis is placed today.

Renaissance elements had begun to arrive in England by the 1460s in the form of Italian illuminated manuscripts and, later, the decorations of printed books. Motifs from such sources passed easily to other media. The arrival of the Florentine sculptor Pietro Torrigiani, by 1511, brought Renaissance sculptural and ornamental styles as well as new techniques and uses of material. Cardinal Wolsey, who frequently went to France and the Low Countries, seems to have played a significant part in introducing Renaissance decorative motifs into the decoration of prominent permanent buildings. Most notable are the famous terracotta roundels of Roman emperors at Hampton Court, made in 1521 by Giovanni da Maiano, an Italian sculptor working in England. Significantly, they were probably economical versions of the more expensive stone portraits found on French royal buildings; even cheaper heads of Roman 'conquerors', probably made in papier mâché or plaster, were supplied by Maiano for Henry VIII's temporary 'Disguising House' for negotiations with the French in 1527. For Henry, the display of lavish and gilded classical imagery and ornament was a matter of politics, actively emulating that of his rival Francis I.

The sheer wealth of Henry VIII meant that none of his courtiers could match him in terms of expenditure, and after about 1530 the court was certainly taking the lead in taste, with its fully integrated Renaissance-style interiors on the French model. A few courtiers are known to have adopted some of these ideas in their own dwellings – for instance, Charles Brandon, the Duke of Suffolk, who had married Henry VIII's sister Mary. Both his houses, at Suffolk Place in Southwark (probably nearing completion in 1522) and Westhorpe in Suffolk (built in about 1525–35), used moulded terracotta decorations with 'antick' motifs. Another notable courtier, Sir William Sandys, Lord Chamberlain from 1526, had richly furnished king's and queen's apartments at his country house, the Vyne, Hampshire, linked by a long gallery, just like the latest arrangements at Hampton Court. The gallery was fully panelled in Gothic linenfold, but incorporating 'antique' motifs and a fine Renaissance-style coat of arms, perhaps by a court carver. In the chapel are ceramic paving tiles, imported from Antwerp, likewise decorated with 'antick' motifs. Renaissance motifs also occur in the stained glass made in Bruges for Sandys's chantry chapel in Basingstoke.

11

12

11 Decorative roundel at Hampton Court Palace, showing the Emperor Hadrian, 1521. By Giovanni da Maiano. Terracotta, formerly painted.

12 Panelling and doorway of the gallery at the Vyne, Hampshire, about 1518–26. The royal arms are flanked by the crest and shield of Sir William Sandys.

THE COURT OF HENRY VIII

Maurice Howard

The court of Henry VIII was essentially a great household that moved from place to place, as determined by seasonal activities, government business, the insatiable desire to hunt well-stocked forests and the fear of pestilence. The enormous amount of building initiated by the King meant that, by the end of his reign, more than 50 buildings could house the court. Some of these were new; some were refurbished palaces; others were houses sequestered from courtiers who had fallen from favour, or sets of lodgings adapted from parts of suppressed monasteries. Greater palaces, like Whitehall and Hampton Court, both once owned by Cardinal Wolsey, could house the whole court

of several hundred people; others, like Nonsuch Palace, served as grand hunting lodges for the King, his guests and perhaps 50 servants.

The court was the place where the King's largesse, his 'magnificence', was displayed and his rivalry with European monarchs – especially Francis I of France – was played out in court ceremonial. On special occasions, such as the entertainment of the Emperor Charles V in 1522 or the Greenwich Revels of 1527, the court was the setting for great hospitality, with the building of richly decorated temporary structures in wood or canvas. Yet it is the sense of the everyday

13. Letters patent with a miniature portrait of Henry VIII, 1524. The portrait probably painted by Lucas Horenbout, also known as Hornebolte. Illuminated parchment. VAM MSL.6-1999.

maintenance of court life that comes across most strongly in the inventory of Henry's goods taken at his death in 1547.

A good many furnishings, household goods and clothes moved with the King. The court's surroundings were constantly redefined by the hanging of tapestries (more than 2,000 were recorded in 1547) in the great public rooms of each palace. The imagery of tapestry was the chief means by which the virtues of the sovereign, his military exploits and the dispensing of justice were praised through the choice of apposite classical and biblical stories. Other signs of the King's presence were his heraldry and personal badges, not only on furniture and fittings, but on the clothes worn by his servants. Alongside this, Henry increased the number of private apartments to which he could retire and it was here that more personal items were kept: the tools of daily life and administration, as well as the illuminated devotional texts and ingenious trinkets that made up the 'gift' culture of the court. The giving of presents between King and courtiers at New Year prompted the flow into court life of the latest fashions in ornament and design.

14. The Great Hall, Hampton Court Palace, London, built 1532–4 for Henry VIII.

15. Cap badge, about 1536–40. Embossed and chased gold. [diam. 4.7cm]. VAM 630-1884.

16. Stained glass showing the arms of Henry VIII and Jane Seymour, about 1536–40. Said to have come from Nonsuch Palace, Surrey. Painted and fired in England. Clear, pot-metal and flashed glass painted with brown enamel and yellow stain. [h. 45.7cm]. VAM C.454-1919.

17. Door lock, about 1539–47. Probably made by Henry Romayne(s), lockmaker to Henry VIII. Formerly on the door to the great hall of Beddington Place, Sutton, London. Gilded wrought iron. [h. 22.4cm]. VAM M.397-1921

18. Detail of a tapestry showing the story of David and Bathsheba, about 1510–15. Made in Brussels and owned by Henry VIII. Musée National de la Renaissance, Ecouen.

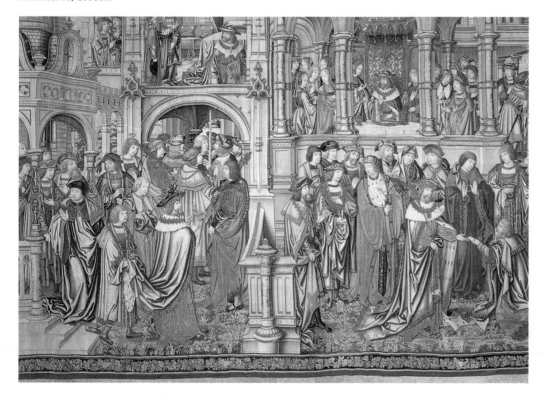

19. *Anne of Cleves*, 1539. By Hans Holbein the Younger. Watercolour on vellum in a contemporary turned ivory box. VAM P.153-1910.

20. Detail of a design for a royal tent, possibly for the Field of Cloth of Gold, about 1520. Watercolour on paper. The British Library.

21 Design for a gold cup for Jane Seymour, third wife of Henry VIII, 1536. By Hans Holbein the Younger. Pen, ink and wash. Ashmolean Museum.

22 Design for a fireplace for Henry VIII, about 1540. By Hans Holbein the Younger. Pen and ink and wash. The British Museum.

6. Taste and trade

The direct employment of foreign artists and craftspeople was one of the most effective ways of getting fashionable ideas from abroad. Henry VIII worked hard to entice them from rival courts, and King James V's French masons profoundly affected the style of Scottish architecture. While a number of such immigrants were French or Italian, many more came from the Low Countries, bringing Italian Renaissance forms with them. Such artists were frequently employed in a variety of fields, transferring ideas across different media, as with the Horenbout (or Hornebolte) family of illuminators from Ghent. Gerard Horenbout was also a painter and designer of tapestries, ecclesiastical vestments and stained glass. His son Luke became a pioneering miniaturist, while Wolsey's Renaissance-style seals may have been designed in the family workshop.

The German painter Hans Holbein the Younger spent two periods in England working for Henry VIII and his court. Expanding well beyond portrait painting, he designed goldsmith's work and jewellery, as well as temporary and permanent decorations and murals, and even woodcuts for the new Protestant religious books. Holbein's portraits of the German merchants of the steelyard remind us that immigrant artists' closest connections were with the more permanent foreign community whose activities as importers, or as makers, provided most of England's requirements for luxury goods, ranging from Italian silks to Flemish goldsmiths' work, right up to the middle of the seventeenth century.

7. A group of classical patrons

Henry VIII's death in 1547 marked a shift in the mechanisms of taste that was to last some 50 years, in which the lead passed from the court to the courtiers. The earliest evidence comes in the reign of his successor, the boy-king Edward VI. It was marked by a remarkable episode of stylistic innovation in architecture, namely the first serious attempt to adopt classical architecture as a system rather than a collection of disparate elements. The principal sponsor was a Protestant group around the Lord Protector himself, Edward Seymour, Duke of Somerset. Somerset was engaged in at least five building projects in the few years up to his execution in 1552, but the most important in terms of design was Somerset House in London. The pioneering French style of Somerset House can be traced in the houses of several of Somerset's associates – sometimes extending into the reign of Elizabeth I – including Sir William Sharington's Lacock in Wiltshire, Thomas Seymour's (the Protector's brother) Sudeley Castle in Gloucestershire and the Duke of Northumberland's Dudley Castle in the West Midlands. The link between them was the mason John Chapman, who went on to Longleat in Wiltshire, built by the Protector's secretary Sir John Thynne, where he developed the ideas of Somerset House. Northumberland was the employer of John Shute, whose pioneering book, *The First and Chief Groundes of Architecture*, was published in 1563. That the engraved plates in Shute's book were not directly reflected in built structures was significant only of a change in taste, for by this date printed images had become a key factor in taking design forward.

23

23 *Somerset House, The Strand, London*, built 1547–52. Detail from a plan and elevation by John Thorpe, drawn after 1611. The building was demolished in about 1777 to make way for the present Somerset House. Pen and ink. Trustees of the Sir John Soane Museum.

24 *Henry Howard, Earl of Surrey*, about 1546. Attributed to
William Scrots. Most of the ornamental frame with the
figures is inspired by a French Fontainebleau-school print of
the 1540s. Oil on panel. National Portrait Gallery, London.

8. Prints and taste

The invention of movable type, of printed images in woodcut, engraving and etching in books and as separate sheets had an incalculably great effect on the spread of visual ideas and aesthetic theory throughout Europe from the middle of the fifteenth century. For England, entirely dependent for its novel notions on sources from abroad, print became an especially important wellspring of new ideas after about 1560, but the presence of printed images before that date, if less directly influential, is well attested. The earliest ornament design book to be published in England, a set of moresques by Thomas Geminus, a Frenchman, was published in 1548. Significantly, it was aimed at embroiderers, many of whom were amateurs in constant need of new patterns, and at goldsmiths, who of all craftspeople had perhaps the greatest requirement to stay in the vanguard of fashion. But an English publication was exceptional, for up to the 1660s most printed visual source material came from abroad. Foreign prints lie behind the ornamental elements in portraits of the Archbishop Thomas Cranmer and Henry Howard, Earl of Surrey. Painted slightly earlier than Geminus's pattern book, they show a remarkably rapid adoption of very up-to-date motifs of the type that were used by Francis I in the palace of Fontainebleau.

The years 1560–1620 saw the peak of the influence of the foreign print in British design, matching exactly the fashion for Flemish Mannerist ornament and its associated figure subjects, notably narrative biblical stories and scenes from classical mythology. The objects affected covered a huge range, both of type and quality. All the external decoration of Wollaton Hall in Nottinghamshire, built in the 1580s and designed by Robert Smythson, was copied from a single set of images in Hans Vredeman de Vries's *Architectura*, published in 1577. Another print by him of about 1565 supplied elements in the embroidered Shrewsbury Hanging, worked by Bess of Hardwick and Mary, Queen of Scots in the 1570s. But prints were expensive. The Abbott family of Devon plasterers, and the professional embroiderer Thomas Trevelyon, had to copy prints for their own use.

The final effect was the same. Such a concentrated use of images from prints was a reflection of the need to provide ideas for a notably complex and ornament-laden style. But there would probably have been no demand for prints had high design, formerly limited to the court sphere, not been becoming less exclusive. It is significant that the end of the stream of print-derived decoration in the 1620s coincided with the return of the court to an exclusive style – that of Inigo Jones – and the development outside the court of other styles.

25

26

25 Motif for plasterwork, showing a cartouche adapted from a plate in a set of prints by Benedetto Battini, 1553. By a member of the Abbott family, probably John Abbott. Pen and ink. Devon County Record Office.

26 *A strapwork cartouche*. Plate from a set of cartouches by Benedetto Battini, published in Antwerp in 1553. Engraving on blue paper, coloured by hand. VAM 14357.9.

PRINTS AS SOURCES FOR DESIGN

Elizabeth Miller

In the sixteenth and seventeenth centuries there were a number of ways in which craftspeople could secure information about new designs – from finished objects, models, drawings or prints. Prints were the newest method of communicating design. They had originated in continental Europe in about 1400, but it was in the sixteenth century that they came increasingly to be used as sources for design in Britain.

The starting point for making a print was a flat piece of wood or a sheet of copper. Using knives and gouges on the piece of wood, and pointed tools or the action of acid on the copper, ridges were created in the wood or grooves in the copper to produce a reversed version of the desired image. These ridges or grooves were then coated or filled with ink. A blank piece of paper was pressed up against the inked wood or copper and, when the paper was peeled away, it had been printed with the image.

With each new inking, the transfer of ink from the wood or copper was repeated to produce multiple copies of the same print. Eventually the piece of wood or metal began to wear down, but not before hundreds or even thousands of copies of the print had

27. The Ill-Assorted Couple, about 1495. By Albrecht Dürer. Engraving. VAM E.648-1940.

28. Misericord, Henry VII's chapel, Westminster Abbey, London. Finished about 1519. Adapted from Albrecht Dürer's The Ill-Assorted Couple, 1495.

29. Title-page to a play, Nobody And Somebody, 1606. Printed in London for John Trundle. Woodcut on paper. VAM NAL Dyce 6967.

30. Figure of Nobody, 1680–5. Adapted from the title-page to the play Nobody And Somebody. Made in Southwark or Lambeth, London. Tin-glazed earthenware (delftware). [h. 24.5cm]. VAM C.4-1982.

31. *A Ewer,* 1531. Engraved by Agostino Veneziano and published in Rome by Antonio Salamanca. Engraving. VAM 16842.

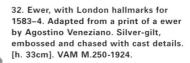

32. Ewer, with London hallmarks for 1583–4. Adapted from a print of a ewer by Agostino Veneziano. Silver-gilt, embossed and chased with cast details. [h. 33cm]. VAM M.250-1924.

33. *Abraham and the Angels,* 1585. Engraved after Maarten de Vos. From *Thesaurus Sacrarium,* published in Antwerp by Gerarde de Jode. Engraving. Fitzwilliam Museum, Cambridge.

been created. It was the existence of multiple copies of the same print that made printmaking such an effective method of spreading visual information over large distances in a short space of time, to an extent that had previously been impossible.

Prints were made of a vast variety of subjects. They were relatively inexpensive to make and buy, compared to drawings and paintings, and were light and easily transported. Some prints were produced specifically as design sources for craftspeople, but makers could – and did – draw on any print that suited their purpose. The borrowing of ideas from prints could take many forms. A two-dimensional print could be used either for the design of another flat object, as certainly happened with embroidery, or for the creation of a three-dimensional object. Sometimes the whole printed design source was reproduced in another material. Alternatively, a detail of a print could be selected for use in the design of part of a new object, or parts of two or more prints could be combined in one item.

Prints came to provide a vast pool of imagery, which makers based in Britain could trawl for the latest visual ideas from some of Europe's greatest artists and designers.

34. Detail of a cushion cover, 1640–70. The main scene adapted from a print after Maarten de Vos. The other elements taken from English prints. Non-professional embroidery over outlines drawn by a professional pattern-drawer. Linen canvas embroidered in wool and silk. [h. 55.9cm]. VAM 443-1865.

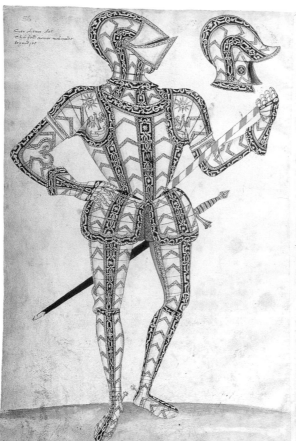

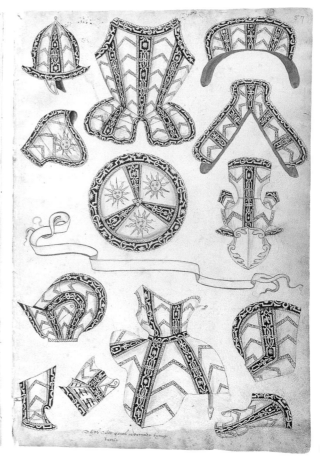

35

36

9. Art and politics

The period from the accession of Queen Elizabeth in 1558 to her death in 1603 was marked by an extraordinary visual culture among her leading courtiers. The Queen herself built little and, having inherited her father's vast store of goods and furnishings, was modest in her expenditure, but she was surrounded by an entire court culture in which she was increasingly celebrated as the Virgin Queen, especially from about 1580. Courtiers, as her knights, vied for her favour at annual accession-day jousts, wearing armour simultaneously real and fantastic, decorated with their emblems. The court was the nation's greatest concentration of heraldry and emblems in an age when symbolism carried all the meaning of works of art. At every level, the chivalric ideal was celebrated, with court administrators shown lying in full armour on their tombs.

According to the custom of the day, all that was the courtier's was the Queen's. This was especially so during the court's annual summer 'progress' around their country seats. While Henry VIII had also made progresses, those of Queen Elizabeth were unprecedented in their scale and the courtiers' responses to them. At Kenilworth, in 1575, for instance, Lord Robert Dudley presented her first with a vast banquet in a marquee. Later she was greeted by guns and trumpeters and by figures in fantastic costume, led by an Arthurian 'Lady of the Lake' seated on a 'movable island', reciting verses in her honour. Several days of hunting, dancing, masques and other festivities followed. The decisive move from court to courtiers is most clearly shown, however, in

35 Pendant: the Drake Jewel, the miniature dated 1588. Made in London. This jewel, given to the naval hero Sir Francis Drake, contains a portrait of Elizabeth I by Nicholas Hilliard. Courtiers frequently wore the Queen's portrait. The phoenix was the Queen's symbol. Enamelled gold with sardonyx cameo, table-cut rubies and diamonds, hung with pearls. Miniature painted in watercolour on vellum. VAM. Anonymous loan.

37

their huge 'prodigy' houses. A number of them, like Wollaton, Longleat and Burghley, survive, but even bigger structures, most notably Lord Burghley's Theobalds in Hertfordshire, have disappeared.

Far too big for the immediate domestic needs of their owners (who also had many other properties), these houses were first and foremost political statements, serving as permanent expressions of status and public office, but also, when necessary, as surrogate palaces during the Queen's progresses. The prodigy houses were remarkable exercises in taste. Many used the same Flemish Mannerist ornamental vocabulary as the applied arts of the period (and, indeed, showed a remarkable unity of style with them). But in terms of architectural design they were often novel and experimental, reflecting the need to combine the conflicting messages of chivalry and long ancestral lineage with expressions of more up-to-date (and foreign) learning, as well as the practical requirements of ceremony and status.

At Burghley, the central courtyard is surrounded by classical triumphal arches, balconies and colonnades, functioning like an arena for shows, but is topped by a huge stone pyramid supported by the family arms.

At Hardwick Hall, constructed in the 1590s, the builder and owner, Bess of Hardwick, is announced by her initials on the skyline, surmounted by a countess's coronet. Although the general impression of bays and towers recalls great courtyard houses of about 1500, huge quantities of expensive glass announce that this is a modern, outward-looking house. The increasing height of the windows clearly reveals the increasing status of the rooms within. Entrance is made through the earliest classical entrance colonnade in England, while a classical balustrade runs around the top. The interiors give us a good idea of the colourful, textile-rich rooms to which other less wealthy patrons would aspire. Bess, however, had hopes of a royal visit (which never happened) as well as a granddaughter, Arabella Stuart, with some claim to the throne. The state rooms are arranged in a sequence as in a royal palace, leading to the royal bedchamber, while their decorations carry the royal arms and an iconography related to Queen Elizabeth, subtly linked to emblems signifying Bess herself.

38

39

38 The entrance front of Hardwick Hall, Derbyshire, built 1591–7. Designed by Robert Smythson for Elizabeth Hardwick, Countess of Shrewsbury.

39 The courtyard at Burghley House, Lincolnshire, 1755. By John Haynes. Built 1555–85 for William Cecil. Pen and wash. The Burghley House Collection.

36 Design for armour and extra pieces, for Sir Henry Lee, 1570–5. Probably drawn by Jacob Halder, a German armourer and master workman of the Royal Armouries of Greenwich. Halder decorated the plain German cavalry armour and added pieces adapting it for infantry use and the tournament. The decoration throughout incorporates Lee's badges of the sun and falcon. Watercolour on paper. VAM D.599-1894.

37 *George Clifford, 3rd Earl of Cumberland*, about 1590. By Nicholas Hilliard. Clifford was the Queen's champion, defending her honour at the annual accession-day tilts. The combatant knights wore fancy dress: Clifford's represents the knight of Pendragon Castle – he came in riding on a horse dressed as a dragon. Watercolour on vellum laid on panel. © National Maritime Museum, London.

THE EARLY STUART COURT

Nick Humphrey

Both James I and VI and his son, Charles I, were extremely interested in art and design. They employed foreign artists and craftspeople and built up the royal collections, as well as promoting the pioneering work of Inigo Jones. Although now chiefly celebrated as an architect for his classical buildings, Jones became established at the Jacobean court as a designer – particularly of masques for Anne of Denmark. His fantastic, Italianate stage-sets, machinery and costumes for members of the court were developed in hundreds of pen-and-ink sketches. His principal building, the Whitehall Banqueting House (1619–22), was intended by James I as a formal reception chamber. The rigorous proportions and balance of Jones's modified Roman basilica interior

and the Palladian façade contrasted sharply with the confusion of the Tudor Whitehall Palace. Within, Peter Paul Rubens's paintings of the life and apotheosis of James I, fixed into the compartmentalized ceiling in 1635, made explicit the building's projection of royal authority and harmony.

The promotion of tapestry was another royal endeavour. Hugely costly, tapestry production served economic, political and aesthetic ends. The Mortlake factory established in 1619 by Sir Francis Crane, using Flemish weavers, was sponsored by the Crown in emulation of Henri IV of France's Gobelin workshops. In 1623 Charles I acquired for Mortlake seven of Raphael's tapestry cartoons for the *Acts of the Apostles*, made in 1515–16.

The growing reputation of the English court encouraged foreign artists and craftspeople to come to London. The bronze founder Francesco Fanelli received a royal pension and styled himself Sculptor to the King. Orazio Gentileschi came from Paris, aged 62, and painted the allegorical ceiling canvases for the Queen's House, Henrietta Maria's riverside villa at Greenwich. Rubens's pupil Anthony Van Dyck superseded Daniel Mytens as the preferred court portraitist.

Encouraged by the example of his elder brother Henry, and by courtier-connoisseurs like the first Duke of Buckingham and the second Earl of Arundel, Charles was a knowledgeable and enthusiastic collector, though financially constrained during the period of personal rule from 1629 to 1640. In 1627 he secured through his shrewd agents a great prize for £18,000, the collections of the Duke of Mantua, bringing to London more of the Venetian paintings he loved, as well as outstanding contemporary works, important antique sculpture and Andrea Mantegna's *Triumphs of Caesar*. The last were retained by Cromwell when most of the royal art collections were sold in 1649.

40. The interior of the Banqueting House at Whitehall, London, 1619–22. Designed by Inigo Jones.

41. *Charles I, Queen Henrietta Maria, Prince Charles and Princess Mary,* 1632. By Sir Anthony Van Dyck. Oil on canvas. © The Royal Collection.

42. Tapestry, *The Miraculous Draught of Fishes from the Acts of the Apostles*, 1637–8. The central scene designed by Raphael. Woven at the Mortlake tapestry factory, London. Made for Philip Herbert, Earl of Pembroke. VAM Loan: Buccleuch. I.

43. *Saint George and the Dragon*, about 1640. By Francesco Fanelli. Cast bronze. [h. 19.1cm]. VAM A.5-1953.

44. Two costume designs for the King and Queen, for the masque, from *Salmacida Spolia*, written by Sir William D'Avenant, 1640. By Inigo Jones. Pen and brown ink, one over grey wash. Devonshire Collection, Chatsworth.

10. A new court

The triumphal entry of James I and VI into London in 1604 was a public celebration unmatched since the days of Henry VIII. Seven great arches were the stages for orations and songs composed by celebrated dramatists. Clothed in Flemish Mannerist ornament (and based on those used for the entry into Antwerp of Archduke Albert and the Infanta Isabella in 1599), the arches were nevertheless designed to modular proportions answering the musical harmonies. This great event marked the return of the court to the centre of visual culture. From the start, more money was spent: the pageantry of the entry alone cost more than was expended on all such events during the reign of Elizabeth I, while James immediately set about replacing with modern plate the 14,000 troy ounces (435 kilograms) of old silver that he had given away at the accession. The size of the royal family was a key factor, with separate palaces being fitted out for the King, Queen and Henry, Prince of Wales.

James I and VI's international outlook, coinciding with a period of peace in Europe, finally opened up British visual culture to the Renaissance tradition in architecture and the visual arts. This process was pursued, in different ways, by a number of individuals at court, including James I and Queen Anne, the connoisseur and collector Earl of Arundel and the court architect Inigo Jones. It was continued by Charles I and his queen, Henrietta Maria. Jones, who worked for all these patrons, was a key figure. As well as being a brilliant and

IGNATII IONES MAG: BRIT: ARCHITECTI GE-
NERALIS,- VERA EFFIGIES,

Anth: van Dyck Eques pinxit,   *W: Hollar fecit, aqua forti,*

45

original architect, he was a court designer in the European tradition, able to turn his hand to most designing tasks; starting with masque designs, he moved on to buildings and then interiors. His great aim, as expressed in 1606 by his friend the antiquarian Edmund Bolton, was that 'all that is praiseworthy in the elegant arts of the ancients, may some day insinuate themselves across the Alps into our England'. This aim was shown as much in his masque designs, which introduced numerous ideas from Italy and France, as in his buildings, which for the first time in England showed a proper understanding of the nature of classical architecture.

45 *Inigo Jones*, 1655. By Wenceslaus Hollar after a drawing of 1640 by Sir Anthony Van Dyck. Engraving. VAM Circ.116-1967.

46 *The Pegme of the Dutchmen*, a triumphal arch made for the procession of James I and VI through the City of London in March 1604. Engraved by William Kip and published by Stephen Harrison as part of the set, *Arch's of Triumph*, 1604. Engraving. VAM 14008.

11. Art at court

The Stuart court was the first in Britain to patronize and collect painting and sculpture for their own sake, rather than for their subjects. Charles I, especially, raced to make up for artistic lost ground by seeking to employ the most famous artists from abroad. For a few years, until they were dispersed under the Commonwealth, the art collections of the British court exceeded in quality those of most foreign competitors. The new pastime of collecting Italian and other modern painting and sculpture was matched by the habit (also of Italian origin) of assembling collections of classical sculpture and other antiquities, rarities and 'objects of virtue'.

Most active in this field was the second Earl of Arundel, one of the key figures in the intended revival in the arts and learning. The Earl's collections, built up from 1612, included inlaid Italian furniture, a famous collection of paintings by Holbein, the celebrated 'Arundel marbles' and more than 200 albums of Italian Renaissance drawings. The trips to the continent that formed a vital part of Arundel's artistic education were pioneering examples of the Grand Tour, an experience that was to become key in forming the tastes of the ruling classes. In 1613 Arundel took with him Inigo Jones, to whom this Italian trip was crucial. He met Vincenzo Scamozzi, the stylistic disciple of Andrea Palladio, acquired Palladio drawings and studied his buildings systematically at first hand, acquiring a profound critical knowledge of classical architecture.

In 1615 Jones took up the post of Surveyor of the King's Works, in charge of all royal building activity. He was an architect of recognizably modern type, a single controlling mind able to work out a whole building on paper and see it built as it was drawn. This was something completely new in Britain – not because of Jones's brilliance (undoubted though it was), but because before the advent of the symmetrical certainties and systems of classicism, with its logically related plans, elevations and sections, it was simply not possible to be certain of built outcomes. This new approach, which did not reach all building until about 1700, had a profound effect on the origination and transmission of design ideas, enabling architects to be certain of their intended results, and allowing architectural ideas to travel without distortion via books and prints.

47 *Thomas Howard, 2nd (Howard) Earl of Arundel and Surrey*, about 1618. By Daniel Mytens. The Earl points to the sculpture gallery on the first floor of Arundel House, London. Some of the statues had been brought back from Italy in 1614. Oil on canvas. National Portrait Gallery, London.

The sophisticated clarity, proportion and appropriate grandeur of Jones's few buildings were at first appreciated only by a tiny cultured élite, but their effect was like a time-bomb. The Banqueting House (1619–22) was the prototype for palace-like government buildings from the 1660s onwards. The Queen's House at Greenwich (1616–35) and the Prince's Lodging at Newmarket (1619–21) became the touchstones of the neo-Palladian revival a hundred years later. But it was in urban building that Jones's ideas were to have the greatest immediate impact. The arcaded scheme at Covent Garden (1631–7), put up by the Earl of Bedford, was one of the origins of the London square and quickly established the idea of the classical terraced building. Details of Jonesian origin, such as the iron balcony or 'pergula' (which, according to the antiquary John Bagford, 'country folks were much wont to gaze upon'), became part of the builder's baroque composite style now known as 'artisan Mannerism'.

In the broadest sense, a classical form of building, however varied in detail, had become the norm by about 1660. By this stage, too, as James Cleland wrote as early as 1607 in *The institution of a young noble man*, 'the principles of architecture . . . [are] also necessary for a gentleman to be known', as was a knowledge of painting and sculpture. This educational process was assisted by a steadily increasing number of books in English about architecture and the visual arts from about 1600, and especially after 1660. Up to 1715 they were, significantly, nearly all translations of French or Italian texts. One of the few exceptions was *Elements of Architecture* of 1624 by Sir Henry Wotton, the

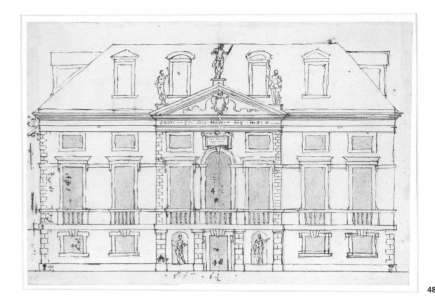

48

ambassador in Venice. Experience abroad was seen as essential for designing buildings, especially after 1660, when Sir Roger Pratt advised that 'if you be not able to handsomely contrive it [a suitable design] yourself', then it was necessary to get at least a sketch 'from some ingenious gentleman who has seen much of that kind abroad', as well as to have read the right books. The only buildings considered worth inspecting in England were the Banqueting House and Inigo Jones's colonnade at St Paul's Cathedral.

49

48 *Design for the Prince's Lodging, Newmarket Palace, Suffolk*, 1619. By Inigo Jones. Pen, ink and wash. RIBA Library Drawings Collection.

49 *Covent Garden on a Market Day*, about 1756–8. By Samuel Scott. Inigo Jones designed the arcaded buildings on the right (1631–7) and the church of St Paul on the left (1631–3). The Museum of London.

12. Fashion from abroad: the court of Charles II

Pratt was one of many who had been forced abroad by the political events of the 1640s and 1650s. On his return he became an influential gentleman architect (see Chapter 2), notably through his house for the Earl of Clarendon in Piccadilly.

The shift in taste that occurred after the King's return in 1660 is clearly shown in two reactions to Clarendon House. Firstly, to John Evelyn, Pratt's friend and fellow continental traveller, it was simply 'the best contriv'd, most useful, most graceful, and magnificent house in England. I except not Audley-end [a house he had admired in 1654]; which though larger, and full of gaudy & barbarous ornaments, does not gratify judicious spectators'. Samuel Pepys, too, changed his opinion of Audley End, praising the huge Jacobean house in 1660, but, after visiting Clarendon House in 1667, finding it old-fashioned after the 'nobleness' and 'furniture and pictures' of the London house: 'the ceilings are not so good as I took them to be, being nothing so well wrought as my Lord Chancellor's are; and though the figure of the house without be extraordinary good, yet the staircase is exceeding poor'.

Pepys's concentration on the interiors of both buildings, and his continuing approval of the *exterior* of Audley End, reminds us that one of the principal effects of Charles II's exile and triumphant return was the introduction of new forms of interior decoration and ornament. These were created in emulation of foreign courts, and especially that of France. The survival of great courtier houses like Chatsworth and Petworth and the destruction or alteration of all Charles II's significant palace projects, including Wren's royal palace at Winchester and most of the great baroque interiors of the 1670s at Windsor Castle, have obscured the pioneering nature of court building and decoration. Only the reduced echoes still seen at Windsor and at the Scottish Palace of Holyroodhouse serve to remind us of the achievements in plaster and paint that were so influential.

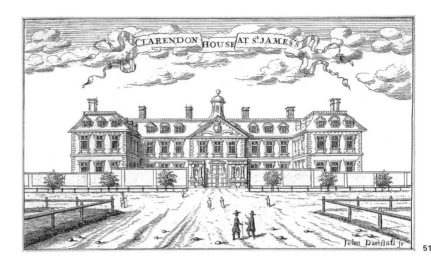

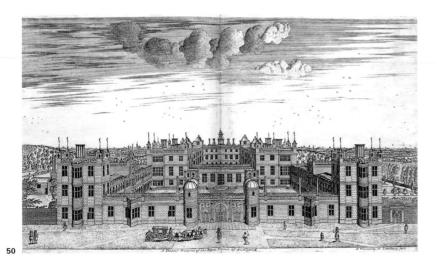

50 Audley End, Essex, built 1603–14. Engraved by Henry Winstanley, about 1676. Engraving. VAM E.343-1902.

51 Clarendon House, Piccadilly, London, built about 1670. By John Dunstall. Clarendon House, designed by Sir Roger Pratt, was built in 1664–7 and demolished in 1683. Etching. VAM E.426-1898.

52 The Great Hall at Audley End, Essex, built 1603–14.

53

55

54

The accessibility of Charles II's court, in contrast to that of Charles I, not only opened it up to censure on moral grounds, but exposed private royal tastes to a greater number of people. Evelyn was shocked at the luxury displayed therein, although he approved of appropriate grandeur on the exteriors of royal buildings. Writing in 1683 about the dressing room of the King's mistress, the Duchess of Portsmouth, he commented:

> . . . what ingag'd my curiosity, was the rich & splendid furniture of this woman's apartment, now once or twice puld down and rebuilt, to satisfie her prodigal and expensive pleasures . . . : Here I saw the new fabrique of *French Tapissry*, for design, tendernesse of worke, & incomparable imitation of the best paintings; beyond anything, I had ever beheld . . . Then for *Japon Cabinets*, *Skreenes*, *Pendule* Clocks, Huge *Vasas* of wrought plate, *Tables*, *Stands*, *Chimny furniture*, *Sconces*, *branches*, *Braseras* &c they were all of massive silver and without number, besides of his Majesties best paintings . . .

But Evelyn was in the minority, for by this stage the royal lead was eagerly being followed by courtiers, who were busily ordering state beds and creating apartments *en enfilade*. At Ham House, which, Evelyn said, was 'furnished like a great Prince's', the Duke of Lauderdale created these features in rooms

53 The king's ante-chamber, the Palace of Holyroodhouse, Edinburgh. Holyroodhouse was enlarged and remodelled in 1671–9 to the designs of Sir William Bruce. The plasterwork was by John Houlbert and George Dunsterfield.

54 The Queen's closet, Ham House, London, about 1675.

built in the 1670s. Some 25 great state beds survive from this period up to about 1700. In the 1680s courtiers, who had left off large building projects since the early years of the century, started to put up country houses on a palatial scale. The earliest, the Earl of Devonshire at Chatsworth, employed all the carvers, painters, smiths and other craftspeople being used on the royal works, although other noblemen did not stint on importing their own craftspeople and painters from France, as the Duke of Montagu did for Montagu House in the early 1690s. However, royal influence was not simply a matter of art and design, but of complete court etiquette. The King played a key role in introducing as court dress the wearing of the Persian vest in deliberate opposition to French fashion, during hostilities with France in 1666, in order that, according to Lord Halifax, 'we might look like a more distinct people'.

Foreign artists and craftspeople became especially important in the process of creating the Franco-Dutch court style after 1660.

Sometimes opposition from the London trade guilds was overcome by their employment in the royal office of the Great Wardrobe, which was outside guild control. Perhaps significantly (in view of Evelyn's comments), the Flemish painter Sir Peter Lely was largely employed to paint private images of Charles II's mistresses, while the English painter John Michael Wright did the King's state portraits. Antonio Verrio (brought to England by the Duke of Montagu in 1672) introduced the art of *trompe l'oeil* baroque mural painting.

Foreign craftspeople became especially evident in the 1680s, when the accession of William and Mary made Britain a particularly suitable destination for several thousand Huguenots fleeing France, following the revocation of the Edict of Nantes in 1685, which took away their protection. The high technical expertise of Huguenot goldsmiths, gunmakers, clockmakers, silk weavers, ironsmiths and others was at least as important as

55 *The Duchess of Portsmouth*, about 1679. By Sir Peter Lely. Oil on canvas. Atkinson Art Gallery, Southport.

56 The chapel, Chatsworth House, Derbyshire, built 1688–93. Painting by Louis Laguerre, Ricard and Antonio Verrio. Carving by Caius Gabriel Cibber, Samuel Watson and Grinling Gibbons.

57 *Charles II*, 1671. By John Michael Wright. Oil on canvas. © The Royal Collection.

THE MELVILLE BED

Tessa Murdoch

The accession of William and Mary in 1689 inspired a new confidence in the monarchy. A spate of rebuilding and redecoration of the royal palaces was imitated by leading courtiers and officers of state. This resulted in a crop of grand British houses in the baroque style.

In 1689 George Melville was appointed Secretary of State for Scotland and in 1690 William III made him an earl. From 1691 Melville held other lesser offices of state with lucrative salaries. In 1697 he commissioned a palatial residence, Melville House, Fife, from the leading Scottish architect James Smith.

The highlight of the State Apartment on the first floor was the State Bedroom, with its magnificent bed hung with crimson Genoa velvet and lined with ivory Chinese damask. Like the entrance doorway and the carved overmantels, the State Bed was decorated with symbols of Melville's authority – earl's coronets – and personalized with ciphers of his initials and those of his wife, Catherine. The marriage was of dynastic importance; she was the daughter of Alexander, first Earl of Leven, and brought that title into the Melville family.

The bed was inspired by the work of Daniel Marot, the French-trained designer to William and Mary, whose work in interiors and garden layouts Lord Melville would have seen during his exile in Holland in the 1680s. Marot's designs, published from 1687, provided a rich source for contemporary craftspeople. The bed

58. *George, 1st Earl of Melville*, **1691. By Sir John Baptiste de Medina. Oil on canvas. Scottish National Portrait Gallery.**

is attributed to the French émigré upholsterer Francis Lapiere, who worked in Pall Mall, St James's, London.

As the dominant piece of furniture in the palatial, but often rarely used apartments of state that became a feature of noble houses in the late seventeenth century, beds of this kind were not intended for regular sleeping. Rather they symbolized their owner's wealth, noble rank and exalted connections. On the few occasions they were used, it was by illustrious visitors, usually royalty. Then they became a majestic theatrical setting where the visitor received privileged guests according to strict rules of precedence. Only the prodigiously wealthy could afford to spend so much on a little-used symbol of their eminent status.

59. Headboard of the State Bed from Melville House.

60. *Catherine, 1st Countess of Melville*, **1691. By Sir John Baptiste de Medina. Oil on canvas. In a private Scottish collection.**

61. The State Bed from Melville House, Fife, about 1700. Probably upholstered by Francis Lapiere and assembled in London. Bed stock of oak, tester of pine, hangings of crimson Italian velvet with ivory Chinese silk linings, embroidered with crimson braid and fringe. [h. 462.3cm]. VAM W.35-1949.

62

the fashions they brought, allowing them to keep up with changing French tastes through networks of their compatriots on the continent. The immigrants also added to the growing quantity of ornament prints published in England after 1660. Their mixed nature, a combination of reissues of old sets and copies of new ones from abroad, is a clear indication of a great demand for guidance in the new styles.

13. Classicism established

The years after 1660 fulfilled the aspirations of Charles I and Inigo Jones to create a new national architecture expressed in the classical style. This was principally the achievement of Sir Christopher Wren. We should not be surprised, given the period's importance as a cradle of experimental science, that Wren began as a distinguished scientist, Professor of Astronomy and founder of the Royal Society, for contemporaries like Evelyn believed that architecture was 'the flower and crown as it were of all the sciences mathematical'. Indeed, it was Wren's work as a scientist that first attracted the King's attention in 1660, leading to his eventual appointment as Surveyor General of the King's Works in 1668. Wren was a brilliant empirical designer, capable of working in a number of different classical styles drawn from a wide range of sources. Most significantly, he operated almost entirely in the public arena. Some of his designs, such as most of his palace schemes, were either never built or were truncated in their execution, but his built public work, and especially St Paul's Cathedral and the City churches after the Fire of London, affected church building right into the nineteenth century and secular building up to the 1720s, establishing a consistent public architecture in Britain for the first time.

This process went hand-in-hand with the development of the King's Office of Works, which became, in effect, a training school for architects, builders and other craftspeople. The consequences were profound. In the long term it represented the first step towards the creation of a real architectural profession; more immediately it was a mechanism for the spread of design ideas through the subsequent work of the participating masons and other master craftspeople, both for exteriors and interiors. While the craftspeople and builders followed Wren's style, leading to the creation of a national school, his assistants and distinguished colleagues, like Nicholas Hawksmoor and Sir John Vanbrugh, went their own way stylistically, creating a new and dramatic baroque style.

An Act of God can also be said to have had a profound and long-term effect on architecture and planning. A few days after most of the City had been burned down in the Great Fire of 1666, Wren presented the King with a scheme to rebuild London on a regular plan. This came to nothing, but in the same year Wren, Pratt and the royal architect Hugh May were among the commissioners considering the rebuilding and helped to draft the Rebuilding Act of 1667. This was the first of many statutes that regulated building in the City of London (and, after 1774, beyond it as well), marking the true end of haphazard medieval building and

63

---

62 Dish and ewer, with London hallmarks for 1705–6. Made and engraved by Philip Rollos and supplied by John Charleton, Master of the Jewel Office, as ambassadorial plate for Thomas Wentworth, Baron Raby and third Earl of Strafford, as Ambassador Extraordinary to the King of Prussia. Silver-gilt, engraved and cast with applied ornament. VAM M.23-1963.

63 *Designs for an écuelle and lid*, 1694. By C. de Moelder. Plate from the set *Proper Ornaments to be Engrav'd on Plate*. The ecuelle (porringer) was introduced into Britain by Huguenot craftspeople. Engraving and stipple engraving. VAM E.386-1926.

64

65

66

design practices, which had been the subject of fitful regulation for some 60 years. Among other things, the Act established four sorts of flat-fronted house, related in height to the width of the street and with a fixed number of floors at fixed distances. The purpose of regulation was not simply to allow in light and air (and prevent fire) but to control appropriate occupation, from the houses of the first, two-storey sort in 'by-streets and lanes' to the 'Citizens of Extraordinary quality' in the third sort, 'fronting high and principal streets'. A sumptuary law by another name, it was created at a time when other forms of consumption were beginning to move away from such controls, as taste moved into the Georgian period. But that is another story.

64 St Paul's Cathedral. London, built 1675–1710. Designed by Sir Christopher Wren.

65 *Sir Christopher Wren*, 1711. By Sir Godfrey Kneller. Oil on canvas. National Portrait Gallery, London.

66 No. 10, Neville's Court, London, built about 1680–1700. A house of the second sort, as established by the Rebuilding Act of 1667.

CHAPTER 4

Tudor and Stuart Britain, 1500–1714
Fashionable living

MAURICE HOWARD

1. The impact of change

In the modern world we have got used to the idea that our lives are subject to change. We may mix and match the fashions of a few years ago with those of the present, but we all accept that the houses we live in, the goods amassed there and the clothes that we wear will look fundamentally different at one end of our lives from the other.

In the sixteenth and seventeenth centuries people in Britain had to come to terms with the impact of change in new and challenging ways. The Reformation radically changed fundamentals of belief and systems of authority within the Church and redistributed between one-quarter and one-third of the country's land. The great inflation of about 1550 challenged previous certainties about economic stability. The political upheavals of the seventeenth century saw a king executed and another forced into exile, with permanent impact on the power of the monarchy. All these moves suggested that political, economic and social structures were impermanent and encouraged a new, sober judgement on change in matters of everyday life.

1 Paycocke's House, Great Coggeshall, Essex, built about 1500 for Thomas Paycocke, chief clothier of the town.

2 *Sir Thomas More and his family*, 1527–8. By Hans Holbein the Younger. Preparatory drawing for a lost life-size painting. This is one of very few contemporary depictions of an early 16th-century English domestic interior. Pen and ink. Öffentliche Kunstsammlung, Basel.

In his *Description of England*, first published in 1577, the Essex clergyman William Harrison perceived change in terms of economic prosperity expanding down through the social classes; barons, the lowest rank of nobility, could now, he argued, afford new houses of a scale formerly reserved for great princes, and 'inferior artificers and many farmers' have 'learned also to garnish their cupboards with plate, their joint beds with tapestry and silk hangings, and their tables with carpets and fine napery, whereby the wealth of our country . . . doth infinitely appear'. By the time Daniel Defoe compiled *A Tour through the Whole Island of Great Britain* in the 1720s, the change that Harrison had described was being explained in terms of great cycles of the rise and fall of cities, important families, harbours and manufactures, but his comments were also infused with a sense of the new 'Empire' of Great Britain as a net exporter of ideas and products, in command of change and thus of its destiny.

When examining the houses and disposable goods that made up the day-to-day of people's lives it is important to stress two things, firstly about quantity and availability, and secondly about the dominant market. One of the ways of gauging the greater availability of objects in the home is to judge aspects of use, and it does appear that while a great many items in the house of about 1500 might be new (or certainly renewable, according to the dictates of fashion), the vast majority were objects that were in daily use; few things were superfluous or decorative. By 1700 many more objects were kept for the sake of decoration and for their value as collectable items; indeed, among the most wealthy the growth of collecting, and the discrimination that went with that development of taste, forms a key feature of the story of the arts in the seventeenth century.

In the early seventeenth century a handful of leading collectors gathered antique sculpture and other antiquities, alongside paintings and drawings recognized as great achievements of the Italian and Flemish schools of artists. By 1700 collecting had expanded to include contemporary work and examples from a range of the decorative arts. The first collections of contemporary delftware were being assembled, led by the example of Queen Mary II, celebrating the finest and rarest manufactures that were on offer. Netherlandish delftware had already been copied by English factories at Lambeth and Bristol.

William Harrison used the evidence of houses as an indicator of improved living conditions. He especially noted the greater adoption of permanent materials, the importance of larger living spaces and the rethinking of parts of the house in relation to each other: 'The ancient manors and houses of our gentlemen are yet, and for the most part, of strong timber . . . Howbeit, such as be lately builded are commonly either of brick or hard stone or both, their rooms large and comely, and houses of office [i.e. kitchens, rooms for storage, stables] further distant from their lodgings.' He was writing, however, only at the beginning of a great upturn in building activity. The period from about 1570 has often been described as an age of the 'Great Rebuilding' of the country's domestic housing, which continued until the early eighteenth century, interrupted to some extent by the disruption of the civil war of 1640–60.

3 *A Magnificent Mansion lately standing in Crutched Friars*, 1792. By J. T. Smith. Showing the courtyard of an elaborate London house of about 1600. Engraving. Corporation of London.

2. House planning

The initial phase of this regeneration witnessed great changes in the interior planning of houses, which reflected greater prosperity for some, new ideas about privacy and convenience and, in the grandest houses, new concepts of demonstrating wealth and splendour for entertaining and impressing one's peer group. Various styles of exterior architecture were successively employed – sometimes to express, at other times to disguise, changes within. After about 1660, however, a second phase of great rebuilding saw the emergence of a new conformity of style in the exterior of houses in both town and country. This evolved from the architectural logic of the classical style, with its symmetry and proportion, its clear sense of how to express the more and less important parts of a building through a standard vocabulary of ornament. This overlay of classicism proved the ultimate means of harmonizing external order with the new internal arrangements of houses.

In the largest houses, built for the nobility and the wealthiest of gentry landowners, the increase in the number of room spaces marked a greater concern for privacy, for separating masters and servants and thereby abandoning the provision of the communal living spaces that had marked great houses at an earlier period. The hall, once a communal living and often sleeping space, had by this time become more of a vestibule, a circulation or crossing point between the various rooms of the house. There was also a sense of other rooms now having specialist functions.

In the first half of the sixteenth century great houses were often built around courtyards, essentially planned as separate ranges with different roles in servicing the house. There was no sense of external symmetry or order, save that afforded by the material employed: brick largely in the south and east of England, stone in the West Country and in Scotland. The building was understood externally by a kind of applied sign language indicating the various parts: coats of arms over gateways, bay windows to important rooms and tower structures. These last often had an added floor to indicate the owner's privacy and as a place for the security of goods. The concern for heraldry to denote both the hierarchy of the house and the importance of its owner found its way also, within the house, into stained glass, wall hangings and fittings such as tiles.

5

4

6

4 The south front of Belton House, Lincolnshire, built 1685–6 for Sir John Brownlow.

5 Armorial floor tile, 1500–21. Made in the Worcester area for Edward Stafford, Duke of Buckingham, for use at Thornbury Castle, Gloucestershire. Red earthenware, stamped and filled with white clay slip. VAM 1098-1892.

6 Stained-glass panel from Beaupré Hall, Cambridgeshire, about 1570. It shows the arms of the 16th-century owner's great-grandfather, stressing his ancestry. Clear, flashed and pot-metal glass painted with brown enamel and yellow stain. VAM C.60-1946.

The later sixteenth century saw grand houses with just as large a floor area, but now integrated into compact blocks, with courtyards increasingly abandoned and a clear articulation of separate floor levels. The demarcation of functions of the house by floor level eventually prompted the regular application of classical orders to the exterior. It was members of the gentry and of the wealthy urban middling class who led the way in the demand for compact houses in both town and country. Compactness and consistency of floor levels led in turn, both externally and internally, to a new concept of design. Rooms that once would have been arranged with purely functional considerations in mind, leading off each other where practical needs determined and with larger or smaller windows according to the room's importance, were now arranged in *enfilade*, with doors from one room to another aligned to create a regular vista. This regularity meant that conventions of decoration and furnishing could become more standardized and the furnishings of each particular space more *en suite* with each other. The earlier loose association of internal spaces had by 1700 become organized into sets of rooms.

It was in Scotland that the modern form of 'hall' was first given a correct, descriptive name, for it there became known as the 'lobby', indicating its function as vestibule. In Scotland the word 'hall' usually meant a grand reception room, more akin to the space in England known as a 'great chamber'. This room was often reserved in great houses for special occasions and would, in the grandest houses, serve as the place of reception for visitors of high rank, perhaps for dining in at particular times of year and even as a

15

16

15 The winter parlour, Canons Ashby, Northamptonshire, with painted decoration of the 1590s.

16 The long gallery, Haddon Hall, Derbyshire, built about 1600. This gallery was built as an extension to an earlier courtyard house, forming one side of a second court and overlooking the gardens.

place for the lying-in-state of the dead body of a high-ranking owner. The great chamber was on the upper floor of the house, while a downstairs room retained the name 'parlour' well into the seventeenth century and was the family room of common daily life. 'Drawing room' generally supplanted the term 'great chamber' in the seventeenth century, though a number of drawing rooms proliferated in larger houses. Sometimes the word 'saloon' – derived from the French *salon* and denoting the predominance of French fashions in interior furnishing – was used for the chief reception room.

Throughout the sixteenth century and in many parts of the country even beyond 1600, particularly in rural areas or less fashionable country houses, inventories of household possessions tell us that many rooms in the house still contained beds. Some great houses had a 'best' bedchamber, indicating a room probably reserved for visitors, but a significant development of the seventeenth century was the emergence of a 'state' bedchamber: part of a sequence of rooms, for which an especially grand bed would be commissioned. The bedchamber would be preceded by at least one room for private reception by an important visitor, and followed by a small, inner room closer to the bedroom – the whole set of rooms making up an 'apartment', a term derived from the French, with whom the idea began. In the largest houses two suites of such rooms were provided for the honoured visitor and for his wife, the plan of these matching rooms echoing each other across the main floor of the house. One remarkable feature attending this development, however, was the disappearance of regular provision, in new houses after about 1550, for sanitation. Late medieval and early Tudor houses usually had garderobe offshoots acting as lavatories wherever they were needed, disgorging into moats or into a pit that was periodically emptied. The increase of formality in architecture meant that these 'necessaries' as outshoots from the building were more difficult to place and disguise (though sometimes the sides of huge fireplace projections were used). Greater privacy may have meant that inner closets could now provide the place for a personal close stool, attended to by the servant who slept nearby.

The greater formality of planning the important rooms of a house was tied to a greater expectation of daily ceremonial in the household and, on the occasion of important visits, places that could be shown as a sign of family status. One especially notable feature of the greater country houses of these two centuries (and even of larger town houses where this proved convenient) was the provision of a long gallery. This originated as a means of access into the gardens, along the sides of courtyards linking parts of the building to one another or running alongside a sequence of rooms to provide a communal passage of communication. By the Elizabethan and Jacobean period long galleries were on a grand scale, in the largest houses being built high in the house underneath the roof to overlook parkland and forest, and usually containing some of the finest family possessions, including portraits.

3. Wall and ceiling decoration

The fitting out of a house began from practical concerns, but increasingly offered a choice of materials as the period progressed. Wall coverings were important for the exclusion of draughts. Panelling, in oak and usually painted throughout this period, developed from a piecemeal art of small panels attached to battens, the panels often being decorated with a pattern of folded cloth, later called 'linenfold'. From the later sixteenth century inlaid woods were more often employed and the arrangement of panelling became grander, devised architecturally with dado and cornice, perhaps also with pilasters in the main field, thus echoing the order of exterior architecture, especially for large rooms such as main drawing rooms (or saloons) and long galleries. In this new architectural scheme the fireplace became a focal point, with the generally lower fireplaces of early Tudor times now giving way to larger, grander fire openings with overmantels, carrying heraldry or allegorical subjects, in carved wood or alabaster.

As an alternative to panelling, textile hangings might cover a wall. The wealth of hangings was certainly the most distinctive feature of a room, especially when associated with textiles on accompanying furniture, and often gave the name to a particular room in the house to distinguish it from others.

17

17 Detail of a panelled room known as the 'Haynes Grange Room', created about 1585–1620, perhaps for Chicksands Priory, Bedfordshire. The interior architecture created here partly followed woodcuts for Sebastiano Serlio's third book on architecture (first published 1540), in which he described the interior of the Pantheon in Rome. This photograph shows the panelling as re-erected at the Victoria and Albert Museum in 1929. VAM W.1-1929.

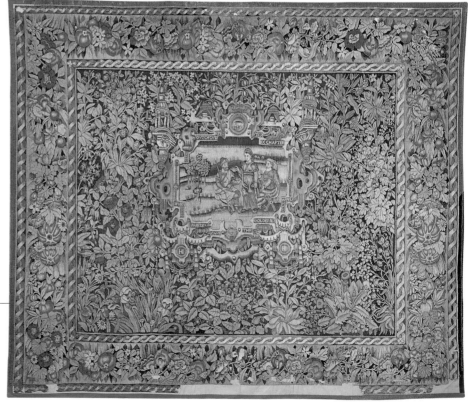

18 Tapestry showing the arms of the Earl of Leicester, about 1585. Probably made at one of the Sheldon tapestry workshops in Warwickshire or Worcestershire, for Leicester House, near the Thames, the London house of Robert Dudley, Earl of Leicester. Tapestry woven in wool and silk. [h. 290cm]. VAM T.320-1977.

19 Tapestry showing the Judgement of Paris, about 1595. Made at one of the Sheldon tapestry workshops in Warwickshire or Worcestershire, for Chastleton House, Oxfordshire. Tapestry woven in wool and silk. [h. 321cm]. VAM T.310-1920.

At the highest end of the market, tapestry, imported from Flanders or subsequently supplied by the Mortlake tapestry factory founded in the reign of James I and VI, carried grand themes, still sometimes biblical (though with a narrower choice of subjects and stories, after the Reformation discouraged the depiction of certain mystical Christian themes) or from classical literature or ancient history. Dense landscapes set in the heart of woodland evoked the necessary pastime of hunting, which was so integral to life on the country estate. Cheaper stained and painted cloths hung in less important rooms, or throughout the main living spaces in less important houses. Style changed much less in these over two centuries, so that the few surviving fragments of this material are often difficult to date. There was a vogue in the seventeenth century for hangings of gilded or painted leather, usually imported from the Low Countries. However, the great revolution in wall coverings came with the fashion for silks or damasks (reversible fabrics of silk or linen with a woven patterned surface), so that hangings of these materials could be bought by the yard and applied to any wall space, fixed to the frames that made up the architecture of each wall of the room. Between 1679 and 1683 the ante-chamber to the Queen's Bedroom at Ham House was fitted with 'foure pieces of blewe Damusk, impaned and bordered wth. blew velvet embroidered with gould and fringed'.

20 Detail of a wall hanging imitating panelling, about 1600. Painted for the upper room of The Lockers, Hemel Hempstead, Hertfordshire. Tempera on canvas panels, painted. VAM W.41-1952.

21 Wall hanging, about 1720. Made for Jenkyn Place, Bentley, Hampshire. Distemper on canvas, painted and possibly partly printed. [h. 152cm]. VAM. Anonymous loan.

22 Leather panel, about 1670. Attributed to Martinus Van den Heuvel the Younger, owner of the gilt leather firm, Compagnie van Goudleermaken of Amsterdam. Embossed leather with metallic finish, paint and coloured glazes. [h. 86cm]. VAM W.67-1911.

23 The painted chamber, Gladstone's
Land, Edinburgh. The painted ceiling in
this upstairs room of a merchant's house
dates from 1617–20.

24 The great chamber, Canons Ashby, Northamptonshire. The plaster ceiling was installed shortly after 1632.

Wallpaper first appeared in England in the early sixteenth century in small printed sheets, but the technology developed so that longer lengths were being produced by the end of the seventeenth century. In John Houghton's *A Collection of Letters for the Improvement of Husbandry and Trade* of 1689 the author describes the older tradition of small sheets, but goes on, ' . . . there are some other done in Rolls in long sheets of thick paper made for the Purpose whose sheets are pasted together to be so long as the Height of a Room, and they are managed like Woolen hangings, and there is a great Variety, with curious Cuts, which are Cheap, and if kept from Wet, very lasting'. Wallpaper was sufficiently established that a tax was first imposed in 1712.

Above the wall-plate level in especially grand rooms, the frieze might be painted in the early sixteenth century; examples survive with rough but vigorous work in the antique style, but increasingly the frieze was a field garnished with plasterwork, which later extended to ceilings. After a period in the early sixteenth century when ceilings were decorated with wooden battens or ribs – filled, in the case of the royal palaces of Henry VIII, with decorative *all'antica* ornament in papier mâché or pressed leather – the fashion for plaster ceilings became popular after about 1570, with the first appearance of plaster ceilings with hanging pendants. These ceilings carried family heraldry and often emblematic devices, or representations of the months, the seasons or the worthies. A particularly rich tradition of lavishly painted, sometimes emblematic ceilings developed in Scotland between about 1570 and 1640, but there painted directly on to the wooden beams of the most important rooms in the house. By the mid-seventeenth century the taste had changed in both England and Scotland to the use of plasterwork for geometrically divided compartments, now usually banishing emblems in favour of wreaths of fruit and flowers and heavy classical mouldings.

4. Furnishings

Sixteenth-century inventories, recording all the movable goods of the house at a critical point in its history (usually the death of the owner), list a variety of objects, but with a proliferation throughout the house which suggests that things were much moved around. Furniture at this time, predominantly of oak, fulfilled the basic requirements of seating, surfaces for eating and storage, with a sufficiency of soft furnishings in the form of cushions and table carpets to render the surfaces more comfortable and luxurious. Fairly simple wooden furniture (items such as framed chests and cupboards, gate-leg tables and panel-backed chairs) remained the staple furnishing of modest houses throughout the seventeenth century, individualized and regionalized by the use of distinctive geometric motifs, or sometimes with biblical or other

25 Armchair, about 1540. Carved and joined oak. VAM W.39-1920.

inscriptions. Furniture with leather seats and backs was a feature of the mid-century period. Walnut furniture became fashionable for the wealthier classes, as did, by the 1670s, furniture covered with marquetry: a decorative veneer applied to the surface and made up of pieces of wood and perhaps other materials, like ivory or bone, to form a pictorial or patterned mosaic.

For seating, the seventeenth century saw a great increase in upholstered furniture, with whole sets of chairs, footstools and benches being commissioned, notably accompanying a state bed. Indeed, in the decades after 1660, so expensive and dominant were the upholstered items in a room of state that the upholsterer in effect became the designer of the interior furnishings as a whole. High-backed cane chairs were often used in dining rooms, halls and vestibules where people waited and in everyday living parlours.

26 Cushion cover with the arms of Sandys and Windsor, impaling vines, probably 1550s. Linen canvas embroidered with silk and metal thread in long-armed cross and tent stitches, laid and couched work. VAM T.51 1978.

27 Draw-table, about 1600. Made in England, though the design of the bulbous legs is Flemish and German in origin. Inlaid and carved oak, sycamore, holly and bog-oak. VAM 384-1898.

28 Gate-leg table, about 1700–10. Elm, turned and joined. VAM W.37-1938.

One significant area of textile production – that of embroidery – remained firmly within the domestic sphere. The appropriateness of the task of embroidery at home is stressed from the late sixteenth century onwards in conduct books for women and it was a task carried out, it seems, by women of all classes, from Mary, Queen of Scots and Bess of Hardwick to the daughters of the professional class. While much sixteenth-century embroidery was for clothes and hangings, in the seventeenth century boxes, caskets and mirror surrounds were worked. Mirrors are especially interesting, given their expense (home-produced mirrors were of poor quality and the best were imported from Venice) and their association with the sin of vanity. Surrounding the mirror with an uplifting embroidered narrative or image therefore turned the object into a moral lesson for maker and viewer alike. Particularly popular during the reign of Charles II were images of the King and Queen flanking mirrors.

29 Chair, 1695–1705. Made in England. Carved and turned walnut with cane seat and back. VAM W.35-1936.

30 Armchair, about 1670. Probably made in France for Ham House, London. Beech, carved, gilded and silvered with traces of coloured glazes. VAM HH.81:1-1948.

31 Mirror frame, 1660–80. The king and queen represented are probably Charles II and Catherine of Braganza, his wife. Border of satin embroidered with silk and metal thread; framed in wood painted to imitate lacquer. VAM 351-1886.

TEXTILES FOR THE HOME

Sara Pennell

The importance that people in the sixteenth and seventeenth centuries accorded to textiles as domestic furnishings is captured by William Harrison's observation in 1577 that even artificers and farmers now furnished their 'beds with tapestry and silk hangings, and their tables with carpets and fine napery'. These had been the traditional prerogatives of the noble household. Their spread down the social scale was visible evidence of an improvement in living standards among the middling groups in the population.

Textiles had a vital practical function at a time when interiors consisted of timber floors, wainscoted walls and rooms often lacking hearths. Practicality did not, however, preclude decoration and luxury. The most exclusive (often imported) fabrics, like cloth-of-gold, remained the preserve of kings and courtiers. Yet by the close of the sixteenth century a growing indigenous industry using skills drawn from continental Europe was producing a versatile range of furnishing textiles – light woollens and wool-linen mixes, such as

32. Hangings on a bed at Doddington Hall, Lincolnshire, 1680. Crewelwork.

dornixes, dyed with novel dyestuffs. Carpets from Persia and Turkey introduced yet more colour and pattern, as did Indian painted fabrics ('pintadoes'), the precursors of the chintzes and calicoes that flourished a century later.

How these textiles were used illustrates the flexibility of furnishings in the era before fixed seat upholstery and wallpapers. The elaborately embroidered cushions that softened wooden seat furniture, the carpets that dressed tables – all were eminently mobile. Even costly tapestries like Charles I's Mortlake sets travelled from palace to palace, as occasion demanded. Domestic textiles were 'mobile' in another sense, too, as one of the major forms of wealth bequeathed down the generations. Surviving crewelwork bed curtains made by Abigail Pett may indeed be the set belonging to the 'complete bed' that she left in her will, dated 1706.

Needleworking was considered an appropriate 'knowledge' to be learned by women who aspired to good housewifery, not least because its products were considered

33. *The Somerset House Conference*, about 1604. Painted by an unknown artist. The scene shows the signing of an Anglo-Spanish peace treaty in Somerset House, London, a royal property. Turkish carpets cover the table and floor, and Flemish tapestries the walls. The delegates are seated on upholstered chairs. Oil on canvas. National Portrait Gallery, London.

valuable ornaments to the domestic environment. However, considerable application was needed to embroider a complete set of bed curtains. Sometimes it deserted even the most dedicated needlewoman. In 1657 the wealthy lawyer Heneage Finch reported that his wife had nearly completed a set of bed curtains, but as for the matching carpet and seating, 'I should despayr of seeing an end of them.' Such industry notwithstanding, domestically produced textiles were often used alongside ready-made products throughout the Tudor–Stuart period. The commercial availability of popular designs in books, prints and ready-drawn patterns sold by booksellers also meant that motifs used by professional embroiderers were accessible to domestic needleworkers.

35. Detail of a cushion cover, about 1550–1600. Perhaps made for a stool or chair. Woven silk satin ground, with applied work in velvet, cloth-of-silver and silk; embroidered details
in silk, metal thread and sequins. VAM T.22-1947.

36. Tapestry showing the story of Vulcan and Venus, 1620–5. Woven in the Mortlake tapestry factory, London. The design is taken from 16th-century Brussels tapestries. From a set made for Charles, Prince of Wales, later Charles I. Woven wool, silk and metal thread. [h. 453cm]. VAM T.170-1978.

34. Bed hanging, 1680–1700. Embroidered by Abigail Pett, who put her name on an associated valance. The foliage influenced by imported Indian textiles. Embroidered in crewel wool on a linen and cotton ground. [h. 195.6cm]. VAM T.13-1929.

5. Buying in town

Shopping for goods for the home and personal attire was one of the primary attractions of the great urban centres. London led the way, but many provincial cities and towns also increased their trade in goods hugely in this period. Some places, like Canterbury, that had been great centres of pilgrimage in earlier times needed to diversify after the Reformation and became places of leisure by the end of the seventeenth century, attracting local wealthy gentry and the nobility. Through great centres of trade, goods from around the world became increasingly the common currency of luxury buying.

Sir Thomas Smith, scholar and political writer, remarked as early as 1549 that within the last 20 years perhaps a dozen haberdashers' shops in London had grown to such a number that 'from the towere to westminster alonge, everie streate is full of them; and their shoppes glisters and shine of glasses, as well lookinge as drinckinge, yea all mannor of vesselles of the same stuffe, painted cuses, gaye daggers, knives, swordes, and girdles'. The building of the Gresham's (later named the Royal) Exchange in 1578 and then the New Exchange, built as a speculative venture by Sir Robert Cecil in 1609, created the equivalent of shopping malls in Elizabethan and Jacobean London, with many small booths gathered together under one roof. In other parts of the city it is noticeable that retail spaces became larger at this time. The capital was of course the chief distribution point for foreign goods, and for a considerable time there was much anxiety about the unfavourable balance of trade. Elizabeth I's chief minister William Cecil noted the 'excess of silkes . . . of wyne and spice' (wine imports quadrupled during Elizabeth's 45-year reign) and believed that their promotion was a way of 'consent to the robbery of the realm'.

Provincial cities like Gloucester became suppliers for a large network of part-time shops in rural areas within a 24–30 kilometre radius, as well as serving the local gentry who visited to buy. While Gloucester depended heavily on Bristol for foreign imports, it is true to say that London fashions in a whole range of goods, from clothes to domestic fixtures and the ordering of funerary monuments, were especially dominant by 1700, with the result that it is more difficult to characterize and identify regional styles of goods than it is from the period around 1500.

37

38

37 Casting bottle, about 1540–50. Made in England by an unknown goldsmith, using the maker's mark of a cusped I. For the keeping and sprinkling of perfumed water. Silver, chased, embossed and engraved. VAM 451-1865.

38 Detail of a fringe, about 1600–30. Made in Italy or possibly England. A trimming for upholstered furniture. Silk, gold and silver thread. [w. 8.5cm]. VAM T.270-1965.

By 1700 shops were being designed with interior architectonic features like stage sets, and glazed windows allowed a view from the outside. There were anxieties about the increasing popularity of shopping turning it from a necessary activity to one of leisure. Women were seen as especially prone to the temptations of shopping, particularly where clothes were concerned. A character in Ben Jonson's play *Epicene* warns another of the danger of marriage and of women's lust for consumer goods: 'She must have that rich gown for such a great day, a new one for the next, a richer for the third; be served in silver; have the chamber filled with a succession of grooms, footmen, ushers and other messengers, besides embroiderers, jewellers, tire-women, sempsters [seam-stresses], feathermen, perfumers.' As so often in a patriarchal society, women got the blame for a general unease about society's indulgences. It is interesting, too, that the desire for the latest fashion in dress heads the list of these 'sins' of excess.

39 Tobacco box, with London hallmarks for 1655–6. Mark of 'IS'. The luxury of tobacco stimulated expensive accessories such as this box. Silver, engraved. [h. 2.4cm]. VAM M.695-1926.

40 Trade card for the Blue Paper warehouse, Aldermanbury, London, about 1710. The proprietor, Abraham Price, stands at the door of his shop. The process of wallpaper printing is depicted at the top left. Engraving. Bodleian Library.

6. Dress codes

Like extravagant building, excessive attention and expenditure on dress invoke the threat of severe punishment in the Bible, which was the authoritative support for much of the high moral tone taken by the critics of luxury. One of their major anxieties concerned the possible assumption of habits of dress above the station of the individual. The sumptuary laws of sixteenth-century England sought to control dress by regulating who could wear what fabric, what colour, in what place and on what occasion. While the repeated issuing of these laws throughout the century suggests that they were difficult to enforce, they do remind us that apparel and its decoration were significant means of understanding rank and status in public places.

In the last proclamation of Elizabeth I's reign, issued in 1597, expensive fabrics were predictably reserved for the upper ranks of society: for men, satin, damask, grosgrain (a coarse fabric invariably containing some silk) and taffeta in hose and doublet were forbidden to those under the degree of a gentleman bearing arms, for instance. Interestingly too, significant accoutrements signifying power were also to be controlled: lace mixed with gold or silver, spurs, swords, rapiers, daggers, wood knives, hangers, buckles or studs of gilt could be worn only by the son of a baron, or higher. Many of the items listed here remind us of the constant government concern about public order and with keeping weapons out of the hands of the lower classes. Court officials, of whatever origin, were exempted from most of these constraints. Most revealingly, those under the degree of baron were forbidden to wear woollen cloth made out of the country, suggesting an eye on the need to control the import of foreign fashions. That the sumptuary laws were governed by political expediency is quite apparent from the fact that after 1600 they ceased to be renewed.

Sixteenth-century fashionable dress was dominated by foreign styles, especially at the royal court, where foreign ambassadors were expected to comment on appearances and attest to the richness of apparel being superior to that of their own countries. The pointed gable hood, which was common to female dress in the first half of the century, was sometimes supplanted by the fashionable French hood, first seen at the court of Francis 1 in the 1540s; this was rounded, set further back and followed the shape of the head. Yet dress was customized to some extent through the choice of material and a love of certain motifs; floral motifs, often emblematic of love or of loyalty to a particular patron, constantly reappeared in English fashions throughout the sixteenth century.

Dress was characterized by the emphasis of certain prominent features – the framing of the head and hands by elaborate necklines, ruffs and cuffs – yet by the denial of the basic body shape. In the case of men, the physical bulk of the upper body was expressed by the wide-shouldered fashions of the first half of the century. The shoulders were narrowed by tighter-fitting doublets in the

41

second half of the century, when male fashions increasingly emphasized (even fetishized) the legs. For women, clothes divided the body into a series of geometric shapes, particularly the triangle of the bodice and the wide skirt, emphasized towards the mid-century by a triangular opening at the front to reveal the underskirt beneath. While the basic shapes of major garments often stayed in fashion for 20 or 30 years, particular additions to dress (what we would now term accessories) put the wearer in the height of fashion. Thus jewellery, hats, gloves and fans, for example, often help to date the dress in a portrait because these things would be especially sensitive to the latest influences from home and abroad.

Clothes for both sexes were covered with surface detail. From about 1510 outer garments were often slashed to reveal the linen beneath. Renaissance ornament, particularly patterns of the moresque design, was applied to underskirts, in the black patterned edging of necklines and the cuffs to shirts, and on the front of the doublet. Occasionally aspects of male and female dress influenced each other. In the 1560s and 1570s women sometimes wore tall, sober hats after the male fashion, and the bodices of their dresses were

41 *Margaret Laton*, about 1620. Probably painted in London by Marcus Gheeraerts the Younger (see *2:27 for her jacket*). Oil on oak panel. VAM E.214-1994.

sometimes influenced by the fastenings of male doublets. Men in the 1580s wore earrings and wore their hair longer. Spanish fashions were especially dominant in about 1600 and encouraged the apogee of elaborate dress for men, with wide, baggy breeches known as 'slops', ruffs (or more commonly by this time starched high collars) framing the head and cutting it off from the body, and a wealth of trimmings and ornament.

Dress took a different turn from about the 1620s, when French influence began to dominate, especially through the leading role played by Charles I's queen, Henrietta Maria. The contours of clothes were softened, plain satins of duller colours were now in evidence and the spiky lace of earlier times gave way to soft bobbin lace. All this reflected a move away from the use of highly patterned materials echoing contemporary heraldry, as a sign of rank and class, towards a sense of demeanour, of knowing how to conduct oneself in these looser fashions to convey a sign of good breeding and education in appropriate manners. Men abandoned shoes with elaborate pompons for boots made of soft Cordoba leather and fashionable women dressed with a careful sense of disorder that was positively *déshabillé*.

43

42 *Anne Erskine, Countess of Rothes and her daughters, Lady Margaret and Lady Mary Leslie*, 1626. By George Jamesone. Oil on canvas. Scottish National Portrait Gallery.

43 *A woman, possibly Elizabeth Capell, the Countess of Caernarvon*, 1653–7. By Richard Gibson. Watercolour on vellum, put down on pasteboard. Fruitwood frame. VAM P.15-1926.

LORD AND LADY CLAPHAM

Susan North

Lord and Lady Clapham are accurate and unique documents of dress history; their clothes are perfect miniatures of fashions of the 1690s Such elaborate and expensive dolls were not children's toys. They were made for the amusement of older girls and women, in the same manner as the 'baby houses' or doll houses of the late seventeenth century.

Lady Clapham's formal garments include a mantua, a type of woman's gown introduced in the 1670s. It is made from white Chinese silk damask trimmed with lace and worn with a matching petticoat. Underneath she wears linen petticoats and boned stays, which give her torso the tubular shape fashionable in the 1690s. Lord Clapham's coat, waistcoat and breeches represent the three-piece outfit introduced by Charles II in the 1660s. Over the next three centuries this ensemble would evolve into the modern business suit. At this period the three garments were not expected to match. Lord Clapham's coat is made of scarlet English wool; his waistcoat and breeches of white silk, probably French, elaborately patterned in silver thread.

Both Lord and Lady Clapham have nightgowns made from silk imported from China. The nightgown was a new item of dress added to the wardrobes of wealthy men and women in the 1670s; it was not worn to bed, but for relaxing in private at home. These

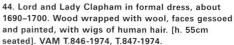

informal gowns were Western variations of the Japanese kimono, whose influence in Europe came through the Dutch East India Company. The man's nightgown is almost an exact copy of the kimono in cut and construction, being a simple T-shaped garment. It would have been

44. Lord and Lady Clapham in formal dress, about 1690–1700. Wood wrapped with wool, faces gessoed and painted, with wigs of human hair. [h. 55cm seated]. VAM T.846-1974, T.847-1974.

worn over the shirt and breeches. The gathers at the back neck and a tuck on either shoulder of Lady Clapham's nightgown illustrate the modifications made in order to accommodate the matching petticoat worn underneath.

What is exceptional about the dolls and their clothes is that they preserve many accessories that do not survive as full-sized garments, as well as illustrating the order in which the garments were worn. Lady Clapham's outfit even includes a mask of the sort worn at the masked balls that were so popular in the seventeenth and eighteenth centuries. Made of cardboard lined with vellum and covered with black silk, it was kept in place by means of a bead attached inside, which was held between the teeth.

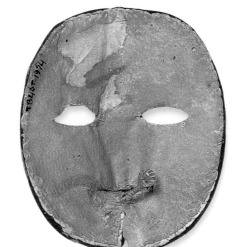

45. Lady Clapham's mask. VAM T.846:T-1974.

46. The back of Lady Clapham's mask. VAM T.846:T-1974.

47. Lady Clapham in her shift, stockings, garters, shoes, underpetticoat and 'pocket' (a separate garment). VAM T.846: A,B,C,G,H,I,J,K&L-1974.

48. Lord Clapham in his shirt, stockings, garters, shoes and breeches. VAM T.847:A,B,F,G,H,I&J-1974.

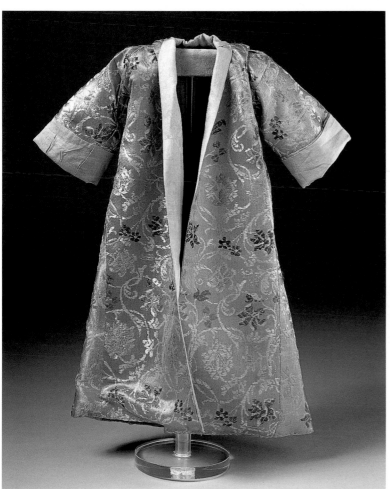

49. Lady Clapham's nightgown. VAM T.846:N-1974.

50. Lord Clapham's nightgown. VAM T.847:N-1974.

In the later years of the seventeenth century rigidity again entered women's fashion with the wearing of boned bodices, then boned stays and, in the 1690s, the introduction of the bustle at the back of the gown. But an informal looseness persisted, especially with the emergence of the mantua in the 1670s, a loose gown that draped over the rigid foundation garments. Men's fashion also became more formalized, yet in a comfortable and malleable way that was to introduce a basic convention lasting down to modern times. The development of the ensemble of a vest or waistcoat (first knee-length, but later raised to waist-high) along with knee breeches and top coat became the origin of the three-piece suit. Both sexes enjoyed more casual wear.

These developments broadly followed the fashions set in France, despite the attempts of Charles II to develop a distinctively English style of dress for men in the 1660s, employing exclusively English materials. Yet for all the powerful influence exercised by French modes, by the start of the eighteenth century British fashion, especially for men, had a reputation for sobriety compared with the most extravagant of continental fashion. By 1722 a travel guide was to point out that 'the dress of the English is like the French but not so gaudy; they generally go plain but in the best cloths and stuffs'. It added that 'they wear embroidery and laces on their cloathes on solemn days, but they don't make it their daily wear, as the French do'.

This picture of changing fashions tells but one half of the story, for the expense of luxurious apparel meant that there was a thriving trade in second-hand clothes and the refashioning of fabrics at all times. Some clothes were passed on through wills; items trimmed with fur in particular often headed the list of gifts to family, friends or business associates. In her will of 1531 Margaret Heron, of Hackney (now part of London, but then in the county of Middlesex), left her 'gowne of blacke satten furrid' to her son John and her kirtles (also gowns) to her sister, god-daughter and other women she knew. At this time, immediately before the worst excesses of stripping churches of their furnishings during the Reformation, people often left expensive fabrics to the Church, so Margaret Heron also left a gown of tawny velvet to make a vestment or cope. References in the Assize records to the theft of clothing, not just of expensive items but of fine linen from washing lines, testify to an unofficial circulation of goods. Fabric could also be reworked and refashioned if its original expense was worth the effort; goldsmiths were known to buy materials with gold thread, or silver and gold trimmings, to recover the precious metal they contained.

51 A pair of stays, 1660–70. Probably made in England. This under-garment was essential for the flat-fronted female silhouette, yet the material, sleeves and front lacing suggest that it was meant to be seen when dressed informally. Pink watered silk, backed with linen, stiffened with whalebone and trimmed with pink silk ribbons. VAM T.14 1951.

7. The outside world

One of the messages conveyed by items of dress depicted in sixteenth- and seventeenth-century portraits was the presence of the wearer in public or private spaces; such signals would have been clearly understood at the time but are now of a subtlety that is lost to us. The wearing of one glove, for example, and the carrying of the other may have indicated that the sitter was about to move from home to a public place. A more obvious, yet still domestic, way of representing the outside world in portraits was to suggest the presence of a garden in the background and to one side of the picture. In the early sixteenth century most gardens, even at great houses, were relatively small; they tended to be seen as private enclosures and might lead to walks along walls, give access to ancillary buildings or even the means for the owner to reach the local church, as at Thornbury Castle near the Bristol Channel, built by the Duke of Buckingham in the years before his execution in 1521. In his house at Chelsea, Sir Thomas More had a garden retreat for study and contemplation.

54

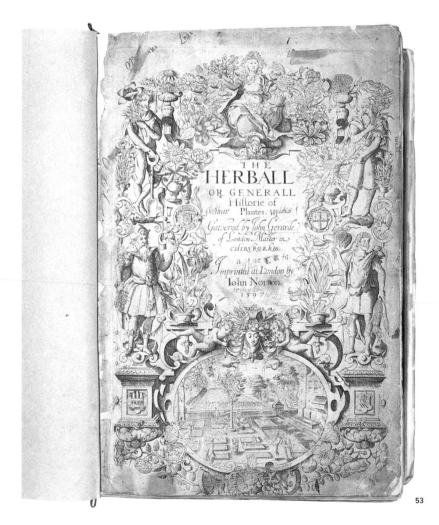

53

Early Tudor enclosed gardens often had knot gardens, arbours, mounds from which to view the surroundings, and topiary. The garden was a source of pleasure, but also of food and herbs for medicinal use and for the banishment of smells from the house – hence their portrayal in books known as herbals, a sort of treatise on plants with advice on their usefulness. By the later sixteenth century gardens were often larger, spread out from one or more sides of a great house and were increasingly designed at the same time as the building, or certainly envisaged alongside it. This was the period when the first distinctive 'garden' side to the house, distinct in architectural character from the main entrance front, began to appear, sometimes with a terrace or loggia linking the two. Garden buildings at this period often explored new ideas in building design; small structures in ingenious geometric shapes might serve as places of retreat or as 'banqueting houses' where the owner and guests took sweetmeats after the main meal of the day. Ingenuity extended also to water features.

---

52 Wedding suit, 1673. Made for James, Duke of York (later James II and VII) for his wedding to Mary of Modena. Wool embroidered with silver and silver-gilt thread and lined with red silk. VAM T.711-1995.

53 *The Herball, or Generall Historie of Plantes* by John Gerarde, 1597 Printed by Edmund Bollifant and published by John Norton. Engraving. VAM 86.F.92.

54 Detail of *Sir Thomas More, his family and descendants*, 1593–4. Probably by Rowland Lockey after an earlier painting by Hans Holbein. This is thought to represent Sir Thomas More's garden at his house in Chelsea, created in the 1520s, with his brick study or retreat. Watercolour on vellum, stuck on card. VAM P.15-1973.

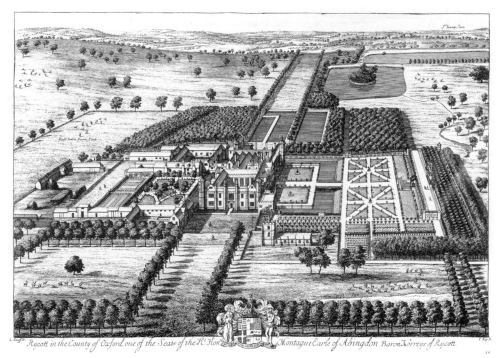

Greater formality appeared with the seventeenth century, inspired by Italian example. The century's concept of formality meant that the act of looking at the garden – already significant in the sense that great sixteenth-century houses often had rooftop walks – became more important than the exploration of it. Gardens were viewed from the first-floor state apartment. Vistas were created towards garden features. The knot gardens of the sixteenth century gave way to the terraced *parterres* of the seventeenth, some of these known as *parterres de broderie*, filled with flowers, grass and gravel, and edged with box, to create flowing patterns. Garden statuary, sometimes original works imported from Italy, but more often copies of antique sculpture, became central features of planned garden design. Towards the end of the seventeenth century long, formal canals and large, circular basins became common, influenced by French and Dutch example. More elaborate waterworks, such as fountains and cascades, were also popular. Older gardens were modernized, sometimes using remaining parts of a medieval moat to turn a once defensive necessity into a pleasurable, reflective surface.

Also significant is the way in which the concept of the garden was extended into the public sphere, as public gardens became places of resort and encounter. Hyde Park in London was still used for hunting at the time of James I and VI, but during the reign of his son, Charles I, it became a parade ground for the coaches of the wealthy. At this time the Mulberry Gardens in the royal parks of London and the commercially run Spring Gardens were intended as places of simple natural pleasures, but became places of scandal.

It was relayed to the Earl of Strafford in 1634 that:

> The Bowling in the Spring Garden was by the King's Command put down for one day . . . continual bibbling and drinking of wine all day long under the trees, two or three quarrels every week. It was grown scandalous and insufferable; besides, my Lord Digby being reprehended for striking in the King's garden, he answered that he took it for a common bowling place where all paid money for their coming in.

In 1661 John Evelyn went to see the New Spring Garden at Lambeth, also a commercial entertainment, which he described as 'a pretty contrived plantation'. This garden formed the beginnings of the famous establishment later called the Vauxhall Gardens, described by a foreign visitor in 1710 as consisting 'entirely of avenues and covered walks . . . and green huts, in which one can get a glass of wine, snuff and other things, although everything is very dear and bad'.

55 The water garden, Westbury Court, Gloucestershire, 1696–1705.

56 *Rycote House*. Plate from *Britannia Illustrata*, 1707. By Johannes Kip and Leonard Knyff. The Tudor house has been given new formal gardens and the moat turned into a water feature. Engraving. Corporation of London.

8. Coffee houses as places of debate

Other places of public resort were the coffee houses that were proliferating by 1700, a new venue of indoor social interaction to supplement the long-established inns and taverns. One of the earliest known examples opened in Oxford in 1650. Most provincial towns had one or two by the end of the century, but in London the numbers ran to hundreds. In 1719 they were described by a French traveller as 'extremely convenient. You have all manner of news there; you have a good fire, which you may sit by as long as you please; you have a dish of coffee; you meet your friends for the transaction of business, and all for a penny, if you don't care to spend more.'

This novel environment was, for its frequenters, an alternative to domestic social life, and a new range of objects emerged to serve the pursuits that went on there. Coffee pots and coffee dishes sat alongside newspapers and tobacco pipes. The reputation of the coffee house for serious discussion made it the most significant debating place of the early eighteenth century. The poet Oliver Goldsmith described how he saw clergymen writing their sermons there; the journalist Joseph Addison sat in them writing for the *Spectator*; and the painter William Hogarth's father set up a coffee house where Latin was to be spoken. They were predominantly, given the exclusion of women from public political debate, male preserves. They represent, however, the mark of a fundamental shift in British society. In 1500 the church remained the most obvious place of public assembly. Throughout the seventeenth century, as the voices of religious dissent sought to control the excesses of what they saw as a tyrannical monarchy, the Puritan chapel became the focus of debate and 'the citadel of seventeenth-century freedoms'. By 1700 it was the coffee house that had become, in the words of Abbé Prévost, the 'seat of English liberty', where discussion of everything from politics to social mores was open to a mix of classes and religious denominations.

58

57 Detail of *Arthur, 1st Baron Capel and his family*, about 1639. By Cornelius Johnson (Cornelis Jonson van Ceulen I). This garden at Little Hadham, Hertfordshire, was laid out in the 1630s. Oil on canvas. National Portrait Gallery, London.

58 *A London coffee house*, about 1700. By an anonymous artist. Body-colour. The British Museum.

CHAPTER 5

Tudor and Stuart Britain, 1500–1714

What was new?

JOHN STYLES

1. Unnecessary foreign wares

When in 1549, in his *Discourse of the Common Weal of this Realm of England*, Sir Thomas Smith railed against the haberdashers' shops that had recently proliferated in London, his anger centred on the attractive imported goods they stocked in such profusion – 'French or Milan caps, glasses, daggers, swords, girdles, and such things.' Many of these goods were, Smith complained, mere fripperies, made from cheap materials – paper, pins, needles, knives, hats, caps, brooches, buttons, laces, gloves, tables, playing cards, puppets, hawks' bells, earthen wares – yet in importing them, the kingdom wasted its resources. England was 'overburdened with unnecessary forrayn wares', things 'that we might ether clene spare, or els make them within oure owne realme'.

The annoyance expressed by Smith at the rising tide of foreign imports exposes an ambivalence in English attitudes towards innovation during the Tudor period. On the one hand, it betrays a suspicion that many of the small, often decorated consumer goods being imported in ever-increasing quantities were wasteful and unnecessary extravagances. On the other hand, it reveals a dismay at England's inability to make such goods and resentment at the lost opportunities that their import represented for English workers. Disapproval of superfluous novelties was to persist throughout the rest of the Tudor and Stuart period, though it did little to prevent them being bought and enjoyed in growing quantities. By contrast, dismay at the country's dependence on foreigners to supply those novelties became an important force propelling innovation in design and the decorative arts.

Innovation in high-design goods in the sixteenth and seventeenth centuries was mainly a matter of imports and import substitution – the long drawn-out process by which the British learned to make decorative goods that were already familiar as imports, but required techniques and materials they had previously been unable to master. Britain was artistically and industrially

2

1 Uncut playing cards, about 1500. French. Card printed from woodblocks and hand-coloured. VAM E.988-1920.

2 German stoneware pot with English mounts, about 1550–60. Stoneware with silver-gilt mounts. VAM 2119-1855.

3 *John Rose, the Royal Gardener, presenting Charles II with the first pineapple grown in England*, 1787. By Thomas Hewart after a 17th-century painting at Houghton Hall attributed to Henry Danckerts. Pineapples originated in South America. Oil on canvas. VAM HH.191-1948.

backward by the standards of her continental neighbours. Innovation characteristically involved an extended process whereby goods were initially imported in their indigenous foreign forms, then tailored by their overseas makers to British tastes, then copied crudely in Britain and finally manufactured proficiently by the British. This broad sequence can be observed across a whole range of decorative goods, from German stoneware jugs to Indian decorated cottons.

The fact that innovation in design and the decorative arts came mainly from abroad should come as no surprise to us. After all, this was a period when almost every aspect of British life was becoming less provincial and more cosmopolitan. Take botanical knowledge. At the start of the sixteenth century the number of plant species known in Europe was approximately 500, not very different from the number known to the ancient Romans. By the time the English botanist John Ray compiled his catalogue of plants two centuries later nearly 20,000 species had been identified, mainly as a consequence of the European exploration of the extra-European world.

An equivalent process can be observed at work in the English language. The unsurpassed power and richness of the language used by Shakespeare and the translators of the King James Bible testify to a huge expansion in its vocabulary, the result of borrowings from Greek and Latin, from French, Italian and Dutch. As in design and the decorative arts, there were those who resented foreign imports. They wanted new words to be coined exclusively from English roots. But the poet Philip Sidney, writing at the end of the sixteenth century, defended these linguistic borrowings as a form of creative eclecticism that ultimately strengthened the English language. 'Some will say it is a mingled language. And why not,' he went on, 'so much the better, taking the best of both.'

The same could have been said of foreign innovations in design and the decorative arts. The British, eager to acquire new kinds of high-design goods that came from abroad, but resentful at the scale of imports, endeavoured to make the same goods themselves. More often than not, the initial intention was simply to produce British copies of foreign products. After all, copying and imitation had few negative connotations at this period. Originality, in its uncompromising modern sense, was not necessarily prized. Yet the mix of skills and raw materials, ideas and tastes that prevailed in Britain and its colonies often demanded adaptations that amounted to substantial innovations in themselves. Silver teapots, wine glasses made from lead glass, Christopher Wren's London churches – all these reworked elements that originally came from abroad into things that came to be regarded as distinctively English.

2. Spurs to innovation

Innovation in design and the decorative arts faced many obstacles in the sixteenth and seventeenth centuries. Politicians, as we have seen, worried about excessive imports of unnecessary trifles. Moralists feared that an inordinate interest in new and beautiful things would divert people's attention from God, or, worse still, seduce them into worshipping God in the wrong way. Established manufacturers and their workers made strenuous efforts to prevent both the introduction of new goods that might threaten their livelihoods and the settlement of immigrants with new skills. In an age that set great store by precedent and custom, it was hard to shake people from their established likes and dislikes. Furniture and textiles might be prized as much for their associations with stability, order and hierarchy as for being new, fashionable and up-to-date.

Yet novelty, in certain guises, was attractive to many; this was not confined to kings and their courtiers, who, in an age of competitive royal magnificence, could hardly avoid monitoring the ever-changing extravagances of foreign courts. It was a hunger for fashionable clothes that drove the sister of a humble Lancashire clergyman, Adam Martindale, to London against her parents' wishes in the 1620s. In explanation, her brother pointed out that 'freeholders' daughters were then confined to their felts, petticoats and waistcoats, cross handkerchiefs about their necks, and white cross clothes upon their heads, with coifs under them wrought with black silk or worsted'. He concluded, with more than a hint of irritation, 'these limitations I suppose she did not very well approve'. Manufacturers were well aware of the popular appetite for novelty. The historian Thomas Fuller explained how the use of a new name could stimulate sales of the colourful Norwich-made worsted cloths popular among the 'middling sort' of the population in the mid-seventeenth century. When particular designs of cloth 'begin to tire of sale', customers' interest could be 'quickened with a new name'. Not surprisingly, novelties introduced in one material were quickly copied in another, like the multi-coloured decorative motifs that appeared on large Staffordshire earthenware dishes about 1670, mimicking recent developments in the decoration of dishes made from both tin-glazed earthenware and pewter.

4 Dish decorated with the figure of a mermaid, 1670–89. Made by Thomas Toft in Staffordshire. Earthenware, lead-glazed, with trailed slip decoration. [diam. 44cm]. VAM 299-1869.

Moreover, the arguments against innovation offered by the enemies of novelty, both religious and secular, did not go uncontested. New inventions designed to bring about improvements in material life were consistent with God's purpose, argued the farmer and inventor Cressy Dymock in 1651. 'The reformation of states in civil affairs for the most part, is not compassed without violence and disturbances: but inventions make all men happy without either injury or damage to any one single person. Furthermore, new inventions are as it were new creations, and imitations of God's own works.' Inventions like printing, clocks and gunpowder, which had been unknown to the ancient Romans, were cited as evidence of the superiority of the modern over the ancient world.

A belief in the human capacity for intellectual innovation was fundamental to the new kind of experimental science that flourished in seventeenth-century Britain, notably in the work of Isaac Newton and Robert Boyle. One of the most influential statements of this belief was Francis Bacon's demand that God's works should be studied in order to achieve a 'knowledge of causes, and secret motions of things; and the enlarging of the bounds of human empire, to the effecting of all things possible'. The Royal Society, which was founded in 1660 with this broad purpose in mind, was committed to securing practical benefits from advances in scientific knowledge.

Crucial to the establishment of the Royal Society was a patriotic desire for national advancement. Its founders hoped 'to render England the glory of the western world, by making it the seat of the best knowledge, as well as it may be the seat of the greatest trade'. In the sixteenth century Britain's rulers became increasingly receptive to the notion that they should take responsibility for 'the weal and advancement of the state'. As a result, governments began to give more active support to the establishment of new industries, especially those that would reduce imports and provide employment. From the middle of the sixteenth century the English government encouraged the settlement of Protestant refugees from continental Europe who possessed skills in short supply in England. 'We ought to favour the straungers from whome wee learned so great benifites,' argued one writer, 'because wee are not so good devisers as followers of others'. Government also granted monopoly privileges to entrepreneurs prepared to invest in new forms of manufacturing, which often included restrictions on competing imports.

6

These policies had considerable success. New kinds of decorative manufactures were established in England, including the making of colourful woollen cloths of the kind woven in the Low Countries, known as the 'new draperies'; silk fabrics in the Italian style; tin-glazed ceramics using the techniques of Italian majolica and Dutch delftware; and crystal glass in the Venetian manner. But the effects of government policies on innovation in the later sixteenth and early seventeenth centuries were far from consistent. Governments were as interested in raising revenue and placating vested interests as they were in reducing imports and promoting employment. Sometimes they refused monopoly privileges to successful innovators, as in the case of William Lee, the Nottinghamshire clergyman who invented the first hand-powered knitting machine in the 1580s.

Often state-sponsored attempts at import substitution failed, none more spectacularly than the scheme to have all English woollen cloth dyed prior to export, promoted in 1614 by Sir William Cockayne, an immensely wealthy merchant, financier and London alderman. Sometimes immigrant settlers failed to perform their allotted role of passing on their skills to natives, like the German swordsmiths who settled at Hounslow in the 1620s. Occasionally

---

5 Barometer, about 1700. Designed and made by Daniel Quare. Experiments in London and Holland during this period resulted in an improved vacuum, which helped to make barometers more reliable. Turned ivory, ebonized wood and engraved brass [h. 103.5cm]. VAM W.64-1926.

6 Dish depicting Frederick, King of Bohemia, with his wife and children, about 1627. Made in Southwark, London. Frederick of Bohemia was the husband of Elizabeth, the daughter of James I and VI. Deposed from the Bohemian throne, he became a popular Protestant hero in England. Tin-glazed earthenware. VAM C.38-1928.

opposition to imports had the perverse consequence of inhibiting the introduction of promising new materials, like the ban imposed in 1581 on the import of logwood, the new dyestuff for blacks and blues from the Caribbean, which was unjustifiably condemned as 'false and deceitful'.

A variety of official efforts to encourage import substitution continued throughout the seventeenth century. But there were changes of emphasis. After the civil war the granting of monopoly privileges was restricted, because they had become an issue in the quarrel between King and Parliament. Henceforth, protection from competition was provided for a limited period only to those who could prove themselves to be innovators, under a system that was to become the basis of modern patent law. Towards the end of the Stuart era official support for British manufactures came to focus increasingly on tariffs and other trade controls that facilitated exports and restricted imports. By 1714 a situation had developed whereby most foreign manufactures were subject to heavy import tariffs – so high, in the case of France, that a legal import trade was virtually impossible. Moreover, the import of certain goods (Indian decorated cotton textiles and French alamode silks, for example) was prohibited. Imports of manufactured goods now began to stagnate and even started to decline.

3. How things were made

Innovation in design and the decorative arts was inextricably linked to changes in the ways things were made. At the start of the sixteenth century most people in Britain lived in the countryside and were engaged in agriculture in one way or another. For the majority, material possessions were few, and their meagre stock of manufactured goods was largely made by craftspeople in the local village or town. Indeed, many of the items they possessed – in particular textiles – were manufactured, at least in part, in their own homes for their own use. The wealthier sections of the population, especially the nobility and the gentry, owned many more objects made at a distance, including decorative luxuries from abroad, like linen damask tablecloths from the Low Countries and Italian silk velvet garments. Nevertheless, by the standards that would prevail at the end of the seventeenth century, their possessions were often sparse. The wealthy too relied heavily on craftspeople in their localities: in the 1470s the Eyres, a gentry family from Hassop in Derbyshire, obtained most of their woollen cloth from local weavers, fullers and dyers. Wool and flax were spun, and hangings and garments embroidered, by the women of such families and their servants. At all levels of society, households and localities displayed a marked degree of self-sufficiency, even when it came to decorative goods.

The manufacturing enterprises that produced goods for sale in the early sixteenth century tended to be very small. In the countryside, most consisted of a self-employed craftsperson – a tailor, a weaver or a shoemaker – who worked with the assistance of his family or an apprentice, using a few, simple tools. Even in London and other large towns, where more specialized manufacturing trades like goldsmithing might serve a regional or national market among the better-off, many master craftspeople worked single-handed. In an affluent London trade, like the making of pewter plates and drinking vessels, the vast majority of craftspeople employed no more than three workers. Only in the manufacture of woollen cloth, the single major export industry, were enterprises with large numbers of employees at all familiar, and then only in some rural areas. In parts of Suffolk, Essex and the West Country master clothiers put out wool to hundreds of spinners and yarn to scores of weavers to work up in their homes for a wage, often on a part-time basis.

7 Bowl, early 16th century.
Made in England or Flanders. Pewter.
VAM M.37-1945.

SKILLS FROM EUROPE, 1500–1600

Sara Pennell

Prior to 1500 the major ports and cities in England and Scotland accommodated small foreign populations, consisting mainly of merchants trading with continental Europe and immigrant craftspeople, chiefly employed in leather working, tailoring and brewing. This small-scale foreign presence grew dramatically during the sixteenth century. Religious persecution of continental Protestants was one impetus to immigration. French and Dutch Reformed churches were established in London after 1550. By 1571 there were perhaps 10,000 foreigners (or 'strangers' as they were called) in London alone, comprising 10 per cent of the

city's population. But persecution alone does not account for the rise in such numbers. Continental craft techniques and skills were much coveted in England, particularly in areas like glassmaking, where indigenous products were crude and imported wares answered the demand for high-quality goods.

The English government actively promoted the settlement of skilled foreign artisans in certain trades. Dutch and Flemish weavers were recruited to settle in East Anglia and the south-east, where they boosted flagging textile industries by helping to develop light woollen-mix fabrics, the so-called 'New Draperies'. Jacomo Verzelini, a Venetian glassmaker who helped establish the Crutched Friars glasshouse in London, was also encouraged to stay and pass on his expertise. A 1574 royal grant gave him a 21-year monopoly over the English manufacture and supply of Venetian-style glasswares.

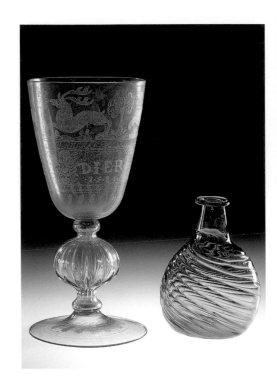

9. Left: wine glass, 1581. Probably made in London by Jacomo Verzelini, perhaps engraved by Anthony de Lysle. Engraved soda glass. [h. 21.2cm]. VAM C.523-1936. Right: flask, about 1580–1620. A typical example of native English glassmaking. Glass, mould-blown and 'wrythen' (twisted into a spiral). VAM C.1-1910.

8. *Londinium Feracissimi Angliae Regni Metropolis*. Map of the cities of London and Westminster from *Civitates Orbis Terrarum*, 1572. By Georg Braun and Franz Hogenberg. Printed in Antwerp. Bishopsgate, where many 'strangers' settled, is on the north-east edge of the built-up area shown on this map. Southwark is on the south bank of the River Thames. Woodcut and wash. Corporation of London.

The arrival of the 'strangers' was not universally welcomed. Fear of competition aroused hostility from the many guilds that controlled the organization of manufacturing in the City of London. They tried to restrict the places where immigrants could work and the people they could employ. To escape guild controls, many immigrants settled in areas like Bishopsgate and Southwark beyond the City walls, or pursued relatively 'young' trades such as printing, which as yet had little formal organization in London. Royal and aristocratic patronage likewise helped to protect foreign workers, such as the German armourers who settled in Greenwich.

It was primarily immigrants who enabled home-produced luxury goods like glasswares and armour to replace imports. Unlike native craftspeople, the 'strangers' were able to use new continental forms of ornament and design and brought with them technical skills (for example, in instrument making and printing) that were unmatched by most English artisans. The rate of immigration had peaked by the end of the sixteenth century, but immigrants continued to play an important role in high-design manufacturing throughout the seventeenth century. In 1607, for instance, the Goldsmiths' Company, the guild that represented native London goldsmiths, was still complaining that 'aliens and strangers [are] in better reputation and request than that of our own nation'.

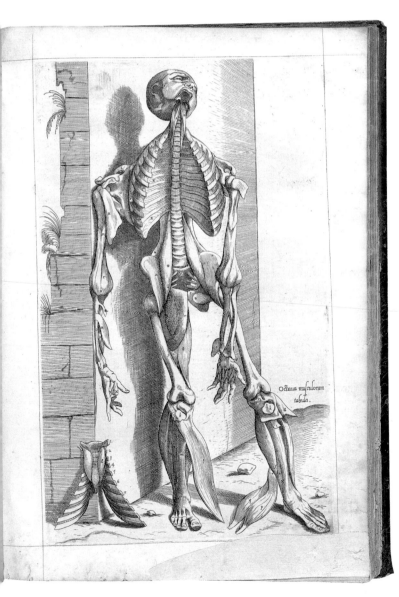

10. *Octava muscularum tabula*. Illustration in *Compendiosa totus anatomie delineatio*, 1545, written by Thomas Geminus, who was in England from about 1540. The text and illustrations taken from *De humani corporis fabrica* (Basel, 1543) by Andreas Vesalius. Printed in London by John Herford. Engraving. VAM RC.T.18.

11. Astronomical clock, dated 1588. Made in London by Francis Nowe, who was born in Brabant, the Netherlands. In 1571 he came to London, where he died in 1593. The earliest dated English clock. Engraved gilt-brass case, the movement a late 17th-century replacement. VAM M.39:1&2-1959.

12. Standing cup, with London hallmarks for 1611–12. Marked 'TvL' in monogram: made by an immigrant craftsman, perhaps by Thierry (Dierick) Luckemans. Silver-gilt, decorated with bands of applied wire (filigree), wire-work panels, chasing and engraving. VAM 5964:1&2-1859.

JOHN DWIGHT

Robin Hildyard

In the seventeenth century the nationalistic desire to become independent of foreign imports such as Venetian glass, Chinese porcelain and German brown stoneware came to be combined with a new, more systematic approach to scientific research. After the failure of attempts to make stoneware at Woolwich and Southampton, it became apparent that only systematic experiment by an inspired chemist could unravel the complex secrets of high-fired ceramics.

The talents of John Dwight (about 1633–1703), the second son of an Oxfordshire yeoman, were recognized early. He studied law and chemistry at Oxford, later becoming legal adviser to the Church while pursuing his ceramic researches at Wigan. In 1672 he obtained a patent for 'Porcelane…as also…the stone ware vulgarly known as Cologne ware', and built a pottery at Fulham, then on the outskirts of London. His life of unceasing experimentation may be compared to those of

13. Left: *Lydia Dwight resurrected*, about 1674. John Dwight's daughter Lydia died at the age of six. Right: *John Dwight*, about 1673–5. Made by an unknown modeller at John Dwight's Fulham factory. Modelled and salt-glazed stoneware. VAM 1054-1871, 1053-1871.

Johann Friedrich Böttger, founder of the Meissen porcelain factory in Saxony in 1710, and Josiah Wedgwood, the eighteenth-century Staffordshire potter.

Initially Dwight hired experienced potters at Fulham and attempted to make every kind of pottery covered by his patent: tavern bottles and mugs, like those imported from Germany; porcelain and red stonewares, like those

imported from China; and his own innovative figures, which, with their dense body and tight-fitting glaze, had the capacity to simulate bronze. His stoneware bottles bore personalized medallions to compete with the newly invented glass wine bottles. Since the clay for his patented red stoneware was found only in Staffordshire, he allowed the Elers brothers there to make teapots, globular

14. *Neptune*, about 1673–5. Made by an unknown modeller at John Dwight's Fulham factory. Modelled stoneware with a wash to imitate bronze. VAM C.393-1920.

15. Three bottles. From left to right: about 1640–50, made in Woolwich; dated 1674, made in Southampton by William Killigrew; about 1675–80, made at John Dwight's Fulham factory. Salt-glazed stoneware. VAM C.1-1994, C.110-1995, C.59-1967.

16. Centre: 'gorge' mug, 17th century. Made in Westerwald, Germany. Left and right: fragments of two 'gorge' mugs, about 1675. Made at John Dwight's Fulham factory. Salt-glazed stoneware with applied and moulded decoration and partially painted in cobalt blue and manganese purple. VAM Circ.627-1926, 414/852-1885.

'gorges' for strong beer, and coffee and chocolate capuchines, but he also manufactured these objects himself at Fulham in refined brown and white stoneware.

Dwight's innovations represented major advances in European ceramics, especially his superior clay bodies incorporating Dorset clay and ground flint, and his use of marbled, splashed oxide, 'scratch-blue' and fine applied sprig decoration. For hot drinks, his stonewares proved vastly superior to soft lead-glazed English slipware and delftware. His innovations went on to form the basis for the great rise of the Staffordshire potteries in the eighteenth century. As for the magical porcelain, only his failure to find the vital China Stone in Cornwall prevented him from being the first European to crack the secret.

17. Centre: bottle, about 1685. [h. 17.2cm]. Left and right: two 'gorge' mugs, dated 1682 and about 1680–5. Made at John Dwight's Fulham factory. Salt-glazed stoneware with applied marbling and sprig-moulded decoration; silver mounts. VAM C.101-1938, 414/853-1885, 896-1905.

18. Left: capuchine and mug, about 1695. Made by David and John Philip Elers at Bradwell Wood, Staffordshire.
Right: capuchine and mug, about 1700. Made in the Dehua kilns in Fujian Province, China. Red stoneware and white porcelain. VAM C.100-1938, C.159-1932, 3588-1901, 3749-1901.

With the introduction of many entirely new and more sophisticated kinds of manufacturing in the later sixteenth and seventeenth centuries, the scale of industrial enterprises expanded. The rise of the large enterprise was most obvious in trades that required a concentration of expensive plant and machinery on a single site: the 70 water-powered paper mills that lined the rivers of south-east England and the Midlands by the late seventeenth century; the 26 London glass houses of the same period with their coal-fired furnaces; the potteries of Southwark and Lambeth, where colourful tin-glazed plates and bowls were made. Such plants could employ scores or, in exceptional cases, hundreds of workers. More than 200 people worked in the East India Company's shipyard at Blackwall Yard on the Thames in the 1620s. Setting up equipment like water wheels and coal-fired furnaces required a large outlay, but it is important to emphasize that the bulk of the work was still reliant on human eye and muscle. Potters' wheels were turned by foot; wood for ships was sawn by hand; glass was blown by mouth. These single-site establishments, moreover, were not the only kind of large enterprises producing decorative goods at this time. More common were businesses employing sometimes hundreds of people in their own homes under the putting-out system, increasingly as full-time workers. By the early eighteenth century they could be found in town and country, undertaking the manufacture of a vast range of decorative products – silks, linens and lace; stockings, hats and gloves; buttons, buckles and watches.

Most producers of decorative goods continued, however, to work on a small scale. Even in London, where the high-design trades requiring the greatest skills were concentrated, production was largely organized in workshops housing only a handful of workers. But these workshops did not operate in isolation. As Joseph Moxon noted in his *Mechanick Exercises* in 1678, 'One trade may borrow many Eminent Helps in work of another Trade.' In a number of trades,

20

19

19 Detail from an engraved invitation to a church service for members of the Goldsmiths' Company, 1701. This engraving does not provide an accurate depiction of a London goldsmith's workshop, but illustrates the range of activities that might be conducted there and the tools employed. Engraving. © The Worshipful Company of Goldsmiths.

specialist retailers abandoned production to concentrate on assembling an attractive array of goods for their customers from a variety of makers. Such were the upholders who emerged in the later seventeenth century to provide a comprehensive furnishing service for the homes of the wealthy. At the same time workshops in the high-design trades increasingly came to specialize in particular types of work, subcontracting some tasks to other workshops. The leading Restoration London goldsmith, Thomas Fowle, subcontracted gilding, engraving, planishing, burnishing and the making of jewellery, flatware, casters and chafing dishes. The practice was to become even more widespread in the eighteenth century, when it was claimed to give the London high-design trades an advantage over their continental competitors who had to rely on multi-skilled, non-specialist workers.

Guild controls in London generally proved ineffective against subcontracting, especially after the mid-seventeenth century. Most urban trades in the sixteenth and seventeenth centuries were organized in guilds, which policed entry into the trade and training for it. In London the number of guilds increased during this period, but despite their wealth and political influence, many of them exercised relatively little control over the aesthetic quality of the goods their members produced. In the late sixteenth and early seventeenth centuries the Goldsmiths' Company, for example, intermittently tried to make young workers produce a masterpiece to demonstrate their all-round command of the skills of the trade, a common guild requirement on the continent, but the policy appears to have been widely flouted and was abandoned in the 1630s.

20 *The East India Company's Yard at Deptford*, London, about 1660. By an unknown artist. Oil on canvas.
© National Maritime Museum, London.

Increasing specialization in manufacturing at this time had other consequences. Households became less self-sufficient, with a decline in the amount of woollen and linen cloth made for the household's own use and a corresponding rise in purchases of an expanding range of ready-woven cloth. Yet at the same time women in wealthier households seem to have undertaken ever-more elaborate decorative needlework for domestic use, although they sometimes drew on the services of professional embroiderers. New forms of embroidery emerged, such as the sewing of figurative and narrative scenes on domestic objects like mirror surrounds, cushions and boxes.

21 *William Broderick, the King's Embroiderer*, 1614. By an unknown artist. Oil on panel. Wandsworth Museum.

22 Embroidered casket, 1671. Martha Edlin embroidered this when she was 11 years old. The panels may have been supplied to her ready-drawn and sent to a casket maker to be assembled after she had embroidered them. Wood covered in panels of satin, embroidered with coloured silks and metal thread. [h. 24.5cm]. VAM T.432-1990

23 Sampler, 1668. This is the earliest surviving piece of needlework from a group by Martha Edlin, the daughter of a landowning family, completed when she was eight years old. It was normal for young women in prosperous families to learn needlework in the 17th century. Samplers were made to show the development of their skills through a range of stitches and techniques. Linen embroidered in silks. VAM T.433-1990.

24 A page of patterns for embroidery motifs, 1632. Plate from Richard Shorleyker's *A Scholehouse for the Needle*, 1632. This plate shows patterns for the isolated naturalistic motifs that were a characteristically English form of embroidery. Initially they were based on illustrations in herbals, but by the early 17th century patterns were being supplied by print sellers specifically for the use of embroiderers. VAM 95.O.50.

4. New materials and new techniques

A steady stream of decorative artefacts made from new materials and employing new manufacturing techniques flowed into Tudor and Stuart Britain. One current in this flow was the arrival of previously unknown or unfamiliar materials and techniques from the world beyond Europe – porcelain from China, lacquer from Japan, cotton chintz from India, carpets from Turkey, dyestuffs like cochineal and logwood from the Americas. A second current was import substitution, by which the British learned to make previously unattainable decorative goods. These were predominantly goods originally supplied from continental Europe: the tapestries, swords, firearms, brasswares, woollens, linens, silks, glass, ceramics and myriad other items

25

that were so frequently listed by Tudor statesmen exasperated at England's dependence on foreigners. A third current – the least powerful one, but nevertheless an important precursor of developments in the eighteenth and nineteenth centuries – was the development in Britain of new materials like lead glass and of new techniques like William Lee's knitting machine.

Of course import substitution was not confined to goods previously made in Europe. The British tried to mimic almost all the new manufactured goods from the industrially advanced areas of Asia. In some cases, most notably in the making of porcelain, they failed. Even a talented chemist like John Dwight, who in the second half of the seventeenth century successfully mastered the German techniques for making stoneware ceramics, proved unequal to the task. It was only in the mid-eighteenth century that the British began to make porcelain. However, in the case of many other Asian manufactures, like lacquer and carpets, the British succeeded before the end of the seventeenth century in producing imitations that could sell, at least in the home market. The history of Indian cotton chintzes in Britain illustrates the whole sequence, from early imports to British manufacture.

25 Goblet and cover, about 1695. Made in England. This tall goblet was probably intended for ceremonial or communal drinking. Lead glass. [h. 36cm]. VAM C.536-1936.

27

26

26 Japanned chair, about 1700. Made in England. It has a curving back splat and cabriole legs, a new style that may have been influenced by Chinese furniture. It is painted or japanned in imitation of red Chinese lacquer. Beech wood japanned in gold and green on a red ground; modern upholstery. VAM W.44-1938.

27 Japanese box, about 1600. Wood covered in black lacquer, with gold Hiramaki lacquer and shell. VAM W.450-1922.

GOODS FROM THE INDIES

Dinah Winch

In Tudor and Stuart Britain much of Asia and the Americas was known indiscriminately as 'The Indies'. The use of the term was not simply a matter of poor geographical knowledge. It reflected how the different parts of the globe that were opened up to direct European trade from the late fifteenth century came to be endowed with a shared exotic allure. This was particularly evident in the great demand for goods brought from 'The Indies' to Europe. Decorative items and curiosities from Asia – primarily India, China and Japan – had long been a by-product of the lucrative trade in spices. However, after the founding of the Dutch and English East India Companies at the start of the seventeenth century, the expansion of trade and cultural exchange began to have a significant effect on the design of goods produced in both Britain and 'The Indies'.

Goods that had once been cabinet pieces, above all porcelain, became common enough to be in daily use in wealthy households. Asian producers of luxury commodities developed export styles to cater for the expanding European market. The decoration of Japanese export lacquer was self-consciously exotic, in contrast to the sparser aesthetic of goods produced for the domestic Japanese market. Similarly, Indian producers adapted both Indian and European designs on printed cottons to suit European tastes. The flowering tree design, which was an amalgam of Asian and European patterns, featured on both Indian and British textiles. The success of Asian artefacts stimulated British production of

28. Mounted bowl, the porcelain made in China, 1522–66, the mounts in London, with hallmarks for 1599–1600. Painted hard-paste porcelain in silver-gilt mounts. [h. 13.9cm]. VAM M.945-1983.

29. Comb case and comb, 1673. Made in Jamaica. Carved and engraved tortoiseshell. [h. 19.5cm]. VAM 524-1877.

30. Panel for a room, about 1696. By Robert Robinson. Oil on wood. VAM P.6-1954.

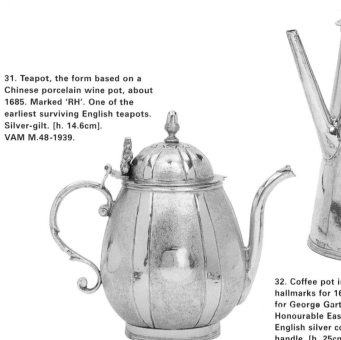

31. Teapot, the form based on a Chinese porcelain wine pot, about 1685. Marked 'RH'. One of the earliest surviving English teapots. Silver-gilt. [h. 14.6cm]. VAM M.48-1939.

32. Coffee pot imitating a Turkish form, with London hallmarks for 1681–2. Maker's mark of 'GG', probably for George Garthorne. Given by Richard Sterne to the Honourable East India Company. The earliest known English silver coffee pot. Silver, with leather-covered handle. [h. 25cm]. VAM M.398-1921.

34. Detail of a bed curtain, 1690–1710. Made in England. The pattern influenced by Indian painted textiles. Linen and cotton twill, embroidered with wool. VAM 72C-1897.

imitations, such as japanned wares and delftware. These were given the necessary exotic appeal by simulating Asian manufacturing processes (as in the case of japanning) and by combining colours and motifs in ways that appeared Asian to European eyes. The new beverages of tea and coffee adapted vessel forms from the countries in which they originated.

While Europeans did not import decorative goods from the Americas in anything like the quantity they brought from Asia, the Americas did have an impact on British decorative arts.

They were an increasingly important source of commodities such as silver, gold, precious stones, hardwoods and dyes. The imagery of the American goods and peoples had a significant effect on British design as it became incorporated into the multi-layered imagery of the non-European world. The fusion of the fantastic East and West is often lavishly illustrated in early chinoiserie decoration. In the late seventeenth century whole decorative schemes employing such imagery were devised as showcases for imported objects such as porcelain and lacquer.

33. Cabinet, about 1700. Made in England imitating Japanese examples built for export. Japanned wood. VAM W.9:1-1936.

35. Detail of a hanging, about 1700. Made in western India for the European market. Painted and dyed cotton (chintz). VAM IS.156-1953.

The principal objectives of the founders of the English East India Company in 1600 were to sell English woollens in Asia and to secure a direct supply of spices from south-east Asia. For centuries India had been renowned for the supply of cotton textiles with fast and brilliant dye-colours to the lands around the Indian Ocean, but in its early years the East India Company imported few Indian textiles for use in England. Those few were luxury items, such as quilts and hangings, that sold or were given away as curiosities. Gradually the company began to develop a market in England for fine Indian decorated cottons for use as table and bed linens, wall hangings and other household furnishings, but the quantity imported remained small before 1660. One of the key limitations here was their design. Before the middle of the seventeenth century the company's agents in India bought cottons that had been painted, printed or embroidered according to the requirements of Indian and other Asian consumers. Such designs had only a limited appeal in England.

The crucial innovation came in 1643, when the company began to require its agents in India to insist that the designs on the cloth be changed to accord with English taste. Those quilts 'which hereafter you shall send we desire may be with more white ground, and the flowers and branch to be in colours in the middle of the quilt as the painter pleases, whereas now most part of your quilts come with sad red grounds which are not so well accepted here'. In other words, the Indian preference for a pattern against a coloured ground was now reversed in favour of the European taste for a pattern in silhouette against a white ground. In the 1660s the company went one step further and began

to send sample patterns for chintz, quilts and hangings for the Indian workers to copy. The result was the use of two-dimensional forms and motifs that were perceived in England as Indian, but which in fact came to India from England. The late seventeenth-century Indian chintzes that became so popular for women's garments may have retained an exotic allure for their English wearers, but the range of patterns and motifs they employed often had more to do with English constructions of the exotic than with Indian visual culture.

36 Long cushion cover, first quarter of the 17th century. A piece of English embroidery employing some of the chinoiserie motifs usually associated with the Tree of Life designs found on 17th-century Indian cottons. It predates most imported Indian cottons, however, suggesting that the source for such designs was English. Linen canvas embroidered with silk; wool and metal thread mainly in tent stitch. [l. 100cm]. VAM 816-1893.

37 Painted cotton coverlet, mid-17th century. Made in the Deccan, western India, for the Indian market. It has a red ground of the sort that the East India Company rejected for export to Europe. Painted and dyed cotton. [l. 89.5cm]. VAM IS.34-1969.

The design of these two hangings, one made in India and the other in England, derives from the same source. They are not identical. One is the reverse of the other and they differ in a number of minor respects. Nevertheless, they are both clearly adaptations of a single original design, probably taken from a pattern book of the kind published in 17th-century England for the use of embroiderers. It was patterns of this kind that the East India Company sent to India from the 1660s to be used in the manufacture of decorated cotton cloth for sale in England (see also 5:34 and 35).

38 Detail of a bed or wall hanging, about 1700. Made in Gujarat, western India, for the English market. Cotton embroidered with silk; chain stitch. VAM IS.155-1953.

39 Detail of a crewelwork bed hanging, about 1680. Embroidered in England. Linen and cotton embroidered with wool. © 2000 Museum of Fine Arts, Boston.

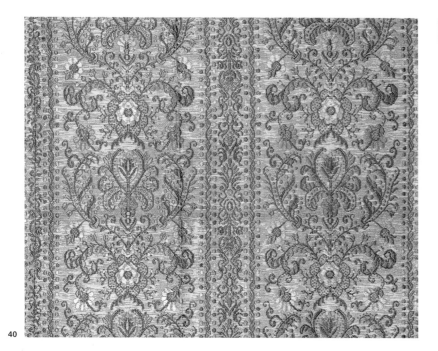

This reworking of designs was necessary because the East India Company was entering a market in which it faced stiff competition from a variety of new European decorated cloths, including woven silks and the light worsted cloths known in England as the 'new draperies', as well as from various styles of embroidery. Indeed, sixteenth- and seventeenth-century Europe witnessed a tide of innovation in decorated fabrics of many kinds.

In the face of this competition, the East India Company's policy of dictating design from London was enormously successful. By the 1680s its imports from India were running at more than one million pieces of cloth a year, many of them decorated fabrics intended for furnishing or clothing. This rising tide of imports was the cause of much resentment in England. One response was to imitate the Indian technique of printing fast colours on either cotton or linen cloth. The technique was already being successfully employed in the London area by the 1670s. By the early years of the eighteenth century the East India Company was complaining that printing could be done in England at half the price charged for Indian goods and in better colours and patterns. A second response was the campaign by British manufacturers of silks and light worsted cloths (themselves both import substitutes) to have all dyed or decorated cottons, whether imported from India or not, banned outright. The campaign culminated in 1721 in a legal prohibition that was to last 50 years.

40 Detail of a woven silk, third quarter of the 17th century. Probably woven in England. VAM T.14-1922.

41 Detail of a striped worsted, early 18th century. Woven at Norwich or Spitalfields, London. Part of a Portuguese chasuble. Portugal was an important export market for English worsteds. Combed wool, woven. VAM T.287-1962.

42 Printed cotton 'calico', 1690–1700. Made in England or the Netherlands. The scale of its design suggests that it was intended for bed hangings. Cotton, block-printed. VAM 12-1884.

Like cotton printing, the history of the making of fine, decorative glass in Tudor and Stuart Britain began with imports and attempts to copy them. Unlike cotton printing, it culminated in radical innovations in the kind of material used and in the appearance of the objects made from it. In part these innovations were the result of British inventiveness. In the sixteenth century the British, like most Europeans, imported drinking glasses from Venice made of the clear cristallo glass for which that city was renowned. British-made glass was crude, green and opaque. Italians introduced the manufacture of crystal glass to Antwerp early in the century and in 1567 a Protestant refugee glass maker from Antwerp, Jean Carré, arrived in England, at roughly the same time as many other skilled Antwerp craftspeople escaping religious persecution, including various silk and woollen weavers. Within a year Carré had started manufacturing crystal glass in the Venetian manner at Crutched Friars in London. Subsequently he imported nine Venetian glass workers, one of whom, Jacomo Verzelini, took over the business. In 1574 Verzelini was granted a 21-year monopoly to make drinking glasses of the Venetian type, protected by a ban on Venetian imports.

With the aid of its monopoly, the business prospered. By the early seventeenth century, after Verzelini's retirement, it was managed by an English glass maker, William Robson, suggesting that the Venetians' skills had been successfully transferred to native workers. By 1620 the Venetian ambassador was complaining that English crystal glass rivalled the Venetian product in quality, although large quantities of Venetian glass were also being imported: more than 10,000 glasses in 1626. It was at this period that the first major British technical innovation occurred – the introduction of coal fuel. Previously glass had been made using wood to heat the raw materials to the very high temperatures required, but in the early seventeenth century a method was developed of preventing the molten glass coming into contact with the fuel, using closed clay pots. This allowed coal, which was abundant in Britain, to be used to fuel the glass furnaces, in spite of its noxious impurities. The subsequent shift of the whole industry to coal firing was exceptionally rapid, because in 1615 the government, desperate for revenue, transferred the monopoly of glass making to the promoters of the new process and banned the use of other fuels. It is important to stress, however, that this change would almost certainly have happened eventually without government intervention. One of the most significant technological developments in Stuart Britain was the shift to coal and coke firing for the smelting and refining of copper, lead, brass and a host of other materials used in the high-design trades.

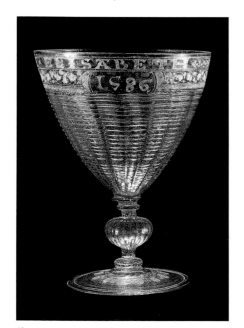

43

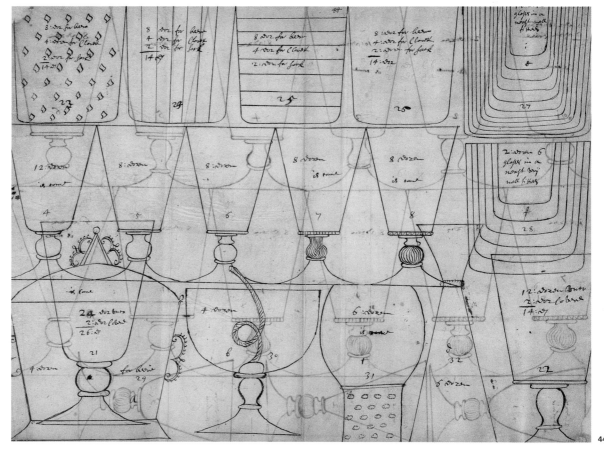

44

43 Goblet, 1586. Made in London by Jacomo Verzelini. Engraved by Anthony de Lysle. Glass with mould-blown stem, gilt, trailed decoration and diamond-point engraving. VAM C.226-1983.

44 Page of a manuscript containing letters and drawings of glass designs, sent by John Greene of London to his Venetian agent Alessio Morelli, 17 September 1669. The drawings are specifications for the drinking glasses that Greene was ordering from Venice. Ink and paper. The British Library.

The new fuel contributed to the success of two significant innovations in objects made from glass. The British made a major contribution to each of them. The first was the development of the glass wine bottle, the result of the discovery that if the pots used to hold the molten glass were left uncovered in the coal-fired furnaces, a dark, almost black glass resulted that excluded light and was ideal for storing wine. The second was lead glass. In 1674 George Ravenscroft, a wealthy English merchant in the Venetian trade who had set up a glass house in the Savoy area in London, sought a patent for a process to make 'a particular sort of Christaline Glasse resembling Rock Cristall'. Ravenscroft's glass was distinctive because it contained large quantities of lead oxide. The use of lead in glass was not new – the Venetians were familiar with its use in the manufacture of paste jewels, and all over Europe glassmakers in the mid-seventeenth century were looking for ways to make a heavier, more sturdy glass. But Ravenscroft helped perfect and market the new kind of glass, drawing on techniques introduced shortly before in the Netherlands. The new technique spread widely in British glass-houses even before Ravenscroft's patent expired in 1681. Lead glass was heavy, slow-cooling and impossible to blow thinly or to ornament with fine pulled threads. It resulted in a style of drinking glass and other vessels with bold, simple forms and little decoration that came to be seen as distinctively British, although a British preference for simplicity was already apparent in the glass the Venetians were supplying to London before Ravenscroft's innovation.

46

45

45 Wine bottles, 1660–1720. Made in England. Right: free-blown glass, 1660–70. Centre: free-blown glass, stamped with a dated seal, 1693. Left: blown and rolled glass, stamped with a dated seal, 1720. VAM C.382-1993, C.383-1993, C.113-1945.

46 Wine glass, 1700–10. Made in England. Lead glass with baluster stem. VAM C.233-1912.

5. New products

Innovation in the Tudor and Stuart period was not just a matter of new techniques and materials. Britain also saw the appearance of an astonishing number of artefacts that were new in kind, irrespective of how they were made or what they were made from. They included punch bowls and wallpaper, upholstered chairs and longcase clocks, bookcases and snuff boxes. Some, like the clay tobacco pipe, were among the many new products that emerged as a result of Britain's engagement with the world beyond Europe. Some, like the newspaper, took advantage of the opportunity to sell information offered by the new technologies of printing and paper making. Others, like the 30-piece silver toilet services given to many noblewomen on marriage, reflected the way that apparently intimate activities like gettting dressed became occasions for spectacular display in grand seventeenth-century houses. But there was more to the novelty of these objects than just the circumstances that called them into being. They challenged previous assumptions about product identity – about *how* things were to be used and how one object might differ from another.

48

47 Bookcase, about 1695. Probably made by a London joiner. From the library at Dyrham Park, Gloucestershire, the house of William Blathwayt. Oak, crown glass and iron. VAM W.12-1927.

48 Wallpaper, about 1550–75. From Besford Court, Worcestershire. Made in England. Printed with woodblocks. VAM E.3593-1913.

THE BOOK

Rowan Watson

Printing with movable type was invented by the German goldsmith, Johann Gutenberg, at Mainz in Germany in the 1450s. William Caxton probably encountered the new technology when on business in Germany and Flanders; he imported it to London in 1476. Nonetheless, Britain continued to rely heavily on books published abroad. Until the Protestant Reformation in the 1530s, books for personal devotions (especially Books of Hours) were mostly imported. In terms of design, continental printing set standards that English printers emulated.

The works of Caxton and his successors employed the same letter shapes and page design as handwritten books, but most English ornament and illustration appeared crude when compared to continental products. Gothic types were widely used – popular works such as almanacs were printed with them until after the seventeenth century. Roman type, which was first used in England in 1508, and italic fonts became more common after the mid-sixteenth century.

49. *The Golden Legend*, **1527. By Jacobus de Voragine; translated by William Caxton. Printed in London by Wynkyn de Worde. Illustrated with woodcuts. VAM 86.F.93.**

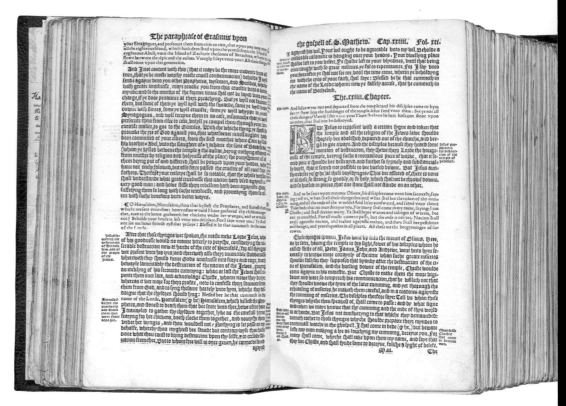

50. *The first tome or volume of the Paraphrases of Erasmus upon the Newe Testament*, **1551. By Desiderius Erasmus. Published in London by Edward Whitechurche. VAM 86.F.91.**

The use of avant-garde Renaissance ornament in books became increasingly common as the sixteenth century progressed, through the use of woodcuts, but books relating to religious matters reflected the Anglican preference after the 1530s for the word and text, rather than the image. Nevertheless, the official Bible of 1539 had a carefully composed frontispiece that demonstrated pictorially Henry VIII's position as head of the Church and, for some works, images remained essential. John Foxe's *Book of Martyrs* (first edition 1563) needed images for accounts of Protestants who had died for their faith. Puritans were, however, on the whole hostile to images for religious works. In 1640 Archbishop Laud was attacked for sanctioning the publication of bibles with images, although prints to stick into bibles were available for those of the high-church persuasion.

Illustrations printed with engraved metal plates (often engraved in the Low Countries) began to be used in books in the latter part of the sixteenth century, although engraved title-pages replete with allegorical and emblematic allusions, usually arranged around a Roman arch, only became common after 1600. The superior quality of engraved images ensured that they were widely used in the seventeenth century: maps, scientific and antiquarian books and manuals of all kinds could now be systematically illustrated to unprecedented levels of quality.

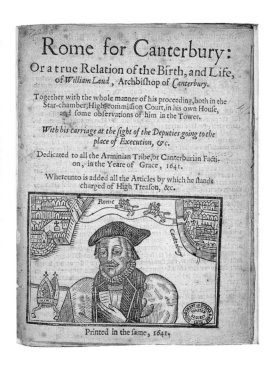

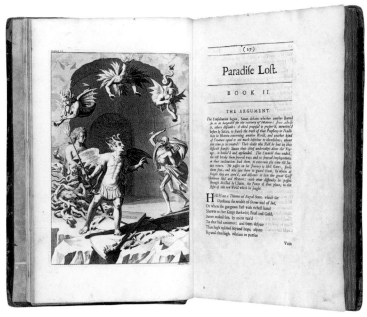

52. *Paradise Lost. A poem in twelve books*, 4th edition, 1688. By John Milton. Illustrations engraved by Michael Burgesse after designs by John Baptist Medina. Printed in London by Miles Flesher. Published by Richard Bentley and Jacob Tonson. VAM Dyce:6606.

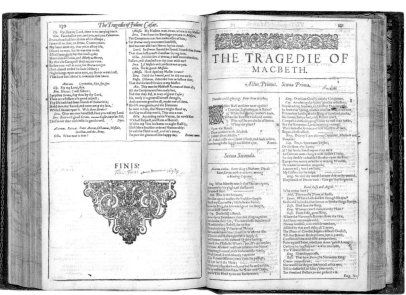

54. *Mr William Shakespeares comedies, histories & tragedies. Published according to the true originall copies*, 1623 (The 'First Folio'). By William Shakespeare. Printed in London by Isaac Jaggard and Edward Blount. VAM Forster:7884.

From the 1620s entrepreneurial publishers such as John Wright specialized in cheap ballads, news pamphlets, plays and 'penny books'; by 1700 the chapbook, often illustrated with a woodcut, was delivered around the kingdom by pedlars and travelling salesmen, who supplemented a distributive network established by publishers and booksellers.

55. *The second volume of the ecclesiastical history contaynyng the Actes and monumentes*, 1596, popularly known as *Foxe's Book of Martyrs*. By John Foxe. Printed in London by Peter Short, assignee of Richard Day. Illustrated with woodcuts. VAM 86.G.55.

53. Title-page and frontispiece of *An epicede or funerall song on the most disastrous death of . . . Henry Prince of Wales*, 1612. By George Chapman. Printed in London by Thomas Snodham. Published by John Budge, London. Letter-press, with an engraving by William Hole. VAM Dyce:2040.

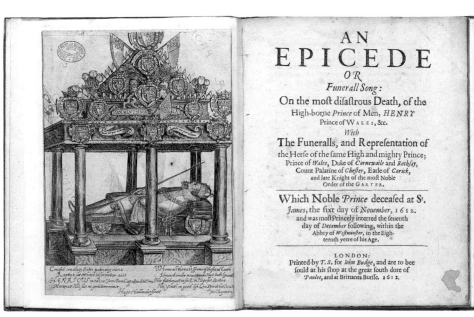

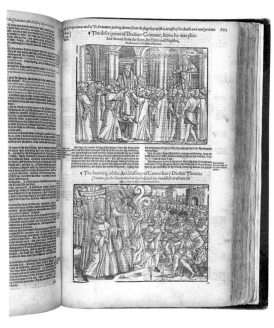

56

57

56 The Calverley toilet service, with London hallmarks for 1683–4. Maker's mark of William Fowle. The reliefs on the lids cast from plaquettes by Guglielmo della Porta. The service consists of one mirror frame, two tazzas, two large round boxes with lids and two small round boxes with lids, two rectangular boxes with lids, two large vessels with lids and two small vases with lids, and one pincushion. Silver, cast and chased. VAM 240-1879.

57 Detail of the front page of *The Post Man* newspaper, no. 1024, 3–6 October 1702. Printed in London. Letter-press and woodcut. The British Library.

Numb. 1024 CCCC

The Post Man:

And the Historical Account, &c.

From **Saturday** October 3, to **Tuesday** October 6, 1702.

Milan, Sept. 27.

ON Sunday last, being the anniversary of the Birth of the Queen of *Spain*, the Princess of *Vaudemont* gave a noble entertainment to the Persons of the chief Quality of both Sexes. Letters from the Camp near *Luzara* say, that the King of *Spain* in

a readiness to fall upon their Rear if possible, for we are incamped within a Musket shot of their Works, yet the Country is so difficult, by reason of Canals, Ditches and little Brooks, that 'tis very likely they will decamp without any Action. Our Parties obtain frequent advantages over them, and have brought several Prisoners since our last. One of them seiz'd 3 days ago 7 large Boats going down the Po, to be imployed for the Bridge near *Gonsuls*; they killed 7 French men therein, and brought away a War

Tobacco pipes were disposable, rarely being reused more than three or four times, and had constantly to be replaced. So too did the newspaper, but its disposability arose from the fact that old news would not sell. It was one of a number of seventeenth-century innovations that traded on built-in obsolescence. Like the introduction of seasonal changes in the design of fashionable silk fabrics, the newspaper intensified the distinction between the old and the new, accelerating the commercial cycle and organizing it on a regular basis, weekly or even daily. But this was not the only tactic for ensuring sales by manipulating product identity. The silver toilet service represented another tactic, binding the customer to a single supplier by providing objects in standardized sets that matched in terms of material, form and decoration.

These new kinds of ephemerality and standardization demonstrate how the ever-growing variety of artefacts in circulation pushed Tudor and Stuart manufacturers towards new ways of making their products distinctive. The pressures on them could be considerable. An innovation made from one material might threaten the livelihoods of producers in other materials. Yet, at the same time, it might provide inventive manufacturers in those materials with an opportunity to extend their range.

One of the most striking instances of this process is the development of the silver teapot in London between 1660 and 1714. As tea slowly became an established commodity in Britain from the 1660s, it was made mainly in ceramic teapots and wine pots that were imported from China. Asian porcelain pots were imitated in tin-glazed earthenware by London delftware potters, and red stoneware teapots from Yixing in China were imitated by John Dwight at Fulham and by the Elers brothers at their factories at Vauxhall and in Staffordshire. But at roughly the same time as these English imitations were being undertaken in ceramic materials, there occurred a much more radical reformulation of the Chinese teapot form as a silver object, which had no immediate direct precedents either in China or in England.

58 Tobacco pipe, 17th century. Made in England. Pipe clay. The Museum of London.

59 Chinese pear-shaped stoneware teapot, 1650–60. Red stoneware teapots of this kind were produced at Yixing in China and imported to Europe by the Dutch during the 17th century. Unglazed red stoneware. [h. 7.5cm]. VAM C.871-1936.

60 Teapot imitating Chinese stoneware teapots, 1690–8. Made by David and John Philip Elers at Bradwell Wood, Staffordshire. Slip-cast, unglazed red stoneware with moulded panels and unfired gilding. [h. 8.9cm]. VAM C.4-1932.

As has often subsequently been the case with new artefacts, there was initially a marked indeterminacy about the form of these new silver teapots. It was not until the start of the eighteenth century that some degree of design stability was achieved as a limited range of type forms became dominant. The first surviving English silver teapot was presented to the directors of the East India Company in 1670 by George, Lord Berkeley. Its shape had no obvious Chinese or Japanese parallels and it was much larger than most East Asian teapots (which were mostly less than 15cm in height). However, it closely resembled the typical coffee pot used in London coffee houses of the period. At this date, although both tea and coffee were recent novelties, coffee drinking had become much better established. In coffee houses, large pots with lids in the Turkish style, like the lid of the East India Company teapot, were used for serving numerous customers.

Other silver teapots made in London in the 1660s and 1670s were much smaller. None survive, but they probably resembled the pear-shaped silver teapots of the 1680s, which weighed under 285g, were less than 15cm tall and loosely followed the forms of Chinese

ceramic tea and wine pots (*see 5:31*). By the first two decades of the eighteenth century, when tea consumption began to increase rapidly, silver teapot design had stabilized around this smaller size of pot, with two forms dominant – the plain, squat, pear shape and the globular, 'bullet' shape. Both survive in smooth and polygonal versions; both derived from Chinese ceramic forms, although the techniques of manufacture and the overall visual effect were radically different from Chinese teapots. They were much more suited than the East India Company teapot for making tea in limited quantities, for drinking by individuals or small groups, and they were immensely successful.

---

61 Still life with Chinese blue-and-white porcelain teapot, silver jar and candlestick, about 1695. Probably painted in London, by an unknown artist. Oil on canvas. VAM P.2-1939.

62 An English pear-shaped teapot, with London hallmarks for 1713–14. Maker's mark of Thomas Folkingham. Silver, with replacement wooden handle. [h. 14cm]. VAM M.224-1930.

63 Detail of a tile panel showing a coffee-house boy with a coffee pot, late 17th century. Tin-glazed earthenware. The Museum of London.

64 The first surviving English silver teapot, with London hallmarks for 1670–1. Maker's mark of TL. Engraved with the arms of the East India Company and of Lord Berkeley. Silver, engraved; handle of leather and wood. [h. 35cm]. VAM M.399-1921.

SILVERWARES

Helen Clifford

Between 1500 and 1714 developments in silverware were driven more by social and political changes at home, and new ideas from continental Europe, than by technical innovation. The greatest single influence was the Protestant Reformation. It witnessed a change in the character of church plate, from the smaller Catholic chalice to the larger Protestant communion cup, and was accompanied by a demand for secular plate, buoyed by economic prosperity among the élite. As a result there was an increase not only in the number of dining, drinking and dressing wares being made, but also in their variety.

Increased demand stimulated the appearance of novel kinds of objects, such as tankards, casting bottles and spice plates. Older forms, like the standing salt, were replaced by smaller, cheaper designs, like the bell salt, which appears in inventories from the 1530s. Their manufacture (comprising two tapering sections) required no great technical ability, and they could easily be chased and engraved with the latest Renaissance strapwork ornament. Most of the new forms were based on French and Dutch models, although the steeple cup, which appears in royal plate inventories from the 1570s, was peculiarly English and was intended to enhance the splendour of the buffet display. Some continental habits, like the use of the fork – common in court circles in Italy in the 1530s – took longer to arrive in England. The earliest-known English example, a silver fork of 1632, is based on a continental design source.

67. Bell salt, with London hallmarks for 1594–5. Marked 'NR' conjoined over four pellets in a plain shield. Chased silver-gilt. VAM 283:1&2-1893.

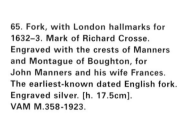

65. Fork, with London hallmarks for 1632–3. Mark of Richard Crosse. Engraved with the crests of Manners and Montague of Boughton, for John Manners and his wife Frances. The earliest-known dated English fork. Engraved silver. [h. 17.5cm]. VAM M.358-1923.

66. Communion cup and cover, about 1571–4. Mark of John Jones of Exeter. Silver, with gilded interior, die-struck and punched foot-rings and wires on base; engraving on band around cup and on cover. VAM 4636-1858.

The design and decoration of English silver were generally unadventurous. The main exception was an early flickering of the Dutch auricular style. It first reached England just before the civil war, although it did not become more widespread until the Restoration of Charles II in 1660. The muscular dissolving borders of the silver-gilt porringer of about 1665 are a high-quality example of the style. The Restoration coincided with the spread of new French modes of dining, which required refinements in silver tableware. It also saw the introduction of silver serving equipment for new beverages, such as tea, coffee, chocolate and punch. It was at this period, too, that silver objects began to proliferate in the bedroom, with the introduction of toilet services. The arrival of large numbers of skilled French Protestant goldsmiths – the Huguenots – after 1685 helped the goldsmiths' trade in England satisfy the demand for the new objects, since they brought with them innovatory forms, like the helmet-shaped ewer, and decorative techniques, like cut-card work.

68. Font cup, with London hallmarks for 1500–1. Mark of a device in a shaped shield; originally the property of the Campion family of Danny, Sussex. Silver-gilt. VAM M.249-1924.

71. Porringer, about 1665. Mark of a star above an escallop with six pellets. Engraved with the arms of Anthony Ashley Cooper, later Earl of Shaftesbury. Embossed and chased silver-gilt. VAM M.104-1984.

70. Steeple cup, with London hallmarks for 1625–6. Marked 'TF', possibly the mark of Thomas Flynt. Given by Richard Chester to the Corporation of Trinity House in 1632. Chased and embossed silver-gilt. VAM M.244-1924.

69. Helmet-shaped ewer, with London hallmarks for 1700–1. Mark of David Willaume. Engraved with arms of the diplomat and public servant, the Honourable and Reverend Richard Hill of Hawkestone, Shropshire. Silver-gilt with cast details and applied cut-card work, ornamented in relief. VAM 822-1890.

72. Silver wire-work purse, 1630–50. Silver-gilt filigree with silk lining and tassels. VAM M.17-1989.

73 *Sovereign of the Seas*, 1637. By John
Payne. Hand-coloured engraving. © National
Maritime Museum, London.

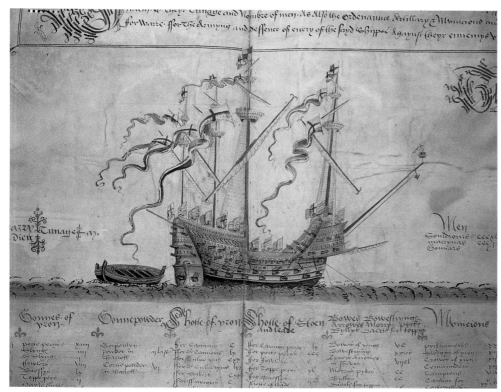

The development of the silver teapot was a response to the new and competitive market for hot-drink utensils, but not all competition in Tudor and Stuart Britain was commercial. Another new British artefact of the seventeenth century – the three-deck warship – is testimony to competitiveness of a very different sort: the military and propaganda struggle between European states. The *Sovereign of the Seas*, completed in 1637 for Charles I, was the first great warship to be built with three gun decks. Charles's predecessors had also built great ships, like Henry VIII's *Henri Grâce à Dieu* and James I and VI's *Prince Royal*. Often considerations of royal prestige had been as influential as strict naval necessity. Prestige certainly loomed large when Charles I informed the leading English shipbuilder, Phineas Pett, of his 'princely resolution for the building of a great new ship'. The *Sovereign of the Seas* was designed to impress. She was huge and, in contrast to the *Prince Royal* of 1610, also designed by Pett, she was a genuine three-decker. She carried a massive armament of 102 guns, almost twice the earlier ship's 55, and outgunned her Dutch and French rivals.

Built at a cost of £65,587, the *Sovereign of the Seas* was extraordinarily expensive, ten times the price of the average 40- to 50-gun warship. Part of this expense arose from the cost of the ship's decoration. Great naval vessels in the seventeenth century were always highly decorated, especially at the bow and stern, but the decorative work on the *Sovereign of the Seas* was exceptional, costing £6,691 alone, executed by the carvers John and Mathias Christmas.

Her figurehead was King Edgar the Peaceful on horseback; her stern carried figures of Victory, Neptune, Jason, Jupiter and Hercules. In service, much of this decoration had to be removed to improve her stability, but its cost and elaboration confirmed the importance that Charles I ascribed to the arts in projecting the dignity and majesty of his kingship in all its aspects. Like the tapestries made at Mortlake or Van Dyck's royal portraits, the *Sovereign of the Seas* was an exercise in the aesthetics of royal power.

Critics among shipbuilders warned that 'the art or wit of man cannot build a ship fit for service with three tier of ordnance', but their views dissuaded neither the King nor Pett, a designer who in some respects stood outside the dominant tradition of the craftsman-shipwright. The result was a vessel that was far less manoeuvrable than most of her predecessors and one that concentrated a much greater proportion of her firepower in the broadside, rather than fore and aft. In the sixteenth century, when naval tactics emphasized turning and boarding, these characteristics would have been a disadvantage. But in the Anglo-Dutch War of 1652–4 the British developed the devastating new tactic of fighting in a single line of battle, in which each ship had to hold its position. *Sovereign of the Seas* was well suited to this, and she became the vessel that set the pattern for the three-deckers built in large numbers in the second half of the seventeenth century. Ships of this configuration were to remain the most powerful naval vessels and, indeed, the largest ships in the world, until steam replaced sail in the nineteenth century.

74 *Henri Grâce à Dieu*, 1545–6. Detail from the Anthony Anthony Roll. Built for Henry VIII in 1514, she was rebuilt between 1536 and 1539. Watercolour on vellum. Pepys Library, Magdalene College, Cambridge.

75 Medal, 1639. Cast in London by the Frenchman Nicolas Briot. Charles I issued medals to promote his royal authority and to publicize his policies, including his maritime ambitions. This medal, depicting on its reverse a naval vessel in full sail, asserted his sovereign authority over the English Channel. The inscription reads NEC META MIHI QVAE TERMINVS ORBI (Nor to me is that a limit, which is boundary to the world). Cast silver. VAM 949-1901.

The pattern of innovation in design and the decorative arts experienced in Tudor and Stuart Britain, combining imports from abroad with native inventiveness, was not new. Innovations in the material culture of Venice and Florence in the fifteenth century, or Antwerp and Paris in the sixteenth, derived from a similar combination of external and internal sources. Britain was a latecomer, often soaking up new influences from southern Europe and Asia at second or third hand. But in the seventeenth century, especially, her location on Europe's favoured north-west seaboard, her aggressive trading policy and her resources (both human and natural) worked to produce an immensely successful commercial economy. In this fertile soil it was possible for the manufacture of high-design goods, previously lacking in sophistication, to approach the highest western European standards of aesthetics and technique. Nevertheless, it was only to be in the course of the century after 1714 – the year when the last Stuart monarch, Queen Anne, died – that Britain came to share in setting those standards.

76 *Peter Pett and the Sovereign of the Seas,* about 1660. By Sir Peter Lely. The painting shows the elaborately carved stern of the ship after rebuilding in 1660, when she was renamed the *Royal Sovereign*. The shipwright Peter Pett, the builder of *Sovereign of the Seas*, was the son of the ship's designer, Phineas Pett. Oil on canvas. © National Maritime Museum, London.

Georgian Britain

1714–1837

CHAPTER 6

Georgian Britain, 1714–1837

Introduction

JOHN STYLES

1 previous pages (left):
Crayfish salt cellar, 1752–6. Made at
the Chelsea porcelain factory, London.
Possibly modelled by Nicholas Sprimont.
Soft-paste porcelain, painted in enamels.
[h. 5cm]. VAM C.73-1938.

2 previous pages (right):
Cabinet, about 1776. Designed by Robert
Adam and made by the firm of John
Mayhew and William Ince, London, with
pietra dura plaques made in Florence
by Baccio Cappelli and mounts made
in Birmingham by Matthew Boulton.
Commissioned by Elizabeth, Duchess of
Manchester. Mahogany, oak, satinwood,
rosewood, pietra dura, ormolu mounts.
VAM W.43.1949.

1. Georgian preoccupations

In 1715 the Scottish lawyer and architect Colen Campbell published a book
of architectural prints entitled *Vitruvius Britannicus*. Its title points to two of
its most important features. The mention of Vitruvius, the architectural author
whose writings had survived from ancient Rome, demonstrates Campbell's
obsession with classical accuracy. The reference to Britain testifies to the book's
patriotic rejection of French influence on architecture, which, Campbell
believed, had been excessive under the later Stuart monarchs. Against the
French, Campbell held up two men as models of classical purity in
architectural design – the seventeenth-century English court architect Inigo
Jones and the sixteenth-century Italian architect, Andrea Palladio, who inspired
much of Jones's work.

Prominent among the prints in *Vitruvius Britannicus* was an engraving of
Campbell's own design for Wanstead House, a palatial mansion then being
built in the neo-Palladian style in the Essex countryside, close to the outskirts
of London (*see* 7:8). Campbell designed Wanstead for Sir Richard Child, the
heir to an East India Company fortune, but it was the young nobleman,
the third Earl of Burlington, who was to become Campbell's principal patron.
Burlington promoted Campbell's ideas and developed them, giving Campbell's
new approach to architecture a cachet that was both intellectual and social, and
which could not have been supplied by Campbell himself.

Vitruvius Britannicus was to become the single most influential work
of architecture published in the Georgian era; and Wanstead its single
most influential building. Emerging together, in the immediate aftermath of
George I's coronation in 1714, the book and the house embody a number
of the Georgian period's deepest cultural preoccupations. Between them they
exemplify many of the imperatives that were to shape design and architecture
in Georgian Britain – the hunger for authentic classical precedent; the cultural

3 Detail of *Wanstead House,* about
1780. By George Robertson. The house
designed by Colen Campbell. Built
1715–20 for Sir Richard Child. Pen, ink
and wash. VAM E.2517-1938.

3

The reasons for French mastery of European design and decorative arts at the start of the eighteenth century were many, but two in particular stand out. Firstly, the sheer size of the country and its resources, from which an opulent ruling élite benefited disproportionately. In terms of population, France in 1700 was the largest western European country, with about 20 million people. Great Britain, by contrast, had little more than six million. Despite the poverty of much of the French peasantry, the country's ruling élite was large and immensely wealthy, constituting a sizeable market for expensive, luxury goods. The second reason for French supremacy lay in the success of Louis XIV's deliberate policy of cultural domination. European monarchs in the baroque age were well accustomed to competing by means of elaborate displays of splendour and magnificence. Louis XIV raised such theatricality to new levels of sophistication. Not only did his royal palace at Versailles dwarf the architectural achievements of other European monarchs, but it served as a showcase for the products of French high-design industries, like Gobelin tapestries and Lyons silk textiles. These industries were themselves in several cases the creations of the French state and benefited from state subsidies. In addition, the state provided specialist training for designers.

Rivalry with France was a crucial element in Georgian Britain's rise to international prominence in design and the decorative arts. As in many such rivalries, the British copied a great deal from the French, despite their virulent Francophobia. The British imported both French stylistic ideas, such as rococo and aspects of neo-classicism, and French workers, most prominently the Protestant Huguenots. But they did not borrow the French policy of systematic royal promotion of the visual arts. In a constitutional monarchy of the British eighteenth-century type it was hardly possible to do so. The third Earl of Shaftesbury argued in his *Letter concerning the Art, or Science of Design*, written on the eve of the accession of George I, that under a free constitution it was undesirable, inappropriate and futile for the monarch to dictate taste. Anyway, most of the kings descended from the royal house of Hanover were unsuited to the task, both in their personalities and their interests. Royal palaces continued to be refurnished and rebuilt; foreign ambassadors and the British nobility continued to attend at court. Yet neither George I's court nor those of his two successors (his son, George II, and his great-grandson, George III) were crucial sites of national cultural display, in the manner of Versailles. Indeed, the only Hanoverian king who exhibited a special interest in design and the decorative arts was George IV. His trend-setting activities as Prince of Wales, Prince Regent and ultimately King included the building or rebuilding of Carlton House, London, and the Pavilion at Brighton. But by this stage his was only one influence among many. By the end of the eighteenth century cultural leadership had become dispersed among a multiplicity of designers and craftspeople, manufacturers and shopkeepers, noble patrons and Grub Street critics.

4. Commerce

To understand Britain's increasing international reputation in design and the decorative arts in the Georgian period we need, therefore, to look beyond the royal court. The sources of Britain's success in this sphere lay ultimately in the economy, in particular in the achievements of British commerce and manufacture. Already regarded as a wealthy country at the start of the eighteenth century, Britain was to be the most successful European economy of the eighteenth and early nineteenth centuries. On almost every front British output outpaced that of its major rivals.

Take agriculture, which was still, at the beginning of the Georgian period, the largest single sector of the economy. Between the start of the eighteenth century and the 1830s the output of British agriculture grew rapidly enough to go on feeding the population without much recourse to imports, even though the number of people nearly tripled, from little more than six million to well over 16 million. Yet agriculture was not the most consistently dynamic area of the economy. It was commerce and manufacturing that grew most rapidly.

The best evidence for this lies in the spectacular expansion of towns, the key centres for trade and industry, and communications. London was already, in 1700, the largest city in western Europe, with about 575,000 people, approximately one-tenth of the country's population. Paris was the second-largest western European city, with 510,000 people. Among the rest of the cities of western Europe, only Amsterdam and Naples had populations over 200,000. London's size reflected its triple role as the capital city, the leading port and the country's largest industrial centre. It was the arbiter of fashionable taste, the natural habitat of the *beau monde* and its seductively designed shops

13

14

13 Trade card of Martha Cole and Martha Houghton, at the Sun in St Paul's Churchyard, London, about 1720–30. Engraved by B. Cole. At the start of the Georgian period fashionable London shops were already using carefully designed interiors to lure customers. This trade card depicts a shop fitted out with a mirror and a glazed partition, where well-dressed female customers enjoy the comforts of an open fire and an elegant stool. Engraving. VAM E.2299-1987.

14 *The Thames and the City of London from Richmond House*, about 1747. By Antonio Canaletto for the second Duke of Richmond. Oil on canvas. By courtesy of the Trustees of the Goodwood Collection.

dominated the retailing of high-design goods. It enjoyed these same advantages 130 years later, when its population had more than tripled to well over one and a half million people, some of them accommodated in the spacious houses that surrounded the new streets and squares laid out in the classical style, with many more living in mean one- or two-room lodgings.

However, this figure still represented only about one-tenth of the country's (by then) much larger population. It was not in London, but elsewhere in Britain – in the English provinces, in Wales and in Scotland – that the most dramatic urban growth took place during the Georgian era. There towns grew far more rapidly than London, although none of them came close to rivalling London in terms of sheer size. In 1831 London was still eight times larger than Glasgow or Liverpool, the country's next largest towns.

15 *Messrs Harding, Howell & Co. of Pall Mall*, 1809. Plate from Rudolph Ackermann's *Repository of Arts*, vol. 1, no. 3, March 1809. Harding, Howell & Co.'s Grand Fashionable Magazine opened in Schomberg House, Pall Mall, London, in 1796. An early precursor of the department store, its spacious and elegant ground floor, shown here, was divided into four departments separated by glazed partitions. The first sold furs and fans, the second haberdashery, the third jewellery, clocks and perfumery, and the fourth millinery and dresses. Upstairs was a refreshment room. Etching and aquatint. VAM 11.RC.R.1.

16 *Bloomsbury Square, London*, about 1787. By Edward Dayes. Etching and aquatint. The Museum of London.

17

17 *The Distressed Poet*, 1736. By William Hogarth. The sparsely furnished London garret lodging of an impoverished poet and his family. The arrival of a truculent milkmaid demanding to be paid underscores his distressed circumstances. Oil on canvas. Birmingham Museums and Art Gallery.

The towns that grew most quickly were ports like Bristol and Liverpool, Whitehaven and Glasgow, centres of industry like Manchester, Leeds and Merthyr Tydfil, and leisure resorts like Bath, Brighton and Scarborough. It was as a consequence of their growth, not of the growth of London, that by 1851 more than half the population of Britain lived in towns. In 1700 less than one-fifth had done so.

The growth of towns was encouraged by the rapid improvement of the means of communication between them. In contrast to many continental European states, Britain had no internal customs duties or other barriers to internal trade. The country formed one large, uninterrupted market, ringed by a fence of customs duties, designed to defend British manufactures from foreign competition. Within the customs ring, trade was facilitated by a succession of transport innovations, almost all based on commercial rather than

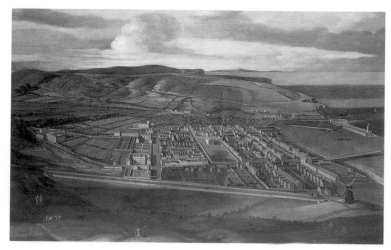

19

18

18 *Leeds*, 1816. By J. M. W. Turner.
Watercolour. Yale Center for British Art,
Paul Mellon Collection.

19 *Prospect of Whitehaven from
Brackenthwaite*, 1736. By Matthias Read.
Oil on canvas. The Beacon, Whitehaven.

government investment. Rivers were made navigable and, from the 1760s, a new network of canals was built. Roads were improved by establishing turnpike trusts, which charged tolls to pay for the cost of rebuilding. In 1750 there were barely more than 3,000 miles (4,827km) of turnpike road; by the 1830s 20,000 miles (32,180km) of road had been turnpiked. The consequences were dramatic. In 1700 it took 90 hours to get from Manchester to London; in 1800 it took just 33. Some, of course, disapproved. 'I wish with all my heart,' moaned the conservative John Byng at the end of the eighteenth century, 'that half the turnpike roads of the kingdom were ploughed up, which have imported London manners and depopulated the country.' For men like Byng, worse was soon to come. The first passenger railway, from Stockton to Darlington in County Durham, was opened in 1825; by 1838, 743 miles (1,195km) of track had been laid.

20 *North Parade, Bath*, about 1777. By Thomas Malton junior. The second and third buildings from the left were Assembly Rooms. Watercolour. VAM 1723-1871.

21 *Greenwich Railway. View from the Surrey Canal*, 1836. By G. F. Bragg. The new London–Greenwich railway on its continuous viaduct as it crosses the Surrey Canal. Lithograph. Ironbridge Gorge Museum Trust.

Improvements in communication were not simply a matter of the physical movement of goods and people. Just as significant was the development of new media for the circulation of information. The most important of these were the newspaper and the periodical, although we should not ignore the poster, the handbill and the trade card. For much of the half century before 1695, only one newspaper had been allowed to circulate. This was the weekly *London Gazette*, which had a semi-official status. After restrictions were lifted in 1695, newspapers began to be published as purely commercial enterprises in greater and greater numbers. The first daily paper, *The Daily Courant*, appeared in London in 1702; by 1792 there were 16 London dailies. London newspapers and periodicals were widely read in the provinces, but local newspapers also sprang up in almost every major provincial town. Both newspapers and periodicals played a significant role in the development of design and the decorative arts. In addition to political news, they carried advertising for a wide range of goods and also articles that commented on almost every aspect of cultural life. Indeed, by the later Georgian period, journals such as Rudolph Ackermann's *Repository of Arts, Literature, Commerce, Manufactures, Fashion and the Politics* (1806–29) were almost entirely devoted to high-design goods.

The growth of population in the port towns, especially those on the western seaboard that faced the Atlantic and the world beyond Europe, reflected the importance of international trade and colonies to Britain's economy. Throughout the Georgian period, no other major European economy was more heavily committed to international trade than the British, with the single exception of the Netherlands, a country in economic decline. Britain's self-image was that of a trading nation. 'Our trade,' announced Lord Carteret in 1739, 'is our chief support.' Indeed, so dedicated were Britons to the cult of trade that Thomas Mortimer, the historian, could describe commerce in 1762 as 'the great idol of this nation, and to which she sacrifices every other consideration'. The common seaman, notoriously truculent and uncouth, was fêted as the epitome of British courage and the mainstay of Britain's prosperity. The Royal Navy, which secured the trade routes, was the focus of national pride. Victorious admirals like Vernon, Rodney and Nelson were national heroes.

22 Poster advertising the programme at Astley's circus, 1833. Philip Astley founded his circus in London in 1768. It became a leading British innovator in advertising, pioneering large posters printed in an arresting variety of display typefaces, with different-coloured inks and woodcut and wood-engraved illustrations. Woodcut and letter-press. [h. 74cm]. VAM S.2-1983.

25

24 Plate showing Emma Hamilton as Britannia unveiling a bust of Admiral Nelson, 1806. Made at the Coalport porcelain factory, Shropshire, and painted by Thomas Baxter junior in the London workshop of Thomas Baxter senior. Hard-paste porcelain, painted in enamel colours. VAM C.67-1984.

25 *A Thames–side Quay*, about 1757. By Samuel Scott. The mark 'UEIC' on the bale in the foreground is for the United East India Company. Oil on canvas. VAM FA.249.

Trade followed the flag. Britain was at war for more than one-third of the period from 1714 to 1837, and was largely victorious, with the notable exception of the American War of Independence (1776–83). In all these wars France was the principal enemy, while trade and colonies figured prominently among the causes of conflict. In the eighteenth century, especially, colonies offered unrivalled opportunities for the expansion of trade. They might serve as exclusive markets for manufactured exports, like Britain's North American territories with their fast-growing populations of European and African descent. They might serve as sources of exotic manufactures, like muslins and ivory wares from India; or as suppliers of tropical foodstuffs, like the West Indian sugar islands. Indeed, it was the West Indies that were the jewels in the imperial crown in the eighteenth century and the object of the most intense colonial rivalry among the European powers. Throughout the Caribbean, on islands owned by the British, the French, the Spanish, the Dutch and

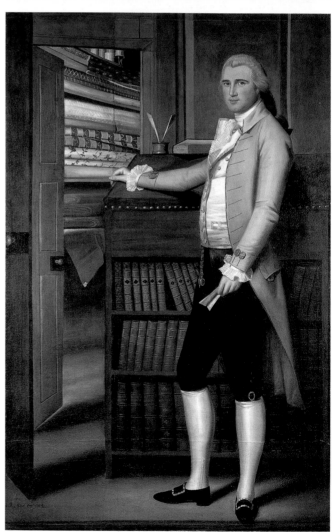

26 *A View of Charles Town*, 1774. By Thomas Leitch. At this period Charleston in South Carolina was one of the most prosperous ports in the British North American colonies. Oil on canvas. Courtesy of the Museum of Early Southern Decorative Arts, Winston-Salem.

27 Work box in the shape of a cottage, 1790–1800. Made in Vizagapatam, India, for the English market. The country cottage symbolized rustic simplicity and uncorrupted Englishness, yet this example was made in India. Wood veneered with ivory. [h. 15.5cm]. VAM W.20-1951.

28 *Elija Boardman*, 1789. By Ralph Earl. Boardman, depicted in his shop, was a dry-goods merchant in New Milford, Connecticut. His large stock of patterned textiles would have been mainly imported from Britain. Oil on canvas. © 2001. The Metropolitan Museum of Art, New York.

29

30

other European powers, huge numbers of slaves from Africa toiled on sugar plantations. They laboured to satisfy the insatiable appetite for sweetness among European consumers and to generate spectacular wealth for their European owners. It was only towards the end of the Georgian era, in 1833, that slavery was abolished in the British territories, at a time when the significance of the West Indian colonies for the British economy was reduced. Nevertheless, the colonies as a whole continued to make an important contribution to the success of British commerce through the later Georgian years. The United States of America may have been lost in 1783, but thereafter Britain went on to conquer new territories – in India, Africa and Australia.

British trade grew enormously between the start of the eighteenth century and the middle of the nineteenth. Not only did the volume of trade expand perhaps thirtyfold, but the geographical extent of British commerce and the variety of goods traded also increased. All this contributed to the huge growth in national wealth that took place during the Georgian era. Changing patterns of trade register the growing international status of British manufactures. They also register a growing international respect for British design and decorative arts. Between the sixteenth and nineteenth centuries Britain underwent a long drawn-out transformation that saw a peripheral and relatively unsophisticated economy transformed into the manufacturing workshop of the world. A country that had exported mainly raw materials and semi-finished goods now became one whose exports consisted principally of high-quality, finished manufactures. It was the Georgian period that witnessed the decisive shift from one pattern of trade to the other.

---

29 Medallion for the Society for the Abolition of the Slave Trade, about 1787. Modelled by William Hackwood. Made at Josiah Wedgwood's factory, Etruria, Staffordshire. The design was taken from the Society's seal and bears the words 'AM I NOT A MAN AND A BROTHER'. The medallions were given to the society's members. Wedgwood was a keen supporter of the campaign to abolish slavery. White jasper ware, with black relief, mounted in gilt-metal. [h. 3cm]. VAM 414:1304-1885.

30 *Francis Williams, The Jamaican Scholar*, about 1745. By an unknown artist. Williams was a mathematician and poet. Educated in England, he returned to Jamaica to set up a school in Spanish Town. He is shown in his study, with a Jamaican landscape in the background. The population of Jamaica in the 18th century consisted overwhelmingly of people of African descent, almost all of them slaves. Williams was a member of a tiny minority of free blacks. Oil on canvas. VAM P.83-1928.

31

We can observe one element of this shift in the destinations of manufactured exports. In 1700 the principal market was Europe, and woollen cloth remained by far the most important product exported, just as it had been for more than two centuries. By the early 1770s, on the eve of the American Revolution, there had been striking changes. Europe had been overtaken as a market by Britain's colonies on the American mainland and in the West Indies. Woollen textiles remained important, but the range of products exported had widened to include Spitalfields silks, Lancashire printed cottons, Staffordshire pots, Bristol glasswares and a huge diversity of small metal goods, from humble nails to fine silverware. By the 1830s the destinations and the mix of exports had changed again. Now approximately one-third of exports went to Europe, one-third to the United States, Canada and the West Indies, and one-third to the rest of the non-European world. As for the mix of goods, cotton was now king, with cotton cloth and yarn accounting for just under half of all exports, although the remainder included almost every kind of manufactured product imaginable at the time, such was Britain's manufacturing prowess.

Imports displayed equally dynamic changes. At the start of the eighteenth century about one-third of all imports consisted of manufactured goods – silk and cotton textiles from India, porcelain from China, lacquered wares from Japan, linen cloth from Germany and bar iron from Sweden. But as British manufacturing flourished and a government policy of high tariffs restricted manufactured imports, they became less and less important. By the eve of Victoria's reign manufactured goods constituted only a tiny proportion of British imports, which increasingly comprised foodstuffs and raw materials. Britain remained largely self-sufficient in the foods produced in a temperate climate, so it was exotic foodstuffs from beyond Europe that were imported – tea from China and sugar from the slave plantations of the British West Indies. Raw materials to feed Britain's growing workshops were initially imported mainly from Europe – timber and flax from the Baltic, raw silk and dyestuffs from the Mediterranean. As the Georgian era progressed, however, more and more raw materials came from further afield – mahogany for fine furniture from the Caribbean, raw cotton for the Lancashire mills from the slave plantations in the newly independent United States, raw silk from China and, by the 1830s, wool from the new British colonies in Australia.

32

31 Commemorative jug, about 1825. Probably made by J. & R. Clews in Cobridge, Staffordshire, for export to the United States. The scene on the jug is entitled 'Landing of Gen. Lafayette at Castle Garden New York 16 August 1824'. Lead-glazed earthenware, transfer-printed. VAM C.38-1974.

32 Armorial plate, about 1772. Made at the Jingdezhen kilns, China, and decorated either there or in Canton, for export to Britain. It bears the arms of Pitt, Earl of Chatham, impaling those of Grenville, copied from an English pattern. Porcelain, decorated in overglaze enamels and gilt. VAM C.71-1932.

33 *Paul Crespin*, about 1730. By an unknown artist. Crespin was born in London in 1694, the son of a Huguenot immigrant, and became one of the capital's leading goldsmiths. Oil on canvas. VAM P.29-1985.

5. Manufacturing

The key to these shifts in patterns of trade was a progressive increase in the output, range and sophistication of British manufactures that continued through the Georgian period. The innovations associated with the Industrial Revolution after 1760 – innovations principally in steam power and textile machinery – made a critical contribution to this process of improvement. But it is important to emphasize that it was a process that was already well advanced by the mid-eighteenth century and one that extended to a far wider range of industries than those conventionally associated with the Industrial Revolution.

Consider the experience of the high-design industries during the first half of the eighteenth century. Already, at the start of the century, the range and the quality of skills that were available in Britain had grown significantly by comparison with the early seventeenth century. By the accession of George I in 1714, Britain was manufacturing virtually the whole range of high-design products that the country had previously imported, from stoneware jugs to decorated cotton textiles, from engraved prints to lacquered cabinets, although notable exceptions, such as porcelain, remained. Yet British high-design manufactures displayed important weaknesses at this stage. Often British producers could not match the quality of their European equivalents, so high-design manufactures remained heavily dependent on immigrant designers and makers from all over Europe – from France, the Low Countries, Germany, Switzerland, Italy and Sweden. Most prominent were the Huguenots – exiled French Protestants and their immediate descendants – like the silversmith Paul Crespin and the silk designer and manufacturer James Leman. What most of these foreigners shared, irrespective of their trade or country of origin, was the freehand drawing skills that were the key to eighteenth-century design, skills that were in lamentably short supply among native Britons. Also a weakness was the narrowness of indigenous innovation. It was in only a handful of fields that Britain enjoyed a reputation as a leading innovator at the start of the eighteenth century, most notably in the manufacture of clocks, watches and scientific instruments. During the second half of the eighteenth century, most of these weaknesses were successfully addressed. Britain became widely admired across Europe for the quality of products such as ceramics, decorative metalwares and prints. It was regarded as a leading innovator in fields like coach building, printed textiles and men's fashion. The country's reliance on foreign designers and makers was much reduced.

The Industrial Revolution of 1760–1850 was, therefore, part of a wider process of improvement in British manufacturing that continued through the Georgian period, and not its cause. The Industrial Revolution is usually associated with two sets of inventions – James Watt's rotary steam engine and the cotton-spinning machines developed by James Hargreaves, Richard Arkwright and Samuel Crompton – which were brought together in a new kind of productive unit: the factory. The impact of these inventions was immense. Cotton became the largest single British manufacturing industry by

34 *Sir Richard Arkwright*, 1789–90. By Joseph Wright. Prominently displayed on the table beside Arkwright is a set of cotton-spinning rollers, a crucial part of the spinning machine that he patented in 1769, which earned him an immense fortune. Oil on canvas. Private collection.

34

35

35 *Morning View of Coalbrookdale*, 1777. By William Williams. Smelting iron by means of coke was invented by Abraham Darby at Coalbrookdale, Shropshire, in 1709, but the major expansion of iron making with coke began there only after 1750. In the last quarter of the 18th century the furnaces belching smoke and flame and the new iron bridge across the gorge of the River Severn became wonders of the age, much visited and depicted in paintings and prints. Oil on canvas. Clive House Museum, Shrewsbury.

the early nineteenth century. Steam engines were used not just to drive many new factories, but to pump water out of mines, to provide the blast in iron works and to power ships and railway locomotives. It is, however, important to stress just how limited was the direct impact of the new steam-powered technologies on the making of high-design goods. Outside of cotton and woollen textiles, most high-design artefacts continued to be made at the start of Victoria's reign largely by hand tools and hand-driven machines (stamps, presses, lathes and the like). The workshop remained much more characteristic of these trades than the factory reverberating to the din of steam-powered machinery.

36 *Carding, Drawing and Roving*, 1835. By Thomas Allom. Engraved by J. Carter. Plate from *History of the Cotton Manufacture in Great Britain* by Edward Baines, 1835. Engraving. VAM 43.D.88.

37 *The Collier*, 1814. By George Walker. Etched by R. and D. Havell. Plate from *The Costume of Yorkshire* by George Walker, 1814. Steam power is used here both at the mine and to move coal on the wagonway. Etching and aquatint. VAM 11.RC.F.19.

Ceramics, glasswares, small decorative metalwares, furniture: in 1837, and indeed well into the final decades of the nineteenth century, their manufacture remained overwhelmingly a hand trade. But this is not to say that such industries were unaffected by technical change. Hand making was itself transformed by innovations in technique, such as transfer printing on ceramics and glass pressing, and by new materials, such as mahogany, Sheffield plate and steel furniture springs. Innovations of these kinds in what remained fundamentally hand trades could make high-design goods cheaper and encourage the proliferation of new varieties of object.

39

6. People

Who provided the market for the surge of artefacts that poured forth from workshop and factory alike? Overseas markets may have grown faster, but it was British consumers who bought the bulk of British manufactured goods throughout the Georgian period. Not only did the number of these consumers more than treble as population growth took off from the mid-eighteenth century, but they became better off, at almost every social level. Nevertheless, this remained a profoundly unequal society. At the top were the nobility, whose wealth came from their ownership of a considerable proportion of the nation's land. There were very few of them. In England and Wales the 160 peers of 1688 had risen to some 350 by 1832 – a mere handful compared with the 120,000 nobles in France on the eve of the Revolution in the 1780s or the half million in Spain. On the continent, where nobles were numerous, it was far from unusual for them to be impoverished. In Britain, where nobles were few, almost all were fabulously wealthy, and becoming more so. The nobility benefited not only from growing agricultural profitability after 1760, but indirectly, through their ownership of urban and industrial property, from the expansion of trade and manufacturing. Consequently they had a huge impact on the aesthetic life of the nation. Nobles could afford to travel throughout their country and the continent, collecting art works and antiquities as they went. They built, rebuilt and refurnished enormous houses in London and the country-side, which were often the equal of royal palaces in the smaller European states. They patronized artists and artisans, shopkeepers and showmen. But, however wealthy and influential the nobility was, their numbers were far too small to soak up all the high-design consumer goods that British manufacturers produced in ever greater quantities. This role fell principally to their immediate inferiors, the burgeoning middling ranks in the British social hierarchy.

38

38 *John Cuff*, 1772. By Johann Zoffany. Cuff was master of the Worshipful Company of Spectacle Makers in 1748. He is depicted in his workshop with an assistant, at his bench, surrounded by his tools, polishing a lens. Oil on canvas. © The Royal Collection.

39 *Sheffield Cutler*, 1814. By George Walker. Etched by R. and D. Havell. Plate from *The Costume of Yorkshire* by George Walker, 1814. Etching and aquatint. VAM 11.RC.F.19.

40 *Marriage à la Mode. The Tête à Tête*, 1745. By William Hogarth. In his second painting from the *Marriage à la Mode* series, Hogarth ridicules the excesses of noble splendour, in particular the style of William Kent in interior decoration, the rococo, and the cult of Old Masters and the antique. Oil on canvas. © Tate, London, 2001.

41

42

Immediately below the nobility on the social ladder lay the massed ranks of the moderately wealthy. By the early nineteenth century they were numbered in hundreds of thousands and were growing faster than the rest of the population. In some respects they were not a homogeneous group. Their wealth came from a number of different and sometimes antagonistic sources – from land, trade, manufacturing, the professions. These differences were the occasion of myriad petty snobberies, as were differences in the sheer scale of their wealth. The middling group in British society embraced a huge range of incomes, from merchants, bankers, industrialists and landed gentry, whose wealth occasionally matched that of the nobility, to shopkeepers, farmers, workshop masters and country curates, whose incomes might not be very much greater than that of a skilled workman. It was also deeply divided in matters of religion between Anglicans and Nonconformists.

Nevertheless, the various elements that made up the middling group in Georgian Britain did have a number of things in common. They formed a much larger proportion of the British population than was the case in the rest of Europe – in France, unlike Britain, noted one British traveller in the 1780s, 'you go at once from beggary to profusion'. They were also becoming increasingly urban. They enjoyed more than their fair share of the fruits of Britain's economic success when compared with their inferiors among the labouring classes. And, most importantly for design and the decorative arts, they shared an aspiration to a genteel way of life that found much of its expression in owning, using and displaying the right goods. It was they, above all, who

sustained that growing multitude of manufacturers producing the high-design objects that comprised the essential props of gentility – porcelain tea sets, mahogany dining tables, wine decanters, patterned floor carpets, creamware dining services. English manufactured products, it was pointed out by the writer on economics Josiah Tucker in the mid-eighteenth century:

> are more adapted for the demands of peasants and mechanics, in order to appear in warm circumstances, for farmers, freeholders, tradesmen and manufacturers in middling life; and for wholesale dealers, merchants, and for all persons of landed estates to appear in genteel life; than for the magnificence of palaces or the cabinets of princes. Thus it is . . . that the English of those several denominations have better conveniences in their houses, and affect to have more in quantity of clean, neat furniture, and a greater variety, such as carpets, screens, window curtains, chamber bells, polished brass locks, fenders etc . . . than are to be found in any other country of Europe.

41 *The Duet*, 1749. By Arthur Devis. Devis was famous for portraits like this showing genteel families in polite poses. Although the detailed settings did not always represent real interiors, they reflected the social rank and aspirations of his sitters, who were usually wealthy landed gentry, professionals or merchants. Oil on canvas. VAM P.31-1955.

43

Those in the middle ranks of British society may have enjoyed a disproportionate share of the fruits of Georgian economic success, but that does not mean we should ignore the significance as a market for consumer goods of those beneath them in the social ladder – those frequently described in the eighteenth century as the 'labouring poor'. After all, the working classes comprised a large majority of the population. Their experience of the Georgian years was a mixed one. At some periods (especially before the 1780s) and in some regions (especially in the industrial areas of the north and west) they enjoyed periods of modest prosperity. At other times and in other places they suffered terrible hardships, as a result of impossibly high prices for basic foodstuffs, falling wages and mass unemployment. Especially hard were the long years of war with France from 1793 to 1815 and their aftermath. The

44

42 *Grace before a Meal*, about 1725. By Joseph Van Aken. A moderately prosperous middle-ranking family prepares to eat. The sparsely furnished interior is typical of the possessions of small shopkeepers, craftspeople and farmers at the start of the Georgian period. Oil on canvas. Ashmolean Museum.

43 Detail of a bill advertising Packer's Royal Furniture Gloss, 1793. Two well-dressed women are depicted sitting in a genteel, but not opulent, interior. Their polite conversation turns on the merits of the furniture, but quickly transmutes into an advertising pitch for Packer's polish. Engraving. The British Museum.

44 *A Cottage Interior*, 1793. By William Redmore Bigg. The teapot, tea bowl and saucer, the side-table, chair and clock suggest a modest degree of material comfort. By the end of the 18th century it was not uncommon for the labouring poor to own possessions of this sort. Oil on canvas. VAM 199-1885.

45

worst privations were endured by the farm workers of eastern and southern England. Nevertheless, as the prices of manufactured goods fell, even the labouring poor were able to indulge in some of the aesthetic and social pleasures of decorative goods, albeit of an inexpensive kind. At the end of the eighteenth century, in contrast to its beginning, printed cotton gowns were commonly owned by working women and silver watches by many labouring men. Clocks and earthenware teapots were familiar adornments of their living rooms. Indeed, the labouring poor could aspire to a certain plebeian gentility, even if those aspirations were often dashed by unemployment, unforeseen price hikes or ill health. 'I made shift,' remembered one old man, looking back to 1741 when he was a poor, 17-year-old apprentice stocking maker at Nottingham, 'with a little over-work, and a little credit, to raise a genteel suit of clothes, fully adequate to the sphere in which I moved.'

45 *Plucking a Turkey*, 1770s. By Henry Walton. A young woman, probably a servant, at work. She wears a cotton or linen bedgown printed in lilac with white spots and a fashionable cap with a silk ribbon. Oil on canvas. © Tate, London, 2001.

46 *The Imports of Great Britain from France*, 1757 Drawn and engraved by Louis-Philippe Boitard. Inscribed 'Humbly Address'd to the Laudable Associations of Anti-Gallicans, and the generous promoters of the British Arts and Manufactories'. A Thames-side quay, upstream from the Tower of London: dancing masters, hairdressers, milliners and other purveyors of effeminacy disembark, while on the quay are imported French wines, cheeses and luxury goods. Etching and engraving. The British Museum.

7. Culture

Georgian Britons often prided themselves on being a distinctively commercial people. This is not surprising, because in Britain so many goods and services were subject to commercialized forms of supply. This was particularly striking in the arts. In continental Europe, facilities from the academies that trained artists to the factories that manufactured porcelain were often creations of the state. In Britain, they were all overwhelmingly commercial in character. Nevertheless, the kind of successful commercial society that the British had made caused its creators great unease. At the heart of that unease lay the conviction that increasing wealth – what they called luxury – would lead to political corruption, military enfeeblement, debauched morals and ultimately national decline. Among the educated, who idolized the civilizations of ancient Greece and Rome, the decline and fall of the Roman empire presented a terrible warning of where luxury could lead. For many, the growing consumption of high-design goods offered prime evidence of luxury's inexorable advance. This was certainly the critic John Dennis's opinion in his *Vice and Luxury Public Mischiefs* of 1724:

> When the plague of luxury is once become epidemical and has thoroughly infected a nation, when there is a general contention who shall out do and outshine his neighbour in the pomp and splendour of it; in the pomp and splendour of buildings, furniture, gardens, apparel, equipage, and sumptuous tables, when that respect is paid to vice and folly, which to wisdom and virtue is only due; then riches, the food and support of luxury, are fraught with insatiable avarice, and to obtain them, the most solemn obligations are infringed, the most sacred trusts are violated.

This view exercised a powerful grip on the public imagination throughout the eighteenth century, though it did little to inhibit the growth of national wealth. It fuelled intense British suspicion of French design, which epitomized luxury in its most enticing but most corrupting form. It promoted widespread admiration for the virtues of the simple, rustic life. Later in the eighteenth century it also encouraged a deep, moralizing suspicion of aristocratic excess. It did not go uncontested, however. It was argued, most powerfully by the Scottish philosophers David Hume and Adam Smith, that commerce, far from

46

47 *A Perspective View of the inside of the Grand Assembly Room in Blake Street, York*

that seemed to many to have been responsible for the disastrous civil strife of the seventeenth century. Politeness did not deny the legitimacy of social rank, but it required the different ranks to mix with each other in an agreeable manner. Hence the rule made early in the eighteenth century by Beau Nash, the Master of Ceremonies at the resort city of Bath, that nobles should treat lesser visitors with the same courtesy they usually reserved for each other. 'That ease and open access,' wrote the poet Oliver Goldsmith of Nash's rule, 'our gentry brought back to the metropolis, and thus the whole kingdom by degrees became more refined by lessons originally derived from him.'

Ease and open access were principles that lay at the heart of politeness and explain why it touched so many aspects of eighteenth-century life. 'Polite science' was science that was accessible to a wide public through lectures and demonstrations, not hidden away in the laboratory. 'Polite literature' could be read with understanding and enjoyment by a broad, educated public, in contrast to the obscure, impenetrable writings of pedants. 'Polite entertainments' were those that encouraged polite forms of social mixing and were accessible to anyone who could pay the entry charge. Typical examples were assemblies, concerts and pleasure gardens, like those at Vauxhall and Ranelagh in London. They were run sometimes as commercial enterprises, sometimes by individuals who clubbed together to raise a subscription. The club or association was one of the characteristic Georgian institutions, and many, though not all, were dedicated to polite purposes.

undermining public morality, political freedom and national advancement, could promote all of them, and in addition polish public taste where matters of artistic judgement were concerned. Increasingly, it was this view that prevailed among the powerful and the wealthy in the later Georgian years. Nevertheless, a deep suspicion of the corrupting potential of wealth and commerce persisted among those who advocated a more democratic polity and society.

In the everyday lives of the upper and middling groups in British society many of these anxieties were worked out through the code of manners known as politeness. Just as Georgian Britons frequently chose to characterize themselves as a commercial people, so too they often described themselves as a polite people. Politeness in the eighteenth century meant much more than mere etiquette. It was an all-embracing philosophy of manners, a model of how people should behave to one another. It promoted openness and accessibility in social behaviour, but at the same time set demanding standards as to precisely how people should behave. Politeness demanded that people should make themselves agreeable to others. This was one of its great attractions, because it offered an alternative to the uncompromising religious fanaticism

47 *A Perspective View of the inside of the Grand Assembly Room in Blake Street, York*, 1759. Drawn and engraved by William Lindley. The interior of the magnificent assembly room at York designed by the Earl of Burlington and opened in 1732. Rococo carved work and mouldings were added in the 1750s. Engraving. York City Art Gallery.

48 *The Court of Equity or Convivial City Meeting*, 1779. By Robert Dighton. Engraved by Robert Laurie. This print depicts a room at the Globe Tavern, Fleet Street, London, where a club is meeting. Those present include a printer, a printseller, a silversmith, an auctioneer and (at the far right at the back) the artist Robert Dighton himself. Mezzotint. VAM E.540-1976.

Much of the appeal of politeness lay, therefore, in its inclusivity. It had a particular appeal for women, because its stress 'on the art of pleasing in conversation' set limits on male boorishness. But for all its inclusivity, politeness was far from being a democratic code of manners. It defined itself against plebeian vulgarity and provincial grossness. It aimed to create people of decorum, taste and refinement who could be agreeable in the correct way. Politeness did not require its followers to be genteel by birth, merely that when in company

49

they behave in a genteel manner. For many, such performances had to be learned. Instruction was widely available, though at a price, from the growing numbers of dancing masters, music teachers and drawing tutors, as well as from a host of advice books. Politeness also required the purchase of equipment. Many of the high-design goods that British manufacturers made so readily accessible to a broad group of consumers – upholstered sofas and knives and forks, tea services and snuff boxes – were indispensable props in the genteel

performances that constituted politeness, whether in the dining room or the assembly room. Your gentility was judged by whether you owned the right items, whether they were sufficiently genteel in their design and whether you were capable of using them in the correct way.

Politeness did not carry all before it. Many felt that its stress on performance led to artificiality, insincerity and dishonesty. From the mid-eighteenth century it was opposed by the cult of sensibility, which stressed authenticity rather than display, sincerity of emotion rather than performance, rustic simplicity rather than metropolitan polish. Sensibility had important consequences for the arts. It focused artistic interest on wild and authentic nature – the Cumbrian mountains, the Welsh hills, the Scottish Highlands – and, in the process, came to redefine what was quintessentially British. It promoted the idea that people's responses to works of art should rely less on intellectual discrimination and more on overwhelming, spontaneous inner feeling. Here lay the roots of the full-blown Romantic view of art that achieved such a widespread currency by the early nineteenth century. In practice, however, sensibility and politeness managed to coexist as cultural ideals for most of the Georgian period.

50

49 *The Complement RETIRING*, 1737. By Bartholomew Dandridge. Engraved by Louis-Philippe Boitard. Plate from *The Rudiments of Genteel Behaviour: An Introduction to the Methods of attaining a graceful Attitude, an agreeable Motion, an easy Air and a genteel behaviour* by François Nivelon, 1737. Engraving. VAM L.766-1876.

50 *Conway Castle, North Wales, by Moonlight*, 1794. By Julius Caesar Ibbetson the Elder. By the late 18th century the Welsh landscape was becoming popular with tourists, who appreciated its wild and sublime grandeur. Artists such as Ibbetson took advantage of this taste, capitalizing on the growing interest in native landscape. Oil on panel. VAM 377-1888.

8. Towards Victoria: the later Georgian years

By the time Victoria ascended the throne in 1837 Britain was the dominant world power. It owed this status to the continuing vitality of the British economy and to the country's victory in the long wars with revolutionary and later Napoleonic France, between 1793 and 1815. It still basked in the glory of admiration for all things British – the veritable anglomania – that had swept Europe in the second half of the eighteenth century. Yet economic, military and cultural success was accompanied by a new political and moral unease that was to have immensely important consequences for design and the decorative arts. Among the educated classes, confidence in Britain's achievement was tempered by fears that the nation was in the grip of a soulless, inhuman materialism, productive of undreamt riches for the few, but physical squalor and moral degradation for the many. Foreign visitors, too, began to express the view that Britain's success had been bought at too high a price. Heinrich Heine, the German poet, caught the pessimistic note in 1827. 'The perfection of machines, which are everywhere in use here and have taken over so many human functions, has for me something uncanny,' he wrote. 'The certainty, the exactness, the madness, the precision of life in England fills me with not less anxiety; for just as the machines in England seem like human beings, so the human beings there seem like machines.' Eight years later the French historian Alexis de Tocqueville visited Manchester. 'From this foul drain the greatest stream of human industry flows out to fertilize the whole world,' he observed with dismay, 'from this filthy sewer pure gold flows. Here humanity attains its most complete development and its most brutish; here civilization works its miracles, and civilized man is turned back almost into a savage.'

Among the British, such doubts reflected the rise of a new moral earnestness from the 1780s, encouraged by the spread of evangelical religious belief at every social level. They also reflected dismay at the conditions of life in many of the new industrial towns and a growing fear among the prosperous of the urban working classes. The prosperous responded by electing mainly Tory governments, opposed to reform, from the 1780s to the 1820s. The threat posed by the lower classes of the rapidly growing towns was both a political and an economic one. It had its origins in demands for the extension of political rights that were encouraged, in the later eighteenth century, by the American and French Revolutions. The threat intensified after the defeat of Napoleon at the Battle of Waterloo in 1815. Resentment mounted among the working classes at their failure to secure an adequate share of the fruits of economic growth and at the refusal of governments to alleviate the distress of those suffering the consequences of technological change. It was reinforced by the fact that when political reform did at last arrive, in the guise of the Great Reform Act of 1832, the working classes were excluded. The Great Reform Act extended the vote only to sections of the middle classes.

Educated men and women at the end of the Georgian era responded in a variety of ways to these doubts about the world they had created. Many retained a degree of confidence in the capacity of a commercial society, well administered, to improve the lives of the population. Some advocated much more radical moves towards democratic politics and social equality. Others rejected modern society and sought refuge in a vision of a medieval past untainted by commerce. There was wide agreement, however, that society's ills required a response that was self-consciously moral in character. This powerful sense of a moral agenda was to be a defining characteristic of British life during Victoria's reign – one that was to have an especially powerful impact on the development of design and the decorative arts.

52

---

51 *The Gough Family*, 1741. By William Verelst. This painting shows Captain Harry Gough of the East India Company with his family. The Goughs were a wealthy merchant family who had built their fortune on trade with India and China and were consolidating their position through the gradual acquisition of land. They are shown taking tea, displaying their taste and wealth. The painter has taken care to show that the silver tea kettle has a coat of arms on the side. Oil on canvas. VAM Anonymous Loan.

52 *Cotton Factories, Union Street, Manchester*, 1831. By Samuel Austin. Engraved by McGahey. Plate from *Lancashire Illustrated* by S. Austin, J. Harwood and G. and C. Pyne, 1831. The plate depicts the factories of Messrs McConnel and Co. Engraving. VAM 233.A.6.

CHAPTER 7

Georgian Britain, 1714–1837

Style

MICHAEL SNODIN

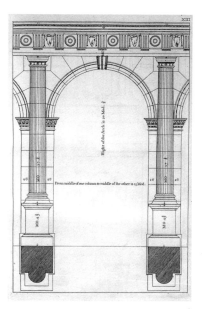

1. A matter of choice

The story of style from 1714 to 1837 is one of complexity and rapid change. To an extent this is deceptive, for the dizzying range of Georgian styles can be grouped broadly into two distinct tendencies. The dominant trend was based on ancient Roman and Greek architecture and decoration, and its Renaissance interpretations. It included the baroque, neo-Palladian and neo-classical styles. From time to time it was matched by anti-classical styles, including the rococo, neo-Gothic and chinoiserie. The mere possibility of such choice was a sign of profound changes in attitudes to style, for it allowed style and ornament to carry the kinds of meanings and feelings that mark our experience of them today. As far as we know, this was something new, for earlier viewers and consumers had tended to 'read' the meaning of a piece of decoration or design principally through its heraldry and symbolic content, rather than its ornamental forms. With style now being 'read' in formal terms, it became an indicator of other areas, including taste, social position, religious affiliation, political allegiance and national pride. The expansion in available styles was greatly encouraged by the opening up of the market for manufactured goods to the growing middle classes. This became especially evident from the 1770s onwards, as styled goods became increasingly available through improved marketing and labour-saving means of production, which reduced the reliance on craft skills.

The Georgian period also saw the establishment of nationwide styles. The growing sense of nationhood, and Britain's increasing power in the world, was matched by a conscious desire to create national styles, normally set by trends in London. Although continental Europe, and especially France, continued to be a touchstone for taste and style, some of the new national styles, like the neo-classicism of Robert Adam, were both admired and imitated abroad.

1 *A Common Council man of Candlestick Ward and his wife on a visit to Mr Deputy – at his Modern Built villa near Clapham*, 1771. By an unknown artist. The social pretensions and flawed taste of City of London merchants is here satirized. To Mr Deputy's suburban house, a plain clapboard cottage, have been added disparate neo-Palladian, Gothic and chinoiserie elements. Hand-coloured engraving. Courtesy of the Lewis Walpole Library, Yale University.

2 *The Tuscan Order*. Plate from *The four books of Andrea Palladio's Architecture*, translated and published by Isaac Ware, 1738. Engraving. VAM 62.B.19.

1

2. British baroque

A new monarch seldom means a new style, and the accession of George I in 1714 was no exception. The baroque style, which from the 1680s was being employed across architecture, interiors and movable objects, continued into the 1730s. Its greatest architectural expressions, Castle Howard and Blenheim Palace, had already been built or were under construction. At Blenheim, Sir John Vanbrugh put up the only British palace to rival in scale Louis XIV's Versailles, a composition of immense spatial drama intended to express the nation's pride in the Duke of Marlborough's victories in the War of the Spanish Succession. At a more modest level, from about 1700, many new houses were baroque in their varied sense of scale, elaborate skylines, occasional breaking of the classical rules or the addition of a few Italian details taken from a book. They shared a growing taste for the imposing and monumental, assisted by the

increasing use on façades of classical pediments and a preference for giant orders of columns, rising from the ground to the roof.

In the background was a growing interest in classical architecture and the buildings and ideas of the Italian Renaissance architect Andrea Palladio, whose work (and publications) had inspired the buildings of Inigo Jones 75 years before. Eventually this trend resulted in the triumph of the neo-Palladian style, but up to the 1730s it was a mixed story, with nominally baroque architects increasingly taking on Palladian ideas. Chief among these was James Gibbs, who had, unusually, trained in Italy, under the baroque architect Carlo Fontana. In Britain, in such characteristic buildings as St Martin-in-the-Fields in London and the Radcliffe Camera in Oxford, Gibbs developed a modest baroque style based on a Palladian framework. The publication in 1728 of his *Book of Architecture*, packed with ornamental details as well as designs for buildings, brought his style to thousands of ordinary builders in Britain and the colonies, setting a notion of 'Georgian' style that is still with us today.

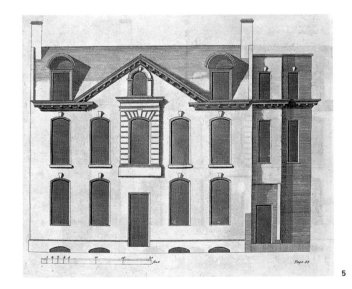

3 *The South-West Prospect of St Martins-in-the-Fields, London*, 1738. Engraved by William Henry Toms after Robert West. James Gibbs's church, built 1722–6, became a model for new churches in Britain and the colonies. Engraving. VAM E.1688-1888.

4 Wine cooler, with London hallmarks for 1719–20. Mark of Anthony Nelme. Magnificent equipment like this was the focal point of the baroque dining room. Made for Thomas Parker, later first Earl Macclesfield, for Shirburn Castle, Oxfordshire. Parker was made Lord Chancellor in 1718. Silver. VAM M.27-1998.

5 *A baroque-style house*. Plate from *An Essay in Defence of Ancient Architecture* by Robert Morris, 1728. Engraving. VAM 33.B.1.

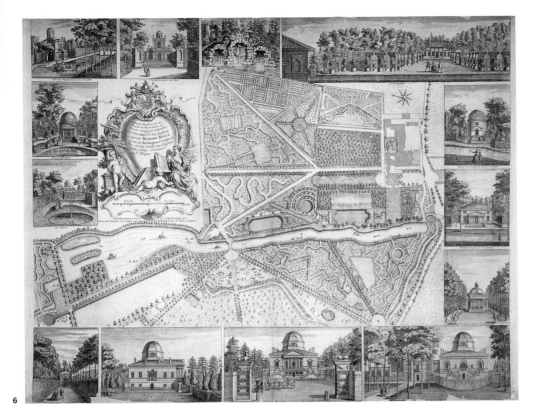

3. Neo-Palladianism

In 1728 the neo-Palladian architect Robert Morris delivered a withering attack on a baroque house built four years earlier:

> There is not a single object in the whole execution, but is in a direct opposition to the rules of ancient architecture: for instance, look on the pediment what a false bearing, or rather what bearing at all has it? How irregular is it in the disposition, how contrary even to the most common notions in the pitch of it, the roof; with the windows, how disproportionate are they with their ill dispos'd pediments, the returns of the cornice in every part, the irregular breaks, and likewise the disagreeable affinity they have to each other?

Morris's attack, published in his *Essay in Defence of Ancient Architecture*, not only reveals his humble background, but also shows the power of the neo-Palladian revolution, with its captivating mantra of classical rules, first clearly demonstrated by Colen Campbell and later taken up to huge effect by Lord Burlington. The composition of Campbell's design for the great country house of Wanstead was indebted to Castle Howard, but its detail made it Palladian rather than baroque (*see 7:8*). The great pedimented entrance portico, the alternately arched and pedimented windows, the rusticated basement in rough blocks and the end pavilions lit by three-part Venetian windows were all to become key neo-Palladian features. Above all, the composition relied for its effect on the careful balance between the blank, untextured wall surface and the window openings, giving it a sense of combined grandeur and repose.

Neo-Palladian buildings were intimately linked to the gardens that surrounded them. At first such gardens (like that at Lord Burlington's villa at Chiswick), filled with small classical buildings and complicated paths, were designed to recall the gardens described in the great literary works of classical antiquity. As no such ancient gardens survived, the models used were often taken from more modern Italian examples. Although they now seem rather artificial, the asymmetry of these gardens was in marked contrast to the grand symmetrical gardens of the baroque, making them part of a trend towards the natural in British gardening, which began about 1700. In a more simplified form such neo-Palladian gardens, like that at Stourhead, were designed as a circuit, with temples and other buildings set in relationship to a lake (*see 8:11*). Stourhead is an evocation of a classical arcadia, a vision of harmony and order. But its likeness to an Italian landscape painting is no accident, for such paintings, by the seventeenth-century artist Claude Lorraine and others, lay at the heart of the true 'natural' gardening promoted from the 1750s by Lancelot 'Capability' Brown. The natural or 'open' style of gardening, so perfectly suited to setting off the clarity of neo-Palladian architecture, was a genuine innovation, involving nothing less than the creation of an ideal landscape. In that sense it was just as artificial as the earlier style, since it always involved the introduction of water and sometimes extensive topographical remodelling.

6 *Plan du Jardin & Vüe des Maisons de Chiswick*, 1736. Designed and engraved by Jean Rocque. Etching and engraving. VAM E.352-1944.

7 *Croome Court, Worcestershire*, 1758–9. By Richard Wilson. George, sixth Earl of Coventry, employed Lancelot 'Capability' Brown to landscape the grounds around his neo-Palladian house, also designed by Brown and created from an earlier building, 1751–2. Oil on canvas. Croome Estate Trustees.

NEO-PALLADIANISM

Michael Snodin

The West Front of Wanstead in Essex the Seat of Sr Richard Child Baronet Hereditary Warden of Waltham Forest &c. Col. Campbell Inv. et Delin. To whom this Plate is most humbly Inscrib'd. *Scale of 40 Feet.* *Extends 260.* *Elevation de L'Entrée du Chateau de WANSTED dans la Comté D'ESSEX appartenant à Mr CHILD Chevalier.*

Neo-Palladianism was a classical style used in architecture and interiors, which emerged fully in about 1715 and was in use up to about 1800. It was based on the forms and ornament of ancient Roman buildings, the work of Andrea Palladio and other Italian Renaissance architects, and the seventeenth-century architecture of Inigo Jones, who also admired Palladio. It first emerged in the work of the Scottish architect Colen Campbell. His book *Vitruvius Britannicus* (1715) featured his pioneering house at Wanstead, but similar great neo-Palladian houses were not to appear for another 15 years. In that time neo-Palladianism acquired a much more persuasive champion, the architect Lord Burlington, who, first in the company of Campbell and later with others, set the character of the neo-Palladian style. From a scholarly amalgam of Italian and Jonesian sources, Burlington formed a classically correct style that was uniquely British. It was as applicable to the smallest terraced house as it was to the grandest mansion, setting the pattern for British architecture for the next 100 years. For Burlington's followers, neo-Palladianism also had a special meaning, signalling a link between the virtues and power of ancient

8. Wanstead House, London, built about 1714–20. Designed by Colen Campbell for Sir Richard Child. Plate from *Vitruvius Britannicus* by Colen Campbell, Vol. 1, 1715 (this plate from the 1731 edition), published by the author. Engraving. VAM 34.G.182.

Rome and the culture of Italy and the culture, political systems and power of the burgeoning British nation.

Burlington's own designs were mainly for small buildings, the most characteristic being an extension to his own house at Chiswick. Begun in 1725, it was based partly on Palladio's Villa Rotonda at Vicenza. It established the idea of the small independent villa, a house type that came to invade every suburb some 100 years later. As with many neo-Palladian buildings, the plain exterior contrasted with richly decorated interiors. These were not based on Palladio's own designs, but on details from ancient Roman buildings, combined with fireplaces, ceilings and other details taken from Inigo Jones.

9. Console table, 1727–32. Designed by William Kent for the gallery at Chiswick House and perhaps made in London by John Boson. Carved and gilded pine and Siena marble. [h. 88.9cm]. VAM W.14-1971.

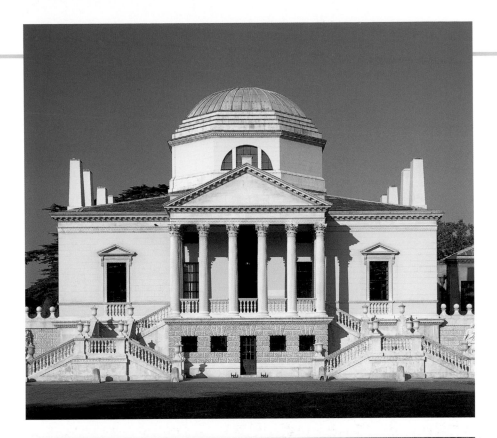

10. The entrance front of Chiswick House, London, 1725–9. Designed by Richard Boyle, third Earl of Burlington.

While the walls of most of the rooms were hung with woven textiles, the central saloon was plastered and painted, and enlivened with sober sculptural ornament, a pioneering and highly influential concept. The interiors were designed by Burlington's assistant and protégé, William Kent, who was also responsible for designing furniture and other movable items for subsequent neo-Palladian interiors. Again there was no accessible precedent in Palladio, so Kent, who was trained as a painter but had a brilliant and poetic imagination in a number of design fields, devised new models derived equally from Italian baroque examples and ancient Roman sculptural ideas.

11. Design for a chimneypiece at Oatlands Palace, Surrey, 1636. By Inigo Jones. Pen and brown ink over black chalk. RIBA Library Drawings Collection.

12. The Gallery, Chiswick House, London, 1725–9. Designed by Richard Boyle, third Earl of Burlington, and William Kent.

4. The neo-Palladian interior

In their interiors, Lord Burlington and his interior designer William Kent aimed to depart from current baroque fashions: tall, vertically panelled rooms, often in wood, or the more expensive, dramatically painted interiors rich with Italian plasterwork and extravagantly 'incorrect' mouldings. It is interesting to compare the interiors of Burlington's villa at Chiswick with a room designed by James Gibbs at about the same date. While the Chiswick ceilings are beamed in the Inigo Jones manner, Gibbs employs a baroque ceiling of curved mouldings made by Italian plasterworkers and enclosing Italian paintings. While Burlington's chimneypieces and other details are faithfully copied from Jones and Palladio, Gibbs employs his own repertoire of forms related to – but developing – Jonesian ideas.

The same opposition can be seen in furniture and other movable items. William Kent's blocky designs were very different in style from the leading luxury furniture style of the day, still indebted to the ideas of Daniel Marot from the 1690s, or the more modest pieces reflecting the broken pediments, pilasters and other architectural elements of the baroque interior. Neither furniture nor interiors in Kent's heavy style were to remain fashionable much beyond 1750. The main reason was the arrival in the 1730s of a new anti-classical style, the rococo.

5. The rococo

Rococo was a style without rules. In France it was known as the *genre pittoresque* (picturesque manner) and in Britain simply as 'modern', clearly signalling its break with the ancient classical norms. While classicism was based on the architectural orders, with their measured proportions and fixed hierarchy of ornamentation, rococo had only the asymmetrical pictorial composition known as the *morceau de fantaisie*, an infinitely variable exercise in illogicality. The nearest the rococo ever came to a theoretical justification was William Hogarth's *Analysis of Beauty* (1753), which isolated the serpentine 'line of beauty and grace' as the essence of aesthetic beauty: 'there is scarce a room in any house whatever, where one does not see a waving line employed in some way or other'. It was no accident that the same line was linked to drawing exercises for the essential element of British rococo design, the curled acanthus or 'raffle leaf' (*see 8:17*).

The anti-classical nature of rococo and its perceived origins in the craft workshop were by the 1730s provoking counterattacks by French academic critics. In 1755 the miniaturist (and friend of Hogarth) André Rouquet was attacking 'the taste called *contrast* . . . which men of indifferent taste adopt without feeling, and apply without judgement'. A year later the neo-Palladian architect Isaac Ware was deploring rococo as the product of the French, 'a frivolous people we are too apt to imitate . . . It consists of crooked lines like

13 Ceiling from the drawing room of No. 11 Henrietta Place, London, about 1727–30. Designed by James Gibbs, with plaster-work by Giuseppe Artari and Giovanni Bagutti. As re-installed in the Victoria and Albert Museum. VAM W.5-1960.

14 Design for a rococo-style interior, about 1755. By John Linnell. Pen, ink and watercolour. VAM E.263-1929.

C's and ƆC's, the Gothick is hardly more contemptible'. The rococo style joined such undesirable French imports as dancing masters, smelly cheeses and effete manners, all offensive to robust Englishmen. But the opposition could only be beaten by emulation, especially in the field of luxury goods. Although anti-French groups like the Anti-Gallican Society, founded in 1745, sought to oppose the 'insidious arts of the French Nation', their keenest supporters, like the carver and drawing master Thomas Johnson, were among the most enthusiastic exponents of the rococo style.

6. Gothic and chinoiserie

Rococo was a natural partner for two other styles, Gothic and chinoiserie. To critics like Isaac Ware all three were 'unmeaning' – that is, confused and without system. This did nothing to halt their popularity, which reached a peak in the years around 1750. They could be used either separately or together. At Claydon House, Buckinghamshire, there were adjacent Gothic, Chinese and French (or rococo) rooms, while all three styles were frequently combined in a single piece of furniture. In architecture, the medieval forms of the Gothic style had occasionally been revived earlier, even by such distinguished classicists as Sir Christopher Wren, and it had never entirely disappeared from certain traditional environments, such as the Oxford and Cambridge colleges. What happened in the 1730s was new, for Gothic began to be treated as a historical style with a meaning, both playful and deeply serious. Early Gothic buildings in gardens and pioneering domestic projects, such as Horace Walpole's house of Strawberry Hill, were intended both to be decorative and to suggest through their style a link with a specifically British history. From such serious beginnings, however, Gothic was quickly adopted as a popular style, abetted by the publishers of architectural books, who even attempted to impose upon it the rule of classical orders. It was not until the 1770s that an increasingly serious antiquarian study of medieval architecture led to neo-Gothic buildings accurate in their details, if not in their overall design.

The years around 1750, which saw the height of the rage for Gothic and rococo, also witnessed the peak of popular interest in chinoiserie. A style evoking an imaginary China had been popular since the 1690s. At that time it chiefly involved the display and use of items from China, India and Japan in sympathetic and evocative surroundings, sometimes created by covering walls with lacquer, paint or paper. While the enthusiasm for East Asian and Indian things increased over the next 50 years, the forms of consumption changed, and a new style emerged that was based on scenes and motifs on lacquer and porcelain, but which was purely European and could be applied to objects outside those traditional materials.

15 *Fontaine Glacée*, 1736. Plate from the set *Livre nouveau de Douze Morceaux de Fantaisie*, 1736, engraved by Jean-Baptiste Guelard after Jacques de Lajoue. Etching and engraving. VAM 229678.3.

16 *Bureau bookcase*, 1754. Engraved by Matthias Darly after Thomas Chippendale the Elder. Plate from *The Gentleman and Cabinet Maker's Director* by Thomas Chippendale, 1754. While the upper part is Gothic – vaguely recalling medieval window tracery – the legs are rococo and the finial Chinese. Engraving. VAM RC.CC.11.

ROCOCO STYLE

Hilary Young

The rococo was an ornamental style that had a long genesis, but which emerged as a distinct style in France during the 1720s and 1730s. Key elements were C- and S-scrolls, and an amorphous, organic, shell-like substance known as rocaille. These were frequently used in combination with fish, shells and other marine motifs. Compositions were often markedly asymmetric and featured illogical combinations of scale. Naturalistic fruit and flowers were introduced, notably in ceramics and on silks, and the style was used in combination with Chinese and Gothic motifs.

The style flourished in English design between about 1740 and 1770, but was rarely taken up for architecture. Its chief promoters in Britain were artists, craftspeople and entrepreneurs from the middle ranks of society, rather than architects and their noble patrons. Rococo was used for both luxury and utilitarian goods – it appears in grand furnishings and silver, for example, but also on inexpensive pottery and ephemeral prints.

The rococo first appeared in England in silver and engravings of ornament of the 1730s. Immigrant artists and craftspeople, including Huguenot refugees from France, played a key role in its dissemination. Its seedbed was the St Martin's Lane Academy, with which the book illustrator Hubert-François Gravelot and the painters Andien de Clermont and William Hogarth were all associated.

19. Two-handled cup, with London hallmarks for 1759–60. Mark of Thomas Heming. Silver-gilt. [h. 39.5cm]. VAM M.41-1959.

20. Trade card of Henry Patten, razor maker and cutler, about 1750. Engraved by Edward Warner after Henry Copland, London. VAM E.571-1976.

17. Inkstand, with London hallmarks for 1738–9. Mark of Paul de Lamerie. Silver-gilt. Duke of Marlborough.

18. Design for a brocaded silk tobine, 1749. By Anna Maria Garthwaite for the London weaver Daniel Vautier. Watercolour on paper. VAM 5987.1.

21. Chimneypiece, about 1750. From Winchester House, Putney, London. Carved pine with marble and glass. [h. 321.9cm]. VAM 738-1897.

22. Plate, about 1756. Transfer-printed with a scene from *The Aeneid*, after a drawing by Hubert-François Bourguignon, called Gravelot. Made at the Bow factory, London. Soft-paste porcelain with transfer-printed decoration and enamelled border. [diam. 19.7cm]. VAM C.217-1940.

23. 'French' chair, about 1710–65. Designed and made by Matthias Lock. Lime and pine wood, carved and gilded; modern silk damask upholstery. [h. 104cm]. VAM W.1-1973.

Gravelot's figure style and his elegant handling of rococo scrollwork were highly influential in Britain. However, a more spiky and distinctively British form of rococo scrollwork was introduced in the prints of cartouches and mirror frames that Henry Copland and Matthias Lock published from 1742. This style was widely adopted for woodcarving and other decorative work and subsequently dominated British rococo design until the mid-1760s. However, British designers continued to imitate contemporary French work for silver, porcelain and furniture that were being made for the top end of the market.

Many pattern books of rococo ornament of the type issued by Lock and Copland were published in England in the 1740s and 1750s. These were largely intended for craftspeople and designers and were hugely influential in disseminating rococo idioms. Their popularity stemmed from the complexity of the style, which placed great demands on the design and modelling skills of British craftspeople. Many felt that the nation lacked the design skills necessary to compete with imported French goods, which led to initiatives to improve design standards during the years when the rococo was current in Britain.

24

This formal interest was signalled as early as 1683 when Sir William Temple recognized asymmetry and 'beauty without order' (which he called by an apparently Chinese word, 'Sharawagdi') as a characteristic of the design of lacquer screens, porcelain and 'Indian Gowns', as well as of Chinese gardens. It was not, however, until the 1730s that true chinoiserie was born, a child of the rococo style, with which it shared similar fantastic and asymmetrical elements. It was only to be expected that such style plurality, especially when it was so eagerly taken up by the nouveaux riches, should be satirized in books and newspapers. In fact the Chinese style was thought to be particularly appropriate for bedrooms at the highest social level, hung with Chinese wallpaper, decorated with ceramics and housing a chinoiserie bed. This was attested by Sir William Chambers, whose *Designs of Chinese Buildings, Furniture, Dresses, Machines, and Utensils* (1757) attempted to regulate the Chinese mania by supplying the reading public with examples taken from his own observations in China.

Chambers put theory into practice in 1761 by designing for Princess Augusta at Kew Gardens the first pagoda built in Europe and the most permanent of many garden buildings in the Chinese style. At Kew the pagoda joined an 'Alhambra', a 'Mosque', a Gothic 'cathedral' and a range of classical temples, turning the gardens into a demonstration of world architectural styles. While such stylistic mixes in other contexts drew snobbish ridicule, they were all expressions of a generally more relaxed attitude towards rule-breaking in style, easing the arrival of neo-classicism in the late 1750s.

25

24 *A view of the wilderness, with the Alhambra, the Pagoda and the Mosque in the Royal Gardens at Kew*, 1763. All of these were built between 1758 and 1762. Anonymous engraver after William Marlow. Hand-coloured engraving. VAM 29428.A.

25 Pier glass in the chinoiserie style, about 1758–60. Similar to designs by the carver and gilder Thomas Johnson. Carved gilded wood. [h. 329cm]. VAM W.23-1949.

7. Neo-classicism

Neo-classicism was known to contemporaries as the 'antique manner'. As a European style it had complex roots linked to Italy and Greece and the archaeological rediscovery of antiquity, combined with a reassessment of Renaissance design. A return to the antique had, of course, been part of art and design since the fifteenth century, but now it was directed at creating an eternally valid 'true style'. It was not simply a matter of motifs, but also of a search for the ideal, characterized in its purest form by a high moral seriousness in stark opposition to the frivolous, hedonistic nature of the rococo. Nor was it a matter of strict architectural rules and proportions, but of reactions to the antique on the level of emotion and imaginative aesthetic enquiry. This not only gave neo-classicism the freedom to develop beyond the models that inspired it, towards forms and treatments that the ancients would hardly have recognized, but allowed the parallel use of other, seemingly diametrically opposed styles, such as Gothic.

Neo-classicism was as much about the rediscovery and reassessment of ancient painting and sculpture as it was about architecture and design. The result was a style of remarkable homogeneity, in which two- and three-dimensional classical figures, used in a more or less scholarly manner, became an integral part of the vocabulary of architecture, interior decoration and the applied arts, matching the actual ancient (or not so ancient) sculpture that was sent home following the Italian Grand Tour of many an English milord. The archaeological tendency also meant that neo-classicism became a total style, extending beyond architecture and interiors to fixed and movable objects of all types, from furniture to silver.

26

26 Chimneypiece, about 1775. Designed by Sir William Chambers and probably made by Joseph Wilton. Commissioned by Granville Leveson Gower, second Earl Gower, for the great drawing room at Gower House, Whitehall, London. Carrara marble. [h. 190cm]. VAM A.1-1998.

8. British neo-classicism

Robert Adam, James Stuart and Sir William Chambers, the architect founders of British neo-classicism, had all been in Rome during the exciting years around 1750, when French students and others were laying the ground for the style. The British approach nevertheless turned out to be very different from neo-classical developments on the continent, for Britain – unlike the rest of Europe – already possessed in its neo-Palladian architecture and interior decoration a controlled and simple classical style. Indeed, some examples of neo-Palladianism, like Lord Burlington's Assembly Rooms at York (a re-creation of Vitruvius's Egyptian Hall as envisaged by Palladio), can be described as neo-classical in the true sense (*see 6:47*). Thus, while neo-classical ideas transformed the ornament, and even the forms, of objects both large and small, architecture and interiors at first tended to take only the decorative devices, adding them to fundamentally neo-Palladian structures.

Robert Adam claimed, in 1773, to have effected in buildings 'a remarkable improvement in the form, convenience, and relief of apartments; a greater movement and variety in the outside composition, and in the decoration of the inside an almost total change'. The last was certainly true, for Adam's version of neo-classicism set off a revolution in style. His distinctive decorative system used a limited range of ornament, brilliantly distilled from ancient and Renaissance sources, chiefly wall paintings and room decorations. By the very early 1760s Adam had developed a form of interior decoration that sought to suggest the rooms of the ancients, but adapted to modern uses. Ceilings and walls, and often floors (in the form of inlays or carpet), were covered with continuous areas of small-scale ornament, which played down architectural definition and were frequently based on the antique form of decoration known as the grotesque. A genre of ancient Roman painted wall decoration, the grotesque had been codified into a usable form by Raphael in the sixteenth century and had continued in use with gradual changes. Neo-classical designers sought to purify the form by re-establishing the link with ancient Roman painting through the earliest systematic excavations of ancient domestic sites, including (from 1748) the buried cities of Pompeii and Herculaneum, as well as by going back to Raphael. The use of colour in ancient interiors inspired Adam, in a radical departure from neo-Palladian precedent, to introduce strong colours into his own designs

Adam's own theory of design was based on the principle of 'movement', the rise and fall and advancement and recession of forms, ultimately derived from the buildings of Burlington and Kent, but clothed in columns, decorated pilasters and other ancient devices. The idea was matched in his interiors by their manner of arranging sequences of rooms that were different in plan, often punctuated by three-dimensional effects in the form of detached columns (*see 8:36*). The concentration on visual and scenic effects, at the expense of stately logic, matched the growing engagement with the idea of the Picturesque, which by the end of the century was to dominate all fields of design.

27 View of the gallery, or library, at Syon House, London, 1763–73. By an unknown artist for Robert Adam. The Syon gallery was created by Adam for the Duke and Duchess of Northumberland. Pen, ink and wash. VAM E.1063-1940.

27

9. Coordinated design

Although notions of coordinated design had occurred before the neo-classical period, most notably in the furniture and interiors of Daniel Marot in about 1700 and in those of William Kent, they had never before been so widespread in British design. The process was encouraged by the relative ease with which repetitious and regular neo-classical ornament (and Adam ornament in particular) could be produced in flat pattern or low relief, and standardized simple shapes could be fitted together in interestingly different combinations. Ideally, modern objects, both practical and decorative, would imitate antique prototypes. When these could not be found, as was frequently the case, a few key antique forms were adapted. The most important were the vase and the tripod, both powerful and appealing signals of antiquity.

Among the first neo-classical objects to be made in Britain were an ormolu vase and tripod, both designed by James Stuart before 1760. The vase, characteristically, concealed its function as a plate warmer, and was an original composition. The tripod was a perfume burner, its design taken from the finial of the choragic monument of Lysicrates in Athens (*see 7:35*). Stuart had seen the monument in 1751 and illustrated it in his book (written with Nicholas Revett), *The Antiquities of Athens*, published in 1762, the first accurate survey of classical Greek remains. In 1762 Robert Adam incorporated both objects in his scheme for the dining room at Kedleston Hall (a project he took over from Stuart), a characteristically unified neo-classical scheme incorporating furniture, utensils and decoration. Tripods continued to be a rich source of design ideas in many fields.

Vases became an acknowledged mania. They were especially exploited by manufacturers like Josiah Wedgwood and Matthew Boulton, who vigorously plundered sources ranging from Renaissance prints to excavated Greek pottery in order to satisfy an insatiable market for vases as ornaments. Among their chief sources were the illustrated volumes published in 1766–7 by Sir William Hamilton on his collection of antiquities in Naples, *Catalogue of Etruscan, Greek, and Roman Antiquities* by Baron d'Hancarville. This was aimed at instructing craftspeople and artists, and was immediately taken up by Wedgwood, who not only named his factory Etruria, but celebrated its opening in 1769 by making a set of vases after d'Hancarville's illustrations.

Neo-classicism took some 10 years to spread beyond the fashionable élite. Even Adam was content to add a neo-classical spin to sofas of rococo form and chair types devised by William Kent, although his fixed furniture, such as pier tables and glasses, was more often strictly architectural in design. By the early 1770s full-blown neo-classical furniture had penetrated the general market, and in 1774 the architect John Carter could describe a pair of Adam-style grotesque panels shown in *The Builder's Magazine* as being 'in the present reigning taste'. Such characteristic ornament was translated into inlay and paint on furniture and as sparkling 'bright-cut' engraving on silver, while figures in cameo were found on all sorts of objects, from chimneypieces to jewellery.

28

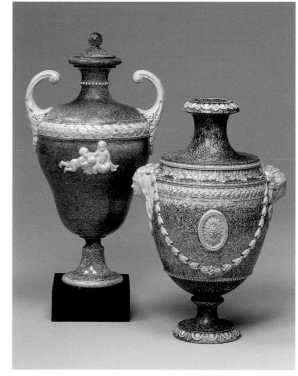

29

28 Detail of a design for the dining-room alcove, Kedleston Hall, Derbyshire, drawn 1762. Designed by Robert Adam. Pen, ink and watercolour. The National Trust, Kedleston Hall.

29 Left: vase, about 1773–5. Made at Josiah Wedgwood's factory, Etruria, Staffordshire. White 'terracotta stoneware', with applied reliefs and 'pebble' glaze. Right: vase, about 1770–80. Probably made by Humphrey Palmer or his successor James Neale at the Church Works, Hanley, Staffordshire. Creamware, with applied medallion and 'porphyry' glaze. [h. 25.08cm]. VAM 2386-1901 and 304-1869.

NEO-CLASSICISM

Hilary Young

Neo-classicism was a style that emerged in Britain and France in the 1750s; it affected all the visual arts and flourished into the early years of the nineteenth century. Its birth and rapid spread were the result of a renewed passion for the remains of the classical past and a dissatisfaction with the rococo style. Initially confined to a small circle of collectors and patrons, this interest in antiquity was fuelled by a number of publications championing ancient art, publicizing archaeological discoveries at Herculaneum in Italy, Palmyra in Syria and elsewhere. They also illustrated major collections of antique engraved gems, vases and sculpture.

Architects pioneered the style in Britain, and in its earliest, most vigorous phase the decorative vocabulary of neo-classicism was architectural. The pioneering neo-classical

30. *Design for a dining room*, about 1770–5. By James Wyatt. Pencil, pen, ink and watercolour on paper. VAM 7231.35.

artists and designers were consciously creating an emphatically modern style based on the remains of the classical past.

The architects who introduced the style in Britain were James 'Athenian' Stuart, Sir William Chambers and Robert Adam, all of whom had studied in Rome and travelled widely. Chambers's and Adam's designs were disseminated by their folio publications of 1759 and 1773 respectively. By the 1770s Adam's early robust, archaeologically inspired manner had given way to a more delicate and attenuated style, which was taken up and further developed by James Wyatt. All these men designed coordinated interior schemes, sometimes with furniture and silver to match.

31. Table, 1769. Designed by Sir William Chambers for his own use and made in London by Georg Haupt. Oak and pine carcase veneered with satinwood; the top inlaid with ebony veneer and samples of jasper, onyx, lapis lazuli, quartz and serpentine. VAM W.38-1977.

32. *Thetis and Her Nymphs Rising from the Sea to console Achilles for the loss of Patroclus*, about 1778. Carved in Rome by Thomas Banks. Marble. [h. 91.4cm]. VAM A.15-1984.

33. Armchair, about 1790. Supplied by the firm of Seddon and Shackleton to Daniel Tupper of Hauteville House, St Peter Port, Guernsey. Painted satinwood. VAM W.2-1968.

34. Armchair, 1764–5. Designed by Robert Adam and made in London in the workshop of Thomas Chippendale for 19 Arlington Street, London, the house of Sir Lawrence Dundas. Gilded beechwood and walnut; replacement upholstery. VAM W.1-1937.

The designs and decorative language of the leading architects were imitated and freely adapted by craftspeople and manufacturers, effecting a revolution in English design around 1770. In silver of the 1770s, for example, rococo ornament was replaced by plain areas of silver set against narrow bands of classical motifs. Some designers, however, combined rococo and neo-classical elements, creating an elegant hybrid style. Wedgwood and other manufacturers took up the 'antique' vase as a fashionable sign of the new style. Changes in manufacturing technologies encouraged the taste for plainness during the final decades of the century, as seen in Sheffield plate. What had begun life as a learned and exclusive style confined to a small social élite was enjoying a wide market by the 1780s, when Birmingham and Sheffield metalwork and Staffordshire pottery in neo-classical styles were being made for nationwide markets and for export.

35. Perfume burner, about 1760. Designed by James Stuart and made by Diederich Nicolaus Anderson. Cut and chased ormolu; marble stand. [h. 53.97cm]. VAM M.46-1948.

36. Water jug, about 1785. Probably made in Sheffield. Copper plated with silver (Sheffield plate). VAM M.207-1920.

10. After Adam

In architecture, the Adam style was quickly taken up and developed by others. It was refined in the hands of architects like James Wyatt, while acute observers like Horace Walpole began to tire of the Adam brothers' 'gingerbread and sippets of embroidery'.

A bolder approach had already been proposed by Adam's great rival, the royal architect Sir William Chambers, who designed in a stately amalgam of neo-Palladianism and ideas learned in Rome and Paris. Chambers's biggest project, Somerset House, housing the new Royal Academy as well as civil servants, conspicuously brought the style before the public. Its deep masonry basements were a built demonstration of the ideas of the architect Giovanni

37 The Bank Stock Office, Bank of England, London, built 1792–4. Designed by Sir John Soane. Drawn by Joseph Michael Gandy, 1798. Pen, ink and watercolour. Trustees of the Sir John Soane Museum.

38 Detail of *The Strand*, *London*, about 1796. By Thomas Malton. On the right is Somerset House, designed by Sir William Chambers and built 1776–96. The comparatively narrow street front of the building opens into a huge courtyard, giving onto the Thames. In the middle distance of this view is James Gibbs's Church of St Mary-le-Strand, built 1714–17. Watercolour. VAM 1725-1871.

Battista Piranesi, at whose feet both Chambers and Adam had sat when in Rome. Piranesi's sensationalist prints of huge Roman structures and ponderous neo-classical inventions led architects all over Europe to use simpler, more dramatic forms, which became increasingly separate from strict classical precedent.

Britain was not exempt from this tendency, and in the buildings of George Dance junior from the mid-1760s, and of his brilliant pupil Sir John Soane from the 1780s, a new type of poetic architecture developed, employing elemental geometric forms. The same trend towards simplification showed itself in other forms of design from the 1780s onwards. At the highest level neo-classical styles were imported from France, marking a return to the historical tendency for Britain to follow the French lead in matters of design.

At Carlton House, designed by Henry Holland for the Prince of Wales from 1783 onwards, a French-style exterior enclosed a French interior, ornamented and supplied with furniture by French decorators and craftspeople. By 1785 Horace Walpole was admiring its 'august simplicity . . . it is the taste and propriety that strike. Every ornament is at a proper distance, and not one too large, but all delicate and new, with more freedom and variety than Greek [i.e. Adam-style] ornaments; and although probably borrowed from the Hôtel de Condé and other new Palaces, not one that is rather classic than French.' A similar 'august simplicity' showed itself in a wide range of more modest applications in furniture (for instance, the designs shown by George Hepplewhite and Thomas Sheraton), and in ceramics and metalwork. Often these designs were admirably suited to production by means of the new, mainly hand-powered machines that proliferated in the Georgian era.

39 *The hall, Carlton House, London*, about 1819. By Charles Wild. Part of the alterations to Carlton House, designed for the Prince of Wales by Henry Holland, carried out 1785–9. Watercolour. © The Royal Collection.

40 Kettle and stand, about 1795. Made in Sheffield. Copper plated with silver (Sheffield plate). [h. 33cm]. VAM M.637-1936.

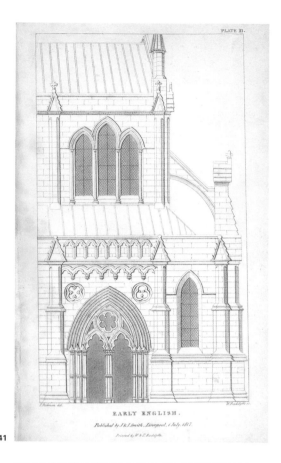

11. Style plurality

The 1790s marked a turning point in the way styles were viewed and used. For the first time a whole group of historical and non-European styles, including Gothic, Chinese and two newcomers, Indian and Egyptian, became legitimate alternatives to classicism, opening the door to a wave of style plurality that continued to the end of the nineteenth century. This development was condemned by many contemporary commentators as a frenetic striving for novelty (fed as it was by the first style and fashion magazines), but was nevertheless very different from the superficially similar style plurality of 40 years before, for now all styles, both classical and non-classical, were treated with a new seriousness, both in their application and their accuracy.

The application of style came increasingly to be based on the notion of association – the idea that a certain style might conjure up certain thoughts or feelings. This led naturally to a code of appropriateness. A learned institution might, for instance, be housed in the sober and majestic style of the Greek Revival but never in Chinese, while the Prince Regent's summer palace at Brighton was an exercise in extravagant exoticism. Patriotism during the Napoleonic Wars also played its part; Egyptian motifs were reminders of British victories, while the Gothic style recalled ancient British values and virtues during the years of international insecurity.

At the same time, the treatment of style became ever more accurate in its detail. Classical styles were spurred on by new archaeology. Non-European styles were promoted by illustrated accounts of foreign travels, like Baron Denon's *Voyage dans la Basse et la Haute Egypte*, published in London in 1802. In 1817 Thomas Rickman's *An Attempt to Discriminate the Styles of English Architecture from the Conquest to the Reformation* established the stylistic nomenclature of medieval architecture that is still in use today. The new stylistic accuracy encouraged the idea of coordinated design, pushing it from architecture and decoration to movables of all sorts, including furniture and even clothes.

41 *Early English*. Plate from *An Attempt to Discriminate the Styles of English Architecture from the Conquest to the Reformation* by Thomas Rickman, 1817. Published by Longman, Hurst, Rees, Orme and Brown. Engraving. VAM 34.E.66.

42 The Royal Institution, Edinburgh, built in the Greek Revival style, 1822–6. Designed by William Henry Playfair.

12. The Picturesque

Central to the whole approach to style and design from about 1790 was the notion of the Picturesque, which combined a heightened sense of history with a tendency to see things in specifically pictorial terms. Picturesque theory – as expounded, for instance, in Sir Uvedale Price's *Essay on the Picturesque as Compared with the Sublime and the Beautiful* (1794) – was heir to various investigations into aesthetics that had begun to appear from the 1720s onwards, most especially in Edmund Burke's writing on the sublime in the 1750s. Burke had explored the idea of extreme emotional reactions to nature and works of art derived from purely visual criteria. In Picturesque theory, irregular ancient buildings combined with agreeably rough natural landscapes to produce an emotional reaction, partly through their forms and partly through historical associations.

43 *Ludlow Castle, Shropshire*, 1778.
By William Hodges. Oil on canvas.
VAM 43-1880.

43

Translated into real terms, the Picturesque meant Humphry Repton's landscape gardens. They depended on a single viewpoint and were demonstrated by pictures from that viewpoint, both before and after construction. Equally Picturesque were John Nash's plans for London, with the great curve of Regent's Street (*see 8:59*) leading up to the Repton-like Regent's Park, surrounded by 'villages' of small houses in varied styles (including rustic Italian and Gothic), as well as palace-like classical terraced houses peering enticingly through the trees. The scenic effect of the

Regent's Park architecture was symptomatic of the whole Picturesque movement, which was about appearances rather than solid substance; a similar insubstantial approach was found in other areas of design, including furniture and interiors, which were deeply concerned with imitation materials and heightened optical effects.

Greater historical and archaeological knowledge, and the visual emphasis of the Picturesque, encouraged the idea that architecture and the fine and applied arts were intimately linked. In creating his house-museum, filled with sculpture and paintings in dramatically lit interiors, Sir John Soane was aiming to demonstrate 'the unity of the arts'. The house-museum of the banker and collector Thomas Hope in Duchess Street, London, aimed at a visual totality based on the use of a symbolic programme. Of the room centred on John Flaxman's statue of Aurora and Cephalus, Hope wrote:

44

> the whole surrounding decoration has been rendered, in some degree, analogous to these personages, and to the face of nature at the moment when . . . the goddess of the morn is supposed to announce the approaching day . . . The sides of the room display, in satin curtains, draped in ample folds over panels of looking-glass, and edged with black velvet, the fiery hue which fringes the clouds just before sunrise: and in a ceiling of cooler sky blue are sown, amidst a few still unextinguished luminaries of the night, the roses which the harbinger of the day . . . spreads on every side about her.

The furniture was decorated with appropriate symbolic motifs, including emblems of the night, medallions of the god of sleep, owls and stars.

45

44 *The Aurora room, at the house of Thomas Hope, Duchess Street, London*. Plate from *Houschold Furniture and Interior Decoration executed from Designs by Thomas Hope*, 1807. Engraving. VAM FW.10D/2.

45 *Cumberland Terrace, Regent's Park, London*, 1827. Planned by John Nash, executed by James Thompson, built 1826. Engraved by James Tingle after Thomas Hosmer Shepherd. Plate from *Metropolitan Improvements* by James Elmes, 1827. Engraving. VAM 237.F.44.

13. The growth of the medieval

The enhanced status of medieval styles as alternatives to the classical was most clearly shown by the new Commissioners' churches, built with one million pounds from the government from 1818 onwards. Planned as simple preaching boxes, they could be either Greek or Gothic; that most were the latter was due more to the cheapness of Gothic than to any aesthetic preference. The symmetrical plans of the Commissioners' churches ran counter to the most complete handling of Gothic style, for anti-classical irregularity had become a key characteristic of the Gothic from the much-publicized Strawberry Hill onwards. At Downton Castle, in 1772, Richard Payne Knight, a major theorist of the Picturesque, built the first irregular castle, set in a naturally wild landscape. Downton had classical interiors, but James Wyatt's Lee Priory of 1783–90, which had never been a medieval religious site, was Gothic both inside and out.

From the 1790s large, irregularly planned Gothic country houses were built in considerable numbers, the most spectacular being Fonthill Abbey, designed by James Wyatt for the collector and West Indian plantation-owner William Beckford. The message of such houses was one of ancient lineage (in Beckford's case invented), feudal land ownership and the romance of Old England. According to the purpose, several styles were on offer: Humphry Repton listed Castle Gothic (as at Downton), Abbey Gothic (used at Fonthill) and Manor House. It was the last, a revival of the Tudor late-Gothic style of the early sixteenth century, that came to be the most popular and expanded to

46 *St Nicholas's Church, Lower Tooting, London*, 1832. By C. Rosenberg after Thomas William Atkinson. The church, designed by Atkinson, replaced a medieval church behind it, which had become too small for a rapidly growing congregation. Hand-coloured aquatint. Wandsworth Museum.

47 *Fonthill Abbey, Wiltshire*, 1822. By J. Barnett after John Chessell Buckler. The Abbey was designed by James Wyatt and built 1796–1818. The tower, 273ft (83 metres) high, fell down in 1825. Etching. VAM 29635.415.

48

embrace furniture and fittings as well as architecture, eventually being adopted as a suitably national style for the huge project of the Palace of Westminster, built from 1840. The biggest Gothic project before Westminster was the comprehensive restoration and enhancement of the castle at Windsor under Sir Jeffry Wyatville, a nephew of James Wyatt. Its rich interiors, completed in 1828, showed an entirely characteristic combination of gilt Gothic detail and luxurious modern textile furnishings. At a less exalted level, Gothic styles became especially popular in the cheaper forms of metalwork.

From about 1810 the medieval repertoire expanded chronologically in both directions. At one end it grew to encompass pre-Gothic Norman styles and at the other Elizabethan, Jacobean and even the Restoration styles of the later seventeenth century. The second group was especially associated with 'antiquarian interiors' of the type first promoted by Horace Walpole at Strawberry Hill from the 1750s onwards. At Fonthill Abbey, filled with a dazzling array of art objects of the highest quality, chiefly from the continent, the great Gothic galleries were furnished with new pieces in a variant of the Jacobean style, while among Beckford's collections of precious objects were the earliest examples of the revived continental Renaissance style. By the later 1830s the Elizabethan and Jacobean styles had become conflated into a 'Jacobethan' style, which eventually ousted Tudor-Gothic as the chief indicator of the 'Olden Days', a position it still holds today.

50

50 Chair, 1815–18. Probably designed by Richard Bridgens and made in the workshop of George Bullock. Commissioned by Sir Godfrey Vassal Webster for Battle Abbey, Sussex. The chair was intended to recall Jacobean and Restoration examples. Oak, painted and gilded, with gilt-brass mounts; the replacement upholstery based on the original. [h. 101cm]. VAM W.53-1980.

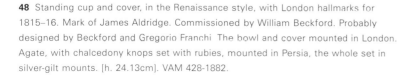

49

48 Standing cup and cover, in the Renaissance style, with London hallmarks for 1815–16. Mark of James Aldridge. Commissioned by William Beckford. Probably designed by Beckford and Gregorio Franchi. The bowl and cover mounted in London. Agate, with chalcedony knops set with rubies, mounted in Persia, the whole set in silver-gilt mounts. [h. 24.13cm]. VAM 428-1882.

49 Armchair, about 1823. Probably designed by Augustus Charles Pugin and possibly made by Gillow & Co. Made for the drawing room at Eaton Hall, Cheshire, designed for the second Earl Grosvenor. The huge Gothic house at Eaton was extravagantly furnished in much the same manner as Windsor Castle. Mahogany, gilded; modern upholstery. [h. 94cm]. VAM W.22-1959.

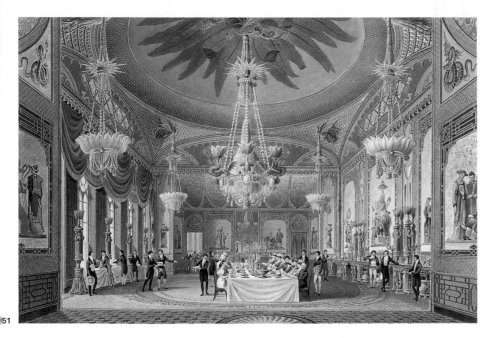

14. Exotic styles

Non-European styles were used in two ways. The first was as part of a popular and generalized exoticism, of the type that had long been part of public spectacle and the theatre. Transfer-printed plates and printed textiles, for instance, combined vaguely Indian, Chinese and even Italian scenes and motifs. Ceramics were also the context for the most popular chinoiserie design of this period, the decoration known as the Willow Pattern. Loosely derived from painted Chinese porcelain of the late eighteenth century, it had no precise Chinese origin, while the famous 'Chinese tale' that still accompanies it was invented as a marketing tool by a ceramic manufacturer in the 1830s.

The second, purer approach to exoticism was marked by the move to greater stylistic accuracy. As with Gothic, the various styles were adapted to certain characteristic uses. Chinese was a domestic style and, except for garden buildings, was not used on external architecture. Significantly, rococo-derived chinoiserie furniture was replaced by furniture that incorporated Chinese motifs into classical forms, or by pieces that were really Chinese or imitations of them. The first approach was adopted in the famous Chinese rooms at the Prince of Wales's Carlton House, which were decorated by imported French artists and filled with French furniture. The second type of furniture was found in the Prince's pavilion at Brighton, which appears as a Chinese fantasy without parallel, but in fact employs on a huge and extravagant scale many of the decorative techniques used on Chinese export goods and real Chinese buildings. The extraordinary Mogul-inspired exterior of the Pavilion had relatively few parallels, and they, significantly, were usually made for nabobs: men who had returned to Britain with fortunes made in India.

The Egyptian style, unlike the Chinese and Indian, was a Europe-wide craze. While isolated examples of Egyptian motifs had been part of earlier neo-classicism, archaeological surveys linked to Napoleon's campaigns in Egypt produced evidence of an ancient and mysterious civilization, raising it to the status of a historical style. Egyptian gods and hieroglyphs provided a whole new range of useful symbols to give meaning to objects and buildings. In architecture, the massive dignity and pure lines of Egyptian remains, and their predominantly sepulchral and solemn nature, made the style especially useful for public structures, from cemetery gateways to suspension bridges. At a more popular level, the striking Egyptian façade of William Bullock's Museum in Piccadilly, London, signalled the history and wonders within, as well as spawning several direct imitations and a rash of novel shop fronts.

---

51 *The Banqueting Room, Royal Pavilion, Brighton*, created 1815–17. Designed by Robert Jones. Plate from *The Royal Pavilion at Brighton* by John Nash, 1826. Etching and aquatint, hand coloured. VAM 100.B.32.

52 Willow Pattern plate, dated 1818. Possibly made at the Spode factory, Stoke-on-Trent, Staffordshire. Earthenware, cobalt-blue printed under a lead glaze. [diam. 22.54cm]. VAM C.231-1934.

53 Mantel clock, about 1807–8. Made by Benjamin Lewis Vulliamy. The design of the clock, except for the sphinxes, taken from plates in *Voyage dans la Basse et la Haute Egypte* by Baron Dominique Vivant Denon, published in Paris and London, 1802. Black marble, with mounts of ormolu and patinated bronze, gilt dial. [h. 22.86cm]. VAM M.119-1966.

EXOTICISM AND HISTORICISM

Frances Collard

Designs influenced by exotic and historical sources were very fashionable between 1714 and 1837 in Britain. Artists, architects, designers, makers and manufacturers produced an extensive range of motifs, forms and patterns to satisfy a sophisticated and eager market. This interest intensified at the end of the eighteenth century, establishing exotic and historical styles on an equal footing with the leading style of neo-classicism.

54. Furnishing chintz, possibly for a window blind, about 1830–5. Printed cotton. VAM T.354-1972.

The range of exotic styles included Chinese, Egyptian, Moorish and Hindu, but the most popular style throughout the Georgian period was the Chinese; Egyptian and Indian designs became fashionable only in about 1800. Historicism, or the interest in and reinterpretation of British historical styles, included Gothic, Norman, Tudor and Elizabethan styles, with Gothic being the most prominent.

The Chinese style was used right across the applied arts, as well as in interior decoration and garden buildings and furniture. John Linnell's chairs for Badminton House are starkly original and innovative, with panels of painted lattice replacing the usual carved back and arms.

Designers or architects often combined elements from more than one style. The most elaborate example is the Royal Pavilion at Brighton, built in a mixture of Indian, Moorish and Chinese architectural styles. Originally designed in the neo-classical style in 1787 by Henry Holland for the Prince of Wales, the building was transformed in 1815–23 by the architect John Nash. For Indian architectural details, he borrowed William and Thomas Daniell's book, *Oriental Scenery*, from the Prince's library. Nash incorporated tent-roofs, Mogul domes, Islamic arches and perforated screens, based on Indian *jalis*, into the east front of the Pavilion. The interiors underwent several phases of chinoiserie decoration, designed by Frederick Crace and Robert Jones.

55. Design for a chair for the bedroom at Badminton House, Gloucestershire, about 1754. By John Linnell. Watercolour. VAM E.71-1929.

56. Bureau bookcase in the Gothic, classical and Egyptian styles, 1808–10. Probably designed and made by George Oakley of Oakley and Evans, Old Bond Street, London. The doors contain watercolour views of the River Clyde, dated 1808, by James Baynes. Mahogany, veneered with zebrawood and satinwood, inlaid with box; mahogany mouldings, ormolu mounts. [h. 158.5cm]. VAM W.15-1930.

57. Wallpaper border in the Egyptian style, about 1806. From the drawing room at Crawley House, Bedfordshire. Coloured print from woodblocks and flock. VAM E.2498&A-1966.

58. The Royal Pavilion, Brighton. Remodelled by John Nash, 1815–23.

Historical styles, particularly the Gothic Revival, were also plundered for ideas. Forms and motifs borrowed from architectural sources included arches, ruins, fan vaulting, stained glass and columns. Furniture designers and makers incorporated Gothic or Norman arches into the backs of chairs; more appropriately, chintz for blinds was printed with designs of stained-glass windows.

Designers and manufacturers sometimes combined both exotic and historical motifs in the same design. Furnishing textiles were printed with Chinese pagodas and medieval ruins. Exotic motifs were used as decorative details. Gothic glazing bars and pilasters with Egyptian heads decorated a bookcase made of zebrawood, an imported exotic timber.

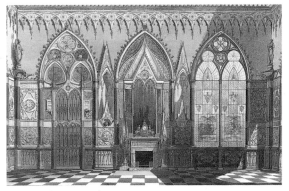

59. *Design for a Gothic Saloon*, 1810. Designed by Gaetano Landi. Plate from *Architectural Decorations* by Gaetano Landi, 1810. Published in London. Hand-coloured aquatint. VAM 57.K.9.

60. *Parlor chairs fronts & profiles*, in the Norman style, 1807. Designed by George Smith. Plate from *A Collection of Designs for Household Furniture and Interior Decoration* by George Smith, 1808. Published in London by J. Taylor. Hand-coloured etching and aquatint. VAM II.RC.S.2.

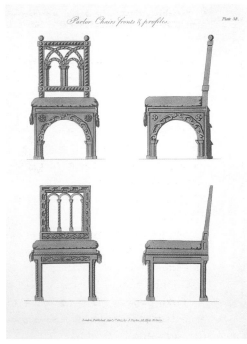

15. Classical varieties

Two broadly defined varieties of classicism emerged in about 1800: Greek and Roman. Both marked a shift from what were seen as the light, insignificant forms of earlier neo-classicism and benefited from a greater archaeological correctness. James Stuart had built the first European Greek Revival buildings in the 1750s, but it was not until 1800 that a Greek architectural style appeared employing simple elements like the baseless Doric order and adopting the forms of peripteral temples. In Britain it became widely popular after about 1810, eventually replacing neo-Palladianism in most official architecture. Greek-style interiors, in parallel with the contemporary Empire style in France, employed ideas derived from a wide range of sources – Greek, Roman and even, on occasion, Egyptian. All were marked by an attention to archaeology, precision of detail and purity of line. This last, which had long been a key element in neo-classicism, was emphasized by the practice of showing designs in outline only, even in the case of brightly coloured interiors like those of Thomas Hope. The archaeological drive led to furniture, vessels and even clothes being copied and adapted from ancient models, or being formed, either in whole or in part, in the shape of classical motifs. By the 1830s a restrained Greek style had become the norm for modest furniture and furnishings.

61

61 *The Library-Drawing Room at Bromley Hill House, Kent*, 1816. By John Chessell Buckler. Bromley Hill, with its Greek-style Library-Drawing Room, was the country house of the politician and connoisseur Sir Charles Long, later Lord Farnborough. Corporation of London.

62 Chair, about 1805. Probably designed and made by James Newton, for Soho House, Birmingham, the home of Matthew Boulton. A direct copy of the ancient Greek Klismos chair. Mahogany with a cane seat. [h. 89cm]. VAM W.2-1988

63

64

62

65

Like the Greek Revival, the Roman style had equivalents in the rest of Europe. Characterized by a magnificent heaviness and attention to sculptural detail, it was especially suitable for the grandest interiors. The sources of the style lay in a re-examination of Roman imperial architecture and sculptural fragments. Silver and metalwork, adopting the forms of ancient stone vases, were often taken from those illustrated in Piranesi's *Vasi, Candelabri, Cippi* of 1778, giving it a suitable sculptural drama, while furniture borrowed ideas from ancient stone seats and table legs.

63 Plate from *A Series of twenty-nine designs of Modern Costume Drawn and Engraved by Henry Moses, Esq.*, 1823 (first published in 1812). The dresses are adapted from ancient Greek models, the pole screen from an ancient shield. *Designs of Modern Costume* closely reflected Thomas Hope's ideas on the Greek style. VAM 24.B.189.

64 Ice pail, 1809–10. Mark of Paul Storr. Retailed by the royal goldsmiths, Rundell, Bridge and Rundell. The form is taken from the famous Medici vase (a stone vase of the first century AD) in the Uffizi Gallery, Florence. Silver-gilt. [h. 34.7cm]. VAM M.48C-1982.

65 Stool, about 1800. Designed by Charles Heathcote Tatham and possibly made by Marsh and Tatham. The stool imitates an ancient marble seat seen by Tatham in Italy, and recorded in his *Etchings of Ancient Ornamental Architecture*, 1799. Beechwood, painted white and gold to imitate marble. VAM W.2-1975.

16. Pluralism absorbed

The 1820s saw the start of a synthesis of historical styles into new wholes. In the hands of Charles Robert Cockerell, a great scholar of Greek architecture, a classical style emerged that incorporated ideas from Italian sixteenth-century architects and Sir Christopher Wren. Italian vernacular styles, which had been part of irregular Picturesque architecture since John Nash's villas of about 1800, grew up at Hope's The Deepdene. Sir Charles Barry's Travellers' Club in London's Pall Mall of 1829 reintroduced Italian sixteenth-century *palazzo* forms and the same style achieved truly palatial proportions in his Trentham Hall, Staffordshire, begun in 1838.

This eclecticism was paralleled by developments in interior decoration. A fashion for collecting baroque objects, including French late-seventeenth-century furniture, German ivories and English silver, had been boosted by the quantities of material coming from the continent after the French Revolution. This fashion probably helped to prepare the ground for the gradual reappearance of the rococo style in objects and interiors from the 1820s onwards. The most admired models were French: one of the first examples of the revived style, a silver tureen of 1812, copied a French example of the 1730s. Ceramics and textiles were profoundly affected. Although there were few examples of complete rococo interiors, baroque and rococo elements were frequently added to a Roman framework. The French rococo furniture style, confusingly described as either Louis XIV or Louis XV, began the climb that was to make it the preferred British style from the 1840s to 1900. However, its story belongs in that period.

66 The Deepdene, Surrey. *View from the Hall: entrance towards turret etc*, 1825–6 By William Henry Bartlett. The Deepdene, designed by Thomas Hope and William Atkinson, was built in 1818–19 and 1823. Watercolour. London Borough of Lambeth Archives Department.

67

68 The Elizabeth saloon, Belvoir Castle, Rutland, decorated in the rococo style 1824–8. Designed for Elizabeth, Duchess of Rutland, by Benjamin Dean Wyatt and Matthew Cotes Wyatt. Some of the panelling was taken from a French château. The ceiling painting by Matthew Cotes Wyatt.

67 Vase, about 1826. Designed in a rococo style by Thomas Brameld, painted by Edwin Steele. Made at the Rockingham pottery, Yorkshire. Porcelain, painted and gilded. VAM 47-1869.

68

CHAPTER 8

Georgian Britain, 1714–1837

Who led taste?

MICHAEL SNODIN

1. The development of taste

The Georgian years witnessed a fundamental transformation in the ways that taste in design and the decorative arts was created and transmitted. For centuries high design existed to serve and reinforce a social system with the monarch at its head, and its consumption – at least in its most expensive form – was limited largely to those at the top. Below that level, consumption and display were expected to reflect social rank. By 1714 this was changing. Shifts in political power from the Crown to Parliament and the nobility meant that the personal tastes of the monarch counted far less. In place of a court focused on the monarch, a range of centres of taste formation emerged. Important elements in this process were a steady increase in manufactured goods and of the number of people able to consume them, as well as the arrival of new cultural ideas. These included the identification of a group of activities as 'fine arts', also called 'the elegant arts' or 'arts of taste'. They included music and poetry, painting and sculpture, architecture and garden design, which were thought to involve the emotions. At a lower level, although not in terms of consumption, stood the 'useful' or 'mechanical arts', among which were what we now call the applied or decorative arts. Both the fine and the useful arts played a key role, as arenas for the exercise of taste, in the creation of a distinctive 'polite' culture. As this spread, so did the arts, taking high design to vastly greater numbers of people. A variety of taste makers participated in this process, but they naturally included the nobility and gentry. Their consumption of fashion goods was often eagerly emulated further down the social scale, with sometimes confusing results: 'In a few years we shall have no common folk at all.' The process was also geographical, for while London remained the centre of style, new design ideas passed rapidly to provincial centres, aided by better roads, newspapers and prints, and by shopkeepers visiting London.

By the end of the Georgian period, recognizably modern forces of taste formation were well in place. On the one hand, there was the commercial tendency, dedicated to maximizing selling and promoting the cycle of fashion. On the other, official and unofficial bodies worked to control a national taste that they considered to be corrupted by the forces of commerce. The positions taken by these two groups had emerged early in the eighteenth century. Commentators had begun to argue that the increase of goods – of 'luxury' – across society could have moral consequences. Only by the exercise of taste through 'politeness' could consumption be controlled. One critical voice was the Whig philosopher Anthony Ashley Cooper, the third Earl of Shaftesbury. In his *Letter concerning the Art, or Science of Design* of 1712 he deplored the courtly taste of 'the long reign of luxury under King Charles II', suggesting that the free spirit of the nation, and more particularly of its nobility, would most effectively promote the arts and foster national taste.

1 The hall at Holkham Hall, Norfolk, begun 1734. Designed by William Kent. One of the major neo-Palladian houses, Holkham was built for Thomas Coke, Earl of Leicester, a great collector of antique sculpture.

THE DUKE AND DUCHESS OF NORTHUMBERLAND, ARISTOCRATIC PATRONS

Rachel Kennedy

The Duke and Duchess of Northumberland were one of the wealthiest couples in mid-eighteenth-century Britain: Elizabeth Seymour Percy was heir in her own right to six of England's oldest baronies, while her husband Sir Hugh Smithson owned estates in Yorkshire and Middlesex, as well as Northumberland House in London.

Like many other wealthy landed families in Britain, they divided their time between their estates in Northumberland and London, where the Duke was a Member of Parliament and later a member of the House of Lords. Like other members of the nobility, both the Duke and Duchess held royal appointments at the courts of George II and George III, but it was in their shared role as patrons of the fine and decorative arts that they are chiefly remembered today.

The Duke's interest in art began in his youth on the Grand Tour when he first started to collect antique sculpture and Old Master paintings. In addition, he commissioned works of art from artists whom he met in Italy and was one of Antonio Canaletto's first patrons on his arrival in England in 1746. The Duchess preferred northern European art and travelled abroad to buy paintings. In 1771 she acquired what she described as her 'best Teniers' and observed of a private collection of ivories, enamels and miniatures, 'I really think my own Collection of Ivorys at least equal to any which I saw there.' She chose the Gothic style when making architectural improvements to her family seat, Alnwick Castle in Northumberland, where a medieval rather than a neo-classical interior was thought to better reflect her historical Percy lineage.

One of the Duke and Duchess's most prestigious projects was the refurbishment of Northumberland House in London, for which Robert Adam designed a magnificent drawing room and picture gallery. He also designed neo-classical interiors and furnishings for Syon House in London, where the Great Hall contains a copy of the antique sculpture *The Dying Gaul*, commissioned by the Duchess.

The Northumberlands became leaders of taste through their patronage of fashionable architects and artists like Adam, Canaletto and Reynolds. However, the couple's deliberately ostentatious displays of wealth, frequently exhibited at the social events they hosted in London and at Alnwick, sometimes attracted criticism. Even the Duchess's Gothic-loving friend, Horace Walpole, declared that her excessive love of entertainment and jewellery made her 'coarse' and 'junketaceous'.

2. Left: *Hugh, 1st Duke of Northumberland*. By James Barry. Oil on canvas. Far left: *Elizabeth, 1st Duchess of Northumberland*. By Sir Joshua Reynolds. Oil on canvas. Collection of the Duke of Northumberland.

3. The Glass Drawing Room at Northumberland House, London, 1870s. By an anonymous artist. The drawing room designed by Robert Adam, 1770–5, enlarged about 1820. Watercolour. Collection of the Duke of Northumberland.

4. The Great Hall, Syon House, London, 1762–9. Designed by Robert Adam.

5. *Alnwick Castle, Northumberland*, 1752. By Antonio Canaletto. Oil on canvas. Collection of the Duke of Northumberland.

2. Lord Burlington and neo-Palladianism

Shaftesbury's ideas were reflected in the work of Richard Boyle, the third Earl of Burlington and the chief promoter of neo-Palladian architectural style. Burlington's architectural success derived from his position as a general leader of taste and was closely linked to contemporary politics. Although some recent commentators have suggested that he was a Jacobite, many of his connections were with the ruling Whig group of grandees, who supported the Hanoverian succession and monopolized political power. His supreme reputation as the 'Apollo of the Arts' derived from twice having made the Grand Tour and from his active promotion of Italian ideas in music, painting, literature and architecture. By the mid-1720s his own style was established among his friends and relatives. His associated position at court, meanwhile, meant that he could place his protégés in key positions on the Board of Works, which dealt with all government building. These included his main assistant, William Kent, as well as Henry Flitcroft (nicknamed Burlington Harry), John Vardy and Isaac Ware.

Neo-Palladianism's domination of ordinary urban architecture began with Burlington's own building schemes on the fields behind his house in London. It was finally achieved through the activities of hundreds of small builders using the pocket handbooks that began to come out in large numbers from the mid-1720s. While Burlington himself played no part in their publication, they frequently took their illustrations from more expensive publications that he sponsored. The most important of these was Isaac Ware's translation of Palladio's *Four Books of Architecture*, published in 1738 (*see 7:2*).

Earl of Burlington.

7

6

6 The Horse Guards, London, built 1751–9. Designed by William Kent and built under the direction of the Board of Works.

7 *Richard Boyle, 3rd Earl of Burlington and 4th Earl of Cork*, 1717–19. By Jonathan Richardson. In the background is Burlington's first building, the Bagnio or Casina, in the gardens of Chiswick House, London. Oil on canvas. National Portrait Gallery, London.

8 Frontispiece to *The chimney piece Maker's Daily Assistant* by John Crunden, Thomas Milton and Placido Columbani, 1766. Designed by Isaac Taylor, engraved by R. Pranker. In this pattern-book frontispiece, a client and his architect discuss a design while a carpenter puts up a neo-Palladian chimneypiece. A bust of Inigo Jones presides over the scene. Engraving. VAM 34.B.62.

The work and influence of the architect James Gibbs revealingly demonstrate the strengths and weaknesses of the Burlingtonian revolution. Gibbs was a covert Catholic and politically suspect, as both a Tory and a Scot. In the reign of Queen Anne, the influence of the Catholic Earl of Mar had briefly gained Gibbs a place as one of the surveyors for the scheme to build fifty new London churches, leading to his St Mary-le-Strand and St Martin-in-the-Fields. His unusual Italian training and a customer base of Tory magnates led to a career as a successful independent architect, while his flexible baroque style allowed him to absorb neo-Palladian elements. In 1728 he published his *Book of Architecture*, the first book to be devoted to the work of a single British architect. It was immensely influential in Britain and the British colonies, not only for its designs for whole buildings but for its decorative and other useful details, especially in interiors, a field not well covered in publications by the Burlington group.

9

8

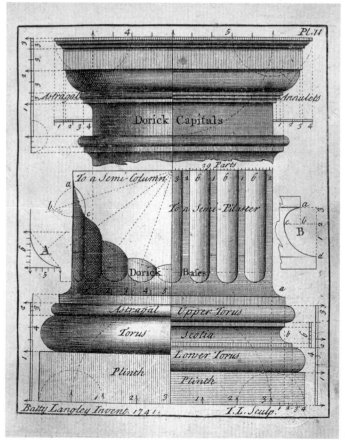

10

9 *James Gibbs*, signed and dated 1726. By John Michael Rysbrack. Marble. VAM A.6-1988.

10 *The Doric Order*. Plate from *The Builder's Jewel, or, The Youth's Instructor, & workman's remembrancer* by Batty Langley and Thomas Langley, 1741. Engraving. VAM L.1146-1981.

The importance of Italy in the careers of Gibbs and Burlington shows how the Grand Tour had become the key experience in the acquisition of taste. While such tours always took in Paris and often Germany, the most prized destination was Italy. The power of Italy for generations of young men brought up on classical literature is hard to imagine today. There, at the actual sites of classical mystery and myth, they absorbed the glories of classical culture and the virtue associated with the contemplation of ancient art, as well as the knowledge of works of art that made them virtuosi. Returning laden with paintings, sculpture, books, Italian silks, exotic furniture and ideas about architecture, culture and luxurious living, they became the leading taste makers. Their Italian spoils filled their new neo-Palladian houses. Their grounds, modelled on contemporary Italy, ancient Rome and the paintings of Claude Lorraine, were dotted with temples symbolic of classical ideals and filled with portraits of the owner, his friends and political supporters. In this setting, ideas of ancient virtue could be linked to notions of British history and British liberty, free of the shackles of an oppressive monarchy. By such means Burlington's modern classical style turned into something quintessentially British.

The dominating taste of Lord Burlington and his circle was not without its critics. They included William Hogarth, who, in his popular print *Masquerades and Operas*, satirized the Italianate nature of Burlington's patronage and promotion of

11 *The gardens at Stourhead, Wiltshire, from the West*, about 1770. By Copplestone Warre Bamfylde. The gardens were created 1741–72. Watercolour. VAM E.360-1949.

12 *The Painter and his Pug*, 1745. By William Hogarth. On the palette is Hogarth's 'line of beauty and grace'. Oil on canvas. © Tate, London, 2001.

the arts. In the foreground he attacks the Italian opera promoted by Burlington, while English plays are being carted off in a wheelbarrow as waste paper. In the background is the gate of Burlington House, inscribed 'Accademy of Arts'. It is surmounted by the figure of William Kent, palette in hand, at whom figures of Raphael and Michelangelo gaze up in admiration. While Hogarth may have had a personal motive in attacking Burlington (his future father-in-law, the mural painter Sir James Thornhill, was competing for commissions with Kent), he had a continuing interest in drawing British taste away from foreign influences and especially from a love of foreign artists. His most effective initiative was the revival in 1735 of the private academy of painting and sculpture at St Martin's Lane, originally founded in 1720.

Until the foundation of the Royal Academy in 1768, the Academy in St Martin's Lane, London, was the chief school for British artists. It taught principally drawing and included working from a living model. But these exercises were aimed at the useful, as well as the fine, arts. In 1745 the instructors included not only the history painter Francis Hayman and the French sculptor Louis François Roubiliac, but also the Swiss gold chaser George Michael Moser, the medallist Richard Yeo and the French illustrator and draughtsman Hubert Gravelot. In stylistic terms, the most important was certainly Gravelot, whose ornamental style and elegant figure draughtsmanship were taken up by the other members, making the academy one of the principal

engines for the introduction of the rococo style in the 1740s. But this loose-knit group of taste makers operated in a very different way from the rather remote, if single-minded, operations of Lord Burlington. They were part of a network of artists and craftspeople working in London's West End and congregating in its coffee houses, especially Slaughter's (also in St Martin's Lane). Many academy pupils must have come from the workshops of the surrounding furniture makers, goldsmiths and other trades as well as neighbouring artists' studios. Its known pupils included the famous furniture designer and maker John Linnell and the architect James Paine, both of whom designed in the rococo style.

13 *Masquerades and Operas* or *'The Bad taste of the Town'*, 1724. By William Hogarth. Etching and engraving. VAM F.188:152.

14 Detail of a design for a candlestick, with a figure of Daphne, about 1740. By George Michael Moser. The candlestick was matched by another with the stem formed as a figure of Apollo. Key elements in this candlestick are taken from prints by Gilles-Marie Oppenord and the goldsmith Juste-Aurèle Meissonnier. Pen, ink and wash. VAM E.4895-1968.

3. Rococo and the printed pattern book

The complex and irregular three-dimensional forms of the rococo style, and its emphasis on variety and invention, made great demands on the drawing and design skills of craftspeople. It was therefore no accident that from the mid-1730s the previously thin and hesitant stream of English engraved ornament rapidly grew to a flood that did not abate until the 1770s. For the first time in Britain most of the prints were original designs rather than copies of continental productions, acknowledging a specifically English variant of the rococo style then emerging from the craft workshops. They were primarily made by crafts-people, especially woodcarvers, a number of whom – like Matthias Lock and Thomas Johnson – were also drawing masters. Rather than copying such prints entire, carvers mined them for ideas, cutting them up and adding their own notions. The rococo style also arrived in the form of engraved trade cards, at that time reaching an unprecedented size and elaboration. As trade-card motifs can be found on tablets and

16

gravestones, porcelain, maps, metal tickets and many other types of object, they probably transmitted rococo design ideas more effectively than any other type of printed ornament.

The most influential single set of pattern prints, however, was put out as a book of furniture designs. *The Gentleman and Cabinet Maker's Director* by Thomas Chippendale the Elder (his son, also a furniture designer, was also called Thomas) was published first in parts and then as a collected edition in 1754, with the full apparatus of dedication (to the Earl of Northumberland), frontispiece and text, followed by 106 engraved plates drawn by Chippendale. The *Director* broke new ground in being both a source of design ideas and a pattern book for his potential customers. Its 308 subscribers, who sponsored its publication, included noblemen and architects as well as major furniture makers. They would have appreciated its large, impressive format, which mimicked that of expensive architectural books. It was, however, among smaller furniture makers, mostly outside London, that the patterns had their greatest effect.

4. Promoting design, and a national crisis

By the mid-eighteenth century design and aesthetic theory had become a subject of intense debate. The ideas in Hogarth's *Analysis of Beauty* (1755) were developed in Edmund Burke's *Philosophical Inquiry into the Origin of our Ideas of the Sublime and Beautiful* (1756). Theory was joined to practice in Mayhew and Ince's *The Universal System of Household Furniture* (1759), which was prefaced by an exercise 'for young practitioners in drawing', showing 'a Systematical Order of Raffle Leaf from the Line of Beauty', from the fundamental design principle set forth in Hogarth's *Analysis*. But most concern was shown for the consequences of poor national taste in international competitiveness. As an Irish commentator on the silk trade in Dublin commented in the middle of the century, 'as we depend upon England for matters of fashion, so England for the like matters depends upon France, where many schools and academies are established, at the public expence, for carrying those manufactures to their highest perfection.' The deficiency was made up by foreign immigrants from all over Europe – from France, the Low Countries, Germany, Switzerland, Italy and Sweden. In Birmingham alone in 1759, '30 or 40 Frenchmen and Germans are constantly employed in drawing and designing'.

15 Trade card of Peter Griffin, map and print seller, London, 1746–9. Among the large range of prints (both political and satirical) and a drawing book is Matthias Lock's *A Book of Ornaments*, 1745, shown at the bottom right. Engraving. The British Museum.

16 *Design for a mirror*. Plate from *Six Sconces* by Matthias Lock, 1744. Etching. VAM 27811·6

A common solution was the establishment of societies for the encouragement of the arts and manufacture and to promote design training, often through prizes. The aim was to improve drawing and, by that means, invention in design. As the commentator R. Campbell observed in 1747, 'he who first hits upon any new Whim is sure to make by the Invention before it becomes common in the Trade; but he that must always wait for a new Fashion till it comes from *Paris*, or is hit upon by his Neighbour, is never likely to grow rich or eminent in his Way'. The first example in the British Isles was set up in Dublin in 1731, with similar societies in Glasgow and Edinburgh in 1753.

In London the Anti-Gallican Society gave premiums, while the Society for the Encouragement of Arts, Manufactures and Commerce, still in existence as the Royal Society of Arts, was founded in 1754. William Shipley, its principal promoter, sought to exclude fine arts from the society's concerns, aiming instead to encourage 'ingenious mechanics, such as carvers, joiners, upholsterers, cabinet makers', in the belief that an improvement in taste would lead to general refinement, as well as usefully relieving unemployment. The society gave prizes for design exercises in specific fields. The competition entrants were chiefly teenagers from private drawing schools, who covered both textile and three-dimensional design.

The establishment of such societies was matched by calls for the founding of a national academy of the visual arts. In 1755 a group of leading artists, headed by Francis Hayman, unsuccessfully proposed to the Society of Arts and the Society of Dilettanti an academy 'for the improvement of the arts in general' and the 'refining of taste'. It would cover architecture (both internal and external), painting and sculpture, engraving and chasing, and planting and gardening, but would also recognize the 'Subordinate branches of design: namely utensils of all sorts, plate [silver] and cabinet-work, patterns of skills [silk design], jewelling, garniture, carriage-building and equipage, down even to toys and trinkets'. In the event, when a Royal Academy was eventually founded, in 1768, architecture was in, but the applied arts were out. A state-supported system of schools of design was not to appear for another 60 years, the training of designers lying meanwhile in the hands of private drawing masters and enlightened manufacturers.

17 *A Systematical Order of Raffle Leaf from the Line of Beauty*. Plate from *The Universal System of Household Furniture* by William Ince and John Mayhew, 1759. Engraved by Matthias Darley. Engraving. VAM RC.CC.14.

18 *Design for a clock*, 1759. By William Herbert. This drawing for a competition run by the Society for the Encouragement of Arts, Manufactures and Commerce won the second prize in its class: 'For the best drawing or compositions of ornaments, being original designs, fit for Weavers, Callico Printers, or any Art or manufacture, by Youths under the age of twenty'. Herbert was a pupil of Francis Vivares. Pen, ink and wash. Royal Society of Arts.

THOMAS CHIPPENDALE AND THE LONDON FURNITURE MAKERS

Tessa Murdoch

By 1754, when Thomas Chippendale the Elder (1718–79) had settled in St Martin's Lane and had published the first edition of his *Gentleman and Cabinet Maker's Director*, the West End of London was the centre of the London furniture trade. Many of the workshops were large, and as a German visitor to London noted in 1767, 'the master himself no longer touches a tool. Instead he oversees the work of his forty journeymen.' Established close to the royal court, the seat of government and a fashionable residential area, the leading cabinet makers, carvers and upholsterers were well placed to make furniture of new and fashionable design for the nobility, gentry and the growing merchant classes.

Chippendale's design ideas reached a much wider audience through the *Director*, which came out in parts that were eagerly awaited by regional and metropolitan cabinet makers. In 1760 Richard Gillow of Lancaster urged his cousin James in London to send 'Chippindale's additional Number as soon as possible'. Such published designs could then be adapted to suit an individual. Gillow wrote to a client in 1765 about some library bookcases: 'if any of Chippindales designs be more agreeable, I have his Book and can execute 'em & adapt them to the places they are for'.

Chippendale's neighbours in St Martin's Lane included John Channon, an Exeter-trained maker, whose bookcases of 1740 for Sir William Courtenay's library at Powderham Castle in Devon were decorated with brass inlay inspired by continental practice. William Vile and John Cobb specialized in quality carcase furniture, embellished with exquisite carving – then regarded as the highest skill associated with the furniture trade. They supplied King George III and Queen Charlotte with cabinets for their collections of medals and jewellery.

Carved woodwork or composite substitutes such as papier mâché lent themselves to both spirited rococo and disciplined neo-classical ornament. The demand for flat decoration to harmonize with neo-classical interiors led to a revival of marquetry techniques, as used on Chippendale's desk for Edwin Lascelles of Harewood House in Yorkshire, his most important patron. A complex decorative effect could be achieved more cheaply with painted furniture. Painted chairs were appropriate for occasional use in bedrooms and drawing rooms. A decorator's sample – a rare survival – demonstrates how patterns for colour and form were shared.

19. Panel showing alternative schemes for decorating a painted shield-back chair, about 1790. Painted oak. [h. 53cm]. VAM W.11-1993.

20. Bookcase, 1740. Made at the workshop of John Channon in St Martin's Lane, London, for the library of Sir William Courtenay at Powderham Castle, Devon. Veneered in padouk wood with carved and gilt decoration. VAM W.1-1987.

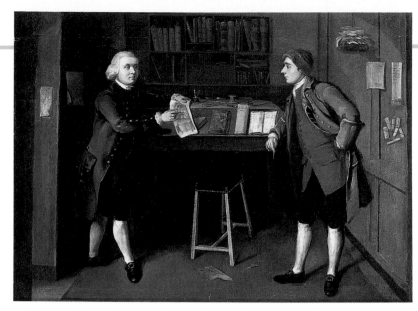

21. *A cabinet maker's office*, about 1770. By an unknown artist. Oil on canvas. VAM P.1-1961.

22. *A Variety of New-Pattern Chairs*, 1754. Plate xii in *The Gentleman and Cabinet Maker's Director* by Thomas Chippendale the Elder, 1754. By Matthias Darly after Chippendale. Engraving. VAM RC.CC.11.

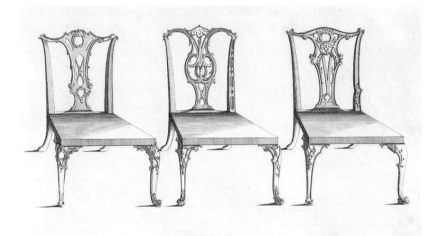

23. Medal cabinet, 1760–1. Made by the firm of William Vile and John Cobb for George III. Mahogany. [h. 200.5cm]. VAM W.11-1963.

24. Chair, about 1754. Inscription beneath the splat reads '6 pedistals for Chipendel's backs'. Splat taken from Plate xii in Chippendale's *Director*. Mahogany, carved; modern upholstery. VAM W.67-1940.

25. Bureau dressing table, 1771–5. Made by the firm of Thomas Chippendale the Elder in St Martin's Lane, London, for Edwin Lascelles for Harewood House, Yorkshire. Rosewood and marquetry of other woods on a carcase of pine, oak and mahogany. VAM W.55-1928.

5. Public art and design

The foundation of the Royal Academy was one move in a trend towards the general opening up of visual culture. In today's world, bombarded with visual stimuli of all types, it is difficult to imagine the situation before about 1730. With the notable exception of what could be seen in churches, paintings and sculpture were largely invisible, locked up in private houses, and high-design decorative schemes and objects were accessible only to the few. Paintings could also be seen in salerooms or at picture dealers, but works of art were most easily consumed second hand through prints. From about 1700 the world of the printed image, encompassing illustrated books and printed ephemera as well as loose prints, underwent a huge expansion. This exposed a wide public, including craftspeople and those learning the ways of politeness, to art and new ideas in design. The essentially commercial character of the print world was paralleled in other areas, most notably in the field of public entertainment.

One of the most significant developments in such visual culture was at the Vauxhall Pleasure Gardens in London. Opened by the 1660s, they had sunk into scandal as a venue for prostitution and debauchery by the 1720s. For the gardens' new proprietor, Jonathan Tyers, raising their tone was an astute commercial move answering the rising demand for polite entertainment. In addition to introducing new attractions and improving the buildings, including adding a new orchestra to provide the essential music, he set up what was in effect the first public art exhibition in England. The first move, in 1738, was the erection of a statue of the composer George Frederick Handel, by the sculptor Roubiliac. While public sculpture of living monarchs was not unknown, commoners were generally shown only on their tombs after death. But here was a living composer of the popular Italian opera, portrayed in relaxed dress as a modern Orpheus or Apollo. Tyers's intentions were made clear in a newspaper article published just before the statue's installation. The civilizing qualities of Handel's music would be enhanced by the effigy of the composer himself, set next to the orchestra 'where his harmony has so often charm'd even the greatest crouds into the profoundest calm and most decent behaviour'.

A month after it was unveiled, the statue was illustrated in a songsheet decorated by Gravelot. Some two years later more art appeared in the gardens, in the form of large paintings of moral and literary subjects by Hayman and after Hogarth. This move is usually attributed to the influence of Hogarth, and certainly involved the St Martin's Lane group, which also made itself felt in other ways: the metal tickets for the gardens were designed by Yeo, and the rococo relief wall ornament of the Music Room was designed by Moser. The 1740 art initiative at Vauxhall was probably a response to the recently opened Ranelagh Gardens, on the other bank of the Thames. Ranelagh, which became the most fashionable of the pleasure gardens, pioneered a new type of public spectacle. It contained no art, but its huge rotunda presented a remarkable architectural interior. It was unmatched in size and design among secular public buildings until the opening in 1772 of the Pantheon in Oxford Street, described by the musical historian Charles Burney as 'the most elegant structure in Europe, if not on the globe'. The effect on taste of such public spaces must have been considerable: the Pantheon, for instance, was probably the most easily accessible neo-classical structure in London at a time when the style was just taking hold among the general public.

26

26 *Jonathan Tyers*, about 1740. By Louis François Roubiliac. Terracotta. [h. 71.1cm]. VAM A.94-1927.

27 *Vauxhall Gardens showing the grand walk at the entrance of the garden and the orchestra with musick playing*, about 1751. By Johann Sebastian Muller after Samuel Wale. The statue of Handel is to the right of the orchestra; paintings are hung on the walls of the supper boxes to the left. The daylight in this scene is misleading – Vauxhall was an evening and night-time venue. Etching and engraving, coloured by hand. VAM W.27BB-1947.

28 *View of the Pantheon, London*, about 1772. Attributed to William Hodges and Johann Zoffany. The Pantheon, built 1769–72, was designed by James Wyatt. Oil on canvas. © Leeds Museums and Galleries.

29

In 1781 the Royal Academy moved into purpose-built premises in Somerset House on the Strand in London, designed by the academy's treasurer and co-founder, the architect Sir William Chambers. Although it served as a civil-service office block and a home for the learned societies, Somerset House's consciously neo-Palladian exteriors marked it out as a national monument. The premises of the Royal Academy at Somerset House were a place to see and be seen, like the pleasure gardens, theatres, assembly rooms, concert halls, exhibitions and other settings for the social round. All these were, to varying degrees, also taste-forming spaces, but the academy was significantly different, for by virtue of its location and ambitions it had a national status. In this context it was notable that it was controlled not by connoisseurs like the Society of Dilettanti (who had refused to support the fledgling academy of 1755) but by the member artists and architects, who designed and decorated the rooms, thus establishing themselves as arbiters of taste.

29 *Portraits of their Majesty's and the Royal Family viewing the exhibition of The Royal Academy 1788.* Etched and engraved by Pierre Antoine Martini. The portraits drawn by John Henry Ramberg. Etching, stipple etching and engraving. VAM E.3648-1923.

6. Neo-classical networks

The neo-classical stylistic revolution showed very clearly the forces of taste formation that were in place by the 1760s. It emerged and spread via the operation of a network of overlapping and mutually reinforcing interests, involving designers, enterprising manufacturers and men and women of taste. The activities of three key personalities make the process clear: the architect Robert Adam and the manufacturers Josiah Wedgwood and Matthew Boulton.

Adam stamped his version of neo-classicism upon the nation, but the story is a revealing one. His letters from Italy in 1757 show that he had decided to become the most prominent architect in Britain. This was a normal aspiration for a young British architect on the Grand Tour, but Adam was unusual in wanting to bring to Britain what he called the 'one true grand and simple style'. Unlike Burlington, Adam did not have a ready-made network of noble friends and relations and was too busy learning to draw to make the contacts that would provide clients for his future practice. This was in marked contrast to William Chambers, whose path he briefly crossed and whom Adam immediately recognized as a future rival. But what he lacked in contacts, Adam made up for in drive and determination, combined with a strong dash of good luck.

On his return to Britain in 1758 Adam took properly furnished rooms at a good address to display his Italian drawings. The fashionable world soon flocked to see them and they played a key part at a crucial meeting with Lord Scarsdale, at which Adam secured the management of Scarsdale's grounds at Kedleston Hall. Later, at dinner with Scarsdale, Adam showed him more drawings. Scarsdale was particularly excited by a grand Roman design, 'the Nabob's palace'. The following year Adam was invited to Kedleston, where a house by the neo-Palladian architects Mathew Brettingham and James Paine was already under construction. James Stuart, another pioneer of neo-classicism, was working on the interiors (*see 8:33*). Unlike Adam, he had actually been to Greece and published a book on the subject. Adam was nevertheless able to have him dismissed on the grounds of his designing ability, attacking Stuart's pioneering neo-classical designs as 'so excessively and ridiculously bad they beggared all description'. Adam's Scottish origins also played a crucial part, for it was his good fortune that several of the ministers of the future George III, who came to the throne in 1760, were his countrymen. A number became his clients, and one, Lord Bute, lay behind his appointment as royal architect, together with Chambers. But Adam's success with his noble clients does not fully explain the widespread adoption of his style. For that we must look at the nature of the style, at the Adam firm and his publications.

30

30 *Robert Adam*, about 1770–5. Attributed to George Willison. Oil on canvas. National Portrait Gallery, London.

31 *Sir William Chambers*, 1788. By Carl Fredrik von Breda. Oil on canvas. Royal Institute of British Architects.

31

Two aspects of his style were crucial. Notwithstanding Adam's concern with architectonic concepts of visual 'movement', the essence of the style lay in the use of ornament. This was acknowledged by Robert's brother and architectural partner James, who called ornament the 'great secret in architecture', and by Sir John Soane, who looked back in 1812 to when Adam had introduced ' . . . a light and fanciful style of decoration . . . This taste soon became general; everything was Adamitic . . .' The second aspect was Adam's insistence on stylistic coherence across every element of his interiors. Total control of the client was achieved by the production of enticing drawings setting down every detail. As everything had to be in the new style, nothing could be 'off the peg'. Thus makers in many fields (like the cabinet makers Mayhew and Ince) experienced the new style directly from Adam's own designs or (like Thomas Chippendale) were obliged to produce their own versions for Adam interiors. Either way, it was only a matter of time before the style passed to customers who were not Adam's clients.

Interestingly, Robert Adam at first experienced difficulty in getting things done in the way he required – for instance, finding it impossible to get ceiling plasterers to work in the 'stiff angly manner' he had seen in Italy. The solution was to import Italian artists for decorative painting, and to train workers in other trades. As with the workmen who carried out the decoration of the churches designed by Sir Christopher Wren and his office, the small group of

33

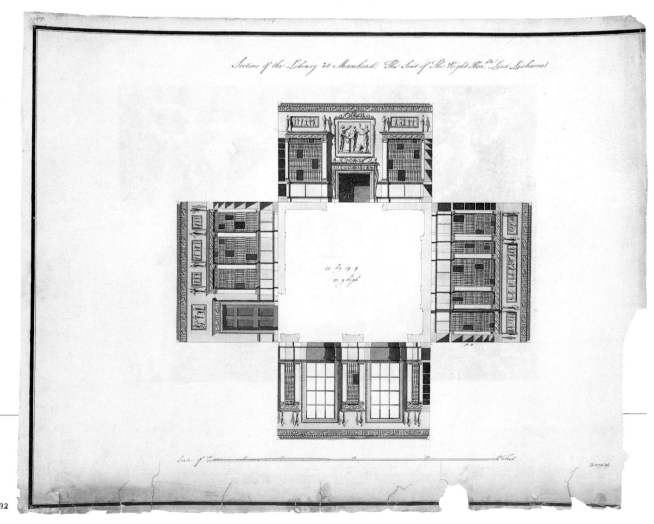

Section of the Library at Mamhead, The Seat of The Right Hon.ble Lord Lisburne

32

34

32 *Design for the walls of a library for Mamhead House, Devon*, 1766. Designed by Robert Adam, the drawing by an Adam office draughtsman. This and fig. 34 were drawings made for the client, Lord Lisburn. Pen, ink and wash. VAM D. 2174-1896.

33 *Design for decorating a state room at Kedleston, Derbyshire*, about 1757–8. By James Stuart. Pen, ink and wash. The National Trust, Kedleston Hall.

34 *Design for the ceiling of a drawing room for Mamhead House, Devon*, 1766. Designed by Robert Adam, the drawing by an Adam office draughtsman. Pen, ink, water and body-colour. VAM D.2171-1896.

35

Adam building craftspeople, such as the plastering family of Rose, inevitably carried the style beyond their Adam commissions. The activities of the Adam firm had the same effect. Robert was not only the senior partner in a large architects' practice, but also the creative genius behind a huge family building firm busy with urban speculation. William Adam & Company, set up in 1764, owned brick works, patented a form of exterior cement and at one point employed some 3,000 workmen. Only a national bank crash prevented it from reaping success from the vast Thameside development at the Adelphi (named for the word 'brothers' in Greek).

The Adams' lavish publication, *The Works in Architecture*, published in parts from 1773, played a significant but less than obvious role in the dissemination

of their style. Its characteristically boastful text, which credited the complete change in national taste to the brothers, certainly established their reputation for the future. The illustrations encouraged the idea of the total interior, for they were soon followed by print sets clearly reflecting the same idea.

On the other hand, isolated examples of Adam style and other neo-classical style decoration had begun to appear in ornament prints from the mid-1760s. These were mainly produced not by craftspeople but by a new breed of professional draughtsmen or designers, like Matthias Darly, or by self-professed architects, like John Crunden, whose publication of 1766, entitled the *Chimney-piece Maker's Daily Assistant*, contained perhaps the first example of the style in print.

---

35 *The London riverfront between Westminster and the Adelphi*, about 1771 2. By William Marlow. On the right is the Royal Terrace of the Adelphi development under construction. Oil on canvas. The Museum of London.

36 *View of the Third Drawing Room at Derby House*, 1777. Engraved by B. Pastorini after Robert Adam. Plate from *The Works in Architecture of Robert and James Adam*, volume II, 1779. Adam remodelled the interior of Derby House, Grosvenor Square, London, for Lord Stanley, 1773–4. Engraving. VAM 11.RC.GG.2.

37

38

36

39

7. Boulton and Wedgwood

Enterprising manufacturers played a key role in the spread of neo-classicism. Especially important were the Birmingham metalworker Matthew Boulton and the Staffordshire potter Josiah Wedgwood, who were friends as well as occasional commercial rivals. Operating far from the centre of fashion in London, their ingenious methods of obtaining new ideas and of selling clearly show how the market in fashionable goods worked. It was not a matter of originality in design, but of recognizing the key importance of the nobility as consumers, as Boulton wrote to the Earl of Findlater in 1776: 'I only wish to excell in the execution of that taste which my employers must approve'. But the real purpose of having such customers was to increase the consumption of high-design goods lower down the social scale. Wedgwood's 'Queen's Ware' was one example, while Boulton happily copied for sale a clock originally made for the King and designed by Chambers, the King's architect.

---

37 *Matthew Boulton*, 1814. By Peter Rouw the Younger. Wax. VAM 1858-1871.

38 *Section of a room with Greek Ornaments*, 1770. Plate by Matthias Darly. The garlanded medallions and rosettes strongly resemble the decoration of interiors by Sir William Chambers. Engraving. VAM E.2252-1908.

39 Table clock, 1772. Made by Matthew Boulton, after a design by Sir William Chambers, from the moulds prepared for a clock supplied to George III in 1771. It was bought for Sir George Cornewall of Moccas Court, Herefordshire. Ormolu, Derbyshire flourspar and glass. Courtauld Institute Gallery, London.

JOSIAH WEDGWOOD

Hilary Young

The remarkable success of the potter Josiah Wedgwood (1730–95) can be attributed to a unique combination of personal qualities. Firstly, he had a rare grasp of the chemistry and physics of the potter's craft: this, and his passion for experimentation, led him to invent or improve a number of ceramic materials and glazes. Secondly, he was sensitive to shifts in fashion and he responded by introducing new designs and product lines, the excellence of which won him a leading place in the market. Finally, he possessed exceptional entrepreneurial skills and had the vision and daring to promote his wares in a bold and often innovative manner.

The crucial years were 1768–80, when he was in partnership with the cultivated Liverpool merchant Thomas Bentley, who introduced Wedgwood to a circle of antiquarians, architects and collectors. Under their influence he adopted the classical styles then becoming fashionable in interior decoration. These men allowed Wedgwood to copy designs from their books and antiquities and did what they could to promote his wares. Striving to make modern pottery in the revived classical taste, Wedgwood introduced new materials, notably Jasper and Black Basalt, and such novel pottery goods as vases, chimney tablets and portrait medallions. These were almost the first items made in English pottery that were intended to be viewed and valued as works of art.

42. *Sir William Hamilton*, about 1772. Modelled by Joachim Smith and made at Josiah Wedgwood's factory, Etruria, Staffordshire. Unglazed white stoneware. [h. 16.51cm]. VAM 275-1966.

43. Teapot, 1785–90. The reliefs designed by Lady Templetown. Made at Josiah Wedgwood's factory, Etruria, Staffordshire. Jasper with green dip and applied reliefs. VAM 414:1152&A-1885.

40. Volute krater vase, about 1785. Made at Josiah Wedgwood's factory, Etruria, Staffordshire. Black Basalt with 'encaustic' enamel painting. [h. 87.31cm]. VAM 2419-1901.

41. Punch bowl, about 1795. Made at Josiah Wedgwood's factory, Etruria, Staffordshire. Creamware ('Queen's Ware') painted in enamels. VAM 3229-1853.

Much of Wedgwood's success stemmed from his flair for marketing and publicity. Early in his career he capitalized on a royal commission to market his improved creamware pottery as 'Queen's Ware', realizing the importance of the correct connotations for his wares. Wedgwood marked his pottery with his name: this became accepted as a guarantee of high quality, enabling him to charge higher prices than his

45. *The Wedgwood Family in the grounds of Etruria Hall*, 1780. By George Stubbs. Oil on canvas. The Wedgwood Museum, Barlaston.

46. Dish painted with a view of the lake at West Wycombe Park, Buckinghamshire, 1773. Made at Josiah Wedgwood's factory, Etruria, Staffordshire, and painted at his decorating studio in Chelsea, London. From the 'Frog Service' made for Catherine the Great of Russia. Creamware ('Queen's Ware'), painted in enamels. VAM C.74-1931.

competitors. He opened exclusive London showrooms, where he entertained and cultivated the custom of 'shoals of ladies'. Here he held exhibitions of his finest work and most prestigious commissions, notably the 'Frog Service', made for Catherine the Great, and his copy of the Portland Vase. He consistently targeted above all the wealthy, believing that the 'middling sort' would follow the example of their 'betters'. Wedgwood was the first British potter to publish trade catalogues, which were issued in English and foreign-language editions. These helped him win huge export markets, which accounted for an astonishing 80 per cent of his business by the 1780s.

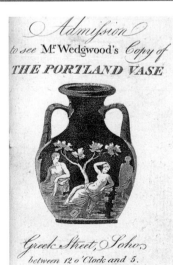

44. Ticket to the exhibition of the copy of the Portland Vase at Wedgwood's showroom, 1790. Engraving and aquatint. VAM 96.M.23.

Wedgwood and Boulton moved towards the antique style in the late 1760s, seeking ideas for new designs everywhere. Taking them from rivals was an old trick. Boulton visited London 'toyshops' and silver retailers and bought or had drawn what he saw. But copying cut both ways, and Boulton suggested that his proposed private London showroom should have curtained showcases to guard against spies or 'pimps' from Sheffield, Birmingham and London. Objects and works of art were also to be seen in private collections. In 1770, for example, Boulton waited on the Duke and Duchess of Northumberland. After drinking chocolate together, the Duke showed Boulton 'his great picture gallery and many of his curiositys. He made me sit down with him till 3 o'clock and talked about various arts.'

Both Boulton and Wedgwood bought or borrowed the all-important illustrated source books on antiquity. Wedgwood was particularly careful to cultivate 'the legislators of taste'. These included Sir William Hamilton, whom he flattered with a cameo portrait. Hamilton in turn responded by attributing the diffusion of 'a purer taste of forms and ornaments' to the products of the Wedgwood factory, modestly downplaying the effect created by his own collection of antiquities and its publication in 1766–7 in a book written by Baron d'Hancarville.

Noble clients could give access to architects, and vice versa. Wedgwood saw the importance of having fashionable architects as 'proper sponcors', regretting in a letter to his partner Bentley that 'we were really unfortunate in the introduction of our jasper into public notice, that we could not prevail upon the architects to be godfathers to our child'. Ideally, architects would also be directly involved in the design of products. A scheme in which the Adam brothers were to design Boulton's goods (and set up a London showroom together) unfortunately came to nothing. Sir William Chambers, however, designed Boulton's ormolu and James Wyatt formed a distinctive neo-classical style for his silver. An essential part of Wedgwood's design policy was the employment of skilled modellers, who included the young John Flaxman, later to become the leading sculptor of his generation.

But the ultimate impact of both Wedgwood's products and those of Boulton was the result of brilliant marketing. Assiduous courting of the nobility and gentry through direct contact and the establishment of showrooms and auction sales in London were matched by the production of printed catalogues of the firms' more ordinary products. Wedgwood's Etruria factory in Staffordshire and Boulton's Soho works in Birmingham were also promoted as fashionable and instructive tourist sights in their own right, attracting huge numbers of British and foreign visitors, who could buy the goods as well as see them made, assisted by the wonderful technology of water and steam power.

47

8. Shops and shopping

Boulton's and Wedgwood's showrooms, exhibitions and auction sales joined a rapidly increasing number of similar events drawing the London crowds, including museums of curiosities and art exhibitions, both temporary and permanent. Part of the general movement towards a more sophisticated polite culture, they became leading areas of taste promotion. Shops were increasingly significant. Since the late seventeenth century they had been becoming more fashionably decorated inside. At the same time glazed shop-window displays turned London's chief shopping streets into a major tourist sight, as a German visitor, Johanna Schopenhauer, observed in 1803: 'The brilliant displays of silverware, the beautiful draperies of muslin . . . behind large plate glass windows, the fairy-tale glitter of the crystal shops, all this bewitches the visitor.' Fashions, new styles and the products of a new breed of 'artistic manufacturer' were also brought to the public through fashion magazines and the first British style magazines. Among the latter was Rudolph Ackermann's *The Repository of Arts*, begun in 1809. As with such magazines today, it was

47 Painting on an ancient Greek vase. Plate from *Catalogue of Etruscan, Greek and Roman Antiquities from the cabinet of the Hon. W. Hamilton*, vol. I, by Pierre Hugues d'Hancarville, 1766–7. Coloured etching. VAM 64.G.44.

48 *Interior of the Shakespeare Gallery, London*, 1790. By Francis Wheatley. The gallery was created in 1789 to promote history painting, by exhibiting Shakespearean subjects and having them engraved. The fashionable crowd shown here includes the Dukes of York and Clarence, the Duchess of Devonshire and Sir Joshua Reynolds. Watercolour. VAM 1719-187.

49 *The Strand from the corner of Villiers Street, London*, 1824. By George Scharf. Watercolour over pencil with black ink. The British Museum.

48

49

Prince played a very active role: indeed, Porter said when taxed with overspending, 'I have not added or *branched* out into a single thing that was not plan'd by the Prince himself (not *me*).' Carlton House was demolished in 1827, but by then the chief royal residence had become Buckingham House, which was rebuilt as Buckingham Palace, with interiors richly decorated in a heavy Roman style. Every detail, said Nash, 'is the subject of a distinct drawing, submitted for previous approbation'. At Brighton, Holland built the Prince a classical 'marine pavilion'. The whole house was eventually converted into the Chinese style inside, with reconstructed exteriors in the Mogul manner. 'I do not believe that, since the days of Heliogabalus, there has been such magnificence and such luxury,' wrote the Princess Lieven. At Windsor, the Gothic style was adopted for furniture in the castle, which was comprehensively restored with new suites of state rooms and given the impressive silhouette that we see today. A simple lodge was also converted by Nash into a huge thatched *cottage orné*.

62

61

61 The Royal Lodge, Windsor, 1828. Designed by John Nash, built 1813–16. Hand-coloured aquatint. © The Royal Collection.

62 Model of the Marble Arch, London, about 1826. Perhaps after a wood and clay original model. Designed by John Nash and John Flaxman. The Marble Arch, now at the north end of Park Lane, was originally erected in front of Nash's Buckingham Palace. Plaster. VAM A.14-1939.

They actively publicized their royal link, not only at their shop in Ludgate Hill, but also on every piece they made, which bore their title, in Latin, as goldsmiths to the Prince and King. They became the biggest, most influential manufacturing goldsmiths in the country.

This firm clearly demonstrates the changes in status and practice of craftspeople and retailers, and the rising position of the applied arts since the mid-eighteenth century. An earlier goldsmithing firm like that of Paul de Lamerie was certainly innovatory in pioneering the rococo style in silver, but it did not make artistic claims for its products. Rundells, on the other hand, saw advantages in being artistic. As well as useful plate, they made pure art works, like the Shield of Achilles, John Flaxman's reconstruction of a famous ancient work described by Homer. Although this was a risky speculation, it certainly enhanced the status of the firm, as the reaction of the *European Magazine* testified on a visit to Rundells: 'It appears that, highly to the credit of the taste, discernment, and liberality of Messrs Rundell and Bridge, this has been entirely a speculation of their own.' Even in their more useful silver (the *European Magazine*'s 'many gorgeous and valuable articles'), the trend towards more sculptural design based on ancient forms demanded unprecedented levels of artistic skill in design and execution. Rundells responded by setting up their own design studio, headed for many years by the sculptor John Theed. In addition to Flaxman (who had worked for Wedgwood), it employed the sculptors Edward Baily and Sir Francis Chantrey, and the painter and book illustrator Thomas Stothard.

The Prince's collecting of paintings and *objets d'art* also had a profound influence on national taste. He led the trend away from the Italian Old Masters and Grand Tour objects of the past towards an interest in more modern French products, seventeenth-century Dutch painting and modern British art. His patronage also played a key role in encouraging the manufacture of British luxury goods. The most characteristic example was that of the royal goldsmiths, Rundell, Bridge and Rundell, who set about remaking and expanding the royal plate from 1806. Royal patronage had, of course, long been important to makers and retailers, but Rundells typified a new trend.

63 *The premises of Rundell, Bridge and Rundell, Ludgate Hill, London*, 1826. By John Clement Mead. The shop, designed by Mead, was built in 1825. Watercolour. Corporation of London.

64 The Shield of Achilles, with London hallmarks for 1821–2. Mark of Phillip Rundell. Designed and modelled by John Flaxman, and made by Rundell, Bridge and Rundell. © The Royal Collection.

10. Taste reform

Extremes of taste and fashion in the years around 1800 were matched by an unprecedented amount of criticism. While Jane Austen satirized the horrors of the Gothic novel in *Northanger Abbey*, brilliant caricatures by James Gillray and others linked the Prince Regent's stylistic excesses to his financial extravagance, his unpopularity and his immorality. The extraordinary performance of George IV's coronation in 1821, with its side-show of the excluded but popular Queen Caroline, only confirmed these notions. With typical royal attention to detail, the entire cast was clothed in historicizing dress, while the accoutrements were designed to match. The coronation helped to establish a fatal link between bad taste and immorality, which lay at the root of the design debates of the Victorian era. It was the last coronation on such a scale until the needs of Empire created another in 1911.

But the move towards design reform had begun some 20 years earlier in the work of Thomas Hope (whose London house is discussed in Chapter 7). Hope was a new kind of patron. Like Lord Burlington, he aimed single-handedly to influence and reform fashionable artistic taste, but his banking background and his very public methods reflected the shifts in the consumption of visual culture towards the ever-growing urban, business élite. Hope's interests encompassed literature as well as visual culture, from furniture and paintings to gardens and architecture. His London house at Duchess Street was a demonstration (open to the public) of his ideas in art, taste and decoration. In 1807 he published *Household Furniture and Decoration Executed from Designs by Thomas Hope*, illustrating the interiors and contents of the house (*see 7:44*). The illustrations alone would have made it a new kind of design book, but it was also accompanied by a polemical text setting out Hope's reforming manifesto on design and craftsmanship.

Hope's London house, the illustrations in his *Household Furniture* and *Designs of Modern Costume* (1812), which he inspired (*see 7:63*), were the main agents for the general adoption of the pure classical style during the Regency period. In the long term, however, it was Hope's text that was most significant, setting out, as his son Alexander wrote in 1862, ' . . . the idea of art-manufacture, of allying beauty of form to the wants and productions of common life'. By promoting craftsmanship, avoiding the excesses of the division of labour and by employing (according to Thomas Hope) 'the talent of the professor of the more liberal arts; the draughtsman, the modeller, the painter, and the sculptor', it would be possible to give not only 'new food to the industry of the poor, but new decorum to the expenditure of the rich'. The resulting rise in design standards would lead 'not only towards ultimately increasing the welfare and the commerce of the nation, but refining the intellectual and sensible enjoyments of the individual'. The continuing story of these ideas belongs in the Victorian era.

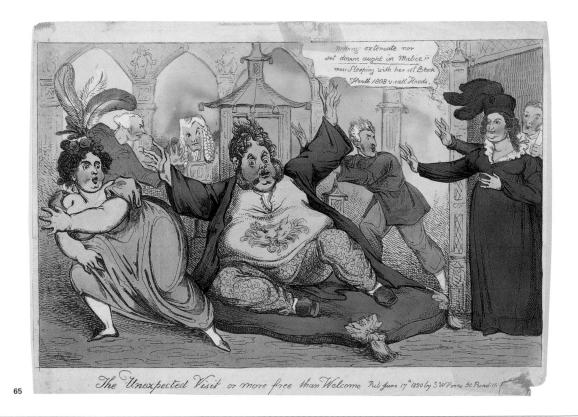

65

65 *The Unexpected Visit, or more free than Welcome*, 1820. By William Heath. The rejected Queen Caroline arrives in Brighton, surprising the Prince Regent and his mistress Lady Conyingham. Hand-coloured etching. Corporation of London.

66 *The Coronation Banquet of George IV*, 1821–2. By George Jones. Oil on canvas. © The Royal Collection.

CHAPTER 9

Georgian Britain, 1714–1837

Fashionable living

MICHAEL SNODIN

1. The spread of luxury

In 1771 Tobias Smollett, in his novel *Humphry Clinker*, looked back on a changed London. He did not like what he saw. 'In the space of seven years I am credibly informed that eleven thousand houses have been built in one quarter of Westminster . . . Pimlico and Knightsbridge are now almost joined to Chelsea and Kensington; and if this infatuation continues for half a century, I suppose the whole county of Middlesex will be covered with brick.' According to Smollett, 'the daily increase in this enormous mass' had been created by a single 'grand source of luxury and corruption' – the spread of the trappings and habits of elegant living from the nobility to the merchants and professionals of London, and thence to social ranks lower down:

> About five and twenty years ago, very few, even of the most opulent citizens of London, kept any equipage, or even any servants in livery. Their tables produced nothing but plain boiled and roasted, with a bottle of port and a tankard of beer. At present, every trader in any degree of credit, every broker and attorney, maintains a couple of footmen, a coachman, and postilion. He has his own town-house, and his country house, his coach, and his post-chaise. His wife and daughters appear in the richest stuffs, bespangled with diamonds. They frequent the court, the opera, the theatre, and the masquerade. They hold assemblies at their own houses; they make sumptuous entertainments, and treat with the richest wines . . . The substantial tradesman, who was wont to pass his evening at the ale house for fourpence half-penny, now spends three shillings at the tavern, while his wife keeps card-tables at home; she must likewise have fine clothes, her chaise, or pad, with country lodgings, and go three times a week to public diversions . . . The gayest places of public entertainment are filled with fashionable figures; which, upon inquiry, will be found to be journeymen tailors, serving men, and abigails [ladies' maids], disguised like their betters.

Smollett's attack on luxuries as both morally dangerous and socially destabilizing was an old refrain. In 1755, the time to which he was looking back, the newspaper *The World* had followed a similar line: 'Thanks to the foolish vanity which prompts us to imitate our superiors . . . every tradesman is a merchant, every merchant is a gentleman, and every gentleman one of the nobles. We are a nation of gentry.' These shifts in consumption were among the most characteristic features of the Georgian period, in which

2

the civilizing codes of gentility and polite living spread from the upper to the middling classes, and sometimes beyond. As Smollett suggests, the effects were to be seen in every aspect of life, from building to eating and drinking, from clothes to modes of travel, the last a significant cost item: maintaining an equipage of coach and horses could cost as much as running a helicopter today. It was not simply a matter of consumption, but of the closest attention to manners and deportment, as Lord Chesterfield made clear when writing to his son in 1751: 'take particular care that the motions of your hands and arms be easy and graceful, for the genteelness of a man consists more in them than in anything else . . . '

---

1 Detail of *A Millener's Shop. Mrs Monopolize, the Butcher's wife, purchasing a modern Head Dress*, 1772. Coloured mezzotint on glass. VAM E.620-1997.

2 *To Offer or Receive*. Plate from *The Rudiments of Genteel Behaviour: An introduction to the Method of attaining a graceful Attitude, an agreeable Motion, an easy Air and a Genteel behaviour* by François Nivelon, 1737. Engraved by Louis-Philippe Boitard after Bartholomew Dandridge. Engraving. VAM L.766-1876.

The chief arena for such manners, and of the increased sociability that they promoted, was the rapidly expanding and changing area of entertainment, both public and private. Greater sociability was especially linked to a progressive decrease in heavy formality. This applied to public areas such as Vauxhall Gardens, but also to the more private sphere, in which genteel activities like tea drinking (and the accompanying conversation) grew into an important social ceremony, while the noble ceremonials of formal dining tended to decline.

2. Changing spaces

In the private sphere, the demands of genteel sociability were closely reflected in house planning and furnishing. One of the key factors was the development of new forms of social gathering, in particular the 'assembly', which had both private and public forms. The early private assemblies were small and decorous affairs; in 1751 they were defined as a 'stated and general meeting of polite persons of both sexes, for the sake of conversation, gallantry, news and play'. By then, however, assemblies were sometimes being called 'routs' – 'a colossal

3 The music room from Norfolk House, London, 1748–56. Designed by the architect, Matthew Brettingham, Thomas Clark and Giovanni Battista Borra. V&M W.70-1938.

caricature of an assembly', involving dancing, conversation and cards. The lack of large enough rooms soon began to make itself felt, although in older country houses an existing room could sometimes be adapted as the desired 'Great Room'. At Temple Newsam House, Yorkshire, between 1738 and 1745, the seventh Viscount Irwin and his wife Anne altered, refurnished and redecorated the virtually derelict Jacobean Long Gallery in the latest neo-Palladian and rococo styles as a great room for company. The movable furniture consisted of 20 chairs, two settees, a daybed, two pier tables and eight candlestands. The fixed decorations were two pairs of pier tables, two wall sconces and 83 pictures.

In new country houses more radical solutions were possible: a case in point was the Palladian-style Houghton Hall, Norfolk, begun in 1722. Instead of adopting the linear baroque enfilade of multi-room apartments extending from one or two great state rooms, the plan of the first floor wrapped four 'apartments' around the great hall and saloon. Two of the apartments could be joined to the hall and saloon as public spaces. By 1731 one apartment included one of the earliest state dining rooms, not only ousting the hall or saloon as the setting for great dinners, but also starting a process of equalization in the status of rooms. In London, as the architect Isaac Ware noted disapprovingly in *A Complete Body of Architecture* in 1755, the solution was more difficult: 'In houses which have been some time built, and have not an out of proportion room, the common practice is to build one on to them: this always hangs from one end or sticks to one side, of the house . . . The custom of routs has introduced this absurd practice.'

A better answer came with Norfolk House in London's St James's Square. On the first floor the Duchess of Norfolk's state bedchamber and a dressing room, together with an ante-room, a music room, two reception rooms and a great room formed a circuit around the main staircase. The whole run was in use at the opening assembly in 1756. 'All the earth was there,' wrote Horace Walpole, 'you would have thought there had been a comet, everybody was gazing in the air and treading on each other's toes. You never saw such a scene of magnificence and taste. The tapestry, the embroidered bed, the illumination, the glasses, the lightness and the novelty of the ornaments and ceilings are delightful.' As the army captain William Farrington noted, 'Every room was furnished with a different colour, which used to be reckoned absurd, but this I suppose to be the standard.' The decorations were equally varied, with different ceilings and wall treatments and an 'entirely Chinese' dressing room, but apart from a general increase in magnificence in the great room, marked by its decoration with tapestries, the general aim was equality of use. Cards could be played in any room, and the dining tables and seating were equally movable.

4 The Picture Gallery, Temple Newsam House, Leeds, created 1738–45.

TAKING TEA

Rachel Kennedy

Tea was introduced to Britain in the mid-seventeenth century. Samuel Pepys noted the first time he encountered tea in his diary in 1660, describing it as 'a China drink of which I never had drank before'. Within a century the practice of 'taking tea' had become a widespread national custom.

It was not until the early eighteenth century that tea overtook coffee and chocolate as the nation's favourite hot drink. It became enormously popular for several reasons: it was easier to prepare than either coffee or chocolate; it could thus be served anywhere, from large social events such as public balls and concerts to more intimate gatherings among family and friends; above all, by the early eighteenth century it was cheaper than the alternatives.

At first, though, tea had been prohibitively expensive and only the very wealthy could afford to buy it. The tea paraphernalia or 'equipage' required to indulge in this pastime reflected the drink's early social exclusivity. Tea caddies, tea services, kettles and stands were made from expensive materials, such as silver, and were considered luxury items. Equipages were commissioned from leading craftspeople of the day and might be embellished with the owner's family crest or

5. *A Family of Three at Tea*, about 1727. By Richard Collins, possibly painted in Leicestershire or Lincolnshire. Oil on canvas. VAM P.9-1934.

6. Tea tray, 1743. Probably made in London. Tin-glazed earthenware. [diam. 35.5cm]. VAM 3864-1901.

7. Teawares, 1683–1731. From left to right: sugar bowl, with London hallmark for 1730–1. Mark of Edward Cornock. [h. 8cm]. Tea caddy, with London hallmarks for 1722–3. Mark of Bowles Nash. Tea bowls and saucers, about 1683–1722. Made in the Jingdezhen kilns in Jiangxi Province, China. Spoon tray, with London hallmarks for 1722–3. Teapot, with London hallmark for 1705–6. Mark of Simon Pantin (about 1680). Silver, and porcelain decorated in underglaze cobalt blue. VAM M.164-1939, M.180-1919, C.777-1910, C.778-1910, M.318-1962, M.172-C-1919.

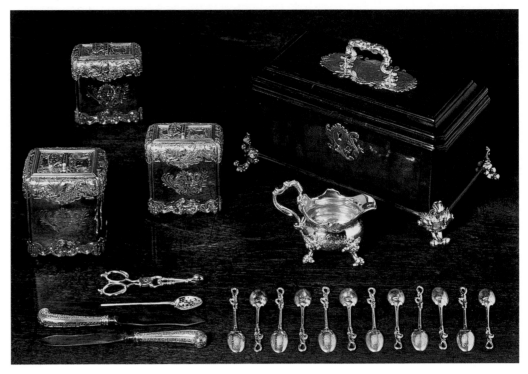

8. Tea equipage, with London hallmarks for 1735–6. Marks of Paul de Lamerie. Engraved with the arms of Jean Daniel Boissier and Suzanne Judith Berchere. Silver. © Leeds City Museums and Galleries.

9. Kettle, probably 1730–2. Made in London in the workshop of Charles Kandler for the banker Littleton Pointz Meynell. Cast, chased and engraved silver with basketwork handle. VAM M.49-1939.

10. Chelsea tea service, about 1759–69. Made at the Chelsea porcelain factory, London. Soft-paste porcelain and painted in enamel colours and gilt. Marrow scoop, 1748–9. Teaspoons, about 1730–80. Sugar nips, about 1750. Silver. VAM 517-522-1902, 144-1903, M.65-1910, M.39&41-1928, M.11-1976, 1118-1902, Circ.8386-1956.

coat of arms. Specialist tea wares were also imported from China and Japan. As tea became cheaper, British potters began to make tea wares in cheaper materials. In the second half of the eighteenth century tea drinking became universal.

By the start of the Georgian period the habit of taking tea had become particularly associated with women. Men tended to drink coffee in coffee houses. Collecting Chinese porcelain, of the kind imported into Britain for drinking tea, was already regarded as an especially female activity. But the association between women and tea may also have arisen because taking tea fitted so well with the new custom of visiting, which developed in the late seventeenth century, especially in London. Tea could easily be served by the mistress of the house herself to a group of female friends around a small, intimate tea table. So close was the link between women and tea during the Georgian period that the tea table itself came to be regarded by some writers as a symbol of unwelcome female power and influence. Several artists played with this idea, such as the caricaturist George Cruikshank, who portrayed tea-drinking women as dangerous gossips or 'slandering elves'.

11. *A Curious Junto of Slandering Elves*, early 19th century. Copy by an unknown artist after a caricature by George Cruikshank, from a drawing by E.H.L. Hand-coloured engraving. VAM E.501-1955.

3. Neo-Palladian planning

The Palladian notion of the *piano nobile* meant that the most important rooms at Norfolk House were on the first floor. The more everyday rooms on the ground floor included the Duke's bedroom and dressing room and the everyday dining and drawing rooms. The example of Norfolk House helped to free the log-jam of formal planning for both town and country houses. On constricted town-house sites, neo-classical architects like Robert Adam and Sir William Chambers devised ingenious sequences of grand public rooms, varied both in shape and decoration and precisely adapted to their role as a glittering setting for a nocturnal assembly or morning levee. Adam took particular credit for this development, noting that 'the parade, convenience, and social pleasures of life, being better understood, are more strictly attended to in the arrangement and disposition of apartments'. A key element was the staircase. Usually top-lit, it became a processional way to the great rooms above. In smaller urban houses the same precepts held, for they increasingly had to accommodate large social gatherings. The standard internal arrangement for terraced houses – two rooms and a closet on each floor – was adapted to fit the concept of the *piano nobile*. On the first floor lay the drawing room and sometimes the dining room, but the latter was more often on the ground floor. The hall and staircase that linked them often impressed foreign visitors by their neatness, relatively large size and carpeted stairs. Bedrooms, too, could be on the first floor and were often provided with closets or dressing rooms that functioned as more intimate social spaces.

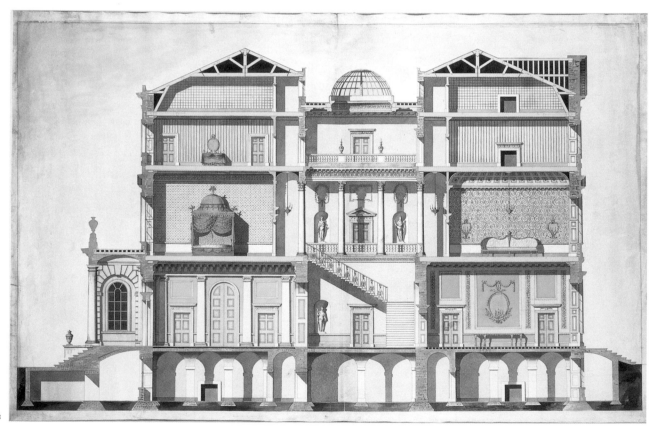

12 The staircase hall, Fairfax House, York, about 1755–62. Designed by John Carr of York for the ninth Viscount Fairfax.

13 *Design for a town mansion*, 1774. By John Yenn. Pen, ink and watercolour. © Royal Academy of Arts.

Central to the Palladian style was a hierarchy of decorative treatment. This stemmed from the notion of the classical orders, ranked in status, as described by Vitruvius and elaborated by Palladio and other Renaissance theorists. In a design for a town mansion by Chambers's pupil, John Yenn, the basement is Doric, the most primitive of all the orders. The entrance porch is Tuscan and leads into an Ionic hall. This connects with a top-lit staircase, in which a ring of Corinthian columns announces the *piano nobile* and the state bedroom and drawing room, or saloon, with its coved ceiling. A smaller house, lacking columns or pilasters, would express the same hierarchy in mouldings and ceiling heights.

Yenn's general decorative finishes reflect contemporary ideas on the appropriate treatments for certain types of room. The entrance hall is a grand introduction for the even nobler staircase. But as both places are not for lingering in, except by servants, their walls comprise plain plaster with minimal ornament. The great dining or eating room off the stairs is plastered in panels. The room's relatively austere stateliness reflects not only the concern that soft wall coverings absorbed food smells but also the idea that this was a male sphere. This was linked to the custom of drinking in the dining room at the end of dinner after the women retired to the drawing room. The dining room tended to become, by extension, the locus of family history, where silver and older portraits were displayed, and somewhere that changed less quickly with shifts in taste. The drawing room or great room, by contrast, came to be regarded as part of the feminine sphere. It was the seat of taste and fashion and the chief setting for large social gatherings. Yenn's drawing room announces its superior status with walls hung in patterned textiles and its feminine function with an elegant sofa.

Yenn's state bedchamber is less profusely decorated, but in reality such grand bedchambers were often elaborately furnished with textiles, with the curtains matching the bed hangings and the walls hung with tapestries or Chinese wallpaper. The attached dressing rooms, not shown by Yenn, were often just as richly and curiously decorated. They were the site of business or social meetings, which took place while the occupant dressed. Yenn's upper bedrooms, though better furnished than the servant's bedrooms in the attic, show that even in grand houses ordinary family bedrooms could be relatively modest in design.

4. Floors, walls and furniture

In 1749 the architect John Wood, who began Bath's transformation into the elegant city we see today, described the advances in furniture and furnishing that he had observed since the 1720s. His list of signs of modernity in a provincial context emphasized solidity, quality and expense: floors, made of the 'finest clean Deals or Dutch Oak Boards', were for the first time carpeted, while 'the Rooms were all Wainscoted and Painted in a costly and handsome Manner; Marble slabbs and even Chimney Pieces, became common; the Doors in general were not only made thick and substantial, but they had the best sort of Brass Locks put on them'. The furniture told the same story: 'Walnut Tree Chairs, some with Leather, and some with Damask or Worked Bottoms supplied the place of such as were Seated with Cane or Rushes.' Oak tables and chests of drawers were exchanged for mahogany or walnut ones, while 'handsome Glasses were added to the Dressing Tables, nor did proper Chimneys or peers [spaces between the windows] of any of the rooms long remain without Well Framed Mirrors of no inconsiderable Size; and the Furniture for every Chief Chimney was composed of a Brass Fender, with Tongs, Poker, and shovel agreeable to it'.

14 *Mr B. Finds Pamela Writing*, 1743–4. By Joseph Highmore, from a set of four scenes from *Pamela, or Virtue Rewarded* by Samuel Richardson, published in 1740–1. The room shown, though probably imaginary, has many of the features listed by John Wood in 1749. Oil on canvas. © Tate, London, 2001.

15 *The Lady's Last Stake*, 1759. By William Hogarth. The walls are hung with woven silk damask. Oil on canvas. [Overall size: 91.6 x 105.6cm]. Albright-Knox Art Gallery, Buffalo, New York. Gift of Seymour H. Knox, Jr, 1945.

16

Wood's insistence on the modernity of wainscot in 1749 would have surprised fashionable Londoners. Wainscot had been introduced to replace textile hangings; by 1750 it was itself being ousted in grander rooms by woven textiles, especially damasks, or their imitations in wallpaper. Wallpaper was becoming increasingly important. For two centuries it had imitated more expensive forms of wall covering, especially textiles. By the 1740s it was intensely fashionable, eventually displacing not only wainscoting but also moulded and modelled plasterwork. Much of its appeal lay in its high-quality colour printing, enabling it to match closely the surrounding curtains and upholstery.

As Wood's remarks show, a decoratively treated fireplace was relatively uncommon in ordinary homes until neo-Palladianism introduced standard types of chimneypiece. These not only provided an area for the display of ornaments, but also formed the decorative focus in standard room compositions. Elegant as neo-Palladian fire surrounds were, the grates remained very inefficient, although coal burning allowed for more attractive designs. Although cast-iron stoves were introduced to heat larger areas, it was not until the early 1800s that the Rumford grate, or 'stove', increased the efficiency of the ordinary fireplace.

5. From formal to informal

Wood's comments also indicate the arrival into more ordinary contexts of two features that had been developing in great houses for some 40 years: an increased use of soft seating and the introduction of sets of furniture of matched design, formally arranged. This not only emphasized the architectural character of room design, but also reflected changing room functions and social customs. Thus by the 1740s the spaces, or 'piers', between windows were often filled with mirrors and matching fixed pier tables. Seating, including chairs and sofas (the latter now more numerous than before), was arranged around the walls when not in use, set against the protective chair-rail. Tables were stored out of sight or against the wall when not needed.

Towards the end of the eighteenth century a new informality became evident in house planning and furnishing. This was partly the product of ideas of the Picturesque, which encouraged asymmetry and an easy connection between the interior of the house and the 'natural' park or garden outside. Humphry Repton, in his *Fragments on the Theory and Practice of Landscape Gardening* of 1816, used his famous before-and-after technique, and a verse, to illustrate the effects of the new informality. The 'cedar parlour's formal gloom' had become the new 'living room', 'where guests to whim, to task or fancy true/Scatter'd in groups their different plans pursue'. The ideal place for the principal rooms became the ground floor, 'so that you may instantly be outdoors', as Mrs Powys noted approvingly at Longford Castle in 1776.

17

16 Wallpaper from Doddington Hall, Lincolnshire, about 1760. Colour print from woodblocks. VAM E.474-1914.

17 *Mrs Congreve and her children*, 1782. By Philip Reinagle. The seating is arranged around the walls, except for the armchair, which is temporarily pulled up in front of the fire. Oil on canvas. National Gallery of Ireland.

In Jane Austen's *Persuasion*, the daughters of the house informalize the wainscotted 'old fashioned square parlour, with small carpet and shiny floor' through sheer activity, 'gradually giving the proper air of confusion by the grand piano forte and harp, flower-stands and little tables placed in every direction'. Such activities demanded light furniture of new types, like 'the nest of tables for ladies' described by Robert Southey in 1807: ' . . . you would take them for play things, from their slenderness and size, if you did not see how useful they find them for their work'. 'Quartetto' tables were part of a new range of multi-functional furniture, which had of course existed for a long time; the bureau-bookcase, a compact combination of bookcase, desk and chest of drawers, was an innovation of the first half of the eighteenth century. But the general increase in such furniture matched a heightened demand for elegant high-design goods intended for use in confined spaces.

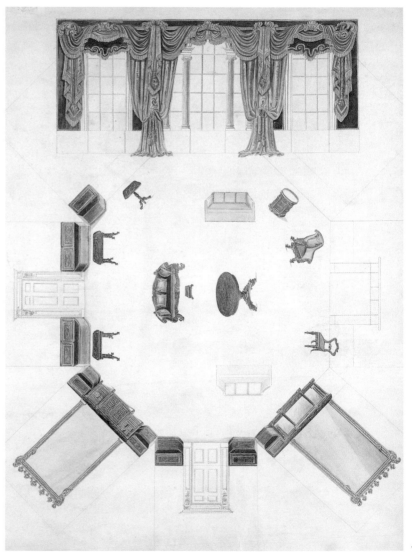

At Petworth House, Sussex, built in the 1690s, the state apartments were already on the ground floor. In the late 1770s the windows were lengthened, allowing direct access to a new terrace. With no *piano nobile*, all the bedrooms could be placed upstairs. In the extra space, the ground floor developed as a set of principal rooms with distinct functions. Many of the room-types were new, including breakfast rooms, billiard rooms and conservatories. Designs for their permanent furnishing show drawing rooms filled with comfortable, heavy sofas and tables and chairs, arranged in informal conversational groups, while dining rooms introduced massive permanent tables and monumental sideboards.

18 *The cedar parlour and the modern living room.* By Humphry Repton. Plate from *Illustrations from Fragments on the Theory and Practice of Landscape Gardening*, 1816. The transition from living room to exterior was eased by an attached conservatory. Aquatint. The British Library.

19 *Design for furnishing an octagonal drawing room*, about 1825. Made for Gillow & Co. Pen, ink and watercolour. VAM E.42-1952.

NORTHUMBERLAND HOUSE, STRAND : THE STAIRCASE.   [See p. 993, ante.

20

21

Meanwhile, in London's West End, a handful of great houses were being brought to a state of hitherto unparalleled opulence. At Northumberland House, in the early 1820s, especially large sums were spent on lighting, by then a key consideration, as dinners, routs and balls were all held after dark. At a more modest level, the shift from afternoon to evening dining was reflected in the widespread adoption of the previously unusual branched candlestick for the table. The need to increase the number of reflective surfaces also led to the insertion of mirrors and refractive glass wherever possible. At Northumberland House, £720 – about the annual income of a lesser-ranking landed gentleman – was spent on enriching the four gallery chandeliers with 64,000 'spangles etc'. While these were lit by candles, and other lights by oil, the two three-metre candelabra on the stairs (£2,000) were lit by gas, which had been introduced as street lighting in 1809. Especially valued for lighting factories and shops, gas was rare in domestic contexts until the 1840s.

20 A set of quartetto tables, about 1800. Rosewood, with green-stained legs. By courtesy of H. Blairman & Sons, Ltd.

21 *The staircase at Northumberland House, London,* fitted out in 1823. Illustration from *The Builder,* December 1873, engraved by F. George Williams after J. R. Brown. Wood engraving. VAM PP.19.G.

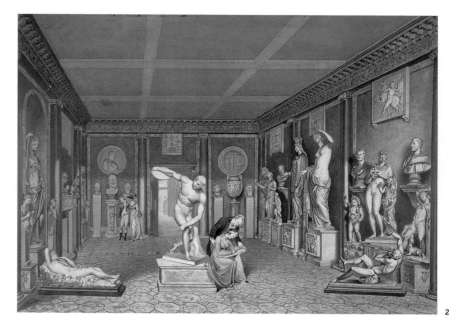

6. Special rooms for special needs: collecting art

Among the pictures in Lord Irwin's saloon at Temple Newsam in 1750 were the best of the 40 paintings bought in Venice in 1705 by his grandfather, 'to furnish my great rambling house'. Pictures had long adorned the walls of great houses, but they had been mainly portraits and their display was usually more dynastic and political than artistic in intention. Before 1700 collecting art for its own sake was a connoisseurial activity limited largely to the few who had been abroad, and especially on the Grand Tour. But with increasing numbers of people going on the Grand Tour, the collecting of Italian painting and ancient sculpture became an essential demonstration of taste, and their display a significant form of decoration in the grandest spaces of the neo-Palladian house. Those who had not travelled bought works through dealers or salerooms in London, which were singled out by William Hogarth and others as feeding an obsession with badly painted (and probably fake) Old Masters at the expense of modern British art.

The rising prestige of British painting and sculpture in the second half of the eighteenth century, and the study of the aesthetics of ancient art associated with neo-classicism, had an impact in both public and private spaces. Private sculpture galleries, largely inspired by Roman examples, were a case in point. One of the pioneering ventures, the Duke of Richmond's gallery of plaster casts at Richmond House, London, set up in 1758, was for the use of students. From 1774 the collector Charles Townley filled his London house with a great collection of antique art. The dining room was specially adapted for its display, the walls being set out with columns imitating porphyry. Galleries built specifically to take the spoils of the Grand Tour became a feature of country houses, like that at Newby Hall, Yorkshire, designed by Robert Adam, and the gallery at Woburn Abbey, Buckinghamshire, which culminated in a temple for Canova's *Three Graces*.

22 *Project for the decoration of the saloon at Houghton Hall, Norfolk*, 1725. By William Kent. Sir Robert Walpole's great picture collection was sold to Catherine the Great of Russia in 1779. Pen, ink and wash. Private collection.

23 *The Great Library, Cassiobury Park, Hertfordshire*, about 1815. By Augustus Charles Pugin. Figures engraved by Meyer, aquatint by F. Lewis. From *The History and description of Cassiobury Park* by John Britton, 1837. Etching and aquatint. Stapleton Collection.

24 *The Dining Room at Charles Townley's house at 7, Park Street, Westminster*, 1794. By William Chambers. Watercolour. The British Museum.

But owners could be fickle in their tastes. In 1771 the Earl of Shelburne, on a visit to Rome, decided to turn his projected music room at Shelburne House, in London's Berkeley Square, into a sculpture gallery. A design was commissioned, and the painter and antiquary Gavin Hamilton was contracted to dig up statues for the next four years. A year later the Earl changed his mind; the space was to become a library for his remarkable collection of books, manuscripts and other material. The shift is not as surprising as it may at first seem, for libraries, suitably decorated with busts of writers and other significant figures, had become an important demonstration of taste, growing from a private scholarly sanctum into a large and useful social space.

Sculpture galleries, too, served a social function: the gallery at Petworth House, formed in 1754–63, was frequently used for large dinners for the tenantry and local yeomanry. In 1824 a large top-lit picture gallery was added. Significantly only 24 of the pictures were Old Masters, the remaining 67 being modern British and American works, which were displayed alongside modern sculpture. The gallery's purpose was the serious display of art, and it borrowed many features from the Dulwich Picture Gallery, opened in 1811 as Britain's first public art gallery. In other contexts, notably the great London houses from about 1820, richly decorated picture galleries became the principal social room.

25

25 *The North Gallery, Petworth House, Sussex*, about 1827. By J. M. W. Turner. Watercolour and gouache. © Tate, London, 2001.

COLLECTING AND THE GRAND TOUR

Malcolm Baker

By 1730 a tour through France to Rome was already well established as part of a British nobleman's education. As well as allowing young men to complement their knowledge of Greek and Latin texts with first-hand experience of the monuments and antiquities of ancient Rome, a 'voyage to Italy' was seen as a progress through 'the common stages of the journey of life'. As the classical scholar Conyers Middleton put it in 1729, 'At our setting out through France, the pleasures that we find, like those of our youth, are of the gay fluttering kind, which grow by degrees, as we advance towards Italy, more solid, manly, and rational, but attain not their full perfection until we reach Rome.' Later in the century the tour extended as far south as Naples and the newly excavated sites of Pompeii and Herculaneum and attracted increasing numbers of men (and women) of more modest means.

Tutors as well as guide books were available to indicate what antiquities and works of art were to be particularly admired – whether

26. Cabinet, about 1743. Designed by Horace Walpole, perhaps in collaboration with William Kent, for his collection of miniatures. The figures on the top by James Francis Verskovis show the sculptor François Duquesnoy and the architects Andrea Palladio and Inigo Jones. The reliefs on the front, made in Rome by Andrea Pozzo, show classical subjects. The cabinet attributed to William Hallett. Veneered with padouk on a pine carcase with oak drawer linings, carved ivory plaques and figures. [h. 156cm]. VAM W.52-1925.

antique sculpture, the paintings of Raphael or the marbles being carved in the studios of contemporary sculptors. The Grand Tour served to consolidate and expand the canon of antique sculpture that was regarded as the height of aesthetic achievement for both connoisseurs and those many artists who flocked to Rome and Florence. Some major works were bought by the wealthy British, but as it became steadily more difficult to export such pieces, collectors made do with marble copies, plaster casts and even smaller-scale reproductions in ivory, which could be mounted in furniture made at home.

27. *Antonio Canova in his Studio with Henry Tresham and a Plaster Model for his sculpture of 'Cupid Awakening Psyche'*, about 1788–9. By Hugh Douglas Hamilton. Tresham, a painter and dealer, was in Rome accompanying Colonel John Campbell, who had commissioned *Cupid Awakening Psyche*. Pastel on paper. VAM E.406-1998.

28. *The Three Graces*, 1814–17. By Antonio Canova.
Carved in Rome for John, sixth Duke of Bedford.
In 1819 it was installed in a specially built Temple of
the Graces at Woburn Abbey, Bedfordshire. Marble.
[h. 173cm]. VAM A.4-1994.

29. *Edward Howard with
his dog, leaning against a
parapet overlooking the
Roman campagna*, 1764–6.
By Pompeo Batoni. Edward
Howard was the son of
Lord Philip Howard. Oil on
canvas. VAM W.36:1-1949.

Another way of importing antiquities was to
have them included in a portrait of oneself by
a fashionable Roman painter, such as Pompeo
Batoni; set in a neo-classical British interior,
this would serve as a record of a visit usually
made only once in a lifetime, and as a
demonstration of the owner's taste and
cultivation. British visitors took advantage of
the wealth of art in Italy – foreign as well as
Italian – to purchase and commission many
modern neo-classical works of sculpture and
painting, the most distinguished being
sculptures such as Canova's *Three Graces*.

30

7. Collecting and the antiquarian interior

Collecting was also taking place across a broader field. A key event was the publication in 1784 of *The Description of Strawberry Hill*, an illustrated account of Horace Walpole's villa in Twickenham. Walpole was the younger son of Sir Robert Walpole of Houghton. He had catalogued his father's great collection of Old Masters, but his own collecting interests went beyond art and classical antiquities, to ceramics, metalwork, arms and armour, enamels, *objets de vertu* and engraved portraits, often collected more for their associational or historical value than for their beauty. Except that it excluded natural history specimens, Walpole's collection was in a direct line of descent from the cabinets of curiosities and prototype museums of the previous two centuries – places that were, as he wrote, 'an Hospital for everything that is *singular*'.

Walpole's innovation was to combine his collection with his domestic environment. While some rooms were consistently thematic, most contained a mix of objects of widely differing origin, quality and date. In the Refectory or Great Parlour, the furniture included a remarkably forward-looking set in the

31

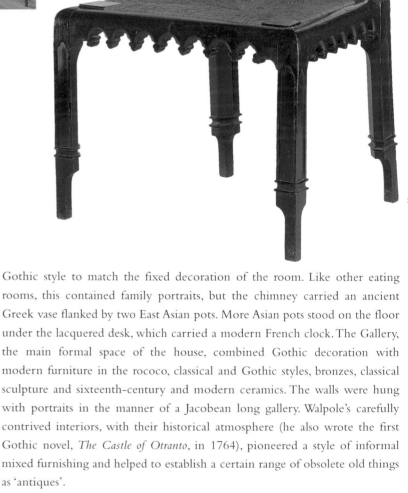

32

Gothic style to match the fixed decoration of the room. Like other eating rooms, this contained family portraits, but the chimney carried an ancient Greek vase flanked by two East Asian pots. More Asian pots stood on the floor under the lacquered desk, which carried a modern French clock. The Gallery, the main formal space of the house, combined Gothic decoration with modern furniture in the rococo, classical and Gothic styles, bronzes, classical sculpture and sixteenth-century and modern ceramics. The walls were hung with portraits in the manner of a Jacobean long gallery. Walpole's carefully contrived interiors, with their historical atmosphere (he also wrote the first Gothic novel, *The Castle of Otranto*, in 1764), pioneered a style of informal mixed furnishing and helped to establish a certain range of obsolete old things as 'antiques'.

30 *The Refectory or Great Parlour, Strawberry Hill*, 1788. By John Carter. Watercolour. Courtesy of the Lewis Walpole Library, Yale University.

31 Cravat, about 1690. By Grinling Gibbons. Walpole greatly admired the work of Gibbons, who carved lace as an exercise in virtuosity. The cravat was kept in the Tribune at Strawberry Hill. Limewood. [h. 24cm]. VAM W.181-1928.

32 Chair, 1755. Designed by Horace Walpole and Richard Bentley. Probably made by the firm of William Hallett, Senior, for the Great Parlour at Strawberry Hill. Beechwood, painted black to imitate ebony; modern replacement rush seat. The back formerly carried a finial. [h. 125cm]. VAM W.29-1979.

33 *The Antiquary's Cell*, 1835. By Edward William Cooke. To make the painting, Cooke collected material from antique dealers in London's Wardour Street and elsewhere. Oil on panel. VAM FA.42.

34 *The Gallery at Strawberry Hill*, 1781. By Thomas Sandby and Edward Edwards. Watercolour. VAM D.1837-1904.

DINNER PARTY OF FOURTEEN.

Plate I. First Course.

1.— Soup	5.— Tongue	A. Epergne	a. 2 Wine Glasses
2.— Fish	6.— Chickens	B. Wine Coolers	to each person
3.— Vegetables	7.— Asparagus	C. Water Carafts	b. Attendants, or
4.— Melted Butter	8.— Fish Sauce	D. Branch Candlesticks	Waiters

No Plates, or Wine Decanters are introduced to prevent crowding, they being

35

8. Special rooms for special needs: eating and drinking

For a member of the fashionable élite like Walpole, the term Great Parlour was probably used self-consciously to convey the idea of an old-fashioned great house. However, in the houses of the merely genteel, in both town and country, parlours performed the same function as the drawing rooms of the fashionable, although they had far less money spent on their furnishing and equipment than dining rooms did. In addition to a sideboard, a table and a set of chairs meant to last a lifetime, at least two sets of eating wares and utensils had to be provided. Elizabeth Shackleton of Colne in Lancashire, the widow of a landowner and now the wife of a merchant, divided her ware and equipment for eating and drinking clearly into 'common' and 'best', used in different combinations of utensils and spaces according to the occasion. Servants and tenants would eat in the kitchen on common ware, while superior tradesmen and -women, such as milliners and mantua makers, would be given tea in the parlour or dining room, but on the same common ware. Only guests of Mrs Shackleton's status, or above, used the dining room adorned with silver and laid with the best blue-and-white Chinese export dinner service on a damask tablecloth.

Increasingly genteel modes of eating and drinking were marked by a huge rise in the number of specialized vessels and utensils, as well as in the range of materials employed in their manufacture. Many of these new types were French in inspiration, following the fashion for service *à la française*, which required diners to help themselves or their companions to food already set out on the table. Of the new types of vessel, those introduced by 1730 included bottle coolers, tureens for soup and boats for sauce. By the end of the century a wide range of specialized smaller items had appeared, including dishes for pickle and asparagus, cruets for a new range of sauces and novel implements, from soup ladles to fish servers. New breakfast equipment included toast racks

35 *A dinner party of fourteen: The first course.* Diagram from *The Footman's Guide* by James Williams, 1840. VAM 215.D.65.

36 Wine cooler, with London hallmarks for 1727–8. Marks of Paul de Lamerie and Paul Crespin. Britannia Standard Silver. [h. 26.5cm]. VAM M.1-1990.

36

37

and egg stands. The custom of drinking after dinner, with the tablecloth removed, created the bottle holder or coaster, an item unknown on the continent. The most impressive object was the centrepiece, a complex structure that could be adapted to the main and dessert courses. Its decorative function was enhanced by the addition of either sugar or porcelain figures to the table, especially during the dessert course. By 1800 a mirrored stage-like plateau had been added.

The spread of genteel dining was greatly aided by the arrival of new materials. From the 1760s fused 'Sheffield' plate brought the look of silver to many tables, while the range of materials that was available for plates and other vessels was increased to include porcelain (either British-made or imported from China or the continent) and cream-coloured earthenware. This last material had the most profound effect on dining. Since the 1760s it had replaced, according to George Robertson in 1829, 'the old, clumsy Dutch delft-ware, and the more ancient pewter plates' at Scottish farmers' tables: 'being fully as cheap as any of those kinds of table service mentioned, . . . [it] was highly agreeable to the females of the house'.

38

37 Centrepiece, with London hallmarks for 1743–4. Mark of Paul de Lamerie. Given as a wedding present to Sir Roger and Lady Newdigate in 1743. It is here set up with dishes for the presentation of dessert. For the main course the central bowl served as a tureen and the branches supported candles. [h. 25.3cm]. Silver. VAM M.149-1919.

38 Top, from left to right: pewter plate, about 1760–1800. Possibly made in London by John Townsend and Thomas Giffen. Creamware ('Queen's Ware') plate, transfer-printed in black enamel, about 1780–90. Made at Josiah Wedgwood's factory, Etruria, Staffordshire. Bottom, from left to right: soft-paste porcelain plate, painted in underglaze blue, about 1780–90. Made at the Caughley porcelain factory, Shropshire. Soft-paste porcelain plate, painted in enamels and gilt, about 1773. Made at the Derby porcelain factory, part of a service sold to Philip Egerton of Oulton, Cheshire. Porcelain plate, decorated in overglaze enamels and gilt. Qing dynasty, about 1772. Made in China, the porcelain made at the Jingdezhen kilns and the decoration either added there or in Canton. VAM M.41-1945, 2302-1901, C.151-1921, C.23-1978, C.71-1932.

SPITALFIELDS SILKS AND THE SPREAD OF FASHION

Clare Browne

39. *Design for a woven silk,* **1708. By James Leman for his father, the master weaver, Peter Leman. Commissioned by the mercer Isaac Wittington. Watercolour. VAM E.1861.52-1991.**

During the later seventeenth century the European market for fashionable dress silks had been dominated by material from France. The developing English industry expanded to meet this competition. It was significantly helped by refugee Huguenot families, who contributed both textile skills and business acumen. Huguenots were among large numbers, both from within England and from abroad, attracted to the capital, and by 1700 the London silk industry had spread east from the City to Spitalfields. Until the 1770s there was almost continuous progress in its production, stimulated by a considerable export market and constant innovation in fashionable design.

The Spitalfields designers and weavers had to keep up with changes in fashion and technical advances in France in order to earn a share of the market, but English silks came to develop their own individual style. One of the leading designers in the early eighteenth century was also a manufacturer, James Leman. Born into a weaving family of Huguenot descent, he produced his own accomplished designs from his early years of apprenticeship to his father, and as a master weaver later commissioned them from other leading pattern drawers.

The silks designed and woven in Spitalfields in the middle years of the eighteenth century displayed a particularly English interpretation of the rococo style, with a realistic depiction of botanical details in flowers scattered across an open or subtly patterned ground, usually in an asymmetrical arrangement, and with clear, true colours. Anna Maria Garthwaite's designs from the 1740s epitomize this style. She worked freelance, selling her work to a number of the leading London mercers and master weavers for a period of 30 years. More than 800 of her dated silk designs survive, vividly illustrating the progression of fashionable taste in dress silks during those years.

40. *Lady Walpole Wemyss,* **1754. By Allan Ramsay. Oil on canvas. In the collection of the Earl of Wemyss.**

41. Silk dress fabric, 1749. Designed by Anna Maria Garthwaite for the master weaver Daniel Vautier. Brocaded silk. VAM T.192-1996.

42. Detail of a waistcoat, about 1734. Made from silk woven in Spitalfields, London. Silk brocaded with coloured silks and silver thread. VAM T.72-1951.

43. *Sir Thomas Kennedy of Culzean, 9th Earl of Cassilis*, 1746. By William Mosman. Oil on canvas. National Trust for Scotland, Culzean Castle.

The complex patterns and variety of surface effects achieved in the silks were fully exploited in fashions for both men and women. Satins, damasks, lightweight taffetas treated to achieve a high lustre (known as lustrings or lutestrings), heavier paduasoys and gros de Tours, cut and uncut velvets, tissues with different textures of gold and silver thread – all of these could be brocaded, or 'flowered', in brightly coloured silks or with more gold and silver for extra visual impact. Women's sack-back dresses with their pleated lengths of silk falling from the shoulders and men's long waistcoats, often the focal points of their outfits, allowed the intricate, balanced designs to be seen to full effect.

44. Detail of a sack-back gown, about 1755–60. Made from silk woven in Spitalfields, London. VAM T.426-1990.

9. Consuming taste

'Not Rachel, weeping for her children, could show more sorrow than Mrs Garrick,' wrote the actor David Garrick in 1775 to his influential friend Guy Cooper. 'Not weeping for her children for children she has none . . . What does she weep for then? It is for the loss of a chintz bed and curtains . . . she had prepared paper, chairs, etc. for this favourite token of Indian Gratitude.' A gift from 'the Gentlemen at Calcutta', the chintz was impounded by Customs under an Act of 1721 forbidding the import of Indian cottons. Eva Maria Garrick was unlucky, but such experiences were not unusual among people of fashion trying to import foreign luxuries, for fines or high duties controlled other luxuries, including French porcelain and furniture.

The Garricks were a fashionable couple, whose social and cultural circles ranged from the Duke of Devonshire to William Hogarth. Of relatively humble background and unencumbered by inherited goods, they were keen consumers of the latest fashions, from clothes to architecture, and avid collectors of books and modern paintings. In 1772 they took a London house in the best part of the new Adelphi development, beside that of its designer, Robert Adam, before the rest of scheme was completely built (*see 8:35*). The Adam interiors were matched by Chippendale furniture, while the movable goods included a remarkably large best tea and coffee set in the same fashionable style. Three years later Adam modernized the Garricks' villa at Hampton, further up the River Thames. Chippendale was probably again responsible for the suite for the chinoiserie best bedroom (which eventually received the troublesome chintz), combining imitation lacquer with the latest neo-classical styling.

46

45

47

45 Bed hanging, about 1775. The cotton made in a factory of the English East India Company at Masulipatam in Madras, India. Used by David Garrick and his wife for the principal bedroom of their villa at Hampton, Middlesex. Painted cotton. VAM W.70i-1916.

46 Tea and coffee service, with London hallmarks for 1774–5. Marks of James Young and Orlando Jackson. Commissioned by David Garrick and engraved with the arms of Garrick and his wife. Silver. VAM M.24-1973.

47 Robe and petticoat, 1760–5. Robe made in England of silk woven and painted in China. Owned and worn by Mrs David Garrick, née Eva Maria Veigel. Chinese painted silk. VAM T.593-1999.

48

50

49

48 Bergère chair, about 1772. One of a pair, supplied by Thomas Chippendale to Mr and Mrs David Garrick for their drawing room at No. 6 Royal Terrace, Adelphi, London. Painted beech; modern upholstery. [h. 96.5cm]. VAM W.41-1977.

49 Ceiling about 1772. Designed by Robert Adam, painted by Antonio Zucchi and possibly David Adamson. Removed from the drawing room of No. 6 Royal Terrace, Adelphi. Plaster and painted paper; the decorative parts partially restored after being painted over. VAM W.43-1936.

50 *David Garrick and his Wife by the Temple to Shakespeare at Hampton*, 1762. By Johann Zoffany. Oil on canvas. Yale Center for British Art, Paul Mellon Collection.

Mrs Garrick was not exceptional in taking charge of the furnishings at Hampton. Just as households at all social levels (except the very highest) were managed chiefly by women, so genteel women often took the leading role in choosing household furniture and furnishings, as they did other household goods. For Mrs Shackleton of Colne – self-consciously genteel, but lower down the social and fashion scale than Mrs Garrick – such choices may have stopped at the expensive suite of dining furniture that was ordered by her husband from the successful cabinet makers Gillows of Lancaster, but did include smaller, locally made pieces of furniture. At the top end of society the active role of women could include dealing directly with architects, as Lady Shelburne did with the normally dominating Robert Adam over Shelburne House: ' . . . with [Mr Adam] I consulted on the furniture for our painted antichamber, and determined that it should be pea green and satin spotted with white and trimmed with a pink and white fringe, it was entirely my own thought and met with his entire approbation'. On the other hand, it was with her husband that Lady Shelburne visited suppliers:

. . . we went first to Zucchi's, where we saw some ornaments for our ceilings, and a large architecture painting for our antichamber, with which, however, my Lord is not particularly pleased. From there to Mayhew and Inch [Ince] where is some beautiful cabinet work and two pretty glass cases . . . From thence to Cipriani's where we saw some beautiful drawings and crayon pictures and where Lord Shelburne bespoke some to be copied for me, to complete my dressing room . . . From thence to Zuccarelli's where we also saw some large pictures doing for us and from thence home it being half past four.

Outside the metropolis, learning about fashion and acquiring fashionable goods was a more complex business. Elizabeth Shackleton, like many genteel provincial consumers, used friends and relatives living in London to advise and act for her in the purchase of such items as tableware. London contacts, newspapers and a network of observant informants in the bigger northern towns, like York and Pontefract, kept her well apprised of the latest in fashionable dress. Such local centres had their own social calendars, some being

---

51 Trade card of Phillips Garden, working goldsmith and jeweller, about 1750. A man and a woman are shown shopping together at a fashionable London goldsmith's. Engraving. The British Museum.

52 Page from an album of textile cuttings and printed fashion sources put together by Barbara Johnson. At the top left is a cutting from a sack (a loose, tube-shaped dress) made for attending the races at Stamford, Lincolnshire, in June 1767. VAM T.219-1973.

linked, like London, to a 'season' (that at the spa of Tunbridge Wells occurred in the summer) or to regular events, like the races or the assizes, which naturally brought people together.

The London season, which ran from November to May, was set by the timing of the court and Parliament. Although by the end of the eighteenth century an actress like Mrs Abington could set tastes in fashionable dress, the key events in the London fashion calendar continued to be those associated with the court. Especially important were the balls and 'drawing rooms' marking the King's and Queen's birthdays, at which the dazzling clothes worn were described in great detail in the newspapers. The textiles used were just as closely observed as the changing cut and other details. In the case of silks, their patterns changed at least twice a year. Clothes worn at court were at the top of a carefully graduated scale of fashionable clothing divided into two main areas: the formal 'dress' and more everyday, although often no less elaborate, 'undress'. In addition there were special clothes for riding and various types of gowns and hats for relaxation. The cut and cloth of clothes, as well as hats, hair, wigs and accessories, announced the social position of the wearer, as Lord Chesterfield acidly observed: 'A gentleman is every man who, with a tolerable suit of clothes, a sword by his side, and a watch and snuff box in his pockets, asserts himself to be gentleman . . .'

While court dress became to some extent fossilized, retaining into the 1820s the very wide hoops of the 1750s, it shared a general tendency towards the informal. In the 1780s the relaxed lines of informal 'chemise gowns' found their way into women's 'undress'. At the same time, men's 'undress' was gradually taking on a new simplicity under the influence of everyday country riding and sporting wear. This culminated in the restrained elegance codified by George 'Beau' Brummell. His chief aim, according to his biographer, ' . . . was to avoid anything marked; one of his aphorisms being that the severest mortification that [a] gentleman could incur was to attract attention in the street by his outward appearance'. The result was a simplified form of men's dress with close-fitting coats and pantaloons, the immediate ancestor of the modern suit. While a small élite followed every seasonal shift in taste, the reaction of Mrs Shackleton and many like her was to resist the dictates of fashion by maintaining a middle course. But even for her, clothing was the element most subservient to changes in taste, with tableware coming next and furniture, which was expected to go on for a lifetime, last. The kind of sudden shift to genteel manners and consumption that became the common butt of metropolitan satire must have been extremely rare.

53

54

53 Mantua and petticoat, about 1740–5. English. This mantua was made to be worn over the very wide hoops characteristic of the mid-18th century. Silk embroidered with coloured silk and silver thread. [h. 170cm]. VAM T.260-1969.

54 *Farmer Giles and his Wife shewing off the daughter Betty to their Neighbours on her return from School*, 1809. By James Gillray, after an amateur. The drawing room of 'Cheese Hall' is fashionably decorated, while 16-year-old Betty's genteel accomplishments are much in evidence. Hand-coloured etching. VAM 1232(73)-1882.

PUBLIC ENTERTAINMENTS

Kate Newnham

The Georgian period saw the emergence in Britain of a new kind of public entertainment, the commercial pleasure ground. There, for a modest admission charge, visitors could promenade, listen to music and take refreshments. This new form of leisure brought people together in an environment expressly designed to promote gentility and politeness. There were 64 pleasure grounds recorded in London alone, the most successful of which – Vauxhall, Marylebone and Ranelagh Gardens – were imitated in towns across Britain and Europe.

Horace Walpole described Ranelagh when it opened in 1742. 'There is a vast amphitheatre, finely gilt, painted and illuminated, into which everybody that loves eating, drinking, staring, or crowding is admitted for twelvepence.' He remarked, too, on the unprecedented social mingling that took place, embracing the nobility and gentry as well as the various ranks of London's middle classes.

Of all the pleasure grounds, Vauxhall Gardens was the longest-lasting and the most famous. It was built on the site of the old 'Spring Gardens' on the south bank of the River Thames near Lambeth. The area of park and woodland had been open to the public since the 1660s, but had gained a dubious reputation. In 1728 the young entrepreneur

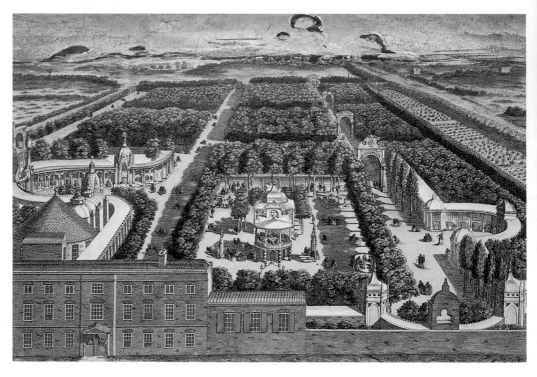

55. *A General Prospect of Vauxhall Gardens, shewing at one View the disposition of the whole Gardens*, 1751. By Johan Sebastian Muller after Samuel Wale. Hand-coloured engraving. VAM E.809-1903.

Jonathan Tyers bought the lease to the land, made improvements and reopened the pleasure grounds in 1732 as a more refined attraction. The high wall round the gardens and entrance gate enabled him to control the number of visitors and extract admission charges from them.

Each evening, from late spring to early autumn, two programmes of orchestral and vocal music were performed, with works by leading composers of the day, such as George Frederick Handel, William Boyce and Thomas Arne. On 21 April 1749 a crowd of 12,000 attended a rehearsal of Handel's *Music for the Royal Fireworks*, stopping the traffic for three hours. Between the programmes, visitors could explore the five hectares of gravel walks, pavilions and triumphal arches or take a meal in one of about 50 'supper-boxes'. The Irish writer Oliver Goldsmith wrote in 1760, 'I found every sense overpaid with more than expected pleasure; the lights every where glimmering through the scarcely-moving trees; the full-bodied concert bursting on the stillness of the night.'

56. *Vauxhall Gardens*, 1784. Madame Weischel singing to a crowd including Dr Johnson and the Prince of Wales. By Thomas Rowlandson. Watercolour. VAM P.13-1967.

59. *Interior of the Rotunda at Ranelagh*, 1754. By Antonio Canaletto. Oil on canvas. © The National Gallery, London.

58. *George Frederick Handel*, 1738. By Louis François Roubiliac. Made for Vauxhall Gardens. Marble. [h. 153.5cm]. VAM A.3-1965.

57. *The Milkmaid's Garland, or Humours of Mayday*. Painting for a supper box at Vauxhall Gardens, 1741–2. By Francis Hayman. Oil on canvas. VAM P.12-1947.

10. Public arenas

Christian Goede, a German visitor to London between 1802 and 1804, noted that in Bond Street, London's chief area for luxury goods, the foot pavement was 'so perfectly covered with elegantly dressed people as to make it difficult to move', while 'the gentlemen pass up and down the street on horseback so as to see and be seen'. Shopping was but one of a growing number of public cultural activities in which fashionable town dwellers could indulge, as Tobias Smollett made clear in his attack on the citizens of London. To his 'Court, the opera, the theatre, and the masquerade' should be added public assemblies, clubs, circulating libraries, exhibitions and pleasure gardens. As Goede's comments about the fashionable West End of London suggest, the regular planning of Georgian towns tended to encourage genteel sociability. In cities like London, Bath and Edinburgh, as well as smaller towns, the refined and unified appearance of the classical street façades was matched by the airy squares and crescents in which they were laid out. Such outdoor spaces had a definite social purpose. In London, according to Goede, the squares 'fill with ladies in morning dress, presenting lovely groups to the observation of the passengers'. After shopping, 'all the world hurries to Hyde Park' to promenade until about four or five in the afternoon, the end of the fashionable 'morning'. In smaller cities a 'town walk' sometimes served the same function. The chief purpose of these activities – both outdoor and indoor – was to observe, and be observed by, the fashionable. At indoor entertainments like the theatre this was made possible by lighting the auditorium as much as the stage.

As the eighteenth century advanced, the social rituals of the London season, with their emphasis on polite visual culture, were increasingly matched by similar

---

60 *Stand coachman, or the Haughty Lady well fitted*, 1750. By an unknown artist. The print depicts a traffic incident outside the toy shop of Mrs Chenevix at Charing Cross, London. Items of stock are shown carefully displayed in the shop's windows to catch the attention of the throng of passers-by, many of them well dressed. Engraving. The British Museum.

61 *A London Street Scene*, 1835. By John O. Parry. The array of posters exemplifies the huge range of sensational entertainment available at the end of the Georgian period. Oil on canvas. The Alfred Dunhill Museum and Archive.

experiences on country estates, with their neo-Palladian houses and their landscape gardens. Such gardens of the mid-century provided more fully developed versions of the mix of buildings and walks to be found in London pleasure gardens. Their circuitous paths, dotted with buildings and other convenient resting places, were intended to promote philosophical contemplation, as well as providing an opportunity for exercise and sociability. Later landscape parks, with their invisible sunk fences and artfully remodelled topography, drew the whole visible countryside into fashionable culture. Getting into the real countryside for reasons other than sport became for the first time a widespread genteel activity. But such cultural tourism was not restricted to the well-trodden round of picturesque sights. Between 1765 and 1775 Elizabeth Shackleton was far from unusual in setting out to see such modern wonders as the Leeds cloth hall, the new turnpike road and the locks on the Leeds to Liverpool canal.

62 *The Prospect Before Us*, 1791. By Thomas Rowlandson. A performance of the ballet *Amphion et Thalie* at the King's Theatre at the Pantheon, London. Hand-coloured etching. VAM Beard collection.

63 Detail of *Buckingham House, St James's Park*, 1790. By Edward Dayes. Hyde Park took over from St James's Park (and the Mall) as the principal place of fashionable parade in London. Buckingham House was acquired in 1762 as the royal family home. Watercolour. VAM 1756-1871.

CULTURAL TOURISM AND THE APPRECIATION OF THE NATIVE LANDSCAPE

Malcolm Baker

64. *A scene on the River Wye*, 1770. Plate from *Observations on the River Wye* by William Gilpin, 1789. By Francis Jukes. Hand-coloured aquatint. VAM L.1860-1914.

65. *The Ruins of Rievaulx Abbey, Yorkshire*, 1803. By John Sell Cotman. Watercolour. VAM FA.496.

The idea of Britishness entered public thinking during the eighteenth century and became defined in large part through contrast with the French. One expression of it was the cult of national heroes, such as Nelson and Wellington; another was a growing appreciation of Britain's native landscape. With the French Revolution of 1789 and subsequent wars with France, continental travel became more difficult and tourists began to enthuse about the scenery of Wales and the Lake District.

The tourist parodied by Thomas Rowlandson in his illustrations to William Combe's three

66. A Claude glass in its case, 1775–1800. Blackened mirror glass. [h. 21cm]. VAM P.18-1972.

volumes of tours by 'Dr Syntax', *Dr Syntax in search of the Picturesque*, *Dr Syntax in search of Consolation* and *Dr Syntax in search of a Wife*, stood for those many visitors who set out for these regions, keen to see antiquities and the remains of a national past and to record Britain's native scenery in their own drawings. A model was provided by William Gilpin's *Observations...Relative Chiefly to Picturesque Beauty*, which played a crucial role in forming a taste for the 'picturesque' landscape, with its qualities of roughness, irregularity and variety. One effect was to replace the idea of landscape as property with the notion of scenery as native land.

Amateur artists such as Lady Farnborough executed 'sketchbooks' with finished views of sites celebrated for their antiquarian or natural interest, often drawing with the help of a Claude glass (a tinted, curved mirror named after the painter Claude Lorraine), which concentrated the composition. Such images represent the British countryside seen through the eyes of an increasingly urban population at a time when the rural economy was in a state

67. *Dr Syntax drawing a waterfall at Ambleside.* By Thomas Rowlandson. Watercolour. VAM Dyce 813.

of flux. These same subjects also attracted the attention of professional artists, especially those like Thomas Girtin and John Sell Cotman, who developed the watercolour into a major and distinctively British genre suitable for ambitious compositions that were prominently exhibited at the Royal Academy. This tradition of British landscape painting reached its apogee in works such as John Constable's *Salisbury Cathedral*, which continues to epitomize a certain notion of Britishness. However, these were images of nature intended for exhibition to urban viewers – landscape as elevated public art.

68. *View of Arundel Church*, from a sketchbook with finished views of Sussex towns and villages, 1800–25. By Amelia Long, Lady Farnborough. Pencil and ink wash. VAM E.21080-1957.

69. *Salisbury Cathedral from the Bishop's Grounds*, 1823. By John Constable. Commissioned by John Fisher, Bishop of Salisbury. Oil on canvas. VAM FA.33.

N.º

72

73.

74.

75.

76.

77.

78.

79.

80.

81

82

83.

Card.
N.º 7.

Fine Martineques, 18 In.ᵉ 32 yds.
From N.º 63 to N.º 67.

CHAPTER 10

Georgian Britain, 1714–1837

What was new?

JOHN STYLES

1. The view from abroad

In 1784 François Lacombe, the author of a guide book for French visitors to London, listed 'the objects that no people can furnish in such a range and quality as the English', along with the goods that the English exported 'in profusion' to France, much 'to the shame of the ministry at Versailles'. The list was a long one, testimony to Britain's growing industrial might, especially as most of the goods could reach their customers in France only by being smuggled through French customs. It included a host of high-design products – cotton, woollen and silk textiles, decorative metal buttons and boxes produced in Birmingham, iron railings and grates, scientific instruments, clocks, furniture such as tea stands and mahogany tables, tin-glazed pottery and the new white earthenware, and even coaches.

1 Page of a textile sample book for the Spanish and Portuguese markets, 1763. Produced for John Kelly, a Norwich worsted manufacturer. The export of worsted dress and furnishing fabrics was very important to the textile industry in Norwich. This book is the 'counter-part', or matching copy, of one sent to Seville and Lisbon, where customers would order from the numbered samples. Worsted (wool) samples mounted on paper. VAM 67-1885.

2 An unknown man, 1780s. By John Russell. The man in this portrait wears a full complement of the steel buttons fashionable in the 1780s. Pastel on paper. VAM P.33-1952.

3 Snuff box, about 1765–75. Made in the West Midlands, probably Birmingham. Enamelled copper painted in colours on a green ground with raised dots and cartouches, in a chased gilt-metal mount. [h. 3.5cm]. VAM C.470-1914.

5 *Voiture Inversable*, 1782. Drawn by G. Robertson. Engraved by Peter Benazech. An advertisement in French for the non-overturning carriage invented by the British coach maker John March of Grosvenor Place, London. Engraving. VAM 19402.

The list demonstrates the vast improvement in Britain's reputation as a producer and exporter of quality manufactures that had taken place since the seventeenth century. At the same time it registers the wealth of innovation – in products, materials, manufacturing techniques and design – that transformed British manufactures during the Georgian era. Lacombe's list embraces many novel kinds of artefact, from cut glass to creamware dinner services. It also includes products – both old and new – that employed new materials, like mahogany or Turkey red dye; new techniques, like transfer printing or power spinning of yarn; and new design ideas, like those developed in the Staffordshire potteries or the coach-building workshops of London. Above all, the list reveals Georgian Britain's capacity for invention and improvement, a phenomenon that astonished, delighted and sometimes, as in Lacombe's case, disturbed foreigners.

This tide of innovation bears witness to profound changes in the ways things were made in Britain. In retrospect, our view of these changes has been dominated by the new steam engines and textile machines that, brought together within the forbidding walls of the factory, have come to define the Industrial Revolution for subsequent generations. Yet it was only in the 1830s

and 1840s that the notion of an Industrial Revolution, defined in this way, was developed. Even then, its currency was largely confined to continental European observers, concerned to analyse Britain's extraordinary economic success so that they could learn from it. It was they who coined the term 'Industrial Revolution', making an analogy between the social transformation wrought by the French Revolution on the continent at the end of the eighteenth century and what they regarded as an equivalent transformation wrought by the new manufacturing technologies invented in Britain at

4 Automaton clock made for the China trade, about 1780. By William Carpenter. Clocks like this one were mostly produced for the Chinese market. Clock case, mechanized figures and bells, made from gilt-brass with enamelled and glass paste decoration. [h. 88.9cm]. VAM M.1108-1926.

6 Cut-glass cruets in a cruet frame, with London hallmarks for 1789–90. Frame with mark of John Scofield. Silver-gilt frame with cast and engraved decoration; cut lead-glass cruets. VAM M.46-1960.

7 *Arkwright's Cotton Mills by Night*, about 1782–3. Painted by Joseph Wright. An atmospheric night-time depiction of the two water-powered mills erected by Richard Arkwright in 1771 and 1776 on the banks of the River Derwent at Cromford in Derbyshire to house his cotton spinning machines. Oil on canvas. Private collection.

the same period. The French economist Adolphe Blanqui wrote in an appropriately apocalyptic vein in 1837:

> Just as the French Revolution witnessed great social experiences of earth-shaking proportions, England began to undergo the same process on the terrain of industry. The end of the eighteenth century was signalled by admirable discoveries which were destined to change the face of the world and increase in an unforeseen manner the power of their inventors. The conditions of labour underwent the most profound alteration since the origin of societies. Two machines, henceforth immortal, the steam-engine and the spinning machine, overthrew the old commercial system and gave birth, almost at the same moment, to material goods and social questions unknown to our fathers.

Those Britons who lived through the period did not perceive these developments as an Industrial Revolution in the quite the way Blanqui did. This is not to suggest that they were blind to the manufacturing changes that were taking place all around them. On the contrary, they were obsessed with these changes. Indeed many, like the Luddite machine breakers, were violently hostile to them. For much of the Georgian period, however, those who wrote about innovation tended to treat it as something affecting a wide range of industries and processes, rather than focusing on the all-transforming effects of just two innovations, the steam engine and the spinning machine. The characteristic view was captured by the potter Josiah Wedgwood in 1766 when he wrote to a friend about 'the extensive capability of our manufacture for further improvement'.

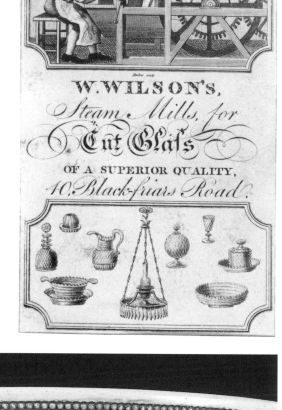

A glance at Lacombe's list of the most competitive British products indicates why the British tended to take a broad and inclusive view of the country's burgeoning industrial innovations. Published in a decade when the new textile machines were beginning to be introduced in some numbers and the first rotary steam engines were being installed, the list contains only three types of goods whose manufacture was to be fundamentally changed over subsequent decades by these particular technologies – cotton textiles, some types of woollen textiles and cast-iron railings and grates. This was because the range of industries transformed by the application of steam and powered machinery was narrow, confined principally to textiles and the production of raw iron. The other manufactured goods in Lacombe's list continued to be made by hand tools or hand-driven machines for the rest of the Georgian era and, in many cases, on into Victoria's reign. This was especially true of the more intricate, fashionable high-design goods. Their manufacture demanded a combination of great manual dexterity and frequent changes in specification, which often proved impossible to mechanize. The persistence of hand techniques does not, however, indicate a lack of innovation. In the case of almost all the hand-made products mentioned by Lacombe (as well as many other artefacts that he did not mention, including entirely new kinds of goods), hand making was itself profoundly changed by innovations in technique, materials and design.

8 Balcony from 12 John Adam Street, Adelphi, London, 1775. Designed by the Adam brothers and probably made by Carron Iron Co., near Falkirk, Scotland. Cast iron. VAM M.429-1936.

9 Trade card for the steam-powered glass-cutting mills of W. Wilson, Blackfriars Road, London, about 1807. Glass cutting was one of the few high-design manufactures to which steam power was applied, although much of the skill remained with the operator. Steam power facilitated deep cutting, but tended to limit the range of cutting styles. Engraving. Corning Museum of Glass.

10 Detail of a bowl, about 1770. Made at the Leeds pottery. The bowl depicts the process of hand throwing in a pottery factory. Turning the potter's 'great' wheel was traditionally a job for boys. Creamware with red enamel decoration. VAM C.22-1978.

2. The size and organization of manufacturing enterprises

Innovation in design and the decorative arts in Georgian Britain was predominantly market-driven. All the manufactured goods on Lacombe's list were produced by commercial firms. The pattern of innovation reflected the commercial opportunities identified by entrepreneurs and inventors and their capacity to use the ideas, skills and resources available in Britain to exploit those opportunities. Britain did not have the state-sponsored manufactories producing prestigious high-design goods that existed in a number of continental European countries, like the Gobelin tapestry works in Paris or the Meissen factory near Dresden in Saxony, where the European discovery of the secret of porcelain was applied for the first time.

This is not to suggest that other influences were unimportant. Innovation benefited in a variety of ways from the protection and encouragement of the British state. The state provided tariff barriers that protected British industries from foreign competition; ferocious laws against the export of machinery and the emigration of skilled workers; a patent system designed to ensure that inventors reaped their due rewards from their new ideas; and, in 1787, the first copyright legislation for design, which gave three months' protection to patterns for printed textiles. Innovation also benefited from a cultural milieu that encouraged the country's élite to take an active interest in scientific, technical and artistic improvement. It became fashionable to visit industrial sites, attend scientific lectures and art exhibitions, join philosophical societies and sponsor design competitions. Nevertheless, the main driving force propelling innovation in materials, techniques, products and design remained commercial profit.

Yet commerce had many faces. Understandably, our received image of commercial manufacturing during the Industrial Revolution tends to be dominated by the big cotton factory, with its hundreds of workers toiling to the rhythm of powered machines. But commercial manufacturing in Britain during the Georgian era was extremely diverse, both in its scale and in the ways that businesses were organized. There is little doubt that the largest industrial firms and their plant grew bigger. The application of the new powered technologies in iron works and textile mills accounts for a good deal of this increase in scale. The 85 largest Lancashire cotton mills in 1841 each employed 500 or more workers. Nevertheless, in most sectors of manufacturing the majority of enterprises continued to remain small. Even in 1841 nearly half of Lancashire's 975 cotton mills employed fewer than 100 workers. Elsewhere textile factories tended to be smaller still.

The small size of most businesses should not blind us to the growing scale of the web of commercial relationships that entwined them. Men like the independent village linen weaver, working up locally grown materials on an artisanal, jobbing basis for his neighbours, became fewer. Even the smallest manufacturing firms were enmeshed in chains of supply and demand that became ever more extensive. To secure both raw materials and customers they came to rely increasingly on the packhorse tracks, turnpike roads and canals that carried goods to every corner of Britain, and on the fleets of British

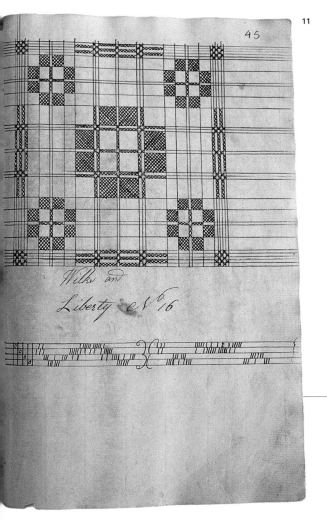

11

12

11 *Wilks and Liberty No. 16*, late 18th century. A design for a woven linen cloth drawn by the jobbing linen weaver Ralph Watson of Aiskew, near Bedale, North Yorkshire. From the book of designs compiled by Watson, which he circulated among his local customers to secure orders. Ink on paper. North Yorkshire County Record Office.

12 Printed cotton dress fabric, about 1790. Possibly designed by William Kilburn, one of the London-based designers of printed textiles who lobbied Parliament for copyright legislation in 1787. VAM T.84-1991.

merchant vessels that plied the sea routes to continental Europe and beyond. Increasingly, therefore, purchasers of manufactured goods were reliant on distant, anonymous suppliers. This trend was already well established at the start of the Georgian period and was noted by the author Daniel Defoe in 1726: 'Suppose the poorest countryman wants to be clothed, or suppose it be a gentleman wants to clothe one of his servants, whether a footman in a livery or suppose it be any servant in ordinary apparel, yet he shall, in some part, employ almost every one of the manufacturing counties of England, for making up one ordinary suit of clothes.' The same was true of the household furnishings of a country grocer's family: 'It is scarce credible to how many counties of England, and how remote, the furniture of but a mean house must send them; and how many people are everywhere employed about it.'

Large manufacturing enterprises had, of course, existed long before the emergence of the first water-powered cotton-spinning factories in the 1770s and after that date they were not confined to industries that employed the new powered technologies. There were many large firms that made goods with a high visual design content exclusively by means of hand techniques. In the silk industry of Spitalfields in London, for instance, where the finest patterned fabrics for men's and women's clothes were woven, some master manufacturers in the first half of the eighteenth century employed hundreds of hand-loom weavers. John Sabatier, one of the leading masters, recalled that he began 'to trade for himself in the year 1750, and then employed about fifty looms; that afterwards took a partner, and increased his looms to one hundred'.

Each loom required the labour of three or four workers. Many of these weavers were employed on piece rates in their own homes under the putting-out system, under which the master manufacturer retained ownership of the raw materials, but put them out to the employee to work up into a finished product. This form of organization was widespread and embraced more women workers than men. It was characteristic of the production of most textiles, including woollens, worsteds, linens and lace, and of the manufacture of ready-made clothes like stockings, shoes, hats and gloves. It was also widespread in many branches of metalworking, including watches, buttons, buckles and domestic utensils.

13 *Matthew Boulton's Soho Works*, about 1781. Aquatint. Birmingham City Archives.

14 *Woman spinning*, 1814. By George Walker. Etched by R. and D. Havell. Plate from *The Costume of Yorkshire* by George Walker, 1814. A woman spins by hand at the fireside in her home. Etching and aquatint. VAM 11.RC.F.19.

Equally large enterprises in the high-design sector were organized as single-site manufactories employing skilled hand labour. The new porcelain factories built in the 1740s and 1750s used little or no powered machinery, but employed hundreds of workers. Earlier, the tin-glaze potteries of Lambeth in London and of Bristol had employed similarly large numbers. In 1786 the London furniture maker George Seddon employed 400 workers in a building with six wings. Around Birmingham the larger workshops making japanned goods, buttons and other decorative metalwares employed 200 or 300 workmen in the 1760s. The largest of all, Matthew Boulton's Soho works, employed more than 600 people soon after it opened in 1766.

Large single-site manufactories like this aroused huge public interest in the eighteenth century, appealing to the taste among the educated for scientific knowledge and national advancement. High-design products were, however, most commonly made by producers working on a smaller scale. In some cases, like the Sheffield cutlery trade, goods of this kind were manufactured by individuals who ran independent businesses virtually alone – buying their raw materials, working them up in a workroom in their own houses, with the assistance perhaps of a single apprentice, and then selling the finished product to dealers who coordinated sales throughout Britain and beyond. But the scale of enterprise associated with high-design trades was typically somewhat larger than this, characteristically taking the form of a free-standing workshop, run by a master manufacturer employing waged workers and apprentices, who were usually numbered in single figures or tens, not hundreds. This sort of business was found in an enormous range of industries, from goldsmithing to coach building, from type founding to cabinet making. Workshops of this kind could be found in most major towns in Britain, but it was London that had the greatest concentration, despite a tendency for some high-design trades, such as cotton printing, to move away from the capital to the provinces.

15 *China Painters: The Painting Room of Mr Baxter, no. 1 Goldsmith Street, Gough Square*, 1810. By Thomas Baxter junior. Baxter senior was a painter and gilder who in 1797 set up a porcelain-decorating workshop in London, buying porcelain blanks directly from the manufacturers. The standing figure is Thomas Baxter junior; his father is the seated figure decorating a saucer. For the plate depicted in the foreground, *see 6:24*. Watercolour over pencil. VAM 782-1894.

16 *View of Mr Hatchett's Capital House in Long Acre*, 1783. By John Miller. This engraving depicts the workshop of John Hatchett, the coach maker, in Long Acre, London, the centre of the coach-building trade. Coaches can be seen on display inside the open street front of the workshop. Engraving. Corporation of London.

THE PRINTED ILLUSTRATED CATALOGUE

Helen Clifford

The origin of the printed trade catalogue lies in the engraved books of patterns produced in continental Europe in the sixteenth and seventeenth centuries. These were sources of ornament for use by makers of all kinds of high-design goods. Out of them developed publications like Thomas Chippendale's path-breaking *The Gentleman and Cabinet Maker's Director* of 1754, which served not just as a source of designs for other cabinet makers, but as an advertisement to wealthy customers of his cabinet-making business. Trade catalogues, by contrast, were intended for use by travelling salesmen and wholesale merchants, who acted as intermediaries between manufacturer and retailer. Their role became indispensable as high-design goods came increasingly to be made in long runs, according to a fixed range of pre-determined designs. In this respect, illustrated catalogues resembled the sample cards and swatches that textile manufacturers circulated in exactly the same manner. As with illustrated catalogues, textile samples showing the

19. Page from a catalogue of 'Queen's Ware' made by Josiah Wedgwood, Etruria, Staffordshire, 1774. Engraved by John Pye. Engraving. The Wedgwood Museum, Barlaston.

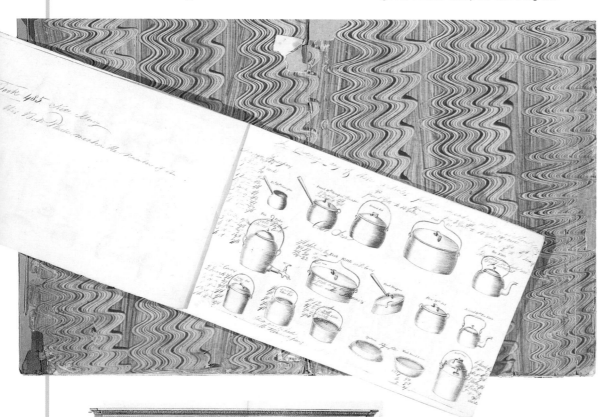

17. Front: page from a Birmingham iron-founder's catalogue, about 1810. Engraving. VAM E.124-1896. Back: binding of a catalogue of decorative furniture mounts, about 1770–80. Published in Birmingham. Marked 'HFils & B'. Marbled paper. VAM E.1038-1059-1899.

18. *Chimney-piece complete.* Page from a catalogue of composition ornament, about 1785. Engraving. VAM E.1483-1907.

range of designs that a firm could produce were sent out to distant wholesale customers, both in Britain and overseas. The firm's production schedule was then set up according to the orders received.

The first British printed trade catalogues were for metalwares, particularly brass, and seem to have emerged in the mid-1760s. Birmingham was the leader in brass production and it can be assumed that many of these early catalogues were connected with Midlands firms. But the range of products marketed by means of catalogues quickly expanded. Josiah Wedgwood produced his first 'Queen's Ware' catalogue in 1774. Catalogues were usually anonymous, because it was often in the interest of wholesale merchants to keep their sources secret; they were marketing tools in frequent, hard use, and it is rare for the original binding, like the one illustrated above left, to survive. The catalogue whose binding appears in this illustration reveals enough about its user – 'HFils & B' – to show that it was intended for a foreign market.

20. Commode with English brass mounts, about 1766. Made in Amsterdam by Andries Bongen. Oak veneered with rosewood and other woods. Courtesy of the Amsterdam Historical Museum.

21. *To Make a compleat Commode sett*, 1780–5. Page from a brass-founder's trade catalogue. Probably made in Birmingham. Engraving. VAM E.2324-1910.

Such catalogues reveal a great deal about the market for high-design goods and the ways in which visual information was transmitted. English catalogues were rarely coloured, unlike later French examples; and some were crude. Early printed Sheffield-plate catalogues were simply engraved versions of earlier hand-drawn designs. Some provided a full-sized image of the objects for sale, and occasionally these can be matched with surviving objects, like the brass corner mounts and escutcheons on a Dutch commode of about 1766. Many catalogues simultaneously illustrated objects in a variety of styles, from the rococo to neo-classical, to suit the widest possible range of consumer preferences.

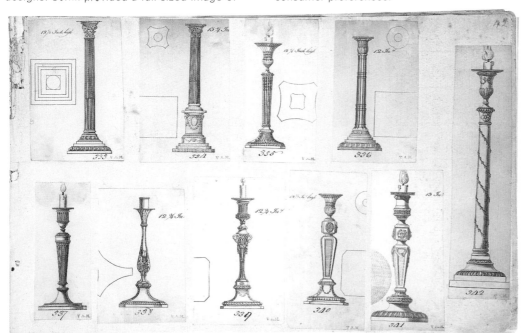

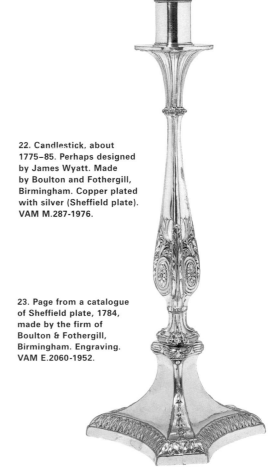

22. Candlestick, about 1775–85. Perhaps designed by James Wyatt. Made by Boulton and Fothergill, Birmingham. Copper plated with silver (Sheffield plate). VAM M.287-1976.

23. Page from a catalogue of Sheffield plate, 1784, made by the firm of Boulton & Fothergill, Birmingham. Engraving. VAM E.2060-1952.

3. Craft skill and the division of labour

Diverse though British manufacturing may have been in terms of the size of firms and the way they were organized, it did have a number of common features. Foreigners were especially alert to these. As Britain in the early Georgian years became an initiator of industrial innovation, rather than an importer of innovations from overseas, foreigners were attracted to discover the secrets of British industrial success. They identified a number of distinctive features of British manufacturing that seemed to make it so competitive. Among the characteristics most often mentioned were British inventiveness, British manufacturers' dedication to producing goods to high specifications for the middle and lower levels of the market, the use of coal as the prime source of heat for a host of manufacturing processes, the widespread application of labour-saving machinery (both hand- and power-driven) and the intensity of the division of labour between workers.

This last characteristic made a particular impact. Le Turc, a French industrial spy, reported in 1786 that 'there is no country where labour is so divided as here. No worker can explain to you the chain of operations, being perpetually occupied with one small part: listen to him on anything outside that and you will be burdened with error. This division is well-intentioned, thus resulting in inexpensive handwork [and] the perfection of the work.' Intense specialization of skills and work tasks was found throughout British manufacturing, but it was in the high-design industries in particular that the division of labour marked Britain out from her European neighbours. On the continent, guild regulations often insisted on a comprehensive training for skilled workers and imposed restrictions on the master manufacturers' ability to subcontract work to specialists. In London and other leading centres of high-design manufacture, guild regulation of the organization of production and the content of training was ineffectual by the Georgian period. The author of a review of the London trades recognized this in 1747 when he pointed out that:

> the goldsmith employs several distinct workmen, almost as many as there are different articles in his shop; for in this great city there are hands that excel in every branch, and are constantly employed but in that one of which they are masters. This gives us an advantage over many foreign nations in this article, as they are obliged to employ the same hand in every branch of the trade, and it is impossible to expect that a man employed in such an infinite variety can finish his work to any perfection, at least, not so much as he who is constantly employed in one thing.

As this description makes clear, there was a division of labour not simply within a single workshop, but between different workshops. Typical of the larger London goldsmiths was the firm of Parker and Wakelin, whose retail shop was in Panton Street, off the Haymarket in the West End. The firm operated a network of 75 subcontractors in the 1760s, most of them specialists in particular processes or in the making of specific types of object. What was true of goldsmithing was equally true of a host of other high-design trades, including those that made goods on a bespoke basis to individual customers' requirements, like the coach makers, and those that produced a limited range of products in batches to pre-set specifications, like the hatters. Subcontracting work outside the main workshop was the norm throughout the high-design sector, especially in London. It provided access to skills that were not required frequently enough to justify employment of a full-time specialist worker in the master's workshop. It also enabled masters to limit their own manufacturing activities or even to become pure retailers, while still handling a wide range of product types.

24

24 Tea canister, about 1765. Mark of John Parker and Edward Wakelin. This canister was sold through Parker and Wakelin's shop, but making it was the work of their subcontractors. James Ansill and Stephen Gilbert supplied the silver cubes for the tea tubs, as well as the cast finials; William Lestourgeon provided locks and lead linings; Robert Clee engraved them; Edward Smith made mahogany cases, when required. Silver, engraved, with applied castings. VAM Lonsdale: Loan:84.

25 Set of 12 plates depicting the division of labour in the manufacture of porcelain, 1813. From *The process of making China. Illustrated with twelve engravings, descriptive of the works of the Royal China Manufactory, Worcester*, 1813. The booklet was published by permission of the owners of the Royal Worcester Manufactory 'for the information of youth'. Engravings. VAM 60.S.145.

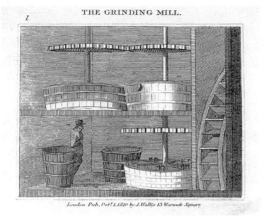

THE GRINDING MILL.

London Pub. Oct. 1.1810 by J.Wallis 13 Warwick Square

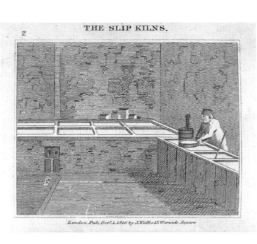

THE SLIP KILNS.

London Pub. Oct. 1. 1810 by J.Wallis 13 Warwick Square

TEMPERING THE CLAY.

London Pub. Oct. 1.1810 by J.Wallis 13 Warwick Square

FORMING ON THE WHEEL.

London Pub. Oct. 1.1810 by J.Wallis 13 Warwick Square

TURNING.

London Pub. Oct. 1.1810 by J.Wallis 13 Warwick Square

MODELLING.

London Pub. Oct. 1.1810 by J.Wallis 13 Warwick Square

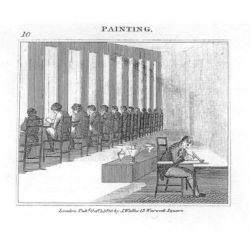

THE BISCUIT KILN.

London Pub. Oct. 1.1810 by J.Wallis 13 Warwick Square

DIPPING OR GLAZING.

London Pub. Oct. 1.1810 by J.Wallis 13 Warwick Square

THE GLAZE KILN.

London Pub. Oct. 1.1810 by J.Wallis 13 Warwick Square

PAINTING.

London Pub. Oct. 1.1810 by J.Wallis 13 Warwick Square

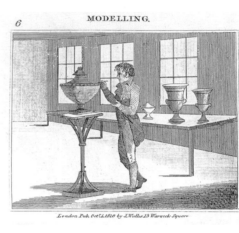

ENAMELLING KILN.

London Pub. Oct. 1.1810 by J.Wallis 13 Warwick Square

BURNISHING.

London Pub. Oct. 1.1810 by J.Wallis 13 Warwick Square

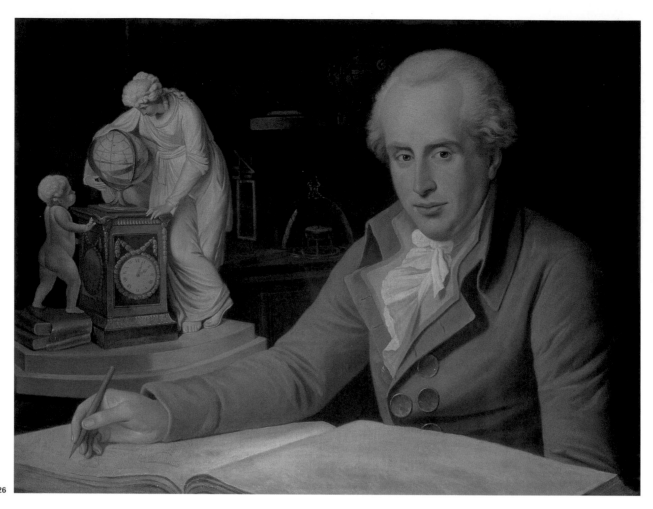

26

We often assume that the masters of Georgian workshops personally made the fine objects we now associate with their names. But famous individuals like Paul de Lamerie in goldsmithing or Thomas Chippendale in furniture making should be regarded first and foremost not as master craftsmen but as master manufacturers – entrepreneurs who organized production. When their businesses were at their height they can have handled – let alone crafted – very few of the large numbers of objects they sold that we now associate with their names.

Individuals like these may have played a part, often a key part, in designing the goods they sold, or at least in selecting and authorizing their design. Nonetheless, the work of hand crafting each object fell to a chain of specialist workers, each of whom was dedicated to the efficient execution of a limited task and was not necessarily under the master's direct supervision. Under these circumstances, determining the look of the object – its design – became one more specialist process. In most of the high-design trades it was not the creative work of an individual multi-skilled artisan who designed and made an object from start to finish.

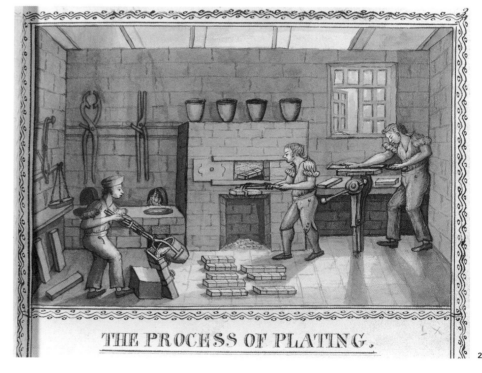

27

26 *Benjamin Vulliamy*, about 1790. By an unknown artist. Vulliamy is pictured in his shop in Pall Mall, next to one of the sculptural clocks he sold from the 1780s. He was best known as one of London's leading clock and watch makers at the end of the 18th century, but his firm also supplied ornamental plate, silver goods, other ornamental metalwares, diamonds and pearls. The firm's records show that most of the manufactured goods he sold were produced by subcontractors. Oil on canvas. Worshipful Company of Clockmakers.

27 *The Process of Plating*, 1830–2. Drawing in a manuscript by R. M. Hirst, 'A short account of the founders of the silver and plated establishments in Sheffield', 1830–2. The drawing depicts the making of Sheffield plate. Left: copper ingots being cast. Centre: silver sheets being fused to copper ingots in an oven. Right: ingots being filed. Ink on paper. Sheffield City Libraries.

4. New materials

New materials were crucial to the burgeoning success of the high-design manufactures in Georgian Britain. They enabled manufacturers to make an ever-widening range of products, especially those produced to high specifications for the middle and lower levels of the market, a phenomenon that struck foreigners as being distinctively British. One such material was pinchbeck, an alloy of copper and zinc invented early in the eighteenth century that looked like gold, but at a fraction of its price. It was named after its inventor, Christopher Pinchbeck, a London watch and toy maker, and was much used for watch cases and jewellery. Sheffield plate, a fusion of silver and copper discovered in 1742, was another. It is a particularly impressive example, because objects made from Sheffield plate were visually indistinguishable from a huge range of pure-silver objects three or four times their price.

In the seventeenth century innovation in materials had often been a matter of import substitution – discovering how to make things that had previously been made abroad and imported into Britain. This process continued during the Georgian period, most prominently in the case of porcelain, where a whole new British industry was developed from the 1740s and seized much of the domestic market for this most prestigious of high-design products, from east Asian and European imports. But new materials continued to flow from overseas, particularly from the world beyond Europe as British trade and imperial conquest flourished. Mahogany – by the later eighteenth century the quintessential British furniture timber – is a prime example.

At the start of the eighteenth century British furniture makers were already very dependent on imported raw materials, especially walnut, then the most highly prized decorative timber. Mahogany grew extensively in the West Indies, including Jamaica, which became a British colony in 1655. Before the 1720s, however, hardly any mahogany was imported. Yet by 1792 mahogany worth nearly £80,000 and weighing about 7,000 tonnes was being imported into England annually and it had become the dominant timber used to make fine furniture. Imports of walnut had virtually ceased. Mahogany had a number of practical and stylistic characteristics that made it attractive. It was available in sizes large enough to make the dining tables that became an increasingly prominent feature of British high-style interiors. It could take the high polish required to show off table silver. It carved well, developed a deep, dignified colour and had the allure of the exotic.

However, mahogany's phenomenal success was not simply a matter of the wood's intrinsic qualities or the result of a change in public taste. It owed as much, if not more, to the economics of transatlantic shipping and the imperatives of government colonial policy. Crucial was the passing of the Naval Stores Act of 1721, which allowed West Indian timber to be imported free of duty, in order to improve the profitability of transatlantic shipping. This Act made it worthwhile for mahogany to be carried on ships returning from the West Indies to Britain when alternative, more lucrative cargoes were unavailable. The concerns of furniture and furniture makers played no actual part in this decision. It was simply a case of imperial economics shaping innovation in taste.

28 Sheffield plate dessert spoon, about 1800. The silver on this spoon has worn to reveal the copper underneath. Copper plated with silver. [l. 22 cm]. VAM M.47-1992.

29 Mahogany tripod tea table, 1737–8. Probably made in London by Frederick Hintz. The scalloped edges were designed to protect the tea wares, and the hinged top meant that the table could be placed flat against the wall when not in use. Mahogany with inlaid brass and mother of pearl. VAM W.3-1965.

PORCELAIN

Hilary Young

Although porcelain had been made on the continent for almost half a century, Britain did not succeed in making it until about 1745. The first factories were established at Chelsea, Limehouse and Bow in London, but many others followed soon after 1750. It is clear from the sudden birth and expansion of the industry that the possibility of making this white-bodied translucent ceramic material aroused an enormous amount of interest in mid-eighteenth-century Britain.

The earliest English wares were not true (or 'hard-paste') porcelains, but were imitations ('soft-pastes') made with a variety of ingredients in place of china clay and china stone. Bow's recipe included bone ash, which resulted in a tough, utilitarian material; Worcester used soaprock, which enabled exceptionally fine potting; other factories, such as Chelsea, made glassy-bodied wares suitable for light or ornamental use. It was not until 1767–8, at Plymouth, that an English factory succeeded in making hard-paste. Movement of workers and industrial espionage soon ensured that potting technologies spread from one factory to another.

30. Vase, about 1760–5. Made at the Chelsea porcelain factory, London. Soft-paste porcelain, painted in enamels and with tooled and burnished gilding. VAM C.8-1996.

33. Scent flask, about 1749–59. Made at the factory of Charles Gouyn, London. Soft-paste porcelain, painted in enamels, with gem-set gilt-metal mounts. VAM 2000-1855.

31. Salt cellar in the form of a crayfish and shell, about 1752–6 (Chelsea factory mark between about 1752 and 1758). Possibly modelled by Nicholas Sprimont, the design first made in silver by Sprimont in 1742–3 and repeated at his Chelsea porcelain factory, London, after 1745. Soft-paste porcelain, painted in enamels. [h. 5cm]. VAM C.73-1938.

32. Dish, about 1765. Made at the Bow porcelain factory, London. Soft-paste porcelain, transfer-printed in brown and painted in enamels. VAM 414:59/A-1885.

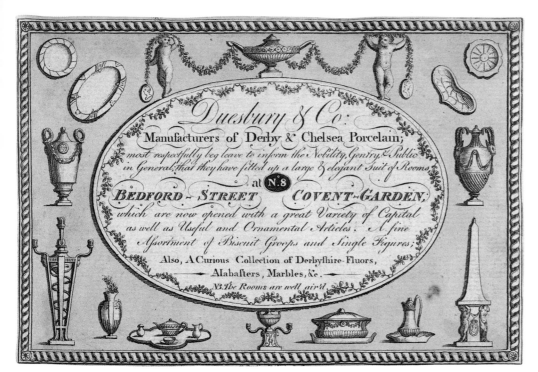

34. Trade card of Duesbury & Co., manufacturers of Derby and Chelsea porcelain, London, about 1775. Hand-coloured engraving. VAM E.1638-1907.

35. Figures of shepherds. Left: about 1750, modelled by Johann Joachim Kaendler and made at the Meissen porcelain factory, Germany. Hard-paste porcelain, painted in enamels and gilt. VAM C.147-1931. Right: about 1754, made at the Bow porcelain factory, London, imitating Meissen. Soft-paste porcelain, painted in enamels and gilt. VAM C.144-1931.

Much English porcelain was painted in cobalt blue before glazing, in the manner of imported Chinese wares; this was a relatively cheap method of decoration. Porcelain was also decorated by painting over the glaze in enamels (metallic oxides in a glassy medium) and by transfer printing. Both techniques were new to the English ceramic industry. Transfer printing was invented in Birmingham around 1750; at its best it allowed high-quality decoration at a low cost per unit. It involved printing an image on to a sheet of paper or gelatin, which was then used to transfer the design to the ware. Gilding was painted and fired-on, and at Chelsea it was often elaborately tooled in the manner of the French royal factory at Sèvres.

36. Plate, about 1755. Made at the Bow porcelain factory, London. Soft-paste porcelain, painted in underglaze blue. VAM C.595-1924.

Pottery figures had long been made in England, but the porcelain figure of the second half of the eighteenth century was a new and distinct ceramic genre. The conventions adopted for English porcelain figures were taken largely from Meissen figures, and many early English figures and wares were in fact directly copied from Meissen examples. After about 1760 Sèvres set the fashions for English porcelain luxury wares. Chinese blue-and-white wares were also copied throughout the second half of the eighteenth century, particularly for cheaper lines. There was no copyright protecting ceramic designs during this period and English factories did not hesitate to plagiarize the patterns of their rivals.

But in the Georgian period more and more new materials came to be invented in Britain. Often invention was a matter of chance. It was while repairing a knife handle that Thomas Boulsover, a Sheffield cutler, found that copper and silver fused under pressure, the key discovery that led to the creation of Sheffield plate. Much invention proceeded by a process of trial and error, developing recipes for dyestuffs or metal alloys in a manner more akin to cookery than modern laboratory science. Nevertheless, the rage for scientific enquiry among a broad, educated public did encourage the application of systematic techniques to the process of innovation. One of the most prominent exponents of such techniques was the Staffordshire potter Josiah Wedgwood, who believed that 'everything gives way to experiment'. During the 1750s, while still in his twenties, he embarked on a series of experiments to 'try for some more solid improvement, as well in the *Body*, as the *Glazes*, the *Colours*, and the *Form* of the articles of our manufacture'. These experiments resulted first in the development of a fine, transparent green glaze and in improvements in the variegated wares that imitated natural stones.

Next, in the late 1750s, Wedgwood turned his attention to improving the lead-glazed creamwares that had been invented in Staffordshire in the 1730s, combining a white English stoneware body and a lead glaze. His improved creamware was to be immensely influential, not least because of his own inspired marketing and the patronage of Queen Charlotte. By the early nineteenth century creamware made by the Wedgwood firm and other potteries had become the standard ceramic material for tableware among the middle and upper ranks of British society. Wedgwood went on, in the 1760s and 1770s, to develop more new or improved stoneware bodies. These

37 Tureen, cover and stand, about 1790–5. Made at Josiah Wedgwood's factory, Etruria, Staffordshire. Creamware ('Queen's Ware'), painted in enamels. VAM 344-1854.

38 Tea canister, cover and bowl, probably early 1760s. Probably made in Staffordshire by Josiah Wedgwood or Thomas Whieldon. Cream-coloured earthenware, with a green and orange-yellow lead glaze. VAM Schr.II.295.

39 Plate from *Designs for Sundry Articles of Queen's or Cream-Colour'd Earthen-Ware, Manufactured by Hartley, Greens and Co. at Leeds Pottery,* published in Leeds, 1794. The pattern book of the creamware products of the Leeds Pottery, one of the leading firms producing creamware for British and overseas customers in the 1790s, with title-pages and descriptive lists of the contents in English, French and Dutch. Engraving. VAM 96.A.41.

included black basalt and jasper, intended for use in ornamental pieces in the new neo-classical style, such as vases, plaques and portrait medallions. Perfecting jasper required thousands of meticulously recorded experiments, as well as the development of a specialized kiln and a thermometer to measure kiln temperatures. Wedgwood's life-long commitment to a systematic, experimental approach towards innovation was recognized in 1783 when he was elected a Fellow of the Royal Society.

41

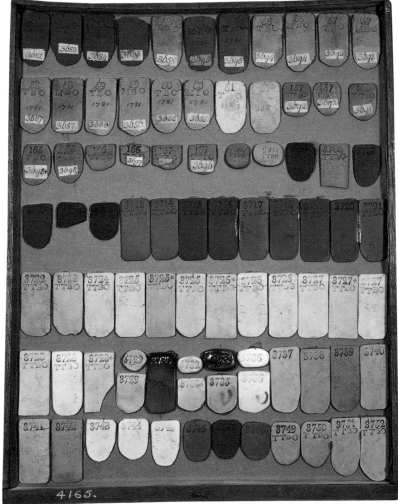

40

5. New techniques

It was innovation in the way things were made that had the greatest impact on foreign visitors to Britain during the Georgian era. They identified two features of Georgian manufacturing as especially distinctive. The first was the use of coal, and its derivative coke, in virtually the whole range of industrial processes where heat was required, from the refining of metals to the firing of pottery kilns. For continental Europeans, familiar with the use of wood or charcoal for such purposes, this seemed odd, especially as coal was notorious for containing noxious impurities that could easily damage delicate, expensive materials. Readily accessible coal deposits were relatively rare on the continent, but coal was abundant in Britain. Its use freed British manufacturers from reliance on limited and increasingly expensive supplies of timber fuel.

In the course of the Georgian period it also became clear that coke allowed the processing of basic materials on a much larger scale, and therefore more cheaply, than was possible with charcoal. The development of huge blast furnaces for converting iron ore into pig iron, like those built at the Cyfarthfa works in Merthyr Tydfil in the 1790s, would have been impossible without the use of coke. Smelting iron ore with coke only became widespread after 1750, allowing a huge increase in the production of cast-iron grates and other decorative ironwares. But the initial breakthrough in iron smelting with coke had been made by Abraham Darby at Coalbrookdale in Shropshire in 1709 and it is important to remember that iron was almost the last of the major metals to be converted to smelting with a coal-based fuel. The application of coal and coke firing to the smelting and refining of copper, lead, brass and a host of other materials used in high-design manufactures had already been completed during the century before the accession of George I in 1714, principally by means of the reverberatory furnace, which separated the fuel

42

---

40 Tray of Josiah Wedgwood's jasper trials, about 1773–6. Each trial piece is marked with a number that corresponds to an entry in Wedgwood's 'Experiment Book'. Jasper trial pieces, mounted in a wooden tray. Wedgwood Museum, Barlaston.

41 Buckle with a jasper plaque, about 1780–90. Cut steel and jasper. VAM M.3-1969.

42 *Cyfarthfa Ironworks*, about 1795. By Julius Caesar Ibbetson the Elder. Men working hot iron at the Cyfarthfa ironworks, Merthyr Tydfil, south Wales, one of the largest ironworks of the period. Watercolour. Cyfarthfa Castle Museum and Art Gallery.

43

44

and its impurities from the material. The fact that this innovation began to excite the general attention of overseas commentators only in the Georgian period is testimony to the novelty of foreign interest in British manufacturing.

The second characteristic of Georgian manufacturing that foreigners picked out was the widespread use of labour-saving machinery. Specialist machinery combined with an intense division of labour could cut costs, not just by increasing output per worker, but also by simplifying tasks so that at least some processes could be taken over by lowly paid child or female workers. At the same time, the use of machinery ensured much greater consistency in the quality of the finished product. These features of British manufacturing were already stimulating foreign admiration well before the invention of the powered textile machines of the second half of the eighteenth century. The French priest Jean-Bernard le Blanc pointed out in 1747 that:

> England has more than any other country of those machines so useful to the state, which really multiply men by lessening their work; and by means of which one man can execute that which would take up thirty without such assistance. Thus by turning a wheel, a boy of ten years old gives a hundred things of steel, all at the same time, that beautiful polish, which few of our French workmen can imitate.

Labour-saving machinery was not confined to the metal trades. New hand-powered mechanical devices proliferated in textiles, too, from the flying shuttle invented by the Lancashire reedmaker John Kay in 1733, to speed up weaving, to the improvement to the stocking frame enabling it to knit ribbed stockings, patented in 1758 by the Derbyshire farmer Jedediah Strutt. Ironically, some of the much-admired hand machines and devices used in the Birmingham light-metal trades for making buttons, buckles, small boxes and other decorative

items were already in use throughout Europe in mints, particularly mills for rolling metal into sheets, and fly presses and dies for stamping ornament on to soft metals. In a number of continental countries, including France, their use outside the mint for commercial purposes was restricted to safeguard the integrity of the coinage. Britain imposed no such restrictions, despite the circulation of distressingly large quantities of counterfeit coin, and such machinery was progressively improved and elaborated. Of course, not all labour-saving innovations involved machines, whether hand- or power-driven. Transfer printing, a hand technique invented in the early 1750s, did not require elaborate machinery. Nevertheless, it enabled highly sophisticated engraved decoration to be reproduced at a very low cost per unit, providing an alternative to the labour-intensive process of individually painting each object.

43 Hob grate, about 1790. Cast iron with steel fire grate. VAM M.424-1936.

44 Transfer-printed enamel plaques of the Gunning sisters: Elizabeth, Duchess of Hamilton and later Argyll, and Maria, Countess of Coventry, probably 1752. Transfer-printed decoration probably engraved by John Brooks after 1751 pastel portraits by Francis Cotes. Transfer printing was probably first developed in Birmingham around 1751. It was initially used to decorate enamelled plaques like these. The technique rapidly spread to other centres for the decoration of ceramics and enamels. White enamel on copper, transfer-printed in black with some overpainting also in black; gilt-metal frames. [h. 14cm]. VAM 414:1410-1885, 414:1411-1885.

If the extensive employment of labour-saving machines excited foreigners' attention throughout the Georgian period, it was powered machinery that came to dominate foreign perceptions of British manufacturing by the later Georgian years. The focus of attention was the power-driven machinery developed to spin cotton. This is not surprising. Although this chapter has emphasized that steam power and powered machinery had only a limited direct impact on the making of most Georgian high-design goods, their effect on the manufacture of British cotton textiles was immense. The two initial inventions in spinning, based on different principles, were made in the 1760s – the spinning jenny, invented by James Hargreaves, a hand loom weaver from Oswaldtwistle in Lancashire, and the water frame, invented by Richard Arkwright, a barber and wig-maker from nearby Preston.

The first cotton spinning factories relied on water, horse or, in the case of the spinning jenny, human muscle power, but from the 1790s the largest urban cotton mills began to install the new rotary steam engines invented by the Scot, James Watt. Power spinning brought about a massive reduction in the price of cotton cloth, which underpinned the astonishingly rapid growth experienced by the cotton industry in the late eighteenth century. By the early nineteenth century cotton textiles had overtaken woollen textiles – the traditional British staple – as the largest single manufacturing industry. Moreover, despite the fact that the weaving and finishing branches of cotton manufacture were still not completely mechanized at the end of the Georgian period, the earlier innovations in spinning had already transformed their production and reduced the cost of almost every type of cotton fabric, from plain coarse sheeting to the finest patterned cloths. As a result, during the late eighteenth and early nineteenth centuries cotton garments tended to replace many items of clothing made from linen, silk and wool in the wardrobes of rich and poor alike.

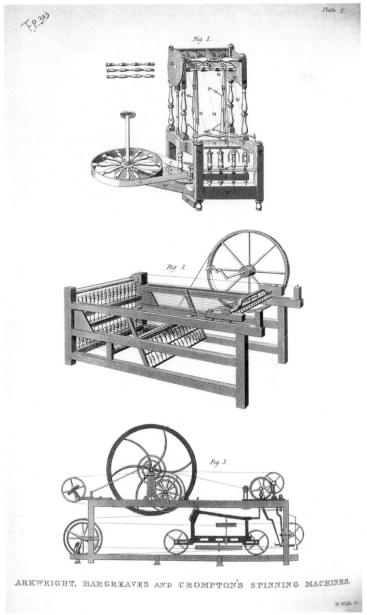

ARKWRIGHT, HARGREAVES AND CROMPTON'S SPINNING MACHINES.

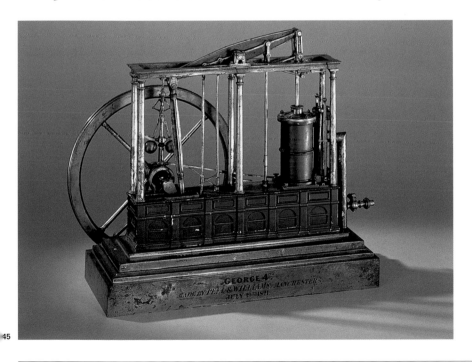

45 Model of a beam engine, 1821. Made by Peel and Williams of Manchester for the coronation of George IV. This model of a stationary steam engine incorporates the separate condenser and governor invented by James Watt. The linear motion of the piston is translated into a rotary motion, enabling engines of this kind to power factories. Iron and steel. [h. 41cm]. Science Museum, London.

46 *Arkwright, Hargreaves and Crompton's Spinning Machines,* 1857. Engraved by W. Willis. Plate from *History of the Worsted Manufacture in England* by John James, 1857. From top to bottom: Richard Arkwright's water frame of 1769; James Hargreaves's spinning jenny of 1764; Samuel Crompton's spinning mule of 1779. Engraving. VAM 43.E.8.

PRINTED TEXTILES

Clare Browne

By the mid-eighteenth century woodblock printing on cotton and linen textiles had developed to a high standard, even though the home market was affected by legislation protecting the silk and wool industries. The dyeing techniques used to produce the strong, fast colours on imported Indian chintzes, which had dazzled European customers in the seventeenth century, had been mastered and colour ranges were further developed with the introduction of 'pencilling' of indigo in the 1730s and 'china blue' by the early 1740s. A commentator on the state of British textile arts in 1756 wrote, 'chintz...can imitate the richest silk brocades, with a great variety of beautiful colours'.

Until this time, textile printing from engraved metal plates was restricted to the use of non-washable printers' ink. Francis Nixon from Drumcondra in Ireland was the first manufacturer to adapt the technique so that a mordant or dye could be printed from copper plates. He was advertising 'printed Linens, done from Metal Plates (a method never before practised)' in Dublin in 1752, and by 1757 he had brought the technique to England, joining in partnership with George Amyand at Phippsbridge in Surrey. Fine engraved designs on a large scale were now possible, and with the outstanding results that the technique achieved it was quickly adopted by textile printers around London. For the next 30 years plate-printed furnishings of high quality in terms of both design and production were manufactured at printworks like Bromley Hall. The standard of woodblock cutting also continued to be refined, achieving a crispness of detail that could realize the fine drawing of designers such as William Kilburn.

47. Page from a pattern book of printed textile designs, 1760–1800. From the factory run by members of the Ollive, Talwin and Foster families at Bromley Hall, London. The design taken from illustrations by William Kilburn in *Flora Londiniesis*, by William Curtis, 1777. Impression on paper from a copper plate. VAM E.458-1955.

48. Cuttings of dress fabrics, including printed cottons, 1780–1. From an album of textile cuttings and printed fashion sources put together by Barbara Johnson, 1746–1822. VAM T. 219-1973.

49. Furnishing fabric, 1803. Designed by I. Pincott. Printed at Bannister Hall, Lancashire. Block-printed cotton. VAM T.556-1997.

51. Furnishing fabric, 1770s. Printed by Nixon & Company, Phippsbridge, Surrey, using a copper plate engraved by Henry Roberts, originally for John Collins at Woolmers, Hertfordshire, 1765. Cotton, plate-printed in china blue. VAM T.612-1996.

52. Furnishing fabric, 1769. Made by Robert Jones & Co., Old Ford, London. Linen and cotton, plate-printed with additional colours added by block-printing and pencilling. VAM T.140-1934.

In 1783 a patent for printing from engraved metal rollers was taken out by Thomas Bell. The technique was initially confined to small patterned dress prints, but its potential for reducing labour costs and speeding up production was developed in the early nineteenth century, particularly in Lancashire. By 1815 roller printing was being used for larger-scale patterns, both furnishings and dress, alongside woodblock-printed chintzes, which had continued in popularity.

Chemical discoveries were also contributing to the change in appearance of printed textiles, whose colours had previously been achieved with vegetable dyes. Resist and discharge printing were developed and mineral colours were introduced, such as Ilett's single green – the first solid green available to British printers – and chrome yellow. In different combinations the new dyes and processes were fully exploited and incorporated into the increasing mechanization of the industry.

50. Furnishing fabric, 1818. Printed by Samuel Matley and Son, Hodge, Cheshire. Roller-printed cotton using Ilett's single green. VAM Circ.248-1956.

53. Detail from a design for printed cotton, about 1790. By William Kilburn. Body colour. VAM E.894-1978.

Power spinning triumphed even in the manufacture of fine muslins. At the start of the 1780s, as part of a general shift towards simpler styles in dress, muslin became fashionable for women's gowns and accessories. It was the most prized and expensive cotton fabric of the period, capable of the soft, light, flowing drape required for the styles of women's gown that predominated from 1780 to 1820. In the early 1780s almost all the muslin used in Britain was supplied from India by the East India Company. Muslin was woven from exceptionally fine yarn, but neither British hand spinners nor the new spinning machines could produce the degree of fineness regularly achieved by Indian hand spinners.

The invention of the spinning mule changed all this. The mule, invented in 1779 by Samuel Crompton, a jenny-spinner from Bolton in Lancashire, and so-called because it combined elements from the spinning jenny and the water frame, could spin exceptionally fine yarn. Initially hand machines (like the

54 *Lady Elizabeth Foster*, 1784. By Angelica Kauffmann. The sitter wears a muslin chemise dress. Oil on canvas. The National Trust, Ickworth House.

55 Muslin dress, about 1800. Fabric woven in India, dress made up in England. Through their cut, drape and colour these dresses made deliberate reference to the costume of classical Greece and Rome. Muslin embroidered in cotton thread. VAM T.785-1913.

spinning jenny), mules were being driven by water and steam power by the 1790s to produce ever-finer yarns. British-made muslins woven from mule-spun yarn began to drive out lower-quality Indian imports in the 1780s. In 1788 the East India Company reported, 'we are convinced however successfully the [British] manufacturers may have imitated the goods of the lower descriptions, that they will still find it very difficult to combat the high estimation in which our fine goods are held'. The Company was wrong. By the early nineteenth century the British could compete with the highest-quality Indian cloth. Rudolf Ackermann's *Repository of Arts*, the bible of high fashion, noted in 1810 that 'the improved state of the British manufacture of muslin goods, has, for some time, enabled many persons to substitute British for India, and so well have they been imitated, that even many inexperienced vendors themselves have not been able to distinguish them whilst new. From these combined causes, for two or three years past, the Indian goods have sunk in the estimation of the public.'

6. New products

Intimately linked with innovations in materials and technique was a proliferation of new high-design products. Sometimes their novelty amounted to little more than minor variations in established product lines, intended to satisfy the public appetite for novelty or exploit a new fashion. Others, like creamware pottery, transfer-printed ceramics and copper plate-printed fabric, represented genuinely new kinds of decorated artefact. But perhaps the most characteristic form of product innovation in the Georgian period was the multiplication of new varieties of existing artefacts. This process can be observed in furniture, where a whole range of multi-purpose, adjustable designs was developed in the late eighteenth and early nineteenth centuries – dining tables with flap tops and extensions, combined writing and work tables for ladies, dressing tables with a variety of concealed, adjustable mirrors. The same process was visible in coach building.

56 *Mule Spinning*, 1835. Drawn by Thomas Allom. Engraved by J. W. Lowry. Plate from *History of the Cotton Manufacture in Great Britain* by Edward Baines, 1835. Engraving. VAM 43.D.88.

57 Work and games table, about 1820. This multi-functional table was designed for a woman's use. Below the hinged reading surface is a backgammon board, and embroidery materials could be stored in the hanging bag. Rosewood, with mounts and stringing lines of brass; replacement upholstery. VAM W.60-1931.

57

SILVERWARES

Helen Clifford

In the Georgian period silver maintained its position at the top of the status-conferring hierarchy of materials, while becoming available to a wider audience as a result of new techniques of manufacture. At the same time it faced a number of challenges. These came from cheaper, imitative materials like Sheffield plate, from new finishes like japanning for cheaper metalwares and from materials like porcelain, which could be substituted for silver in many of its uses.

The introduction of the flatting mill in the 1720s meant that goldsmiths could cut costs by reducing the weight of silver used to make their products. The tea canister known as a 'tub' could, for example, be made from flatted silver using a fraction of the metal employed in its predecessors, whether cast or raised and embossed. Die-stamping, introduced in the 1730s, and fly-pressing were well suited to producing the geometric shapes and repeat architectural motifs associated with neo-classicism. These new hand-operated machines allowed lighter, cheaper wares to be made in the most fashionable styles.

60. Buttons engraved with hunting scenes, about 1750. Probably made in Sheffield. Copper plated with silver (Sheffield plate). Courtesy of Gordon Crosskey.

Although silver substitutes like French plate and paktong had been known since the late seventeenth century, difficulties in manufacture meant that they did not offer much competition to silver. This changed with the invention of Sheffield plate, a sandwich of copper between first one and then two layers of silver, discovered in 1742 by Thomas Boulsover, a Sheffield cutler. The process was first applied to buttons, until Thomas Hancock realized the potential for large objects like candlesticks, which could be stamped with the same dies as were used for silver. In terms of design, weight and surface texture there was no difference between silver and Sheffield plate, save that objects made from the latter might cost as little as one-fifth of the price of the same object made in solid silver.

58. Detail of a dessert basket, with London hallmarks for 1774–5. Mark of Burrage Davenport. Silver, cut out by hand. VAM 756:1-1877.

59. Detail of a dessert basket, with London hallmarks for 1776–7. Mark of Ann Chesterman. Stamped out by means of a fly press. VAM 755:1-1877.

New kinds of silver objects proliferated. The refinement of dining demanded new types of specialized equipment. Tureens, sauce boats and centrepieces, derived from French forms, were introduced from the 1720s; in the 1740s urn-shaped peppers and mustards replaced casters. Smallwares such as funnels, strainers and waiters or trays became more prevalent, and new objects like bottle stands and tickets emerged. Many could be made by means of hand-operated machines. Alongside them were new gadgets, like the cucumber slicer and the tea fountain. John Wadham's patent of 1774 for the tea fountain used an iron to heat the water, thereby liberating the tea kettle from the constraints of a bottom burner and enabling it to adopt the fashionable urn shape.

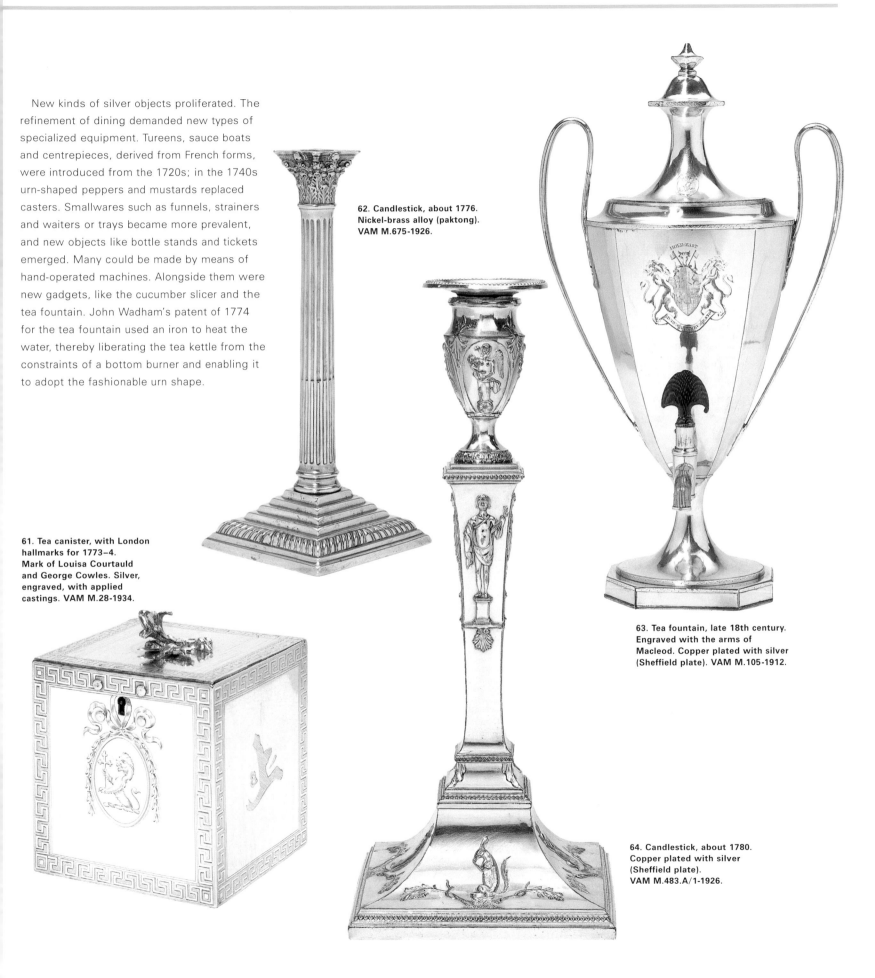

62. Candlestick, about 1776.
Nickel-brass alloy (paktong).
VAM M.675-1926.

61. Tea canister, with London hallmarks for 1773–4. Mark of Louisa Courtauld and George Cowles. Silver, engraved, with applied castings. VAM M.28-1934.

63. Tea fountain, late 18th century. Engraved with the arms of Macleod. Copper plated with silver (Sheffield plate). VAM M.105-1912.

64. Candlestick, about 1780. Copper plated with silver (Sheffield plate). VAM M.483.A/1-1926.

Victorian Britain

1837–1901

CHAPTER 11

Victorian Britain, 1837–1901

Introduction

JOHN STYLES

1. The workshop of the world

The Great Exhibition of the Works of Industry of all Nations, held in London's Hyde Park in the summer of 1851, marked the high-water mark of British economic power. Britain in the middle of the nineteenth century was the globe's pre-eminent manufacturing nation, quite literally the workshop of the world. It commanded a far larger proportion of world trade in manufactured goods than any of its major competitor countries. Yet the Exhibition was not simply an exercise in British industrial triumphalism. Indeed, the concerns that inspired its founders, attracted its six million visitors and animated its critics reveal a combination of pride in British economic success and unease about the economic and cultural sustainability of that success, which was characteristically Victorian.

The Exhibition attracted immense audiences, ranging from the landed nobility to the more affluent, skilled sections of the working classes. More women attended than men. Many visitors – probably most – enjoyed it principally as a spectacle. It offered a gargantuan celebration of modernity, progress, civilization and internationalism, as its British organizers conceived them, enclosed within the technological wizardry of a structure made almost entirely from glass and iron – the Crystal Palace. The very fact that this, the first truly international exhibition, took place in London could hardly fail to highlight Britain's economic and technological superiority. But the Exhibition also affirmed a number of other aspects of mid-nineteenth-century British life. It provided a powerful endorsement for the British policy of peaceful international competition through free trade. It demonstrated public support for Queen Victoria and her husband, Prince Albert, who was one of the Exhibition's foremost promoters. And the good behaviour of its humbler visitors calmed fears among the comfortably-off that a resumption of the working-class political agitations of the 1840s was imminent.

1 previous pages (left):
Detail of a clock, 1896–1901. Designed and probably painted by C. F. A. Voysey, case probably made by Frederick Coote, movement stamped by Camerer, Kuss & Co., London. Painted and gilded mahogany; movement of brass and steel. VAM W.5-1998.

2 previous pages (right):
Vase with a portrait of Queen Victoria, 1851. Made by Charles Meigh & Son, in Hanley, Staffordshire. Stoneware with relief moulding, gilding and painted decoration in enamels. VAM Circ.374-1963.

3 Detail of *The Opening of the Great Exhibition by Queen Victoria on 1st May 1851*, 1851–2. By Henry Courtney Selous. Oil on canvas. VAM 329-1889.

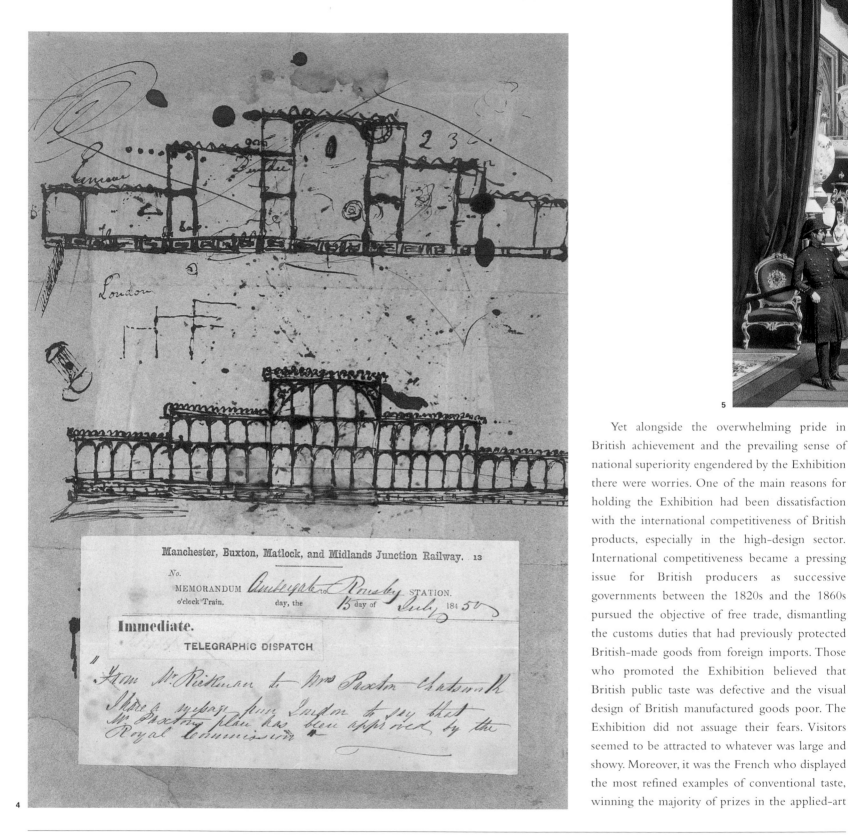

Yet alongside the overwhelming pride in British achievement and the prevailing sense of national superiority engendered by the Exhibition there were worries. One of the main reasons for holding the Exhibition had been dissatisfaction with the international competitiveness of British products, especially in the high-design sector. International competitiveness became a pressing issue for British producers as successive governments between the 1820s and the 1860s pursued the objective of free trade, dismantling the customs duties that had previously protected British-made goods from foreign imports. Those who promoted the Exhibition believed that British public taste was defective and the visual design of British manufactured goods poor. The Exhibition did not assuage their fears. Visitors seemed to be attracted to whatever was large and showy. Moreover, it was the French who displayed the most refined examples of conventional taste, winning the majority of prizes in the applied-art

4 First sketch for the Crystal Palace, 11 June 1850. By Sir Joseph Paxton. This sketch was drawn on blotting paper by the architect while he was attending a Midland Railway board meeting in Derby. It was converted into proper drawings within a week. Pen and ink on pink blotting paper, mounted on a sheet of wove paper with a telegram form. VAM E.575-1985.

categories. 'French superiority in artistic industries is no longer in doubt,' remarked one French journalist, 'even in the eyes of the English.' In machinery, where Britain was undoubtedly dominant, American, French and German technology challenged the British in a number of fields. And beyond the barrage of journalistic approval that greeted the Exhibition were heard other, more critical voices. Radicals attacked its failure to acknowledge the workers who toiled in workshop and factory to create the exhibits. Conservatives, like the writer Thomas Carlyle, contemptuous of an urban, industrial, mass society, dismissed the Exhibition as a 'congregation of empty, windy mortals'. Cultural critics, like John Ruskin, argued that artefacts made by machinery without the creative involvement of the worker could have no aesthetic value. For Ruskin, the Crystal Palace was mere technology. 'We suppose ourselves to have invented a new style of architecture,' he complained, 'when we have magnified a conservatory.'

The Victorian era was one of immense self-confidence, but it was a self-confidence sometimes assailed by doubts. Victorian Britain experienced a paradoxical alliance of material optimism and spiritual disquiet. Nowhere was this ambivalence more acute than in the field of design and the decorative arts. In the contradictory reactions to the Great Exhibition we find rehearsed the controversies – economic and social, aesthetic and moral – that were to engage designers and artists for the rest of Victoria's reign.

2. State and nation

Queen Victoria ascended the throne in 1837 at the age of 18. Her two immediate royal predecessors and uncles, the unpopular George IV and his brother William IV, had both died without surviving legitimate children. Victoria's great popularity towards the end of her reign, most obvious at the Royal Jubilees of 1887 and 1897, masks the extent to which support for the monarchy had previously waxed and waned, and, to some extent, did so throughout her reign.

Victorian Britain resembled most other European states of the period in that it was a monarchy. At the end of Victoria's reign in 1901 the vast majority of Europeans were subjects of kingdoms or empires, just as they had been at its start, more than 60 years earlier. But none of these nineteenth-century European monarchies escaped the consequences of the French Revolution of 1789. Despite the rapid demise of the revolutionary regime in France, the demands it unleashed – that each state should represent a distinct national population and that all the people of that nation should have a say in its government – were to affect Europe for the whole of the nineteenth century and beyond. In the case of France itself, these demands led eventually, in 1870, to the permanent replacement of kings and emperors by a republic. In the cases of Italy and Germany, which had for centuries been divided into a patchwork of small and medium-sized political entities, a series of wars in the 1850s and 1860s resulted in their unification as large nation states, ruled by monarchs.

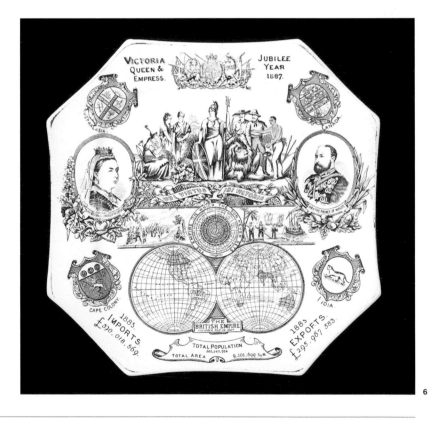

6

5 *France No. 3*, 1852. From *Dickinson's comprehensive pictures of the Great Exhibition of 1851*, 1854 (second edition; first published 1852). Designed by Joseph Nash; printed and published by Dickinson Brothers, London. This view shows the French section at the Exhibition. Colour lithograph with some watercolour and varnish retouching. VAM 19536:5.

6 Plate, made in 1887; design registered in 1886. Made by Wallis Gimson & Co., Lane Delph Pottery, Fenton, Staffordshire. This popular type of Golden Jubilee item was sold in Britain and exported to India and other parts of the Empire. The plate displays statistics that boast of a successful trading nation and imperial power. Earthenware, lead-glazed, transfer-printed. VAM Circ.198-1966.

QUEEN VICTORIA AND HER FAMILY

Suzanne Fagence Cooper

From the moment she ascended the throne in 1837, Queen Victoria (1837–1901) enjoyed an unprecedented hold on the public imagination. Her portrait was found in magazines and advertisements, on sheet music and, of course, on that recent innovation, the postage stamp. Her marriage to Albert, the Prince Consort, in 1840 reinforced her position and the fashionable couple patronized the arts and sciences. The Queen would regularly buy paintings from the annual Royal Academy exhibitions and helped to establish the reputations of artists such as William Powell Frith and Lady Butler. Prince Albert was also enthusiastic about modern art, even turning his hand to modelling statuettes of his favourite dogs. His personal involvement in coordinating the Great Exhibition of 1851 helped to ensure the success of the project. As their nine children grew up, their marriages strengthened Britain's relationship with other European states: the Princess Royal, also called Victoria, became the wife of the German Kaiser,

7. Music cover: *The Queen and Prince Albert's Polka*, about 1840. Designed by John Brandard. Printed by M. & N. Hanhart. Published by Jullien, London. Colour lithograph. VAM E.828-1959.

8. *The First of May 1851*. By Franz Xavier Winterhalter. The Duke of Wellington presenting a birthday gift to the Prince Arthur on the opening day of the Great Exhibition. Oil on canvas. © The Royal Collection.

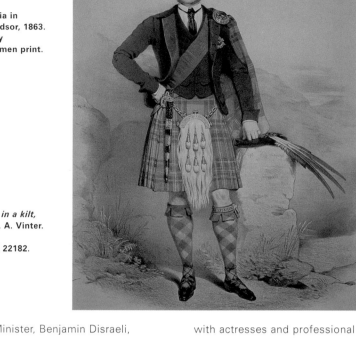

10. Queen Victoria in mourning at Windsor, 1863. *Carte de visite* by Bambridge. Albumen print. VAM 3517-1953.

11. *Prince Albert in a kilt,* about 1850. By J. A. Vinter. after K. Macleay. Lithograph. VAM 22182.

Frederick III; and Prince Alfred married the only daughter of Tsar Alexander II of Russia.

The royal family became a role-model for domestic virtue and affection. The Prince Consort led the way in popularizing the German tradition of celebrating Christmas, introducing the Christmas tree to the royal festivities. In 1852 the royal couple bought an estate at Balmoral in the Scottish Highlands and established new fashions for Scottish tartan and holidays hunting on the moors. Albert's death in December 1861 left the Queen devastated. She went into mourning and largely withdrew from political life. During this time she developed an attachment to one of the ghillies from Balmoral, John Brown.

The Prime Minister, Benjamin Disraeli, gradually became a friend and ally and tried to persuade her to return to her duties. It was thanks to him that the Queen was declared Empress of India in 1876. Although she did not personally visit her imperial territories, the Prince of Wales travelled to India as her representative. Both the Prince and Princess of Wales remained popular figures throughout Victoria's reign, despite rumours of his affairs with actresses and professional beauties like Lillie Langtry. The death of his son, the Duke of Clarence, in 1892 was generally mourned.

The celebration of the Queen's Golden Jubilee in 1887 and Diamond Jubilee 10 years later brought her back into public view, re-establishing Victoria as a great figurehead for Britain and its expanding Empire. When she died on the Isle of Wight on 22 January 1901 the nation mourned the end of an era.

9. Scrapbook containing pictures of the Duke of Clarence, Queen Victoria and the Prince and Princess of Wales, about 1880. VAM 60.W.191.

The changes experienced by France, Italy and Germany were especially dramatic, but no European country in the nineteenth century escaped demands for national self-expression and popular involvement in government, often leading to bloody revolutions. Most European monarchies made some attempt, however reluctant, to accommodate these pressures by establishing parliaments and similar representative bodies. But it was the hunger for national self-expression that was to have a particular impact on design and the decorative arts. Across Europe, the embattled advocates of a multitude of nationalisms promoted peasant crafts and folk art as key elements of national identity.

Victorian Britain was not immune to these pressures, although the political power of the British monarch was already very limited at the start of Victoria's reign. Political authority resided principally with the elected Members of Parliament. Yet even after the changes introduced by the Great Reform Act of 1832, Parliament was elected by only a tiny proportion of the British population – a mere 15 per cent of all adult men – among whom the wealthy were heavily over-represented. Despite mass campaigns to secure a democratic constitution, such as those organized by the working-class Chartists in the 1830s and 1840s, it was only very slowly and reluctantly that the governing classes granted the vote to broader sections of the population. The parliamentary Reform Acts of 1867 and 1884 progressively

extended the right to vote to men from the more affluent sections of the working classes, but when Victoria died Britain was far from being a democracy. In 1901 two-fifths of adult men were still not eligible to vote, nor were any women. The defining characteristic of the Victorian polity was representative government without democracy.

The emergence of suppressed nationalisms also had its impact on Victorian Britain, most obviously in its relations with Ireland. Before the nineteenth century Great Britain and Ireland had shared a monarch, but had enjoyed separate parliaments. The Act of Union of 1801 finally integrated the two parliaments to form a single United Kingdom of Great Britain and Ireland. Large sections of Irish opinion, especially Irish Catholic opinion, were never reconciled to this arrangement. Campaigns for Irish autonomy were to punctuate Victoria's reign. Towards its end, they became increasingly associated with the efforts of cultural nationalists to construct an ethnically pure Irish identity, unsullied by Anglo-Saxon

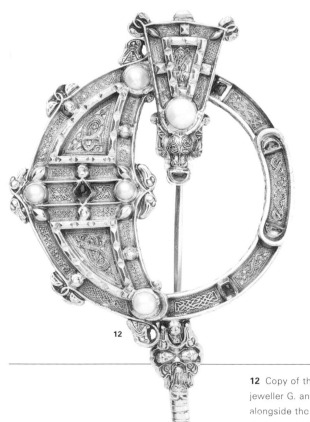

12 Copy of the Royal Tara Brooch, about 1851. Made by the Dublin jeweller G. and S. Waterhouse and exhibited at the Great Exhibition, 1851, alongside the early medieval Irish original that had been discovered the previous year near Drogheda, Ireland. Oxidized silver, partially gilded and set with diamonds, amethysts and river pearls. VAM 920-1852.

13 Tartan bag, about 1850. Embroidered silk, trimmed with silk cords and tassels. VAM T.67-1961.

influences. Their efforts focused on the promotion of the Irish language, Gaelic sports and decorative art employing medieval Irish forms and motifs.

In the other territories that comprised the United Kingdom there was little pressure for political separation, but cultural nationalisms flourished within the context of a broader commitment to Britain. As in the rest of nineteenth-century Europe, the search for the essential characteristics of the nation and its people led to those peripheral rural areas that seemed least contaminated by modern commerce. Elements of rural life were selected for imaginative reconstruction into a national culture of questionable authenticity. In Scotland, a rapidly industrializing country, national identity in the Victorian era came to focus on an idealized version of the life and history of the rural Highlands, with particular emphasis on tartan, the kilt and the baronial style of architecture. Victoria and Albert's enthusiasm for their Highland estate at Balmoral gave added respectability to this romanticized version of Scottish identity. In Wales, cultural nationalism was more heavily concentrated on the Welsh language, still widely spoken in rural areas, but an idealized national costume also enjoyed considerable popularity. In England, it was more common for national identity to reside simply in an outward-looking celebration of British commercial and imperial success. Nevertheless, it is possible to detect here, too, a search for the essence of race and nation in a romanticized rural past, especially in the rediscovery of an old English vernacular architecture.

14 A page from a sketchbook depicting girls wearing Welsh hats, 1800–50. By an unknown artist. Pencil on paper. VAM E.3243-1931.

15 Frontispiece from *News from Nowhere* by William Morris, 1892. It depicts Kelmscott Manor, Oxfordshire, the 16th-century English vernacular house that Morris rented in 1871 and described as 'a heaven on earth'. Woodcut. VAM 883-1893.

16

In continental Europe, the rise of nationalism led to warfare, in particular the wars that forged Germany and Italy into nation states during the mid-Victorian years. For most of Victoria's reign, Britain's direct involvement in these and other conflicts on the continent remained diplomatic rather than military. With the exception of the brief Crimean War, fought against Russia between 1854 and 1856, Victorian Britain enjoyed a long peace with its European neighbours. Britain's capacity to remain aloof, though not entirely disengaged, from continental quarrels was most obviously a reflection of the strength of her navy and the weakness of her army. It also reflected a widely held British belief in the country's superiority over her continental neighbours – a superiority that was simultaneously economic, political and moral. Those who governed Victorian Britain did not flinch from competition with her European neighbours, but they preferred the peaceful competition of the international market to military engagements on the battlefield.

16 *The Channel Squadron*, 1898. By Eduardo de Martino. Britain sustained her naval supremacy during the Victorian transition from sail to steam. By the end of the 19th century the Royal Navy's capital ships were steam-powered, armour-plated and relied on the firepower of a relatively small number of heavy guns. Oil on canvas. © National Maritime Museum, London.

17 *Imperial Federation Map of the World*, 1886. From *The Graphic*, 24 July 1886. Colour lithograph. VAM PP.8.D-E.

17

3. Empire

The long Victorian peace did not extend to the wider world beyond Europe. There the process of British imperial expansion by threat and force that had characterized the later Georgian years continued unabated. In an age of rampant imperialism, Victorian Britain was the world's greatest imperial power. By the end of Victoria's reign, it controlled one-quarter of the world's surface and one-fifth of its population. As the leading conservative politician, Benjamin Disraeli, declared in 1866, 'there is no power that interferes more than England. She interferes in Asia, because she is really more an Asiatic Power than a European. She interferes in Australia, in Africa, and New Zealand.' Yet there was no single motive at work behind the seizure of new territories. In some cases, like Hong Kong in 1842, the objective was to open up new markets for British trade. In others, like the annexations in India that followed what the British called the Mutiny of 1857, the aim was to consolidate and safeguard existing territories in the face of local opposition. In yet others, like West Africa, the goal was to forestall the expansion of rival European powers.

The immediate causes of imperial expansion were, therefore, diverse. Nevertheless it would be wrong to ignore the cumulative power of the imperial imperative. The complaints of liberal politicians like William Gladstone, that colonial expansion was often pointless and expensive, did little to stop it, even when the complaints came from politicians who themselves controlled the levers of government. A powerful predisposition towards imperial expansion held sway both in Britain itself and among British officials stationed across the non-European world. It was grounded in a belief in the universal benefits of open trade and Christian (and more especially British) civilization. It drew on the conviction that Britain had a right to safeguard its existing colonial possessions against native peoples and other European powers. It reflected the fact that expansion was relatively painless, given the extraordinary and unprecedented superiority of European military technologies over those available to non-European peoples. It was fuelled by a long-standing belief that the non-white races were intellectually and culturally inferior and might require not just guidance, but also subjection. This belief found renewed vigour after the publication of Charles Darwin's *On the Origin of Species* in 1859, when a vulgarized version of Darwin's theory of the evolution of species was applied to human racial groups, conveniently suggesting that the white races were superior as the result of a process of natural selection. The new, harsher, pseudo-scientific racism played well in the chorus of imperial enthusiasm that dominated the final decades of Victoria's reign.

19

18 'Jubilee' wallpaper, 1887. From the stock of F. Scott & Son, 26 High Street, Hawick, Roxburghshire. Colour print from engraved rollers. VAM E.791-1970.

19 Charles Darwin, about 1860. By Julia Margaret Cameron. Albumen print. VAM 14-1939.

THE BRITISH EMPIRE, 1848 AND 1902

John Styles

In 1848, in the early years of Victoria's reign, Britain was already the world's greatest imperial power, controlling more people and territory across the globe than any of its European competitors. The British Empire continued to expand up to the end of the Boer War in 1902, especially in India, Africa and the Pacific, although it was not to achieve its greatest territorial extent until after 1918. Territorial expansion was accompanied by the rationalization of imperial government and, in the later Victorian years, by an increasingly jingoistic celebration of Empire, both in Britain and overseas. Formal control of British India was finally transferred from the East India Company to the British Crown in the aftermath of the Indian Mutiny of 1857; Queen Victoria was declared Empress of India in 1876. Self-government was granted to the colonies of white settlement in Canada, Australia and New Zealand, but elsewhere emerging demands for political representation from native peoples were resisted.

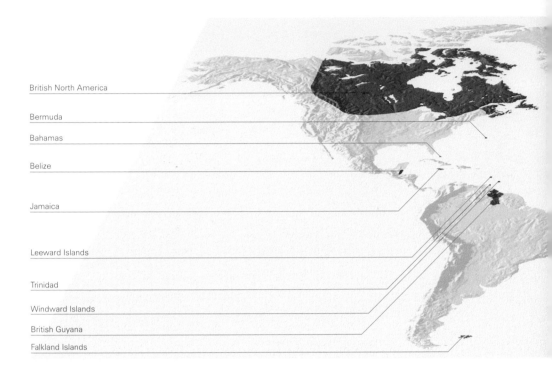

British North America

Bermuda

Bahamas

Belize

Jamaica

Leeward Islands

Trinidad

Windward Islands

British Guyana

Falkland Islands

Asce
Tristan da Cu
South Georgi

Canada

Bermuda

Bahamas

Belize

Jamaica

Leeward Islands

Ducie I.

Pitcairn I.

Trinidad

Windward Islands

British Guyana

Falkland Islands

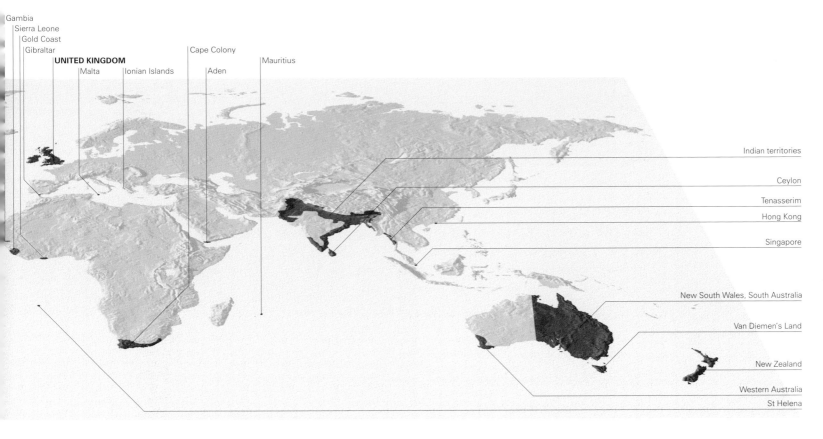

Gambia
Sierra Leone
Gold Coast
Gibraltar
UNITED KINGDOM
Malta
Ionian Islands
Cape Colony
Aden
Mauritius

Indian territories
Ceylon
Tenasserim
Hong Kong
Singapore
New South Wales, South Australia
Van Diemen's Land
New Zealand
Western Australia
St Helena

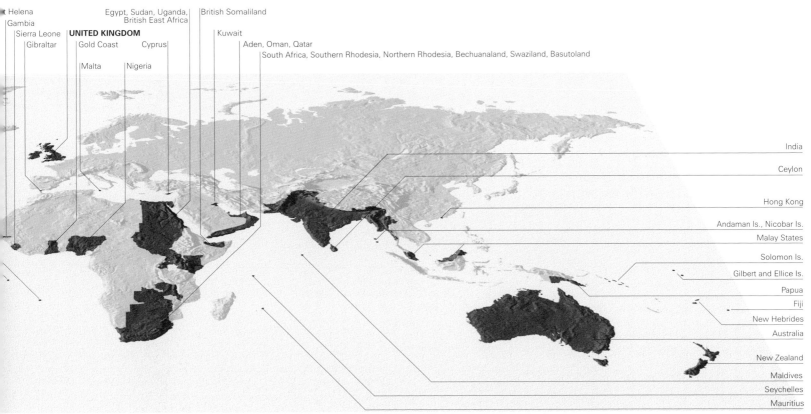

Helena
Gambia
Sierra Leone
Gibraltar
UNITED KINGDOM
Gold Coast
Cyprus
Malta
Nigeria
Egypt, Sudan, Uganda, British East Africa
Kuwait
British Somaliland
Aden, Oman, Qatar
South Africa, Southern Rhodesia, Northern Rhodesia, Bechuanaland, Swaziland, Basutoland

India
Ceylon
Hong Kong
Andaman Is., Nicobar Is.
Malay States
Solomon Is.
Gilbert and Ellice Is.
Papua
Fiji
New Hebrides
Australia
New Zealand
Maldives
Seychelles
Mauritius

Nevertheless, it would be wrong to imagine that Victorian attitudes to the peoples and cultures of the non-European world amounted simply to brutal racist disdain. The new biological racism was never as influential in Britain as in many of her European neighbours. Indeed, in design and the decorative arts it is the consistent Victorian enthusiasm for non-European objects that is most striking. Islamic ceramics, Indian textiles and Japanese prints may have been products of what were regarded as less commercially advanced civilizations, but in the eyes of Victorian designers and critics this was precisely what accounted for their aesthetic superiority. In their use of colour, form and decoration these objects surpassed what many regarded as the unprincipled disorder of a European decorative art corrupted by a ceaseless search for mere commercial novelty.

20 Embroidered muslin from Madras, 1868. From *The Textile Fabrics of India* by James Forbes-Watson, vol. VII, 1868. A page from one of the volumes of Indian textile samples assembled by Forbes-Watson, copies of which were supplied to museums and schools of design throughout Britain with the aim of improving British textile design. Cotton muslin with gold embroidery mounted on paper. VAM Indian and South-East Asian Department Library.

21 Left: jug, about 1600. Made at Iznik in Turkey (Anatolia). Siliceous-glazed earthenware, painted. Right: bottle, about 1862. Made by Minton & Co., Stoke-on-Trent. Bone china, painted in underglaze and overglaze colours. Large manufacturers such as Minton & Co. produced ceramics in the fashionable Turkish or Persian (Iranian) style. Shapes, colours and decoration were taken from historical examples, often found in museums and private collections of the 1860s. VAM 728-1893, 8098-1963.

4. Manufacturing

In the 1850s and 1860s Britain made close to half of all the manufactured goods that were traded around the world. It was at one and the same time the world's greatest manufacturing and trading nation. In almost every category of manufactured good and at almost every level of the market the British were perceived by their foreign rivals as immensely effective competitors. With British-made goods so dominant in world trade, British design and decorative arts could hardly fail to have a huge international impact. But British mastery of trade and manufactures was not absolute. Competitors like the French were able to find solace in the superiority of their expensive textiles, furniture and ceramics. The British agonized over the aesthetic shortcomings of their high-design goods. To assess the role of design and the decorative arts in the workshop of the world, we need to examine the elements that made up the British industrial economy in its Victorian heyday.

The most effective way to do this is to consider Britain's trade in manufactured goods. For most of Victoria's reign, Britain was more reliant on overseas markets for manufactured goods than rivals like France, Germany or the United States, and it exported a greater share of its industrial output. But its main manufactured exports consisted of a very slim range of goods, principally cotton yarn and cloth (much of it plain), and iron and steel in the form of sheets, bars, rails and wire. These were the products of that remarkably narrow, but hugely successful range of industries that were the principal users

22 *The Wealth of England: the Bessemer Convertor*, 1895. By W. H. Titcomb. The painting depicts the interior of a steelworks at Rotherham, Yorkshire. The English inventor and industrialist Henry Bessemer developed a process in the 1850s for converting iron into steel by blowing air through molten iron. It was the first of a number of technical innovations that enabled steel to be produced cheaply and in vast quantities. As a consequence, by the end of the 19th century steel had replaced iron in most of its uses. Oil on canvas. Sheffield Industrial Museums Trust Ltd.

23

of steam power. In other words, Britain's decisive advantage over her competitors lay in the products of factory and furnace; in the export of what were often semi-finished goods, produced by the coal-based technologies that the British had developed so successfully during the period 1760–1850. Her advantage was not so decisive when it came to the multitude of finished consumer goods that relied heavily on qualities of visual design and skilled hand labour. In the manufacture of these goods – the products of workshop and sweatshop – steam power was either not used at all (as in the manufacture of glasswares) or only for one or two out of a long sequence of different processes (as in pottery and furniture). As far as goods of this kind were concerned, Britain was often a successful exporter, but not a dominant one. The economist W. S. Jevons noted the implications of this when he compared the economies of Britain and continental Europe in the 1860s. 'Great Britain,' he argued, was 'capable for the present of indefinitely producing all products depending on the use of coal'. Europe, by contrast, was 'capable of an

24

23 *Apsley Pellatt's Falcon Glassworks, Southwark, London*, about 1840. By an unknown artist. Oil on canvas. The Museum of London.

24 *The Dinner Hour, Wigan, Lancashire*, 1874. By Eyre Crowe. The painting depicts the mainly female workforce of Wigan's steam-powered cotton mills. Oil on canvas. Manchester City Art Gallery.

25 *Launching a buoy on the Great Eastern*, 1866. By Robert Dudley. Plate from *The Atlantic Telegraph* by W. H. Russell, published in London, 1866. The plate shows a buoy being launched to mark the spot where the Atlantic telegraph cable had been grappled and mended during the third, successful attempt to lay a transatlantic cable. Colour lithograph. Science Museum, London.

indefinite production of artistic, luxurious, or semi-tropical products, but debarred by comparative want of coal from competition with us'.

The limitations of British industrial dominance become clearer still if we examine the destinations of British manufactured exports during the Victorian era. Increasingly these went to the less developed parts of the non-European world, including Britain's own colonies. The proportion of exports that went to the developed economies of Germany and the United States declined, while the proportion that went to the less sophisticated economies of Africa and Asia rose, with India in particular becoming more and more important. This shift was not necessarily to the disadvantage of the British economy as a whole, at least in the short term. It was an element in that broader Victorian process of globalization, facilitated by innovations like the telegraph, the railway, the steam ship and refrigeration, which resulted in ever more complex patterns of economic specialization throughout the world. Asian and African markets were buoyant, growing and profitable. But competition in these markets was less intense. They were less likely than the developed countries to

26 *Modelling*, 1874. From *The Graphic*, 7 November 1874. The modelling room at Elkington and Co. of Birmingham, manufacturers of silver plate. Wood engraving. VAM PP.8.D.

27 *The Slitting Room for Pens*, 1851. From the *Illustrated London News*, 22 February 1851. Women workers in the factory of Messrs Hinks, Wells and Co. of Birmingham, steel-pen manufacturers, slit pen-nibs using hand-operated machines. Wood engraving. VAM PP.10.

require goods that were at the international cutting-edge of design and product innovation. Even when they imported goods with a high visual design content, it was a content that was often tailored to very specific local tastes and conditions, like the printed cottons made in Lancashire solely for the Indian market.

It would be wrong to regard this shift towards less sophisticated markets simply as evidence for the shortcomings of British manufacturing. Partly it resulted from the erection of high tariff barriers in the developed world. The international trend to free trade, promoted by the British in the middle years of the nineteenth century, was reversed after 1870. Though Britain remained loyal to free trade, other developed countries became more protectionist in the increasingly nationalist and imperialist climate of the late Victorian years. By the late 1890s, for example, Bradford manufacturers of worsted cloth for men's coats and suits had to pay a customs duty that was greater than the cloth's original value when they exported it to the United States. As a consequence, Americans were obliged to pay more than twice as much as purchasers in

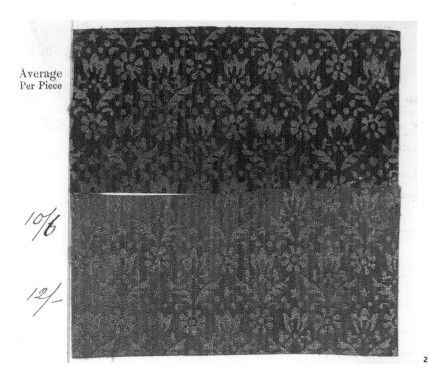

Britain to acquire the same cloth. Exports collapsed. Partly, too, the shift towards less sophisticated markets reflected the vast sums British financiers invested in the less developed countries, both within the Empire and beyond. Much of this investment paid for building railways, harbours and other infrastructure that soaked up the products of British heavy industry.

But it is striking that the shift in British exports to less developed markets in Africa and Asia went hand-in-hand with increasing British imports of manufactured goods from Europe and North America. At the start of Victoria's reign, Britain had imported very few manufactured goods. The growth of manufactured imports suggests that the workshop of the world was becoming increasingly uncompetitive in a number of industries as Victoria grew older. British-made products that suffered at the hands of foreign imports included high-design goods like woven silk fabrics, fine worsted cloth, porcelain and hand-blown wine glasses and decanters. Moreover, this trend was not confined to established industries. Britain also lagged behind her industrialized competitors in a number of the new technologies of the late nineteenth century – electrical goods, dyestuffs, small machines for office and home, such as the typewriter and sewing machine, and, at the very end of the Victorian era, the motor car. Nevertheless, it is important to stress that at no point in Victoria's reign was the overall contribution of British manufacturing to national wealth and trade seriously threatened. Industrial output and industrial exports grew enormously. Still, there was a real economic justification for the anxieties about the quality of British high-design goods that so exercised many Victorians and did so much to promote design education.

28 Poster for the Empire typewriter, 1897. By Lucien Faure. Colour lithograph. VAM Circ.586-1962.

29 Samples of 'goldings', 1888. 'Goldings' were an expensive cotton cloth, printed with a gold pigment, produced in Lancashire for the Indian market. These examples were printed at the Abbey Print Works, Whalley, Lancashire, on 11 October 1888. Printed cotton. Lancashire County Record Office.

5. People

During the reign of Queen Victoria, Britain was the richest country the world had ever known. By the time of her death a progressive increase in national wealth had brought at least some benefits to almost every section of the country's ever-growing population, which doubled from less than 19 million in 1841 to 37 million in 1901. As more and more people came to enjoy increased spending power, the domestic markets for a multiplicity of decorative goods expanded enormously. At the same time, these markets became ever more minutely graded according to wealth and status, with manufacturers producing household goods like clocks and coffee pots to a huge range of specifications, carefully contrived for every taste and pocket. For this remained a profoundly unequal society, one in which even minor distinctions of income, occupation or belief were signalled by the clothes one wore or the way one furnished one's home.

The Victorian era was the first in which it was common to think about society in terms of broad social classes constituted by patterns of work and ownership – the working class, the middle class and the upper class. Few Victorians, at any social level, wholeheartedly embraced the socialists' belief in class exploitation and the inevitability of class conflict. The social distinctions that most concerned them were often ones of status or manners, which did not fit straightforwardly into the grand class categories – distinctions between skilled workers and white-collar clerks with similar incomes, or between the respectable and the rough. Nevertheless, the vocabulary of class distinction was widely employed, albeit with little precision or consistency. Its ubiquity is evidence of the aggressiveness of economic and other inequalities in the Victorian era. The resulting snobberies, anxieties and resentments were very keenly felt.

The summit of the Victorian social pyramid was inhabited by a small but mixed group of astonishingly wealthy families, whose riches derived from land, commerce and manufacturing. The most surprising feature of this élite of wealth, given that Britain had become a predominantly urban nation by the early years of Victoria's reign, was the continuing prominence of rural landowners. The landed aristocracy – as the landed super-rich were increasingly referred to in the nineteenth century – was never precisely defined, but was loosely coterminous with the 4,000 people who in 1873 owned well over half the land in England and Wales, and their Scottish equivalents. These people and their families retained an extraordinarily powerful influence on national politics and London high society. Their significance for design and the decorative arts was immense, most obviously because, before the agricultural depression of the 1870s, many of them went on building and rebuilding vast country houses. These became ever larger and more expensively furnished, incorporating the most up-to-date notions of design, comfort, convenience and sanitation. Remodelling houses like the

30 A page from *A Catalogue of Christmas, New Year's, Birthday and Wedding Presents*, 1860–70. Published by Silber and Fleming of London, silversmiths. Engraving. VAM TC.C. Box 2.

31 *Epsom Races*, 1847. From the *Illustrated London News*, 22 May 1847. The engravings depict the three classes of railway-excursion passengers on their way to the races at Epsom in Surrey. Wood engraving. VAM PP.10.

35

Among the utterly impoverished of the urban slums, ragged clothes and bare rooms with a few sticks of broken furniture were common enough. Nevertheless, British workers were, on average, better housed than their German and French equivalents and, from the middle of Victoria's reign, experienced significant improvements in their purchasing power. Even in the poorer working-class households there existed a powerful desire to make a show, to mark out a place in the local pecking order, where status was judged by the ability to possess goods. Walter Besant, the social reformer, described the

35 *A cottage interior*, about 1883. By Alfred Edward Emslie. The walls of this sparsely furnished interior are decorated with framed pictures, cheap prints and fans. Albumen print. VAM E.8822-1994.

6. The urban condition

For all but the very early years of Victoria's reign most British men and women lived in towns; 1851 was the first year in which less than half the British people were recorded as living in the countryside; by 1901 the urban share of the population had grown to three-quarters. Of course, the urban experience was not unfamiliar to the British. At Victoria's accession, London had already been western Europe's largest city for a century and a half. It remained the world's largest city for the whole of the nineteenth century, with approximately a million people at its start and four and a half million at its end. Nevertheless, the fact that for the first time in human history the majority of the inhabitants of a large and populous nation like Britain had ceased to live in the countryside was a momentous one, evoking feelings of both pride and foreboding. Above all, it contributed to the Victorians' acute sense of their own modernity, their sense that humanity's ever-growing power over nature was remaking their world in ways that seemed to have no historical precedent.

two-room tenements of the East End of London at the end of Victoria's reign, where one of the rooms would contain little more than a table, chairs and a chest of drawers:

> On this chest stands a structure of artificial flowers under a glass shade. This is a sacred symbol of respectability . . . On each side of the glass shade are arranged the cups and saucers, plates and drinking glasses, belonging to the family. There are also exhibited with pride all the bottles of medicine recently taken by the various members.

Among workers in skilled or specialist occupations with high earnings, much more impressive forms of display could be achieved. Here, the front room or parlour was the ultimate symbol of respectability, where all the most flamboyant and expensive possessions were located – heavy mahogany furniture, a mirror, patterned linoleum, perhaps even a piano. Middle-class social reformers, like Mrs Samuel Barnett in 1906, disapproved on grounds of both economy and taste:

> In most rooms there is too much furniture and there are too many ornaments . . . I have counted as many as seventeen ornaments on one mantelpiece – three, or perhaps five are ample. She who aims to be thrifty will fight against yielding to the artificially developed instinct to possess.

Yet it is far from clear that the desire to possess such objects needed to be developed artificially. It was a well-entrenched feature of a working-class culture that placed a high value on these and other forms of conspicuous consumption.

36 A Scottish working-class living room, about 1880. The respectable Scottish working-class family depicted in this carefully posed photograph has relatively few domestic possessions, but what it has are carefully arranged and displayed. Hamilton Museum.

37 *Ludgate Hill and St Paul's*, 1887. By William Logsdail. This painting suggests the hectic pace of life in the world's largest city towards the end of the 19th century. Oil on canvas. Private collection.

CHAPTER 12

Style

MICHAEL SNODIN

1. The great style debate

In 1840 the decorators Henry and Aaron Arrowsmith calmly observed in *The House Decorator and Painter's Guide* that 'the present age is distinguished from all others in having no style which can properly be called its own'. They went on to set out a tempting menu of historical and exotic possibilities, including 'Greek, Roman, Arabesque, Pompeian, Gothic, Cinque Cento, François Premier, and the more modern French'. For other people the lack of a style unique to the age was the most visible sign of a need for design reform. Ornament, they felt, had simply got out of control, and a return to basic principles was needed. The next 60 years were to be marked by a search, by government, critics, architects, artists and designers, to come up not only with a single style appropriate to the modern world but the means to achieve it. The solutions ranged from a government educational programme, based on the study of historical ornament, to the all-encompassing ideas of the Arts and Crafts movement in the 1880s, in which style was incorporated into a complete attitude towards designing and making.

In the end, this reforming drive did nothing to reduce the number of styles on offer. In fact its diverse approaches contributed to making the Victorian period the most stylistically eclectic episode in British history, a veritable bazaar of style, aided by ever-increasing access to cheap, mechanically produced goods. The Victorian treatment of style depended on the idea of synthesis, in which elements from different sources were combined into a new and coherent whole, eventually losing any link with their stylistic parents. The synthetic styles thus produced reflected a hitherto unparalleled knowledge of historical and non-European ornament and design, a fundamentally romantic approach to history and ornament, and a fascination with complexity and intricacy. Significantly, the Victorians' own style names were usually more atmospheric than accurately descriptive. It is hard for us

2

now to distinguish between two very similar neo-rococo chairs of 1851, called respectively Louis XIV and Louis XV. Similarly, the 'Queen Anne' style of the 1870s and 1880s was a charming hotchpotch of various English vernacular ideas taken from the sixteenth to the eighteenth centuries, sharpened by a dash of Japan.

The great Victorian style debate is exemplified by two books and an exhibition. A. W. N. Pugin's *Contrasts; or a Parallel between the noble edifices of the fourteenth and fifteenth centuries and similar buildings of the present day*, published in 1836, was the first work to attach strongly moral, religious and social values to a specific style (*see 13:40*). Pugin was not simply promoting the ideas and values

---

1 Detail of *Design for the interior of Breidenbach's shop, New Bond Street, London*, 1853. By Robert Lewis Roumieu. Breidenbach's, perfumier and distiller of eau-de-cologne to Queen Victoria, was fitted out in a synthesis of French rococo and Italian baroque elements. Pen, ink and watercolour. RIBA Library Drawings Collection.

2 *A design for the side of a room in the Louis Quatorze style*. Plate from *The House Decorator and Painter's Guide* by Henry and Aaron Arrowsmith, 1840. Hand-coloured etching and aquatint. VAM 47.N.34.

of the Middle Ages as a model for the nineteenth century, but was also saying that its style – medieval Gothic correctly treated – was the only true (and Christian) style. Gothic never shook off this moral load, and similar readings were soon being attached to other styles, especially those that opposed it.

Owen Jones's *The Grammar of Ornament*, published in 1856, marked an equally profound shift in the way that styles were perceived, but one that was directly opposed to the moral strain of Pugin. Promoted by the government's design education establishment, the *Grammar*, with its 100 coloured plates categorized by period and style, for the first time presented ornament (and therefore style) as a universal formal language, capable of being analysed and scientifically applied. Jones went on to set out a number of general principles of design and application of ornament, for his aim was not to promote historical revivals but to show how artists should, 'by an attentive examination of the principles which pervade all works of the past, and which have excited universal admiration, be led to the creation of new forms equally beautiful'. Although some of the principles were derived from Pugin, they were wholly free of Pugin's moral drive, except in so far as Jones saw all admiration of natural form as praise of the Creator.

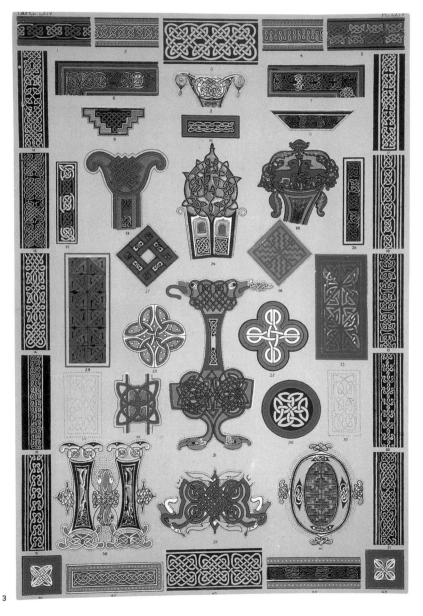

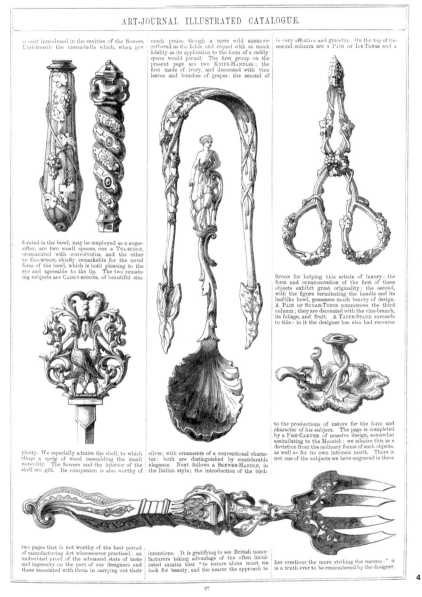

3 *Celtic No. 2.* Plate from *The Grammar of Ornament* by Owen Jones, 1856. Coloured lithograph. VAM L.1625-1986.

4 A page from the *Official descriptive and illustrated catalogue of the Great Exhibition*, 1851. 'There is not one of the subjects we have engraved in these two pages that is not worthy of the best period of manufacturing Art wheresoever practised.' VAM PP. 6.B.

The third key event was the Great Exhibition of 1851. Today, its contents are often held to exemplify the sheer confusion of Victorian design. The art manufactures on display are unfavourably compared with the great iron and glass structure of the Crystal Palace itself, a logical piece of engineering in a which historical style seems to have had no place. Contemporary reactions were very similar, at least among design-reforming critics like Ralph Nicholson Wornum. His essay on the 'The Exhibition as a lesson in Taste' regretted the departure from the Greek and Roman 'taste so active fifty years ago' and the 'endless specimens of the prevailing gorgeous taste of the present day, which gives the eye no resting-place, and presents no idea to the mind, from the want of individuality in its gorged designs'. As a lecturer in the Government School of Design, set up in 1837, Wornum was expressing a particular design-reform agenda which echoed that of the official drive to improve national design. This stemmed originally from a Parliamentary Select Committee, which reported in 1836 that British manufactures were losing the export race, principally because of the low quality of their design. The Exhibition showed that it was not simply a matter of exports but of the reform of national taste itself.

2. From Regency to Victorian: classical style

By 1837 almost all the historical styles that were to dominate Victoria's reign were already in use. The classical style, known as 'Greek', was dominant in public interiors and public architecture. Increasingly linear and abstract, it was attacked by Pugin in 1836 as the 'New Square style'. Its days were indeed numbered, at any rate for external architecture; in 1833 the critic and gardener John Claudius Loudon had pointed out that the Greek style, while acceptable in town, was unsuitable for country houses, spelling the beginning of the end for the neo-Palladian tradition in British architecture that had begun with Inigo Jones some 200 years earlier. More prophetic was a lusher style that intermixed classical with baroque and rococo elements, which had emerged in interiors of the 1820s. It was matched at a more modest level by a type of sinuously modelled, simplified classicism, which was characteristic of much furniture of the 1830s and 1840s, often accompanied by violently patterned and brightly coloured wallpaper and furnishing textiles. The second classical strain in architecture was the Italianate, a style derived equally from Picturesque villas and Renaissance *palazzi*. At first applied to large country houses and later to the royal residence of Osborne House (partly designed by Prince Albert), it became, from the 1850s up to the 1870s, the standard style for middle-class houses.

---

5 Osborne House, Isle of Wight, built 1845–8. Designed by Prince Albert and Thomas Cubitt.

6 *The Grand Hall and Staircase at Stafford House, London*, about 1843. By Joseph Nash. Stafford House (now called Lancaster House) was begun in 1820 as York House. Benjamin Dean Wyatt completed it from 1827 for the second Marquess of Stafford and his son, the second Duke of Sutherland. The hall and staircase were created in 1825–9 in a classical style with baroque and rococo elements. Watercolour. The Museum of London.

While neo-Palladianism died out in external architecture, in certain circles classical styles continued in favour after 1850, in interiors and household objects, and, reacting to new waves of archaeological discoveries and publications, even took on a greater accuracy. The 'Pompeian' decoration style of the 1860s onwards was matched by accurate (and usable) reproductions of ancient jewellery and furniture. From the 1860s the neo-classical and Empire styles were gradually rediscovered, first of all in exhibition pieces and then less expensively. From the 1870s the interiors of people of 'artistic' taste began to fill up with small, light 'Sheraton' and 'Hepplewhite' furniture (real or reproduction). In the 1890s Adam-style drawing rooms became the fashionable norm.

3. From Regency to Victorian: rococo and naturalism

The mid-eighteenth-century rococo style was first revived in the second decade of the nineteenth century. By the 1820s it was being incorporated into classical interiors. The style was to some extent derived from the English rococo style – notably that of Thomas Chippendale, whose furniture pattern book (as well as those of other English rococo furniture makers and carvers) was being reprinted and reproduced from the 1830s onwards – but was chiefly identified with France and was, indeed, the 'more modern French' style described by the Arrowsmiths. At first presented as a mixed style with the baroque (perhaps accounting for its popular name of 'Louis XIV'), it became in the 1840s a distinctly Louis XV style. In both Britain and France rococo was now the leading style for mainstream luxury decoration, a position that it retains to this day. While it was often used fairly accurately, imaginative variations were emerging by the 1830s, enabling rococo to become the main vehicle for the extravagantly modelled upholstery of the mid-nineteenth century, as well as the origin of the 'balloon back', the most common form of Victorian light chair.

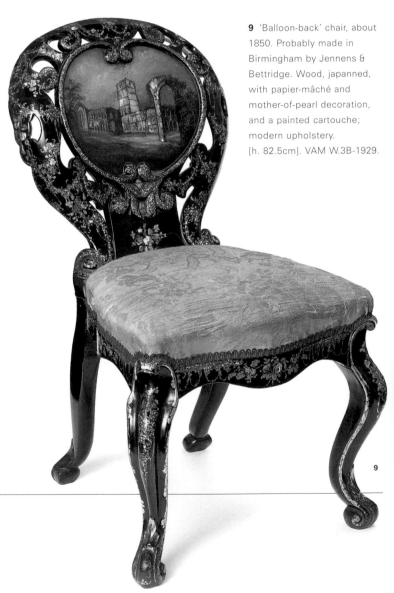

9 'Balloon-back' chair, about 1850. Probably made in Birmingham by Jennens & Bettridge. Wood, japanned, with papier-mâché and mother-of-pearl decoration, and a painted cartouche; modern upholstery.
[h. 82.5cm]. VAM W.3B-1929.

7 The drawing room, 118 Mount Street, London, 1894. Carried out in the 'Adam' style by the decorator Howard Hanks, for a Miss Walford. Photograph by H. Bedford Lemere. Albumen print. VAM 230-1926.

8 Coffee pot, with Sheffield hallmarks for 1872–3. Mark of W. & G. Sissons. The engraved horsemen were taken from the Parthenon marbles. Silver. VAM Circ.98-1961.

10

The plants and other natural forms that were a traditional part of the rococo style played a leading role in the development of naturalism, which became the most characteristic stylistic expression of the middle years of the century. The naturalistic style involved the use of sculptural figures and organic naturalistic ornament, often with a symbolic – or at least story-telling – intent. This trend, which had begun in the early years of the century, reached its peak in the 1840s and 1850s, with silver, ceramics and other materials being treated in a highly sculptural way. At its least extreme, naturalistic elements were added to objects of traditional form, while at its most developed, figures and organic forms created the whole shape of the object. This was something completely new, creating artefacts that broke entirely with historical exemplars.

4. A break with the past

Naturalism was taken up by Henry Cole, the design reformer and later the first Director of the South Kensington Museum, in his designing and making enterprise, called Felix Summerly's Art Manufactures, which began in 1847. Unlike most other expressions of the naturalistic style, the Summerly objects sought to use natural ornament in a manner appropriate to their function. Thus the 'well-spring' water carafe was decorated with a flower band and abstracted water-reed decoration (complete with decoratively disposed roots at the base), while a christening mug was decorated with protective angels.

The Summerly objects were also designed to combine ornament with practicality. The mug was carefully provided with a wide, undecorated lip for drinking, while a papier-mâché wine tray, unlike other products in the same material, had two practical depressions for glassware. The simplicity and logic of these objects becomes apparent when they are compared with expressions of naturalism shown at the 1851 Exhibition, which, although very popular, horrified design commentators with their stylistic freedom and lack of appropriateness. The artist Richard Redgrave, who had designed the 'well-spring' carafe, turned his back on naturalism in his comments on the Exhibition and, like Ralph Wornum, advocated a return to Renaissance styles and design principles.

11

12

10 *View of a Drawing Room in a London town house*, about 1855. By Samuel Rayner. Decorated in the revived rococo style. Watercolour. VAM E.1167-1948.

11 Gas jet lamp in the form of a convolvulus, the design registered in 1848. Made by the firm of R. W. Winfield, Birmingham. This lamp was shown in the Great Exhibition in 1851 and formed part of Henry Cole's display, in 1852, of Examples of False Principles in Decoration. Gilt brass and glass. VAM M.20-1974.

12 'Wellspring' water carafe, 1847–50. Designed by Richard Redgrave and made by J. F. Christy, Stangate Glassworks, Lambeth, London, for Felix Summerly's Art Manufactures. Glass, painted in enamel. VAM 4503-1901.

5. Plants and ornament: Owen Jones and Christopher Dresser

The official disapproval of naturalism did not extend to the use of natural ornament as a whole. The general enthusiasm for plants (so copiously evident in the naturalistic style) was matched by advances in the scientific categorization of nature and a corresponding drive towards a type of botanical ornament that was based on the scientific study of natural forms. Examples like Redgrave's design exercise on the sow-thistle led to a type of botanical ornament that was both highly decorative and sympathetic to the actual behaviour of plants. This reached its most effective form in the work of William Morris and the Arts and Crafts movement. Owen Jones attempted something more profound, maintaining in *The Grammar of Ornament* that nature had a key role to play in creating a new style that was to be separated from architecturally based historicism. If a student were to 'examine for himself the works of the past, compare them with the works of nature, bend his mind to a thorough appreciation of the principles which reign in each, he cannot fail to be himself a creator, and to individualize new forms, instead of reproducing the forms of the past'. It was left to Jones's disciple, the radical designer Christopher Dresser, to carry his hints into practice during the 1860s.

Today Christopher Dresser is perhaps best known for his designs for startlingly functional ceramics and metalwork of the 1870s and 1880s, which sprang from his central idea of fitness or 'adaptation to purpose'. Dresser's notion that it was possible to produce an 'artistic' object entirely without ornament was certainly revolutionary, but his ideas on ornament, based on botany, were equally daring. Both an art and design theorist and a scientific botanist, Dresser had drawn the plates of natural specimens at the end of Jones's *Grammar* and had lectured at the Government School of Design on artistic botany – that is, the application of scientific botany to design, a subject that he himself had invented. Dresser also preached that ornamentation was a fine art, which should 'ennoble and elevate our fellow-creatures'. Certain treatments of form and colour could, for instance, suggest repose, excitement or melancholy. He also believed that there were certain design principles common to all cultures, leading to a list of 'Grades in the Decorative Arts', from natural adaptations (the lowest form of ornament), through 'conventional treatment of natural form' and mental ideas suggested by nature, to the pinnacle of 'purely ideal ornament' – 'utterly an embodiment of mind in

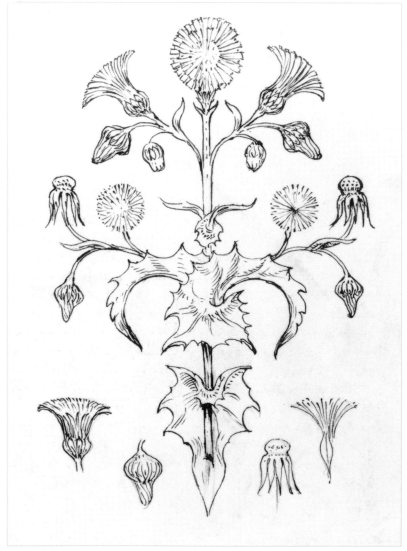

13 *A Study of a Sonchus or Sow Thistle*. By Richard Redgrave. Used as an illustration in his *Manual of Design*, 1876: 'the plant is displayed and flattened, whilst the form of the buds, the seed vessels and the leaves, are examined as new motives for ornaments'. Pen and ink. VAM 8452.B.

form'. From historical and exotic styles he assigned to the highest grade the 'Greek, the Moorish, the Early English, much of the Indian, and many features of the Japanese, and some parts of Egyptian and Renaissance', while in the lowest lay 'our modern floral patterns'. Perhaps the most extraordinary example of his theory was a pattern used on a Wedgwood vase in 1867, in which, he wrote:

> I have sought to embody chiefly the idea of power, energy, force, or vigour; and in order to do this, I have employed such lines as we see in the bursting buds of spring . . . and especially such as are to seen in the spring growth of a luxuriant tropical vegetation: I have also availed myself of those forms to be seen in certain bones of birds which are associated with the organs of flight . . . as well as those observable in the propelling fins of certain species of fish.

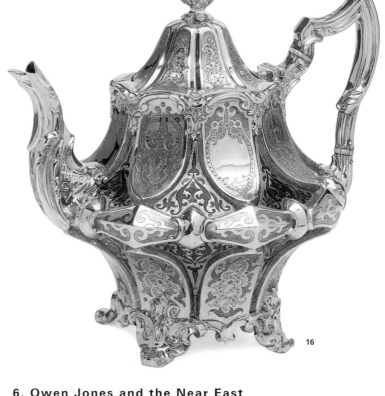

16

6. Owen Jones and the Near East

The original source of Jones's ideas and analysis of ornament was a close study of Islamic architecture and ornament. Islamic ornament in particular suited his reforming notions, as it was both naturalistic and carried out on geometrical principles. Jones's studies culminated in 1842–5 in the publication of the first serious account of Islamic design, *Plans, Elevations, sections and details of the Alhambra*, a study of the famous Moorish palace in Granada, Spain. The book used lavish chromolithographed plates to illustrate the all-important colouring of the palace interiors. The Islamic use of colour lay at the heart of the colour theories in design that Jones was developing. They were matched by contemporary advances in scientific colour theory, as well as by a growth of interest in the use of colour in ancient Greek and Roman architecture. Jones's colour theories were put into practice most famously at the 1851 Exhibition, where he painted the huge ironwork structure a mixture of primary colours calculated to merge into white at a distance.

Jones's publications led to the adoption of Moorish interlaced patterns and other motifs in textiles, tiles and other fields. At a more general level, the Moorish style was adopted for appropriate interiors,

---

14 Vase, 1867. Designed by Christopher Dresser. Made by Josiah Wedgwood and Sons, Etruria, Staffordshire, 1867. Earthenware, transfer printed, painted in enamels. John S.M. Scott, Esq.

15 *Window in the Mirador of Lindaraja, The Alhambra, Granada, Spain*. Plate from *Plans, elevations, sections and details of the Alhambra* by Owen Jones and Jules Goury, 1842–5. Coloured lithograph. VAM 110.P.36.

16 Teapot, with London hallmarks for 1850–1. Made for the Great Exhibition by Joseph Angell. The outline form and feet are rococo in style, but the modelling and other decoration are Near Eastern. Silver, parcel-gilt, with enamel decoration and ivory. VAM M.27-1983.

such as smoking rooms, while carefully selected Moorish and Near Eastern furniture and artefacts became an essential part of the art interior in the 1880s and 1890s. This use of exotic styles, which also included Indian and Japanese elements, was very different from the essentially frivolous and fantastic use of exoticism before 1850. By the final decades of the century their context was that of expanding European empires and their sources were the national displays in international exhibitions. But reactions to these exotic artefacts was far from negative, at least among design reformers. The products of India and Japan were perceived as being closer to their design ideal than anything produced at home. In 1852 the Museum of Manufactures, in buying from the Great Exhibition, spent as much on objects from India as from Europe. At the 1862 exhibition the architect William Burges admired the Japanese display as the 'true medieval court' for its attitudes to craft and design.

7. Gothic style

If any particular style is linked to the Victorian period today it is probably the Gothic Revival. Why should this be? The answer probably lies in the Church, for Gothic was the principal expression of an extraordinarily fervent religious revival. This not only encompassed new churches and their furnishings, but also the more or less vigorous restoration, re-ordering and refurnishing of almost every ancient church in the country in what was seen as the medieval manner. In the domestic architectural field, Gothic was much less in evidence, although it had never fallen out of favour as a suitable style for country houses since its inception in that field in about 1800. By the 1870s mass-produced Gothic details were creeping into ordinary houses. In public and civic buildings, however, Gothic was the leading serious style from the 1850s to the 1870s, although it was in contention with both the classical and the Renaissance styles.

The key event in the establishment of Gothic was the decision, following a disastrous fire in 1834, that the New Palace of Westminster (or Houses of Parliament) should be built in the Gothic or Elizabethan style. The choice was an official recognition that these styles represented the truest expression of British history and national identity. This idea had been growing since the beginning of the century, in tandem with an intensely Romantic attitude to the Middle Ages and the sixteenth century as periods of national glory and social stability. It reached its peak with such events as the Eglinton Tournament of 1839, an attempt by the nobility to re-create a medieval tournament. The same period saw the publication of Tennyson's Arthurian poems and a complete edition of Joseph Nash's *Mansions of England in the Olden Time*, in which the notion of Merry England – with contented peasantry and a benevolent aristocracy – was transplanted into surviving country-house interiors. Nash's imaginary Jacobean and Elizabethan world was backed up by real modern architecture, interiors, furniture and furnishings in the same styles.

17

17 The Victoria Tower, the Palace of Westminster, London, 1867. Built 1840–70. Designed by Sir Charles Barry and A. W. N. Pugin. Photograph by Stephen Ayling. Albumen print from wet collodion on glass negative. VAM 61.115.

18 The smoking room, Cecil Hotel, London, 1896. In the Indian style. The walls are covered with Doulton's tiles. Photograph by H. Bedford Lemere.

8. Pugin and principles

The completed New Palace of Westminster, which is still the largest secular Gothic Revival building in the world, was designed by the architect Charles Barry and the young A.W.N. Pugin, who provided most of the Gothic detail, both inside and out. Pugin's belief in Gothic as a style that could pull Britain back from the brink of social chaos has already been described. His theories were expanded in *The True Principles of Pointed or Christian Architecture*, published in 1841, which contained many of the ideas behind the subsequent treatment of the Gothic style. These went beyond a mere choice of period (although he favoured the 'Decorated' Gothic style of the early fourteenth century). Pugin urged architects and designers to work from the fundamental principles of medieval architecture and design. These included the banishing of features 'not necessary for convenience, construction or propriety' and the revealing of construction (but suitably beautified with ornament), so that a piece of architecture or design should clearly express its purpose, both symbolically and practically. This principle became a cornerstone of Victorian design reform.

In Pugin's own work, these ideas of truth to structure, function and material, and the rejection of 'sham' ('in God's house, everything should be real'), spread beyond architecture. They were applied to furniture in solid wood with revealed pegged construction, and to the employment of a group of manufacturers who could be trusted to make domestic and church furniture and fittings that obeyed his principles. As in architecture, correct ancient models were sought in furniture, metalwork and fittings, not only by Pugin, but also by the Ecclesiological Society, which adopted his ideas and applied them to reforming the interiors of existing churches, as well as influencing the form of new ones. In fact, from the 1840s church architecture and fittings were to take the lead in the Gothic style, culminating in the 1860s in a distinctive and very vigorous type of High Victorian Gothic. This rapidly departed from medieval precedent, taking on a particular nineteenth-century character.

19 *The Cartoon Gallery, Knole, Kent,* 1841. By Joseph Nash. Painted for his *Mansions of England in the Olden Time*, 1839–49. Watercolour. VAM 1037-1873.

THE GOTHIC REVIVAL

Jim Cheshire

During the Victorian period the Gothic style was transformed from an esoteric subject of Romantic contemplation to a major style in architecture and the decorative arts. For some 20 years, from the 1840s to the 1860s, it represented the cutting edge of high design.

The Victorian faith in the culture of the Middle Ages was exemplified early on by Lord Eglinton's re-creation of a medieval tournament at his Scottish castle in 1839. The event symbolized a strong feeling among Tory aristocrats that the utilitarian tendencies of the state had eroded patriotism and chivalry.

The architect Augustus Welby Northmore Pugin was a seminal figure in the history of the Gothic Revival, both as a theorist and as a practising designer. His key contribution was to give the Gothic style a moral impetus through arguments about the rationality of its construction. For Pugin, honesty of design lay in furniture or buildings that revealed their structure or supported the perceived essential properties of the material. These theories had direct stylistic consequences: furniture proudly proclaimed its construction with tusked tenon joints and huge decorative hinges, while veneer, non-structural ornament and 'Brummagen Gothic' were patently false.

21. *The Tournament at Eglinton*. By W. Gordon. From *An account of the tournament at Eglinton, revised and corrected by several of the knights*, 1839, by James Aikman. Published in Edinburgh by H. Paton, carver and gilder. Colour lithograph. VAM L.736-1937.

20. *Patterns of Brummagen Gothic*. From *The True Principles of Pointed or Christian Architecture*, 1841, by A. W. N. Pugin. VAM SC.94:0028.

22. Table, 1852–3. Designed by A. W. N. Pugin and made by John Webb of George Street, Hanover Square, London, for Francis Blanchard at Horsted Place, Sussex. Carved oak. VAM W.26-1972.

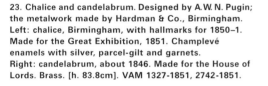

25. *Design for the Town Hall, Manchester*, 1867–8. By Alfred Waterhouse. Pen, ink and watercolour. VAM D.1882–1908.

23. Chalice and candelabrum. Designed by A.W. N. Pugin; the metalwork made by Hardman & Co., Birmingham. Left: chalice, Birmingham, with hallmarks for 1850–1. Made for the Great Exhibition, 1851. Champlevé enamels with silver, parcel-gilt and garnets. Right: candelabrum, about 1846. Made for the House of Lords. Brass. [h. 83.8cm]. VAM 1327-1851, 2742-1851.

24. *The Mediaeval Court*, 1851. By Louis Haghe. From *Dickinson's comprehensive pictures of the Great Exhibition of 1851*, 1854 (second edition; first published 1852). Printed and published by Dickinson Brothers, London, 1854. Colour lithograph. VAM 19536:15.

By the 1850s Gothic had gained momentum as a style for public buildings: all over the country Gothic churches were being built, and Pugin's Medieval Court was acknowledged as a major success of the Great Exhibition. The critic John Ruskin was the great Gothic theorist of the 1850s: he saw Gothic buildings as evidence of the liberty of the craftspeople who made them. For Ruskin, this liberty had been destroyed by capitalism, and Victorian Britain had a duty to restore this freedom to its artisans and artists. Pugin and Ruskin left a theoretical legacy that captivated a generation of Arts and Crafts designers later in the century, but in their hands these theories did not necessarily equate with the Gothic style.

William Burges is typical of the second generation of great Gothic designers: he had little of Pugin's religious or moral zeal and far wider aesthetic interests. Burges's taste was avant-garde: he collected Japanese prints and drew freely on designs from the Islamic world. All these influences are apparent in his extraordinary interiors, where the precise and serious symbolism of the Gothic Revival erupted into weird and wonderful fantasy schemes. As a Gothic designer he was too idiosyncratic to be really influential, but he remains a monument to the glorious disintegration of Gothic as the morally correct style in the later Victorian years.

26

27

26 Interior of the church of All Saints', Margaret Street, London, begun 1849. Designed by William Butterfield.

27 The Albert Memorial, London, built 1864–76. Designed by Sir George Gilbert Scott.

28 *The Winter Smoking Room, Cardiff Castle,* about 1870. By Axel Hermann Haig. The interiors at Cardiff Castle, designed by William Burges, were made from 1865 onwards. This room was decorated as shown. Watercolour. The National Trust, Knightshayes, Devon.

28

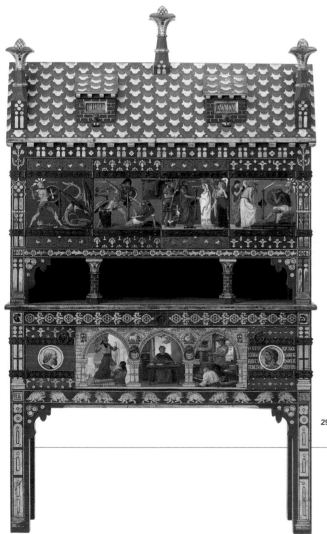

29

9. High Victorian Gothic

The tone for the style was set by the most famous of the ecclesiological churches, All Saints', Margaret Street, in London. Designed by William Butterfield and begun in 1849, it was built in the spirit of Gothic but without copying any particular details. Still standing today, its exterior is of uncompromising London brick and its interior is equally uncompromising, a shiny and almost violent display of machine-polished coloured stone and bright paint in strong patterns. The use of coloured stone, called 'structural polychromy', was first suggested in John Ruskin's *The Seven Lamps of Architecture*. Ruskin had studied its use in Italy, and its subsequent use in Britain ushered in a host of foreign Gothic ideas, which gave High Victorian Gothic its varied character. The machine-made ornament in All Saints' was also highly significant, for this type of Gothic was nothing if not frankly nineteenth-century, even accommodating exposed cast iron.

Perhaps the best-known example of High Victorian Gothic architecture today is Sir George Gilbert Scott's Albert Memorial, which was begun in 1864. Formed like a giant medieval shrine, it used in its decoration the same group of metalworkers, sculptors and others who had worked on the ornamentation and fitting-out of Scott's church work. It was from this group of Gothic architects and the medievalizing art-workers who supplied them with furniture, fittings, stained glass and textiles, metalwork and other furnishings that the first examples of painted 'art' furniture for the home emerged in the 1850s. They derived from medieval furniture and were plentifully supplied with painted decoration and metal trimmings. The most extreme exponent of this approach, the architect William Burges, was fortunate to find an immensely rich client in the mystically inclined third Marquess of Bute, for whom he created, from 1865, a number of extraordinary and completely furnished medieval fantasy buildings. Gothic art furniture of the 1850s developed during the next decade into a type of 'reformed Gothic' furniture, which matched contemporary Gothic architecture in its strong geometric lines and use of colour. Although a minority taste, reformed Gothic furniture played a major role in the earliest 'artistic' interiors of the 1870s, where it was combined with motifs from Japanese sources.

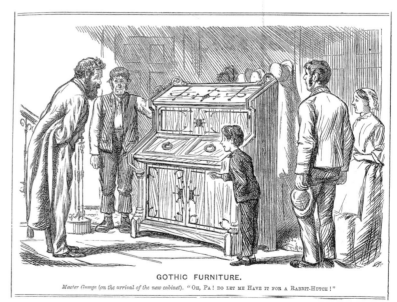

GOTHIC FURNITURE.

Master George (on the arrival of the new cabinet). "OH, PA! DO LET ME HAVE IT FOR A RABBIT-HUTCH!"

30

29 Cabinet, 1858. Designed by William Burges, painted by Edward J. Poynter and made by Harland and Fisher, London, for Herbert George Yatman. Pine and mahogany, painted and gilded. VAM Circ.217-1961.

30 *Gothic Furniture*. Cartoon from *Punch*, 18 November 1865. Ever ready to make fun of new styles, *Punch* here satirizes 'reformed Gothic' furniture. Wood engraving. VAM P.P.8.L.

THE BATTLE OF THE STYLES

Suzanne Fagence Cooper

Victorian designers had a bewildering diversity of styles at their disposal. Historical studies were developing apace, so it was possible for architecture and interiors to imitate classical, Renaissance or Gothic models more accurately. Past styles, moreover, could provide a reassuring appearance of stability and confidence at a time of disruptive social change. The introduction of Japanese and Middle Eastern elements into British design reflected new trading interests and commercial opportunities. London stores such as Liberty's imported exotic textiles, ceramics and metalwork to lend a modern artistic flavour to the drawing room. If a client wanted something more wholeheartedly British, then the simple shapes and restrained decoration of the Arts and Crafts workshops were ideal. The emphasis here was on skilled hand work, which sympathetically revealed the best qualities inherent in the raw material.

31. French-style grand piano, about 1840. Mechanism made by Erard & Co., London. Case designed and made by George Henry Blake for the wife of Thomas, Lord Foley, Baron Kidderminster. Satinwood marquetry with painted and gilded stand. [h. 95.3cm]. © 2001 The Metropolitan Museum of Art.

32. Egyptian-style upright piano, about 1870. Designed by William James and George Ashdown Audsley. Made in the workshop of W. H. and G. H. Dreaper. Ebonized wood, with carving, gilding and paint. National Museums and Galleries on Merseyside.

By the later years of the century all these styles, as well as some eclectic mixtures, battled for public attention in the displays and catalogues of department stores and furniture warehouses. A newly married couple could order a complete Old English dining room or a Louis XV boudoir from any number of Oxford Street stores.

33. The 'Manxman' piano. An Arts and Crafts-style upright piano designed in 1896 by Mackay Hugh Baillie Scott. Made in 1902–3, the mechanism by John Broadwood and Sons, London. Ebonized mahogany with carved wood, pewter, mother-of-pearl; marquetry of stained wood; silver-plated handles and hinges. VAM W.15-1976.

34. Arts and Crafts-style semi-grand piano, 1906–7. Designed by Sir Edwin Lutyens. Made by John Broadwood & Sons, London. Oak. VAM W.38-1984.

35. Oriental-style upright piano, with Japanese and Middle Eastern motifs, 1878. Designed by Henry W. Batley. Made by Collard & Collard, London; the case by James Shoolbred & Co., London. Carved boxwood. VAM W.26-1983.

Archetypal Victorian objects, such as pianos and teapots, were contorted to suit exotic or historical styles, however inappropriate they might be. With pianos, designers also had to wrestle with the problem of their unwieldy size and shape in their efforts to make them fit into their intended domestic surroundings. Technical improvements throughout the nineteenth century made the grandest instruments larger and more sonorous. It was only in the 1880s that design reformers returned to simplified shapes derived from harpsichords.

The piano provided a focus for Victorian social events, and particularly for female display. Consequently there was a strong incentive for the instruments to be lavishly decorated. They became a symbol of respectability among the aspiring middle classes. Wives and daughters relied on servants to do the household chores, so they had leisure time to spend at the piano. Richly decorated pianos dominated middle-class drawing rooms, signifying both their owner's taste and their social status. The eclectic range of motifs applied to these modern instruments – motifs whose origins ranged from the ancient past to the imperial present – represented one of the most distinctive elements of Victorian design.

36. Aesthetic-style grand piano, 1883. Designed by Sir Edward Burne-Jones. Decorated by Kate Faulkner. Made by John Broadwood & Sons, London. Oak, stained, with gilt and silvered gesso decoration. VAM W.23-1927.

10. The battle of the styles

The choice of Gothic for the Palace of Westminster did not go unopposed, and in fact marked the start of an architectural 'battle of the styles', a rivalry between classical and Gothic that ran up to the mid-1870s. It was seen most clearly in public buildings, where it reached its peak in the 1860s, with the newly established corporations of northern industrial towns building rival town halls: classical in Leeds, Gothic in Manchester. Even at the centre of government the battle raged, most famously over the Foreign Office in 1859, where Gilbert Scott was forced by the Prime Minister, Lord Palmerston, to replace his romantically towered Gothic scheme with an equally competent, if less romantic, Italianate scheme with an Osborne-like tower. The interiors were a blaze of colour in paint and stone.

In ecclesiastical architecture the styles divided along broadly denominational lines, with Gothic being chosen by the established Church, classical by the dissenters. The warehouses, offices and other commercial buildings rising in their hundreds in the burgeoning cities took full advantage of the elaborate eclecticism. Here, it was not a battle over principles but a battle for attention. In London at least the rivalry was welcomed by commentators, who saw the mixed styles and materials producing something like the variety seen in historical European city centres, in marked contrast to the plain uniformity (or tedium, as it was then seen) of the Georgian urban scene. In the City of London the classical dominated, with *palazzo*-like office blocks, but Gothic was especially favoured for warehouses, where its use for decoration was combined with cast-iron structures.

37

38

37 The Town Hall Leeds, West Yorkshire, built 1853–8. Designed by Cuthbert Brodrick.

38 The Town Hall, Manchester, Lancashire, built 1867–77. Designed by Alfred Waterhouse.

Perhaps the most vigorous supporter of the classical style was the government design reform machine itself, centred at the Museum and Government School of Design at South Kensington. Although the policy-formers of the South Kensington establishment had adopted many of Pugin's central ideas on design, they believed that Italian Renaissance, rather than Gothic, was the way forward for style, not simply because it included the best examples of the conjunction of art and manufacture, but because it most fully answered their ideas on the principles of design. The whole South Kensington complex from 1857 onwards was a built demonstration of the virtues of the North Italian Renaissance style, with elaborate coloured interiors in mosaic and ceramic in the same style (*see 13:22*). South Kensington largely failed to spread its brand of Renaissance beyond government buildings, but its adventurous experimentation with 'artistic' materials that would survive a corrosive urban atmosphere (notably strongly coloured brick and moulded terracotta), contributed a key element to the emergence of freer styles at the end of the century.

40

11. Art in the home

From about 1860 onwards ideas around the link between art and manufacture, and fine and decorative art, began to change in a way that had profound effects for the development of style. The activities of 'Art furnishers' promoted a new attitude towards design by producing furniture that was thought to have 'artistic' content. At first 'Art furnishing' was a minority taste, exemplified by the early work of William Morris and his associates, whose pioneering art-furnishing company was founded in 1861 as a direct result of Morris's inability to find sufficiently 'artistic' furniture for his own use in the commercial market. In the 1870s (and up to the end of the century) the word 'artistic' became a signal of the latest in design, led by the idea – as expressed in *Building News* in 1872 – that 'art and artistic feeling are as much shown in the design of furniture and other accessories as in what have hitherto been considered the higher or "fine" arts of sculpture and painting'. In architecture, too, 'artistic' ideas took hold among avant-garde 'art' architects, who thought of themselves more as artists (with studios) than as practitioners with drawing offices.

The artistic approach to design involved a highly eclectic and very free attitude to style. It also introduced, for the first time in fashionable interiors, the combination of antique and new furniture. Typically objects from Britain and abroad (and especially the Far East), and in a wide range of styles,

The " Kenilworth "

Occasional Table, in Walnut or Black Wood, very light and strong.

17/6

N.B.—The top of this Table is framed up of six pieces, producing a beautiful and varied effect of grain and colour.

The " Medina "

Five o'clock Tea Table, of richly grained wood in " Liberty " Art Colours, with old Arab Musharabiyeh decoration.

95/-

The " Hampden "

Coffee Table, strong and serviceable. In Walnut or Black Wood, **10/6**
In " Liberty " Art Colours, **15/-**

Liberty & Co.]   [16]   [Regent Street, London.

39

39 Three occasional tables in the *Art Furniture* catalogue of Liberty & Co. of London, 1884. Occasional tables were a sure sign of the artistic. 'Kenilworth', in spite of its name, was Japanese in style; 'Medina' incorporated real Arabic elements; and 'Hampden', with its turned legs, was adopted from cottage furniture. Line-block. VAM Liberty Catalogues (4)-1884.

40 Design for a block of shops and offices, about 1855. By John Burley Waring. Built in iron and glass, with polychromy, in a variation on the Venetian Gothic style. Pencil, water and body-colour. VAM 830:1.

were combined in tasteful harmony. The rooms of pioneers like Morris's collaborator, the artist Dante Gabriel Rossetti, in the 1860s contained light Regency furniture and East Asian blue-and-white porcelain (both to become hallmarks of the artistic interior of the 1870s and 1880s) and an Egyptian-style sofa designed by Rossetti himself. The products of the Morris firm tended to be broadly medieval in character and drawn from sources as diverse as sixteenth- and seventeenth-century botanical book illustrations and Italian fifteenth-century textiles. However, they also included light furniture (some designed by Rossetti) taken from early nineteenth-century models. In architecture, as in interiors and furniture, there was a return to eighteenth- and seventeenth-century styles, with an emphasis on ordinary town and country building. These trends can be broadly divided into two main stylistic areas, although they often overlapped – namely the Aesthetic style and the Old English and Queen Anne styles.

48 *The sitting room at 16 Cheyne Walk, London*, 1882. By Treffy Dunn. Dante Gabriel Rossetti reads to Theodore Watts Dunton. The Regency furniture, paintings and chimneyplace were in the room by 1863. In the corner is a Morris & Co. chair. Watercolour. National Portrait Gallery, London.

49 'Daisy' wallpaper, the design registered in 1864. Designed by William Morris, and based on botanical illustrations. Made for Morris, Marshall, Faulkner & Co. by Jeffrey and Co. Block-printed in distemper colours. VAM E.442-1919.

12. Old English and Queen Anne style

The rediscovery of domestic vernacular architecture was the most significant stylistic development of the second half of the nineteenth century. It began in the 1850s, with houses by such architects as George Devey and the Gothicist William Butterfield, and with Red House, designed in 1859 by Philip Webb for William Morris. These were fundamentally medieval in style, but incorporated later ideas. The Old English style, developed in the 1860s by William Eden Nesfield and Richard Norman Shaw, established a freely composed type of building based on half-timbered Tudor vernacular. Also in the 1860s, at the peak of High Victorian Gothic, another style emerged, which combined ideas from a wide range of modest English and Dutch red-brick buildings of the seventeenth and early eighteenth centuries, using them in a free and informal way. The settled name of this comfortable, adaptable and extremely influential style was Queen Anne, although one of its earliest exponents, the architect John James Stevenson, preferred the name 'Free Classic' or even 'Re-Renaissance'.

51

50

50 *Design for Leyswood, Groombridge, Sussex*, 1868. By Richard Norman Shaw for James William Temple. Pen and ink. RIBA Library Drawings Collection.

51 Red House, Bexleyheath, London, built 1859–60. Designed by Philip Webb for William Morris.

52

The Queen Anne style, mixed in with Old English, was used in the famous 'artistic' suburb of Bedford Park, London, and in much urban building, ultimately leading to a form of public building in the 1890s taken directly from the grand baroque architecture of Sir Christopher Wren. The interior of a Queen Anne house in town might have rooms in styles that were seen as being appropriate to their function, such as a Jacobean hall and dining room, a neo-classical 'Adam-style' drawing room and a Moorish billiard room. But the rooms at Bedford Park tended to have artistic interiors in the Aesthetic style, mixing elements as diverse as Georgian decoration and exotic forms, most notably of Japanese origin.

53

54

52 The Tower House and Queen Anne's Grove, Bedford Park, London, 1882. By M. Trautschold. Bedford Park, begun in 1876, contained buildings designed by a number of architects, but its style was set by Richard Norman Shaw, who designed the Tower House for the estate's developer, Jonathan T. Carr. Colour lithograph. VAM E.4039-1906.

53 *Sketch for a Hall. Modern Jacobean.* Plate from *Decoration and Furniture of Town Houses* by Robert William Edis, 1881. The Chinese jars and sunflower firedogs add an aesthetic touch. VAM 47.E.17.

54 Sideboard, 1867–70. Designed by Edward William Godwin, and made by William Watt and Co., London. A pioneering example of the Anglo-Japanese style. Ebonized mahogany, silver-plated metalwork and panels of embossed leather paper. VAM Circ. 38-1953.

13. Arts and Crafts and the morality of design

The Arts and Crafts movement marked the culmination of the trend towards morality in design that had begun with Pugin in the 1830s. Already by the 1850s the poorly made and sham had come to symbolize bad morals. The artistic movement of the 1870s believed strongly that the contemplation of beauty could by itself have a moral effect, making it possible for Lucy Orrinsmith, writing on interior decoration in 1878, to gush rather optimistically that 'it would be impossible to commit a mean action in a gracefully furnished room'. But for William Morris, the power of beauty was not enough. Although he was an art furnisher, his beliefs were fundamentally different from those of other art furnishers. He believed in the supremacy and moral worth of hand craftsmanship and in the central importance of the designer having a full understanding of the material in which he was designing. The ultimate goal was the general improvement of society.

By the 1880s these ideas had been taken up by a group of younger architects and designers, who had, like Morris, absorbed the notions of Pugin and Ruskin. In stylistic terms, however, they were very different from Morris.

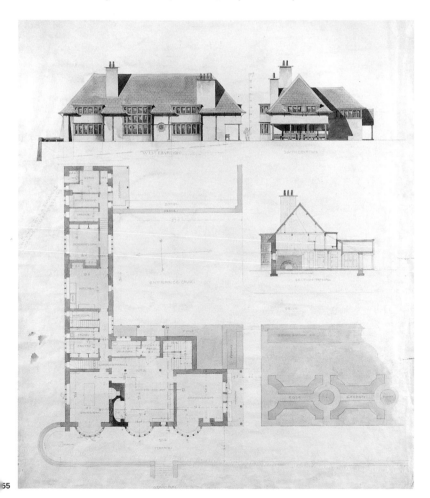

Influenced by Queen Anne style and Aesthetic ideas, they rejected Morris's medieval complexity and deeply coloured richness for a lightness of tone and stylish clarity of outline that were both simple and sophisticated. Unlike the Aesthetic designers, however, their models were resolutely British and centred on the seventeenth and eighteenth centuries, identifying an English tradition of design that, in the words of the architect Arthur Blomfield in 1890, was characterized by 'steadfastness of purpose, reserve in design and thorough workmanship'. The results were often startlingly original, not least in architecture and interiors, which strove to leave behind the 'copyism' of the historicist approach and identify the essence of form. From about 1890 the architect C. F. A. Voysey developed a remarkably pure avant-garde style based on a few perfect forms and motifs impeccably executed, as did the designer Ernest Gimson. In describing Gimson's cottage around 1900, the engraver F. L. Griggs wrote, 'newly cut stone and oak, bright steel and glass, and white walls reflecting the sunshine, nothing but for use and comfort, and all without any sort of make-believe'. In Gimson's simple space, at the very end of the Victorian era, we have travelled very far indeed from the garish, ornament-filled interiors of 50 years before.

55 Design for Broadleys, Cartmel, Lancashire, 1898. By C. F. A. Voysey. Pencil and watercolour. VAM E.252.1913.

56 *Music Room in a House at Crowborough*. By M. H. Baillie Scott. Illustration from *The Studio*, vol. 26, 1902, p.117. Colour halftone. VAM PP 73 A.

57 The interior of Ernest Gimson's cottage at Sapperton, Gloucestershire, about 1904. The armchair was designed by W. R. Lethaby, the table by Gimson himself.

ARTS AND CRAFTS

Linda Parry

Arts and Crafts was an approach to manufacture as well as a style. It developed in Britain during the last quarter of the nineteenth century and took its name from a society formed by a group of artists, designers and craftspeople keen to exhibit their work and provide a forum for the exchange of ideas.

The first exhibition of the Arts and Crafts Exhibition Society was held in London in 1888. It covered all aspects of art and design, from architecture, paintings and sculpture to furniture, textiles, ceramics, glass, metalwork, book binding and illustration, gesso, mosaic,

calligraphy and typography. The work, which was by both amateurs and professionals, was very varied in design, but a strong underlying philosophy controlled the way in which all the exhibits were designed and made. In time, this led to the characteristic style of the Arts and Crafts movement.

Galvanized by William Morris's ideas on the democratization of art and the importance and pleasure of work, Arts and Crafts

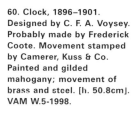

58. *The dining room at the Magpie and Stump, 37 Cheyne Walk, London*, the house of C. R. Ashbee, 1901. Interior designed by Ashbee. Attributed to Fleetwood C. Varley. Pencil and watercolour. VAM E.1903-1990.

59. Armchair, 1892–1904. Designed and possibly made by Ernest Gimson. Made in Pinbury or Sapperton, Gloucestershire. Ash, turned on a pole-lathe, with splats of riven ash; the rush seat is a replacement. VAM Circ.232-1960.

60. Clock, 1896–1901. Designed by C. F. A. Voysey. Probably made by Frederick Coote. Movement stamped by Camerer, Kuss & Co. Painted and gilded mahogany; movement of brass and steel. [h. 50.8cm]. VAM W.5-1998.

exponents increasingly turned away from large, mechanized factories as their main means of manufacture. Instead they set up small workshops, which concentrated not on speed and economy, but on the practical skills of the workers and the pleasure derived from craftsmanship. Importance was placed on the natural beauty of materials. Simple structures and techniques were used that would help to highlight these qualities. Many traditional methods of manufacture were revived. Just as the practice of specialized small-scale production emulated that of medieval guilds, so a nostalgia for the vernacular traditions of the British countryside provided the main inspiration for the design of Arts and Crafts houses, both inside and out.

Many Arts and Crafts followers also sought to live a simple country life, moving out of towns and setting up workshops in rural areas. Some went to areas that could supply the materials for their particular needs. Frequently this provided much-needed work for a local workforce no longer able to secure a living from the land.

Although the style was associated with the countryside, the movement had a strong cosmopolitan base. Many leading exponents were based in cities, and its popularity continued to spread through shops such as Liberty's, which adopted the style as its own. By the end of the century Arts and Crafts ideals had infiltrated the design and manufacture of all the decorative arts in Britain, while its influence in Europe and America was also gaining ground.

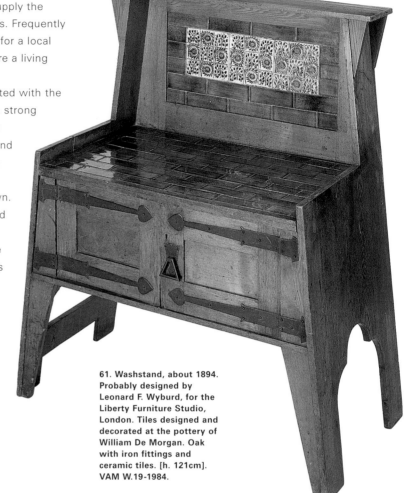

61. Washstand, about 1894. Probably designed by Leonard F. Wyburd, for the Liberty Furniture Studio, London. Tiles designed and decorated at the pottery of William De Morgan. Oak with iron fittings and ceramic tiles. [h. 121cm]. VAM W.19-1984.

62. Vase and cover, 1888–98. Designed by William De Morgan and decorated at the De Morgan pottery, Sand's End, Fulham, London. Earthenware, painted in lustre on a blue background. [h. 30.4cm]. VAM C.413-1919.

63. Detail of a curtain, designed 1896. Designed by C. F. A. Voysey. Made in Darvel, Strathclyde, by Alexander Morton & Co. Sold through Liberty & Co. Woven woollen double cloth. VAM Circ.886-1967.

64

14. Art Nouveau and the Glasgow School

The last significant stylistic development of Queen Victoria's reign took place in Glasgow in Scotland, where a remarkable group of architects and designers, including Charles Rennie Mackintosh, Margaret and Frances Macdonald and Herbert MacNair, came together in about 1893. They devised a new style, which was the closest that advanced British design came to continental Art Nouveau. In fact, Art Nouveau was one of their sources, but others included medievalizing British painting, continental symbolist art, the drawings of Aubrey Beardsley and the designs of C. F. A. Voysey, while their general approach was profoundly affected by the Arts and Crafts movement.

Mackintosh's architecture was a brilliant synthesis of Gothic, old Scottish and other ideas, best shown in his Glasgow School of Art, begun in 1897. Although its work was celebrated abroad, the Glasgow group's influence on British design was small. Together with the Arts and Crafts style and continental Art Nouveau, it fed into the synthetic style, which in the 1890s became the trademark of the London department store of Liberty & Co. The products of the Arts and Crafts movement, and indeed of Liberty's, reached only the upper middle classes. For the rest, all the styles shown in the 1851 Exhibition were still available in their infinite variety.

64 Sheet of sanitary (washable) wallpaper, the design registered in 1895. Made by the firm of David Walker, Middleton, Lancashire. The design combines rococo, Jacobean, classical and naturalistic motifs. Sanitary papers were intended for halls and kitchens, their cheapness making them widely used. Colour-printed from engraved rollers. VAM E.1943-1952.

65 Chair, made about 1900. Originally designed in 1897 by Charles Rennie Mackintosh for Miss Cranston's tearooms, Argyle Street, Glasgow. This example is from a set made for Mackintosh's Glasgow flat. Stained oak; modern upholstery. VAM Circ. 130-1958.

66 The Glasgow School of Art, first phase, 1907–9. Designed by Charles Rennie Mackintosh.

66

67

67 The ladies' drawing room, King's Head Hotel, Sheffield, 1902. An interior in the mixed modern style promoted by Liberty & Co. The chairs carry Glasgow School rose motifs, the cabinet is inspired by Voysey and an Art Nouveau dish is on the table. Photograph by H. Bedford Lemere.

65

3289

3290

3291

3292

3293

3294

3295

3296

3297

3298

3299

3300½

CHAPTER 13

Victorian Britain, 1837–1901

Who led taste?

MICHAEL SNODIN

1. Finding the way

Walk down any antiques market, or leaf through any Victorian shop catalogue or journal, and one of the most characteristic features of the Victorian age is immediately apparent: its staggering range of visual choice. How did the Victorians navigate through this immense quantity of ingenious elaboration? In fact there was no shortage of people eager to help; more ink being spilt on the subject of taste in Victoria's reign than at any time before or since. Commentators included weighty critics like Ruskin, Morris and Pugin, newly professionalized architects and designers, journalists, novelists, interior decorators, teachers, exhibition, museum and gallery organizers, and those who formed government design policy.

In contrast to previous eras, the majority of these putative taste makers were professionals with an axe to grind. Most were reacting to what they saw as a crisis in design, triggered by the end of the old, classically based certainties of the 'rule of taste' linked to an ordered society. These certainties were, they felt, unsustainable in the face of stylistic proliferation, social change and ever-cheaper goods. The resulting confusion was all too easily filled by manufacturers happy to make what the public wanted. Those critics who tried to seize control of the situation believed that the old idea of high design as an expression of social authority had evaporated; on the other hand, it was now available to a huge public and, with the added uplifting ingredient of art, had the potential to be an influence for good in the broadest sense. Although they disagreed, sometimes violently, in their fundamental aims and solutions, all the critics believed that taste had to be controlled – for the good of the consumer, the good of the maker and, ultimately, the good of the nation.

This moral and social imperative set apart the taste-making processes of Victorian Britain from what came before. That is not to say that many of these processes did not have earlier beginnings. The commercial drive that produced the Victorian department store differed only in scale from the great shopping advances of the Regency. Design-conscious art manufacturers, like the potters Minton and Doulton, were building on earlier examples such as Wedgwood and the Regency goldsmiths Rundells. Government design reform initiatives from the 1830s represented the culmination of a century of fitful attempts to raise national design standards in the economic battle against imported manufactured goods, especially those that came from France. The mechanisms of these reforms, the official design schools, the museums of applied art and the various attempts to establish national design standards were, however, entirely new.

The nature of patronage of architecture and design was also shifting. Firstly, compared with the years before 1837, patrons were becoming less important, as architects and designers set themselves up as a professionalized group of self-appointed and self-publicizing taste makers. Rich families with old money, like the Dukes of Devonshire at Chatsworth, who had consumed advanced taste in the past, tended to become conservative, pursuing historicist styles and rarely employing leading designers or architects. The Marquess of Bute, for whom the architect William Burges devised complete medieval environments, was a notable exception (see 12:28). Some of the newer rich, like the Rothschild family, favoured the French style, an international symbol of modern, but conservative, luxury. On the other hand, many newly

---

1 Detail of a page from the *Glass and China Book*, published by Silber and Fleming Ltd, of London, 1880–90. Colour lithograph. VAM A.20.16.

moneyed manufacturers, merchants and entrepreneurs became significant collectors of art, especially in the 1870s and 1880s.

Sir William Armstrong of Newcastle, inventor, engineer and armaments manufacturer, built the great country house of Cragside and filled it with the works of Albert Moore and Dante Gabriel Rossetti, while the Liverpool ship owner Frederick Leyland fitted into his London house the Peacock Room, the most famous Aesthetic-style interior. But such patrons were in the end far less significant leaders of taste than their more modest middle-class counterparts, among whom there were many artists, like William Morris (whose Red House was the focus of design activity by several of his friends) and J. M. Whistler (whose studio house, which was designed by E. W. Godwin, was too radical for the local government officials of the Metropolitan Board of Works).

2

3

2 The south drawing room, Halton House, Buckinghamshire, 1892. The house was finished in 1886 for Alfred de Rothschild, a notable collector of pictures. Photograph by H. Bedford Lemere.

3 The Peacock Room at 47 Prince's Gate, London, 1892. Designed by Thomas Jeckyll and painted by James McNeill Whistler for the shipbuilder Frederick R. Leyland. Photograph by H. Bedford Lemere. Albumen print. VAM PH.240-1926.

4 Design for the White House, Chelsea, London, 1877. By Edward William Godwin. This design was turned down by the Metropolitan Board of Works, which made Godwin add more ornament. Watercolour, pen and ink. VAM E.540-1963.

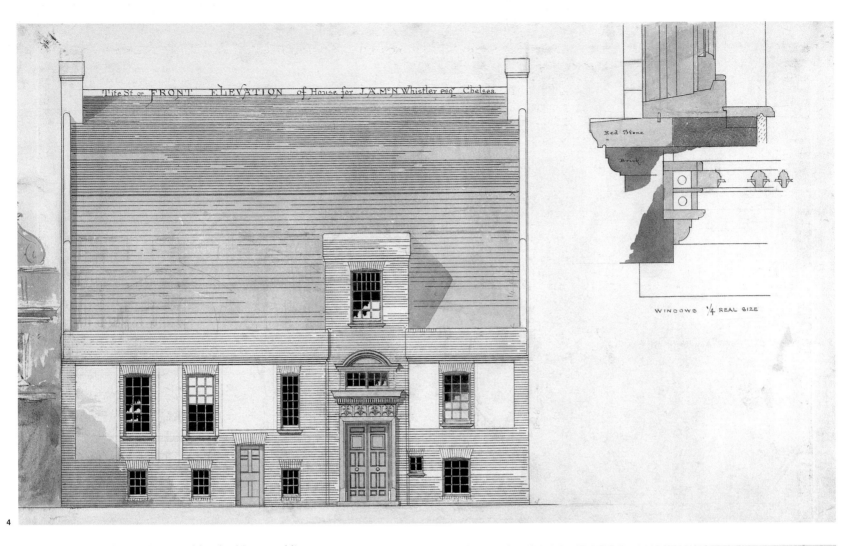

In an age of grandiose public building, public patronage also played a key role in the formation of taste. At South Kensington the government design establishment attempted to create, by example, a classical national style. A newly revived Church of England inspired a mass of building, restoration and furnishing. Other public bodies, like the London School Board, also played a role. Its 'beacons of light' in some of London's poorest districts were built (at least externally) in the very new, 'Queen Anne' style – a symbol of a better lifestyle, which was designed to appeal to the middle-class ratepayer and stamp a clear brand on the school enterprise. While the moral effect on the children is unknown, the schools certainly helped to spread the Queen Anne style to local house builders.

5 The London Board School, Gloucester Road, Camberwell, London, opened in 1875. Designed by Edward Robert Robson. Greater London Photographic Library.

THE CHURCH

Jim Cheshire

Ecclesiastical design was a burning issue for the Victorians. The range of design solutions to the differing denominational demands is aptly illustrated by the contrast between Pugin's idealized interior of 1844 and the 'Tabernacle' built for the immensely popular Baptist preacher Charles Haddon Spurgeon between 1859 and 1861.

The architectural focus of Spurgeon's church is the pulpit – appropriate for a form of worship where the sermon is the focal point of the service. The auditorium seated 6,000 people. The architectural and aesthetic focus of a Puginian church is the east end, where the density of ornament signifies the sacrament of the Eucharist: the focus of the Roman Catholic Mass.

6. *An Altar hung for a Funeral Mass*. Lithographed by H. C. Maguire after A. W. N. Pugin. From *Glossary of Ecclesiastical Ornament and Costume* by Pugin, 1844. Colour lithograph. VAM G.58.G3.

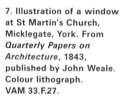

7. Illustration of a window at St Martin's Church, Micklegate, York. From *Quarterly Papers on Architecture*, 1843, published by John Weale. Colour lithograph. VAM 33.F.27.

Attitudes within the Church of England covered almost the whole spectrum between these two poles. The new radicals of the Oxford Movement stressed the Roman Catholic roots of the Anglican Church; their sympathizers in Cambridge took it upon themselves to invent ecclesiology: the 'science' of church building. This combined

8. Left: chalice, with London hallmarks for 1867–8. Designed by William Burges. Made by Jes Barkentin of Barkentin & Krall, London. Silver-gilt, enamels, semi-precious stones and stained glass. [h. 21.4cm]. Background: altar frontal, 1875. Designed by J. P. Seddon. Made by a professional embroiderer for St Andrew's, Wells Street, London. Woven silk damask and velvet embroidered in floss silks in long and short, satin and stem stitches with couched Japanese gold thread, seed pearls and metal ornaments. Right: missal, 1870. Designed by George Henry Birch. Made by Jes Barkentin. Binding: parcel-gilt with enamels and gems. VAM Loan: Kingsbury. 1-1985, Loan: St Andrews.1, Loan: Kingsbury.3.

9. Tiles: The Evangelists, about 1845. Designed by A. W. N Pugin. Made in Stoke-on-Trent, Staffordshire, by Minton & Co. Earthenware with inlaid decoration. [h. 43.4cm]. VAM C.81-1976.

10. Ecclesiastical cope and hood, 1848–50. Designed by A. W. N. Pugin for use at St Augustine's Church, Ramsgate, Kent. Made in London and Birmingham. Silk velvet with velvet appliqué, surface embroidery in silks, with raised, padded and couched work in silks and silver-gilt wire, and thread. VAM T.289–1989 and T.287-1989.

the theology of the Oxford Movement with Pugin's theories and transformed them into churches and church furniture. Opponents of the Oxford Movement, mainly Evangelicals, favoured worship closer to Spurgeon's principles than to Pugin's and portrayed ecclesiological innovations as dangerous and sometimes even illegal. Controversies raged throughout the Victorian period, eventually redefining the relationship between the state and the Church, with the state gaining the upper hand.

Thousands of churches were built or restored by all denominations, but it was the densely decorated churches promoted by ecclesiologists that provided much of the market. Church work surged in the 1840s, but probably did not peak until the 1870s, providing a wealth of opportunities for architects and designers of metalwork, stained glass, tiles and church furniture. The amount of money raised from private sources was enormous. An increased demand for commemorative and memorial products fitted

in well with ecclesiastical products and provided numerous commissions for manufacturers and designers.

During the 1840s journals and books were important in disseminating the new stylistic vocabulary demanded by the increasingly discerning ecclesiastical patron. Ecclesiological societies and commercial publishers produced hundreds of images of historical sources, which the designers transformed into distinctly Victorian products.

With hindsight, we can see many of the developments in Victorian religion as heralding the gradual secularization of British culture, but to the Victorians theirs was the great age of church building, and for us it remains an important period of ecclesiastical design.

11. *Interior of the Metropolitan Tabernacle, London* (detail), 1861. Designed by W. Wilmer Pocock. From *The Builder*, 4 May 1861. Engraving. VAM PP.19.G.

2. Art and commerce

In 1857 Sir Thomas Acland, a friend of John Ruskin, wrote there were 'at least three parties contending in England for the mastery of guidance in the arts'. Firstly, there was the Royal Academy, in which 'the traditions of the past and the tastes of the dilettanti find expression'. Secondly, the Government Schools of Design, with their 'doctrinaire adherence to abstract principles'. Thirdly, there was 'Mr Ruskin and his pre-raphaelite allies – a considerable force of irregulars'. The last two represented the main reactions to the Victorian design crisis. The government design establishment thought that the answer to taste control lay in working with the forces of commerce through a rational programme, although manufacturers, with a keener sense of what the market would bear, were reluctant allies. Ranged against them was a fundamentally anti-commercial tendency, of which Ruskin and Morris were a part, which worked on broader cultural lines, believing in the power of art to transform society. At the start of the Victorian period the first group had the upper hand; by the end, the second was in control. In practice the efforts of both groups were more or less compromised by their reliance on rigid standards of taste, which completely failed to take into account the complexities of a mixed market. Most consumption of visual culture continued to lie outside the charmed circle of the visually approved.

Two of the tangible results of Victorian government involvement in national design issues, and what we would now call design politics, are still with us: the Victoria and Albert Museum, successor to the South Kensington Museum, and the Royal College of Art, whose ancestor, the Government School of Design in London, was founded in 1837. Both the school and the museum, which was originally attached to it, came out of the report of a Parliamentary Select Committee on the arts and their Connexion with Manufactures. It sat in 1835 and 1836, partly to investigate the Royal Academy and partly to 'enquire into the best means of extending the knowledge of the arts and the principles of design among the people (especially the manufacturing population) of the country'. Although the establishment of the Committee should be seen in the context of the general tendency towards enlarging education provision that followed the Great Reform Act of 1832, its main purpose was to improve the design quality of British manufactures in the context of moves towards free trade. The Committee's conclusions were predictable. Witness after witness (including manufacturers, retailers and artists) 'felt themselves compelled to draw a comparison more favourable (in the matter of design) to our foreign rivals, and especially the French, than could have been desired'. Only a system of design schools, both in London and in the manufacturing towns, could, it was asserted, solve the problem.

The resulting London design school – pioneering in the British context – was modelled on those in Germany and France and was appropriately enough run by the Board of Trade. Provincial schools survived only as far as they were supported by local manufacturers. From the start there were problems, principally because of resistance to attempts to limit the schools' teaching to the applied arts, but gradually a curriculum emerged in the London school, which taught (at least in theory) the history and principles of ornament. The arrival in the mid-1840s of Henry Cole transformed the situation, not only of the schools, but also of public visual education in Britain.

12 Teaset, designed 1846, made 1846–71. Designed by Henry Cole for Felix Summerly's Art Manufactures. The set was awarded a silver medal by the Society of Arts. Made by Minton & Co., Stoke-on-Trent, Staffordshire. Earthenware. VAM 2741-4-1901.

13

14

3. Henry Cole and Prince Albert

Even in an age of great men, Henry Cole was an extraordinary figure. Before 1849 he had played a key role in reorganizing the public records and setting up the Penny Post. He applied a similar single-minded approach to his next project, which was nothing less than the reformation of national design and design education along rational and utilitarian lines. To that end he set up his own manufacturing enterprise (Felix Summerly's Art Manufactures) and a propagandizing magazine (the *Journal of Design and Manufacture*) and was the key figure, with Prince Albert, in staging the Great Exhibition. Following that triumph, and after much characteristic manoeuvring behind the scenes, Cole was given control of the School of Design and its museum. With the establishment of the Department of Practical Art and the move of both school and museum to South Kensington, he was able to achieve his ideal.

The 'South Kensington System', a centralized system of art and design education, extended beyond the London school to provincial design schools and right down to elementary schools. Consistency was assured by a rigid curriculum centred on abstract drawing exercises and a scheme of national prizes. The whole system was based on the set of simple and rational design 'principles' formalized by Cole and his team, notably Richard Redgrave and Owen Jones. They were also used in the arrangement, design and decoration of the South Kensington Museum (and its associated institutions in Dublin and Edinburgh), turning them into demonstrations 'by which all classes might be induced to investigate those common principles of taste, which may be traced in the works of excellence of all ages'.

GENERAL PRINCIPLES OF DECORATIVE ART.

The true office of Ornament is the decoration of Utility. Ornament, therefore, ought always to be secondary to Utility.

Ornament should arise out of, and be subservient to Construction.

Ornament requires a specific adaptation to the Material in which it is to be wrought, or to which it is to be applied; from this cause the ornament of one fabric or material is rarely suitable to another without proper re-adaptation.

True Ornament does not consist in the mere imitation of natural objects; but rather in the adaptation of their peculiar beauties of form or colour to decorative purposes controlled by the nature of the material to be decorated, the laws of art, and the necessities of manufacture.

PUBLISHED BY CHAPMAN AND HALL, 193, PICCADILLY, LONDON.

15

---

13 Detail of a plate from *The Drawing Book* by William Dyce, 1842. Dyce, a painter, was Superintendent of the London School of Design. Lithograph. VAM 15561:a 2.

14 Prize drawing of a plaster cast, 1840. Made by R. W. Herman at the Government School of Design. Black and white chalk. VAM E.1967-1909.

15 One of eight placards on design, published by the Department of Science and Art in 1853. They were hung up in the classrooms of the Government School of Design. VAM 52.D.68.

THE GREAT EXHIBITION OF THE WORKS OF INDUSTRY OF ALL NATIONS

Paul Greenhalgh

The Great Exhibition of 1851 transformed everyone's vision of what an exhibition might be. The world's first large-scale temporary international exhibition, or 'expo', it aimed to bring together as complete a range as possible of manufactured produce, across the arts and sciences. Staged in Hyde Park inside the legendary Crystal Palace, a giant iron, wood and glass structure, the exhibition ran for six months from 1 May. It had 6,039,195 visitors, of whom 4,439,419 paid the minimum one-shilling entrance fee. The public were particularly enthralled by the displays of technology, with working steam engines, and by the extraordinary display of raw materials and artworks gathered from the nations in the British Empire.

By the time the exhibition closed it had generated a profit of £186,000, a vast sum in those days. These profits were used to pay for a succession of international exhibitions throughout the century and to found museums at South Kensington, including the Victoria and Albert Museum.

16. *Aeronautic View of The Palace of Industry For All Nations*, 1851. By Charles Burton. Published by Ackermann & Co., London. Colour lithograph. VAM 19614.

Though funded mainly by the private sector, the Great Exhibition was in reality a government initiative to improve standards of design in British manufacturing and to educate the public in matters of taste. The 'taste makers' responsible for it were not a sophisticated aristocratic élite, as they might have been in previous centuries, but civil servants, manufacturers and art teachers. Committed simultaneously to the improvement of manufacturing industry and to the general public, many of them thought that the way forward was to fuse art and industry.

17. *The Agricultural Court*, 1851. By an anonymous artist. Published by Lloyd Brothers & Co. and Simpkin Marshall & Co., London. Colour lithograph with hand colouring. VAM 19538:25.

18. *The Indian Court*, 1852. From *Dickinson's comprehensive pictures of the Great Exhibition of 1851*, 1854 (second edition; first published 1852). Printed and published by Dickinson Brothers, London, 1854. Colour lithograph. VAM 19536:11.

19. Pair of vases, about 1851. Made by Charles Meigh & Son, Hanley, Staffordshire, and exhibited at the Great Exhibition of 1851. Stoneware with relief moulding and painted decoration in enamels and gilding. [h. 101.6cm]. VAM Circ.374-1963 and Circ.418-1963.

20. *The Crystal Palace Transept after the close of the exhibition*, 1852. By Benjamin Brecknell Turner. Albumen print from waxed paper negative. VAM PH.1-1982.

Since 1851 the Crystal Palace itself has consistently been recognized as an architectural masterpiece. Pioneer modernist Le Corbusier looked back on it as the first true work of modern architecture. In contrast to the elegant construction of the building and its delicate ornamental detailing, the objects displayed inside were widely thought to be vulgar and tasteless. Critics then – and later – saw this gathering of high Victoriana as an artistic disaster.

The Great Exhibition triggered a period of design reform in Britain. As a result of the exhibition, art and design criticism grew dramatically as a profession, the taste of its salaried critics being characterized by a rejection of complex, eclectic decoration and an embracing of simpler surfaces and restrained profiles. It seems that positive lessons were taken from the building and negative ones from its contents.

21

23

The buildings were designed in the recommended northern Italian Renaissance style and demonstrated technical experiments in new building materials. Like contemporary churches, their interiors carried instructive and edifying images and mottoes tailored to the contents of the rooms. The whole was a determined attempt to bring high design and high art to the widest possible public.

The most precious objects at South Kensington were, by the late 1860s, contained in a memorial gallery to the Prince Consort. This was entirely appropriate, for Prince Albert was the fairy godfather of the whole enterprise. While Queen Victoria reflected rather than led national taste, Prince Albert worked actively to bring about design reform, linking it to his interest in science and technology. Within the royal sphere, he set an example as a collector and patron of art and architecture. He was also a designer in his own right, conceiving a silver centrepiece and the influential royal seaside villa, Osborne House on the Isle of Wight. The Prince's Germanic taste and foreign connections brought to England experts from abroad, who carried with them advanced theoretical ideas about art and design. These included the art historian Ludwig Gruner and the architect and art-

22

21 The original entrance front of the South Kensington Museum, London, built 1864–6. Designed by Captain Francis Fowke. The terracotta decoration was designed by Godfrey Sykes.

22 *View of the ceramic gallery, South Kensington Museum, London*, 1876–81. By John Watkins. The gallery was designed by F. W. Moody and Godfrey Sykes, and created in 1867–9. The frieze and columns carried names of potters and factories; the stained-glass windows showed ceramic manufacture. Etching. VAM E.370A-1900.

23 Tazza, commemorating the life and work of Prince Albert, 1863. Designed by John Leighton. Made in Stoke-on-Trent, Staffordshire, by William Taylor Copeland. Engraved by Charles Henry James. Glazed earthenware, transfer-printed. [h. 12.8cm]. VAM 715-1899.

SCIENTIA NON HABET INIMICUM NISI IGNORANTEM

24

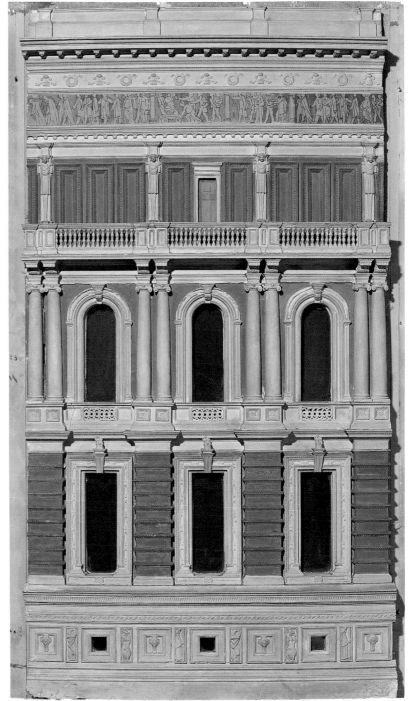

25

historical theorist Gottfried Semper, who taught at the Government School of Design and designed the Duke of Wellington's great funeral car, as well as a neo-Renaissance scheme for South Kensington in 1857. In the event, lack of cash killed Semper's scheme, 'very much . . . to the Prince's disappointment'. When permanent buildings did go up in the 1860s, they were in the Semperian manner, albeit designed by officers of the Royal Engineers.

In the end, however, the Prince was most significant as a committee chairman leading the key design events of the 1840s and 1850s. In 1843 he became chairman of the largely dormant Society of Arts, turning it (together with Cole) into an engine that eventually produced the Great Exhibition of 1851. He was also involved in the Dublin exhibition of 1853 and the Manchester Art Treasures exhibition of 1857. But Prince Albert's greatest contribution was the conception of the idea of 'an establishment, in which, by the application of Science and Art to Industrial pursuits, the Industry of all nations may be raised in the scale of human employment', making permanent the ideals of the Great Exhibition. Bought with the profits of the Exhibition, South Kensington (itself a new name) became such a centre, incorporating art, science and natural history museums, colleges, the Royal Horticultural Society gardens and the Albert Hall, as well as a succession of international exhibitions. Most of the numerous buildings reflected the official style.

24 Sgraffito plaster decoration on the Science Schools, South Kensington (now the Henry Cole Wing, Victoria and Albert Museum). Designed by F. W. Moody and carried out by students of the Art School, formerly the Government School of Design, 1872. Contemporary photograph. VAM Picture Library.

25 Model for the façade of the Royal Albert Hall of Arts and Science, London, 1868. By Major-General Henry Young Darracott Scott. Officers from the Royal Engineers led the building activities at South Kensington. The hall was opened in 1871. Plaster. VAM A.11-1973.

THE SOUTH KENSINGTON MUSEUM

Karen Livingstone

The South Kensington Museum opened in 1857 and was the first public institution in Britain to try to educate directly an audience of students, manufacturers and the general working public through its diverse collections of contemporary art, manufactures and historical decorative art. Its foundation was the result of 20 years of progressive effort to improve standards of taste and manufacture in Britain. Under the administration of Henry Cole and his joint secretary, the artist Richard Redgrave, the museum grew beyond its origins as part of the government initiative to train students of design.

From about 1840 a collection of objects was formed for the Government School of Design, augmented by objects from the Great Exhibition, selected to demonstrate excellence of manufacture. In 1852 the school and museum moved to Marlborough House, where the newly appointed Cole promoted the museum's aim of improving taste by employing a series of principles of art. Tunisian textiles, for example, demonstrated the successful distribution of form and harmony of colour. Cole contrasted these 'true' examples of manufactures with a celebrated but short-lived display of 87 examples of 'False

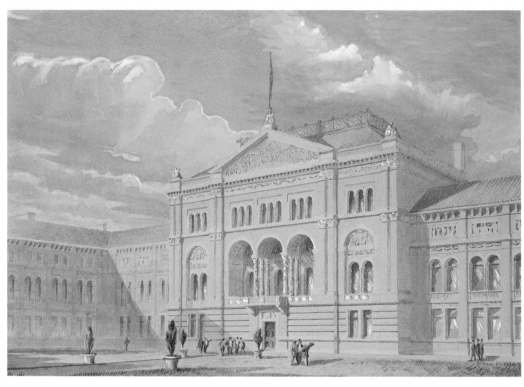

27. Detail of *Sketch for the north side of the quadrangle of the South Kensington Museum*, 1860. By Captain Francis Fowke. Watercolour. VAM E.1318-1927.

Principles in Decoration', to illustrate where British manufacturers were going wrong. The 'chief of the vices' was the 'direct imitation of nature', as illustrated by exhibit 16, a 'furniture chintz' imitating ribbon and roses on a flat surface and lacking symmetrical arrangement.

The main focus of the museum's collections soon began to shift from modern manufactures to medieval and Renaissance decorative arts. Important private collections were purchased or lent to the museum, including the comprehensive Soulages collection. Despite criticism that this kind of historical collection would be of little benefit to manufacturers, some (including the pottery manufacturer Herbert Minton) can be said to have taken inspiration from them.

In 1857 the museum moved to South Kensington, adopting a new name and restating its purpose as the democratic

26. *Henry Cole and Richard Redgrave*, 1854. Attributed to Charles Thurston Thompson. Albumen print. VAM PH.835-1987.

28. Two jugs. Top: late 16th century. In the manner of Bernard Palissy, from the Soulages collection. Lead-glazed earthenware, moulded with applied decoration. [h. 27.5cm]. VAM 7178-1860. Bottom: 1858. Modelled by Hamlet Bourne. Made in Stoke-on-Trent, Staffordshire, by Minton & Co. Earthenware, majolica glazes. VAM 4730-1859.

education of taste. Evening and weekend opening ensured that working people were able to visit. At this date the displays were not confined to works of art. A wide range of displays could be seen, including an Educational Museum, Patented Inventions and Products of the Animal Kingdom. Plans were rapidly laid for new buildings and by about 1860 the South Kensington Museum was presenting a grand public façade, turning itself into a national decorative-arts institution with far-reaching influence.

30. **Objects from the School of Design collection and the Museum at Marlborough House. From left to right: Iznik bottle, about 1600. Made in Turkey. Earthenware. Indian 'Bidri ware' cup with lid, about 1851. Probably made in Bidar, India. Blackened zinc alloy overlaid with silver (bidri). Pilgrim bottle, about 1560. Made in Castel Durante or Urbino, Italy. Tin-glazed earthenware. Bottle, about 1844. Made by Frederic-Jules Rudolphi. Chased, oxidized silver, parcel-gilt. Vase, about 1840. Made by E.-D. Honoré, Paris. Porcelain. VAM 973-1875, 151-1852, 8409-1863, 919-1844, 3101-1846.**

31. *A Room at Marlborough House with the Soulages collection on display*, 1857. By William Linnaeus Casey. Watercolour. VAM AL.7280.

32. Detail of a sash, about 1851. Made in Tunisia. Woven silk. VAM 808-1852.

29. Detail of a furnishing fabric, English, about 1850. This 'furniture chintz' was exhibit 16 in the 'False Principles' display. Roller-printed cotton. VAM T.6-1933.

4. Did South Kensington work?

The efforts of the government design machine had mixed results. They undoubtedly brought art and design to large numbers of the upper artisan class, as well as the middle classes, and in purely social terms this was truly innovatory. As Henry Cole wrote in 1857:

> In the evening, the working man comes to this Museum from his one or two dimly lighted, cheerless, dwelling rooms, in his fustian jacket, with his shirt collars a little trimmed up, accompanied by his threes, and fours and fives of little fustian jackets, a wife, in her best bonnet, and a baby, of course, under her shawl. The looks of surprise and pleasure of the whole party when they first observe the brilliant lighting inside the Museum show what new, acceptable, and wholesome excitement this evening entertainment affords all of them.

But the positive effects in terms of taste were less easy to quantify. In the field of architecture and decoration, the South Kensington buildings were intended to act as a testbed for new forms and techniques. While their dominant neo-Renaissance style in ceramic and iron was emulated in a few hotels and public buildings, the untypical Dutch Kitchen or Grill Room by Sir Edward Poynter and William Morris's Green Dining Room were in the end far more significant, pioneering in the 1860s later forms of aesthetic decoration. In promoting its design principles among manufacturers, South Kensington also had mixed success. Cole claimed that by seeing objects of good taste, the general public would demand more of these goods, eventually persuading manufacturers into supplying better products. The same effect was to be achieved by directly educating manufacturers, designers and manufacturing artisans in the principles of good design.

34

Among consumers, however, progress was not very great. In wallpaper and textiles, for instance, the quite considerable production of approved flat-patterns, after designs by Pugin and Jones, during the 1850s and 1860s hardly dented the popularity of the naturalistic and illusionistic 'French' papers and fabrics, which had been singled out for attack in Cole's short-lived display of False Principles (an exhibition that had to close after opposition from the manufacturers). Nor did Cole's mechanistic 'principles', even though they were partly derived from Pugin, impress critics of South Kensington, like Ruskin and Charles Dickens. In a famous passage in his novel *Hard Times*, Dickens has Cole, thinly disguised as the schoolmaster Thomas Gradgrind, making a little girl cry because she is not allowed to admire the apparently real flowers in the carpet. For Ruskin, the very idea of a rule-bound system offended his notions of architecture and decorative art springing naturally from the mind of the craftsperson in direct relationship with nature.

33

33 *The Grill Room, South Kensington Museum, London*, 1876–81. By John Watkins. The room was designed by Sir Edward Poynter and begun in 1866. The tiles were painted by a class of female students at the Art School, formerly the Government School of Design. The stove, dated 1866, was decorated with Japanese motifs. Etching. VAM E.815-1945.

34 Detail of a furnishing fabric, about 1850. Made in Lancashire, possibly for Jackson and Graham, Furnishers of London. Shown at the Great Exhibition, 1851, and in the display of 'False Principles in Decoration', 1852, as an example of 'Direct imitation of nature': it showed a 'general want of repose'. Roller-printed and glazed cotton. VAM T.11-1933.

35 The Green Dining Room or Morris Room, Victoria and Albert Museum, London. Designed by Phillip Webb, with stained glass and painted panels by Sir Edward Burne-Jones. Decorated by Morris, Marshall, Faulkner & Co, 1866–8.

In raising the consciousness of art, however, and in helping to establish 'art manufactures' (made by 'art workmen') as a distinct type of visual culture, South Kensington had a considerable effect. This concept was entirely new. It elevated the applied arts from mere fashionable furnishings and decorations, subject to shifting patterns of taste, to a new type of high design, distinguished by its incorporation of the ennobling and morally purifying element of art. In the process, high design threw off its role as a social indicator subject to the whims of fashion. It became just as appropriate – or perhaps even more so – in the public context of a church, museum or exhibition as in the home. By contrast, the applied arts of the century leading up to 1850 were seen (at least up to the 1870s) as particularly defective, products of a period when a debased classical style served a frivolous and fashion-dominated aristocracy. The most admired periods were the medieval (as favoured by Pugin, Ruskin and Morris), the Renaissance (South Kensington and the Art Schools) and the golden 'Olden Time' of the Tudors and Stuarts, which had seized the popular imagination as early as the 1820s. All combined the attraction of a pre-industrial, benevolent age, when styles were generated naturally rather than adopted, fashion was (it was believed) unknown, and art existed for its own sake: 'they made it to keep, and we [make it] to sell', as Ruskin wrote.

37 *Augustus Welby Northmore Pugin*, 1845. By John Rogers Herbert. Oil on canvas. Palace of Westminster.

37

38

Linked to this rediscovery was an investigation of ancient methods of making. The leaders in this process were art manufacturers and furnishers, like the potters Minton and Doulton, the metalworkers Hardman and the decorating firm of Crace, who rediscovered old techniques in the fields of pottery, tiles and enamels, and stained (rather than painted) glass and textiles. One interesting outcome was that the manufacturing element often cost far more than the materials, making art manufactures except in precious metals inappropriately expensive. This affected William Morris, who always regretted that his hand-methods inevitably meant that his products were only 'ministering to the swinish luxury of the rich'.

The art manufacturers were spurred on by architects, with whom they often worked in close collaboration, turning churches and public buildings into lavish demonstrations of the art workman. The pioneering figure in this trend was A. W. N. Pugin, who, with other architects, employed Herbert

36 Vase, 1867. Designed and modelled by Victor Etienne Simyan and painted by Thomas Allen. Made by Minton & Co., Stoke-on-Trent, Staffordshire. The technique and some motifs imitate 16th-century maiolica. One of a pair bought by the South Kensington Museum for £158.10 in 1871. Earthenware, painted in enamels and majolica glazes. [h. 121.9cm]. VAM 1047-1871.

36

38 The 'Paradise Lost' shield, 1867. Made by Leonard Morel-Ladeuil for Elkington & Co. It was shown at the Exposition Universelle, Paris, in 1867, winning Morel-Ladeuil a gold medal. Bought by the South Kensington Museum, London, in 1868. The theme was taken from John Milton's *Paradise Lost*. Silver and damascened iron. [h. 87.6cm]. VAM 546-1868.

Minton and chose John Hardman, an obscure button manufacturer, as his chief metalworker. Pugin was also the first architect-designer to make the critical leap from commissioned work to the production of designs for general use. He encouraged J. G. Crace to make and sell his furniture, wallpaper and carpets; as he wrote in 1847: 'We must have a turn at *carpets* next. Let us reform them altogether.' Two years later Pugin was promoting his furniture, reassuring Crace: 'Rely on it, the great sale will be articles that are within the reach of the middling class . . . I am so anxious to produce a sensible style of furniture of good oak, & constructively put together that shall compete with the vile trash made & sold.'

39

39 House of Lords Chamber, Palace of Westminster, London, designed from 1844, completed 1852. Designed by Sir Charles Barry and A. W. N. Pugin.

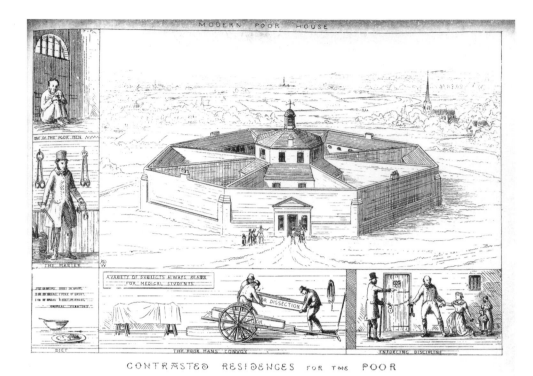

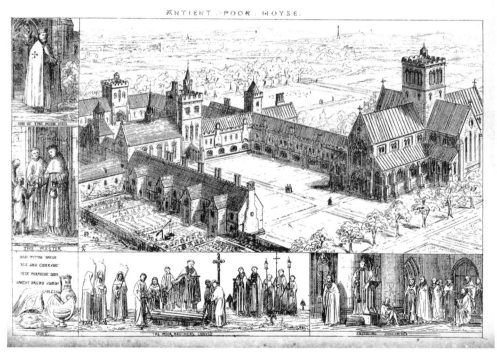

5. Pugin and Ruskin

'I was awakened from my slumber by the thunder of Pugin's writings,' wrote the architect George Gilbert Scott, looking back to the 1830s. The impact of Pugin's brilliant illustrated polemics was far greater than that of his comparatively few built schemes or the products designed by him. For Scott, Pugin's *Contrasts* 'vividly exposed the abject meanness which pervaded the architecture of the day', while *True Principles* 'established a code of rules founded on common sense, utility and truth'. Pugin himself said in 1851 that 'my writings have revolutionized the taste of England'. He was correct, for with Ruskin he was the most influential writer on design of the Victorian period. He was the first to tackle the Victorian style crisis, made Gothic the leading style of the period up to 1870 and introduced the key ideas of honesty in design and workmanship – what he called 'reality' – into Victorian design thinking. The fundamentally religious, indeed sectarian, position of Pugin's ideas did not impede their spread. Several of his central tenets fed into the secular and aggressively utilitarian atmosphere of the government design reform. In the hands of the Anglican reformers of church aesthetics in the Ecclesiological Society (founded as the Cambridge Camden Society), they were turned into a set of rules far more rigid than anything out of South Kensington. The laws were extended beyond buildings in the approved style to fittings and liturgical vessels, transforming the visual language of the established

40 *Contrasted Residences for the Poor*. Plate from *Contrasts* by A. W. N. Pugin, 1836. VAM Loan: Clive Wainwright.

41 John Ruskin, 1894. Photograph taken in Brantwood, Cumbria, by Frederick Hollyer. Salt paper print. VAM PH 7603-1938.

religion in thousands of churches, old and new. Pugin's most significant effect in the long term was on a generation of Gothic architects coming to maturity in the 1850s, like William Morris's collaborator Philip Webb (not to mention Morris himself), setting in train a development that ultimately led to the emergence of the Arts and Crafts movement in the 1880s. The other key figure in this development was John Ruskin.

42

In spite of the notoriously changing nature of his ideas, the subtle eloquence with which Ruskin set them out made him a powerful influence in many fields. On a purely stylistic level there was his advocacy of north Italian Gothic, notably in *The Stones of Venice* (1851–3), as the way out of the Victorian stylistic impasse. This not only led to many buildings being built in the style, but also opened up British architecture to foreign Gothic styles in general, including northern French Gothic, as promoted by the architect Eugène Viollet-le-Duc. Although Ruskin's aesthetic beliefs were rooted in the Christian faith, he preached against Gothic as a purely ecclesiastical style. The civic and commercial nature of many of the Gothic buildings that he studied legitimized modern Gothic in such buildings as town halls and warehouses and in domestic architecture: 'I have had indirect influence on nearly every cheap villa-builder between this [Denmark Hill, his home] and Bromley,' he wrote in 1872.

As an adviser on taste, Ruskin was much in demand. In 1864 he was called to Bradford to lecture on architecture at a time when the style of the town's new Exchange was being decided. In the end he was displeased with the chosen building and altered the printed version of his lecture to reflect his view: 'You may know there are a great many odd styles of architecture about; you don't want to do anything ridiculous; you hear of me, among many others, as a respectable architectural man-milliner; and you send for me, that I may tell you the leading fashion; and what is, in our shops, for the moment, the newest and sweetest thing in pinnacles.'

It was Ruskin's anti-industrial and anti-rationalist approach to aesthetics, rather than his advocacy of a particular style, that had the greatest impact on future developments. His direct appeal to the heart, and his belief in the reforming power of a personalized art and hand-craft based on a study of nature, influenced people as diverse as William Morris, leaders of the Aesthetic movement like Edward Godwin and Oscar Wilde, and members of the Arts and Crafts movement into the years after 1900. Certain texts were more important than others; as Morris wrote about 'The Nature of Gothic' from *The Stones of Venice*: 'To my mind, and I believe to some others, it . . . will be considered one of the very few and inevitable utterances of the century.'

42 *A window of the Palazzo Foscari, Venice*, 1845. By John Ruskin. Made in preparation for *The Stones of Venice*, 1851–3. Pencil and watercolour on paper. VAM D.1726-1908.

43 *The Nature of Gothic*, 1892. By John Ruskin. Printed by William Morris at the Kelmscott Press, Hammersmith, London. Woodblock engraving and letter-press. VAM 95.C.26.

43

The degree to which Ruskin's ideas on hand manufacture filtered through to a more general level is shown in the sales literature of commercial church furnishers. In about 1859 Cox and Sons, as 'church furniture manufacturers', were boasting of their Patent Carving Machines, through which, thanks to the wonders of technology, ' . . . the work is roughed out with great accuracy and expedition (the Cutter making seven thousand revolutions per minute), while the finishing of the more minute parts is carried out by hand labour, so that the result shows precisely the same amount of artistic excellence as if it had been entirely executed by hand'. By 1872 Cox's had subtly shifted the emphasis towards hand manufacture, even though the method of making was probably the same: ' . . . it is desirable to explain that it [the carving machine] is used solely for the purpose of preparation, by the removal of superfluous parts of the material, and shaping it for subsequent hand carving . . . without the artistic excellence of the work being in the slightest degree impaired'.

Specimens of Modern Venetian Table Glass,
manufactured by Salviati & Co.

DECORATIVE PAINTERS,
EMBROIDERIES,
METAL WORK,
STAINED GLASS,
TEXTILE FABRICS,
WOOD AND STONE CARVING.

COX, SONS, BUCKLEY, & CO.
28 and 29 SOUTHAMPTON STREET, STRAND, LONDON, W.C.

6. The Art movement

Cox's change of heart need not have come from a direct reading of Ruskin. The early 1870s saw the emergence into public consciousness of the Art movement, characterized by a new concern to achieve beauty in everyday life, driven by a new wave of literature. Within 10 years aestheticism had become a popular fashion (as well as an object of popular ridicule), a development marked by Gilbert and Sullivan's operetta *Patience* and by the publication of one of the first books to record a contemporary artistic movement as such, Walter Hamilton's *The Aesthetic Movement in England* (1882). Hamilton's analysis was clear: 'the essence of the movement is the union of persons of cultivated taste to define and decide upon what is to be admired'. Given such unpromising beginnings among a tiny clique of artists, architects and self-proclaimed aesthetes, and its very loose nature, the movement's success among the middle classes may at first seem surprising. Nor does the positive tone of most Aesthetic literature suggest that it would be any more effective in changing tastes than the bossy material coming out of South Kensington. The secret of its success was that it was concerned largely with the domestic in architecture and interior decoration and that it was chiefly aimed not at the general public but at a small group of like-minded, moderately wealthy middle-class people wishing to join the exclusive club of the artistic. In a typical piece of polemic of 1881–2 in *The Burlington* magazine the imaginary Mr Philistine Jones, whose dazzling carpets and wallpapers of 1870 'were enough to give a templar a fit of delirium tremens', ' . . . actually has begun to think about the shape of his jugs'.

The pioneering book of the Art movement was Charles Locke Eastlake's *Hints on Household Taste in Furniture, Upholstery and Other Details* (1868). Eastlake's newly coined term, 'Art Furniture', expressed the crucial shift from

44 Advertisement for Cox, Sons, Buckley & Co., London. From the *Handbook to the Ecclesiastical Art Exhibition*, London, 1881. VAM 217.D.21.

45 *Specimens of Modern Venetian Table Glass. Manufactured by Salviati & Co. From Hints on Household Taste in Furniture, Upholstery and Other Details* by Charles Locke Eastlake, 1868. VAM 47.E.13.

individual art manufactures to art applied to the interior as a whole. The book's heady and pioneering mix of a discursive text along Puginian and Ruskinian lines with firm practical and illustrated decorating advice for every aspect of the house drove it to four British editions up to 1878, and six in America between 1872 and 1879. Eastlake set the tone and approach for all the rest, even though the styles they promoted changed considerably, shifting from Eastlake's Gothic to the 'Chippendale'-style furniture of the 1870s. Significantly most of the later books, like those in the *Art at Home* series, were written by women, from the same social group as their audience. Two, Rhoda and Agnes Garrett, were professional interior decorators (then a new career for women); the rest were often linked to artists and the Art movement, such as Lucy Crane (sister of Walter, and author of *Art and the Foundation of Taste*, 1882) and Lucy Orrinsmith (sister of William Morris's associate Charles Faulkner, and author of *The Drawing Room, its Decorations and Furniture*, 1878). Their mixture of aesthetic and practical household advice placed such works close to the growing genre of books of domestic advice, from Mrs Beeton onwards. The two genres actually merged in the hands of slightly later authors, like Jane Panton, author of *From Kitchen to Garret* (1889) and many other books.

7. Commerce and artist

These developments went hand-in-hand with huge growth in commercial outlets of artistic design. These ranged from manufacturers of a single product type, like Doulton's or the Linthorpe art potteries, to art furnishers in general, like Morris and Co., William Watt and Liberty and Co. This growth was matched by an increasingly public profile of individual designers. The example set by Pugin, as both a designer and a journalist and critic on design subjects, was followed by many later avant-garde art designers intent on spreading their ideas, including Owen Jones, Christopher Dresser and E. W. Godwin.

Some manufacturers exploited the links with such avant-garde designers. In the case of William Watt, the firm's links with the pioneering aesthetic designer and architect E. W. Godwin were fully publicized. Its stand at the Paris Exposition of 1878 was jointly designed by Godwin, painted by J. M. Whistler, clearly marked with their names and given the provocative title 'Decorative Harmony in Yellow and Gold'. Such a stunt could not fail to draw attention. The type of close aesthetic control exercised by both Godwin and Whistler, in this and other projects, was matched at a more general level by a tendency for art manufacturers to present their wares in complete settings, both in their showrooms and in illustrated catalogues. Watt's *Art Furniture*, originally published in 1877 with text and illustrations by Godwin, had a design influence far beyond its direct sales function: it was even available in the South

46

46 *View of a Drawing-Room.* Plate from *Suggestions for House Decoration in painting, woodwork and furniture* by Rhoda and Agnes Garrett, 1876. From the *Art at Home* series. VAM 47.D.40.

47 The William Watt stand at the Exposition Universelle, Paris, 1878. Painted by James McNeil Whistler and designed by Edward William Godwin. Photograph by Usine Photographique de Pallencourt, under the direction of H. Klerjot. VAM Picture Library.

47

Kensington loan scheme for books for art schools, joining such basic texts as Owen Jones's *Grammar of Ornament*.

Concerns about originality and authenticity, which lay behind the Design Registration Acts of 1839–43, became especially acute when named designers came to the fore in the 1870s. One solution, the addition of facsimile signatures or other marks of authenticity, was indicative not only of the designers' view of themselves as artists, but of their desire to keep control of the object. Such marks were also exploited by manufacturers. In the case of Doulton Art Pottery, which hired decorators directly from the South Kensington Schools, all the designers had their own mark. Christopher Dresser saw to it that the wide range of products he designed carried his facsimile signature as well as the usual design registration marks. The double function of his signature as an assurance of art value and a means of personal promotion was made clear by the wording of the 1879 prospectus and share certificate of the Linthorpe pottery. This was set up as a producer of cheap pottery at the suggestion of Dresser, who became the firm's 'Art Designer and Art Superintendent': 'Dr Dresser's name, as is well known, is inseparably connected with Art and Designing, and all articles proceeding from the Linthorpe Art Works will bear the facsimile of his Signature, "Chr Dresser" as a trade mark and guarantee of their genuineness, and of their being made in strict accordance with the principles of decorative Art.' Interestingly, in Linthorpe's case, the magic of Dresser's name seems not to have done the trick, for in 1882 the firm turned to less adventurous designs.

49

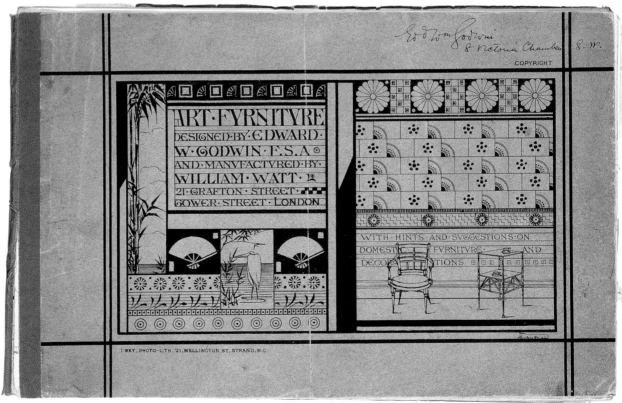

48

---

48 *Art Furniture designed by Edward W. Godwin FSA and manufactured by William Watt, 1877. VAM AAD.4/508-1988.*

49 Vase, 1882. Modelled by Harry Barnard for Doulton & Co., Lambeth, London. Salt-glazed stoneware. [h. 26.5cm]. VAM C.54-1972.

8. Taste and the Arts and Crafts movement

The Arts and Crafts movement could not have happened without the heightened aesthetic consciousness of the 1870s. From the start, however, the movement was much more coherent in its ideas and their presentation than the loose trends of that decade. The official history of the movement is a rather dry tale, beginning in the early 1880s, of societies and guilds of like-minded aesthetes, designers and architects. It accurately reflects the movement's essence, but signally fails to reveal its anti-establishment fervour and the larger-than-life characters that pushed it forward. Ruskin's writings, backed up by the example and ideas of William Morris, were the touchstones of the movement's artistic and social creed. Ruskin had a personal influence on pioneers like the architect and designer Arthur Heygate Mackmurdo. Mackmurdo, Ruskin's companion and assistant in 1874, went on to co-found the Century Guild in 1882. It was created in direct homage to Ruskin's own medievalizing Guild of St George, a group dedicated to rendering 'all branches of art the sphere no longer of the tradesman but of the artist'. The movement acquired a coherent public face, and a name, with the foundation of the Arts and Crafts Exhibition Society in 1887, which grew out of the Art-Workers' Guild, founded in 1884. The Ruskin Reading Class at the philanthropic Toynbee Hall in London's impoverished East End led to the movement's most daring experiment in social engineering, Charles Robert Ashbee's Guild of Handicraft, made up of working-class men and lads from the area.

51 Design for the symbol of the Arts and Crafts Exhibition Society, 1888. By George Heywood Sumner. Pen and ink. VAM E.1097-1993.

52 Salver, with London hallmarks for 1896–7. Designed by Charles Robert Ashbee. Made by the Guild of Handicraft, Essex House, London. Silver. VAM Circ.471-1962.

50 Chair, 1881. Designed by Arthur Heygate Mackmurdo. Probably made by Collinson and Lock, London. A chair of this type was shown by the Century Guild at the International Invention Exhibition in 1885. Mahogany, with an inset fretwork panel; replacement leather upholstery. [h. 97.2cm]. VAM W.29-1982.

WILLIAM MORRIS

Linda Parry

William Morris (1834–96) was one of the most influential of all Victorians. He was a celebrated poet, author and translator, a political activist and one of the early pioneers in the movements concerned with the conservation of ancient buildings and the countryside.

His artistic achievements were equally wide-ranging. Not only was he one of the most popular interior decorators of the nineteenth century, but he and his firm were responsible for designing, making and selling all of the furnishings – stained-glass, wallpapers, tiles, furniture, embroidery, woven and printed textiles, carpets and tapestries – used in his interior schemes. However, his art was not restricted to decoration of the home. A keen calligrapher in his early life, his last artistic endeavour was the founding of the Kelmscott Press, one of the most important private presses of modern times.

53. Detail of jasmine wallpaper, first issued 1872. Designed by William Morris. Printed by Jeffrey & Co. for Morris, Marshall, Faulkner & Co. Block-printed in distemper colour. VAM E.475-1919.

54. *William Morris*, **1877. The London Stereoscopic Co. National Portrait Gallery, London.**

As his reputation as a designer and manufacturer spread through the work of the firms of Morris, Marshall, Faulkner and Co. and, from 1875, Morris & Company, so did his influence on all aspects of the decorative arts. Firms began copying his manner of work, reverting to small units using traditional manufacturing techniques, many of which had disappeared in the earlier years of the nineteenth century in the race for economic and technological expediency. Similarly, fellow designers, keen to capture the simplicity of Morris's floral patterns, turned to the British countryside for their inspiration.

Morris's views on art and life, clearly set out in numerous publications and lectures, found an even wider audience. His belief in the intrinsic value and joy of craft work, and in the need for equality of opportunity, was widely applauded by the new intellectual élite, who were becoming politically sensitive and keen to champion new causes. But his influence also spread to official channels. Morris gave evidence at government inquiries set up to look into the future of art education and the development of industry in Britain.

55. Detail of curtain of *Peacock and Dragon* **woven furnishing, 1878. Designed by William Morris. Made by Morris & Company. Hand-loom jacquard-woven woollen twill. VAM T.64-1933.**

57. The Hall at Red House, Bexleyheath, London, 1859–60. Designed by Philip Webb for William Morris and decorated by Morris.

58. Sussex armchair, designed about 1860. Possibly designed by Philip Webb. Made in London by Morris, Marshall, Faulkner & Co., and later by Morris & Company. Ebonized beech with a rush seat. VAM Circ.288-1960.

Furthermore, as one of the major advisors to the South Kensington Museum for more than 20 years, he suggested which acquisitions represented the best from the past and were, therefore, most useful for study by the designers of the future.

By the late nineteenth century Morris's reputation as one of the most original designers and thinkers of his day had gained wide international recognition. His London shop became a place of pilgrimage for visitors from throughout Britain, Europe, North America, Scandinavia and Australia. His ideas continued to influence the development of the arts in the twentieth century, both at home and abroad.

56. *The Works of Geoffrey Chaucer*, 1896. Designed by William Morris with illustrations by Edward Burne-Jones. Engraved on wood by William Harcourt Hooper. Printed at the Kelmscott Press, Hammersmith, London. VAM L.757-1896.

59. Detail of panel of tiles from Membland Hall, Devon, designed 1876. Designed by William Morris. Made by the firm of William De Morgan. Decorated in Chelsea, London, using tile blanks supplied by the Architectural Pottery, Poole, Dorset. Hand-painted enamels on earthenware. VAM C.36-1972.

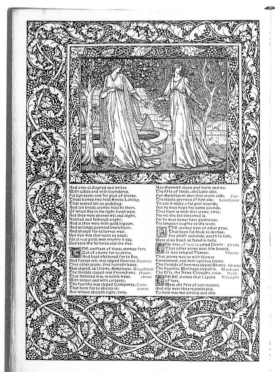

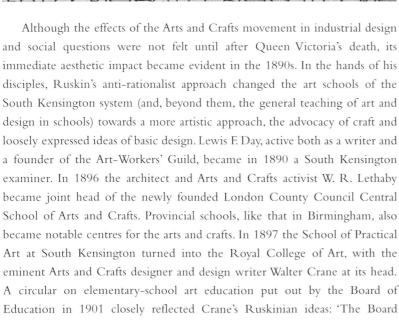

regard instruction in drawing as an important means of cultivating in children a faculty of observing, comparing, recollecting and thinking about all sorts of objects with a view to representing them in an intelligent and careful manner and developing a sense of beauty.' No greater shift from the dry mechanistic exercises of William Dyce's *Drawing Book* of 1842 could be imagined (*see 13:13*). A similarly profound shift from the rule-bound systems of South Kensington is shown in the relaxed approach to pattern design of the architect C.F.A. Voysey, writing in 1896 to the textile manufacturer Alexander Morton on the principles of what he called 'breadth'. Breadth was 'literally the proportion of one scale of richness to another One colour to another One mass to another One curve to another . . . Breadth is on the side of simplicity and repose.'

Public interest in the decorative arts and in the hand-made was shown and promoted in a range of new magazines. Art manufactures had of course long been discussed and illustrated in art magazines. The pioneering *Art Journal* (founded as the *Art Union* in 1839) not only regularly showed and illustrated manufactures, but also published catalogues of the great international

Although the effects of the Arts and Crafts movement in industrial design and social questions were not felt until after Queen Victoria's death, its immediate aesthetic impact became evident in the 1890s. In the hands of his disciples, Ruskin's anti-rationalist approach changed the art schools of the South Kensington system (and, beyond them, the general teaching of art and design in schools) towards a more artistic approach, the advocacy of craft and loosely expressed ideas of basic design. Lewis F. Day, active both as a writer and a founder of the Art-Workers' Guild, became in 1890 a South Kensington examiner. In 1896 the architect and Arts and Crafts activist W. R. Lethaby became joint head of the newly founded London County Council Central School of Arts and Crafts. Provincial schools, like that in Birmingham, also became notable centres for the arts and crafts. In 1897 the School of Practical Art at South Kensington turned into the Royal College of Art, with the eminent Arts and Crafts designer and design writer Walter Crane at its head. A circular on elementary-school art education put out by the Board of Education in 1901 closely reflected Crane's Ruskinian ideas: 'The Board

60 'Panpipes' furnishing fabric, late 1890s. Designed by C. F. A. Voysey, made by Alexander Morton and Co. Woven silk, cotton and wool, double cloth. VAM T.169-1977.

61 Poster for *The Studio*, 1893. Designed by Aubrey Beardsley. Line-block and letter-press. VAM E.451-1895.

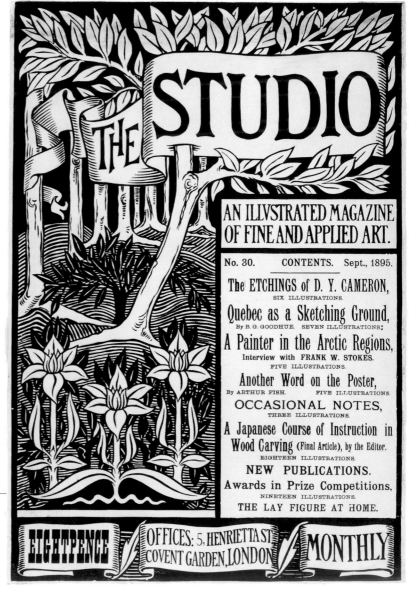

61

exhibitions. But the tone of such journals was largely informational. The Aesthetic movement also produced its own journals, such as *The Burlington* and *The House, An Artistic Monthly for Those who Manage and Beautify the Home* (begun in 1897). The crucial shift was towards journals that promoted the avant-garde and put the fine and applied arts on an equal footing as two sides of the same coin. The most important of these was *The Studio*, founded in 1893. From the start it took an overriding interest in avant-garde applied arts and design, publicizing new work to a wide audience at home and abroad (an American edition began in 1897). But the real influence of this and similar magazines is perhaps most clearly indicated by the arrival of advanced styles in the sphere of commercial furnishing, especially through the firm of Liberty & Co.

62 Cover of the programme for *The Mikado*, Savoy Theatre, London, 1885. Colour lithograph. VAM Theatre Museum.

9. High style goes commercial

Liberty's approach to the commercial promotion of progressive design, and its failure to champion exclusively the hand-made, caused C. R. Ashbee to call them 'Messrs Nobody, Novelty & Co'. Arthur Lasenby Liberty, the founder of the firm, was not a designer but a merchant adventurer and entrepreneur in the old mould. He began in the great shawl and cloak emporium of Farmer and Rogers, setting up an oriental warehouse with purchases from the 1862 exhibition. He became deeply committed to the Art movement, with which he became linked in 1875 through his independent project, East India House, described by Godwin the following year as the 'Anglo Japanese warehouse'. In an astute publicity move, Liberty supplied the textiles for the costumes for Gilbert and Sullivan's *Patience* and was involved in the costumes for *The Mikado*. In 1883 he set up a new shop, selling textiles, furniture and furnishings as well as eastern goods. A year later a costume department was added, with Godwin as consultant, for the sale of artistic 'rational' dress, in direct opposition to conventional fashion. Like the other departments of the shop,

62

the overt aim of 'the new school of dressmaking' was the education of taste, producing its own informative booklets on styles in historical dress. However, it also had a commercial purpose, for it used Liberty's own fabrics, which were too soft for the usual run of dressmakers working in the stiff fashions of Paris.

What made Liberty's exceptional as a department store was its creation, by the 1890s, of a complete package of advanced good taste in a style so unified and distinct that 'Stile Liberty' could become an alternative name for Art Nouveau. One of the keys to this achievement of brand image was the concealment of its designers, many of whom were famous names. Only through such methods could Liberty's produce a style that would respond quickly to the market and tone down the extremes of innovation.

64

63

The great department stores of late Victorian England were the clearest demonstration of the overwhelming range of goods available by 1900, spread by a great tide of commercial propaganda. The type of branded taste control exercised by Liberty's was exceptional, with most other stores aiming to show the largest possible range of goods in the greatest number of styles. Whiteley's in London was known as the Universal Provider. In 1887 it was described in *Modern London*: 'Whiteley's is an immense symposium of the arts and industries of the nation and of the world; a grand review of everything that goes to make life worth living passing in seemingly endless array before critical but bewildered humanity; an international exhibition of the resources and products of the earth and air, flood and field, established as one of the greatest "lions" of the metropolis.' Rather like Harrods today, Whiteley's was a 'sight' – as much an exhibition as a shop. Both impressive and unsettling, it was a clear demonstration that, for all but a select few, 50 or so years of attempts to control Victorian taste had largely failed.

63 Robe, 1895–1900. Made in the 'Artistic and Historic costume studio' of Liberty & Co., London, for a member of the Liberty family. The design was based on 16th-century gowns. Aesthetic sunflowers and pomegranates decorate the brocade; the colours are in the muted 'artistic' range of the 1890s. Silk and cotton brocade with a silk-satin front panel, silk-plush edgings and a taffeta lining. VAM T.57-1976.

65

64 Armchair, 1899–1900. Designed by George Walton. Made for Liberty & Co. by William Birch of High Wycombe, Buckinghamshire. Walton, who began his career in Glasgow, moved to London in 1897, where he was one of a number of independent designers working for Liberty's, which also had its own design studio. Walnut, inlaid with mother-of-pearl. [h. 113.5cm]. VAM W.78-1975.

65 Whiteley's in Westbourne Grove, London, about 1900. A photograph taken at about 4.30 p.m., the fashionable shopping hour for the 'carriage trade'. The Hulton Getty Picture Collection.

66 The unhappy impact of Liberty's in the suburbs. Cartoon by George du Maurier in *Punch*, 20 October 1894. Wood engraving. VAM PP.8.L.

186   PUNCH, OR THE LONDON CHARIVARI.   [OCTOBER 20, 1894.

FELICITOUS QUOTATIONS.

Hostess (of Upper Tooting, showing new house to Friend). "WE'RE VERY PROUD OF THIS ROOM, MRS. HOMINY. OUR OWN LITTLE UPHOLSTERER DID IT UP JUST AS YOU SEE IT, AND ALL OUR FRIENDS THINK IT WAS *LIBERTY!*"
Visitor (sotto voce). "'OH, LIBERTY, LIBERTY, HOW MANY CRIMES ARE COMMITTED IN THY NAME!'"

66

COMMERCIAL PROPAGANDA

Julia Bigham

During the Victorian period an increasing number of ready-made products – ranging from dress to furniture and food – became available to an expanding middle-class market. New types of advertising made the most of contemporaneous improvements in communications. New retailing strategies were devised, including larger shops, some of which had several different departments selling a variety of goods in ever more elaborate displays.

Many of the more radical and avant-garde shops such as Liberty's and Heal's were aimed at an élite market that led taste, yet they too turned to the relatively novel promotional tools of mail-order catalogues and, in the case of Heal's, nationwide press advertising.

The widespread use of pictorial advertising followed the introduction of cheaper methods

ENGLISH SILKS woven exclusively for LIBERTY & CO. Ltd.

The "Alne" Brocaded-Satin.

For Evening-Dresses, Blouses, etc.

The "Alne" Brocaded-Satin is a fashionable and quite inexpensive Satin made entirely of Silk.
The "Alne" Brocaded-Satin is woven in selected designs of dainty and unobtrusive character, both Floral and Geometric. (It can be obtained in either).
The colourings are carefully harmonized, and the rich series of the "Alne" Brocades are all on charming and bright Satin Grounds. 28 inches wide.

Price 2/11 per Yard.

PATTERNS POST FREE.

LIBERTY & CO. LTD.]   15   [LONDON & PARIS.

67. The 'Alne' brocaded satin. From *Liberty Catalogue No. 38*, **1896, published by Liberty & Co., London. Paper and boards. VAM NAL Liberty Catalogues.38.**

of mass printing. Wood engraving and, later in the century, line-block etching were used to illustrate trade catalogues. Increasingly the illustrated press, including the *Illustrated London News* and *The Graphic*, featured advertisements with wood-engraved illustrations.

An important development was the wide-spread use of colour lithography in collectable magazine inserts and, most significantly,

posters. Typographical posters had covered hoardings and blank walls in British cities since the 1820s, but from the 1880s pictorial posters were increasingly in use. During the next decade these became more and more effective, following the rise of advertising agencies offering comprehensive advertising services, and of independent poster designers. At the same time more sophisticated packaging and branding were introduced for consumables. The most heavily advertised products, like Bovril and Colman's Mustard, became household names.

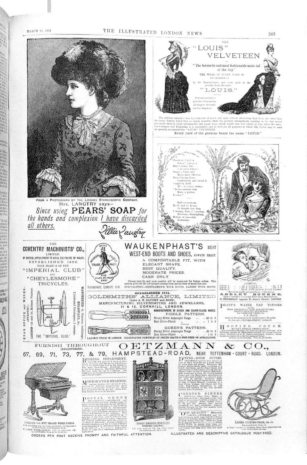

68. Advertisements from the *Illustrated London News*, **15 March 1884. VAM PP.10-1884.**

69. Poster for Edwards' Desiccated Soup, about 1900. Created by the advertising agent S. H. Benson Ltd. Printed by Henry Blacklock & Co., Color Printers, Manchester. Colour lithograph. VAM E.33-1973.

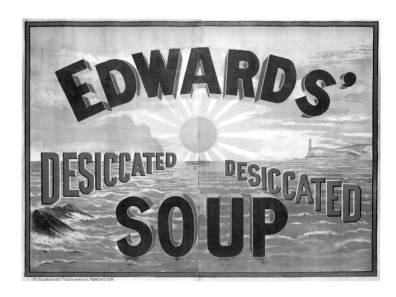

70. *Bubbles*, Pears Soap advertisement from a magazine, 1886. After a painting by Sir John Everett Millais. Colour lithograph. VAM E.2335-1889.

71. Poster for Colman's Mustard, about 1899. Designed in London by John Hassall. Printed by David Allen & Sons. Commissioned by S. H. Benson (advertising agent) for J. & J. Colman Ltd. Colour lithograph. VAM E.23-1973.

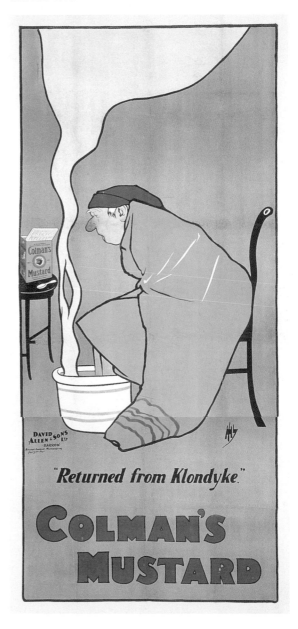

CHAPTER 14

Victorian Britain, 1837–1901

Fashionable living

CHRISTOPHER BREWARD

1. The cult of domesticity

In 1847, just 10 years into the Victorian reign, the political author G. R. Porter noted the increased appearance of carpets in the homes of London shopkeepers. This was presented as proof of the rapid progress made by his compatriots in questions of taste and living standards since the end of the Georgian era. 'In the same houses,' he stated, 'we see not carpets merely, but many articles of furniture which were formerly found in use only among the nobility and gentry: the walls are covered with paintings and engravings, and the apartments contain evidences that some among the inmates cultivate one or more of those elegant accomplishments which tend so delightfully to refine the minds of individuals, and to sweeten the intercourse of families.' For Porter social, technological and material improvements went hand-in-hand, 'producing an increased amount of comfort to the great bulk of people'. Here was an affirmation of a growing national tendency to define moral and spiritual outlook through the choice of home decorations. Four years after Porter's observations, the Registrar-General George Graham could claim with some confidence, in his comments on the results of the 1851 Census, that 'the possession of an entire house is, it is true, strongly desired by every Englishman; for it throws a sharp, well-defined circle round his family and hearth – the shrine of his sorrows, joys, and meditations'.

The idea of the family home played a pivotal role in the organization of life across all levels of Victorian society. From its ordering of the social roles taken by men, women and children to its function as a statement of wealth and status, the private world of the household came to symbolize the distinctive and highly codified nature of nineteenth-century British civilization. In some ways the home was a contradictory space, proclaiming to the outside world the morals and tastes of its inhabitants in the most ostentatious manner, while providing behind the lace blinds of its windows a retreat from the 'vulgar'

2

world of paid labour and public discourse. Its interiors formed a setting for the proliferation of articles that marked the age as one of material excess. At the same time its walls and fences offered quasi-religious protection from the temptations that industrial and commercial life forced on a population increasingly dependent on the symbols of consumer culture as a way of making sense of things.

The concept of 'domesticity' allowed citizens to reconcile these tensions through an idealized way of life that was hierarchical and compartmentalized in the extreme. In the sphere of the home – whether this was located in the country mansion or West End palace of the aristocrat, the suburban villa of the middle classes or the model dwelling of the worker – every surface communicated carefully judged associations that attested to the worthiness of

---

1 Detail from *Evenings at Home*, 1852–3. By George Smith. The family of the administrator and design reformer Henry Cole gather in a room hung with the trophies of his career, protected from the cares of the outside world. Oil on canvas. Private collection.

2 *The Governess*, 1861. By Alice Squire. Even in a relatively humble setting the accoutrements of genteel living are displayed. Carpet, sprigged wallpaper, clean linen, framed prints and fresh flowers attest to the inhabitant's good character. Watercolour. The Geffrye Museum.

the inhabitants. Most especially they showed off the domestic talents of the lady of the house. The rhetoric of domesticity was clearly viewed as a feminine preserve. Men contributed to household concerns and benefited equally from their involvement in the creation of a domestic refuge, but its smooth running was the housewife's prerogative. At the apex of this system sat the family of the Queen, her ordered existence as wife, mother and head of state imposing a model on attempts by all other respectable people to do their duty as subjects, through the proper management of their own homes. Such was the propaganda value of countless images of the first family at leisure in the gardens and state rooms of Windsor, Osborne and Balmoral that the powerful idea of homeliness could even be used to justify the management of a vastly expanding Empire. England itself became a 'home' across the seas to its imperial dominions and Victoria played the role of mother and, later in the century, grandmother to her colonized charges.

It is little wonder then, given its central position in the political and psychic formation of the state and its population, that the image of the Victorian home should retain such powerful associations. In its most stereotypical incarnation, the cluttered surfaces of its fireplaces and tabletops, the over-abundance of draperies and bibelots mark out the claustrophobic later-nineteenth-century household as the prime symbol of the epoch. Its mysterious depths and textured layers can be read now as a closely policed sanctuary of barely disguised neuroses and prejudices. They seem to capture all the most repressive aspects that have subsequently been associated with Victorian life. Yet it is important to remember that the interiors bound up with the cult of nineteenth-century domesticity also offered a stage set where even ordinary members of the population used the objects surrounding them to become new sorts of people and to behave in new ways, fashioning expressive new identities.

Domestic life was undoubtedly promoted as a rather restrictive ideal. Nevertheless beyond the front door other connected spheres of experience encouraged a release from the pressures of home and utilized public spaces as a further arena in which identities might be developed and even tested. A vigorous expansion of organized leisure activities outside the home, which witnessed a transformation in the worlds of shopping, travel excursions and evening entertainments, was justified by its relationship to the private aspirations of family life. Where the influence of the family ideal was absent – scorned at the edges of respectable society, or hidden among the slums of the very poor – alternative cultures fostered

3 *A Toxteth, Liverpool Drawing Room*, 1891. By H. Bedford Lemere. The architectural features of this middle-class drawing room in Liverpool are shrouded in the heavy drapes and trimmings associated with the worst excesses of Victorian decorating taste. The photographs and ornaments turn the mantelpiece into a family shrine.

spectacular forms of fashionable activity. These earned a glamorous sheen precisely because they stood in direct opposition to all that those more conservative notions of the domestic and the 'homely' suggested. The glitter of the demi-monde, which during the nineteenth century attached itself to everything from proletarian East End music hall to the courtesan's Mayfair salon, thus shimmered like a photographic negative, the reverse image of the cosy, but inward-looking spaces associated with the middle-class drawing room. Where these very different worlds were connected, and where both marked a development from the situation in previous periods, was in two areas. First, in the enthusiasm with which they embraced the commercial sphere and its products. Second, in their espousal of a fluid concept of 'lifestyle' as a means of negotiating a whole range of new and challenging social roles. Fashionable culture became the prime measure of where one stood in relation to society. People came to devote more hours than ever before to cultivating these fashionable concerns, both within the home and beyond it.

4 Photograph of an overpainted or retouched photograph of Queen Victoria and her family, 1857. Photographed by Caldesi and Montecchi. Albumen print. VAM 68:021.

5 *The Dancing Platform at Cremorne Gardens*, 1864. By Phoebus Levin. Cremorne was a popular pleasure garden in Chelsea, London, renowned as a meeting place for young men about town and women of loose morals. The vivid garments of the pleasure seekers identify them as inhabiting a world far removed from the safety of the respectable home. Oil on canvas. The Museum of London.

FURNISHING THE HOME

Laura Houliston

Home furnishing, always a priority for the Victorian middle classes, took on a new dynamism after the 1860s. The early Victorian middle-class interior owed much to its late-Georgian predecessor, but by the last 30 years of the nineteenth century there was far greater stylistic diversity.

In the nineteenth century most properties were rented. The artist Mary Ellen Best, daughter of a doctor, is known to have rented a house in York at the start of Victoria's reign and decorated it to her own taste. Possessions and decor in the drawing room were indicators to visiting guests of status, taste and wealth. Her drawing room has many recognizably 'Victorian' aspects, such as the chintz chair covers and buttoned upholstery, but it is strongly rooted in earlier Georgian styles, with features such as the outscrolled arms of the sofa and seat. In the 1850s and 1860s these

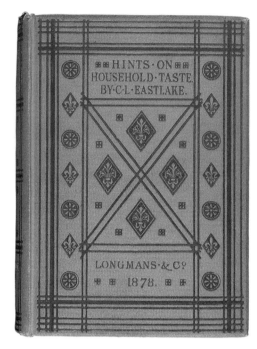

6. *Hints on Household Taste*, 1878. By Charles Eastlake. First published by Longmans & Co., 1868. VAM FW.6G10.

characteristic elements of early-Victorian drawing rooms were supplemented with newly fashionable furnishings, such as clocks in the French eighteenth-century style, polished carved tables, upright pianos, red turkey carpets and wallpaper with naturalistic patterns.

In the course of the Victorian period, reductions in manufacturing costs made a wider range of goods accessible to middle-class consumers. There were also improvements in services, with gas becoming commonplace in middle-class homes in the second half of the century. By 1890 this gave interiors a brightness not previously possible with oil lamps or candles. Shopping took on a new character from the middle of the century, with the spread of large department stores in the West End of London and elsewhere. Identifying, choosing and

7. *Our drawing room at York*, about 1838–40. By Mary Ellen Best. Watercolour. York City Art Gallery.

8. *The Chorale*, 1878. By John Atkinson Grimshaw, showing the artist's home in Scarborough, Yorkshire. Oil on canvas. Private collection.

9. Showcard for Henry Capel's Art Furniture, about 1875. Signed 'BB'. Printed by S. Straker & Sons, London. Photolithograph. VAM 29637:138.

purchasing household items usually fell to the middle-class wife, as creative 'homemaker'. There were increasing numbers of specialist books, manuals and articles to give her advice, many of which came to advocate the new, 'artistic' manner of furnishing. Illustrated catalogues aimed at the middle-class consumer showed ranges of objects and interiors, at prices catering for different budgets. The choice available was staggering.

Under the influence of these developments, the furnishings of middle-class homes became increasingly diverse, with a mixture of styles and a proliferation of objects assembled from across the globe. The Scarborough house of the Yorkshire artist John Atkinson Grimshaw, as painted in 1878, juxtaposes eighteenth-century-style chairs, blue and white Chinese ceramic jars, Japanese fans and a Jacobean-style leaded window. Such juxtapositions were carried furthest in self-consciously 'artistic' interiors like Grimshaw's, but in the later years of the century many middle-class homes followed suit, with rooms full of objects in a variety of reproduction and 'artistic' styles.

10. *'The Newlyn', A set of Plain Oak Furniture.* Illustration by Charles Henry Bourne Quennell, from A *Note on Simplicity of Design*, 1898, by Gleeson White, published by Heal & Son, London. Line-block. VAM AAD/1994/16/3251.

11. *Designs for Furniture and Decorations for Complete House Furnishings*, 1894. Catalogue for Hampton & Sons, London. VAM 505.C.44.

2. Planning the household

As far as the spatial organization of individual houses was concerned, the homes of the very wealthy – the landed rich, who maintained a social supremacy throughout most of the century – provided the stylistic model by which those of lower rank and income might gain an approximation of genteel living as complex as income and space would allow. At the time of the Queen's accession in 1837 roughly 3,000 large working country houses attached to significant estates stood as testament to the enduring political and economic power of landed families in Britain. It is thanks largely to the seriousness with which Victorian landowners took their duties as custodians of these piles that so many have survived virtually intact into the twenty-first century. Consideration for more modern styles of living, in the form of water closets, bathrooms, central heating, gas lighting, hydraulic lifts and mechanized kitchen equipment, was constrained by the unforgiving structures of older buildings

and, after 1870, by the cash drain represented by the huge swathes of land that generally came with them. Such luxuries could be accommodated only in the building of new country houses, of which about 500 were erected (including some remodelling of earlier structures) between 1835 and 1889. Half of these schemes were initiated by families profiting from relatively recent incomes

raised through commerce and industry. Such patrons could only hope to emulate the far-reaching cultural clout of their landed neighbours. Nevertheless, their massive new mansions with all modern conveniences displayed an extraordinary level of comfort and fairly radical new ideas about polite living. They were revolutionary – but in the most discreet manner.

12 *The Last Day in the Old Home*, 1862. By Robert Braithwaite Martineau. The circumstances of modern life often placed landed families in a precarious financial position. Here the high living of a young aristocrat has forced the sale of his old country home and treasured heirlooms. Oil on canvas. © Tate, London, 2001.

13 The Drawing Room, Cragside, Northumberland. Designed by Norman Shaw. Built 1869–84 for the arms manufacturer, Sir William Armstrong. While the imposing neo-Mannerist fireplace, fine panelling and vaulted ceiling recall the traditional country house, upholstered furniture and modern light fittings provide the latest in comfortable living.

14 Ground-floor plan, Bear Wood, Berkshire. The spatial organization of the new country house was a feat of social engineering and rational planning. Rooms were identified according to the sex of their users.

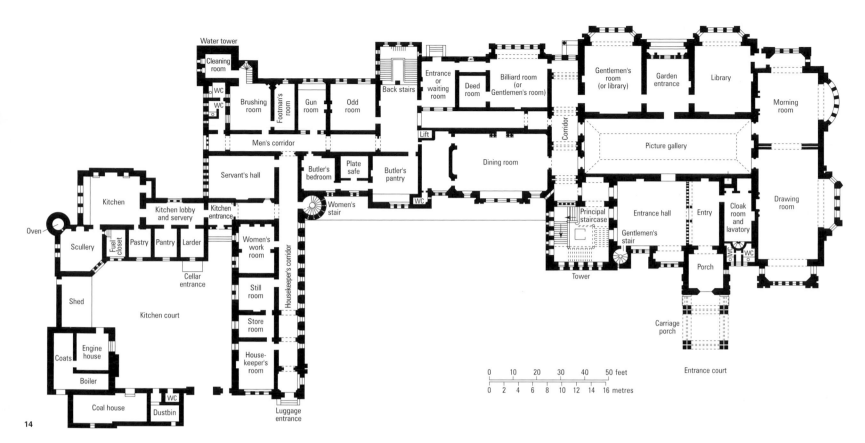

14

It was through this combination of deference to the old established order, whose arcane social rituals acted as a barrier against presumptuous incomers, and an openness to the lessons of modernity that the Victorian country house maintained its primacy as a model for 'correct' domestic arrangements. Many of these arrangements seemed to have common ground with more 'middle-class' notions of decency and propriety. Several of the organizational changes that took place were structural, relating to the spatial relationship of public and private, formal and informal areas. In most houses servants' wings were considerably expanded to support the role of the house as a centre for hospitality and entertainment. Serving staff and younger members of the family were moved out from the attic storeys to self-contained annexes, which also often included provision for nurseries and children's bedrooms. Here, though better provided for, they were also removed from polite eyes. The more socially homogeneous set-up of the eighteenth-century aristocratic household gave way to a class consciousness which dictated that in some houses servants turn to face the wall in the unexpected presence of family members. Children – though an essential component of the family atmosphere that formed a focus of household activities – were similarly side-lined wherever possible until they were old enough for despatch to public school or the care of a governess.

15 *Bear Wood, Berkshire*, 1870. From *The Architect*, 9 July 1870. Drawing by Robert Kerr, lithograph by Kell Bros. Bear Wood was completed in 1870 to designs by Kerr for the newspaper proprietor John Walter. Lithograph. VAM P.P.21.D.

15

This strict segregation of activities and social types was even echoed in the treatment of guests, who found their sleeping quarters diminished in size and separated into men's and women's wings. Old-style private dressing and receiving rooms were largely discarded in favour of communal morning, drawing, garden, music, smoking, reading and billiard rooms where everyone might congregate at specific times of the day. These were also clearly divided according to use, so that the final three rooms retained overtly masculine associations. Any taint of rakish licentiousness was swept away in preference for moral and architectural control. At the centre of the house the family reinforced its symbolic prominence through a revival of the medieval hall. This served as the focus for public events: everything from society balls to servants' dances, from dinners for tenant farmers to parties for local school children. In this sentimental vein the great English country house and its mistress maintained their hold on the popular imagining of English cultural and social life well into the twentieth century, even as the inevitable demise of this way of living was being loudly trumpeted.

These clearly demarcated boundaries whereby the layout of the building reflected the morality of its inhabitants were replicated on a smaller scale in the town houses of the rich, and especially in the suburban dwellings of the middle classes. Similar effects could be discerned in the arrangement of the 'parlour' of the 'respectable' working classes, where the best room of the house

was set aside as a well-tidied shrine, filled with mementoes of family life, prized ornaments, religious ephemera and patriotic memorabilia. By the last quarter of the century many parlours incorporated a piano, the ultimate proof of respectability and a sign of Sunday-evening sociability. Indeed, it is arguable that the refined territories of new lifestyles – aristocratic, middle-class and proletarian – signalled an almost universal acceptance of the morally earnest codes of social behaviour associated with evangelical Christianity. The daughter of a Hertfordshire vicar, recalling a move to a new parish in 1847, presented a description of home life whose abstract considerations were not so far removed from those that might also concern the daughter of a duke or a dustman:

> The house contained a tiled entrance lobby and oak-floored hall, dining room, drawing room and study, three best bedrooms and two dressing rooms, two servants' rooms and two nurseries. These latter were in a wing approached by a baize-covered swing door, and back stairs led down to the kitchen, pantry and a small parish room . . . there were no bathrooms then, and all hot and cold water had to be carried from the kitchen and scullery. But we all had baths each day in spite of that. Oil lamps and candles were used for lighting. Our drawing room was papered with a buff and gilt Fleurs-de-Lys patterned paper. There were book shelves and pier glasses and wool-work ottomans and an upright grand piano with faded red silk fluted across the front and a very fine harp . . . The carpet was red with a buff pattern, and my mother had a davenport sacred to her own use. In the best bedrooms there were four-post beds with damask curtains, though brass beds were by then becoming fashionable . . . Our household consisted of a cook, house parlour maid and a girl.

16 *Design for the Great Hall at Scarisbrick Hall, Lancashire*, 1836. By A. W. N. Pugin. Scarisbrick was remodelled for its rich 19th-century inheritors. The Great Hall was a symbolic focus for the household. Watercolour. RIBA Library Drawings Collection.

17 *Interior of a Cottage at Compton Bassett, Wiltshire*, 1849. By Elizabeth Pearson Dalby. The array of humble possessions reinforces an impression of worthy homeliness. Gouache. © Salisbury and South Wiltshire Museum.

18 *View of a Living Room*, 1909. By C. W. Bodman. By the turn of the century the middle- and working-class parlour had become a show room for inherited furniture and the pursuance of 'respectable' hobbies, including music making, embroidery, flower arranging and painting. Such was the emotional importance of its content that its use was often restricted to Sundays and holidays. Watercolour, pen and ink. VAM E.1273-1984.

19 *Playing at Doctors*, 1863. By Frederick Daniel Hardy. Though slightly frayed at the edges, the interiors of the houses belonging to country vicars and doctors had become a familiar symbol of the 'cosy' middle-class lifestyle by mid-century. Oil on canvas. VAM 1035-1886.

20

Closer in to the rapidly expanding cities, suburban developments of detached, semi-detached and terraced villas followed similar ground-plans, their occupants striving for the same effects, even as space and financial means declined. The trappings of gentility were still in evidence in the jerry-built ribbons of two- and three-storey, narrow and rather dark houses with their italianate or Gothic embellishments, which ringed every sizeable town in Britain by the 1870s.

From the city centre outwards the class hierarchies of Victorian society could be read through the rental value, garden length and room size of a home. Meanwhile the decorative details of mass-produced ornamental brick and stone work, stucco, stained glass and coloured roof tiles on the exterior, and of moulded plaster cornices, volutes and ceiling roses, cast-iron fireplaces, baths and kitchen ranges on the interior, remained constant across a highly variegated social spectrum.

20 *Builders in Clapton Passage, Hackney, London*, 1882. By Alfred Braddock. Nestled between older 18th-century developments and boasting decorative embellishments drawn from a mixture of classical and Gothic sources, the terraced house, constructed by local builders as a speculation, incorporated all the aspirations of a new generation of suburban inhabitants. London Borough of Hackney, Archives Department.

21

Such markers of distinction differed perhaps only in quality and quantity according to the spending power of the respective speculative builder, but some form of elaboration was always present. Thus poorer clerks, schoolteachers, small traders and their families struggled at the inner perimeters to define themselves against the perceived roughness of their working-class neighbours. Professionals in law and medicine, or those whose retail and service businesses guaranteed a substantial income without the need to commute, inhabited larger outlying properties whose grounds had been carved out from the sale of old estates and whose street patterns followed the lanes of ancient villages that had been swallowed up by the urban sprawl. Standing between the successful lawyers and the minor gentry were those stockbrokers and industrial entrepreneurs who peppered the rural hinterlands of urban centres with extravagant domestic edifices that testified to old values and new technologies.

21 *Silver Moonlight*, 1886. By John Atkinson Grimshaw. At the edge of the city, old and new houses in spacious grounds served the domestic needs of urban professionals. Grimshaw delighted in producing composite landscapes based on the prosperous suburbs of northern industrial towns, where crumbling mansions and winding village lanes suggested a more romantic and picturesque conception of modern life. Oil on canvas. Harrogate Museums and Art Gallery.

In between all of these building projects lay the results of earlier booms, and it would be wrong to assume that all Victorians lived in new properties. However, most interiors could be updated to incorporate modern ideas of comfort and hygiene. In 1881 the architect Robert Edis provided encouragement for owners of outmoded Georgian terraces. In his book *The Decoration and Furniture of Town Houses* he suggested that stairwells be brightened with framed drawings, china, leaded lantern lights, flower arrangements and Persian prayer carpets. Dining rooms should be 'designed for use, not show', with well-sprung chairs 'covered with strong, serviceable leather ... in preference to velvet, which is liable to hold dust and to drag the lace of ladies' dresses'. Cumbersome sideboards might be replaced with 'a plain but solidly handsome buffet, arranged for the reception of plate and glass, or for good pieces of china'. In accordance with common practice, 'drawing rooms should be the rooms of all others in which good taste ... should be everywhere apparent'. This meant discarding 'dreary blanks of mere one-tinted paper' for wall displays of 'pleasant objects to look upon' and 'comfortable couches and chairs to lounge and really rest upon'. The mid-century fashion for 'fluffy wool mats ... antimacassars of lace ... [and] bits of Dresden' was to

22 *The drawing room, 3 The Close, Winchester*, about 1900. By B. O. Corfe. The drawing room in the house of Canon A. S. Valpy. During the last quarter of the century the sensitive and 'artistic' homemaker pared down the formal heaviness of previous decades for a lighter touch in which the informality of chintz covers, random piles of books and fine antique furniture betrayed 'superior' taste and learning. Watercolour. VAM E.222-1955.

"YES MOTHER, I COME! I COME!"

23

be pared back so that 'the rooms should, above all, look and be home-like in all their arrangements, with ornaments, books and flowers, not arranged merely for show, but for pleasant study or recreation'. Considerations of health dictated the refitting of bedrooms, which 'should be clear of everything that can collect and hold dust in any form'. Light, simple furniture, including tiled wash-stands, portable dressing tables and deal window seats, together with an avoidance of densely patterned surfaces that 'might be likely to fix themselves upon the tired brain' lent an airiness to cramped attic spaces. Adjoining nurseries could be modernized with flower boxes, washable wallpapers and pasted borders utilizing the colourful Christmas book illustrations of 'Miss Kate Greenaway and Mr Walter Crane'.

24

23 Poster for the play *East Lynne*, about 1895. By an unknown artist. The Victorian house demanded intensive maintenance, and an interest in issues of health dictated that washable and accessible surfaces were introduced, especially in bedrooms such as this, with its iron bed. Lithograph. VAM E.166-1935.

24 *Winter*, 1883. Tile. Designed by Kate Greenaway. Made by T. and R. Boote. Glazed earthenware. VAM Circ.398-1962.

So what distinguished the Victorian period was the relative ease with which middle-class occupants could move between property types and impose their character on empty spaces in the manner that Edis advised. This was a luxury previously reserved for the very rich, or a necessity imposed on the transient poor. Despite the seeming clutter of domestic arrangements, the popularity of renting property over its outright purchase made for a surprisingly mobile urban population, which must have impacted on the increasing turnover and emphasis on portability in styles of furnishing and decoration. Those who bought their own houses were either unusually wealthy or, in the case of the aggressively self-made, déclassé, which led to accusations of fanciful tawdriness against those who used their dwellings as a direct illustration of their wealth (the *arriviste* family with its vulgar tastes was a constant target for satirists like Dickens).

The landlord system ensured that overtly individualized expressions of capital accumulation were kept in check, on the outside of buildings at least. 'Good taste' was more profitably displayed through regular removals to the latest suburban development ('regular' meaning that the middle classes typically took on renewable leases of one to three years, while working-class

tenancies were agreed by the week or month). The constant erection of new streets in the latter half of the nineteenth century offered the house-hunter a range of ready-made external finishes in neo-classical, Gothic and vernacular styles, in districts attuned to minute social gradations that might correspond to shared occupations, religious affiliations, fashionable pretensions or even political sympathies. The freedom of renting also meant that accommodation could be tailored according to stages of the lifecycle, with more or fewer rooms taken on as the family unit expanded and contracted. Furthermore, with an average of only 10 per cent of income given over to the landlord, relatively prosperous Victorians could devote a large proportion of their wealth to other priorities, which included the funding of businesses, the hiring of servants and the education of dependants. This extra money also (and most importantly) went towards the purchase of clothing and furnishings whose opulent surfaces provided a key index of status.

25 *An Ordinary Mantlepiece*, 1878. Illustration from *The Drawing Room; Its Decorations and Furniture* by Lucy Orrinsmith, 1878. While the permanent fittings of rented Victorian houses were often heavy and bulky, new tenants could do much to impose their character on their surroundings with the judicious introduction of ornaments and textiles. Wood engraving. VAM 47.D.38.

3. Accounting for taste

These circumstances both gave rise to an unprecedented multiplication in the number and type of objects on the market. They also opened the floodgates for a deluge of publications that claimed to guide the consumer through an increasingly fraught voyage of self-construction. It seems fair, therefore, to claim that the Victorians – though they would not have recognized the word in its modern sense – were the first generation to succumb to the idea of 'lifestyle'. As the opinions of design reformers and the innovations of producers and retailers impacted on the appearance and use of a proliferation of new objects, this apparent freedom of choice evolved into a highly nuanced value system, whereby the dual influences of morality and fashion dictated that what you purchased really signified who you were. From the 1860s onwards this was true in all spheres of domestic life, from the laying of the dinner table, through the arrangement of pictures on the wall to your choice of wardrobe content. What, when and where you bought, and how you put it to use, said as much about you as the background of your parents or the way you earned your living – and sometimes more. Of course, to an extent this had always been the case, but now, as the pool of consumers widened and diversified, the manufacturers and purveyors of luxury and fashionable goods were far more efficient in ensuring that their products conveyed the appropriate social and cultural messages – messages that were deliberately prone to the vagaries of shifting styles, social habits and 'fads'.

26 *The Awakening Conscience*, 1853. By William Holman Hunt. Every surface of this interior has been chosen by the artist to symbolize the shallow material trappings of a 'kept' woman in her St John's Wood, London, boudoir. Oil on canvas. © Tate, London, 2001.

27 *For Sale*, 1857. By James Collinson. This young woman appears to be the epitome of respectable femininity, fulfilling her charitable duties at a church bazaar. But it is not immediately clear whether it is the table of attractive wares or the woman herself that is for sale. Oil on canvas. Castle Museum and Art Gallery, Nottingham.

28 *Changing Homes*, 1862. By George Elgar Hicks. Not all acquisition was necessarily corrupting. Hicks depicts a proud array of glittering wedding gifts and strikingly coloured upholstery and dress textiles in the comfortable drawing room of an affluent London family. Oil on canvas. The Geffrye Museum.

THE DINING TABLE

Ann Eatwell

The high-Victorian dining table looked very different from that of the Georgian period. The change was prompted by a new method of serving dinner known as *à la russe*, which replaced the earlier service *à la française*. Jane Carlyle (wife of the Scottish writer Thomas Carlyle) describes dining *à la russe* with the novelist Charles Dickens in 1849. 'The dinner was served up in the new fashion – not placed on the table at all – but handed round (by servants) – only the dessert on the table and quantities of artificial flowers.' Inherited silver was replaced by modern glass and ceramics, and on tables set *à la russe* the place setting or cover assumed greater importance. Despite a reluctance to abandon the old style of dining – public debate on the issue even reached the letter pages of *The Times* – by the 1860s polite society had largely embraced the new method of service.

The dinner party was the centrepiece of Victorian social entertaining, especially during the London season, which followed the parliamentary session from April to July. Celebrities were in great demand at such dinners. By June 1879 the author Henry James claimed to have dined out 107 times after the success of his

31. *Dinner at Haddo House*, **1884. By Alfred Edward Emslie. The man in the centre talking to the hostess is Mr Gladstone, the Prime Minister. Oil on canvas. National Portrait Gallery, London.**

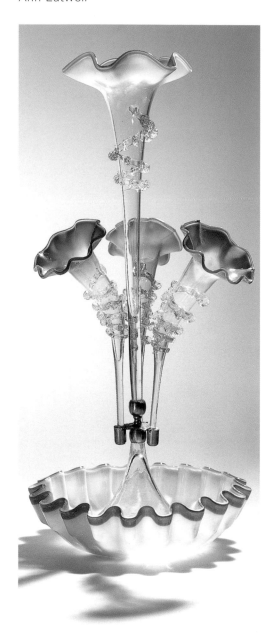

29. Centrepiece, 1890–1900. Possibly made at Stourbridge, West Midlands. Glass and brass. [h. 54.4cm]. VAM Circ.193-1970.

30. Specialist utensils. From left to right: fish knife and fork, with hallmarks for 1902–3. Silver with mother-of-pearl handles. Butter knife, about 1890. Electroplated nickel silver. Asparagus tongs, about 1890. Electroplated nickel silver. Lobster pick. Electroplated nickel silver. Cheese scoop, with London hallmarks for 1894–5. Silver with ivory handle. Grape scissors, late 19th century. Electroplated nickel silver. VAM Circ.102-1953, M.27A-1967, loan: NRM York.1:12-1999, M.26-2000, M.24-1999, M.41-2000.

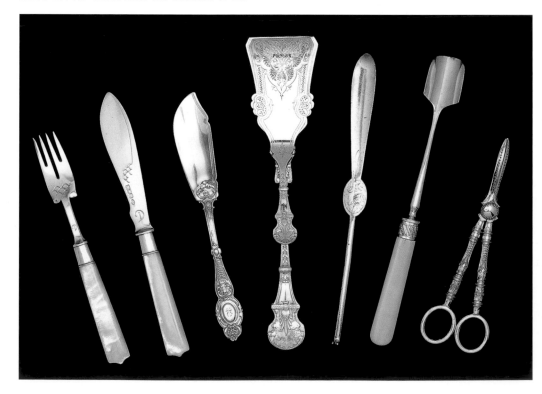

34. Breakfast, hash and soup serving dish with revolving cover, about 1905. Made in Sheffield by Aitkin Brothers. Presented to Captain Frank Johnson by the officers of HM Prison, Pentonville, on his retirement on 2 December 1905. Electroplated nickel silver. VAM M.28-2000.

novel *Daisy Miller*. Many society dinners were reciprocal affairs, described as 'cutlet for cutlet', at which hospitality was returned. Giving a dinner was the middle-class house-wife's contribution to upward social mobility, for a successful dinner could advance her husband's career. It required careful planning of the menu, guest list, table setting and serving of dishes by permanent or hired staff.

Domestic management manuals, such as Mrs Beeton's *Book of Household Management* advised on every aspect of organizing the dinner party, from seasonal menus for serving *à la russe* or *à la française* to the choice of dining equipment and layout of the table

itself. Numerous etiquette books enabled the inexperienced or those with new money to move in good company. Dining etiquette formed an important part of the Victorian code of polite society. *The Manners and Rules of Good Society* (1879) focused on the complicated and changing use of cutlery. With a few exceptions, like eating bread and some kinds of fruit, touching food with the fingers was frowned upon. Diners were presented with a growing – and sometimes confusing – range of specialist utensils for eating particular foods. It was important to be able to recognize lobster picks, asparagus tongs and grape scissors, and to know how to use them correctly.

32. Place setting for dinner, set out according to Mrs Beeton's *Book of Household Management*, 1888. Silver flatware, with hallmarks for 1893–1904. From the outside: table spoon, fish knife, fish fork, knife and fork for first course, knife and fork for main course. Salt cellars, with London hallmarks for 1874–5. Silver and enamel. Glassware, from left to right: comport, about 1864. Swan flower trough, 1870–1900. Champagne, sherry and wine glasses, about 1880–90. VAM M.33-39-2000, M.29-1983, Circ.748-1967, C.270-1987, C.37-2000, C.40-2000, C.36-2000.

33. A dining table. Illustration from *The Book of Household Management* by Isabella Beeton, 1888. Coloured wood engraving. Private collection.

35

In the domestic sphere the effects of expanded consumer options can be traced through an incursion of fashionable styling into home decoration, which reached its peak by the 1880s. Each room in the house could be fitted out through reference to a battery of decorating styles, plundered from historical and global sources to create a virtual index to the aesthetic knowhow of the householder and the traditional function of the space in question. As early as 1865 the journal *London Society* could elaborate on 'seven styles of furniture' that summarized (in a satirical vein) the spectrum of cosmopolitan tastes. The 'dull' style approximated to the traditional manner of decorating the drawing room since the 1840s and symbolized home as a comforting retreat from the world of fashion: 'neatness . . . highly polished round table . . . wax flowers under a glass shade . . . a bit of needlework . . . well-bound books'. The writer of the piece felt that 'one never goes into the room without feeling inclined to yawn, and a sense of depression comes over

36

---

35 *Past and Present No. 1*, 1858. By Augustus Egg. Behind the respectable 'dullness' of the mid-century drawing room all manner of emotional problems might be hidden. This interior has been carefully put together to suggest the fragility of the domestic ideal. In its formal details it shows the prevailing middle-brow taste for dark reds and greens and is perhaps less cluttered than clichéd representations of middle-class rooms might have led us to expect. Oil on canvas. © Tate, London, 2001.

36 *Hush! (The Concert)*, about 1875. By James Tissot. The huge public rooms of great London houses provided the grandiose settings for those formal receptions that marked the social season. Attendance at such events in the correct attire was proof of acceptance into the world of the social élite. Oil on canvas. Manchester City Art Gallery.

one in a few minutes'. The 'upholsterer's' style lacked emotional authenticity and was condemned for its adherence to pattern books. 'The upholsterer goes down with rule and tape . . . and he stamps himself and his shop upon the whole house . . . The drawing room must be white and gold; the dining room red and mahogany; and the library oak and leather.' The 'rich' style took such attitudes to extremes. The author bemoaned that 'heavy massive wealth overpowers it all', and in images of élite interiors, complex draperies, massed reproduction furniture and gilt stucco give some indication of the prevalence of this trend, especially in the cavernous saloons that provided space for the society balls that punctuated the 'season'. In the 1850s and 1860s the 'architectural' style alluded to the taste for all things Gothic. *London Society* associated its use with the furnishing of bedrooms. 'When we saw it we thanked heaven we were not going to sleep in those beds. Imagine the horrors of a nightmare of griffins impaled, or lions rampant, or the ceaselessness of the motto from which one could never escape.' Certainly the ingenious forms of medieval decoration were utilized to disguise objects of more mundane usage, including the technology of bathrooms, water closets and kitchens. The 'antiquarian' style, with its dark panelling and uncomfortable settee 'in which

37

it was supposed some great man had sat a century or two ago', clearly found favour in masculine studies and libraries, while the 'luxurious' and 'meretricious' styles in their sybaritic whimsy came closest to a fusion of the upholsterer's and the couturier's art. In their theatrical showiness, such interiors paid a debt to the new public spaces of hotels, town halls and places of entertainment – the antithesis of the highly personalized and shrine-like inner-sanctum of the drawing room:

> This style abounds in white and gold, and beautifully tinted walls half darkened by rose-coloured blinds, and surrounded by balconies filled with evergreens and bright flowers, and ornamented with arches of creepers . . . there is a great amount of looking glass; a profusion of drapery in the shape of portieres and curtains. The effect is pretty, but it is all more or less a sham . . . It is pretentious, and attempts to pass itself off for something that it is not.

38

37 The guest bedroom in the Tower House, Kensington, London, 1885. From *The House of William Burges* by Richard Popplewell Pullan. Photograph. VAM 51.E.54.

38 The Drawing Room, 34 Grosvenor Square, London, 1890. By H. Bedford Lemere. By the end of the century élite interiors were increasingly being styled with sweeping draperies and trimmings, lush vegetation and neo-rococo furniture, which made it difficult to distinguish the interiors of a fashionable hotel from a private drawing room. Indeed, both were theatrical spaces that permitted a conscious display of fashionability by society women. Albumen print. VAM 186-1926.

39

white china, Japanese paper fans, lacquered screens and all the paraphernalia of the 'artistic' sensibility. In the same year that *The Magazine of Art* was encouraging a rejection of the merely fashionable, Mrs Orrinsmith of Beckenham in her book for middle-class housewives, *The Drawing Room; its decoration and furniture*, was showing readers how to negotiate the blurred boundaries between aestheticism and consumerism:

> To an appreciative mind, not spoiled by the luxury of wealth, what keen pleasure there is in the possession of one new treasure; a Persian tile, an Algerian flower-pot, an old Flemish cup, a piece of Nankin blue . . . not one being costly, yet each in its own way, beautiful and interesting . . . A delight as pure as that of a child with a fresh toy, and superior to that in its lasting power, is open to the aspirant after the beautiful in art.

40

By the 1880s this striving for pretty effects had precipitated the first popular interior-decorating craze, whereby all pretence at creating a moral refuge from the world had become bound up with a desire to express individuality of spirit through the purchase of objects. In the guise of the aesthetic movement, fashion finally made a successful assault on the citadel of middle-class respectability. In its early stages the trend carried traces of moral didacticism through its close association with the political philosophies of Arts and Crafts pioneers like William Morris and Walter Crane. Its proselytizers recommended that the confident individuality expressed in their own bohemian interiors and the discretion to choose honest, well-made artefacts should be enough to construct a pleasing and meaningful environment. In 1878 a correspondent for *The Magazine of Art* urged readers to trust their own instincts: 'If you like white walls have white walls, although your neighbours prefer blue walls, and if you like dark walls don't be afraid of having them, because you hear that a drawing-room should be furnished in the French style.' Such breezy optimism was severely constrained in a world where manufacturers, retailers and publishers were increasingly adept at riding the market. The taste for constructing fantastic settings that played on the imagination was swiftly answered by the commercial provision of blue and

39 *The Dining Room at The Grange, North End Road*, 1898. By Thomas Matthews Rooke. The 'artistic' interior (this one belonging to the painter Edward Burne-Jones in Fulham, London) was at first intended as the antithesis of the fashionable 'decorator's' room. Its self-conscious display of personal treasures promotes the exotic and the quaint over the mass-produced or received notions of good taste. Watercolour. Private collection.

40 *My Aesthetic Love*, 1881. Music cover by Alfred Concanen. By the 1880s the paraphernalia of 'aesthetic' taste was widely available to a broad metropolitan audience. The pretensions of the craze's followers were cruelly lampooned by satirists. Colour lithograph. VAM Enthoven Collection.

41

THE FASHIONS

Expressly designed and prepared for the

Englishwoman's Domestic Magazine.

JULY 1860

42

4. Providing for desires

The commercial success of the aesthetic movement can be attributed to a number of factors. The circulation of definitions and instructions in popular magazines, the promotion of emblems through advertising and other forms of popular culture, and the provision of products in the retail sphere ensured that the trend was brought right into the homes of even the proudly unsophisticated (such as the fictional Mr Pooter of Holloway, London, in the Grossmiths' *Diary of a Nobody*). Mass-market journalism, advertisements and attractively stocked shops were not new phenomena. The important innovations in these industries had been initiated in the eighteenth century. What had changed was the scale and efficiency of their production, and nowhere were the effects more keenly felt than in activities surrounding the acquisition and use of fashionable dress.

For both middle- and upper-class Victorian women, fashion in clothing was on the surface a phenomenon that was firmly associated with Paris, which had long been established as a centre for the luxury trades. In the magazines that provided monthly and later weekly information on the progression of sartorial taste, editors always deferred to the styles being worn in France, and the intricate coloured fashion-plates that accompanied women's journals were generally produced by French publishing companies. However, this Gallic façade disguised an attitude to dressing up that was as closely attuned to British concerns with social differentiation and gentility as the decoration of the home. Periodicals themselves (of which many were launched over the course of the period) were carefully oriented towards the needs of specific classes of readers.

STYLISH OUTDOOR COSTUMES, DESIGNED AT THE MAISON WORTH, PARIS.   **43**

Thus *The Englishwoman's Domestic Magazine*, edited by Samuel and Isabella Beeton, enjoyed a heyday in the 1850s and 1860s as the 'style bible' of middle-class women, each edition being eagerly awaited for its even-tempered advice on the trappings of polite society and its increasingly racy correspondence pages. Its successor, *Myra's Journal of Dress and Fashion*, which dominated the 1870s and 1880s, aimed its content at a broader readership, encouraging those of more straitened financial means to adapt and modernize their wardrobes with the aid of practical patterns and dressmaking tips. Titles such as *The Queen* and *The Season* confined their columns to the concerns of the 'Upper Ten', those aristocratic and plutocratic readers who sought guidance on appropriate wear for fashionable society events and were able to enjoy, and even purchase, the Paris gowns by couturiers like Worth or Doucet that featured in the magazines' pages.

---

41 *He is Dead Too*, about 1888. By Walter Weedon Grossmith. Drawing for an illustration in *The Diary of a Nobody* by George and Weedon Grossmith, 1892. Japanese fans appear even on the walls of the Grossmiths' fictional clerk in unfashionable suburban London. Pen and ink drawing. VAM E.634-1987.

42 *The Fashions. Expressly designed and prepared for the Englishwoman's Domestic Magazine*, July 1860. By Jules David. Engraved and printed in Paris by J. Fourmage. Images of French fashions were made available to the middle-class readership of English women's magazines. Hand-coloured engraving. VAM PP.19.F.

43 *Stylish Outdoor Costumes, designed at the Maison Worth, Paris*, 1895. By Adolphe Charles Sandoz, engraved in Paris by Derbier. From *The Queen. The Lady's Newspaper*, August 1895. For the wealthy reader magazines promoted the creations of Paris designers, including Charles Worth. Engraving. VAM PP.7.C.

44

'Parisian' was also an epithet used by British purveyors of fashionable goods. Corsetiers, milliners and dressmakers, from the élite traders of Bond Street to the back-street concerns of Bolton, all deferred to the superiority of French associations in their promotions. Yet the textile and wholesale industries of Manchester, Glasgow and London benefited from a massive boom during the Victorian period, and the goods they offered carried definite British characteristics at home and in the Empire. In her actual purchases the British consumer was resolutely patriotic. The idea of Paris was really little more than a marketing tool and its broader cultural connotations were in any case rather disreputable! Thus the reasonably fashionable middle-class Englishwoman called on a wide range of local outlets to service her clothing needs over the course of the nineteenth century. Small family drapery and outfitting shops, little changed since the Napoleonic Wars, provided a range of suitable fabrics, accessories, underwear and ready-made items, while the skills of private seamstresses could convert the fantasies of fashion-plates into a more constrained reality. For the richer client a wide range of court dressmakers in the West End were more than capable of producing the elaborately constructed confections of silk, lace and velvet necessary for presentation ceremonies at St James's Palace or the round of 'at homes', musical soirées, fancy-dress parties, dinners and formal balls that constituted the social season.

45

44 *Colworth House, Bedfordshire*,
1850. By Eugène Louis Lami.
Expensively dressed guests socialize
at a Bedfordshire country house.
Watercolour. VAM 169-1880.

45 *Horatio Sparkins*, about 1836. Illustration by George
Cruikshank for *Sketches by Boz* by Charles Dickens, 1836.
The creation of a fashionable wardrobe still depended to a
large degree on the expertise of a range of small traders,
including the draper (seen here) and the dressmaker.
Etching. VAM 9726.6.

The newer city-centre department stores, which had developed from shawl and mantle warehouses in the 1830s and 1840s, probably accounted for a fairly small proportion of the typical consumer's purchases. Nevertheless, their impact on the urban scene and on the practice of shopping was hugely significant. With their spectacular window displays and interior fittings, their guarantee of fixed prices and dependable quality, and their provision of such luxuries as tea rooms, resident orchestras and armies of accommodating staff, London stores such as Peter Robinson in Oxford Street, Harrods in Brompton Road, Whiteley's in Bayswater and Liberty in Regent Street became leviathans of the high street – each appealing to its own constituency of consumers. Improvements in public transport systems ensured that regular trips into town became a crucial social and familial duty for the diligent housewife or hostess. By the 1890s this transformation of metropolitan life and the sense of urban excitement that it engendered had been bolstered by the opening of

47

46

46 *The Bayswater Omnibus*, about 1895. By George William Joy. Shopping for fashionable goods entailed a direct engagement with the noise, visual distractions and social variety of modern urban life. Reliable public transport offered the commercial experience of the metropolis to a growing audience. Oil on canvas. The Museum of London.

47 Oxford Street, London, 1896.

THE RAILWAYS

Jim Cheshire

The Railway Station was one of the most popular paintings of the Victorian period. Its popularity reflected the public's fascination with its subject matter. The *Telegraph* eulogized 'that microcosm of our life journey, the railway platform', while for the *Illustrated London News* the railways represented 'the grandest exponent of the enterprise, the wealth and the intelligence of our race'. Few disputed the central position that the railways held in Victorian culture.

Unlike their European counterparts, British railways were built with private money. The companies formed to finance their construction became enormously powerful through the huge amount of capital invested in them. They were unique in that they had no traditions to conform to. They represented themselves to the public in innovative ways: issuing their staff with fine uniforms, painting carriages and locomotives in distinctive colour schemes and adopting heraldic motifs.

Railway companies used buildings as well as uniforms to create a corporate identity. George Gilbert Scott's great Gothic building at St Pancras announced that the Midland Railway

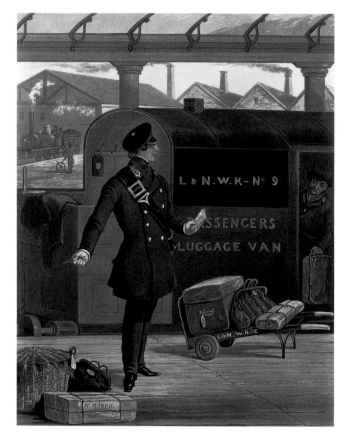

48. *The Guard of 1852*. By J. Harris after Samuel Henry Alken. Aquatint. Corporation of London.

49. *Travelling on the Liverpool and Manchester Railway, 1833*. By John Byam Liston Shaw. Aquatint. Chartered Institute of Transport.

had its own line between London and Yorkshire. It dwarfed the nearby Great Northern Hotel and King's Cross station, the property of the Great Northern Railway company. Fitting out the hotel at St Pancras provided valuable contracts for art manufacturers; Gillows, Elkington, Skidmore and Osler all profited from major contracts.

The Victorian railways provided a conspicuous physical manifestation of Britain's class structure: first-, second- and third-class carriages demarcated degrees of wealth and social standing. 'Parliamentary' trains – introduced after government legislation in 1844 – provided cheap travel for the lower classes, but could be slow and uncomfortable. Nevertheless, by the last quarter of the century the politician John Bright could point out that, although the railway network had increased the power of the rich, 'it has given to the poor a power which they did not at all possess'.

Increased mobility provided new opportunities for work and leisure. Daily commuting now became a possibility, while daytrips and weekend breaks became features of many people's lives. 'Excursion' trains

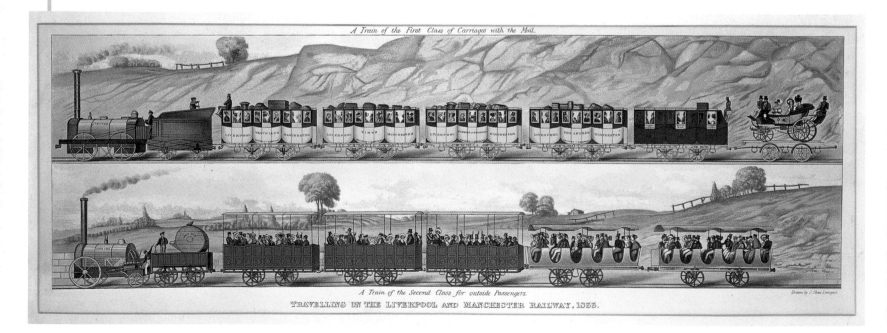

A Train of the First Class of Carriages with the Mail.

A Train of the Second Class for outside Passengers.

TRAVELLING ON THE LIVERPOOL AND MANCHESTER RAILWAY, 1833.

50. *Design for the south elevation of the Grand Midland Hotel, St Pancras Station, London*, about 1865. By Sir George Gilbert Scott. Pen and wash. RIBA Library Drawings Collection.

were laid on for special events. The famous travel agent, Thomas Cook, claimed to have transported 165,000 people to the Great Exhibition between May and October 1851. By 1900 an average person made 30 railway journeys a year and the railways had become part of everyday life. They brought about a revolution in transport and communications that remains one of the most remarkable legacies of the Victorian period.

51. *Design for the Great Hall, Euston Station, London,* 1846–9. By Philip Hardwick. Pen and wash. RIBA Library Drawings Collection.

52. *The Railway Station*, 1862. By William Powell Frith. Oil on canvas. © Royal Holloway and Bedford New College.

opulent restaurants (such as Spiers and Pond), alongside popular cafés (such as the Lyons chain), West End theatres and concert halls (including the Westminster Aquarium and The Empire, Leicester Square), and established pleasure gardens (Cremorne or Rosherville). Concerns such as these provided suitable and largely 'respectable' venues for displays of fashionable taste and social interaction that might previously have taken place within a more domestic context.

A proliferation and fast turnover of fashionable styles also ensured that the social signals given out by dress became increasingly complex as the century wore on. At the onset of Victoria's reign in 1837 the respectable woman's wardrobe echoed a much narrower conception of idealized femininity. Close-fitting bonnets, sleeves and bodices, heavy skirts and enveloping shawls for

daywear in dull plaids and stripes, with equally tightly boned and layered confections in paler whites and pastels for evening, bespoke the gentle submission of the 'angel in the home' – that domestic paragon to which most genteel women aspired (see 14:27). By the 1860s the opportunities afforded by new technologies had introduced bright synthetic dyes, showy sewing-machine-made accessories and the extraordinary lightweight support of the wire crinoline (and later the bustle) to the middle-class wardrobe. In this manner the expanding horizons offered by consumer culture dictated a more

53 *The Oxford Galop*, about 1861. Music cover by T. Packer depicting the interior of the Oxford Music Hall, London, opened in 1861. Colour lithograph. VAM Enthoven Collection.

54 *The Young Widow*, 1877. By Edward Killingworth Johnson. Significant moments in people's lifecycles were marked by the adoption of specific costumes and social habits, which also drew the attention of astute businessmen, from funeral directors to department-store managers. Here the roles of bride and widow have followed each other too quickly for comfort. Watercolour and gouache. VAM E.808-1959.

I CAN'T STAND MRS GREEN'S MOTHER.

WRITTEN BY
HARRY HUNTER.
SUNG BY
LITTLE THOMAS
OF THE MOHAWK MINSTRELS.
COMPOSED BY
WALTER REDMOND.
&
HERBERT CAMPBELL.
Pr 4/

LONDON: FRANCIS BROTHERS & DAY, 351 OXFORD STREET. W.

55

55 *I Can't Stand Mrs Green's Mother*, about 1878. Music cover by Alfred Concanen. The variety and expressive characteristics of consumer culture raised their own problems, not least the potential for conflict that the adoption of new fashions and domestic routines carried between generations and social classes. Colour lithograph. VAM Enthoven Collection.

assertive display of fashionable products (*see 14:5*). Like her mastery of the domestic interior, the housewife had to learn how to use the decoration of her body as a sign of her family's prosperity and good standing. Individual elements of the wardrobe increasingly came to be associated with the specific rituals of respectable life-patterns, so that a woman with pretensions to society might be expected to change several times in the course of a day. This effect found its most concentrated form in the intensified clothing regulations applied to christenings, weddings and deaths in the family. The forbidding strictures of mourning dress reconciled the commercial acumen of crêpe and jet retailers with a supposed rejection of worldly concerns. This was a tension that reflected the opposing forces of display and morality inherent in fashion itself and in attitudes towards feminine culture generally.

If a tightening of the rules was necessary to ensure that an engagement with the dangerous world of fashion did not lead to immorality, then their loosening could also be a sign of the heightened sensibility of the fashion consumer. Echoing the trend towards aesthetic interior decoration, the emergence of 'counter-cultural' modes of dressing from the 1860s and 1870s onwards played an important role in the reordering of clothing habits for ordinary British men and women that was in progress by the end of the century. Aesthetic dress was partly a means of self-identification for those members of the metropolitan upper-middle classes who associated themselves with bohemian pursuits and with progressive political sensitivities, and partly a response to the unhealthiness and the perceived ugliness of contemporary fashionable style. But it introduced a real notion of freedom and common sense into the British wardrobe, with its 'natural' colours, 'tasteful' historicist inspiration and unrestrictive cut. It was, however, mercilessly lampooned at the time. *Punch* offered a typically wry take on what it saw as the absurdities of the

56

trend in a poem published in 1882 to coincide with a joint exhibition of the Rational Dress Society and the Healthy and Artistic Dress Union:

Note robes there for rinking, and gowns for tea-drinking,

For yachting, for climbing, for cricketing too;

The dresses for boating, the new petticoating,

The tunics in brown and the trousers in blue.

The fabrics for frockings, the shoes and the stockings,

And corsets that ne'er will the figure compress:

But in the whole placeful there's little that's graceful

And girlish enough for a Rational Dress!

Masculine clothing had benefited from a more 'rational' design since the end of the previous century. Yet despite the apparent simplicity and uniformity that the respectable male wardrobe seemed to offer, the acquisition and use of its content were just as complex as its female counterpart. With different styles of coat for a variety of professional and leisured contexts and a whole range of accessories, from sticks and gloves to shirts and hats, shopping for men's fashion was a serious business. It called on the skills of tailors, hosiers, outfitters, hatters and shoemakers to furnish a complete suit of clothing. Such was their competence at the top end of the market

56 *A Private View of the Royal Academy*, 1881. By William Powell Frith. The apparent constraints of mainstream fashion were challenged by champions of aesthetic dressing. At the Royal Academy disciples of the Aesthetic movement's 'prophet' Oscar Wilde (centre right) gather round him in corset-free outfits of muted colours and medieval inspiration. Oil on canvas. Private collection.

57

that English tailoring became synonymous with quality throughout the world. Underlying this was a theory of 'gentlemanliness', which bound the 'correct' usage of the male wardrobe to a celebration of moral rectitude, physical endeavour and aesthetic 'good form'. This notion ensured that though a man's dress appeared to reject the ephemerality of fashion, it remained a key indicator of his place in society and his attitude to culture. In its more adventurous forms – for example, when the dapper evening suit was taken up as a badge of belonging for cosmopolitan playboys and dandies in the 1890s, or when the relaxed, sporty lounge suit started to break down the stuffiness implied by morning and frock coats in the same decade – masculine fashion offered a universal template for modern dressing. Women rapidly took up its adaptable components, like the washable shirt and the tailored suit, to form a wardrobe more suitable to the expanded life circumstances of the New Woman in the new century. Like other physical aspects of Victorian life, the man's suit proved to be a flexible barometer of cultural change. Its development illustrated how accomplished nineteenth-century consumers were at reconciling the material plenitude of modern life with their social and emotional needs.

58

57 *Walking in the Zoo*, about 1870. Music cover by Richard Childs. Music-hall stars like 'The Great Vance' provided dapper models of masculine fashion and refute the idea that Victorian men were uninterested in issues of sartorial style. Colour lithograph. VAM Enthoven Collection.

58 *An English family taking tea on the lawn*, about 1900. By an unknown photographer. By the turn of the century many consumers could enjoy a wardrobe that was relatively unconstraining, adaptable to modern pursuits such as cycling, and associated with social, sexual and political emancipation. VAM E.2283:6-1997.

POTTERS
DARWEN

CHAPTER 15

Victorian Britain, 1837–1901

What was new?

JOHN STYLES

1. Novelty

Innovation fascinated the Victorians. Human inventiveness in the fields of technology, art and fashion seemed to have spawned an unprecedented variety of new things. Looking back in 1898, the *Popular Science Monthly* reflected that, 'as the nineteenth century draws to a close, there is no slackening in that onward march of scientific discovery and invention which has been its chief characteristic'. Not that innovation was universally acclaimed. Despite the enthusiasm for the new – and sometimes for the fantastic – that could be found in the ever-more numerous popular magazines, the unceasing tide of innovation unsettled many Victorians. Nowhere was this unease more marked than in design and the decorative arts. Critics complained that public taste had come to be dominated by a wilful striving merely to be different, an aesthetic restlessness that paid little heed to notions of beauty derived from the formal principles of the art academies or to Pugin's notion of honesty of construction. 'Novelty, give us novelty, seems to be the cry,' wrote Henry Cole disapprovingly. In 1849 his *Journal of Design and Manufacture* elaborated:

> There is a morbid craving in the public mind for novelty as mere novelty, without regard to intrinsic goodness; and all manufacturers, in the present mischievous race for competition, are driven to pander to it. It is not sufficient that each manufacturer produces a few patterns of the best sort every season, they must be generated by the score and by the hundreds. We know that one of our first potters brought to town last year upwards of a thousand patterns! There are upwards of six thousand patterns for calico-printing registered annually, and this we estimate to be only a third of the number produced . . . One of the best cotton printers told us that the creation of new patterns was an endless stream. The very instant his hundred new patterns were out he began to engrave others. His designers were working like mill-horses.

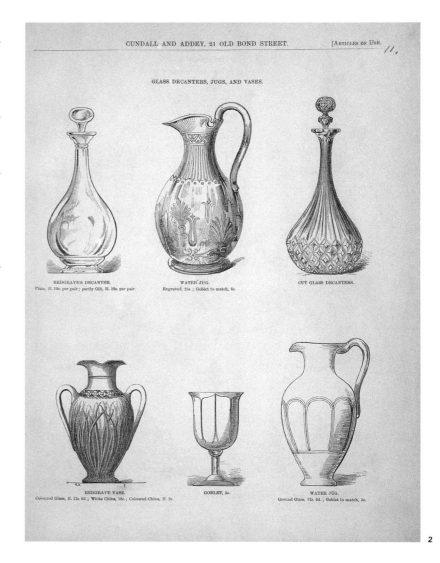

CUNDALL AND ADDEY, 21 OLD BOND STREET. [Articles of Use.

GLASS DECANTERS, JUGS, AND VASES.

REDGRAVE'S DECANTER. Plain, 2*l.* 10*s.* per pair; partly Gilt, 3*l.* 10*s.* per pair.

WATER JUG. Engraved, 25*s.*; Goblet to match, 6*s.*

CUT GLASS DECANTERS.

REDGRAVE VASE. Coloured Glass, 2*l.* 12*s.* 6*d.*; White China, 18*s.*; Coloured China, 2*l.* 2*s.*

GOBLET, 3*s.*

WATER JUG. Ground Glass, 12*s.* 6*d.*; Goblet to match, 3*s.*

---

1 Detail of a wallpaper sample showing a perspective view of a railway station, about 1852. Produced by Potters of Darwen, Lancashire. Wallpaper samples like this in a 'variety of miserable patterns' were included in the exhibit of False Principles in Decoration at the Museum of Ornamental Art, Marlborough House, in 1852. Henry Cole disapproved of this paper because of its false perspective and frequent repeats. Paper, printed from wooblocks. VAM E.558-1980.

2 *Glass decanters, jugs and vases*, 1853. From *A Catalogue of English Art Manufactures, Selected for their Beauty of Design*, published by Cundall and Addey of London, 1853. The objects in the catalogue embodied the principles of good design advocated by Henry Cole and his associates. This page includes a decanter and vase designed by Richard Redgrave, who edited the *Journal of Design and Manufacture* with Cole. Engraving. VAM 37.F.39.

A public appetite for novelties was not, of course, a new phenomenon. The sixteenth, seventeenth and eighteenth centuries had each witnessed the arrival or invention in Britain of multitudes of new things. These innovations were repeatedly accompanied by expressions of concern about the powerful, sometimes irrational grip that new objects exercised on the imaginations and purses of the British population. However, what was distinctive about the nineteenth century was an intense desire to establish an aesthetic distinction between good and bad innovations. This involved drawing an exceptionally stark contrast between 'mere novelty' and 'intrinsic goodness'; between what was described in discussion of design for printed textiles as 'novelty of conception and constant variety of effect' and 'elegance and beauty of execution'. Precisely how this distinction should be defined remained the subject of bitter dispute throughout the Victorian era. Yet these disagreements did little to reduce the appeal of such a distinction as a way of making sense of the tidal wave of new objects that seemed close to overwhelming the human capacity to choose.

By the mid-nineteenth century the growth of national wealth, combined with the accelerating pace of innovation, had brought an unprecedented level of material abundance to broad sections of the population. What and how to choose became the issue of the day, rehearsed in erudite treatises and popular magazines. But it would be wrong to imagine that the Victorian crisis of choice arose simply because innovations in materials and manufacturing techniques made it possible to produce ever-more varied goods at ever cheaper prices.

Many manufacturers undoubtedly believed that by constantly introducing new designs they increased their sales and their profits. Indeed, so great was the pressure on them to differentiate their products by means of design that new laws were introduced between 1839 and 1843 to allow designs to be registered, thereby discouraging piracy. It was at this period too that we begin to observe manufacturers using the names of well-known designers like Christopher Dresser as a selling point. Nevertheless, the crisis of choice cannot be accounted for simply by the desire of businessmen to use design to boost sales. As we have seen, it also reflected the absence of a single, dominant style, at a time when knowledge about historical styles and decorative effects had never been greater or more accessible. It arose out of the competitive anxiety of the ever-increasing population of consumers to use their purchases to improve themselves and their homes. It was fuelled by the conflicting claims about new things with which manufacturers and shopkeepers, designers and critics bombarded the public. Never before had so many people confronted so great a choice of new objects that claimed to be beautiful, but never before had the criteria for making appropriate aesthetic decisions seemed so uncertain.

2. How things were made

The almost miraculous increases in industrial productivity that could flow from the combination of steam power and automatic machinery mesmerized the Victorians. The phenomenon evoked both delight and repulsion, but the powered machine was universally acknowledged as one of the defining characteristics of the age. Yet it was only a narrow range of industries that were utterly transformed by the application of steam power. Indeed, in 1870 transport, in the form of steam ships and railway locomotives, used more steam horsepower than the whole of manufacturing industry. With the exception of cotton and woollen textiles and iron and steel, the impact of steam-powered machinery on British industry was limited before the final decades of the Victorian period. By then, steam was itself beginning to face the challenge of the electric motor as a source of industrial motive power – one that could be applied to small and medium-sized machinery with much more flexibility.

Because powered machinery long remained the exception rather than the norm in many industries, only a small minority of those who toiled in Victorian manufacturing were machine minders. For motive power, much Victorian manufacturing depended on its workers' arms, legs and lungs; for precision, on their keen eyes, steady hands and the almost instinctive

3

3 *The Mill, Saltaire*, about 1853. This sketch of Sir Titus Salt's new worsted mill at Saltaire, Yorkshire, was probably drawn in the Bradford office of its architects, Lockwood and Mawson. It depicts two of the most important mid-19th-century uses of steam power side-by-side – textile manufacturing and the railway. Watercolour and body colour. Salts Estates Ltd.

appreciation of how to combine material and design that came only with long experience. Many industries, such as glass making, used virtually no powered machinery during the whole of the Victorian era. Where it was used, often it was for only one in a long sequence of processes that culminated in the finished product. In the potteries, steam power might be used to mix the clay, but plates, teacups and the myriad other products of the industry continued to be shaped by hand, often on potters' wheels

4 *D'Almaine's Pianoforte Manufactory*, 1830–40. By Thomas Hosmer Shepherd. Pianos are shown being made by hand in this early Victorian factory in Upper Chilton Street, London. Pencil, pen, ink and watercolour. The Museum of London.

5 The upholstery workshop of Harris Lebus, London, 1899. All the work in this late-Victorian upholstery workshop is being undertaken by hand. VAM Furniture and Woodwork Department Library.

CHRISTOPHER DRESSER

Karen Livingstone

As a freelance designer, Christopher Dresser (1834–1904) embodied a new kind of profession. He had a successful studio in London, employing, by 1904, 10 assistants and all five of his daughters. Unusually, Dresser was not a trained architect or professional artist. He studied at the Government School of Design, where he developed an interest in botany and formed influential ideas on nature and ornament from Owen Jones and other prominent lecturers. He began his career as a botanist and lecturer, publishing several books on design, until he started to work full-time as a freelance designer from 1862.

Dresser's inspired approach to marketing his work ensured that his business was successful and that he is remembered as one of the most prolific designers of his age. He toured the country visiting major trade outlets and manufacturers, securing lucrative contracts and selling his designs. His publications – and ventures such as the Art Furnishers' Alliance, with a shop on Bond Street – were intended to promote his work and influence manufacturers. Dresser was one of the earliest designers to have his commercial work accredited to him and his signature marked on the manufactured object. By the height of his career, his name had come to represent a guarantee of 'art

value', forcing him to complain in 1875 that some retailers had started to use his name to sell goods that he had not designed.

Like other designers, Dresser looked to non-European sources for inspiration. Rather than imitating historical styles, he created original forms, such as an earthenware vase with a yellow glaze, drawing on sources as diverse as Chinese and ancient Peruvian pottery, which he know from visits to the British Museum. He visited Japan in 1877 and wrote extensively about what he saw there, consolidating an appreciation of Japanese art and design that was to inform much of his subsequent work.

Dresser's idea of design was utilitarian, aesthetically pleasing and available to a wide buying public. He is notable for responding to new markets and exploiting the properties and manufacturing processes of cheaper materials like electroplate. His most advanced theories on design, such as the correct position of a handle on a teapot, so that it could be lifted without strain and poured without dripping, are set out in publications including *The Principles of Decorative Design*. This approach to function and design as applied to industrial manufacture distinguishes Dresser as one of one of the most exceptional designers of his time.

6. *Christopher Dresser*, about 1861. *Carte de visite* **photograph. The Linnean Society of London.**

7. Tea service, about 1880. Designed by Christopher Dresser. Made by James Dixon & Sons, Sheffield. Electroplated nickel silver VAM Circ.279-1961.

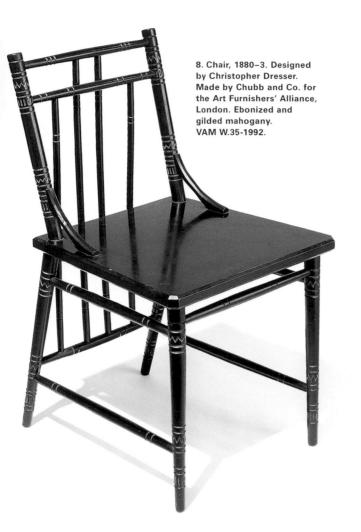

8. Chair, 1880–3. Designed by Christopher Dresser. Made by Chubb and Co. for the Art Furnishers' Alliance, London. Ebonized and gilded mahogany. VAM W.35-1992.

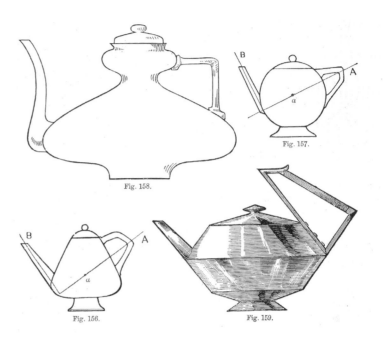

9. Detail of an illustration showing the correct position of handles, from *The Principles of Decorative Design*, 1873. By Christopher Dresser. VAM 58.C.8.

10. The ethnographical galleries at the British Museum showing Peruvian pottery as Christopher Dresser would have seen it, 1880s. The British Museum.

11. Vase, about 1892–6. Designed by Christopher Dresser. Probably made at the pottery of William Ault in Swadlincote, Derbyshire. Earthenware with coloured glaze. [h. 22.1cm]. VAM C.27-1971.

that were themselves turned by hand or foot. Even where machines like lathes were powered by steam, as in some branches of the furniture and the metal trades, the quality of the finished product owed everything to the skill of the worker. 'Steam,' it was pointed out in 1850 in the *Morning Chronicle*, was, under such circumstances, 'only the motive power, for a man must still be employed to "turn"'. Dependence on skilled hand labour meant that British high-design goods were far more vulnerable to foreign competition than staple products like iron or cotton textiles, whose production relied on steam-powered machinery.

There were a number of reasons for the limited extent to which steam power was applied in Victorian manufacturing. One was the abundance of cheap, skilled hand labour in a country with a long history of industrial work and a rapidly growing population. Another was the visual intricacy of so many consumer goods and the constant, rapid changes they underwent to satisfy the Victorian love of novelty. Often it was cheaper for a manufacturer to employ workers whose hand skills were admirably flexible than to invest in cumbersome, expensive machines that were difficult to adjust to new product lines. 'In Birmingham,' the publisher Charles Knight observed in 1846, 'the adjustments required by the ever-varying tastes and wants of the age can be effected only by men's fingers.' Similar comments continued to be made up to the end of the century.

It would be wrong to dismiss this phenomenon simply as the survival of antiquated hand skills in those circumstances where steam power could not be profitably applied. The coming of the steam engine did not stifle inventiveness in the hand industries. Indeed, Victorian capitalism created many more hand skills than it destroyed. In workshops across the land, new hand techniques were constantly being developed, accompanied by the use of new materials and novel ways of organizing work, all of which could bring about significant reductions in the cost of hand-made goods. It is worth remembering that the 300,000 panes of glass which covered that acclaimed symbol of Victorian

12 *A Pottery Shop*, mid-19th century. By Alfred Morgan. A depiction of work in the 19th-century pottery industry; though highly idealized, it indicates the predominance of hand processes. Oil on canvas. VAM E.1632-1989.

13 *The Pen Grinding Room*, 1851. From the *Illustrated London News*, 22 February 1851. Women workers in the factory of Messrs Hinks, Wells and Co. of Birmingham, steel-pen manufacturers, grind pen-nibs on machines turned by power from a steam engine. Large-scale manufacturing of steel-nib pens was an innovation of the 1830s. Specialized machines, both hand- and power-driven, were developed to make them. Wood engraving. VAM P.P.10.

modernity, the Crystal Palace of 1851, were all blown by hand, employing a new technique introduced by Messrs Chance Brothers of Smethwick in the West Midlands. In terms of volume and standardization, this was a kind of mass production, but emphatically not one that required the powered production lines and automatic machine tools that came to define mass production of the twentieth century.

Even where steam power played virtually no part in the manufacturing process, the scale of enterprise could be huge. In the 1880s the plant of Sowerby's Ellison Glass Works Limited at Gateshead in County Durham was the largest pressed-glass manufactory in the world. It employed nearly 1,000 workers, producing vast quantities of decorated drinking glasses, decanters, salt cellars, cake and fruit dishes, plates and a variety of objects in opaque glass. The Sowerby's works was not as big as the largest integrated textile factories, like Titus Salt's worsted mill at Saltaire outside Bradford in Yorkshire, with its 3,000 employees. Nevertheless, Sowerby's and a number of other pressed-glass works employed considerably more workers than the average textile mill. At Sowerby's each employee worked an eight-hour shift, making up to 1,200 tumblers a day. Yet this work was all performed on hand-operated presses that

14 Advertisement for Sowerby's Ellison Glass Works Limited, 1890. From *The Pottery Gazette and Glass Trade Review*, 1 September 1890. The advertisement for this Gateshead glass-pressing firm includes a panoramic view of the works and an illustration of some of its products. Engraving and letter-press. VAM PP.25.A.

15 Plate, 1887. Made by Sowerby & Co., Ellison Glass Works, Gateshead. Press-moulded glass was a perfect medium for commemorative pieces, like this plate, produced for Queen Victoria's Golden Jubilee. Pieces could be produced quickly and in large quantities from a single mould. Pressed glass. VAM Circ.716-1966.

16 Celery vase, 1887. Made by Sowerby & Co., Ellison Glass Works, Gateshead. This type of ornamental glass with moulded decoration was inexpensive and enjoyed a large market both at home and abroad. Pressed glass. VAM C.263-1987.

were themselves a nineteenth-century innovation. Glass pressing originated in the United States in the 1820s and was introduced into Britain in the 1830s. It enabled decorative glassware to be produced at a much lower cost than the slower and more skilled method of blowing the glass to the required shape and then decorating it by diamond cutting. Steam power was not applied until 1894, when Sowerby's introduced their own patent steam pressing process.

The pace of work at Sowerby's Gateshead plant was not set by the remorseless turning of the belt drives that transmitted power from steam engine to machines in a typical Victorian textile mill. But we should not therefore assume that the men who worked the glass presses at Gateshead laboured any less intensively than their counterparts in the textile factories of Lancashire and Yorkshire. The pace of their work was driven by piece rates – payment by results. A degree of skill was involved, but each worker had to perform a specialized task over and over again at a fast enough pace to earn an adequate day's pay. This pattern – monotonous, highly specialized and often physically demanding work, driven at a hard pace – could be found not just in the larger plants using hand machinery, but in many smaller Victorian workplaces that served the insatiable public demand for decorative goods of all kinds. Indeed, Victorian workplaces tended, in the main, to be small and in 1899 the average British workshop employed only

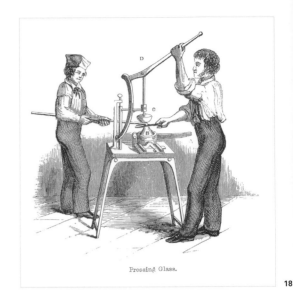

Pressing Glass.

18

17

29 male employees. By that date, even the largest British industrial plants, in steel making, ship building, locomotive building and armaments, were small by American or German standards. And of course there were many workers, especially women, who worked on their own account at home, or in tiny garret workshops, the notorious sweatshops where seamstresses laboured for 12 hours a day, paid by the shirt or the frill.

When critics like John Ruskin and William Morris attacked the capitalist division of labour for degrading workers and depriving their work of creativity, they had in mind this pressured, monotonous hand work as much as the machine-paced labour of those who toiled in the steam-powered factories. Morris himself was, of course, from 1881 the owner of a manufactory at Merton Abbey in Surrey, on the outskirts of London, which used exclusively hand techniques and employed more than 100 workers. He enjoyed a reputation as an excellent employer who paid well and encouraged his workers in their skills. Nevertheless in most respects conditions at Merton Abbey were

20

19

not so different from those at many other Victorian workplaces where paternalist employers strove to provide good conditions for their workers, as far as commercial competition would allow. Titus Salt's textile factory at Saltaire was one of the most famous examples of such paternalism. Most of Morris's workers at Merton Abbey were paid on a piecework basis, 'according to the custom of their trade'; their working day was not noticeably shorter than elsewhere; and hand processes were used to give Morris the artistic control over his products that he felt was essential, and not to provide the workers with creative self-expression. Morris himself regretted that these conditions fell far short of his own socialist-medieval ideal, which was fully realized only among small groups of often affluent Arts and Crafts enthusiasts. But conditions at Merton Abbey reflected the pressures that commercial competition forced on the most paternalist of employers, even those like Morris who cornered a niche market among the extremely well-off.

20 Block-printing chintzes at William Morris's Merton Abbey works, early 20th century. Illustration from Morris and Co.'s catalogue, *Printed Linens and Cottons*, about 1912. VAM Textiles and Dress Department Library.

---

17 The weaving shed at John Butterworth and Sons, Dale Mill, Waterfoot, Lancashire, about 1900. The belt drives transmitted power from the steam engine to the looms. Lancashire County Library, Rawtenstall Local Studies collection.

18 *Pressing Glass*, 1849. From *Curiosities of Glass Making* by Apsley Pellatt, 1849. The engraving depicts an early hand-operated glass-pressing machine. A gather of molten glass (B) is dropped into the mould. The man operating the lever then lowers the metal plunger (C) into the mould to shape the glass. Wood engraving. VAM 89.J.50.

19 *The Sempstress*, 1846. By Richard Redgrave. Redgrave was inspired by Thomas Hood's poem, 'Song of the Shirt', especially the lines 'Oh! men with sisters dear, Oh! men with mothers and wives, It is not linen you're wearing out, But human creatures' lives.' Oil on canvas. The Forbes Magazine Collection, New York.

3. New materials

A flood of new, improved and often cheaper materials had a profound effect on Victorian design. The introduction of substances like linoleum (invented in 1860 and used for floor coverings), celluloid (invented in 1862 and used for combs, cutlery handles and shirt collars) and the cheap steel that resulted from the inventions of Henry Bessemer in the 1850s and replaced iron in many of its uses, hugely expanded the repertoire of materials from which existing types of object could be made. Consumers appreciated the superior functional properties that new materials could offer, such as improved durability or greater ease of cleaning, as well as the widening of choice. But enlarging choice in this way simply intensified the pre-existing quandary as to the appropriate form and decoration for such objects. When a supremely malleable and easily ornamented material like papier mâché came into vogue for furniture, as it did in the early Victorian years, the design critics were horrified at the results.

Increasingly it was from the laboratory that new materials emerged in the course of the Victorian era, the products of systematic research involving the chemical reformulation of geological and biological substances. Fundamental scientific research did not sweep the board – linoleum, for instance, consisted simply of a combination of linseed oil with resin and cork dust, applied to a woven backing of cotton or flax. Nevertheless, laboratory-based research came to be regarded as the most effective way to generate major innovations, although the discoveries that emerged from the laboratory were not always those that had been envisaged. A prime example of a serendipitous scientific discovery was synthetic dyes.

21

22

---

21 Sardine fork with a celluloid handle, late 19th century. Fork, electroplated nickel silver, engraved and beaded; handle of celluloid. VAM M.32-2000.

22 Linoleum, 1875. Designed by William Morris. Manufacturer unknown. Printed Corticine floor covering. VAM Circ.527-1953.

23 *The Fashions. Expressly designed and prepared for the Englishwoman's Domestic Magazine*, December 1860. By Jules David. Engraved and printed in Paris by Lamoureux and J. De Beauvais. The new aniline dyes were ideally suited to producing fabrics in the purple and red colours depicted here. Hand-coloured lithograph. VAM E.267-1942.

COAL TAR DYES.
SPECIMENS OF FABRICS DYED WITH
Simpson, Maule & Nicholson's
COLORS.

Concentrated Regina Purple.

Concentrated Violet with a little Roseine.

Phosphine. *Roseine.* *Regina Purple.* *Violet.*

Phosphine. *Printers Roseine.* *Regina Purple.* *No 2 Violet.*

No 1 Blue. *Blue.* *No 2. Blue & Violet.* *Concentrated Printers Roseine.*

SPECIMENS OF FABRICS DYED WITH
Perkin & Son's Colors.

Before 1856 virtually all dyes came directly from natural (mainly vegetable) materials: blues from indigo, reds from madder and cochineal, weld yellows from the wild mignonette. In that year William Perkin, the 18-year-old son of an east London builder, was a student at the Royal College of Chemistry, recently established in London under Prince Albert's patronage. Encouraged by the college's director to find a synthetic substitute for the anti-malarial drug quinine, Perkin produced a black tar from aniline and potassium dichromate. It lacked the anti-malarial properties he was seeking, but turned out to be effective as a dye, producing the colour that became known as aniline purple or mauve. Perkin's new synthetic dye was an immediate success. It was fast and resisted exposure to light. Remarkably, it proved suitable for dyeing silk, the most prestigious material for women's dresses.

Perkin left the college to set up a factory near London to produce the new dye in bulk and make his fortune. His raw material was the coal tar that was available in vast quantities as an undesirable by-product of the huge industry that manufactured gas from coal. Soon other coal-tar-based synthetic colours were invented, in particular magenta, a vivid red. All these new, synthetic dyes were characterized by an unprecedented brilliance and intensity and were taken up with enthusiasm by British women. Their invention did not create the fashion for crinolines in luminescent, gaudy colours, but certainly encouraged it to ever-greater extremes. 'The exaggeration of the dresses of the ladies or young girls belonging to the wealthy middle class is offensive,' complained Hippolyte Taine, a French visitor to Hyde Park in the 1860s, picking out for particular condemnation 'gowns of violet silk with dazzling reflections' and 'gloves of immaculate whiteness or bright violet'. 'The glare is terrible,' he concluded.

24

THE FASHIONS Expressly designed and prepared for the *Englishwoman's Domestic Magazine.*

DECEMBER 1860 E.267-1942.

23

24 Coal-tar dyes, 1862. Samples of aniline-dyed cloth from *The Practical Mechanic's Journal: Record of the Great Exhibition*, 1862. Dyed fabric samples on paper. VAM PP.23.E.

FURNITURE

Frances Collard

New materials underpinned many of the major innovations in Victorian furniture. Some were extremely unconventional, such as coal or Derbyshire slate, and were used on a very limited scale; others, like papier mâché and metal, had an enormous impact.

Although used for tables, trays and boxes from the 1770s, papier mâché was not suitable for larger pieces of furniture until the introduction of improved moulding techniques between 1836 and 1851. Sideboards and cabinets, or chairs and sofas that were intended for heavy use, were constructed of papier mâché on a wooden or metal frame. The Birmingham firm of Jennens & Bettridge was one of the largest and most celebrated manufacturers, as illustrated by their stand at the 1851 Great Exhibition. Their innovations included the development of decorative techniques and of papier mâché for ship interiors and railway carriages.

The search for new materials combined with the Victorian interest in home decoration to prompt the introduction of frames, swags and friezes made of moulded leather instead of the conventional carved wood. These were exhibited in 1851 by Messrs Esquilant & Co. of London and were recommended for their cheapness and durability, particularly for the interiors of steam ships. The same techniques were used for leather leaves and flowers applied to the support of a table by Messrs Morant of London.

One material developed by the metal industry but of great interest to furniture makers was hollow metal tubing, made either from brass or from iron and brass. This was particularly important for bed manufacturers, who produced numerous different designs, marketed through illustrated catalogues. Birmingham became such an important centre that by 1875 almost 6,000 beds were being produced every week, half of which were sent for export.

25. Seat furniture designed by Filmer and Son, London. From the *Illustrated Catalogue of the Universal Exhibition*, 1868. Wood engraving. VAM PP.6.B.

26. Wine tray and decanter. Designed by Richard Redgrave for Felix Summerly's Art Manufactures. Tray, originally produced 1847; this example 1865. Made in Birmingham by the firm of Jennens & Bettridge. Papier mâché, japanned, gilded with appliqué of mother-of-pearl. [h. 40cm]. Decanter, 1848. Made in Stourbridge by W. H. B. & J. Richardson. Glass, wheel-cut and gilded. VAM 132-1865, C.108-1992,

27. Rocking chair, 1840-50. possibly made by the firm of R.W. Winfield, Birmingham. Steel tube, japanned and gilded. VAM Circ. 20-1961.

28. *The Hardware Display*, 1852. From *Dickinson's comprehensive pictures of the Great Exhibition of 1851*, 1854 (second edition; first published 1852). Printed and published by Dickinson Brothers, London, 1854. The Jennens & Bettridge stand is on the right. Colour lithograph with hand-colouring. VAM 46.K4.

29. Star of Brunswick table, 1851. Designed and manufactured by Henry Eyles in Bath. Plaque made by Messrs Chamberlain and Co. in Worcester. Table of walnut, carved and with inlay of pollard oak. Plaque of Worcester porcelain. VAM W.40-1952.

Manufacturers of upholstered furniture also benefited from improvements in other trades. Although springs are recorded in upholstery from the mid-eighteenth century, they were not widely used until the 1830s when spiral steel springs became commercially viable, as noted by John Loudon in his *Encyclopaedia of Cottage, Farm and Villa Architecture and Furniture* (1833). The characteristic deep buttoning of Victorian sofas and chairs was dependent on the use of springs and the innovations in design and construction that flowed from their introduction.

30. *Design for a brass bed*, about 1885. Made for Robert Lloyd Crosbie & Co., Birmingham. Pencil, chalk, water and body colour. VAM E.2820-1995.

By the 1870s the British textile industry had almost entirely gone over to the new synthetic dyes, now available across the colour spectrum. They were cheaper than natural dyes, easier to use and, because of their quick-drying properties, especially suited to mechanical roller printing. Between 1868 and 1878 imports of the natural dyestuff madder fell by 90 per cent. Some resisted the change, in particular William Morris, who characteristically felt that 'every one of these colours is hideous in itself, whereas all the old dyes are in themselves beautiful colours'. In the 1870s he set about reviving the use of the old dyeing techniques for his own products, although not without considerable difficulty. Ironically, by this time Britain was lagging behind Germany in the invention and production of synthetic dyes. In chemistry, as in electricity, the Germans proved able to sustain a much more productive relationship between science and industry than the British.

4. New techniques

The rapid pace of innovation in materials in the Victorian era was more than matched by the proliferation of new manufacturing techniques. Steam power became ever more widespread as Victoria's reign proceeded, but it was virtually unknown for whole industries to be transformed from hand production to production by powered machinery at one go. Some new techniques did have a dramatic effect, however. Silver plating by electricity, for instance, patented in 1840 by George Richard Elkington of Birmingham and his cousin and partner, Henry Elkington, invoked an entirely new power source and rapidly transformed a major high-design industry. Within a decade, electroplating had effectively killed off the making of Sheffield plate, the previously dominant technique for plating base metals with silver. But the sudden change brought about by electroplating was unusual. It was much more common for innovation in technique to be an incremental process, often a matter of piecemeal improvements to existing tools and machines or of profound changes in one branch of an industry, while other branches remained untouched. Nor did new techniques necessarily result in dramatic changes in the appearance of the goods they were used to make. The introduction of colour printing by means of lithography in the 1840s did enable books to be illustrated in colour on a scale and with a quality of reproduction that were unprecedented. However, as the introduction of electroplating demonstrates, it was common for new techniques to be introduced with the aim of making existing objects more cheaply or with greater consistency of quality, not in order to change the way they looked. If significant changes in design did sometimes emerge from such innovations, often it was only in the longer term.

31

32

31 Detail of 'Bird and vine' fabric, 1879. Designed by William Morris. Manufactured by Morris & Co. Wool dyed with natural dyestuffs, jacquard woven. VAM T.14-1919.

32 Teapot, 1853. Made by Elkington and Co., Birmingham. Electroplated nickel silver; cast and applied handle with ivory insulators; cast and applied spout. VAM M.239-1984

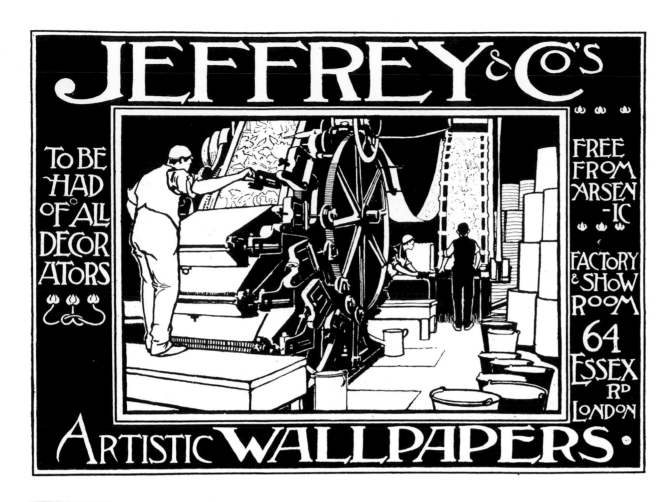

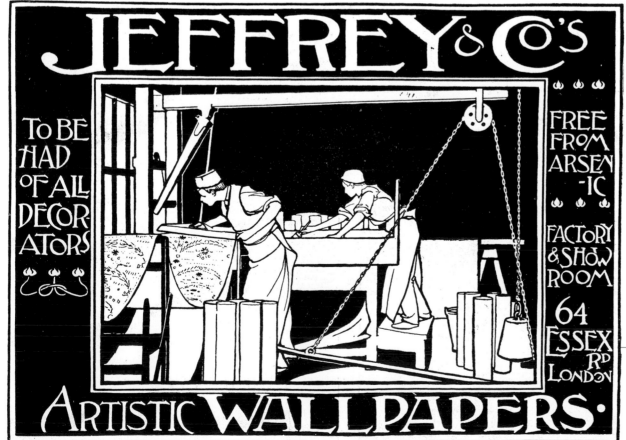

33 Letter-heads of Jeffrey and Co.,
1899. These two letter-heads date
from the same year and indicate that
Jeffrey and Co., manufacturers of artistic
wallpapers, used machine printing and
hand-block printing side-by-side in
their London factory at the end of the
Victorian era. Woodblock print.
VAM E.42A(2)-1945.

33

Many of these characteristic features of Victorian innovation can be observed in the various attempts to introduce powered machinery into the making of furniture. These took two main forms: firstly, and more successfully, the use of powered machinery in basic preparatory processes like veneer cutting, sawing and planing; secondly, and more ambitiously, attempts to use machines to produce decoration, particularly carved work.

The introduction of machinery into the preparatory processes began in the middle years of the nineteenth century, principally in the large, comprehensive London cabinet-making firms that made the highest-quality furniture in the greatest variety of styles. West End firms like Holland and Sons, Jackson and Graham, and Seddon and Company bought steam engines and equipped their workshops with steam-powered veneer cutters, lathes, vertical and circular saws and mortising machines. The result was a hybrid system of manufacture,

which a trade-union report in 1874 described as 'machine-assisted hand production'. Much of the drudgery of preparation was removed. A workman noted in 1867 that 'in shape work, the wood is cut by machinery as well as by hand, and very close and fine, so in cleaning of it only requires the scraper and glass paper to finish'. In the 1880s it could still be said that West End work 'is always supposed to be entirely by hand', although 'the influence of the more rapid methods of machinery begins to make itself felt'. But evidence to a Royal Commission in 1884 pointed out that 'these machines are no drawback to cabinet manufacture. They do all the hard work and still a good cabinet-maker is more essential than ever. The hard work is performed by the machine, but still the work for a good tradesman is left.'

Hand work remained essential because many of the finishing and assembly processes were so difficult to mechanize. For West End firms producing individual pieces of furniture or small batches on a bespoke basis, the highly skilled worker, specialized but capable of adjusting his skills to all kinds of new designs, was indispensable. Of course, West End firms often subcontracted to cheaper East End workshops, which employed less expensive labour, but there the nature of the work (as opposed to the rates of pay) was not necessarily so different. After all, many of the benefits of machinery were available to smaller producers. They could buy materials prepared by means of powered machinery, like veneers, from specialist firms. At the same time they could use small treadle-operated machines, like circular saws and band saws, that did not require steam power. In addition, as Charles Booth's survey of London pointed out in the 1880s, investment in expensive powered machines was inappropriate 'in a market in which workers are so numerous and labour so cheap as in the East End of London'.

34

35

34 Cabinet, 1878. Designed by Bruce Talbert; made by Jackson and Graham, London. This cabinet won the Grand Prize at the Paris International Exhibition of 1878. Jackson and Graham was a high-class West End cabinet-making firm with steam-powered machines. Ebony, inlaid with decorative woods and ivory. VAM W.18-1981.

View of an INTERIOR as recently embellished with the CARVED WOODS supplied by
THE PATENT WOOD CARVING COMPANY
5 Henrietta Street, Covent Garden.

37

The impact that these innovations had on the way furniture looked is questionable. Steam-powered machinery took over the production of veneers during the first half of the nineteenth century, but this was as much a response to the popularity of veneered surfaces as it was its cause. The paper-thin veneers produced by the rotary-knife cutting machine introduced later in the century were cheaper even than their power-sawn predecessors. But it is not clear that machine veneer cutting always resulted in lower prices for furniture. Sometimes it simply encouraged furniture makers to incorporate more expensive, exotic woods in their products.

Similarly, the use of machinery to make decoration, particularly carved work, did not necessarily result in lower prices. The early years of Victoria's reign saw a boom in the popularity of revived period styles. 'A taste has of late years arisen for carved furniture of the Tudor, Louis Quatorze and Renaissance periods,' reported the *Art Union* in 1841. Wood carving was, however, one of the most time-consuming and expensive methods of decorating furniture. There was thus a powerful incentive to develop machinery that could carve furniture quickly and cheaply. A variety of solutions were introduced, including steam-powered cutting tools that carved out the wood by following the shape of a metal template, and iron moulds, heated red-hot, which burned the decoration into the wood. The cutting machines enjoyed some successes, particularly T. B. Jordan's patent machine, which was used for carved work for the new Palace of Westminster, where large amounts of carving were required. Nevertheless, most carving continued to be done by hand. Not only did machine carving itself need hand finishing, but the cost of constantly preparing new metal templates and cutting tools was prohibitive in a trade where the kind of carved work in demand was constantly changing.

38

35 Machine-carved lion, part of a sideboard, 1848–50. Stamped on the back 'JORDAN'S CARVING WORKS 154 STRAND'. Mahogany, machine-carved with hand finishing. VAM W.7-1967.

36 Carving machines in the factory of Harris Lebus, London, 1899. VAM Furniture and Woodwork Department Library.

37 Frontispiece to *Decorations in Wood*, Part 1, the catalogue of the Patent Wood Carving Company, 1845. The company used the hot-iron mould process to simulate carved woodwork. Lithograph. Bodleian Library.

38 Hand carvers finishing machine-made parts in the factory of Harris Lebus, London, 1899. VAM Furniture and Woodwork Department Library.

BOOK ILLUSTRATION AND BINDING

Rowan Watson

Almost all aspects of book production became mechanized during the Victorian period. By the end of the nineteenth century even the process of sewing printed sheets to make quires into a bookblock was done by a powered machine.

Following the example of Thomas Bewick, wood engraving was revived in the 1830s to allow images to be integrated with text; in the 1840s electrotypes and new presses (the platen and cylinder presses) enabled texts with multiple images to be produced in large print-runs. With the establishment of cheap illustrated magazines, such as *Punch* in 1841 and the *Illustrated London News* in 1842, images became a means of guiding the reader's eye and conveying information in conjunction with the text. A veritable army of designers and engravers emerged to serve the printing industry, but wood engraving was superseded by the advent of photographic methods of reproduction at the end of the century. By the 1890s magazines for a mass market, selling for just a few pence, contained densely illustrated articles and advertisements.

The exterior of books was transformed by the development of cloths for binding. Until the early nineteenth century books were normally bound in leather. In the late 1820s, however, experiments began with cloth bindings. Cloths were put over prefabricated covers ('case-bindings'), then stamped with lettering, designs and colours, before being attached to the bookblock. From the late 1830s book covers of all kinds, from gift books and annuals to manuals and stories of exploration, could be appropriately decorated in gold and bright colours on coloured cloth, or with a sober image on a magisterial blue or brown, reflecting the gravity of the text. The new technique of lithography was similarly used to provide decorated covers on paper, as well as illustrations. Colour printing based on lithography (chromolithography) was developed by Owen Jones in the 1830s and was widely used commercially from the 1860s, before giving way to mechanical colour printing based on photography.

40. Case binding of green cloth with a design in gold around a coloured engraving on *Lalla Rookh: an oriental romance* by Thomas Moore. Published by George Routledge, 1868. VAM G.28.E.50.

41. Articles with integrated woodcut illustrations from volume 1 of *Punch, or the London Charivari*, 1841. VAM PP.8.H.

39. 'Illustrated interviews: Mr Hamo Thornycroft, RA' in *The Strand Magazine*, vol. 6, no. 33, September 1893. With halftone illustrations taken from photographs. VAM 1115-1983.

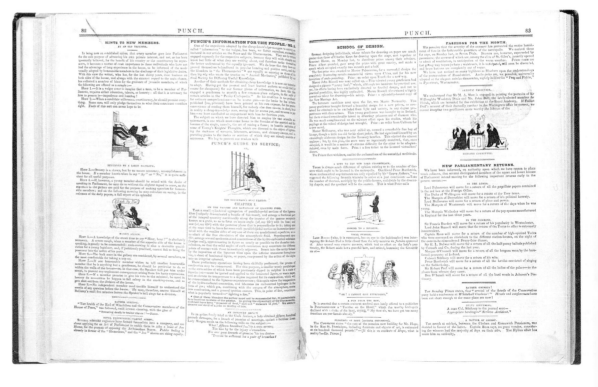

43. Cover design by Samuel Luke Fildes for monthly parts of *The Mystery of Edwin Drood* by Charles Dickens, May, July and August 1870. Woodcut. VAM 42.Z.84.

44. Illustration engraved by John Thompson after a design by Daniel Maclise for 'Morte d'Arthur' in *Poems* by Alfred, Lord Tennyson. Published by Edward Moxon, 1857. Wood engraving. VAM 29.Q.48.

Images on or in books became important for attracting the eye of potential buyers in the bookshop, in the railway bookstall (W. H. Smith was the first in 1848 to see the potential of railway stations for selling as well as distributing books) and in kiosks set up for crowds visiting fairs or major exhibitions. But critics at the end of the century abhorred such displays. In 1899 Gleeson White stated that 'decadence set in with the use of pictures instead of conventional ornament, and the admixture of gold, black and various colours'.

42. Illustration and ornament, designed and engraved by Charles Ricketts for *The Sphinx* by Oscar Wilde. Published by The Bodley Head, 1894. Coloured line-block. VAM L.1524-1902.

45. Cover of *Mrs Brown at the Paris Exhibition* by 'Arthur Sketchley' (George Rose). Published by George Routledge, 1878. Woodcut in three colours. VAM SN.95.0012.

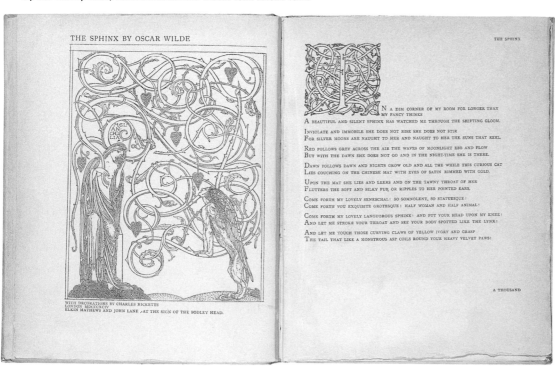

46 Electric desk and wall lamp, 1900. Designed by W. A. S. Benson. Brass. VAM M.957-1983.

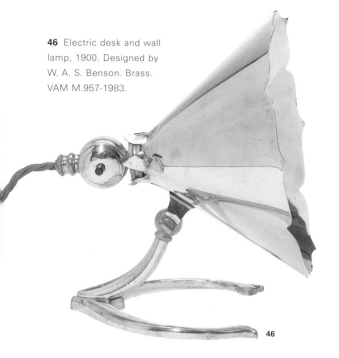

47 Vase, 1862. Figures after designs by Albert Carrier Belleuse. Made by Minton and Co., Stoke on Trent, Staffordshire. Exhibited in London in 1862. This vase is characteristic of the spectacular, technically challenging objects made to win prizes at the new International Exhibitions. Prize-winning pieces were acquired by museums and featured in the advertising of the firm that made them. Bone china, painted and gilded. [h. 95.5cm]. VAM 8111-1863.

5. New products

If innovation in design and the decorative arts in the Victorian era was sustained and sometimes stimulated by new materials and new manufacturing techniques, it was in new products that it found its most spectacular realization. New products, ranging from the cigarette to the ceramic flushing lavatory, from the exhibition piece to the electric lamp, provided the Victorians with tangible evidence of their own modernity, while throwing up new possibilities and new challenges for design and decoration. The pace of product innovation seemed to accelerate, reaching a crescendo in the last quarter of the nineteenth century, the period that saw the invention of (among other things) the electric-filament light bulb, the phonograph, the motor car, moving

49

pictures, the telephone and the safety bicycle. Significantly, only two items in this list of new products originated in Britain – the safety bicycle and the electric light bulb. By the 1870s Germany and the United States, in particular, had become powerful instigators of product innovation, with companies that employed a systematic approach often lacking in Britain.

These new late-Victorian products were widely publicized and stimulated huge public interest. Nevertheless, with the exception of the bicycle, they had limited direct impact on the lives of British people before the end of Victoria's reign, other than for enthusiasts and some of the very wealthy. British homes continued to be lit overwhelmingly by gas; motor cars and the telephone were inaccessible to all but the most privileged; sales of the phonograph were sparse;

and the boom in moving pictures came after Victoria's death. Indeed, it was to take a large part of the twentieth century to develop fully the technical and design potential of the many new products of the late-Victorian years that exploited the possibilities of electrical power and the internal combustion engine.

The new products that became familiar, everyday things before the end of Victoria's reign were principally those invented earlier in the nineteenth century. The list of such products is long and diverse, but two prominent examples – the sewing machine and the railway locomotive – will serve to demonstrate some of the aesthetic challenges posed by the new mechanical objects that so fascinated the Victorian public and Victorian inventors alike.

48 Poster for the Swift Cycle Co. Ltd, late Coventry Machinists' Co. Ltd, Coventry, about 1898. Colour lithograph. VAM E.533-1939.

49 Lord Wimborne in a motor car, 1902. VAM Picture Library.

The sewing machine was an American invention of the 1850s. It was soon being sold in Britain, where the American firm of Singer became the dominant producer in the later nineteenth century, with approximately three-quarters of the market. In the late 1860s the Singer company set up a factory at Clydebank in Scotland, which became the largest sewing-machine factory in the world. By the 1880s the firm was selling 150,000 machines a year in Britain. Originally designed with industrial production in mind, the sewing machine was soon marketed for family use at home. In the United States, Singer's first machine aimed at the family market was launched in 1858. By 1898 Singer was advertising its 'Improved Family' model in Britain as 'the most perfect machine for family use'. In reality, a good half or more of the machines sold to domestic customers went to poorer households, where women used them to boost family incomes by taking in sewing on a freelance basis or by working at home for firms manufacturing ready-made clothes. But vast numbers of sewing machines were also acquired by middle-class households to enable wives to carry out at least some of the family sewing. The incursion of this mechanical object into the sanctum of middle-class Victorian domesticity posed a question that was almost unprecedented in the nineteenth century, but was to become all too familiar in the next: how to reconcile the look of what was obviously a piece of machinery with the carefully contrived aesthetic of the Victorian middle-class interior?

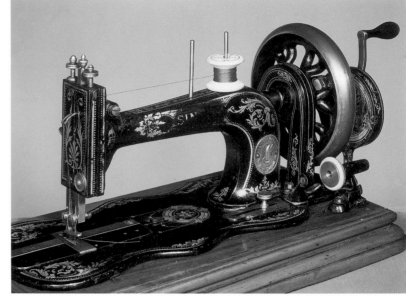

51

The manufacturers of sewing machines were well aware of the problem they faced in domesticating their mechanical product. When the Singer company introduced its 'Family' machine in the United States in 1858, it promoted it as 'a machine of smaller size, and of lighter and more elegant form; a machine decorated in the best style of art; so as to make a beautiful ornament in the parlour or boudoir'. As this promotional statement suggests, domesticating the sewing machine did not usually entail any attempt to disguise entirely its mechanical nature (unlike that other and much older piece of domestic machinery, the clock, which was normally cased). Sewing machines were supplied with polished and sometimes ornamented wooden cases, but the machine itself had to be revealed when in use. Nor did domesticating the sewing machine entail a wholesale departure from the look of the early industrial sewing machine. Like much Victorian industrial equipment, early sewing machines for industrial use were customarily provided with some ornament. The solution at which firms like Singer arrived for their domestic machines involved adjusting their appearance in ways that drew on other, existing objects considered attractive and appropriate in the domestic setting.

50 'Arm and Platform' sewing machine, 1875–92. Designed and manufactured in London by Edward Ward. Iron and steel; ironwork enamelled with decoration in the Greek style. VAM Loan: Science Museum: 101.

51 Singer 'New Family' sewing machine, second half of the 19th century. Designed and first produced in 1865 in the United States by the Singer Manufacturing Company of New York. Iron, steel and wood; ironwork enamelled with decoration in the rococo style. Science Museum, London.

52

flourished. This mode of decoration imitated the practice, well established since the eighteenth century, of coating a variety of small metal objects for the home with painted japanned ornament. In particular, it mimicked the appearance of the lacquered papier-mâché furniture, trays, writing boxes and other domestic objects which were so popular between the 1840s and 1860s, and were themselves often targeted at the female consumer. The ornamental details on sewing machines were almost identical to those on papier-mâché objects, down to the occasional use of mother-of-pearl inlay, much prized by middle-class consumers but deeply disapproved of by the design reformers. Significantly, the aesthetic formula developed for the domestic sewing machine – black enamelled metal surface, brightly polished metal parts, lining and ornament in gold – subsequently became the model for the decorative treatment of those many new mechanical objects for home, office and leisure use that appeared later in the nineteenth century, including the phonograph, the typewriter and the bicycle. It was to remain the dominant aesthetic for such objects into the mid-twentieth century.

The basic structural iron components of all sewing machines were finished in black japanned stove enamel. This was necessary to protect the ironwork, but also provided a lustrous appearance. The metal working parts were brightly polished. In those machines intended for domestic settings, the structural iron components were cast in light, elegant curves, sometimes with moulded ornament; the black enamel that coated the iron parts was always decorated with elaborate ornamental details, usually in gold. Neo-rococo was the chief decorative style employed throughout much of the second half of the nineteenth century, but in an age of stylistic eclecticism other styles also

53

---

52 Work box, about 1850. Made by Jennens and Betteridge, Birmingham. Papier mâché, japanned. VAM W.150-1919.

53 Typewriter, about 1875. Designed in the United States by Christopher Latham Sholes, Carlos Glidden and Samuel Soule between 1866 and 1873. Made in the United States by E. Remington and Sons, Ilion, New York. The machine is shown with the decorative front panel removed. Iron and steel, with decorated enamelled casing. Science Museum, London.

THE PHOTOGRAPH

Mark Haworth-Booth

54. *Man Taking off His Boater*, 1887. Plate from *Animal Locomotion*, by Eadweard Muybridge. Collotype. VAM 558-1889.

A man as old as the century is looking from the window of his Paris hotel in the early 1840s. He is one of the first photographers in the world and is enchanted by what he sees – and what his camera can seize. The boulevard below is dusty and hot. His gaze zooms into details: 'they have just been watering the road, which has produced two broad bands of shade upon it, which unite in the foreground, because, the road being partially under repair (as is seen from the two wheel barrows, &c., &c.), the watering machines have been compelled to cross to the other side'. He glances at 'the forest of chimneys' on the horizon and marvels that each one is perfectly

recorded 'for, the [camera] chronicles whatever it sees, and certainly would delineate a chimney-pot or a chimney-sweeper with the same impartiality as it would the Apollo of Belvedere'.

The man is William Henry Fox Talbot, FRS, inventor of positive/negative photography, and he has just said something of profound importance about his invention. First announced in 1839, it swept the world and

remains in use in the present digital era. Few people 'got' photography in its first decade, except as a way of taking astonishingly fast and accurate portraits (using the French daguerreotype system of photography, also announced in 1839).

Photography progressed much as computers did in the later twentieth century, both being initially the preserve of boffins, then of the scientifically inclined, the financially privileged

55. Plate II from *The Pencil of Nature*, 18– By William Henry Fox Talbot. Calotype VAM R.1.

56. *Horatio & Colin Ross & Old David Dear Fishing at the falls of Rossie*, April 1848. By Horatio Ross. Daguerreotype. VAM PH.245-1946.

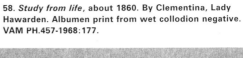

58. *Study from life*, about 1860. By Clementina, Lady Hawarden. Albumen print from wet collodion negative. VAM PH.457-1968:177.

and sometimes the artistically adventurous. Both inventions gradually transformed the world about them, as technical improvements encouraged their take-up for ever broadening purposes. Photography's new standard of authenticity led to the growth of studios, run on factory lines, producing stereoscopic images for home entertainment, portrait miniatures and souvenir views. Both cameras and computers lost their imposing physical bulk and uncertain performance, achieving ease of use and trim, consumer-friendly designs. Both, of course, became essential tools of modern society.

By the end of the nineteenth century photography was in the hands of everyone and was being used for everything. It became as dashing, convenient and fun as that other new craze – cycling. However, it still held the world in the vice of meticulous, enthralled vision celebrated by Henry Talbot as he looked out of that Paris window.

57. Photograph from a family album, 1898. By an anonymous amateur. Platinum print. VAM E.2283-1997.

Mabel Agnes.   Lily Turner.   Laura.

59

If the sewing machine illustrates the way in which the appearance of a new mechanical object was adapted for use in the home, then the Victorian railway locomotive shows how the imperatives of corporate business shaped the look of another new and, in this case, very public mechanical object. The earliest railway locomotives of the 1810s and 1820s were diverse in appearance. It took some time to arrive at the limited range of relatively stable and recognizable types that prevailed from the later 1830s. This was partly a technical matter, but the aesthetics of the railway locomotive were an issue almost from the start. As early as 1827 – just two years after the opening of the first passenger railway – George Stephenson, the father of British railways, and his locomotive-building son Robert were 'endeavouring to reduce the size and ugliness of our travelling engines'.

The solution they came up with – concealing the cylinders, the crucial and most ungainly working parts, underneath the boiler – delighted the renowned engineer of the Great Western Railway, Isambard Kingdom Brunel, who wrote in 1838, 'lastly let me call your attention to the appearance – we have a splendid engine of Stephenson's, it would be a beautiful ornament in the most elegant drawing room'. Among the elements that were so pleasing were the harmonious side-view, achieved by the use of a large central driving wheel with smaller supporting wheels on either side, combined with strong horizontal forms and the balanced verticals of the chimney and the firebox. In motion, there was no evidence of the functioning mechanism, other than the turning of the wheels. This elegance of composition, which had parallels in the carefully contrived aesthetics of British horse-drawn coaches,

59 'Wylam Dilly', 1862. This early railway locomotive was built by William Hedley in 1813 for use at Wylam colliery in Northumberland. It was photographed in 1862 when finally taken out of service. National Railway Museum, York.

60 'Jenny Lind', 1847. An engineering drawing of the 2-2-2 locomotive 'Jenny Lind', designed by David Joy and built by E. B. Wilson's Railway Foundry, Leeds, West Yorkshire, in 1847. Pen and ink and colour wash. National Railway Museum, York.

61 'North Star', 1837. An engineering drawing of the Great Western Railway's 2-2-2 locomotive North Star, designed and built by R. Stephenson and Co., Newcastle-upon-Tyne, in 1837. Pen and ink and colour wash. National Railway Museum, York.

60

combined with the use of neo-classical forms for chimneys, domes and the like, was taken up in many of the locomotives designed at this time. In the 1840s, for instance, the famous 'Jenny Lind' locomotives made by the Leeds firm of E. B. Wilson had fluted safety-valve covers and domes that derived in form and ornament directly from neo-classical architecture.

These aesthetic criteria persisted, and indeed were amplified, as locomotives became bigger and more sophisticated in the second half of the

nineteenth century. But as the century wore on, the look of British railway locomotives came increasingly to diverge from that of their foreign counterparts. This became dramatically obvious at the great international exhibitions. The British considered that their locomotives were uniquely beautiful and they were clear about the reasons. *Railway News*, commenting on the locomotive displays at the Paris Exhibition of 1889, praised the 'magnificent specimens of English locomotives, and their grand simplicity and

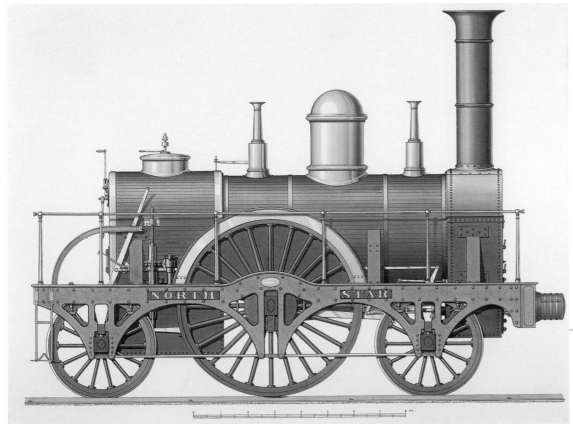

61

repose compare from an English point of view very favourably with the complicated external appearance of the continental exhibitors'. The same criteria were invoked by British critics when the Midland Railway was obliged to buy locomotives from the American Baldwin company during an engineering strike in 1897. 'The ungainly assemblages of iron, etc. that will do duty on the Midland Railway as a goods locomotive' have arrived, reported *The Railway Magazine* in 1897. 'So far as appearances go, no connection can be made between the neat engines designed by Mr Johnson for the Midland Railway and the uncouth machine "made in America".' The contrast was real enough, as is clear from a comparison between one of the Baldwin locomotives – all exposed cylinders, cranks, pipes and valves – and a sleek Midland Railway locomotive with a similar wheel arrangement.

S. W. Johnson's locomotives for the Midland Railway exemplify the distinctive aesthetic that was so prized in Britain and, indeed, often admired abroad. The terms used by the press to describe his most praised design, the single driving-wheel express locomotives that won the Grand Prize at the Paris Exhibitions of 1889 and (in modified form) 1900, were neatness, harmony, compactness, grace, clean lines, beauty of outline and elegance and symmetry in design. What was being identified here was the British stress on proportion in the overall form of the locomotive, on smooth surfaces without applied decoration, on harmonious combinations of flowing curves and straight lines, and on an overall lightness of appearance enhanced by the use of colour and lining. These were all features that had their roots in the aesthetics of the locomotives of the 1830s and 1840s and, before that, in the design of horse-drawn coaches. In contrast to foreign locomotives, in Britain mechanisms were concealed or simplified to achieve a smoothness of line and a minimum of exposed moving parts. By these means the designers of British railway locomotives created a glamorous impression of speed combined with ease. It expressed their locomotives' mechanical efficiency, without having to reveal it.

The distinctive appearance of British locomotives in this period was in large part a consequence of the way British railways were organized. The technical differences between British and foreign locomotives were not decisive. In Britain, in contrast to much of continental Europe, railways were privately owned and competed on many of their routes. And from the 1850s most came to set up their own locomotive works and employ a chief designer. On the continent and in the United States railways normally bought locomotives off the shelf from independent manufacturers. In Britain, therefore, locomotive design had a unique potential to become an element in competition between railway companies. Locomotive styling was accorded a priority that it rarely enjoyed elsewhere. Along with carriage liveries, staff uniforms and insignia, it became a means of identifying and differentiating between railway companies. The design of each company's most glamorous pieces of equipment had become a means of enhancing its corporate identity.

★

The first half of the twentieth century witnessed a universal reaction against Victorian high design, particularly against its fondness for ornament. But the British railway locomotive reveals a different aspect of Victorian design, one that explored the expressive potential of new technologies and new materials. Far from being at odds with twentieth-century developments, this was a theme that would fundamentally shape design in the twentieth century. European modernist designers of the new century espoused an idealized machine aesthetic. American industrial designers developed novel ways of styling mechanical objects to encourage sales and express corporate identity. In their obsession with being modern, both repudiated Victorian ornament. Nevertheless, both owed a profound debt to the Victorian legacy of technological and corporate design.

62 Midland Railway locomotive no. 673. This 4-2-2 locomotive was designed by S. W. Johnson and built in 1897 at the Midland Railway's Derby works. It was this class of locomotive that won the Grand Prize at the Paris Exhibitions of 1889 and 1900, and was described in the press as 'the very beau ideal of symmetry and grace'. The locomotive is shown as restored at the National Railway Museum, York.

63

64

63 Midland Railway locomotive no. 2510, about 1900. This 2-6-0 locomotive was built in the United States in 1899 by Burnham, Williams and Co. at the Baldwin Locomotive Works, Philadelphia, and exported to Britain. Midland Railway Company photograph. National Railway Museum, York.

64 Midland Railway locomotive no. 1757, 'Beatrice', about 1890. This 4-4-0 locomotive was designed by S. W. Johnson and built in 1886 at the Midland Railway's Derby works. It won a Gold Medal at the Royal Jubilee Exhibition at Saltaire, Yorkshire, in 1887. Midland Railway Company photograph. National Railway Museum, York.

Tudor and Stuart Britain
Chronology of Events and Publications, 1485–1714

DATES	POLITICAL EVENTS	DESIGN, ART AND SCIENCE	PUBLICATIONS
1485	Death of Richard III of England, accession of Henry VII		
1492	Christopher Columbus sails to the Americas from Spain		
1498	Vasco da Gama sails to India from Portugal		
1503		Building of Henry VII's chapel at Westminster Abbey begins	
1509	Death of Henry VII of England, accession of Henry VIII		
1511–18	England at war with France		
1513	Death of James IV of Scotland at the Battle of Flodden Field, accession of James V		
1515		King's College chapel, Cambridge, completed	
1517	Martin Luther initiates the Reformation in Germany		
1519–22	Ferdinand Magellan's voyage to circumnavigate the world		
1520	Henry VIII meets Francis I of France at the Field of Cloth of Gold, France		
1522–5	England at war with France		
1533	Henry VIII divorces Catherine of Aragon		
1534	Act of Supremacy ends papal jurisdiction in England		
1535			Miles Coverdale's English translation of the Bible
1536	Union of Wales with England Dissolution of the monasteries		
1542	Death of James V of Scotland, accession of Mary, Queen of Scots		
1543–6	England at war with France		
1547	Death of Henry VIII of England, accession of Edward VI	Building of Somerset House, London, begins	
1548			Thomas Geminus, *Morysse and Damashin renewed and encreased Very profitable for Goldsmythes and Embroiderars*
1549			Sir Thomas Smith, *Discourse of this Common Weal of this Realm of England*
1553	Death of Edward VI of England, accession of Mary I		
1553–8	Roman Catholicism re-established in England		
1557–9	England at war with France		
1557	Loss of Calais		
1558	Death of Mary I of England, accession of Elizabeth I		
1560s	Persecution of Protestants in the Low Countries results in large-scale emigration		
1560	Scottish Parliament abolishes papal jurisdiction and the mass		
1563			John Foxe, *Actes and Monuments* (or *Book of Martyrs*) John Shute, *The First and Chief Groundes of Architecture*
1566		Building of the Royal Exchange, London, begins	
1567		Building of Longleat House, Wiltshire, begins Venetian glass first made in England	
1568	Mary, Queen of Scots exiled in England, accession of James VI		
1577			Hans Vredeman de Vries, *Architectura* William Harrison, *Description of England*
1580s		William Lee invents the knitting frame	
1585–1604	England at war with Spain		
1587	Execution by the English of Mary, Queen of Scots		
1588	Spanish Armada	Staging of the first of William Shakespeare's plays	
1591		Building of Hardwick Hall, Derbyshire, begins	
1594–1603	Nine years war in Ireland		
1599		Globe Theatre built in London	
1600	English East India Company founded		
1603	Death of Elizabeth I of England, accession of James VI of Scotland as James I of England and Ireland		
1607	First permanent English settlement in the Americas at Jamestown, Virginia		
1609		The New Exchange, London, opened	
1611			Authorized version of the Bible English translation of Sebastiano Serlio, *The First Booke of Architecture*

DATES	POLITICAL EVENTS	DESIGN, ART AND SCIENCE	PUBLICATIONS
1612		Coal first used to make glass	
1616		Building of Queen's House, Greenwich, begins	
1619		Building of Banqueting House, Whitehall, begins	
		Mortlake tapestry works established	
1624–30	War with Spain		
1624			Sir Henry Wootton, *Elements of Architecture*
1625	Death of James I and VI, accession of Charles I		
1626–30	War with France		
1627	English settlement of Barbados		
1631		Building of the Piazza at Covent Garden begins	
1632		Anthony Van Dyck settles in England as court painter	
1642–6	English Civil War		
1649	Execution of Charles I		
about 1650		Coal first used to make earthenware	
		Building of Coleshill, Berkshire, begins	
1652–4	First Dutch War		
1655	English capture of Jamaica from Spain		
1657		The first English coffee house opens in Oxford	
1658	Death of Oliver Cromwell, Lord Protector		
1660	Restoration of Charles II	Royal Society established	Samuel Pepys begins his diary
1661	Louis XIV assumes full powers as King of France		Robert Boyle, *The Sceptical Chymist*
1663		Drury Lane Theatre opens in London	
1665–7	Second Dutch War		
1666	Fire of London		
1672		John Dwight establishes his pottery at Fulham	
1672–4	Third Dutch War		
1673		Building of St Paul's Cathedral, London, begins	
1675		Royal Observatory at Greenwich founded	
1678	Popish plot		Joseph Moxon, *Mechanick Exercises*
1679–81	Exclusion crisis		
1680s		Lead, copper and tin first smelted with coal	
1685	Death of Charles II, accession of James II and VII		
	Exodus of Protestant Huguenots from France after Revocation of the Edict of Nantes		
1686		Building of Chatworth House, Derbyshire, begins	
1687			Isaac Newton, *Philosophiae Naturalis Principia Mathematica*
1688	'Glorious Revolution'. Flight of James II and VII		John Stalker and George Parker, *A Treatise of Japanning and Varnishing*
1688–97	Nine Years War		
1689	Accession of William and Mary		
	Bill of Rights		
1690	Toleration Act	Building of Wren's additions to Hampton Court Palace begins	John Locke, *Two Treatises on Government*
1693			Jean Tijou, *A New Book of Drawings, Invented and Designed by Jean Tijou*
1694	Death of Mary II, William III reigns alone		
1695		Lapse of legislation requiring press licensing	
1698		Building of Castle Howard, Yorkshire, begins	
1699		Import of Indian decorated cottons banned	
1701	Act of Settlement		
1702–13	War of Spanish Succession		
1702	Death of William III, accession of Queen Anne		*The Daily Courant*, the first daily newspaper, founded
1707	Act of Union with Scotland	Iron first smelted with coke by Abraham Darby at Coalbrookdale, Shropshire	George Farquhar, *The Beaux' Stratagem*
1709		Copyright Act for books	
1709–11			*The Tatler* magazine published
1711		Sir Godfrey Kneller's drawing academy	Earl of Shaftesbury, *Characteristicks*
1711–12			*The Spectator* magazine published
before 1712		Thomas Newcomen builds his atmospheric steam engine	
1713		East India Company secures right of access to Canton, China	
1714	Death of Queen Anne, accession of George I		Bernard de Mandeville, *The Fable of the Bees*

Georgian Britain
Chronology of Events and Publications, 1714–1837

DATES	POLITICAL EVENTS	DESIGN, ART AND SCIENCE	PUBLICATIONS
1714	Death of Queen Anne, accession of George I		Bernard de Mandeville, *The Fable of the Bees*
1715	First Jacobite Rebellion	Building of Wanstead House, London, begins	Colen Campbell, *Vitruvius Britannicus*
	Death of Louis XIV of France		*The Architecture of A. Palladio*, revised by Giacomo Leoni
1717		Thomas Lombe develops his silk-throwing machine	George Frederick Handel, *Water Music*
1720		St Martin's Lane academy of painting and sculpture founded in London	
1722		Building of Houghton Hall, Norfolk, begins	Daniel Defoe, *Moll Flanders*
		Building of St Martin-in-the-Fields, London, begins	
1725		Building of Chiswick House, London, begins	
1727	Death of George I, accession of George II		William Kent (ed.), *Designs of Inigo Jones*
1728		Jonathan Tyers begins to remodel Vauxhall Gardens, London	James Gibbs, *Book of Architecture*
			Robert Morris, *Essay in Defence of Ancient Architecture*
1729	Methodist Society formed		
1730s		John Kay invents the flying shuttle	
1731		Dublin Society for Improving Husbandry, Manufactures and other Useful Arts established	*Gentleman's Magazine* founded
1732		William Hogarth, *A Harlot's Progress*	
1734		Building of Holkham Hall, Norfolk, begins	
1735		St Martin's Lane Academy, London, established	Bishop George Berkeley, *The Querist*
		Copyright Act for engraved prints	
1738		Herculaneum excavated	Andrea Palladio, *Four Books of Architecture*, English translation by Isaac Ware
1739–48	War of Austrian Succession		
1740s		Benjamin Huntsman invents the crucible steel-making process	
1740		Benjamin Martin introduces the pocket microscope	Samuel Richardson, *Pamela*
1742		Thomas Boulsover discovers Sheffield plate	
1744			Matthias Locke, *Six Sconces*
1745	Second Jacobite Rebellion	Porcelain production begins at the Chelsea factory, London	
		Anti-Gallican Society established	
		William Hogarth, *Marriage à la Mode*	
1748		Building of Strawberry Hill, Twickenham, begins	Samuel Richardson, *Clarissa*
1752	Britain adopts new calendar	Copper plate printing on textiles introduced in Ireland	
		Printed enamel transfers on ceramics introduced	
1753		British Museum founded in London	William Hogarth, *Analysis of Beauty*
1754		Society of Arts established in London	Thomas Chippendale, *The Gentleman and Cabinet Maker's Director*
			Matthias Darley, *A New Book of Chinese Designs*
1756			Edmund Burke, *A Philosophical Inquiry into the Origin of our Ideas of the Sublime and the Beautiful*
1756–63	Seven Years War		
1757		Building of Kedleston Hall, Derbyshire, begins	William Chambers, *Designs of Chinese Buildings, Furniture, Dresses, Machines, and Utensils*
1759			William Chambers, *Treatise on Civil Architecture*
			William Ince and John Mayhew, *The Universal System of Household Furniture*
1760	Death of George II, accession of George III	First public exhibition of paintings at the Society of Arts, London	
1761		Bridgewater canal opens in Lancashire	
1762		Building of Syon House, London, begins	James Stuart and Nicholas Revett, *The Antiquities of Athens*
1763			*The Lady's Magazine* founded
1764		James Hargreaves invents the spinning jenny	Robert Adam, *Ruins of the Palace of the Emperor Diocletian, at Spalatro*
			Horace Walpole, *The Castle of Otranto*
1766	Death of James Stuart, the Old Pretender	Matthew Boulton's Soho works at Birmingham opens	
1766–7			Baron d'Hancarville, *Catalogue of Etruscan, Greek, and Roman Antiquities*
1768		Royal Academy established in London	
1769	Wilkes agitation	Richard Arkwright invents the water frame	Sir Joshua Reynolds, first *Discourse*
		Royal Crescent at Bath completed	
		Josiah Wedgwood's Etruria works in Staffordshire opens	

DATES	POLITICAL EVENTS	DESIGN, ART AND SCIENCE	PUBLICATIONS
1771			*Encyclopaedia Britannica*
1773	Boston Tea Party	Ravenshead plate-glass works opens in Lancashire	
1773–8			Robert and James Adam, *The Works in Architecture of Robert and James Adam*
1775		James Watt invents the rotary steam engine	
1776	American Declaration of Independence		Edward Gibbon, *Decline and Fall of the Roman Empire* Adam Smith, *The Wealth of Nations*
1776–83	American War of Independence		
1779		Samuel Crompton invents the spinning mule First iron bridge at Coalbrookdale, Shropshire, completed	
1780	Gordon riots		
1783		Roller printing on textiles patented Remodelling of Carlton House, London, for the Prince of Wales begins	
1784		Henry Cort's iron-puddling process patented	
1786	Anglo-French trade treaty		
1787		Copyright Act for textile designs	
1788	Death of Charles Edward Stuart, the Young Pretender First British settlement in Australia		George Hepplewhite, *The Cabinet-maker and Upholsterer's Guide*
1789	French Revolution		William Blake, *Songs of Innocence*
1790			Edmund Burke, *Reflections on the French Revolution*
1791			Thomas Paine, *The Rights of Man* Thomas Sheraton, *The Cabinet-maker and Upholsterer's Drawing Book*
1792		John Soane begins to remodel the Bank of England	Mary Wollstonecraft, *Vindication of the Rights of Women*
1792–1815	French Revolutionary and Napoleonic Wars		
1794–1803			Nicolaus von Heideloff's *Gallery of Fashion* published
1795		Building of Fonthill Abbey, Wiltshire, begins	
1798	Battle of the Nile		Robert Malthus, *Essay on the Principal of Population* William Wordsworth and Samuel Taylor Coleridge, *Lyrical Ballads*
1800	Act of Union with Ireland	Robert Owen establishes his model factory at New Lanark, Scotland Henry Maudsley invents the screw-cutting lathe	
1804		Joseph Marie Jacquard patents his punch-card loom in France	
1805	Battle of Trafalgar		
1807	Slave trade abolished in British Territories		Thomas Hope, *Household Furniture and Interior Decoration*
1809–28			Rudolph Ackermann's *Repository of Arts* published
1811	George, Prince of Wales, becomes Prince Regent	Building of Nash's Regent Street, London, begins	
1812	Luddite disturbances	Gas lighting introduced in London streets	
1815	Battle of Waterloo	John Nash's remodelling of Brighton Pavilion begins	
1816			Humphry Repton, *Fragments on the Theory and Practice of Landscape Gardening*
1817			David Ricardo, *Principles of Political Economy* Thomas Rickman, *An Attempt to Discriminate the Styles of English Architecture*
1819	Peterloo Massacre		
1820	Death of George III, accession of George IV	First iron steamship launched	Percy Bysshe Shelley, *Prometheus Unbound*
1821	Queen Caroline Affair		
1822		Charles Macintosh invents the waterproof garment	
1825		Opening of the Stockton–Darlington railway	
1828	Repeal of the Test and Corporation Acts		
1829	Catholic Emancipation		
1830	Death of George IV, accession of William IV	Opening of the Liverpool–Manchester railway	
1831		Charles Darwin begins his voyage on the *Beagle*	
1832	Great Reform Act		Alfred Tennyson, 'The Lady of Shalott'
1833	Slavery abolished in British Territories		
1835		First negative photograph taken by Henry Fox Talbot	
1835–6		Parliamentary Select Committee on the arts and their connection with manufactures	
1836			A. W. N. Pugin, *Contrasts*
1837	Death of William IV, accession of Queen Victoria	Government School of Design, London, founded	

Victorian Britain
Chronology of Events and Publications, 1837–1901

DATES	POLITICAL EVENTS	DESIGN, ART AND SCIENCE	PUBLICATIONS
1837	Death of William IV, accession of Queen Victoria	Government School of Design, London, founded	
1838		London–Birmingham railway opens	
1839	Parliament rejects first Chartist petition	Daguerrotype announced	*Art Union* (later the *Art Journal*) founded
1839–42	War with China		
1839, 1842, 1843		Design Copyright Acts	
1840	Queen Victoria marries Albert of Saxe-Coburg-Gotha	Rowland Hill introduces the postage stamp	
		Building of the new Palace of Westminster, London, begins	
1841			A. W. N. Pugin, *The True Principles of Pointed or Christian Architecture*
			Punch founded
1842–5			Owen Jones, *Plans, elevations, sections and details of the Alhambra*
1842	Parliament rejects second Chartist petition		
1843			Thomas Carlyle, *Past and Present*
1844		The first telegraph line in England is laid	
1845	Irish famine begins	Building of Osborne House, Isle of Wight. begins	Benjamin Disaeli, *Sybil*
1846	Repeal of the Corn Laws		
1847	'Ten Hour' Factory Act	Felix Summerly's Art Manufactures founded	Charlotte Brontë, *Jane Eyre*
			Emily Brontë, *Wuthering Heights*
1848	Chartist demonstration, Kennington Common, London	Queen Victoria's first visit to Balmoral	Karl Marx and Frederick Engels, *The Communist Manifesto*
1849		Building of All Saints' Church, Margaret Street, London, begins	John Ruskin, *The Seven Lamps of Architecture*
1849–52			Henry Cole's *Journal of Design and Manufactures* published
1850		Building of Mentmore Towers, Buckinghamshire, begins	Charles Dickens, *David Copperfield*
		The Germ publishes Pre-Raphelite ideas	
		Isaac Singer produces the first practical sewing machine in the United States	
1851		Great Exhibition in Hyde Park, London	John Ruskin, *The Stones of Venice*
1852		Museum of Ornamental Art, London, founded	*The Englishwoman's Domestic Magazine* founded
1853		Building of Leeds Town Hall begins	
1854			Coventry Patmore, *The Angel in the House: The Betrothal*
1854–6	Crimean War fought against Russia		
1855			Anthony Trollope, *The Warden*
			Daily Telegraph founded
			Elizabeth Gaskell, *North and South*
1856		Henry Bessemer's steel-making process invented	Owen Jones, *The Grammar of Ornament*
		William Perkin prepares the first aniline dye	
		Celluloid first synthesized by Alexander Parkes	
1856–60	War with China		
1857	Indian Mutiny	Manchester Art Treasures Exhibition	
		Science Museum, London, founded	
1858	Japan opened to foreign trade		
1859		Frederick Walton invents linoleum	Charles Darwin, *On the Origin of Species*
		Building of the Foreign Office, London, begins	Isabella Beeton, *Book of Household Management*
		Philip Webb designs Red House, Bexleyheath, for William Morris	John Stuart Mill, *On Liberty*
about 1860		The cigarette invented	
1860		London University establishes degrees in science	
1861	Death of Albert, Prince Consort	HMS *Warrior*, the first all-iron warship, completed	Charles Dickens, *Great Expectations*
		Morris, Marshall, Faulkner & Co. founded	*The Queen* founded
			Ellen Wood, *East Lynne*
1862		International Exhibition, South Kensington, London	
1863		William Whiteley opens his shop in Bayswater, London	Charles Kingsley, *The Water Babies*
		Football Association established in London	
1864		Building of the Albert Memorial begins in London	
		First underground railway opened in London	
1866		The Atlantic telegraph cable is laid	
		Amateur Athletic Club (later Association) founded	

DATES	POLITICAL EVENTS	DESIGN, ART AND SCIENCE	PUBLICATIONS
1867		Building of Manchester Town Hall begins	
1868	Second Reform Act	Building of the Midland Hotel, St Pancras Station, London, begins	Charles Eastlake, *Hints on Household Taste*
	Trades Union Congress founded	C. L. Sholes patents the typewriter in the United States	
		Building of Cardiff Castle begins	
1869	Suez Canal opens	Building of Cragside, Northumberland, begins	Matthew Arnold, *Culture and Anarchy*
			The Architect founded
1870		Building of Eaton Hall, Cheshire, begins	
1871	Bank Holidays introduced	Rugby Football Union founded	*The House Furnisher and Decorator* founded
			Charles Darwin, *The Descent of Man*
1872		Bradford town hall completed	George Eliot, *Middlemarch*
1873			*The Art-Workman. A monthly journal of design for the artist, artificer and manufacturer* founded
			Christopher Dresser, *Principles of Decorative Design*
1875		Trades Marks Act	*Myra's Journal of Dress and Fashion* founded
1876	Queen Victoria declared Empress of India	Alexander Graham Bell patents the telephone in the United States	Agnes and Rhoda Garrett, *Suggestions for House Decoration in Painting, Woodwork and Furniture*
		Building of Bedford Park, London, begins	
1877		Society for the Protection of Ancient Buildings founded	E. W. Godwin for William Watt and Co., *Art Furniture*
		Thomas Edison invents the phonograph in the United States	
		All-England Lawn Tennis Championship first played at Wimbledon	
1878		Joseph Swan demonstrates the electric light bulb	Lucy Orrinsmith, *The Drawing Room*
		Electric street lighting introduced in London	Thomas Hardy, *The Return of the Native*
		Development of Gilchrist-Thomas steel-making process	
1879		First London telephone exchange opens	
1880			Robert Edis, *Decoration and Furniture of Town Houses*
1881		William Morris establishes his Merton Abbey works	W. S. Gilbert and Arthur Sullivan, *Patience*
		Natural History Museum, London, opens	*The Journal of Decorative Art* founded
			Mary Eliza Haweis, *The Art of Decoration*
1882		Electric trams begin to operate in London	Walter Hamilton, *The Aesthetic Movement in England*
		A. H. Mackmurdo founds the Century Guild	
		Building of William Burges's Tower House, London	
1883		Arthur Liberty opens his department store in London	
		Patents, Designs and Trademarks Act	
1884	Third Reform Act	Art-Workers' Guild founded	
		Hiram Maxim invents the automatic machine gun	
		Lewis Waterman invents the fountain pen in the United States	
1885		John Starley introduces the Rover Safety bicycle	W. S. Gilbert and Arthur Sullivan, *The Mikado*
		Karl Benz develops the first petrol-engined motor vehicle in Germany	
1886		Colonial and Indian Exhibition, London	
		John Everett Millais, *Bubbles*	
1887	Queen Victoria's Golden Jubilee	Art and Crafts Exhibition Society founded	
1888		C. R. Ashbee founds the Guild of Handicraft	Jane Ellen Panton, *From Kitchen to Garret. Hints for Young Householders*
		John Dunlop patents the pneumatic tyre	
1890		William Morris establishes the Kelmscott Press	
1891			William Morris, *News from Nowhere*
			Thomas Hardy, *Tess of the D'Urbervilles*
1892		James Dewar invents the vacuum flask	George and Weedon Grossmith, *The Diary of a Nobody*
1893			*The Studio* founded
1894		Lumière brothers invent the cinematograph in France	*The Yellow Book* founded
1895	Trial of Oscar Wilde	The National Trust founded	Oscar Wilde, *The Importance of Being Ernest*
1896		Guglielmo Marconi patents wireless telegraphy	*Daily Mail* founded
1897	Queen Victoria's Diamond Jubilee	Building of Glasgow School of Art begins	*The House* founded
1898		C. F. A. Voysey's Broadley's, Cartmel, Cumbria, built	
1899		South Kensington Museum renamed the Victoria and Albert Museum	
		Felix Hoffman invents aspirin for the Bayer company in Germany	
1899–1902	South African Boer War		
1900			*Daily Express* founded
1901	Death of Queen Victoria, accession of Edward VII		

Tudor and Stuart Britain
Design and the Decorative Arts: A Select Bibliography

1. Introduction

Appleby, J. O., *Economic Thought and Ideology in Seventeenth-Century England* (Princeton, NJ, 1978)

Armitage, D., *The Ideological Origins of the British Empire* (Cambridge, 2000)

Beier, A. L. and Finlay, R. (eds), *London, 1500–1700: The Making of the Metropolis* (1986)

Berry, C. J., *The Idea of Luxury: a Conceptual and Historical Investigation* (Cambridge, 1994)

Braddick, M. J., *State Formation in Early Modern England, c. 1550–1700* (Cambridge, 2000)

Bradshaw, B. and Morrill, J. (eds), *The British Problem c. 1534–1707: State Formation in the British Archipelago* (1996)

Bryson, A., *From Courtesy to Civility: Changing Codes of Conduct in Early Modern England* (Oxford, 1998)

Canny, N. (ed.), *The Oxford History of the British Empire. Vol. I. Origins of Empire: British Overseas Enterprise to the Close of the Seventeenth Century* (Oxford, 1998)

Clay, C. G. A., *Economic Expansion and Social Change: England 1500–1700* (Cambridge, 1984)

Collinson, P., *The Religion of Protestants: The Church in English Society, 1559–1625* (Oxford, 1982)

Corns, T. N., *The Royal Image: Representations of Charles I* (Cambridge, 1999)

Denvir, B., *From the Middle Ages to the Stuarts. Art, Design and Society before 1689* (1988)

Duffy, E., *The Stripping of the Altars. Traditional Religion in England, 1400–1580* (1992)

Durston, C. and Eales, J. (eds), *The Culture of English Puritanism, 1560–1700* (1996)

Dyer, C., *Standards of Living in the later Middle Ages. Social Change in England c. 1200–1520* (Cambridge, 1989)

Earle, P., *The Making of the English Middle Class: Business, Society and Family Life in London, 1660–1730* (1989)

Ellis, S. G. and Barber, S. (eds), *Conquest and Union: Fashioning a British State, 1485–1625* (1995)

Ford, Boris (ed.), *The Cambridge Guide to the Arts in Britain: Vol. 3. Renaissance and Reformation* (1989)

Ford, Boris (ed.), *The Cambridge Guide to the Arts in Britain: Vol. 4. The Seventeenth Century* (1989)

Gaimster, D. and Stamper, P. (eds), *The Age of Transition: The Archeology of English Culture, 1400–1600* (1997)

Green, I., *Print and Protestantism in Early Modern England* (Cambridge, 2000)

Gwynn, R., *Huguenot Heritage. The History and Contribution of the Huguenots in Britain* (Brighton, 2000)

Haigh, C., *English Reformations: Religion, Politics and Society under the Tudors* (Oxford, 1993)

Harte, N. B., 'State Control of Dress and Social Change in Pre-Industrial England', in Coleman, D. C. and John, A. H. (eds), *Trade, Government and Economy in Pre-Industrial England* (1976)

Hoppit, J., *A Land of Liberty? England, 1689–1727* (Oxford, 2000)

Lubbock, J., *The Tyranny of Taste. The Politics of Architecture and Design in Britain, 1550–1960* (1995)

MacCulloch, D., *The Later Reformation in England, 1574–1603* (1990)

McKellar, E., *The Birth of Modern London. The Development and Design of the City, 1660–1720* (Manchester, 1999)

Milton, A., *Catholic and Reformed. The Roman and Protestant Churches in English Protestant Thought* (Cambridge, 1995)

Morrill, J. (ed.), *The Oxford Illustrated History of Tudor and Stuart Britain* (Oxford, 1996)

Orlin, L. C. (ed.), *Material London, ca. 1600* (Philadelphia, PA, 2000)

Palliser, D. M., *The Age of Elizabeth. England Under the Later Tudors, 1547–1603* (1983)

Pointon, M., 'Quakerism and Visual Culture, 1650–1800', *Art History*, 20 (1997)

Porter, R., *London, A Social History* (1994)

Sekora, J., *Luxury: The Concept in Western Thought, Eden to Smollet* (Baltimore, MD, 1977)

Shammas, C., *The Pre-Industrial Consumer in England and America* (Oxford, 1990)

Sharpe, J., *Early Modern England: A Social History, 1550–1760* (1987)

Sharpe, K. and Lake, P. (eds), *Culture and Politics in Early Stuart England* (1994)

Smout, T. C., *A History of the Scottish People, 1560–1830* (Glasgow, 1969)

Spufford, M., *The Great Reclothing of Rural England. Petty Chapmen and their Wares in the Seventeenth Century* (1984)

Walsham, A., *Providence in Early Modern England* (Oxford, 1999)

Watt, T., *Cheap Print and Popular Piety, 1550–1640* (Cambridge, 1993)

Weatherill, L., *Consumer Behaviour and Material Culture in Britain, 1660–1760* (1988)

Williams, P., *The Later Tudors. England, 1547–1603* (Oxford, 1995)

Wrightson, K., *Earthly Necessities. Economic Lives in Early Modern Britain* (2000)

2. Style

Baarsen, R., Jackson-Stops, G., Johnston, P. M. and Dee, E., *Courts and Colonies. The William and Mary Style in Holland, England and America* (1988)

Harris, J. and Higgott, G., *Inigo Jones. Complete Architectural Drawings* (1989)

Harris, J., Orgel, S. and Strong, R. (eds), *The King's Arcadia: Inigo Jones and the Stuart Court* (1973)

Honour, H., *Chinoiserie: The Vision of Cathay* (1961)

Impey, O., *Chinoiserie: The Impact of Oriental Styles on Western Art and Decoration* (1977)

Mowl, T., *Elizabethan and Jacobean Style* (1993)

Peacock, J., *The Stage Designs of Inigo Jones. The European Context* (Cambridge, 1995)

Summerson, J. N., *Architecture in Britain, 1530–1830* (1991)

Summerson, J. N., *Inigo Jones* (1966)

Ward Jackson, P. W., *Some Mainstreams and Tributaries in European Ornament from 1500 to 1750* (1967)

Wells-Cole, A., *Art and Decoration in Elizabethan and Jacobean England: The Influence of Continental Prints, 1558–1625* (1997)

3. Who led taste?

Anglo, S., (ed.), *Chivalry in the Renaissance* (Woodbridge, 1990)

Anglo, S., *Spectacle, Pageantry, and Early Tudor Policy* (Oxford, 1969)

Brown, J., *Kings and Connoisseurs: Collecting Art in Seventeenth-Century Europe* (Princeton, NJ, 1995)

Bucholz, R. O., *The Augustan Court: Queen Anne and the Decline of Court Culture* (Stanford, CA, 1993)

Dunlop, I., *Palaces and Progresses of Elizabeth I* (1962)

Gent, L., *Albion's Classicism: The Visual Arts in England, 1550–1650* (1995)

Girouard, M., *Robert Smythson and the Elizabethan Country House* (1983)

Griffiths, A., *The Print in Stuart Britain, 1603–1689* (1998)

Gunn, S. J. and Lindley, P. G., *Cardinal Wolsey. Church, State and Art* (Cambridge, 1991)

Harris, E., *British Architectural Books and Writers, 1556–1785* (Cambridge, 1990)

Harris, J., *The Artist and the Country House. A History of Country House and Garden View Painting in Britain, 1540–1870* (1979)

Howarth, D. (ed.), *Art and Patronage in the Caroline Courts* (Cambridge, 1993)

Howarth, D., *Images of Rule. Art and Politics in the English Renaissance, 1485–1649* (1997)

Howarth, D., *Lord Arundel and his Circle* (1985)

Jervis, S., *The Penguin Dictionary of Design and Designers* (1984)

Jervis, S., *Printed Furniture Designs before 1650* (1974)

Lytle, G. F. and Orgel, S. (eds), *Patronage in the Renaissance* (Princeton, NJ, 1982)

Maccubbin, R. P. and Hamilton-Phillips, M., *The Age of William III and Mary II: Power, Politics and Patronage, 1688–1702* (Williamsburg, VA, 1989)

Maclean, G., *Culture and Society in the Stuart Restoration: Literature, Drama, History* (Cambridge, 1995)

Murdoch, T., *Boughton House. The English Versailles* (1992)

O'Connell, S., *The Popular Print in England: 1550–1850* (1999)

Orgel, S., *The Illusion of Power: Political Theater in the English Renaissance* (Berkeley, CA, 1975)

Parry, G., *The Golden Age Restor'd. The Culture of the Stuart Court, 1603–42* (1981)

Peck, L. L., *Court, Patronage and Corruption in Early Stuart England* (Boston, MA, 1990)

Sharpe, K., *The Personal Rule of Charles I* (1992)

Starkey, D. (ed.), *Henry VIII, A European Court in England* (1991)

Strong, R. C., *The Cult of Elizabeth: Elizabethan Portraiture and Pageantry* (1977)

Strong, R. C., *Splendour at Court: Renaissance Spectacle and Illusion* (1973)

Thurley, S., *The Royal Palaces of Tudor England: Architecture and Court Life, 1460–1547* (1993)

Veevers, E., *Images of Love and Religion. Queen Henrietta and Court Entertainments* (Cambridge, 1989)

4. Fashionable living

Airs, M., *The Tudor and Jacobean Country House. A Building History* (1995)

Arnold, J., *Queen Elizabeth's Wardrobe Unlock'd* (Leeds, 1988)

Arthur, L., *Embroidery 1600–1700 at the Burrell Collection* (1995)

Ashelford, J., *The Art of Dress. Clothes and Society, 1500–1914* (1996)

Ashelford, J., *Dress in the Age of Elizabeth I* (1988)

Barry, J. (ed.), *The Tudor and Stuart Town, 1530–1688. A Reader in English Urban History* (1990)

Cliffe, J. T., *The World of the Country House in Seventeenth-Century England* (1999)

Cooper, N., *Houses of the Gentry, 1480–1680* (1999)

Cox, N., *The Complete Tradesman: A Study of Retailing, 1550–1820* (Aldershot, 2000)

Croft-Murray, E., *Decorative Painting in England 1537–1837. Vol. 1. Early Tudor to Sir James Thornhill* (1962)

Cumming, V., *A Visual History of Costume: The Seventeenth Century* (1984)

Friedman, A. T., *House and Household in Elizabethan England: Wollaton Hall and the Willoughby Family* (Chicago, IL, 1989)

Girouard, M., *Life in the English Country House: A Social and Architectural History* (1978)

Heal, F. and Holmes, C., *The Gentry in England and Wales, 1500–1700* (1994)

Hearn, K. (ed.), *Dynasties: Painting in Tudor and Jacobean England, 1530–1630* (1995)

Holmes, M., *Elizabethan London* (1969)

Howard, M., *The Early Tudor Country House. Architecture and Politics, 1490–1550* (1987)

Hunt, J. D., *Garden and Grove. The Italian Renaissance Garden and the English Imagination, 1600–1750* (1986)

Jackson-Stops, G. (ed.), *The Fashioning and Functioning of the British Country House* (Washington, DC, 1989)

King, D. and Levey, S. M., *The Victoria and Albert Museum's Textile Collection: Embroidery in Britain from 1200 to 1750* (1993)

Lawrence, A., *Women in England, 1500–1760: A Social History* (1994)

Levey, S. M., *An Elizabethan Inheritance: The Hardwick Hall Textiles* (1998)

Lewellyn, N., *The Art of Death: Visual Culture in the English Death Ritual, c. 1500–c. 1800* (1991)

Mendelson, S. and Crawford, P., *Women in Early Modern England 1550–1720* (Oxford, 1998)

Mercer, E., *English Art, 1553–1625* (Oxford, 1962)

Mertes, K., *The English Noble Household, 1260–1600: Good Governance and Political Rule* (Oxford, 1988)

Platt, C., *The Architecture of Medieval Britain: A Social History* (1990)

Platt, C., *The Great Rebuildings of Tudor and Stuart England: Revolutions in Architectural Taste* (1994)

Schofield, J., *The Building of London: from the Conquest to the Great Fire* (1984)

Strong, R. C., *The Artist and the Garden* (2000)

Strong, R. C., *The Tudor and Stuart Monarchy: Pagentry, Painting, Iconography* (3 vols, Woodbridge, 1995–8)

Thornton, P. K., *Seventeenth-Century Interior Decoration in England, France and Holland* (1978)

Wyman, S. E., *Sociability and Power in Late-Stuart England. The Cultural Worlds of the Verneys, 1660–1720* (Oxford, 1999)

5. What was new?

Archer, M., *Delftware: The Tin-Glazed Earthenware of the British Isles* (1997)

Blake, N. F., *Caxton, England's First Publisher* (1976)

Charleston, R. J., *English Glass and the Glass used in England, c. 400–1940* (1984)

Chaudhuri, K. N., *The Trading World of Asia and the English East India Company, 1660–1760* (Cambridge, 1978)

Feather, J., *A History of British Publishing* (1988)

Gaimster, D., *German Stoneware 1200–1900* (1997)

Glanville, P., *Silver in Tudor and Early Stuart England* (1990)

Godfrey, E. S., *The Development of English Glass Making, 1560–1640* (Oxford, 1975)

Goodman, J., *Tobacco in History: The Cultures of Dependence* (1993)

Goodman, J., Lovejoy, P. E. and Sherratt, A. (eds), *Consuming Habits: Drugs in History and Anthropology* (1995)

Green, C., *John Dwight's Fulham Pottery* (1999)

Harris, J., *Essays in Industry and Technology in the Eighteenth Century: England and France* (Hampshire, 1992)

Harte, N.B. (ed.), *The New Draperies in the Low Countries and England, 1300–1800* (Oxford, 1997)

Hatcher, J. and Barker, T. C., *A History of British Pewter* (1974)

Hellinga, L. and Trapp, J. B. (eds), *The Cambridge History of the Book in Britain, Vol. 3, 1400–1557* (Cambridge, 1999)

Hodnett, E., *Five Centuries of English Book Illustration* (Aldershot, 1988)

Hunter, M., *Science and Society in Restoration England* (Cambridge, 1981)

Irwin, J., 'Origins of the "Oriental Style" in English Decorative Art', *Burlington Magazine*, 97 (1955)

Irwin, J. and Brett, K. B., *Origins of Chintz* (1970)

Lavery, B., *The Ship of the Line* (1983)

Loomes, B., *The Early Clockmakers of Great Britain* (1981)

Mitchell, D., *Goldsmiths, Silversmiths and Bankers. Innovation and the Transfer of Skill, 1550 to 1750* (1995)

North, A., *Pewter at the Victoria and Albert Museum* (1999)

Roger, N. A. M., *The Safeguard of the Sea: A Naval History of Britain: Vol. 1. 660–1649* (1997)

Rothstein, N., *The Victoria and Albert Museum's Textile Collection. Woven Textile Design in Britain to 1750* (1994)

Smith, M. M., *The Title-Page. Its Early Development, 1460–1510* (2000)

Styles, J., 'Product Innovation in Early-Modern London', *Past and Present*, 168 (2000)

Sutherland, J., *The Restoration Newspaper and its Development* (Cambridge, 1986)

Thirsk, J., *Economic Policy and Projects. The Development of a Consumer Society in Early Modern England* (Oxford, 1978)

V&A Museum, *The Needle's Excellency: A Travelling Exhibition* (1973)

Georgian Britain
Design and the Decorative Arts: A Select Bibliography

6. Introduction

Barker-Benfield, G. J., *The Culture of Sensibility: Sex and Society in Eighteenth-Century Britain* (Chicago, IL, 1992)

Barrell, J. (ed.), *Painting and the Politics of Culture: New Essays on British Art, 1700–1850* (Oxford, 1992)

Bermingham, A. and Brewer, J. (eds), *The Consumption of Culture, 1600–1800: Image, Object, Text* (1995)

Berry, C., *The Idea of Luxury: A Conceptual and Historical Investigation* (Cambridge, 1994)

Black, J., *The English Press in the Eighteenth Century* (1987)

Black, J., *Natural and Necessary Enemies. Anglo-French Relations in the Eighteenth Century* (1986)

Breen, T. H., 'An Empire of Goods: The Anglicization of Colonial America, 1690–1776', *Journal of British Studies*, 25 (1986)

Brewer, J., *The Pleasures of the Imagination. English Culture in the Eighteenth Century* (1997)

Brewer, J. and Porter, R. (eds), *Consumption and the World of Goods* (1993)

Canon, J., *Aristocratic Century. The Peerage of Eighteenth-Century England* (Cambridge, 1984)

Clunas, C., *Chinese Export Art and Design* (1987)

Colley, L., *Britons. Forging the Nation, 1707–1837* (1992)

Corfield, P. J., 'Class by Name and Class by Number in Eighteenth-Century Britain', *History*, 72 (1987)

Corfield, P. J., *The Impact of English Towns, 1700–1800* (Oxford, 1982)

Daunton, M., *Progress and Poverty: An Economic and Social History of Britain, 1700–1850* (Oxford, 1995)

Davis, R., *The Industrial Revolution and British Overseas Trade* (Leicester, 1979)

De Vries, J., *European Urbanization, 1500–1800* (1984)

Denvir, B., *The Early Nineteenth Century. Art, Design and Society, 1789–1852* (1984)

Denvir B., *The Eighteenth Century. Art, Design and Society, 1689–1789* (1983)

Hont, I. and Ignatieff, M., *Wealth and Virtue: The Shaping of Political Economy in the Scottish Enlightenment* (Cambridge, 1983)

Houston, R. A., *Social Change in the Age of Enlightenment. Edinburgh, 1660–1760* (Oxford, 1994)

Jaffer, A., *Furniture from British India and Ceylon* (2001)

Jenkins, P., *The Making of a Ruling Class. The Glamorgan Gentry, 1640–1790* (Cambridge, 1983)

Klein, L., 'Property and Politeness in the Early Eighteenth-Century Whig Moralists', in Brewer, J. and Staves, S. (eds), *Early Modern Conceptions of Property* (1995)

Klein, L., *Shaftesbury and the Culture of Politeness: Moral Discourse and Cultural Politics in Early Eighteenth-Century England* (Cambridge, 1994)

Langford, P., *A Polite and Commercial People. England 1727–1783* (Oxford, 1989)

Malcolmson, R. W., *Life and Labour in England, 1700–1800* (1981)

Marshall, P. J. (ed.), *The Oxford History of the British Empire. Vol. II. The Eighteenth Century* (1998)

Mingay, G. E., *English Landed Society in the Eighteenth Century* (1963)

Money, J., *Experience and Identity: Birmingham and the West Midlands, 1760–1800* (Manchester, 1977)

Monod, P. K., *Jacobitism and the English People, 1688–1788* (Cambridge, 1989)

Mullan, J., *Sentiment and Sociability: The Language of Feeling in the Eighteenth Century* (Oxford, 1988)

Newman, G., *The Rise of English Nationalism: A Cultural History* (New York, 1987)

Porter, R., *English Society in the Eighteenth Century* (1982)

Porter, R., *Enlightenment: Britain and the Making of the Modern World* (2000)

Price, R., *British Society, 1680–1880. Dynamism, Containment and Change.* (Cambridge, 1999)

Schofield, R. E., *The Lunar Society of Birmingham. A Social History of Provincial Science and Industry in Eighteenth-Century England* (Oxford, 1963)

Sekora, J., *Luxury. The Concept in Western Thought, Eden to Smollet* (Baltimore, MD, 1977)

Smout, T. C., *A History of the Scottish People, 1560–1830* (Glasgow, 1969)

Spadaforda, D., *The Idea of Progress in Eighteenth-Century Britain* (1990)

Szechi, D., *The Jacobites. Britain and Europe, 1688–1788* (Manchester, 1994)

Thompson, E. P., *The Making of the English Working Class* (1963)

Warman, D., *Imagining the Middle Class: The Political Representations of Class* (Cambridge, 1995)

Weatherill, L., *Consumer Behaviour and Material Culture in Britain, 1660–1760* (1988)

Wilson, K., *The Sense of the People. Politics, Culture and Imperialism in England, 1715–1785* (Cambridge, 1995)

Wilson, R. G., *Gentlemen Merchants. The Merchant Community in Leeds, 1700–1830* (Manchester, 1971)

7. Style

Aldrich, M., *Gothic Revival* (1994)

Barnard, T. and Clark, J. (eds), *Lord Burlington. Architecture, Art and Life* (1995)

Copley, S. and Garside, P. (eds), *The Politics of the Picturesque: Literature, Landscape and Aesthetics since 1770* (Cambridge, 1994)

Crook, J. M., *The Greek Revival: Neo-Classical Attitudes in British Architecture, 1760–1870* (1995)

Curl, J. S., *The Egyptian Revival: An Introductory Study of a Recurring Theme in the History of Taste* (1982)

Friedman, T., *James Gibbs* (1984)

Harris, J., *The Palladian Revival. Lord Burlington, his Villa and the Gardens at Chiswick* (1994)

Harris, J. and Snodin, M. (eds), *Sir William Chambers: Architect to George III* (1996)

Honour, H., *Chinoiserie: The Vision of Cathay* (1961)

Jacobson, D., *Chinoiserie* (1993)

McCarthy, M., *The Origins of the Gothic Revival* (1987)

Morley, J., *Regency Design, 1790–1840: Gardens, Buildings, Interiors, Furniture* (1993)

Parissien, S., *Adam Style* (1992)

Parissien, S., *Palladian Style* (1994)

Paulson, R., *Hogarth* (3 vols, 1991–3)

Richardson, M. and Stevens, M., *John Soane, Architect: Master of Space and Light* (1999)

Snodin, M. (ed.), *Rococo: Art and Design in Hogarth's England* (1984)

Stillman, D., *English Neo-Classical Architecture* (1988)

Stroud, D., *Sir John Soane, Architect* (1984)

Summerson, J. N., *Architecture in Britain, 1530–1830* (1991)

Watkin, D., *Thomas Hope, 1769–1831, and the Neo-Classical Idea* (1968)

Wilson, M. I., *William Kent. Architect, Designer, Painter, Gardener, 1685–1748* (1984)

Wittkower, R., *Palladio and English Palladianism* (1974)

Worsley, G., *Classical Architecture in Britain. The Heroic Age* (1995)

8. Who led taste?

Allen, B., *Francis Hayman, 1708–1776* (1987)

Allen, D. G. C., *William Shipley. Founder of the Royal Society of Arts* (1979)

Altick, R. D., *The Shows of London* (1978)

Baker, M., *Figured in Marble. The Making and Viewing of Eighteenth-Century Sculpture* (2001)

Beard, G. W., *Upholsterers and Interior Furnishing in England, 1530–1840* (New Haven, CT, 1997)

Beattie, J. M., *The English Court in the Reign of George I* (Cambridge, 1967)

Black, J., *The British Abroad: The Grand Tour in the Eighteenth Century* (Stroud, 1992)

Bruntgen, S. H. A., *John Boydell, 1719–1804: A Study of Art Patronage and Publishing in Georgian London* (New York, 1985)

Chard, C., *Grand Tour: Travel Writing and Imaginative Geography, 1600–1830* (Manchester, 1999)

Clayton, T., *The English Print, 1688–1802* (1997)

Collard, F., *Regency Furniture* (Woodbridge, 1985)

Dickinson, H. W., *Matthew Boulton* (1937)

Donald, D., *The Age of Caricature. Satirical Prints in the Age of George III* (1996)

Fleming, J., *Robert Adam and his Circle in Edinburgh and Rome* (1962)

Fox, C., *London World City, 1800–1840* (New Haven, CT, 1992)

Gilbert, C., *The Life and Work of Thomas Chippendale* (1978)

Gilbert, C. and Murdoch, T. (eds), *John Channon and Brass Inlaid Furniture, 1730–1760* (1993)

Ginsburg, M., *An Introduction to Fashion Illustration* (1980)

Goodison, N., *Ormolu. The Work of Matthew Boulton* (1974)

Hallett, M., *The Spectacle of Difference. Graphic Satire in the Age of Hogarth* (1999)

Harris, E., *British Architectural Books and Writers, 1556–1785* (Cambridge, 1990)

Harris, J., *The Artist and the Country House. A History of Country House and Garden View Painting, 1540–1870* (1979)

Hayward, H. and Kirkham, P., *William and John Linnell: Eighteenth-Century London Furniture Makers* (1980)

Ison, W., *Georgian Buildings of Bath, from 1700 to 1830* (1948)

Jervis, S., *The Penguin Dictionary of Design and Designers* (1984)

Lippincott, L., *Selling Art in Georgian London: The Rise of Arthur Pond* (1983)

Moore, A. W., *Norfolk and the Grand Tour: Eighteenth-Century Travellers Abroad and their Souvenirs* (Norwich, 1985)

Myrone, M. and Peltz, L., *Producing the Past: Aspects of Antiquarian Culture and Practice, 1700–1850* (1999)

Pearce, D., *London's Mansions. The Palatial Houses of the Nobility* (1986)

Pears, I., *The Discovery of Painting: The Growth in the Interest in the Arts in England, 1680–1768* (1988)

Pointon, M., *Hanging the Head. Portraiture and Social Formation in Eighteenth-Century England* (1993)

Puetz, A., 'Design Instruction for Artisans in Eighteenth-Century Britain', *Journal of Design History*, 12 (1999)

Reilly, R., *Wedgwood* (1989)

Royal Collections, *Carleton House. The Past Glories of George IV's Palace* (1991)

Sloan, K., *'A Noble Art'. Amateur Artists and Drawing Masters c. 1600–1800* (2000)

Solkin, D. H., *Painting for Money: The Visual Arts and the Public Sphere in Eighteenth-Century England* (1993)

Summerson, J. N., *Georgian London* (1988)

Wainwright, C. (intro.), *George Bullock, Cabinet-Maker* (1988)

Watkin, D., *Athenian Stuart, Pioneer of the Greek Revival* (1982)

White, E., *Pictorial Dictionary of British Eighteenth-Century Furniture Design: The Printed Sources* (Woodbridge, 1990)

Wilton, A. and Bignamini, I., *The Grand Tour: The Lure of Italy in the Eighteenth Century* (1996)

Young, H. (ed.), *The Genius of Wedgwood* (1997)

9. Fashionable living

Andrews, M., *The Search for the Picturesque: Landscape, Aesthetics and Tourism in Britain, 1760–1800* (Aldershot, 1989)

Ashelford, J., *The Art of Dress. Clothes and Society, 1500–1914* (1996)

Ayres, J., *Building the Georgian City* (1998)

Beard, G. W., *Craftsmen and Interior Decoration in England, 1660–1820* (1981)

Borsay, P., *The English Urban Renaissance. Culture and Society in the Provincial Town, 1660–1770* (Oxford, 1989)

Brown, P. B., *In Praise of Hot Liquors: The Study of Chocolate, Coffee and Tea Drinking, 1600–1850* (York, 1995)

Buck, A., *Dress in Eighteenth-Century England* (1980)

Burrows, D. (ed.), *The Cambridge Companion to Handel* (Cambridge, 1997)

Cornforth, J., *English Interiors, 1790–1848: The Quest for Comfort* (1978)

Cruikshank, D. and Burton, N., *Life in the Georgian City* (1990)

Daniels, S., *Fields of Vision: Landscape Imagery and National Identity in England and the United States* (Cambridge, 1993)

Emmerson, R., *British Teapots and Tea Drinking, 1700–1850* (1992)

Fowler, J. and Cornforth, J., *English Decoration in the Eighteenth Century* (1978)

Gere, C., *Nineteenth-Century Decoration: The Art of the Interior* (1989)

Gilbert, C., Lomax, J. and Wells-Cole, A., *Country House Floors, 1660–1850* (Leeds, 1987)

Girouard, M., *Life in the English Country House: A Social and Architectural History* (1978)

Gow, I., *The Scottish Interior. Georgian and Victorian Decor* (Edinburgh, 1992)

Leppert, R., *Music and Image. Domesticity, Ideology and Socio-Cultural Formation in Eighteenth-Century England* (Cambridge, 1988)

McCalman, I. (ed.), *An Oxford Companion to the Romantic Age. British Culture, 1776–1832* (Oxford, 1999)

McKendrick, N., Brewer, J. and Plumb, J. H., *The Birth of a Consumer Society: The Commercialisation of Eighteenth-Century England* (1982)

Mackintosh, I. and Ashton, G. (eds), *The Georgian Playhouse. Actors, Artists, Audiences and Architecture, 1730–1830* (1975)

Moir, E., *The Discovery of Britain: The English Tourists, 1540–1840* (1964)

Oman, C. C. and Hamilton, J., *Wallpapers: A History and Illustrated Catalogue of the Collection of the Victoria and Albert Museum* (1982)

Ousby, I., *The Englishman's England: Taste, Travel and the Rise of Tourism* (Cambridge, 1990)

Rosoman, T., *London Wallpapers. Their Manufacture and Use, 1690–1840* (1992)

Rothstein, N. (ed.), *Barbara Johnson's Album of Fashions and Fabrics* (1987)

Rothstein, N., *Silk Designs of the Eighteenth Century* (1990)

Rutherford, J., *Country House Lighting, 1660–1890* (Leeds, 1992)

Saumarez Smith, C., *Eighteenth-Century Decoration: Design and the Domestic Interior in England* (1993)

Schoeser, M. and Rufey, C., *English and American Textiles from 1790 to the Present* (1989)

Stone, G. W. and Kahrl, G. M., *David Garrick: A Critical Biography* (Carbondale, IL, 1979)

Sykes, C. S., *Private Palaces. Life in the Great London Houses* (1985)

Tinniswood, A., *The Polite Tourist: A History of Country House Visiting* (1998)

Vickery A., *The Gentleman's Daughter. Women's Lives in Georgian England* (1998)

Wainwright, C., *The Romantic Interior. The British Collector at Home, 1750–1850* (1989)

Walsh, C., 'Shop Design and the Display of Goods in Eighteenth-Century London', *Journal of Design History*, 8 (1995)

Wells-Cole, A., *Historic Paper Hangings from Temple Newsam and Other English Houses* (1983)

Williamson, T., *Polite Landscapes: Gardens and Society in Eighteenth-Century England* (1995)

10. What was new?

Archer, M., *Delftware: Tin-Glazed Earthenware of the British Isles* (1997)

Beard, G. W., *Georgian Craftsmen and their Work* (1966)

Berg, M., *The Age of Manufactures, 1700–1820. Industry, Innovation and Work in Britain* (1994)

Berg, M. and Clifford, H., *Consumers and Luxury. Consumer Culture in Europe, 1650–1850* (Manchester, 1999)

Bowatt, A., 'The Commercial Introduction of Mahogany and the Naval Stores Act of 1721', *Furniture History*, 30 (1994)

Chapman, S. D. and Chassagne, S., *European Textile Printers of the Eighteenth Century: A Study of Peel and Oberkampf* (1981)

Charleston, R. J., *English Glass and the Glass used in England, c. 400–1940* (1984)

Craske, M., 'Plan and Control: Design and the Competitive Spirit in Early and Mid-Eighteenth Century England', *Journal of Design History*, 12 (1999)

Edgcumbe, R., *The Art of the Gold Chaser in Eighteenth-Century London* (Oxford, 2000)

Edwards, C., *Eighteenth-Century Furniture* (Manchester, 1996)

Edwards, M. M., *The Growth of the British Cotton Trade, 1780–1815* (Manchester, 1967)

Fores, M., 'The Myth of a British Industrial Revolution', *History*, 66 (1981)

Forty, A., *Objects of Desire. Design and Society, 1750–1980* (1986)

George, M. D., *London Life in the Eighteenth-Century* (1925)

Glanville, P., *Silver in England* (1987)

Hefford, W., *Design for Printed Textiles in England from 1750–1850* (1992)

Hudson, P., *The Industrial Revolution* (1992)

Jones, E. L., 'The Fashion Manipulators: Consumer Tastes and British Industries, 1660–1800', in Cain, L. P. and Uselding, P. J. (eds), *Business Enterprise and Economic Change* (Ohio, 1973)

Kirkham, P., *The London Furniture Trade, 1700–1870* (1988)

Lemire, B., *Fashion's Favourite: The Cotton Trade and the Consumer in Britain, 1660–1800* (Oxford, 1991)

MacLeod, C., *Inventing the Industrial Revolution: The English Patent System, 1660–1800* (Cambridge, 1988)

Marsden, J. and Harris, J., '"O Fair Britannia Hail". The "most superb" State Coach', *Apollo* (February 2001)

Mitchell, D. (ed.), *Goldsmiths, Silversmiths and Bankers. Innovation and the Transfer of Skill, 1550–1750* (1995)

Morton, A. Q. and Wess, J., *Public and Private Science. The George III Collection* (Oxford, 1993)

Rose, M. B. (ed.), *The Lancashire Cotton Industry. A History since 1700* (Preston, 1996)

Rothstein, N., *Woven Textile Design in Britain from 1750–1850* (1995)

Schwarz, L. D., *London in the Age of Industrialisation: Entrepreneurs, Labour Force and Living Conditions, 1700–1850* (Cambridge, 1992)

Smail, J., *Merchants, Markets and Manufacturers. The English Wool Textile Industry in the Eighteenth Century* (Basingstoke, 1999)

Styles, J., 'Manufacturing, Consumption and Design in Eighteenth-Century England', in Brewer, J. and Porter, R. (eds), *Consumption and the World of Goods* (1993)

Tribe, K., *Genealogies of Capitalism* (1981)

Wackernagel, R., 'Carlton House Mews: The State Coach of the Prince of Wales and of the Later Kings of Hanover. A Study in the Late-Eighteenth-Century "Mystery" of Coach Building', *Furniture History*, 31 (1995)

Weatherill, L., *The Pottery Trade and North Staffordshire, 1660–1760* (Manchester, 1971)

Young, H., *English Porcelain, 1745–95: Its Makers, Design, Marketing and Consumption* (1999)

Victorian Britain
Design and the Decorative Arts: A Select Bibliography

11. Introduction

Auerbach, J. A., *The Great Exhibition of 1851: A Nation on Display* (1999)

Berg, M., *The Machinery Question and the Making of Political Economy, 1815–1848* (Cambridge, 1980)

Briggs, A., *Victorian Cities* (1963)

Briggs, A., *Victorian People* (1965)

Cannadine, D., *Class in Britain* (1998)

Cannadine, D., *The Decline and Fall of the British Aristocracy* (1990)

Checkland, S. and O., *Industry and Ethos: Scotland, 1832–1914* (1984)

Collini, S., *Public Moralists. Political Thought and Intellectual Life in Britain, 1850–1930* (Oxford, 1991)

Davis, J. R., *The Great Exhibition* (Stroud, 1999)

Denvir, B., *The Late Victorians: Art, Design and Society, 1852–1910* (1986)

Fraser, W. H., *The Coming of the Mass Market, 1850–1914* (1981)

Harris, J., *Private Lives, Public Spirit: Britain 1870–1914* (Oxford, 1994)

Hilton, B., *The Age of Atonement. The Influence of Evangelicalism on Social and Economic Thought, 1785–1865* (Oxford, 1988)

Hoppen, K. T., *The Mid-Victorian Generation, 1846–1886* (Oxford, 1998)

Hunt, J. D., *The Wider Sea: A Portrait of John Ruskin* (1982)

Irwin, J., *The Kashmir Shawl* (1973)

Johnson, P., 'Conspicuous Consumption and Working-Class Culture in Late Victorian and Edwardian Britain', *Transactions of the Royal Historical Society*, 38 (1988)

Knight, F., *The Nineteenth-Century Church and English Society* (1995)

MacCarthy, F., *William Morris: A Life for our Time* (1994)

MacKenzie, J., *Orientalism: History, Theory and the Arts* (Manchester, 1995)

MacKenzie, J. M. (ed.), *Imperialism and Popular Culture* (Manchester, 1986)

MacKenzie, J. M. (ed.), *The Victorian Vision. Inventing New Britain* (2001)

Parsons, G. and Moore, J. R. (eds), *Religion in Victorian Britain* (4 vols, Manchester, 1988)

Pollard, S., *Britain's Prime and Britain's Decline: The British Economy, 1870–1914* (1989)

Porter, A. (ed.), *The Oxford History of the British Empire: Vol. III. The Nineteenth Century* (Oxford, 1999)

Porter, R., *London. A Social History* (1994)

Rubinstein, W. D., *Men of Property: The Very Wealthy in Britain since the Industrial Revolution* (1981)

Said, E. W., *Orientalism* (1979)

Stedman-Jones, G., *Languages of Class. Studies in English Working Class History, 1832–1982* (Cambridge, 1983)

Stedman-Jones, G., *Outcast London: A Study in the Relationship between Classes in Victorian Society* (Oxford, 1971)

Thompson, D., *The Chartists: Popular Politics in the Industrial Revolution* (1984)

Thompson, D., *Queen Victoria: Gender and Power* (1990)

Thompson, E. P., *William Morris: Romantic to Revolutionary* (1977)

Thompson, F. M. L. (ed.), *The Cambridge Social History of Britain, 1750–1950* (3 vols, Cambridge, 1990)

Thompson, F. M. L., *English Landed Society in the Nineteenth Century* (1963)

Walton, W., *France at the Crystal Palace. Bourgeois Taste and Artisan Manufacture in the Nineteenth Century* (Berkeley, CA, 1992)

Wiener, M. J., *English Culture and the Decline of the Industrial Spirit 1850–1980* (1981)

Wright, D. G. and Jowitt, J. A., *Victorian Bradford* (Bradford, 1981)

12. Style

Aldrich, M., *Gothic Revival* (1994)

Banham, J., MacDonald, S. and Porter, J., *Victorian Interior Design* (1991)

Brooks, C., *The Gothic Revival* (1999)

Cooper, N., *The Opulent Eye. Late Victorian and Edwardian Taste in Interior Design* (1976)

Crawford, A., *Charles Rennie Mackintosh* (1995)

Crook, J. M., *The Dilemma of Style. Architectural Ideas from the Picturesque to the Post-Modern* (1987)

Culme, J., *Nineteenth-Century Silver* (1977)

Darby, M., *The Islamic Perspective: An Aspect of British Architecture and Design in the Nineteenth Century* (1983)

Durant, S., *Ornament. A Survey of Decoration since 1830* (1986)

Gere, C. and Whiteway, M., *Nineteenth-Century Design from Pugin to Mackintosh* (1993)

Girouard, M., *The Return to Camelot: Chivalry and the English Gentleman* (1981)

Girouard, M., *Sweetness and Light. The 'Queen Anne' Movement, 1860–1900* (Oxford, 1977)

Greenhalgh, P. (ed.), *Art Nouveau, 1890–1914* (2000)

Head, R., *The Indian Style* (1986)

Jervis, S. and Wainwright, C., *High Victorian Design* (Ottowa, 1974)

13. Who led taste?

Adburgham, A., *Liberty's. A Biography of a Shop* (1975)

Ames, W., *Prince Albert and Victorian Taste* (1967)

Atterbury, P. and Wainwright, C., *Pugin. A Gothic Passion* (1994)

Bell, Q., *The Schools of Design* (1963)

Brooks, C. and Saint, A. (eds), *The Victorian Church: Architecture and Society* (1995)

Burton, A., *Vision and Accident. The Story of the Victoria and Albert Museum* (1999)

Comino, M., *Gimson and the Barnsleys. 'Wonderful Furniture of a Commonplace Kind'* (1980)

Crawford, A., *C. R. Ashbee, Architect, Designer and Romantic Socialist* (1986)

Crook, J. M., *The Rise of the Nouveaux Riches: Style and Status in Victorian and Edwardian Architecture* (2000)

Crook, J. M., *William Burges and the High Victorian Dream* (1981)

Cunningham, C. C., *Victorian and Edwardian Town Halls* (1981)

Davey, P., *Arts and Crafts Architecture. The Search for Earthly Paradise* (1980)

Durant, S., *Christopher Dresser* (1993)

Franklin, J., *The Gentleman's Country House and its Plan, 1835–1914* (1981)

Frayling, C., *The Royal College of Art. One Hundred and Fifty Years of Art and Design* (1987)

Greenhalgh, P., *Ephemeral Vistas. The Exposition Universelle, Great Exhibitions and World's Fairs, 1851–1939* (1988)

Hitchmough, W., *C. F. A. Voysey* (1995)

Jackson, A., 'Imagining Japan: the Victorian Perception and Acquisition of Japanese Culture', *Journal of Design History*, 5 (1992)

Jervis, S., *The Penguin Dictionary of Design and Designers* (1984)

Kaplan, W. and Cumming, E., *The Arts and Crafts Movement* (1991)

Lambourne, L., *The Aesthetic Movement* (1996)

Lambourne, L., *Utopian Craftsmen: The Arts and Crafts Movement from the Cotswolds to Chicago* (1980)

Lubbock, J., *The Tyranny of Taste. The Politics of Architecture and Design in Britain, 1550–1960* (1995)

McCleod, D. S., *Art and the Victorian Middle Class: Money and the Making of Cultural Identity* (Cambridge, 1996)

Mandler, P., *The Fall and Rise of the English County House* (1997)

Morris, B., *Inspiration for Design. The Influence of the Victoria and Albert Museum* (1986)

Parry, L. (ed.), *William Morris* (Woodbridge, 1996)

Physick, J., *The Victoria and Albert Museum. The History of its Building* (1982)

Physick, J. and Darby, M., 'Marble Halls'. Drawings and Models for Victorian Secular Buildings* (1973)

Soros, S. W. (ed.), *E. W. Godwin. Aesthetic Movement Architect and Designer* (1999)

Steegman, J., *Victorian Taste. A Study of the Arts and Architecture from 1830 to 1870* (1970)

Victoria and Albert Museum, *Victorian Church Art* (1971)

Wainwright, C., *The Romantic Interior. The British Collector at Home, 1750–1850* (1989)

Weiner, D. E. B., *Architecture and Social Reform in Late-Victorian London* (Manchester, 1994)

Wolff, J. and Seed, J. (eds) *The Culture of Capital: Art, Power and the Nineteenth-Century Middle Class* (Manchester, 1988)

14. Fashionable living

Adburgham, A., *Shops and Shopping 1800–1914* (1989)

Ashelford, J., *The Art of Dress. Clothes and Society, 1500–1914* (1996)

Bailey, P., *Leisure and Class in Victorian England: Rational Recreation and the Contest for Control, 1830–1885* (1987)

Beetham, M., *A Magazine of Her Own: Domesticity and Desire in the Women's Magazine 1800–1914* (1996)

Benson, J., *The Rise of Consumer Society in Britain, 1880–1980* (1994)

Branca, P., *Silent Sisterhood: Middle-Class Women in the Victorian Home* (1975)

Breward, C., *The Hidden Consumer: Masculinities, Fashion & City Life 1860–1914* (Manchester, 1999)

Bryden, I. and Floyd, J., *Domestic Space: Reading the Nineteenth-Century Interior* (Manchester, 1999)

Burnett, J., *A Social History of Housing, 1815–1985* (1986)

Byrde, P., *Nineteenth-Century Fashion* (1992)

Campbell Orr, C. (ed.), *Women in the Victorian Art World* (Manchester, 1995)

Cooper, N., *The Opulent Eye* (1976)

Crossick, G. and Jaumain, S. (eds), *Cathedrals of Consumption: The European Department Store 1850–1939* (Aldershot, 1999)

Cunnington, C. W., *English Women's Clothing in the Nineteenth Century* (1937)

Curtin, M., *Propriety and Position: A Study of Victorian Manners* (1987)

Daunton, M. J., *House and Home in the Victorian City: Working Class Housing, 1850–1914* (1983)

Davidoff, L., *The Best Circles: Society, Etiquette and the Season* (1986)

Davidoff, L. and Hall, C., *Family Fortunes: Men and Women of the English Middle Class 1780–1850* (1987)

Davidson, C., *The World of Mary Ellen Best* (1985)

Dyos, H. J. and Wolff, M. (eds), *The Victorian City: Images & Realities* (1973)

Feldman, D., and Stedman-Jones, G. (eds), *Metropolis-London: Histories and Representations since 1800* (1989)

Freeman, M., *Railways and the Victorian Imagination* (1999)

Gere, C., *Nineteenth-Century Decoration: The Art of the Interior* (1989)

Gere, C. and Hoskins, L., *The House Beautiful. Oscar Wilde and the Aesthetic Interior* (2000)

Gernsheim, A., *Victorian & Edwardian Fashion* (New York, 1981)

Ginsburg, M., *Victorian Dress in Photographs* (1982)

Girouard, M., *The Victorian Country House* (Oxford, 1971)

Gloag, J., *Victorian Comfort: A Social History of Design, 1830–1900* (1961)

Goodman, A., *Gilbert and Sullivan's London* (2000)

Gow, I., *The Scottish Interior. Georgian and Victorian Decor* (Edinburgh, 1992)

Hoskins, L. (ed.), *The Papered Wall: The History, Patterns and Technique of Wallpaper* (1994)

Kaplan, J. H. and Stowell, S., *Theatre & Fashion: Oscar Wilde to the Suffragettes* (Cambridge, 1994)

Kidd, A. and Nicholls, D. (eds), *Gender, Civic Culture and Consumerism: Middle Class Identity in Britain, 1800–1940* (Manchester, 1999)

Lambert, M., *Fashion in Photographs, 1860–1880* (1991)

Lancaster, W., *The Department Store: A Social History* (Leicester, 1995)

Levitt, S., *Fashion in Photographs, 1880–1900* (1991)

Loeb, L. A., *Consuming Angels: Advertising and Victorian Women* (Oxford, 1994)

Mason, P., *The English Gentleman: The Rise and Fall of an Ideal* (1982)

Merrill, L., *The Peacock Room: A Cultural Biography* (1998)

Morris, R. J. and Rodger, R. (eds), *The Victorian City: A Reader in British Urban History, 1820–1914* (1993)

Muthesius, S., *The English Terraced House* (1982)

Nead, L., *Victorian Babylon. People, Streets and Images in Nineteenth-Century London* (2000)

Newton, C., *Victorian Designs for the Home* (1999)

Newton, S. M., *Health, Art and Reason: Dress Reforms of the Nineteenth Century* (1974)

Olsen, D. J., *The City as a Work of Art: London, Paris, Vienna* (1986)

Rappaport, E., *Shopping for Pleasure: Women in the Making of London's West End* (Princeton, NJ, 2000)

Richards, T., *The Commodity Culture of Victorian England: Advertising and Spectacle 1851–1914* (Stanford, CA, 1990)

St George, A., *The Descent of Manners: Etiquette, Rules and the Victorians* (1993)

Simpson, M. A. and Lloyd, T. H. (eds), *Middle Class Housing in Britain* (1977)

Sparke, P., *As Long As It's Pink: The Sexual Politics of Taste* (1995)

Storch, R.D. (ed.), *Popular Custom and Culture in Nineteenth-Century England* (1982)

Thompson, F. M. L., *The Rise of Respectable Society: A Social History of Victorian Britain 1830–1900* (1988)

Tosh, J., *A Man's Place: Masculinity and the Middle-Class Home in Victorian England* (1999)

15. What was new?

Anderson, P., *The Printed Image and the Transformation of Popular Culture, 1790–1860* (Oxford, 1991)

Ball, D., *Victorian Publishers' Bindings* (1985)

Braithwaite, J., *S. W. Johnson: Midland Railway Locomotive Engineer Artist* (Skipton, 1985)

Briggs, A., *Victorian Things* (1988)

Burman, B., *The Culture of Sewing. Gender, Consumption and Home Dressmaking* (Oxford, 1999)

Bythell, D., *The Sweated Trades: Outwork in Nineteenth-Century Britain* (1978)

Charleston, R. J., *English Glass and the Glass used in England, c. 400–1940* (1984)

Coe, B. and Haworth-Booth, M., *A Guide to Early Photographic Processes* (1983)

Edwards, C., *Victorian Furniture: Technology and Design* (Manchester, 1993)

Forty, A., *Objects of Desire. Design and Society, 1750–1980* (1986)

Glanville, P., *Silver in England* (1987)

Goldman, P., *Victorian Illustration: The Pre-Raphaelites, the Idyllic school and the High Victorians* (Aldershot, 1996)

Hajdamach, C. R., *British Glass, 1800–1914* (Woodbridge, 1991)

Harrison, R. and Zeitlin, J. (eds), *Divisions of Labour: Skilled Workers and Technological Change in Nineteenth-Century Britain* (Brighton, 1985)

Harvey, C. and Press, J., *William Morris. Design and Enterprise in Victorian Britain* (Manchester, 1991)

Haworth-Booth, M., *The Golden Age of British Photography, 1839–1900* (1984)

Haworth-Booth, M., *Photography: An Independent Art* (1997)

Hoke, D. R., *Ingenious Yankees: The Rise of the American System of Manufacture in the Private Sector* (New York, 1990)

Houfe, S., *Fin de siècle: The Illustrators of the Nineties* (1992)

Hounshell, D., *From the American System to Mass Production, 1800–1932. The Development of Manufacturing Technology in the United States* (Baltimore, MD, 1985)

Jenkins, D. T. and Ponting, K. G., *The British Wool Textile Industry, 1770–1914* (1982)

Joyce, P., *Work, Society and Politics. The Culture of the Factory in Later Victorian England* (1982)

Kirkham, P., *The London Furniture Trade, 1700–1870* (1988)

Lattimore, C. R., *English 19th-Century Press-Moulded Glass* (1979)

Levitt, S., *Victorians Unbuttoned. Registered Designs for Clothing, their Makers and Wearers, 1839–1900* (1986)

McLean, R., *Victorian Book Design and Colour Printing* (1963)

More, C., *Skill and the English Working Class, 1870–1914* (1980)

Parry, L., *British Textiles from 1850–1900* (1993)

Ray, G. N., *The Illustrator and the Book in England from 1790 to 1914* (New York, 1976)

Reed, D., *The Popular Magazine in Britain and the United States, 1880–1960* (1997)

Rose, M. B. (ed.), *The Lancashire Cotton Industry. A History since 1700* (Preston, 1996)

Sabel, C. F. and Zeitlin, J. (eds), *World of Possibilities. Flexibility and Mass Production in Western Industrialization* (Cambridge, 1997)

Samuel, R., 'Workshop of the World: Steam Power and Hand Technology in Mid-Victorian Britain', *History Workshop*, 3 (1977)

Schmiechen, J. A., *Sweated Industries and Sweated Labor. The London Clothing Trades 1860–1914* (1984)

Twyman, M., *Printing, 1770–1970: An Illustrated History of its Development and Uses in England* (1970)

Wakeman, G., *Victorian Book Illustration: The Technical Revolution* (Newton Abbot, 1973)

Picture Credits

New photography of V&A objects illustrated in this publication has been produced by the photographers of the V&A Museum Photographic Studio. Listed below are those who have contributed and their specialist fields:

Christine Smith *Sculpture*
Dominic Naish *Metalwork*
Richard Davis *Ceramics*
Mike Kitcatt, Pip Barnard *Furniture and woodwork*
Ian Thomas, Christine Smith *Textiles*
Sara Hodges, Richard Davis *Glass and stained glass*
Paul Robins *Paintings and books*
Joanna Fernandes, Brenda Norrish *Prints, drawings and photographs*
Ken Jackson *Chief photographer*

Non-V&A illustrations have been provided by the following individuals and institutions:

Albright-Knox Art Gallery, Buffalo, New York. Gift of Seymour H. Knox, Jr 1945 9:15
Courtesy of the Amsterdam Historical Museum 10:20
By courtesy of the Ashmolean Museum 3:21, 6:42
Reproduced by kind permission of Sefton MBC Leisure Services Department, Arts and Cultural Services, Atkinson Art Gallery 3:55
Edward Barnsley Foundation 12:57
Öffentliche Kunstsammlung Basel, Kupferstichkabinett, Martin Bühler 4:2
Birmingham Museums and Art Gallery 4:10, 4:11, 6:17
Reproduced by permission of Birmingham City Archives 10:13
Courtesy of H. Blairman and Sons, Ltd 9:20
Bodleian Library, University of Oxford 4:40, 11:38, 15:37
Courtesy of the British Library Board 1:26, 3:20, 5:44, 5:57, 9:18
© Copyright the British Museum 3:22, 4:58, 6:43, 6:46, 8:15, 8:49, 9:24, 9:51, 9:60, 15:10
Buckinghamshire County Council 11:32
The Burghley House Collection 3:39
Chartered Institute of Transport/Bridgeman Art Library 14:49
By permission of the Duke of Devonshire and the Chatsworth Settlement Trustees 3:44, 3:56
Clive House Museum, Shrewsbury, Shropshire, UK/Bridgeman Art Library 6:35
Corning Museum of Glass, Corning, New York 10:9
Corporation of London Libraries and Guildhall Art Library 4:3, 4:56, 8:63, 8:65, 10:16, 14:48
Guildhall Art Library, Corporation of London, UK/Bridgeman Art Library 5:8, 7:61
Corpus Christi College, Oxford 3:8
The Country Life Picture Library 2:42, 4:9, 9:12
Courtauld Institute Gallery, London 8:39
Croome Estate Trustees 7:7
Courtesy of Gordon Crosskey 10:60
Cyfarthfa Castle Museum and Art Gallery 10:42
Derby Museums and Art Gallery 6:34, 10:7
Devon County Record Office 3:25
Doddington Hall, Lincolnshire 4:32
The Alfred Dunhill Museum and Archive 9:61
© English Heritage 3:52, 7:10, 7:12, 12:5, 12:27
Fitzwilliam Museum, Cambridge 3:33
By permission of the Folger Shakespeare Library 3:2
The Forbes Magazine Collection, New York 15:19

Library of the Religious Society of Friends 1:45
Geffrye Museum, London/Bridgeman Art Library 14:2, 14:28
© The Worshipful Company of Goldsmiths 5:19, 6:11
By Courtesy of the Trustees of the Goodwood Collection 6:14
© Crown Copyright UK Government Art Collection 2:16
Greater London Photographic Library 13:5
London Borough of Hackney, Archives Department 14:20
Harrogate Museums and Art Gallery/Bridgeman Art Library 14:21
© Crown Copyright Historic Royal Palaces 2:61, 3:9, 3:11, 3:14, 3:40, 3:53
Hulton Getty Picture Collection 13:65
Ironbridge Gorge Museum Trust 6:21
Anthony Kersting 1:9, 1:21, 2:1, 2:2, 2:3, 2:4, 2:6, 2:13, 2:17, 2:33, 2:34, 2:36, 2:44, 2:62, 2:63, 2:64, 3:6, 3:64, 4:7, 4:12, 4:16, 7:42, 7:58, 7:68, 8:1, 8:6, 12:66
London Borough of Lambeth Archives Department 7:66
Lancashire County Library, Rawtenstall Local Studies Collection 15:17
Lancashire County Record Office 11:29
© Leeds Museums and Galleries 9:4, 9:8
© Leeds Museums and Galleries/Bridgeman Art Library 8:28
Leeds City Council 12:37
By permission of the Linnean Society of London 15:6
Musée du Louvre 2:15
Mallett and Son Antiques Ltd, London, UK/Bridgeman Art Library 14:8
Manchester City Art Galleries/Bridgeman Art Library 11:24, 14:36
Manchester City Council 12:38
His Grace the Duke of Marlborough and Jarrold Publishing 7:17
The Board of Trustees of the National Museums and Galleries on Merseyside 12:32
© 2001 The Metropolitan Museum of Art, New York 6:28, 12:31
Musée Nationale de la Renaissance, Ecouen. © Photo RMN-Gérard Blot 3:18
Courtesy of the Museum of Early Southern Decorative Arts, Winston-Salem 6:26
Courtesy, Museum of Fine Arts, Boston. Reproduced with permission. © 2000 Museum of Fine Arts, Boston. All rights reserved 5:39
Courtesy of the Museum of London 1:7, 3:49, 5:58, 6:16, 8:35, 8:58, 11:23, 11:41, 12:6; 14:5, 14:46, 15:4
© National Gallery, London 9:59
National Gallery of Ireland, Dublin/Bridgeman Art Library 9:17
The Trustees of the National Library of Scotland 1:23
© National Maritime Museum, London 1:31, 3:37, 5:20, 5:73, 5:76, 6:23, 11:16
National Monuments Record 3:66, 12:18, 12:67, 13:2, 14:3
Courtesy of the National Portrait Gallery, London p.10, 2:30, 3:24, 3:47, 3:65, 4:33, 4:57, 8:7, 8:30, 12:41, 12:48, 13:54, 14:31
National Trust for Scotland 4:23, 9:43
© The National Trust Photographic Library 2:22, 2:39, 2:46, 2:52, 2:65, 3:1, 3:3, 3:12, 3:38, 3:54, 4:1, 4:4, 4:14, 4:15, 4:24, 4:55, 7:28, 8:33, 10:54, 12:28, 14:13
Norfolk Museum Service (Norwich Castle Museum) 1:47
North Yorkshire County Record Office 10:11

Collection of the Duke of Northumberland 8:2, 8:3, 8:4, 8:5
Castle Museum and Art Gallery, Nottingham 14:27
Reproduced by permission of the Palace of Westminster 13:37, 13:39
Pepys Library, Magdalene College, Cambridge 5:74
Private Collection 11:37, 14:1, 14:33, 14:39, 14:56
Private Collection/Bridgeman Art Library 14:56
Private Scottish Collection 3:60
Royal Institute of British Architects 8:31, 12:26
RIBA Library Drawings Collection 2:35, 3:7, 3:48, 7:11, 12:1, 12:50, 14:50, 14:51
© Royal Academy of Arts 9:13
© The Royal Collection 2001, Her Majesty Queen Elizabeth II 2:51, 3:10, 3:41, 3:57, 6:38, 7:39, 8:60, 8:61, 8:66, 11:8
© Royal Holloway and Bedford New College 14:52
Royal Society of Arts 8:18
© Salisbury and South Wiltshire Museum 14:17
Courtesy of the Marquess of Salisbury 2:19
Salts Estates Ltd 15:3
Science and Society Picture Library 10:45, 10:67, 11:25, 15:51, 15:53, 15:59, 15:60, 15:61, 15:62, 15:63, 15:64
Courtesy of John S. M. Scott, Esq., Michael Whiteway, photographer 12:14
Scottish National Portrait Gallery p.10, 3:58
Scottish National Portrait Gallery, Edinburgh, Scotland/Bridgeman Art Library 4:42
Sheffield City Libraries 10:27
Sheffield Industrial Museums Trust, Ltd 11:22
By courtesy of the Trustees of the Sir John Soane Museum 3:23, 7:37
Society of Antiquaries of London 1:3
Sotheby's Picture Library 9:22
South Lanarkshire Council, Museum Development Department 11:36
Stapleton Collection, UK/Bridgeman Art Library 9:23
© Tate, London, 2001 6:40, 6:45, 8:12, 9:14, 9:25, 11:48, 14:12, 14:26, 14:35
Tichborne House, Hampshire/Bridgeman Art Library 1:46
Courtesy of the Lewis Walpole Library, Yale University 7:1, 9:30
Wandsworth Museum 5:21, 7:46
Image by courtesy of the Trustees of the Wedgwood Museum, Barlaston, Staffordshire 8:45, 10:19, 10:40
In the Collection of Earl of Wemyss 9:40
© Dean and Chapter of Westminster 3:28
The Beacon, Whitehaven, and Copeland Borough Council 6:19
Worshipful Company of Clockmakers Collection UK/Bridgeman Art Library 10:26
Worshipful Company of Coachmakers 10:65
Yale Center for British Art, Paul Mellon Collection, USA/Bridgeman Art Library 6:18, 9:50
York City Art Gallery 6:47, 14:7

Every effort has been made to seek permission to reproduce those images whose copyright does not reside with the V&A, and we are grateful to the individuals and institutions who have assisted in this task. Any omissions are entirely unintentional and the details should be addressed to the publishers.

Index

First published by V&A Publications, 2001

V&A Publications
160 Brompton Road
London SW3 1HW

Michael Snodin, John Styles and the contributors assert their moral right to be identified as the authors of this book.

Designed by Janet James
Cartography by bounford.com
Project and production management by Geoff Barlow

Distributed in North America by Harry N. Abrams, Incorporated, New York.

ISBN: 0–8109–6586–0 (Harry N. Abrams, Inc.)

Library of Congress Control Number: 2001088704.

Originated by Bright Arts (HK) Ltd
Printed and bound in Italy by LEGO SpA

Jacket illustrations

Front:
The State Bed from Melville House, Fife, about 1700. VAM W.35-1949.

Back:
(*top*) Chinese porcelain jar with English mounts; jar 1630–40, mounts 1660–70. VAM 308-1962.
(*right*) Robe and petticoat, 1760–5. VAM T.593-1999.
(*bottom*) Clock, 1896–1901. Designed by C. F. A. Voysey. VAM W.5-1998.

Spine:
Stained glass showing the arms of Henry VIII and Jane Seymour, about 1536–40. VAM C.454-1919.

Frontispiece:
Snuff box, about 1765–75. VAM C.470-1914.

Contents page:
Vase and cover, 1888–98. Designed by William De Morgan. VAM C.413-1919.

HARRY N. ABRAMS, Inc.
100 Fifth Avenue
New York, N.Y. 10011
www.abramsbooks.com